OSF Motif® Edition

The **X** *Window System*™

Programming and Applications with **X**t

Second Edition

Douglas A. Young

Silicon Graphics, Inc.
Mountain View, CA

P T R Prentice Hall
Englewood Cliffs, New Jersey 07632

Library of Congress Cataloging in Publication Data

Editorial/Production Supervision: *Mary Rottino*
Buyer: *Alexis R. Heydt*
Acquisitions Editor: *Gregory Doench*
Cover Designer: *Aren Graphics*
Editorial Assistant: *Marcy Levine*

 © 1994 by P T R Prentice Hall
Prentice-Hall, Inc.
A Paramount Communications Company
Englewood Cliffs, New Jersey 07632

The publisher offers discounts on this book when ordered in bulk quantities. For more information, contact Corporate Sales Department, 113 Sylvan Ave., Englewood Cliffs, NJ 07632
Phone: 201-592-2863, FAX: (201) 592-2249

Printed in the United States of America
10 9 8 7 6 5 4 3 2 1

ISBN 0-13-123803-5

Prentice-Hall International (UK) Limited, *London*
Prentice-Hall of Australia Pty. Limited, *Sydney*
Prentice-Hall Canada Inc., *Toronto*
Prentice-Hall Hispanoamericana, S.A., *Mexico*
Prentice-Hall of India Private Limited, *New Delhi*
Prentice-Hall of Japan, Inc., *Tokyo*
Simon & Schuster Asia Pte. Ltd., *Singapore*
Editora Prentice-Hall do Brasil, Ltda., *Rio de Janeiro*

For Teri and D.C.

Contents

Preface   **x1**

Chapter 1   Introduction   **1**

   1.1   The X Server and Xlib   1

   1.2   The Xt Intrinsics   10

   1.3   Motif   14

   1.4   Naming and Coding Conventions   18

   1.5   Summary   22

Chapter 2   Programming with Xt   **23**

   2.1   A Simple Motif Application: memo   23

   2.2   The Xt Programming Model   28

   2.3   Essential Xt Functions   29

   2.4   Handling Input   40

   2.5   Summary   50

Chapter 3   Using the Resource Manager   **51**

   3.1   What Is a Resource?   51

   3.2   Specifying Resources   52

   3.3   Loading the Resource Database   57

   3.4   Widget Resource Conventions   61

   3.5   Using Resource Files: An Example   63

   3.6   Managing Application Resources   68

   3.7   Type Conversion   74

   3.8   Summary   82

Chapter 4   Primitive Motif Widgets   83

4.1   The Core Widget Class   84

4.2   The XmPrimitive Widget Class   85

4.3   The XmLabel Widget Class   86

4.4   Button Widgets   90

4.5   The XmText and XmTextField Widget Classes   101

4.6   The XmList Widget Class   112

4.7   The XmSeparator Widget Class   119

4.8   The XmScrollBar Widget Class   120

4.9   Gadgets   122

4.10   Summary   124

Chapter 5   Manager Widgets   125

5.1   Xt Support for Manager Widgets   127

5.2   The XmManager Widget Class   128

5.3   The XmBulletinBoard Widget Class   129

5.4   The XmRowColumn Widget Class   130

5.5   The XmForm Widget Class   137

5.6   The XmFrame Widget Class   150

5.7   The XmScrolledWindow Widget Class   153

5.8   The XmMainWindow Widget Class   157

5.9   The XmScale Widget Class   160

5.10   The XmPanedWindow Widget Class   166

5.11   Designing Widget Hierarchies   168

5.12   Shell Widgets   171

5.13   Managing Keyboard Focus   176

5.14   Summary   182

Chapter 6   Menus   183

6.1   The Elements of a Menu   183

6.2   Popup Menus   184

6.3   Menu Bars   191

6.4   Accelerators and Mnemonics   199

6.5   Option Menus   202

6.6   A Menu Convenience Package   206

6.7   Supporting Context-Sensitive Help   216

6.8   Summary   222

Chapter 7   Dialogs   **223**

7.1   Xt Support for Dialogs   223

7.2   XmBulletinBoard Support for Dialogs   231

7.3   The XmMessageBox Widget Class   233

7.4   The File Selection Dialog   236

7.5   Creating Custom Dialogs   240

7.6   Summary   248

Chapter 8   Events and Other Input Techniques   **249**

8.1   What Is an Event?   249

8.2   Event Masks   251

8.3   Event Types   251

8.4   Handling Events in Motif Applications   261

8.5   Managing the Event Queue   270

8.6   Using Timeouts   272

8.7   Work Procedures   275

8.8   Handling Other Input Sources   277

8.9   Summary   290

Chapter 9   Using Color   **291**

9.1   The X Color Model   291

9.2   An Example: A Color Palette Editor   303

9.3   Summary   318

Chapter 10   Graphics Contexts   **319**

10.1   Creating Graphics Contexts   319

10.2   Manipulating Graphics Contexts   322

10.3   Graphics Exposures   329

10.4   Regions   329

10.5   Summary   332

Chapter 11   Bitmaps, Pixmaps, and Images   **333**

11.1   Pixmaps   333
11.2   Bitmaps   334
11.3   Copying Between Drawables   335
11.4   Images   342
11.5   Caching Pixmaps   344
11.6   The Xpm Pixmap Format   353
11.7   Summary   362

Chapter 12   Text and Fonts   **363**

12.1   Fonts   363
12.2   Xlib Text Operations   366
12.3   Compound Strings   367
12.4   Compound Text   381
12.5   Summary   381

Chapter 13   Using Xlib Graphics   **382**

13.1   Drawing Points   383
13.2   Drawing Lines   404
13.3   Rectangles, Polygons, and Arcs   410
13.4   Example: A Simple Drawing Program   421
13.5   Summary   454

Chapter 14   Interclient Communication   **455**

14.1   Atoms   456
14.2   Properties   457
14.3   Client Messages   461
14.4   Selections: Cut and Paste   462
14.5   Using the Motif Clipboard   478
14.6   Interacting with the Motif Window Manager   488
14.7   Drag and Drop   494
14.8   Summary   516

Chapter 15   Creating New Widget Classes **517**

15.1   The Architecture of a Widget   518

15.2   The Motif XmPrimitive Widget Class   530

15.3   The Dial Widget: An Example   533

15.4   Summary   559

Chapter 16   Creating Manager Widget Classes **560**

16.1   Architecture of a Composite Widget   561

16.2   The XmManager Widget Class   563

16.3   A Simple Manager Widget: The Row Widget   566

16.4   Summary   585

Chapter 17   Constraint-Based Widget Classes **586**

17.1   Architecture of Constraint Widgets   586

17.2   A Manager Widget Based on Constraints   588

17.3   Summary   620

Getting Source Code   **621**

Index to Example Programs   **623**

Index   **627**

PREFACE

This book is written for programmers who want to write applications for the X Window System using the Motif user interface toolkit. Like the first edition of this book, this new edition focuses on information and techniques most programmers use on a regular basis when writing typical Motif applications. This book introduces Xlib, the Xt Intrinsics, and the OSF/Motif widget set through examples that illustrate how these libraries are used in real programs. By focusing on the aspects of Xlib and Xt that are actually needed by Motif applications, this book presents a single, unified view of Motif programming.

X and Motif have both evolved since the original version of this book was published, and this new edition has been updated to reflect those changes. This edition not only discusses newer features of Motif, like drag and drop and tear-off menus, but also takes advantage of up-to-date X11 and Xt features such as compound text and vararg routines. This book also reflects the current focus of X-based software development in other ways. Some examples in the original edition that no longer represent contemporary practice have been removed, and new examples have been added. Also, earlier editions of this book emphasized Xt more than Motif, because there were still many Xt-based widgets sets in common use, and not everyone was using Motif. Today, Motif has been almost universally adopted as the user interface toolkit of choice for developing X applications and this edition focuses more strongly on the Motif widget set.

Like all books, this book makes some assumptions about the reader's background and experience. All examples are written in ANSI C, and this book assumes the reader is familiar with that language and with developing software in the UNIX environment. Readers who need more background in C or UNIX should consult one of the many good books that address these subjects.

Window systems are inherently graphical in nature, and it would useful for readers to have some familiarity with the basic concepts of bitmapped graphics. Also, before writing applications that run in the X environment, it would be best to have some experience with X as a user. This book assumes the reader is comfortable with X and X-based applications as an end-user. This includes at least some exposure to graphical user interfaces that use common elements like windows, menus, and dialogs. Many good books that address these topics are available for those who need more background or introductory material.

The information in this book is based on X11 Release 5 (X11R5) and the 1.2 release of the Motif widget set. All example programs have been tested with Motif version 1.2.3 on a Silicon Graphics IRIS Indigo workstation, running the IRIX 5.2 release of system software.

ACKNOWLEDGMENTS

Over the years since the publication of the original edition of this book, many people have provided feedback on the examples and other material in that book. Although too numerous to mention, I would like to thank everyone who has taken the time to contact me via e-mail to discuss the material in earlier editions. I have tried to apply your feedback, requests, questions, and suggestions to make this book more useful to everyone.

I would like to thank Oliver Jones for all of his advise over the years. John Pew did a great deal to improve this book while working on an earlier OLIT version. Jerry Smith also helped improve this edition with his suggestions and comments. I would also like to thank the many people who have attended classes and seminars over the past few years in which I tried out most of the material in this book as it evolved to its current form. And finally of course, my most heartfelt thanks goes to my family, who have continually supported all my writing efforts.

Doug Young

Chapter 1

Introduction

This book describes how to develop interactive applications for the X Window System using the Motif user interface toolkit. The X Window System is an industry-standard software system that allows programmers to develop portable graphical user interfaces. Motif is a high-level user-interface toolkit that makes it easier to write applications that use the X Window System.

Programs based on Motif use three main libraries. The first is Xlib, which provides the lowest level interface to the facilities of the window system. The second is the Xt Intrinsics, which is a library that hides many details of Xlib and supports a higher-level programming model. Finally, the Motif library builds on the Xt Intrinsics layer and provides visual components like buttons and scrollbars from which an application's user interface can be built. The examples in this book, like most real applications, use the facilities of all three libraries.

This chapter introduces the basic architecture of X, the Xt Intrinsics, and Motif, and describes how various pieces fit together. Section 1.1 discusses the underlying model of the basic X Window System. Section 1.2 introduces the Xt Intrinsics and Section 1.3 provides a brief overview of Motif.

1.1   The X Server and Xlib

This section introduces some key concepts of the X Window System. Although all examples in this book use the Motif toolkit, it is still important to understand some basic principles that apply to all

X applications. Motif, like most X-based toolkits, depends on the low-level C interface to X known as Xlib. Xlib provides an extensive set of functions that provide complete access to the functionality of the X Window System. This section describes the architecture of the underlying window system and discusses the core facilities provided by X, as supported by Xlib.

The X Window System was originally developed at the Massachusetts Institute of Technology (MIT), with support from the Digital Equipment Corporation (DEC). The name and also some initial design ideas were derived from an earlier window system named W, developed at Stanford University. X was developed at MIT's Laboratory for Computer Science for Project Athena to fulfill that project's need for a distributed, hardware-independent user interface platform. Early versions of X were used primarily within MIT and DEC, but with the release of version 10, many companies began to use X as the basis of commercial products. Today, nearly all UNIX-oriented hardware vendors support X as their primary windowing environment, and X is available for many personal computers as well. Many companies have also begun to produce hardware specifically designed to support the X protocol.

Version 11 of the X Window System has been supported by a consortium of hardware and software vendors who have made a commitment to X as a standard base for user interfaces across each of their product lines. The X Consortium supports and controls the standard specification of the X Window System and provides sample implementations of the X server, Xlib, and the Xt Intrinsics.

One of the most important features of X is its device-independent architecture. X allows programs to display windows that contain text and graphics on any hardware that supports the X protocol without modifying, recompiling, or relinking the application. X's device independence, along with X's position as a widely available industry standard, allows X-based applications to function in a heterogeneous environment consisting of mainframes, workstations, and personal computers.

Another important characteristic of X is that the window system itself does not define any particular user interface style. At the Xlib level, X provides *mechanisms* to support many interface styles rather than enforcing any one *policy*. Many window systems — the one used by Apple's Macintosh, or Microsoft Windows, for example — support a particular style of user interface. In contrast, X provides a flexible set of primitive window operations, but carefully avoids dictating the look or feel of any particular application's user interface.

Instead, X provides a device-independent layer that serves as a base for a variety of interface styles. Therefore, the basic X Window System does not provide user interface components such as the scrollbars, menus, and dialog boxes often found in other window systems. Most applications depend on higher level libraries built on top of the basic X protocol to provide these components. The Motif user interface toolkit is an example of such a high-level library.

The Client-Server Model

The architecture of the X Window System is based on a *client-server* model. A single process, known as the *server,* is responsible for all input and output devices. The server creates and manipulates windows on the screen, produces text and graphics, and handles input devices such as a keyboard and mouse. The server provides a portable layer between all applications and the display hardware. The X server typically runs on a workstation or personal computer, although some vendors offer dedicated X terminals that support X through dedicated hardware or firmware.

An application that uses the facilities provided by the X server is known as a *client*. A client communicates with the X server via a network connection using an asynchronous byte-stream protocol. Multiple clients can be connected to a single server concurrently, and an individual client can also connect to multiple servers.

The X architecture hides most of the details of the device-dependent implementation of the server and the hardware it controls from clients. Any client can communicate with any server, provided both the client and the server obey the X protocol.

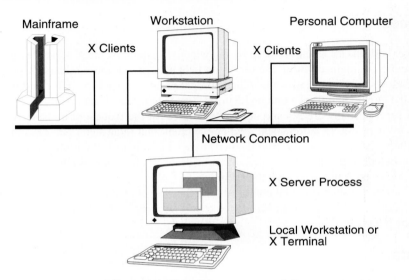

Figure 1.1 The client-server model.

Besides providing device independence, the distributed architecture of X allows the server and clients to run on separate machines located anywhere on a network. This feature has many potential applications. For example, imagine an interactive teaching program that executes on a school's main computer that can display information on inexpensive personal computers at each student's desk. In this scenario, the teaching program is a client that communicates with multiple servers, one for each student's machine. Each student interacts with the program concurrently through a window on his or her local machine. The same program can also be connected to another display at the teacher's desk, which allows the teacher to check the progress of any individual student or the class as a whole. While one window on each student's display provides an interface to the remote teaching program, other windows on a student's machine can provide interfaces to other clients. For example, each student can use a window to interact with an electronic mail system that runs on a central mail server. Still another window can provide an interface to an editor that runs locally on the student's machine.

Displays and Screens

The terms *display* and *screen* are often used interchangeably to refer to the physical device used by a computer to display text and graphics. However, X uses the term *display* to mean a single X server *process*, while a *screen* is a single hardware output device. A single X display can support many screens. X uses the terms *display* and *server* interchangeably. There is normally only one server per central processing unit (CPU).

Before a client can communicate with the X server, the client must open a connection to the server. Once a connection is established, the client can use any of the screens controlled by the server. X provides a security mechanism that allows a server to deny clients that execute on other hosts the right to connect to a display.

Resources

The X server controls all *resources* used by the window system. At the X server level, a resource is a data structure maintained within the server on behalf of one or more clients. X server resources include windows, bitmaps, and fonts. Client programs access each resource through a *resource identifier* (ID). A resource ID is a unique identifier assigned by the X server.

The X server usually creates and destroys resources at the request of a client. Also, the server usually destroys resources automatically when the client that requested them disconnects from the server. X allows clients to specify a *close down mode* which controls the lifetime of server resources allocated on behalf of that client. The default mode destroys all resources allocated for a client when that client breaks its connection with the server.

Server resources should not be confused with the widget resources supported by Xt and Motif (discussed later in this chapter). In Motif, the term "resource" refers to a customizable parameter supported by a widget.

Requests

When a client application needs to use a service provided by the X server, the client sends a *request* to the server. Clients typically request the server to create, destroy, or reconfigure windows, or to display text or graphics in a window. Clients can also request information about the current state of windows or other resources.

The X server normally runs asynchronously with respect to its clients, and all clients run asynchronously with respect to each other. Although the server processes all requests from each particular application in the order in which they arrive, requests are not necessarily processed immediately. Requests from clients are placed in a queue until the server is able to process them, and clients usually do not wait for the server to respond to requests. Applications can request the server to handle requests synchronously, but this approach usually results in poorer performance, because each request to the server requires a round-trip over the connection between the client and the X server. However, it is often useful to run an application in synchronous mode while debugging. The X server always handles certain requests synchronously, and applications need to use care when making these requests to prevent performance problems.

Basic Window Concepts

The most fundamental resource in X is the *window*. A window simply corresponds to a rectangular area of the screen. Unlike windows in some other systems, X windows do not have titlebars, scrollbars or other decorations. An X window appears as a rectangle with a background color or pattern. Each window also has a border whose color, thickness, and pattern can be set independently. Applications can combine multiple windows to create scrollbars, title bars, and other higher-level user interface components.

The X server creates windows in response to requests from clients. The server stores and maintains the data structure that represents a window, while clients refer to the window using the window's ID. Clients can request the X server to alter a window's size, position, color, or other characteristics. Although the server creates each window at the request of a specific client, any client can request the server to manipulate any window, provided the client has access to the window's ID. For example, X window managers use this feature to control the position of all windows on the screen.

The Window Hierarchy

X organizes windows as a hierarchy, known as the *window tree*. The top window in any window tree is known as the *root window*. The X server automatically creates a root window for each screen it controls. The root window occupies an entire physical screen, and cannot be moved or resized. Every window except the root window has a *parent* window (also known as an *ancestor*) and every window can have *children* (also known as *descendents* or *subwindows*). Windows that share the same parent are called *siblings*.

Figure 1.2 and Figure 1.3 show the hierarchical relationship between several windows. Figure 1.2 illustrates how a set of hypothetical windows might appear on the screen, while Figure 1.3 shows the window tree formed by these windows. Windows A and B are children of the root window, while Windows C and E are children of Window A. Window G is a child of Window E. Similarly, windows D and F are children of Window B, and Window H is a child of Window F.

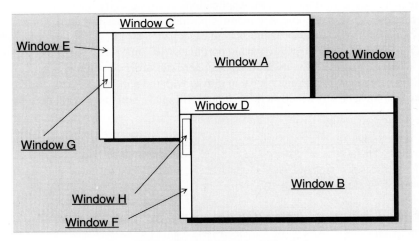

Figure 1.2 A typical window hierarchy.

X places few restrictions on the size or location of a window. One restriction X does enforce is that only the portion of a window that lies within the bounds of its parent is visible; the server *clips* the remaining portions to the boundaries of the parent window.

X allows siblings to overlap in a way that resembles a collection of papers on a desk. The *stacking order* determines which windows or portions of windows appear to be on top (and therefore are visible). If two windows occupy overlapping regions on the screen, the window that is higher in the stacking order completely or partially *obscures* the lower window. For example, in Figure 1.2, Window B is higher in the stacking order than Window A. Clients can request the X server to alter a window's position in the stacking order (for example, raising a window above all other windows). A window's stacking order can only be altered relative to its siblings. Therefore, from a user's viewpoint, a window's descendants raise and lower with the window.

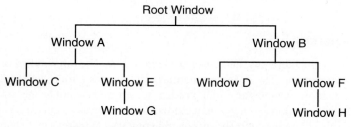

Figure 1.3 Window tree for Figure 1.2.

The X Coordinate System

Each X window, including the root window, has its own integer coordinate system. The coordinate of the upper left corner of each window is *(0, 0)*. The *x* coordinate increases toward the right and the *y* coordinate increases toward the bottom. Applications always specify the coordinate of a point on the screen relative to some window. A window's position (the upper left corner of the window) is always specified relative to the coordinate system of its parent window. For example, in Figure 1.4, Window A's upper left corner is positioned at coordinate *(50, 100)* relative to the coordinate system of the root window. However, the coordinate of upper left corner of window A is *(0, 0)* relative to Window A. Each window's coordinate system moves with the window, which permits applications to place text, graphics, or sub-windows in a window without regard to the window's location within its parent.

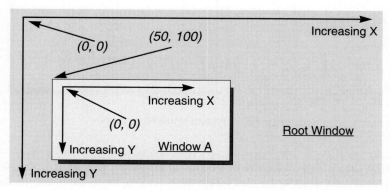

Figure 1.4 The X coordinate system.

Mapping and Window Visibility

Although each X window is associated with a rectangular region on the screen, windows are not necessarily visible to the user all the time. When the server creates a window, it allocates and initializes the data structures that represent the window within the server, but does not invoke the hardware-dependent routines that display the window on the screen. Clients can request the server to display a window by issuing a *map* request. Although a window is considered *mapped* if a client has issued a map request for that window, it still might not be visible for any of the following reasons:

- Another window completely *obscures* the window. The window becomes visible only if it or the obscuring window is moved in such a way that the window is no longer obscured, the obscuring window is removed from the screen, or the stacking order of the two windows changes so that the obscuring window is lower in the stacking order than the other window.

- An ancestor of the window is not mapped. Before a window can appear on the screen, every ancestor of the window must be mapped. A window that is mapped, but has an ancestor that is not mapped, is said to be *unviewable*. An unviewable window becomes *viewable* when all ancestors are mapped.

- The window is completely clipped by an ancestor. If a window is located completely outside the visible boundaries of any ancestor, it is not visible on the screen. The window becomes visible if its ancestor or ancestors are resized to include the region occupied by the window, or if the window is moved to lie within the visible boundaries of its ancestors.

Maintaining Window Contents

In an overlapping window system, each window's contents must be preserved when one window is covered by another window to allow the contents to be restored when the window is no longer obscured. Some window systems maintain and restore the contents of a window automatically, so that applications are unaware of the process.

In X, the responsibility for maintaining the contents of a window lies with the client that uses the window. Some implementations of X support *backing store*, a technique for saving the contents of a window automatically. However, applications must not depend on backing store because there is no guarantee that all server implementations can provide this service for all windows. Saving a copy of the image displayed in each window on the screen places a huge demand on the memory resources of the system on which the server is running. It is usually more efficient for the X server to notify a client when a window is *exposed*, and rely on the client to redisplay the contents of the window.

Every X client must be prepared to recreate the contents of its windows at any time. Although this requirement places some burden on programmers, this requirement is seldom a problem because most applications maintain internal representations of the contents of their windows anyway. In addition, higher-level toolkits like Motif redraw most parts of an application's interface transparently. Backing store is best used to support computationally intensive applications that have difficulty recreating their output quickly. For servers that do not support backing store, such applications usually must resort to saving the current contents of its windows as an off-screen image. Chapter 13 demonstrates this technique.

Many X servers also support *save-unders*. A save-under is a technique that saves the image on the screen, *under* a particular window, so that the image can be restored when the obscuring window is moved to a new location or removed from the screen. The image is saved by taking a snapshot of an area of the screen just before the area is covered by a window. For save-unders to be effective, the state of the screen and all windows on the screen must be held constant between the time the snapshot is taken and the time the image is restored. Save-unders are used primarily when creating popup menus and other small transitory windows to achieve a smooth visual effect.

Events

The X server communicates with clients by sending *events* to client applications. The server generates events as a direct or indirect result of a user action (for example, pressing a key on the keyboard, moving the mouse, or pressing a mouse button). The server also generates events to notify the client of changes in the state of its windows. For example, the server sends a client an `Expose` event when a window's contents needs to be restored. X supports thirty-four types of events, and provides a mechanism that allows clients to simulate additional event types.

The server sends events to a client by placing the event on a first-in, first-out (FIFO) queue that can be read by the client. Each event consists of a packet that reports the type of event, the window in which the event occurred, and other data specific to the particular type of event.

Most X applications are completely *event-driven* and are designed to wait until an event occurs, respond to the event, and then wait for the next event. The event-driven approach provides a natural model for interactive applications. Xt and Motif provide additional support for writing event-drive applications, as discussed in later chapters.

Handling Input

X supports a variety of input devices. Depending on the implementation, a server can support tablets, track balls, scanners, and other data input and pointing devices. The most common input devices are the keyboard, used for textual input, and the mouse, which serves as both a pointing device and a selection device.

The Mouse

A mouse is a device that allows the user to point to locations on the screen and also to issue commands by pressing buttons. The user points to a screen location by controlling the position of an image on the screen known as the *pointer*, or mouse cursor.

The user controls the location of the pointer by moving the mouse on the user's desk. The server maintains the pointer and tracks its current location. Clients can ask the server to report events when the pointer enters or leaves a window, changes position, or when the user presses or releases a mouse button. Clients can also query the server to determine the current position of the pointer, and can change the size and appearance of the pointer as well. Applications often use this ability to change the shape of the pointer to indicate the current state of the application, or to emphasize operations that can be performed in certain parts of an application's interface. For example, the pointer might assume the shape of an arrow when the user selects an object, change to a vertical arrow when the pointer is within a scroll bar, and change to an hourglass when the application is busy.

The pointer also has a *hotspot*. A hotspot is the point within the mouse cursor that defines the precise location of the pointer on the screen. The pointer is said to be *contained* by a window if its hotspot is inside the visible region of the window, or one of its sub-windows. The pointer is *in* the smallest window that contains the hotspot.

The Keyboard

The server generates an event each time a key changes state. The information in the event structure includes a code that identifies which key was pressed or released. Clients can translate key codes into ASCII characters, if desired. Key codes are independent of any particular keyboard arrangement to allow applications to handle a variety of keyboards made by different manufacturers. Applications that use Xt or Motif generally use higher-level mechanism for handling keyboard input and seldom deal with key codes directly.

When a user types at a keyboard, the server sends events to the window that currently has *input focus*. In general, the focus window is the window that contains the pointer, although windows can grab the input focus to change the default behavior. Window managers often provide support for different styles of input focus, and may allow a window to receive keyboard input even when the mouse pointer is not contained by the window. Higher-level toolkits like Xt and Motif also provide additional support for applications that need to control which window has input focus.

Displaying Text and Graphics

X provides very simple support for displaying text and graphics in a window. The X server supports simple 2 dimensional drawing primitives that allow applications to draw points, lines, rectangles, arcs, and polygons. Except for points and lines, these figures can be filled with colors or patterns. X supports 3 dimensional graphics through the use of *server extensions*, which allow the server's capabilities to be extended to add new features.

The server displays text in a variety of fonts. Text can be drawn left-to-right or right-to-left, but cannot be rotated or drawn vertically. There are currently no standard fonts in X, although there are several contributed font sets that are widely available. As of X11R5, X supports the use of scalable fonts, and also can store fonts in a possibly remote location, to be accessed via a font server.

Window Management

In X, a *window manager* is a separate program that allows the user to control the size and location of windows on the screen. An X window manager is an ordinary client application that interacts with the server through events and requests. However, X provides some features intended to allow window managers to control the size and placement of windows. For example, window managers can request that the X server *redirect* requests that deal with the structure of a window to the window manager rather than acting on the requests directly. If an application requests the server to map a window and a window manager has requested that such events be redirected, the X server sends a `MapRequest` event to the window manager. The window manager then has the opportunity to take some action before mapping the window, and can even refuse to map the window.

Some window managers use the ability to redirect requests to place or resize windows according to a set of layout rules. For example, a *tiling* window manager might first rearrange or resize other windows already on the screen to ensure that no windows overlap. Many window managers, including the Motif window manager (mwm), use this feature to add a frame or title bar to the window before mapping it.

Window management is a complex subject that affects not only how users interact with a system, but also how applications interact with each other and with the X server. The *InterClient Communications Conventions Manual* (ICCCM) defines the protocol all window managers and applications must follow to interact properly with each other. In practice, these guidelines mostly concern those few programmers who design window managers and user interface toolkits, or those programmers who choose to program directly with the Xlib C library. Programmers who use the Motif toolkit to write applications seldom deal with the ICCCM protocols directly.

1.2   The Xt Intrinsics

Xlib operates at a level that is lower than the level at which many programmers prefer to work. In relation to the other libraries discussed in this chapter, one could compare Xlib to the assembly code level. Even a program that simply displays a short string on the screen can consist of hundreds of lines of code, if the program conforms to all expected protocols and conventions. The Xt Intrinsics library (often just called "Xt") was designed to make it easier to write X applications by providing more support for the kinds of things programmers want to do with a window system. Xt hides many of the details of Xlib, and automatically supports certain operations expected of all X applications.

Unlike many user interface toolkits, Xt is of little use by itself. In fact, Xt can be best described as a toolkit for building user interface toolkits. Xt defines a model for all applications that use it, and defines an object-oriented architecture for constructing user interface components. Xt defines only a few user interface components itself, and like Xlib, strives to be independent of any particular look and feel. Xt specifies how applications interact with various user interface components, but does not enforce the specific behavior or appearance of any given component.

The user interface components supported by Xt are called *widgets*. Typical widgets include buttons, scrollbars, and menus. A widget is a complex data structure that combines an X window with a set of functions that manipulate that window. In addition to the ID of the X window used by the widget, the widget structure contains additional data needed by these functions.

There are many Xt-based widget sets; the OSF/Motif widget set and the Open Look widget set (known as OLIT, for *Open Look Intrinsic Toolkit*) are both widely-used commercial widget sets based on Xt. The Athena widget set, which is freely available as part of the standard X Window System distribution, is another popular widget set. Most widget sets have more similarities than differences and a programmer who is familiar with one widget set should be able to quickly learn to use any other widget set. All examples in this book are based on the Motif user interface toolkit.

Figure 1.5 shows the architecture of an application based on a widget set and the Xt Intrinsics. Xt and the Motif widget set are smoothly integrated with Xlib, so applications that use the facilities of the higher level library can also use the functions provided by Xlib when needed.

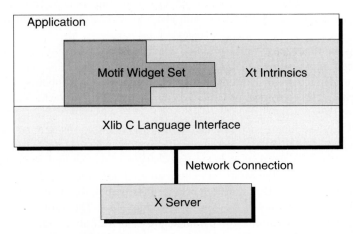

Figure 1.5 Architecture of a Motif/Xt application.

Widgets

All Xt applications use the API supported by Xt to create and manipulate widgets, regardless of the widget set being used. There are fundamentally two types of widgets: *display* widgets and *container* widgets. Display widgets present information to the user or accept input. Buttons, labels, and scrollbars are typical display widgets. Container widgets are used to group other widgets together on the screen. Container widgets can contain display widgets or other container widgets. In this way, widgets form a hierarchy similar to the X window hierarchy, known as a *widget tree*. The root of every widget tree must be a special type of container widget known as a *shell* widget. Shell widgets provide an interface between the application and the window manager.

Widget Classes

Xt defines an object-oriented architecture that supports *objects* and c*lasses* of objects. In nearly any object-oriented system, an object is simply a collection of data along with a set of functions that operate on that data. A *class* is a set of objects that have similar characteristics and usually the same structure. Individual objects are always *instances* of some class. In Xt, the most common type of object is the widget. Each type of widget has a data structure known as a *widget class* that describes the internal structure of widgets of that type.

When using Xt, the function `XtCreateWidget()` creates an instance of a widget class. For example, Motif supports an XmLabel widget class that can be used to display a string. The organization of this type of widget is defined by a structure, `xmLabelWidgetClass`. A specific label widget can be created as follows:

```
Widget label;
label = XtCreateWidget ( "label", xmLabelWidgetClass, parent, NULL, 0 );
```

Here, the widget `label` is an instance of the XmLabel widget class. The widget is created by passing the structure that describes the Motif XmLabel widget class to the Xt function `XtCreate-Widget()`.

Inheritance is another useful object-oriented concept supported by Xt. In most object-oriented systems, a class can inherit some or all the characteristics of another class, in much the same way that people inherit characteristics from their parents. When one class inherits characteristics from another, the inheriting class is known as a *subclass*, while the class from which the subclass inherits is known as a *superclass*.

Programmers can use inheritance to create new widget classes that extend the behavior of an existing widget class. Inheritance is also a useful concept when using existing widget classes because it is possible to characterize the behavior of a type of widget by knowing the classes from which it inherits. For example, the Motif set defines an XmLabel widget class that displays a string or image. Because the XmPushButton is a subclass of XmLabel, the XmPushButton widget class shares many of the characteristics of the XmLabel widget class. The XmPushButton widget class supports many of the same customizable parameters as the XmLabel widget class. However, the XmPushButton class adds some additional behavior to those features inherited from the XmLabel class.

Xt Widget Classes

Xt includes several basic widget classes that serve as superclasses for other widget classes. These widget classes define the architecture used by all other widgets, and also provide some fundamental characteristics inherited by all other widget classes. The widget classes implemented by Xt include:

Core The Core widget class is the most fundamental widget class, and serves as the superclass for all other widget classes. The Core widget class is not meant to be used directly, although it is occasionally used as a blank window in which to display text or graphics. The main purpose of the Core widget class is to provide some basic behavior that is shared by all other widget classes. All widget classes that inherit from Core support a user or programmer-configurable background color, width, height, position, and more.

Composite The Composite widget class is a subclass of the Core widget class, and like Core, is not meant to be used directly by application. All subclasses of the Composite widget class are known as composite widgets. Composite widgets have the ability to contain other widgets as *children*. A composite widget *manages* its children, which primarily means that composite widgets are responsible for determining the physical layout of all managed children. Each composite widget has a geometry manager that controls the location of each child widget according to the composite widget's management policy. Each subclass of Composite can implement its own layout policy.

Constraint The Constraint widget class is a subclass of the Composite widget class, and therefore can also manage children. Constraint widgets manage their children based on some additional information associated with each child. This information often takes the form of some *constraint* on the child's position or size. For example, children can be constrained to some minimum or maximum size, or they can be constrained to a particular location relative to another widget. The Constraint widget class is never used directly by applications.

Shell The Shell widget class is a subclass of the Composite widget class, but can have only one child. Shell widgets are special purpose widgets that provide an interface between other widgets and the window manager. A Shell widget negotiates the geometry of the application's top level window with the window manager, sets the properties required by the window manager, and generally handles the window manager protocol for the application, as defined by the ICCCM.

Xt also supports several subclasses of the Shell widget class. These include the Application-Shell, OverrideShell, and TransientShell widget classes. Each of these widget classes interacts with the window manager in a different way. The ApplicationShell is a "normal" window, which might be used as the main window of an application.

The OverrideShell widget class is completely ignored by window managers. The borders and other decorations that the window manager typically adds to ApplicationShell widgets are not added to OverrideShells. The OverrideShell widget class is useful for popup menus, for example.

The TransientShell widget class is used for windows that are expected to be displayed for a short period of time. For example, a dialog that asks the user a question might be based on the Transient-Shell widget class. Window managers typically do add decorations to transient windows, but often treat them differently than an application's top-level windows. For example, if an application's main window or windows are iconified, any transient windows are usually removed from the screen as well. Transient windows cannot be iconified individually.

Event Dispatching

Xt provides a strong model for how applications handle events sent by the X server. All Xt applications are expected to enter a continuous *event loop*. The Xt event loop continuously retrieves the next available event from the application's event queue and then *dispatches* the event to a widget within the application based on the window in which the event occurred. In many cases, the widget to which the event is dispatched can handle the event without requiring any action on the part of the application.

Xt also supports several mechanisms to allow applications to handle events directly. Xt supports *actions*, which allow applications to register a function with Xt to be called when a specific event or sequence of events occurs. The events are specified using a syntax supported by Xt that is both more flexible and higher level than X server events. For example, an individual key can be specified, as can combinations of keys (Control-Shift-A, for example). The mapping between sequences of events and actions to be performed is known as a *translation table*.

Xt also supports a *callback* mechanism. Callbacks are functions registered with a widget to be called when some widget-specific condition occurs. The condition that causes a callback to be invoked is usually related, at least indirectly, to an event. In some cases, though, the connection is not obvious. For example, the Core widget class supports a list of callbacks to be invoked when a widget is destroyed. Applications can register a function with a widget's destroy callback list, to be called whenever the widget is destroyed. Because all widgets are subclasses of Core, all widgets support this type of callback function.

The third mechanism supported by Xt is known as an *event handler*. An event handler is a function registered with Xt to be called when an X event occurs. Event handlers are the lowest level of these three mechanisms and are primarily intended to be used internally by Xt or within a widget. At times, event handlers are useful in applications. All three of the mechanisms are described in more detail later in this book.

Xt Resources

Although the X server supports data structures known as resources, Xt also uses the term resource to refer to customizable parameters supported by widgets. Xt provides the basic support for setting and retrieving widget resources. Almost every aspect of most widgets' appearance and behavior can be controlled using resources. For example, the Core widget class supports resources that control a widget's background color, width, height, and position. Widget resources can be set programmatically or retrieved from a simple database that allows resource values to be specified outside an application. Many widgets provide convenience functions that can be used to manipulate a widget's behavior, but widgets typically allow all characteristics to be specified through the resource mechanism.

1.3   Motif

Motif is a standard user interface toolkit developed and supported by the Open Software Foundation (OSF) and its member companies. Motif consists of several parts:

- *The Motif widget set* is based on the Xt Intrinsics. The standard Motif widgets include components that support user interaction, such as buttons, sliders, text editors, popup and pulldown menus, and so on. The Motif widget set also includes components that facilitate widget layouts, dialogs that can be used to display error and warning messages, and more.

- *The Motif Style Guide* contains rules and recommendations for achieving visual and behavioral consistency with other Motif applications.

- *The Motif window manager*, mwm, is an ICCCM-compliant window manager whose appearance and behavior complements the Motif widget set.

- *UIL* (User Interface Language) offers an alternative to the C-language programmatic interface for Motif-based applications. UIL is a language that can be used to describe an application's window layout in a separate file from the rest of the program.

This book uses the Motif widget set, and does not discuss UIL. The *Motif Style Guide* is discussed only to a limited extent, although its guidelines influence all Motif applications. Chapter 14 discusses how applications can interact with the window manager.

The Motif widget set contains many components, including scrollbars, menus, buttons, and so on, that can be combined to create user interfaces. Unlike Xlib and Xt (which provide only the underlying mechanisms), the Motif widget set supports a very specific appearance and behavior. Motif has a distinctive three-dimensional appearance and provides strong support for the interface style described in the *Motif Style Guide*.

Unlike Xlib and Xt, Motif is not freely available, but nearly all UNIX companies include Motif as part of their system software. Motif is also available from the OSF and many other sources for a fee. The Motif library is normally found in /usr/lib/libXm.a, and the header files are commonly installed in /usr/include/Xm. Examples in this book are based on Motif Version 1.2, which is based on the X11R5 Xt Intrinsics.

The most noticeable characteristic of the Motif widget set is its three-dimensional, bevelled appearance. Most Motif widgets contain a border whose top and left sides can be set to a different color than the bottom and right sides. By setting these areas to the appropriate colors, a three-dimensional shading effect can be achieved, as shown in Figure 1.6.

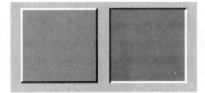

Figure 1.6 The Motif three dimensional shadow effect.

If a widget's top shadow is lighter than its background and the bottom shadow is darker than its background, the widget appears to protrude from the screen, as seen in the widget on the left in Figure 1.6. Reversing these colors makes the widget appear to be recessed into the screen, as demonstrated by the widget on the right side of Figure 1.6. The colors that create this three-dimensional effect can be set by the user or the programmer. By default, Motif automatically generates the appropriate top and bottom shadow colors, based on each widget's background color.

Although the Motif widget set is designed to encourage the programmer to follow the *Motif Style Guide*, most Motif widgets can be heavily customized. So, while Motif encourages a specific style, that style is not strictly enforced by the widget set. Programmers who want their applications to fit smoothly with other Motif-based applications should try to adhere to the conventions described in the style guide as closely as possible.

Motif Widgets

The widget classes provided by Motif can be divided into several categories based on the general functionality they offer. For example, some widgets display information, while others allow widgets to be grouped together in various combinations. The following sections describe the Motif widgets, divided into the following categories:

1. **Display or primitive widgets**. Primitive widgets are simple buttons, labels, text editors, and so on.

2. **Manager or container widgets**. Manager widgets are used to contain, or group, other widgets.

3. **Dialogs**. Dialogs are temporary windows, used to present some information to the user or ask questions.

4. **Menus**. Motif supports popup, pulldown, and option menus that allow the user to select from a set of choices.

5. **Gadgets**. Gadgets were designed to be more efficient versions of the Motif display widgets. Using gadgets in carefully selected situations can improve some program's perfor-

mance, although gadgets have some restrictions that can limit their use.

Display or Primitive Widgets

Motif provides many widgets whose primary purpose is to display information or to interact with the user. These widgets include:

XmArrowButton	XmDrawnButton	XmLabel
XmList	XmPushButton	XmScrollBar
XmSeparator	XmText	XmToggleButton
XmScale	XmCascadeButton	XmTextField

Figure 1.7 shows a collection of Motif primitive widgets.

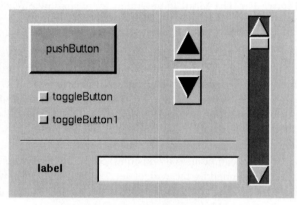

Figure 1.7 Primitive Motif widgets.

Manager or Container Widgets

The Motif widget set provides many widgets that can be used to combine other widgets into composite panels. Composite widgets allow endless combinations of buttons, scrollbars, text panes, and so on, to be grouped together in an application. Complex interfaces are constructed by combining display widgets or collections of display widgets in different arrangements. The layout of each collection of widgets is determined by the container widget that manages that collection.

The Motif container widgets include:

XmDrawingArea	XmFrame	XmMainWindow
XmRowColumn	XmForm	XmScrolledWindow
XmPanedWindow	XmBulletinBoard	

Figure 1.8 shows some layouts created by different Motif manager widgets.

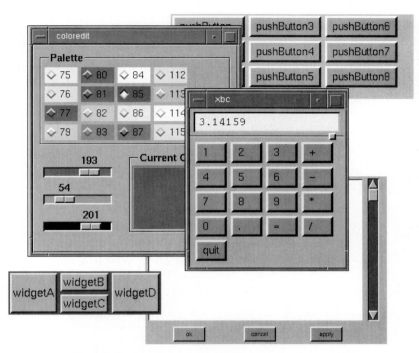

Figure 1.8 Typical window layouts produced using Motif.

Dialogs

Dialogs are temporary windows, usually used to display a message or ask a question of the user. Motif allows applications to design custom dialogs, and provides many commonly needed types of dialogs as ready-made widgets. Figure 1.9 shows some of the pre-defined Motif dialogs.

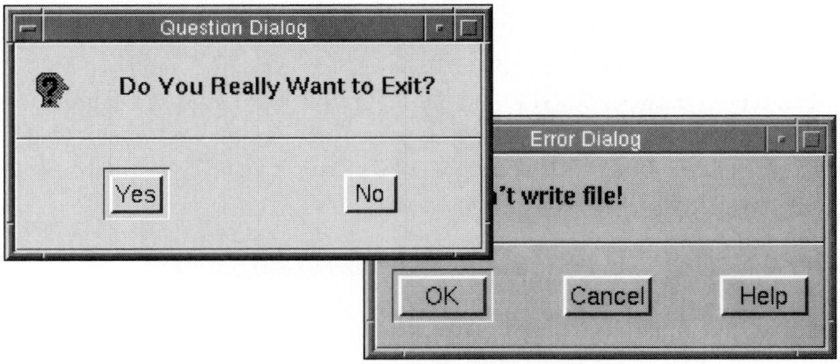

Figure 1.9 Typical Motif dialogs.

Menus

Motif provides several basic types of menus. These are popup menus, pulldown menus, option menus, and menu bars. Figure 1.10 shows a menu bar with a pulldown, cascading menu pane, while Figure 1.11 shows an option menu before and after it is popped up.

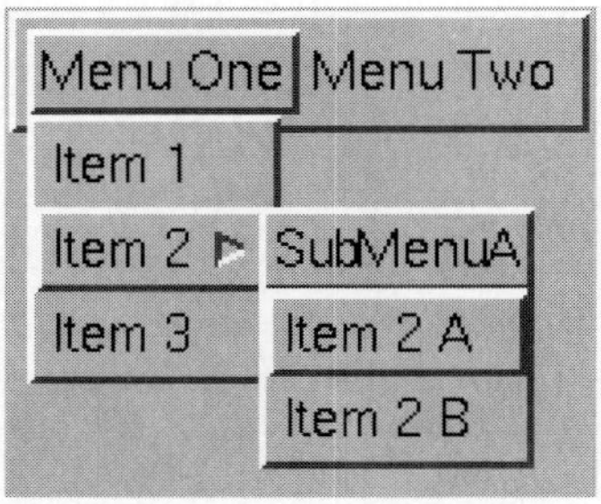

Figure 1.10   A Motif menu bar.

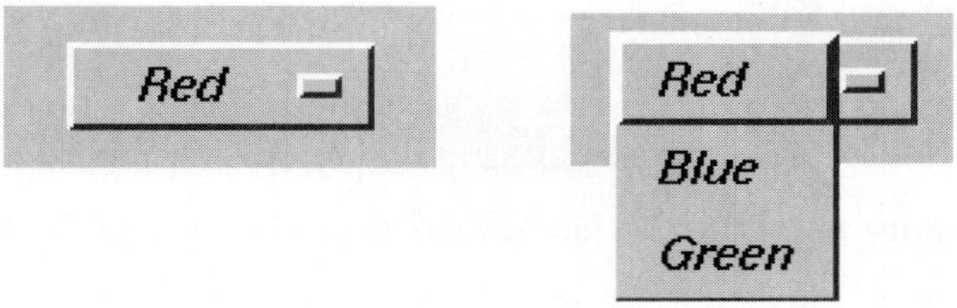

Figure 1.11   An option menu.

1.4   Naming and Coding Conventions

All examples in this book are written in ANSI C. Even readers who have not used ANSI C should find relatively few differences between ANSI C and the older non-ANSI style. The most obvious characteristics of ANSI C is the use of function prototypes to declare all arguments to a function. For example, in older versions of C, a function named `TestFunction()` that had no return value and expected two arguments could be declared simply as:

```
void TestFunction();   /* non-ANSI C declaration */
```

The definition of this function would look like this:

```
void TestFunction ( arg1, arg2 ) /* non-ANSI C Function */
    char *arg1, *arg2;
```

```
{
    /* Empty */
}
```

In ANSI C, function declarations must include the argument types expected by the function, using the form:

```
void TestFunction ( char *arg1, char *arg2 );
```

The argument names are optional, but are useful for those reading the code.

Similarly, when the function is implemented, it must be written as:

```
void TestFunction ( char *arg1, char *arg2 )
{
    /* Empty */
}
```

C has existed for so long that most C code continues to use the older style. However, at this point, nearly all hardware vendors are supporting ANSI C compilers, and Motif, X, and Xt are all written to support applications written using ANSI C. Using ANSI C offers several benefits over the older style, and is used exclusively in this book.

The first time a function is used in this book, the declaration of the function is shown, using the conventions of ANSI C function prototypes. For example, the first time the Xt Intrinsics function `XtAppNextEvent()` is discussed, the full function prototype is shown as:

```
void XtAppNextEvent ( XtAppContext app, XEvent *event )
```

Line Numbering

Most, though not all, code examples in this book form complete programs. To explain the various examples in detail, code may be interspersed with explanatory text. However, all complete examples are organized in files, as they would be written and stored on a system. To make it clear where files end and begin, all examples that represent complete files have line numbers. The line numbers make it easy to refer to a specific line in the code, and also serve to show how the code examples fit together. Lines of code that are intended to be placed in a unique file always start with line 1. Any time a code example begins with line 1, a new file is being started.

Xlib Conventions

Each X library described in this book follows its own naming convention. The names of all Xlib functions and user-accessible data structures begin with the capital letter X, and use a mixed case convention. When function names are composed of more than one word, the first letter of each word is capitalized. For example:

```
XCreateWindow()
XDrawString()
```

All Xlib macros also use a similar mixed case convention, but do not begin with the letter X. For example:

```
DisplayWidth()
ButtonPressMask
```

Xlib also follows some conventions intended to make it easier to remember the argument order used by each Xlib function. The first argument to nearly every Xlib function is a pointer to a `Display` structure. If the function requires a resource identifier as an argument, the resource ID immediately follows the display argument. *Drawable*s precede all other resources. A *drawable* is any resource that can be the object of a graphics request. In X, a drawable can be either a window or a *pixmap* (see Chapter 11). Whenever a function requires both a *source* and a *destination* drawable, the source argument always precedes the destination. When the function parameters include size and location specifications, *x* always precedes *y, width* always precedes *height,* and the *x,y* pair always precedes the *width, height* pair. For example, consider the argument order of the following Xlib function:

```
XDrawRectangle ( Display  *display,
                 Drawable  d,
                 GC        gc,
                 Position  x,
                 Position  y,
                 Dimension width,
                 Dimension height )
```

As specified by the argument ordering conventions, the first argument to `XDrawRect-angle()` is a pointer to a `Display` structure. The next two arguments are identifiers for server resources. The first of these is a drawable, and must precede the second resource, which is a *graphics context* (see Chapter 10). Finally, the *x, y* location precedes the width and height of the rectangle.

Xt Conventions

Xt uses naming conventions similar to those used by Xlib. All functions and macros use mixed case and begin with the letters `Xt`. Unlike Xlib, Xt does not distinguish between functions and macros. For example:

```
XtCreateWidget() /* Function */
XtSetArg()       /* Macro    */
```

Xt also uses string constants to specify names of resources. Defining strings as constants promotes consistency and also assists the programmer by allowing the compiler to detect spelling errors. These resource strings fall into three categories: resource *name strings,* resource *class strings,* and resource *representation strings.* Chapter 3 discusses the meaning of these terms. By convention, Xt composes resource name strings by adding the prefix `XtN` to the string. For example:

```
#define XtNwidth    "width"
```

Resource class strings use the prefix `XtC`:

```
#define XtCBackground    "Background"
```

An Xt resource representation string consists of the prefix `XtR` followed by the string:

```
#define XtRInt    "Int"
```

Motif Conventions

Different widget sets often follow their own conventions for naming functions, types, and variables. For example, nearly all external symbols and functions in the Motif widget set start with the letters `Xm`:

```
XmNlabelPixmap
XmTextGetString()
```

The Motif widget set also uses the `Xm` prefix when defining symbols for the resource strings used by the Motif widgets. For example:

```
#define XmNlabelString    "labelString"
```

In addition, Motif redefines the resource strings provided by Xt, using its own naming conventions. For example, Motif defines the symbol:

```
#define XmNwidth    "width"
```

The string, "width", is also represented by Xt as `XtNwidth`. Motif redefines all resource class strings to use the prefix `XmC`, and all resource representation strings to use the prefix `XmR`. This book uses the Motif versions of these symbols.

The class names of Motif widgets use a mixed case convention, and begin with the letters `Xm`. For example:

```
XmRowColumn
XmPushButton
```

By convention, each widget class pointer consists of the base name of the widget class followed by the word `WidgetClass`. In the Motif widget set, widget class pointers begin with the letters `xm`. For example:

```
xmRowColumnWidgetClass
xmPushButtonWidgetClass
```

1.5   Summary

This chapter presents a high-level overview of the architecture of the X Window System and introduces some basic terminology. X provides a powerful platform that allows programmers to develop sophisticated user interfaces that are portable to any system that supports the X protocol. Several libraries are useful when writing X applications. Xlib provides a low-level interface to the functionality of the X server. Xt provides a higher-level, somewhat object-oriented architecture that is simpler to use. Motif provides a collection of ready-made user interface components, based on the Xt library, that can be used to construct an application's interface.

The next chapter examines several simple programs that use Xt and Motif, while focusing on the core set of functions used by all Motif programs. Later chapters build on this basic information and explore how to use other features of Xlib, Xt and Motif.

Chapter 2

Programming with Xt

All examples in this book are based on the Motif user interface toolkit. However, when programming with Motif, or any Xt-based widget set, programmers primarily use facilities and functions provided by the Xt Intrinsics. Motif provides the specific widgets that appear on the screen, but much of the programmer's task involves using Xt functions to create and manipulate Motif widgets using the programming model defined by Xt. This chapter introduces some of the most commonly used Xt functions and shows how to write some simple Motif applications using these functions.

2.1 A Simple Motif Application: memo

This section presents a very simple Motif application that demonstrates the key features of any Xt application. This first example, a program named memo, displays a string in a window. The string is taken from the application's command line, which make the program useful for displaying brief notes or memos on the screen. The memo program can also be useful as a notifier, a window that can be displayed to post warnings or messages from within shell scripts. The example uses a single Motif widget, an XmLabel widget, to display the string. It also provides a first look at many Xt functions that are used in every Motif application.

```
1     /***********************************************
2      * memo.c: Display a string on the screen
3      ***********************************************/
4     #include <Xm/Xm.h>           /* Required by all Motif widgets */
5     #include <Xm/Label.h>        /* Required by XmLabel widget */
6     #include <stdlib.h>          /* Needed for exit() */
7     #include <stdio.h>           /* Needed to use fprintf */
8
9     void main ( int argc, char **argv )
10    {
11        Widget        shell, msg; /* Widgets created by this application */
12        XtAppContext app;         /* An application context, needed by Xt */
13        XmString      xmstr;      /* Compound string used by Motif */
14
15        /*
16         * Initialize Xt
17         */
18
19        shell = XtAppInitialize ( &app, "Memo", NULL, 0,
20                                  &argc, argv, NULL, NULL, 0 );
21
22        if ( argc != 2 ) /* Make sure there is exactly one argument */
23        {
24            fprintf (stderr, "Usage:  memo message-string\n" );
25            exit ( 1 );
26        }
27
28       /* Convert the first argument to the form expected by Motif */
29
30        xmstr = XmStringCreateLtoR ( argv[1], XmFONTLIST_DEFAULT_TAG );
31
32        /*
33         * Create a Motif XmLabel widget to display the string
34         */
35
36        msg = XtVaCreateManagedWidget ( "message",
37                                        xmLabelWidgetClass, shell,
38                                        XmNlabelString,     xmstr,
39                                        NULL );
40
41        XmStringFree ( xmstr );  /* Free the compound string */
42
43        /*
44         * Realize the shell and enter an event loop.
45         */
46
47        XtRealizeWidget ( shell );
48        XtAppMainLoop ( app );
49    }
```

Let's look briefly at each step of this example. Lines 4 through 7 specify several header files that must be included in the program. Every Motif application must include Xm.h before including any other Motif header files. In addition, each Motif widget has a corresponding header file, which must be included to use the widget. The header file Label.h includes definitions required by the XmLabel widget used in this example. The normal location of these header files is /usr/include/Xm, although the location can vary on different systems. Xm.h automatically includes many other header files, including the file Intrinsic.h, which is required by every Xt application. Intrinsic.h automatically includes various X11 header files, such as Xlib.h, which is required by every X11 application. The Xlib and Xt header files are normally located in /usr/include/X11.

Lines 11 through 13 declare several variables used in this program. The variables shell and msg represent widgets. Although there are many types of widgets (Label, PushButton, ScrollBar, and so on), all variables used to refer to widgets are simply declared as type Widget. Widget is an opaque type, which means that it is a pointer to a structure, whose contents you cannot access. Line 12 declares an XtAppContext. An XtAppContext is another opaque type, intended for use with systems that support multiple threads of execution in a single process. Several Xt functions require an application context as their first argument, although this feature is seldom, if ever, used by Xt applications.

All Motif applications must begin by initializing the Xt Intrinsics, normally by calling the function XtAppInitialize(). The many arguments to XtAppInitialize() include the *class name* of the application, which is "Memo", as well as the command-line arguments for this application. XtAppInitialize() expects to be passed a pointer to argc and the argv array of command-line arguments. Both argc and argv may be modified by XtAppInitialize(). Xt removes any command-line arguments it recognizes from argv and decrements argc accordingly. XtAppInitialize() is discussed in detail on page 29.

The first executable statement of the example, line 19, calls XtAppInitialize() to initialize the Xt Intrinsics, create an application context to be used by the rest of the application, and create a *shell* widget. A shell widget is a special type of widget supported by Xt that provides an interface between other widgets in an application and the window manager. Ordinary widgets cannot be created as direct children of the root window. All non-shell widgets must be direct or indirect children of a shell. A shell widget can contain only one direct child. In this example, the shell is used to contain a label widget that displays the user's string.

Once Xt has had an opportunity to remove certain command-line options, memo tests to see if the proper number of arguments has been provided. If not, the program prints a usage message, and exits. Otherwise, on line 30, memo creates a *compound string* to represent the message given in argv[1]. A compound string is an abstraction used by Motif that supports internationalized strings. Motif almost always uses compound strings rather than character strings. Compound strings are declared as an opaque type, XmString. The function XmStringCreateLtoR() creates a compound string from the data given as its first argument to be displayed using a *character set* specified by the second argument. In this case, the symbol XmFONTLIST_DEFAULT_TAG indicates that this string should be displayed with a default font. Character sets and fonts are discussed in more detail in Chapter 12.

Next, memo calls the function XtVaCreateManagedWidget(). This Xt function, called on line 36, creates a Motif XmLabel widget to display the string retrieved from the command line. The first argument to XtVaCreateManagedWidget() is a string that specifies a name for the new widget. The second argument identifies the type of widget to be created. The symbol `xmLabelWidgetClass` identifies the Motif XmLabel widget class. This identifier, which is known as the widget's *class pointer*, is defined in the Label.h header file included at the beginning of memo.c. The third argument indicates that this widget is to be created as a child of the shell widget returned by `XtAppInitialize()`. The remaining arguments specify optional parameters, called *resources*, that affect how the widget appears or behaves. Any number of resource name/value pairs can be specified, followed by a terminating `NULL`. In this case, only one resource is specified. The symbol `XmNlabelString` identifies the string to be displayed by the XmLabel widget. The XmLabel widget makes a local copy of the string to be displayed, so the space allocated for the compound string should be freed when the string is no longer needed. The function `XmStringFree()`, called on line 41, must be used to free a compound string.

The next step, on line 47, is to *realize* the shell widget by calling `XtRealizeWidget()`. Realizing a widget creates an X window in which the widget can display itself. Realizing a widget also causes the widget's children, in this case the XmLabel widget, to be realized. Finally, `memo` calls `XtAppMainLoop()` on line 48 to begin processing events. `XtAppMainLoop()` contains an endless loop that waits for and processes events. It never returns.

At this point, the message window appears on the screen. The XmLabel widget automatically handles all resize and exposure events that may occur.

The parent/child relationships between widgets created by an Xt program create a hierarchy known as a *widget tree*. Figure 2.1 shows the widget tree formed by the `memo` example. Widget trees are presented in this book with each widget's class name shown in italics below the widget's name. Most, but not all, widget trees directly correspond to the X window hierarchy created by the application. The `memo` widget tree is very simple, but later examples will produce much more complex widget trees.

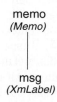

memo
(Memo)

msg
(XmLabel)

Figure 2.1   The widget tree created by `memo`.

Building and Using memo

The `memo` example can be compiled and linked with the various X libraries with the UNIX shell command:

```
cc -o memo memo.c -lXm -lXt -lX11
```

This command compiles the file memo.c and links Xlib, the Xt library, and the Motif library with the resulting binary file to create the program. The ordering of the libraries is significant. All widget libraries must precede the Intrinsics library, which must precede the Xlib library. In some environments, additional libraries may be needed. One commonly needed library is libPW.a, which is required by Motif on some systems. You may also need libXext, which contains Xlib extensions.

The memo program can be executed by typing "memo", along with an argument, in a terminal emulator. For example, executing the command:

```
% memo "Hello World"
```

produces the message window shown in Fig. 2.2. Notice that messages that contain spaces must be enclosed in quotes.

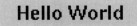

Figure 2.2 The memo message window.

Depending on the window manager used on your system, memo may appear complete with a title bar and other decorations added by the window manager. Fig. 2.3 shows the memo window with a title bar and several other controls added by the Motif window manager, mwm. These additional controls allow you to iconify the application, change its size and shape, and exit the program.

Figure 2.3 The memo window with window manager decorations.

One practical application of memo is to invoke it from a *makefile*. A makefile is a script used by the UNIX make utility, which manages compilation of applications. For example, consider a basic makefile that can be used to build memo itself:

```
##############################
# Makefile for memo.c
##############################
memo:memo.o
     cc -o memo memo.o -lXm -lXt -lX11
     memo "Program Compiled Successfully"
```

Now, the shell command:

```
% make memo
```

builds memo and uses memo itself to announce a successful compilation.

Although `memo` does not appear to provide any way to exit the application, most window managers support some standard way to exit any program. For example, the Motif window manager allows users to issue a quit command from a menu pane attached to the upper left corner of the window manager frame. The window manager uses a protocol defined by the ICCCM to inform the application that it should exit. Although applications can intercept this message and handle it if necessary, simple applications like `memo` usually just allow the application to exit. In this case, the details of the ICCCM window manager protocol are handled by Motif.

2.2   The Xt Programming Model

Xt provides programmers with a well-defined model for writing applications. All X applications are normally designed to be *event-driven*. Programs create an initial set of windows and then enter an event loop. As each event arrives, the program examines the event and processes it according to some logic in the program. Applications based on Xlib usually have a `switch` statement inside an event loop. The `switch` statement looks at the type of each event and performs some action based on the information in the event. If the application uses multiple windows, the program also has to determine in which window the event occurred and take that into consideration. For applications with many windows, such `switch` statements can become quite long and very complex.

Xt builds on the Xlib event model to create what might be called a *dispatch-driven* programming model, in which all events are automatically routed to the appropriate user interface component. Programmers who use Xt write small functions to deal with specific events that occur within each widget. These functions are expected to perform a brief action in response to the event and return quickly to allow the application to handle the next event.

Most applications that use Xt or Motif follow a similar format, and every Xt application performs several basic steps. These are:

1. **Initialize the Intrinsics.** This step establishes a connection to the X server, allocates resources, and initializes the Intrinsics layer. There are several individual Xt functions that can be used to perform various parts of this stage. However, `XtAppInitialize()` can be used to handle all initialization in a single step, as demonstrated in the previous section.

2. **Create widgets.** Every program creates one or more widgets to construct the program's user interface. Normally, the initialization stage creates a shell widget that serves as a container for all other widgets. Additional widgets can be created as needed.

3. **Register callbacks.** Callbacks are application-defined functions that can be used to respond to user actions and events that occur within each widget. The `memo` example in the previous section is so simple that no callbacks are used.

4. **Realize all widgets.** Realizing a widget creates the X window used by the widget. Normally, only the root of a widget hierarchy (a shell) is realized explicitly. `XtRealize-Widget()` traverses the widget tree and realizes all children in the correct order.

5. **Enter an event loop.** Most X applications are completely event-driven, and are designed

to loop indefinitely responding to events. The event loop retrieves events from the X event queue and dispatches the event to the appropriate event handler or callback function associated with the widget in which the event occurred.

Within this basic framework, the details of individual applications may vary widely, of course. However, most applications differ primarily in how they organize widgets and what callbacks and other input handlers they implement. The memo program in the previous section demonstrates most of these steps. Even as later chapters present more sophisticated examples, these basic stages will still be evident.

2.3 Essential Xt Functions

The simple example in Section 2.1 demonstrates several key Xt functions with only minimal explanation. This section discusses these functions in more detail and introduces some other commonly used Xt functions. Besides supporting the programming model described in Section 2.2, these Xt functions provide the primary application programmer's interface (API) used to create and manipulate all widgets, regardless of the widget set being used.

Initialization

Motif applications, like all X applications, must begin by establishing a connection to the X server. Like all Xt applications, Motif applications must also perform some initialization of the Xt Intrinsics before calling any other Xt function. The simplest way to establish a connection to the X server and initialize Xt is to call the function:

```
Widget XtAppInitialize ( XtAppContext    *appContext,
                         const String     className,
                         XrmOptionDescList options,
                         Cardinal          numOptions,
                         Cardinal         *argc,
                         char            **argv,
                         const String     *fallbackResources,
                         ArgList           args,
                         Cardinal          numArgs )
```

XtAppInitialize() is normally called before any other Xt function. This function is a convenience function that performs several steps with a single call. XtAppInitialize() initializes various Xt data structures, opens a connection to the X server, and creates and returns a shell widget. Applications that require more control over the initialization process can call the functions XtToolkitInitialize(), XtCreateApplicationContext(), XtOpen-Display(), and XtAppCreateShell() to perform these steps individually. For most applications, XtAppInitialize() is the preferred choice.

The first argument to `XtAppInitialize()` returns an *application context*, an opaque data structure that is required by many other Xt functions. The application must provide an application context by declaring a variable of type `XtAppContext` and passing its address to `XtApp-Initialize()`. Every application must create one application context. Because many Xt functions require an application context as the first parameter, it is often necessary to declare the application context as a global variable to make it accessible throughout the program.

The second argument to `XtAppInitialize()`, `className`, is a string that specifies the *class* of the application. By convention, the application's class name should be the intended name of the program, with the first letter changed to be upper-case, unless the name of the application starts with the letter X, in which case the first two letters are changed to upper-case. So the class name of a program named "emacs" should be "Emacs", but the class name of a program named "xterm" should be "XTerm". The X resource manager uses the name and class of an application to determine what customizable resources affect the program. Window managers may also use the application's class name in various ways.

The second and third arguments to `XtAppInitialize()` are used to supply a description of additional command-line arguments that should be recognized by the application. All Xt applications recognize a number of common command-line options. (These are discussed in Chapter 3.) The `options` argument allows applications to add application-specific arguments to those already recognized by Xt. If no additional options are required, as in the `memo` example, the `options` argument can be given as `NULL`. Chapter 3 demonstrates how to use Xt to handle an application's additional command-line arguments.

The fifth argument to `XtAppInitialize()` must be the *address* of `argc`, followed by the array `argv`, as passed to the application from the command line. Xt searches the `argv` array for command-line options it recognizes. If any are found, Xt destructively removes them and places them in the application's resource database. The value of `argc` is decremented accordingly.

Most Xt applications have an associated application resource file that specifies the values of various customizable parameters used by the widgets in the application. Typically, the application resource file is found in /usr/lib/X11/app-defaults/<*class*>, where <*class*> is the class name of the application. Some applications need to be sure certain parameters are set to function properly. In this case, the required resource specifications can be passed as a `NULL`-terminated array of strings to `XtAppInitialize()` as *fallback resources*. If the application resource file does not exist, the resources specified in the `fallbackResources` argument are used. If no fallback resources are required, the `fallbackResources` argument can be given as `NULL`. (See Chapter 3 for more information about fallback resources and resource files.)

After initializing the Intrinsics, `XtAppInitialize()` creates and returns an Application-Shell widget. A shell widget serves as a container for other widgets created by the application. The last two arguments to `XtAppInitialize()` allow the program to specify additional arguments, in the form of an `ArgList`, to be passed to the shell widget created by `XtAppInitialize()`. Later sections discuss how to use an `ArgList` to customize widgets.

Creating Widgets

Xt provides several functions that can be used to create any type of widget. The `memo` example in Section 2.1 creates only one widget in addition to the shell, a Motif XmLabel widget that displays a string. The function used in that example, `XtVaCreateManagedWidget()`, is a convenience function that performs several operations with a single call. The most primitive Xt function that can be used to create a widget is `XtCreateWidget()`, which has the following form:

```
Widget XtCreateWidget ( const String    name,
                        WidgetClass     widgetClass,
                        Widget          parent,
                        ArgList         args,
                        Cardinal        numArgs );
```

`XtCreateWidget()` creates and returns a widget, which must be declared as type `Widget` by the program. For example, the following function creates and returns a ScrollBar widget named "scroller" as a child of another widget.

```
Widget CreateScrollBar ( Widget parent )
{
    Widget scroll_bar;

    scroll_bar = XtCreateWidget ( "scroller", xmScrollBarWidgetClass,
                                  parent, NULL, 0 );
    return ( scroll_bar );
}
```

The first argument to `XtCreateWidget()` specifies the name of the widget to be created. A widget's name can be an arbitrary character string, but should ideally be unique, at least within any set of widgets that share the same parent. (The reason for using unique widget names will become clear in Chapter 3.) The widget class is a pointer to the widget class structure declared in the public header file of the widget to be created. In the memo example, the class pointer for the XmLabel widget class was `xmLabelWidgetClass`. In general, the class pointer for a particular widget class can be determined by looking in the widget's header file, or consulting a reference manual for the widget set being used. However, Motif uses a straightforward naming convention that makes it easy to remember the class pointer of any widget class. All class pointers start with the letters xm, followed by the basic class name of the widget (i.e., Label, RowColumn, PushButton), followed by the word WidgetClass. So the class pointer for the XmLabel widget is `xmLabelWidgetClass`, the class pointer for the XmRowColumn widget is `xmRowColumnWidgetClass`, and so on.

The third argument to `XtCreateWidget()` specifies the parent of the new widget. Except for Shell widgets, every widget must have a parent. In the memo example, the shell widget returned by `XtAppInitialize()` serves as a parent for the XmLabel widget. The last two arguments to `XtCreateWidget()` specify an array of additional arguments that modify the widget's appearance or behavior. The purpose and use of these arguments is discussed shortly.

Motif also provides a convenience function for each widget class, which can be used instead of `XtCreateWidget()`. These functions have the form:

```
Widget XmCreate<widgetClass> ( Widget      parent,
                               String      name,
                               ArgList     args,
                               Cardinal    numArgs )
```

where *<widgetClass>* is replaced by the type of widget to be created. For example, the function `XmCreateLabel()` creates a new XmLabel widget, while the function `XmCreateRow-Column()` creates an XmRowColumn widget. Notice that the argument order of these convenience functions differs from the argument order of `XtCreateWidget()`. In `XtCreateWidget()`, the name of the widget precedes the parent, while the convenience functions use the reverse order.

Xt also supports *vararg* versions of many functions, including the widget creation functions. These functions accept a variable number of parameters in place of an `ArgList`. The names of all vararg functions begin with the prefix `XtVa`. One such function is `XtVaCreateWidget()`, which can be used in place of `XtCreateWidget()`. Vararg functions are discussed in more detail in the following section. There are currently no vararg versions of the Motif convenience functions.

Customizing Widgets

Programmers can alter the default behavior of most widgets by providing additional parameters when the widget is created. These additional arguments can be passed to `XtCreateWidget()` or `XtCreateManagedWidget()` using an `ArgList`. An `ArgList` is an array of type `Arg`, which is declared as:

```
typedef struct {
    String   name;
    XtArgVal value;
} Arg, *ArgList;
```

The `name` member of the `Arg` structure is a string that specifies a customizable parameter supported by the widget, while the `value` member indicates a value for the parameter. These customizable widget parameters are called *resources*. If the size of the value stored in the `value` member is less than or equal to the size of `XtArgVal`, the value is stored directly in the `Arg` structure. Otherwise the `value` member of a structure must represent a pointer to the value. The definition of `XtArgVal` is system-dependent, but is generally the size of an address.

`XtCreateWidget()` allows a list of values to be passed to a widget at creation time. The widget compares the resource names in the list against those it recognizes, and copies the corresponding values for its own use.

An `ArgList` can be created as a statically initialized array of `Arg` structures. For example, the width and height of a widget can be specified by creating the following argument list:

```
static Arg args[ ] = {
    { XmNwidth,  300 },
    { XmNheight, 400 },
};
```

This code segment specifies values for two resources in an `Arg` array. The first parameter in each member of the array is a macro defined by Motif to represent a character string. For example, the macros used above might be defined as:

```
#define XmNwidth    "width"
#define XmNheight   "height"
```

Using these macros instead of strings allows the compiler to catch spelling errors that might go unnoticed if character strings were used directly.

The `Arg` array declared above can be used as an argument to `XtCreateWidget()`, like this:

```
XtCreateWidget ( "sample", xmPushButtonWidgetClass,
                 parent, args, XtNumber ( args ) );
```

This statement creates a widget 300 pixels wide and 400 pixels high. The macro `XtNumber()` determines the length of a fixed-size array. Using `XtNumber()` allows the programmer to change the size of the `Arg` array easily and eliminates the use of "magic numbers" in the code to indicate the length of the array. In some programs, the definition of the `Arg` array might be placed in a separate header file, or even used in multiple places, which makes it difficult to keep track of a hard-coded number.

Instead of using a statically initialized array, it is often convenient to create an empty array and to use the following macro to initialize each entry:

```
XtSetArg ( Arg arg, String name, XtArgVal value )
```

`XtSetArg()` is often used with a counter, as shown in the code segment below. Because `XtSetArg()` is a macro that evaluates its first parameter twice, the counter must not be incremented inside the macro.

```
int n;
Arg args[10];

/* Other code ... */
n = 0;
XtSetArg ( args[n], XmNwidth,  200 ); n++;
XtSetArg ( args[n], XmNheight, 300 ); n++;
XtCreateWidget ( name, xmRowColumnWidgetClass, parent, args, n );
```

Using a consistent style such as the one used here helps to minimize mistakes when using `XtSetArg()`.

Using `XtSetArg()` to initialize an `Arg` array has one primary advantage over the static initialization approach described earlier. Using `XtSetArg()` allows the programmer to place the values of the resources used by a widget close to the point in the program where the widget is created. Placing resource declarations near the widgets they affect often produces programs that are easier to understand because it is easier to see which resources have been specified for each widget. On the other hand, lengthy `Arg` lists make a program longer and hide the structure of a program.

Varargs

Instead of constructing an `ArgList`, it is often more convenient to use the vararg versions of various Xt functions. For example, the code segment shown above can be modified to use `XtVaCreateWidget()` as follows:

```
XtVaCreateWidget ( name, xmRowColumnWidgetClass, parent,
                   XmNwidth,   200,
                   XmNheight, 300,  NULL );
```

Any number of resources can be specified in name/value pairs as arguments to `XtVaCreate-Widget()`. The final argument *must* be a NULL to terminate the argument list.

The simplest form of vararg functions uses name/value pairs, as shown above. However, there is a second form that can sometimes be useful. Sometimes resources need to be converted from one form to another before a widget can use them. For example, the character string retrieved from the command line of the `memo` example has to be converted to a compound string, as expected by the Motif XmLabel widget. The `memo` example shows how a compound string can be explicitly created and destroyed. Using an alternate form supported by the Xt vararg functions, Xt can convert between a character string and a compound string automatically.

Using the vararg form, a string to be displayed in an XmLabel widget can be specified as follows:

```
XtVaCreateWidget ( name, xmLabelWidgetClass, parent,
                   XtVaTypedArg, XmNlabelString, XmRString,
                   "hello", strlen ( "hello" ) + 1,
                   NULL );
```

Here, the symbol `XtVaTypedArg` specifies that a typed resource specification follows, rather than a simple name/value pair. The next symbol, `XmNlabelString`, specifies the name of the resource. Next, `XmRString` indicates the type of the value being provided. `XmRString` is a symbol defined by Motif that represents a character string. Finally, the value, in the form of a string, is given, followed by the size of the value, in bytes. This code segment automatically converts the character string "hello" into an equivalent compound string because that is the type expected by the XmLabel widget for its `XmNlabelString` resource. One advantage offered by the Xt vararg functions is that the compound string is freed automatically when it is no longer needed.

Setting Resource Values

Many widget resources can be altered after a widget has been created by constructing an `ArgList` and calling the function:

```
void XtSetValues ( Widget    w,
                   ArgList   args,
                   Cardinal  numArgs )
```

For example, the following code segment specifies a size for an XmRowColumn widget by creating the widget first, and then specifying the desired size:

```
  int    n;
  Arg    args[10];
  Widget rc;

  /* Other code ... */
```

```
rc = XtCreateWidget ( name, xmRowColumnWidgetClass, parent, args, n );
n = 0;
XtSetArg ( args[n], XmNwidth,  200 ); n++;
XtSetArg ( args[n], XmNheight, 300 );n++;
XtSetValues ( rc, args, n );
```

There is also a vararg version of **XtSetValues()**:

```
void XtVaSetValues ( Widget, ... , NULL )
```

Using **XtVaSetValues()**, the above code segment can be written as follows:

```
Widget rc;
/* Other code ... */
rc = XtCreateWidget ( name, xmRowColumnWidgetClass, parent, NULL, 0 );
XtVaSetValues ( rc,
                XmNwidth,  200,
                XmNheight, 300,
                NULL );
```

Both the vararg and non-vararg techniques are useful. The non-vararg variations of Xt functions are particularly useful when the same arguments need to be applied to multiple widgets, and when different parameters are to be passed to the widget depending on the program state. For example, consider the following hypothetical function:

```
void CreateTextFields ( Widget parent, Boolean readOnly )
{
    Widget t1, t2, t3;
    Arg    args[10];
    int    n;

    n = 0;

    if ( readOnly ) /* If readOnly, set additional resources */
    {
        XtSetArg ( args[n], XmNeditable, FALSE ); n++;
        XtSetArg ( args[n], XmNbackground, ReadOnlyPixel ); n++
    }

    /* Create three text fields, passing same arguments to each */

    t1 = XtCreateWidget ( "t1", xmTextWidgetClass, parent, args, n );
    t2 = XtCreateWidget ( "t2", xmTextWidgetClass, parent, args, n );
    t3 = XtCreateWidget ( "t3", xmTextWidgetClass, parent, args, n );
}
```

The **ArgList** form must also be used when using the Motif convenience functions to create widgets because these functions do not have vararg versions. The vararg versions of the various Xt functions are, in general, slightly more expensive that the non-vararg equivalents. It is also easy to introduce serious errors by forgetting the terminating NULL required by these functions. On the other hand, the static Arg arrays used by the non-vararg functions are also a source of errors. The simpler form of the vararg functions can make programs more readable, and these functions are nearly always more convenient to use.

Retrieving Resources

It is often necessary to retrieve the current value of a widget resource. This is easy to do, using the function:

```
XtGetValues ( Widget widget, ArgList arglist, Cardinal nargs )
```

The argument arglist must be an Arg array that specifies pairs of resource names and addresses of variables allocated by the calling function. XtGetValues() retrieves the named resources from the specified widget and copies each item into each given address if the size of the retrieved resource is less than the size of XtArgVal. Otherwise, XtGetValues() stores a pointer to the resource in the location specified by the application.

For example, the following code fragment retrieves the width and height of a widget, and also a character string kept in a hypothetical XmNvalue resource:

```
Arg          args[10];
Dimension    width, height;
char         *str;

int          n = 0;
XtSetArg ( args[n], XmNwidth,  &width ); n++;
XtSetArg ( args[n], XmNheight, &height ); n++;
XtSetArg ( args[n], XmNvalue,  &str ); n++;
XtGetValues ( widget, args, n );
```

When XtGetValues() returns, width and height are initialized to the values of the widget's XmNwidth and XmNheight resources.

Notice that width and height are declared as type Dimension in this code fragment. Declaring variables as the wrong type when retrieving resources is a common error that can result in subtle bugs because Xt copies the data bitwise into the provided address. A common error is to request the width, height, or position of a widget as an int. The width and height of all widgets should be retrieved as type Dimension, while a widget's x,y position must be declared as type Position.

Although width and height contain copies of the widget's resources in the above example, the variable str contains a *pointer* to the widget's XmNvalue resource. This is because the size of Dimension is smaller than or equal to the size of XtArgVal, but the size of the entire character string is greater than the size of XtArgVal. Instead of copying the entire string, XtGetValues() copies the *address* of the resource into str. If the calling application intends to modify this string, it should allocate space for the string and copy it.

In addition to `XtGetValues()`, there is a vararg version, `XtVaGetValues()`, which works similarly. For example, the previous example could also be written:

```
Dimension  width, height;
char       *str;

XtVaGetValues ( widget,
                XmNwidth,  &width,
                XmNheight, &height,
                XmNvalue,  &str,
                NULL );
```

Managing Widgets

All widgets except shell widgets must be *managed* by a parent widget. A widget's parent manages the child's size and location, determines whether or not the child is visible, and may also control input to the child. For example, some widgets arrange their children to form rows and columns, while others group their children into resizable panes. Still others allow the user or the programmer to specify the location of each child widget.

To add a widget to its parent's managed set, applications must call the function:

```
void XtManageChild ( Widget child )
```

It is often more convenient to create and manage a widget in a single step by calling the function:

```
Widget XtCreateManagedWidget ( const String  name,
                               WidgetClass   widgetClass,
                               Widget        parent,
                               ArgList       args,
                               Cardinal      numArgs )
```

There is also a vararg version of this function:

```
Widget XtVaCreateManagedWidget ( const String  name,
                                 WidgetClass   widgetClass,
                                 Widget        parent,
                                 ...,
                                 NULL )
```

These functions are convenient for the programmer, but are not always the best way to create and manage widgets. When a widget is managed, its parent is notified, if the parent is already realized. Often the parent widget must perform some calculation or rearrange its other children to handle the new widget properly. When adding children to a parent that has already been realized, it is more efficient to create a group of widgets first, and then manage them at the same time, by passing an array of widgets to the function:

```
void XtManageChildren ( WidgetList widgetlist, Cardinal numWidgets )
```

A `WidgetList` is simply an array of type `Widget`. Managing multiple children at once reduces the work a parent widget must do, because the widget can compute the layout of all children once rather than each time an individual widget is managed. Managing widgets in groups is only important when adding children to a widget that has already been realized. If a parent widget has not yet been realized, Xt does not notify the parent when children are managed. Instead, the parent is notified all at once when it is realized.

Other Widget Functions

Xt provides many other functions associated with widgets. This section describes a few of the more commonly used functions. Others will be discussed as they are needed in later chapters.

`XtCreateWidget()` allocates and initializes the data structures associated with a widget, but does not create the window in which the widget displays itself. The function:

```
void XtRealizeWidget ( Widget widget )
```

creates a window for a widget. Once `XtRealizeWidget()` is called for a given widget, that widget is said to be *realized*. If a widget has children, `XtRealizeWidget()` also calls itself recursively for each of its children. Notice that it is an error to realize a widget if its parent is unrealized, because the window owned by the parent widget must exist before the child's window can be created. Normally, applications simply call `XtRealizeWidget()` once, giving the top level shell widget as an argument.

It is often useful to know whether a widget is realized, particularly when mixing widgets with Xlib functions that operate on windows. Applications can use the function:

```
Boolean XtIsRealized ( Widget widget )
```

to check if a widget is realized.

Many simple programs create all the widgets used within the application upon start-up and never change the interface while the program is running. However, other applications may need to dynamically create and destroy widgets. The function:

```
void XtDestroyWidget ( Widget widget )
```

destroys a widget and its children, and frees any server resources used by the widget. The X server also automatically frees all resources used by an application, including the window used by each widget when the program exits or otherwise breaks its connection to the server. Therefore, it is not necessary to destroy widgets before exiting.

Many Xt functions require an application context as their first argument, and it is often convenient to declare this structure globally. However, the current application context can be retrieved from any widget using the following function:

```
XtAppContext XtWidgetToApplicationContext ( Widget widget )
```

Most Xt functions operate on widgets. However, Xlib functions cannot deal directly with widgets, and instead require a pointer to a `Display` structure, window IDs, and so on, which are normally hidden from the programmer by Xt and Motif. Xt provides several functions that are useful when combining Xlib and widgets. These functions retrieve the data structures and resource IDs required by Xlib functions from a widget. The function:

```
Display *XtDisplay ( Widget widget )
```

returns a pointer to the Xlib `Display` structure used by the widget, while:

```
Screen *XtScreen ( Widget widget )
```

returns a pointer to the Xlib `Screen` structure used by the widget. The `Display` pointer and `Screen` structure can be retrieved as soon as the widget has been created.

All Xlib graphics functions operate on windows, not widgets. The function:

```
Window XtWindow ( Widget widget )
```

retrieves the ID of the window used by the widget. A widget's window ID will be `NULL` if the widget has not yet been realized. Chapter 13 demonstrates how to mix widgets and Xlib graphics routines.

Event Dispatching

When an event is received by an application, Xt looks up the widget that corresponds to the window in which the event has occurred and looks for a function registered by the widget to respond to the event. If Xt finds such a function, Xt invokes it automatically. The procedure of finding the proper widget and invoking the appropriate function for an event is known as *dispatching* the event. The function:

```
XtDispatchEvent ( XEvent *event )
```

dispatches a single event.

Applications can use the function:

```
void XtAppNextEvent ( XtAppContext app, XEvent *event )
```

to obtain the next event from the X event queue. `XtAppNextEvent()` waits until an event is available in the application's event queue. When an event is available, `XtAppNextEvent()` returns after copying the event at the head of the queue into an event structure supplied by the application. `XtAppNextEvent()` also removes the event from the queue.

Because most Xt applications are entirely event-driven, the heart of nearly every Xt application is a loop that retrieves events from the X event queue and then uses `XtDispatchEvent()` to dispatch the event to the appropriate widget. This event loop can be written as:

```
while ( TRUE )
{
    XEvent event;
    XtAppNextEvent ( &app, event );
    XtDispatchEvent ( &event );
}
```

Because this code segment is almost always identical in every X application, Xt provides it as a function:

```
XtAppMainLoop ( XtAppContext app )
```

Notice that there is no way to exit the Xt main event loop. Applications must arrange another way to exit.

2.4   Handling Input

Like all Motif applications, the example application discussed in Section 2.1 handles many events automatically. The message displayed by the XmLabel widget is redrawn when necessary, and the XmLabel widget automatically repositions the message in the center of the window when the application is resized. It is even possible to exit the program using a window manager menu.

However, memo makes no provision for directly handling user input. This section examines two techniques for handling user input in a Motif application. The first technique is based on an Xt facility known as the *translation manager*, while the second involves registering *callback functions* with the widgets in the application.

Using the Translation Manager

Xt's translation manager is a mechanism that allows programmers as well as end users to specify mappings between user actions and functions provided by a widget or an application. All user actions correspond to events. The translation manager provides a way to specify how certain events or sequences of events should be dispatched.

This section describes a new version of memo that uses the translation manager to define an programmatic response to a user action. This example adds the ability to exit the application when a specific key is typed in the window. Any key can be used, but for purposes of demonstration, memo uses the letter "Q", for "Quit". The basic structure of this example is similar to the memo program described in Section 2.1. Sections of code that are different from the previous version, or completely new, are shown in bold.

```
1   /**************************************************
2    * memo2.c: Display a string on the screen
3    *          Allow users to exit by typing a "Q"
4    **************************************************/
5   #include <Xm/Xm.h>            /* Required by all Motif widgets */
6   #include <Xm/Label.h>         /* Required by XmLabel widget */
7   #include <stdlib.h>           /* Needed for exit() */
8   #include <stdio.h>            /* Needed to use fprintf */
9
10  /* Dclaration of Action function */
11
12  static void QuitAction ( Widget    w,
13                           XEvent    *ev,
14                           String    *params,
15                           Cardinal *numParams );
16
17  /* Register the function quitAction under the symbolic name "bye" */
18
19   static XtActionsRec actionsTable [] = {
20      { "bye",   QuitAction },
21   };
22
23  /* Bind the action "bye()" to typing the key "Q" */
24
25  static char defaultTranslations[] =   "<Key>Q:  bye()";
26
27  void main ( int argc, char **argv )
28  {
29      Widget         shell, msg;
30      XtAppContext   app;
31      XmString       xmstr;
32      XtTranslations transTable; /* Compiled translations */
33
34      /*
35       * Initialize Xt
36       */
37
38      shell = XtAppInitialize ( &app, "Memo",  NULL, 0,
39                                &argc, argv, NULL, NULL, 0 );
40
41      if ( argc != 2 ) /* Make sure there is exactly one argument */
42      {
43          fprintf (stderr, "Usage:  memo message-string\n" );
44          exit ( 1 );
45      }
46
47      /* Register the action functions */
48
49      XtAppAddActions ( app, actionsTable, XtNumber ( actionsTable ) );
```

```
50
51      /* Compile the translation table */
52
53      transTable =  XtParseTranslationTable ( defaultTranslations );
54
55      /* Convert the first argument to the form expected by Motif */
56
57      xmstr = XmStringCreate ( argv[1], XmFONTLIST_DEFAULT_TAG );
58
59      /*
60       * Create the XmLabel widget
61       */
62
63      msg = XtVaCreateManagedWidget ( "message",
64                                       xmLabelWidgetClass, shell,
65                                       XmNlabelString,     xmstr,
66                                       NULL );
67
68      XmStringFree ( xmstr );  /* Free the compound string */
69
70      /*
71       * Merge the new translations with any existing
72       * translations for the label widget.
73       */
74
75      XtAugmentTranslations ( msg, transTable );
76
77      /*
78       * Realize the shell and enter the event loop.
79       */
80
81      XtRealizeWidget ( shell );
82      XtAppMainLoop ( app );
83  }
84
85  static void QuitAction ( Widget    w,
86                           XEvent   *ev,
87                           String   *params,
88                           Cardinal *numParams )
89  {
90      exit ( 0 );
91  }
```

The most interesting parts of this example involve an action table and a translation table. Lines 19 through 21 create a table that relates a name of an action with a function that carries out that action. The resulting action table must be registered with Xt before it can be used.

The function:

```
void XtAppAddActions ( XtAppContext  app,
                       XtActionsRec *actions,
                       Cardinal      numActions )
```

registers an action table. The first argument to `XtAppAddActions()` is an application context. The second argument must be an array of type `XtActionsRec`. This structure consists of a string that defines the public name of an action and a pointer to a function that performs the action.

In this example, the string "`bye()`" is the symbolic name by which the real function is known to the translation manager. The function `QuitAction()` is called whenever the "`bye()`" action is to be executed.

All action functions have the form:

```
void ActionProc ( Widget    w,
                  XEvent   *ev,
                  String   *params,
                  Cardinal *numParams )
```

The first argument to an action procedure specifies the widget for which the function was called, while the second argument provides a pointer to the X event that caused the procedure to be invoked. It is also possible to define additional arguments to be passed to an action procedure. The `params` argument is an array of strings that contains any arguments specified in the translation, while `num_params` indicates the length of the `params` array.

A translation table determines under what circumstances an action procedure may be invoked. In its most basic form, a translation table consists of a list of expressions. Each expression has a left side and a right side, separated by a colon. The left side specifies the user action that invokes the procedure named on the right side. The left side can specify modifier keys and also sequences of events.

Line 25 specifies a simple translation table that binds a user's action (typing the letter "Q") to the action routine named "`bye()`", as defined in the action table. The `bye()` action is specified using a function-like syntax to allow parameters to be passed to the action procedure. For example, assume the translation table used in `memo` was written like this:

```
static char defaultTranslations[] = "<Key>q:    bye(10, Goodbye)";
```

Given this set of translations, if `quitAction()` were to be called, its `params` argument would contain two entries, the string "10" and the string "Goodbye". It would be up to the `QuitAction()` to interpret these arguments.

Translations must be compiled before they can be used. The translations used by the `memo` program are compiled on line 53 using the following function:

```
XtTranslations XtParseTranslationTable ( char * table )
```

Once translations are compiled, they must be registered for a specific widget before they can be used. There are several ways to register translations.

The function:

```
void XtAugmentTranslations ( Widget widget, XtTranslations table )
```

merges the given list of translations with the translations already supported by the widget. `XtAugmentTranslations()` does not override existing translations already associated with that widget.

The function:

```
void XtOverrideTranslations ( Widget widget, XtTranslations table )
```

also registers a translation table with a specific widget. Like `XtAugmentTranslations()`, `XtOverrideTranslations()` merges the given list with those already supported by the widget. However, `XtOverrideTranslations()` replaces existing translations with entries from the new translation list whenever there is a conflict.

Using Callback Functions

Some widget classes provide hooks that allow applications to register functions to be called when some widget-specific condition occurs. These hooks are known as *callback lists* and the application's procedures are known as *callback functions*, or simply *callbacks*, because the widget makes a "call back" to the application-defined function.

Each widget maintains a callback list for each type of callback the widget supports. For example, every type of widget supports a `XmNdestroyCallback` callback list. Each callback function on a widget's `XmNdestroyCallback` list is invoked before the widget is destroyed.

Various widget classes support other callback lists. What callbacks are supported by any particular widget class depends on the behavior of the widget. For example, the Motif XmPushButton widget class supports the following callback lists:

```
XmNactivateCallback        XmNarmCallback          XmNdisarmCallback
```

When the user presses a mouse button while the pointer is inside an XmPushButton widget, the widget invokes all callback functions on the `XmNarmCallback` list. If the user releases the mouse button while the pointer is contained within the XmPushButton widget, the functions on the `XmNactivateCallback` list are called, followed by the functions on the `XmNdisarmCallback` list. If the pointer is not contained by the XmPushButton widget's window when the users releases the mouse button, only the functions on the widget's `XmNdisarmCallback` list are invoked. It is typical to register callbacks for only the `XmNactivateCallback` list, which corresponds to the user pressing and releasing the button. However, the additional callbacks supported by the XmPushButton widget give an application very precise information about changes in a button's state, and are occasionally useful.

Applications can use the following function to add a function to a widget's callback list:

```
void XtAddCallback ( Widget         widget,
                     String         name,
                     XtCallbackProc callback,
                     XtPointer      clientData )
```

The first argument specifies the widget with which a callback is to be registered. The second argument, `name`, specifies the callback list to which a callback is to be added. The third argument must be a pointer to a function to be added to the widget's callback list. Finally, applications can use the `clientData` argument to provide some application-defined data to be passed to the callback function when the callback is invoked.

The form of every callback function must be:

```
void CallbackFunction ( Widget    w,
                        XtPointer clientData,
                        XtPointer callData )
```

Callback functions do not return any useful value, and should be declared as type `void`. The first argument to every callback function is the widget for which the callback was invoked. The second parameter is the `clientData` specified when the callback was registered, using `XtAddCallback()`.

The final argument to a callback function contains data provided by the widget. The type and purpose of this data can be determined by checking the documentation for the specific widget class. In Motif, the `callData` argument is always a pointer to a structure. At a minimum, the call data structure contains a pointer to the X event that directly or indirectly caused the callback to be invoked and a widget-specific code that indicates the reason for the callback. The structure that contains this basic information is defined as:

```
typedef struct {
    int       reason;
    XEvent  *event;
} XmAnyCallbackStruct;
```

Some Motif widget classes use structures that contain additional information, but these structures always contain `reason` and `event` fields as their first two members.

A Callback Example

This section presents a program that demonstrates callback functions. This example is slightly more complex than those presented so far. The program, which is named `xecute`, allows users to confirm an operation before the operation is performed. The operation must be an executable program or shell script. The `xecute` program expects two arguments on the command line, a string and the name of a command to execute. The program displays the string along with two pushbuttons, one labeled "yes", the other labeled "no". If the user pushes the "yes" button, the command specified as the second command-line argument is executed and the program exits. If the user chooses the "no" button, the program exits without executing the command.

The main body of the program is implemented as follows:

```
1     /******************************************************************
2      * xecute.c: Execute a command after the user confirms the action
3      ******************************************************************/
4     #include <Xm/Xm.h>
5     #include <Xm/Label.h>
6     #include <Xm/PushB.h>
7     #include <Xm/BulletinB.h>
8     #include <stdlib.h>
9     #include <stdio.h>
10
11    /* Declarations of callback functions */
12
13    void YesCallback ( Widget w, XtPointer clientData, XtPointer callData );
14    void NoCallback ( Widget w, XtPointer clientData, XtPointer callData );
15
16    void main ( int argc, char **argv )
17    {
18        Widget        shell, msg, bb, yes, no;
19        XtAppContext  app;
20        XmString      xmstr;
21        Dimension     height;
22
23        /*
24         * Initialize Xt
25         */
26
27        shell = XtAppInitialize ( &app, "Xecute", NULL, 0,
28                                  &argc, argv, NULL, NULL, 0 );
29
30        if ( argc != 3 ) /* Make sure there are exactly two arguments */
31        {
32            fprintf (stderr, "Usage:  xecute message-string command\n" );
33            exit ( 1 );
34        }
35
36        /* Create a simple manager widget to hold the other widgets */
37
38        bb = XtVaCreateManagedWidget ( "bboard",
39                                       xmBulletinBoardWidgetClass,
40                                       shell, NULL );
41
42        /* Convert the first argument to the form expected by Motif */
43
44        xmstr = XmStringCreate ( argv[1], XmFONTLIST_DEFAULT_TAG );
45
46        /* Create a label widget as a child of the bulletinboard */
47
48        msg = XtVaCreateManagedWidget ( "message", xmLabelWidgetClass,bb,
49                                        XmNlabelString, xmstr,
```

```
50                                  XmNx, 0,
51                                  XmNy, 0,
52                                  NULL );
53
54      /*
55       * Retrieve the height of the label widget, so we know
56       * where to place the buttons
57       */
58
59      XtVaGetValues ( msg, XmNheight, &height, NULL );
60
61      /*
62       * Create two button widgets for "yes" and "no"
63       */
64
65      yes = XtVaCreateManagedWidget ( "yes", xmPushButtonWidgetClass, bb,
66                                  XmNx, 0,
67                                  XmNy, height + 20,
68                                  NULL );
69
70
71      no = XtVaCreateManagedWidget ( "no", xmPushButtonWidgetClass, bb,
72                                  XmNx, 200,
73                                  XmNy, height + 20,
74                                  NULL );
75
76      /*
77       * Add a callback to each button, for "yes" and "no"
78       * Pass the command to be executed as client data
79       */
80
81      XtAddCallback ( yes, XmNactivateCallback,
82                      YesCallback, ( XtPointer ) argv[2] );
83
84      XtAddCallback ( no, XmNactivateCallback,
85                      NoCallback, NULL );
86
87      /*
88       * Realize the shell and enter the event loop.
89       */
90
91      XtRealizeWidget ( shell );
92      XtAppMainLoop ( app );
93  }
```

The xecute program creates a more complex widget tree than previous examples and uses four Motif widgets. These are: an XmLabel widget that displays a message, two XmPushButton widgets that allow the user to issue commands, and an XmBulletinBoard widget. The XmBulletin-

Board widget is a simple manager widget whose purpose is to contain the other three widgets. Different Motif manager widgets have different layout policies. The XmBulletinBoard widget has one of the simplest layout policies: a specific position must be designated for each child, and the widgets never move or resize. Chapter 5 discusses manager widgets and widget layout in more detail.

Figure 2.4 shows the widget hierarchy created by the `xecute` program.

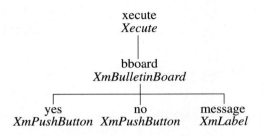

Figure 2.4 The `xecute` widget hierarchy.

Like earlier examples, `xecute` begins by including the Motif header files for all widgets referenced in this file. Lines 4 through 9 include the header files required to use the XmLabel, XmPushButton, and XmBulletinBoard widgets, as well as Xm.h, which is needed by all Motif applications.

Lines 13 and 14 are declarations of functions that will be registered as callbacks. It is necessary to declare these functions before they are referenced, to allow their addresses to be passed to `XtAddCallback()`.

After initializing Xt on line 19, this program checks the number of arguments given on the command line. Two arguments are expected: the message to be displayed, and a command to be executed if the user chooses the "yes" button.

After these preliminary steps are completed, `xecute` constructs the widget tree. An XmBulletinBoard widget is created as a direct child of the shell returned by `XtAppInitialize()`. Because the XmBulletinBoard widget supports more than one child, it can be used to contain all the others.

The next step is to create the Label widget that displays the message. The `XmNx` and `XmNy` resources specify the position of the upper left corner of the Label widget, relative to the BulletinBoard widget. Here, the XmLabel widget is placed in the upper left corner of the XmBulletinBoard widget. Line 59 uses `XtVaGetValues()` to retrieve the height of the XmLabel widget. This value can be used to determine the position of the XmPushButton widgets that are to be placed below the label. Determining the height of the label widget dynamically allows the XmLabel widget's size to vary. For example, the XmLabel widget's height might change if the program displays a multi-line message.

Next, on lines 36 and 71, `xecute` creates two XmPushButton widgets. These widgets are positioned at the bottom of the Label widget, as determined by the value of the `height` variable. The first button is positioned along the left edge (x = 0) of the XmBulletinBoard widget. The second button is arbitrarily placed at x = 200, which should provide enough space for the first button. Figure 2.5 shows the resulting widget layout.

Although the widget layout used by `xecute` is adequate, it is less aesthetically pleasing than it could be, and is also less robust than it should be. For example, the window's contents do not resize when the outer window changes size. If the label on the `yes` button were to be changed to a longer string, this button could overlap the `no` button. Although the layout is less than optimal, better tools and techniques must be discussed before a better solution can be presented. Chapter 5 discusses various techniques for handling window layout, and demonstrates a better way to handle window layout for the `xecute` program.

After creating all the widgets, this example adds two callbacks, one for the `yes` button and one for the `no` button. On lines 81 and 84, `xecute` calls `XtAddCallback()` to register a callback function with each button. This function will be called when the button is activated. Notice that the second command-line argument, `argv[2]`, is given as client data when registering `YesCallback()` as a callback function. The string provides the command that should be executed. Because no command will be executed if the user chooses the "no" button, the client data to the `NoCallback()` function is given as `NULL`.

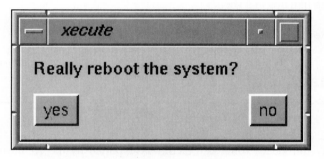

Figure 2.5 The `xecute` window layout.

The `YesCallback()` function is responsible for executing the command specified on the command line. This function casts its `clientData` argument to a string, calls `system()` (a UNIX function that executes a program by name) to execute the program specified by this string, and then exits.

```
94   void YesCallback ( Widget w, XtPointer clientData, XtPointer callData )
95   {
96        /* Cast the clientdata to the expected command string */
97
98        char * cmd = (char *) clientData;
99
100       if ( cmd )
101            system ( cmd ); /* Execute the command */
102
103        exit ( 0 );
104   }
```

The NoCallback() function simply calls exit() to terminate the program with no further actions.

```
105   void NoCallback ( Widget w, XtPointer clientData, XtPointer callData)
106   {
107        /* No action is necessary, just exit. */
108
109        exit ( 0 );
110   }
```

The xecute program can be compiled much like the memo program. It must be compiled and linked with libX11.a, libXt.a and libXm.a:

```
cc -o xecute xecute.c -lXm -lXt -lX11
```

Once compiled, xecute can be used to allow users to confirm potentially dangerous commands. For example, it might be useful to request confirmation before shutting down a system by typing something like this in a shell:

```
% xecute "Really reboot the system?" reboot
```

2.5   Summary

This chapter briefly introduces some key facilities supported by the Xt Intrinsics. Although the programs described in this chapter use Motif, a large part of programming with Motif involves Xt functions. The functions introduced in this chapter form the basis of all examples throughout the remainder of this book. Additional Xt functions are introduced as they are needed.

The following chapter introduces the X resource manager, a facility that provides a simple and consistent way for users to customize applications. It is important to understand how resources work before learning about more complex Motif widgets. Chapter 4 begins to introduce features specific to the Motif widget set. Chapter 5 and later chapters show how to combine widgets to create more complex interfaces.

Chapter 3

Using the Resource Manager

An important part of developing any X-based application involves working with resources. In fact, it is difficult to write any significant Motif application without understanding the X and Xt resource management facilities. Even the simple examples in Chapter 2 used resources, and several key points in that chapter had to be taken on faith until resources could be discussed in more detail. Most users also need to understand something about resource management to customize applications according to their tastes. Before learning about the various Motif widgets and examining more complex examples, it is useful to learn more about how resources work and how applications typically use them.

This chapter explains what resources are and shows how both programmers and users can use the resource manager to customize applications. Sections 3.1 and 3.2 introduce the Xt resource manager and Section 3.3 explains how resources are loaded from various locations. Sections 3.4 and 3.5 discuss conventions for using resources and provide an example. Section 3.6 shows how the Xt resource manager can be used to support application-level resources. The material in Section 3.6 provides some insight as to how the resource manager works, but is needed less often than widget resources. If you are anxious to get started writing applications, you might skip Section 3.6 for now and go on to Chapter 4 after reading Sections 3.1 through 3.5.

3.1 What Is a Resource?

The word *resource* is used in several different ways by different parts of the X Window System. Chapter 1 mentions X *server resources*, such as windows, graphics contexts, and fonts. The X server maintains these resources as private data structures. Clients can refer to these resources using a unique identifier assigned by the server. However, Motif programmers are usually concerned with a different type of resource, the type of widget resource supported by Xt.

Xt uses the term *resource* to refer to customizable data supported by a widget. Xt also allows applications to support user-customization using the same resource management mechanisms used by widgets. Therefore, when using any Xt-based widget set, the term *resource* may refer to any customizable parameter. Some resources, such as colors, fonts, and positions of top-level windows, control the physical appearance of a program's interface, and may be specified by users. Other resources, such as those that define the behavior of individual widgets, are usually specified by programmers.

Xlib provides a simple but powerful mechanism known as the *resource manager* that allows users to control various resources. The resource manager encourages programmers to write customizable applications by providing an easy-to-use mechanism for managing user customizations and specifying default values used by applications. The basic resource manager facilities provided by Xlib allow applications to store and retrieve information from a resource database. Xt provides a higher level interface, built on the Xlib resource manager, that makes it easy for programmers to blend user-specified resources with default values specified by the application or by various widgets.

3.2   Specifying Resources

Every X application maintains a *resource database* that contains user preferences as well as application defaults. Applications can determine the proper value of any given resource at run time by querying the database. This resource database is somewhat different from databases with which you may be familiar. Traditional databases contain information that is completely and precisely specified. Users of such a database generally search for information by making imprecise queries. You might, for example, query a bibliographical database for books about the X Window System by requesting information on "windows." This query could return a possibly large list of books about "windows."

The X resource manager uses a slightly different model. The resource database contains general information about resources used in an application. For example, a user can specify that "All buttons should be red," or "All terminal-emulator windows should be 24 characters high and 80 characters wide." Applications query the database to determine the value of a specific resource for a specific application: "What color should the mail program's quit button be?" or "How wide should my application's command window be?"

The following sections describe the format and rules associated with information in a resource database.

Names and Classes

The resource manager requires that every X application and resource have both a name and a class. The class indicates the general category to which each of these entities belongs, while the name identifies the specific entity. For example, the resource "destroyCallback" names a specific callback list. The class name of this resource, "Callback", identifies a category that includes all callback lists.

Both resource names and resource classes are strings. By convention, resource names generally begin with a lowercase letter, while class names begin with a capital letter. Resource names are often identical to the corresponding resource class names, except for the capitalization. For example, the resource name used to specify a foreground color is "foreground" and the resource class name is "Foreground".

Programmers generally use macros that represent these strings. For example, Motif application should use the symbol `XmNforeground` instead of the string "foreground", and `XmCForeground`, instead of "Foreground". Using these macros allows the compiler to catch spelling errors. Also, Motif defines these macros as pointers to entries in an array of strings, which uses less space than repeating individual strings over and over within a program.

Widgets also have names and classes. The class name of every widget is determined by the programmer who designs the widget, while the application programmer determines the widget's name. For example, the class name of one of the widgets used in the previous chapter was "XmLabel". The `memo` program specifies the XmLabel widget's name as "message".

As noted earlier, applications query the resource database using complete specifications of all desired resources. A resource is completely specified by two strings that together uniquely identify a resource for a particular window or widget. The first string consists of the name of the application, followed by the names of the widgets in the application's widget tree that lie between the top-most shell widget and the widget using the resource, followed by the name of the resource. Each name in the string is separated by a dot ("."). The second string is similar except that it uses class names. Together, these strings specify a unique path through an application's widget tree.

Figure 3.1 and Figure 3.2 show the widget layout and hierarchy of a hypothetical graphics editor named "editor". By convention, the programmer has chosen the class name of the application as "Editor". Figure 3.2 shows the widget tree that corresponds to the widget layout in Figure 3.1, with the class of each widget below the widget's name. The foreground color of `button1` in the upper portion of the window can be specified with the resource name string:

```
editor.panel.commands.button1.foreground
```

and the resource class string:

```
Editor.XmForm.XmRowColumn.XmPushButton.Foreground
```

Notice that the resource name string uniquely identifies `button1`, and differentiates it from the other children of the `commands` widget. This resource string also differentiates `button1` from any other button with the same name but in a different widget hierarchy (such as the `button1` in the `options` widget). The resource class string, however, can potentially apply to many buttons. In this example, the class string represents the foreground color of all XmPushButton widgets managed by both the `commands` widget and the `options` widget.

Applications based on Motif do not have to construct these resource specifications, nor directly query the resource database. Xt provides support that allows each widget to manage its own resources automatically. In the hypothetical editor example, each XmPushButton widget would determine its foreground, background and other colors when the widget is created.

A resource database consists of a set of associations between resource names or class names and the value of a resource. The user can specify these associations in a resource file, such as the.Xdefaults file in the user's home directory. (See Section 3.3 for information on resource files.) Each association consists of a string that contains resource names or class names, followed by a colon, zero or more spaces or tabs, and a value. For example, the following line specifies that the foreground color of `button1` in the `commands` panel should be red:

```
editor.panel.commands.button1.foreground: red
```

The following line specifies the color of all buttons in this application:

```
Editor.XmForm.XmRowColumn.XmPushButton.Foreground: red
```

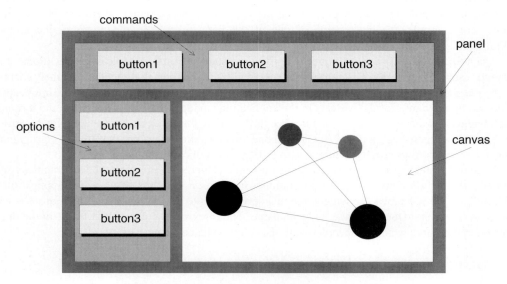

Figure 3.1 Widget layout for resource example.

Although this example specifies resources relative to widgets, the same mechanism can be used to specify resources unrelated to any particular widget or window by using the program name and the resource name. For example the following resource specification:

```
editor.bufsize:     100
```

specifies the value of some resource named "bufsize" used by the program named "editor".

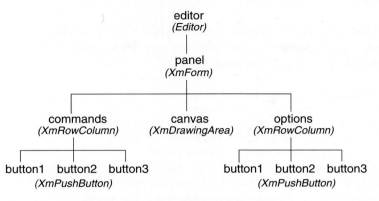

Figure 3.2 Widget tree for Figure 3.1.

The Resource Manager's Matching Algorithm

It is often inconvenient to specify the value of each resource in an application using the complete resource name or resource class specifications, as in the previous examples. The resource manager supports several wildcard characters. An asterisk ("*") matches zero or more resource names or classes, while a "?" character matches any single name or class. (The "?" wildcard character was introduced in X11R5 and is not available in older versions.) For example, continuing to use the editor example whose widget tree is shown in Figure 3.1 and Figure 3.2, the foreground color of `button1` can be specified with:

```
editor*button1*foreground:    red
```

Notice, however, that there are two buttons in this example named `button1`. This resource specification applies to both buttons, because the asterisk matches both `options` and `commands`. A user could indicate the foreground color of `button1` in the `commands` widget with:

```
editor*commands*button1*foreground:    red
```

It is also possible to specify all foreground colors used by the editor application with:

```
editor*foreground:    red
```

The following line specifies the foreground color of the `options` widget and all its children:

```
editor*options*foreground:    red
```

Partial resource specifications can also consist of any combination of resource names and class names. For example, the following line specifies that the foreground color of all widgets that belong to class XmPushButton should be green, regardless of the application:

```
*XmPushButton.foreground:      green
```

Although users can specify resources using incomplete name and class specifications, applications must use complete resource name and resource class specifications when querying the database. At the lowest level, the Xlib function:

```
XrmGetResource ( XrmDatabase db,
                 char        *name,
                 char        *class,
                 char        *typeReturn,
                 XrmValue    *valueReturn )
```

is used to query the database. It returns the value and type of the resource that best matches the complete resource name and class name specification. The resource manager uses a matching algorithm to determine if any entry in the resource database matches the requested resource and returns a type and a value for the query. If no match is found, the returned value is NULL.

The matching algorithm uses several precedence rules to arbitrate between multiple matching entries in the resource database. These rules are:

1. Either the resource name or the class name of each item in the query must match the corresponding item in the database entry. For example, consider a query for the foreground color of button1, using the following resource name and class name specifications:

   ```
   editor.panel.commands.button1.foreground
   ```

   ```
   Editor.XmForm.XmRowColumn.XmPushButton.Foreground
   ```

   This query matches the following resource database entry:

   ```
   editor.XmForm.commands.button1.Foreground: Blue
   ```

   but does not match this entry:

   ```
   editor.XmForm.commands.button1.Highlight:   True
   ```

   because the class name Foreground, specified in the query, does not match the class name, Highlight, in the database.

2. Entries in the database prefixed by a dot (".") are more specific than (and therefore have precedence over) those prefixed by an asterisk ("*") or a "?". Therefore, the database entry:

   ```
   *commands.Background:      green
   ```

   has precedence over:

   ```
   *commands*Background:      red
   ```

   If both these specifications are in the editor application's resource database, the commands widget will have a green background. However, all children of the commands widget (here, button1, button2, and button3) will have a red background.

3. Resource names always have precedence over classes. Therefore, the following entry:

```
*button1.Foreground:    red
```

has precedence over the entry:

```
*XmPushButton.Foreground:    green
```

because the name `button1` is more specific than the class XmPushButton.

4. Both resource names and class names have precedence over an asterisk or a "?". So, this entry:

```
Editor*XmForm*XmPushButton*Foreground: red
```

has precedence over both:

```
Editor*XmForm*foreground: green
```

and:

```
Editor*XmForm.?.foreground: blue
```

because the first entry more completely identifies the path through the widget tree.

5. The resource manager compares database entries left to right, and the first items in a resource specification have precedence over successive items. For example, when determining the foreground color of the buttons in Figure 3.1, the following entry:

```
editor*XmForm*foreground: green
```

has precedence over:

```
editor*XmPushButton*foreground: red
```

6. If the precedence of two entries in the database is equal, the last entry has precedence. For example, if a resource database contains the following two lines:

```
Editor*XmForm*XmPushButton*foreground: green
```

```
Editor*XmForm*XmPushButton*foreground: red
```

the editor program's buttons will be red. Therefore, when multiple resource files are loaded by an application, the files loaded last can override previously loaded files.

Specifying resources takes practice and is often a matter of trial and error, particularly as the number of entries in a resource file grows and the potential for accidental interactions increases.

3.3 Loading the Resource Database

Every Motif application must begin by initializing the Xt Intrinsics and opening a connection to the X server, normally using the convenience function `XtAppInitialize()`. This procedure also creates a resource database and loads it with resource specifications from various resource files. Xt also extracts options specified on the command line and adds them to the resource database. Because the command-line arguments are added last, they override corresponding values specified in any resource file. Motif applications usually do not need to parse command-line arguments themselves. Instead, they use the resource manager interface to obtain the values of command-line arguments.

Xt loads the resource database with specifications from five distinct places. These are the *application defaults file*, the *per-user application defaults file*, the *user's defaults*, the *user's per-host defaults* and the *application's command line*. In the case of multiple, identical specifications, resources in the application defaults file have the lowest precedence, while those retrieved from the command line take the highest precedence. All resource files use the same format as the .Xdefaults file, discussed on page 55. The following sections look at how each of these resource files is found after examining a general mechanism used by Xt for locating files.

Search Paths

Xt uses a flexible mechanism for locating various kinds of files, based on a user-definable search path. An Xt search path consists of a series of patterns separated by colons. When searching for a file, Xt tries sequentially to resolve each pattern in a search path, until a matching file is found or all patterns in the search path are exhausted. The following is a typical search path with three patterns:

```
/usr/lib/X11/%L/%T/%N%S:/usr/lib/X11/%l/%T/%N%S:/usr/lib/X11/%T/%N%S
```

Each pattern in a search path corresponds to a complete path name. Some elements in the search path are file names or directories, while others are special symbols that are replaced at run-time by specific file or directory names. Xt substitutes values for the %<X> characters depending on the type of file desired and the values of various user-configurable parameters. The special characters supported by Xt are %T, %L, %N, %C, %S, %l, %c, and %t.

The %T symbol represents a file *type* and allows Xt to locate different types of files. When searching for resource files, Xt replaces the type field with the string "app-defaults". Other possible types that can be found in different search paths include "bitmap" and "help".

The %L field is derived from the value of the LANG environment variable or the value of an xnlLanguage resource. This allows Xt to identify a different file based on the user's desired language. If LANG is not defined and no xnlLanguage resource has been set, the %L field is ignored.

Xt also supports another way to identify a language-dependent search path. This mechanism relies on the value of an application's xnlLanguage resource. The format of the value of this resource is system-dependent. One possible format for this resource is a string with three parts: a *language* part, a *territory* part, and a *codeset* part. The %l, %t, and %c symbols correspond to these three parts of the xnlLanguage resource. So, the %l in the search path shown above represents just the language part of the xnlLanguage resource.

The %N field represents a file name. For example, when loading a resource file, the %N field is typically replaced by the class name of the application. Some file types may also have a suffix. In such cases, the %S field is replaced by the suffix. Typical suffixes include .txt (text) .dat (data), and .bm (bitmap).

The %C symbol was introduced in X11R5. This symbol is replaced by the value of an application's "customization" resource. The class of this resource is "Customization". Typically, the %N, %S, and %C symbols are used together to represent a file name, for example:

```
%N%C%S
```

The customization resource is intended to support color and monochrome resource files. For example, suppose the value of the editor application's customize resource is "-color" and that the suffix field is ignored. In this case, the above pattern would indicate a file named "Editor-color".

Application Defaults

Xt finds and loads the *application defaults file* by searching a path identified by the environment variable XFILESEARCHPATH. If XFILESEARCHPATH is not defined, Xt uses the following value by default:

```
/usr/lib/X11/%L/%T/%N%S:/usr/lib/X11/%l/%T/%N%S:/usr/lib/X11/%T/%N%S
```

If $LANG is not set and the xnlLanguage resource has not been set, these search paths collapse to:

```
/usr/lib/X11/app-defaults/<class>
```

where *<class>* is the class of the application as given to XtAppInitialize(). Notice that the application defaults file is loaded from the machine on which the application is running, which may differ from the machine on which the X server that displays the program is running.

If no application defaults file is found, Xt loads a set of fallback resources, which can be optionally specified by an application, into the resource database. Fallback resources are specified as a NULL-terminated array of strings, which may be passed to XtAppInitialize(), or set using the function XtAppSetFallbackResources(). Fallback resources provide a way for an application to be sure that certain critical resources are set, even if the application defaults file is not installed properly.

Per-User Application Defaults

After loading, or attempting to load, the application defaults file, Xt searches for a *per-user application* resource file. If the UNIX environment variable XUSERFILESEARCHPATH is set, it is expected to specify a search path, whose form is similar to that used for the XFILESEARCHPATH. If XUSERFILESEARCHPATH is not defined, the default search path is:

```
$XAPPLRESDIR/%L/%N%C:$XAPPLRESDIR/%l/%N%C:\
$XAPPLERESDIR/%N%C:$HOME/%N%C:$XAPPLRESDIR/%L/%N:\
$XAPPLRESDIR/$l/%N:$XAPPLRESDIR/%N/$HOME/%N
```

Here, the various %<X> fields have the same meaning as before, and $XAPPLRESDIR is replaced by the value of that environment variable, if it is defined. If $XAPPLRESDIR is not defined, the default path becomes:

```
$HOME/%L/%N%C:$HOME/%l/%N%C:$HOME/%N%C:\
$HOME/%L/%N:$HOME/%l/%N:$HOME/%N
```

Like the application defaults file, the per-user application defaults are loaded from the machine on which the application is running. All environment variables are also evaluated on the machine on which the client is running.

User's Defaults

Once Xt has tried to locate and load the application defaults and the per-user application defaults files, Xt loads the *user's defaults*. If the root window has a RESOURCE_MANAGER property, the resource manager uses the contents of this property as the user's defaults. The RESOURCE_MANAGER property can be set using the xrdb program. Notice that using the RESOURCE_MANAGER property allows all applications to load the same resources, regardless of the machine on which each application is running because the resources are stored in and loaded from the server. If this property doesn't exist, the resources in the file named .Xdefaults in the user's home directory on the machine on which the client is running are merged into the database.

User's Per-Host Defaults

The final resource file to be loaded is the *user's per-host defaults*. If the environment variable XENVIRONMENT is defined, Xt loads the contents of the file indicated by this environment variable. If this environment variable is not defined, the resource manager looks for the file .Xdefaults-*<host>*, where *<host>* is the name of the machine on which the client is running.

Command-Line Arguments

After processing all resource files, Xt also merges any recognized options from the application's command line into the resource database. XtAppInitialize() removes all recognized options from argv and leaves unrecognized options for the application to process.

Xt supports a standard set of options to ensure that all applications recognize the same command-line arguments. Figure 3.3 lists these standard command-line arguments along with the corresponding resource name used to store the value in a resource file. Each application can also define additional options, which are passed in the option argument to XtAppInitialize(). Section 3.6 discusses the form of these options.

Notice that Xt simply recognizes these standard command-line arguments and places the appropriate value in the application's resource database. Recognizing the command-line argument has nothing to do with whether or not the application actually uses or responds to these resources. For example, Motif widgets use the "fontList" resource to determine the font used to display text. Other widget sets use the "font" resource to determine the font. So, while Xt recognizes the "-font" command-line option, and will place the corresponding value in the resource database, there is no guarantee that the Motif widget set or any other widget set will use that resource at all, or as expected.

The "-xrm" command-line flag allows users to specify an arbitrary string to be placed in the resource database. This flag can be used to specify any resource on the command line, using the same syntax as a resource file. For example:

```
editor -xrm "*foreground:    red"
```

Flag	Resource Name	Type	Example or Effect
+rv	*reverseVideo	None	sets resource to "off"
+synchronous	*synchronous	None	sets resource to "off"
-background	*background	String	-background Black
-bd	*borderColor	String	-bd Black
-bordercolor	*borderColor	String	-bordercolor Black
-bg	*background	String	-bg Red
-borderwidth	.borderWidth	Integer	-borderwidth 2
-bw	.borderWidth	Integer	-bw 2
-display	.display	String	-display expo:0.1
-fg	*foreground	String	-fg Blue
-foreground	*foreground	String	-foreground Blue
-fn	*font	String	-fn 6x13
-font	*font	String	-font 6x13
-geometry	.geometry	String	-geometry =80x24
-iconic	.iconic	None	sets resource to "on"
-name	.name	String	-name Console
-reverse	*reverseVideo	None	sets resource to "on"
-rv	*reverseVideo	None	sets resource to "on"
-selectionTimeout	.selectionTimeout	Integer	-selectionTimeout 5
-synchronous	*synchronous	None	sets resource to "on"
-title	.title	String	-title Console
-xnllanguage	.xnlLanguage	String	-xnlLanguage
-xrm	N.A.	String	-xrm "*fontList: 6x13"

Figure 3.3 Standard command-line options.

3.4   Widget Resource Conventions

Widgets use the resource manager to retrieve resources specified by the user when the widget is created. Applications can also set the value of widgets' resources by passing argument lists to `XtCreateWidget()` or by calling `XtSetValues()` to change the value after the widget is created. Because resources specified by the programmer are applied *after* user-specified resources are retrieved from the resource data base, the programmer's resources override those specified by the user. It is sometimes difficult to determine when a widget resource should be set by an application programmer and when it should be left for end users. The convention used in this book is as follows:

> *Programmers should avoid specifying widget resource values in programs except where absolutely necessary to ensure that an application works correctly.*

Even this guideline leaves room for some variations depending on your definition of "works correctly." For example, it is generally considered to be inappropriate to programmatically specify colors within an application. Not only does hard-coding colors prevent users from choosing colors according to their personal taste, but it may prevent the program from running on monochrome displays. However, imagine a color editor that provides sliders that control the red, green, and blue components of an RGB (Red, Green, Blue) color. (Such a program is described in Chapter 9.) Such a program could set each slider's background to the color component controlled by the slider. In this case, it probably does not make sense to allow the color of each slider to be customized by end-users.

However, programmers should think carefully whenever they are tempted to hard-code resource values into an application. Whenever possible, the programmer should leave decisions regarding fonts, labels, colors, and so on to users. Applications that can be customized by users tend to be more portable. For example, the label displayed by a XmPushButton widget can be set by the user or the programmer. A programmer could probably justify hard-coding the button labels for important functions to prevent the user from using the resource manager to mislabel them. But what if the labels are programmed in English, and the user reads only French? Labels that can be set in a resource database can be changed easily and without access to source code.

Programmers must also be careful not to make any assumptions about what fonts are available in an X environment. There is no standard set of fonts that can be assumed to be available. Furthermore, some displays with limited memory (some X terminals, for example), may support only a limited selection of fonts. Different displays have different screen resolutions and sizes as well, making it important for users to be able to change the fonts used by an application.

Unfortunately, it is difficult to design a program to be customizable by end users and still ensure that it works correctly. For example, if command labels can be redefined by users, there is nothing to prevent the labels of the buttons from being altered in a misleading way. Imagine a situation where the user has inadvertently switched the labels of the "Delete" and "Save" command buttons of an editor. The results could be disastrous. Documenting software that can be radically customized by users is also a difficult problem. Therefore, the approach advocated here is not without flaws.

 One way to make programs customizable, while still providing useful defaults, is to provide an application resource file for every program. Programmers can use the application resource file to specify default resources that the user can override in the .Xdefaults file, if desired. An application resource file also provides a useful place to document the resources and options recognized by an application. Some applications provide multiple application resource files to support monochrome and color displays, high and low resolution displays, and so on. Another approach is to include color and font specifications in the resource file as comments. The user can read this file and use the suggested resources, if desired. The file might also include instructions and suggestions for customizing the application.

Even when it is necessary to hard-code some resources into a program, using a resource file while developing an application makes it easier for the programmer to determine the best value for a resource. Rather than recompiling an application every time a resource needs to be changed, the programmer can simply change the appropriate entries in the resource file and run the program again until the proper value is determined. This prototyping approach is often useful when setting resources that control widget layout. It is unusual (although not unheard of) to allow users to alter the widget layout of an application, and widget layout resources are usually specified programmatically. However, while developing the application, setting widget layout resources in a resource file reduces the amount of time spent recompiling.

Programmers should use common sense when deciding how to control resources. The more customizable an application is, the more easily it can be made to fit the needs of end users. However, users are unlikely to be happy if they must specify values for many resources to make an application behave reasonably. Users normally want a program to be usable by default, and do not want to be required to spend time customizing an application before it can be used. However, many users will want to make minor changes, once they have learned the program, to make it fit smoothly into their environment. Programmers must strike a balance between making programs work correctly, providing ease-of-use, and allowing users to make minor alterations when necessary.

3.5 Using Resource Files: An Example

Most Motif applications use many resources. Typically, applications specify some resources in the program itself. They may also provide an applications default file that contains some resources, and may document some resources to be set by users. Other resources may be completely ignored and left to the discretion of the user. This section looks at a very small, but fairly realistic example program, from the perspective of how resources are typically used.

The example program, shown below, creates the window structure shown in Figure 3.1. The various widgets and resources used in this program are not explained until Chapter 5, but examine the general way various resources are set in the file.

```
1    /****************************************************************
2     * editor.c: An example Motif interface used to discuss resources
3     ****************************************************************/
4    #include <Xm/Xm.h>
5    #include <Xm/DrawingA.h>
6    #include <Xm/RowColumn.h>
7    #include <Xm/PushB.h>
8    #include <Xm/Form.h>
9
10   void main ( int argc, char **argv )
11   {
12       Widget        shell, canvas, panel, commands, options;
13       XtAppContext app;
14
15       /*
16        * Initialize Xt.
17        */
18
19       shell = XtAppInitialize ( &app, "Editor", NULL, 0,
20                                 &argc, argv, NULL, NULL, 0 );
21
22       /*
23        * The overall window layout is handled by an XmForm widget.
24        */
25
```

```
26          panel = XtCreateManagedWidget ( "panel", xmFormWidgetClass,
27                                            shell, NULL, 0 );
28       /*
29        * An XmRowColumn widget holds the buttons along the top
30        * of the window.
31        */
32
33       commands =
34          XtVaCreateManagedWidget ( "commands", xmRowColumnWidgetClass,
35                                     panel,
36                                     XmNnumColumns,       3,
37                                     XmNorientation,      XmVERTICAL,
38                                     XmNtopAttachment,    XmATTACH_FORM,
39                                     XmNrightAttachment,  XmATTACH_FORM,
40                                     XmNleftAttachment,   XmATTACH_FORM,
41                                     XmNbottomAttachment, XmATTACH_NONE,
42                                     NULL );
43       /*
44        * Another XmRowColumn widget contains a column of buttons
45        * along the left side of the window.
46        */
47
48       options =
49          XtVaCreateManagedWidget ( "options", xmRowColumnWidgetClass,
50                                     panel,
51                                     XmNnumColumns,       1,
52                                     XmNorientation,      XmVERTICAL,
53                                     XmNtopAttachment,    XmATTACH_WIDGET,
54                                     XmNtopWidget,        commands,
55                                     XmNrightAttachment,  XmATTACH_NONE,
56                                     XmNleftAttachment,   XmATTACH_FORM,
57                                     XmNbottomAttachment, XmATTACH_FORM,
58                                     NULL );
59       /*
60        * The middle window, in which the application can display
61        * text or graphics is an XmDrawingArea widget.
62        */
63
64       canvas =
65          XtVaCreateManagedWidget ( "canvas", xmDrawingAreaWidgetClass,
66                                     panel,
67                                     XmNtopAttachment,    XmATTACH_WIDGET,
68                                     XmNtopWidget,        commands,
69                                     XmNrightAttachment,  XmATTACH_FORM,
70                                     XmNleftWidget,       options,
71                                     XmNleftAttachment,   XmATTACH_WIDGET,
72                                     XmNbottomAttachment, XmATTACH_FORM,
73                                     NULL );
74
```

```
75    /*
76     * The buttons in the commands and options panels are
77     * created as XmPushButton widgets.
78     */
79
80    XtCreateManagedWidget ( "button1", xmPushButtonWidgetClass,
81                            commands, NULL, 0 );
82    XtCreateManagedWidget ( "button2", xmPushButtonWidgetClass,
83                            commands, NULL, 0 );
84    XtCreateManagedWidget ( "button3", xmPushButtonWidgetClass,
85                            commands, NULL, 0 );
86    XtCreateManagedWidget ( "button1", xmPushButtonWidgetClass,
87                            options, NULL, 0 );
88    XtCreateManagedWidget ( "button2", xmPushButtonWidgetClass,
89                            options, NULL, 0 );
90    XtCreateManagedWidget ( "button3", xmPushButtonWidgetClass,
91                            options, NULL, 0 );
92
93    XtRealizeWidget ( shell );
94    XtAppMainLoop ( app );
95 }
```

Notice that this example program includes several resources that are hard-coded in the program itself. Specifically, the resources that determine the positions and orientation of the various widgets are set programmatically. Although some programmers may wish to allow users to alter the layout of an application's windows, it is not unreasonable to expect that the basic window layout is determined by the application and is not user-configurable.

However, labels and fonts should not be hard-coded into an application because doing so will make the application non-portable. It would be unfortunate if an application would not run on a particular machine, just because a hard-coded font was not available. Labels are even more important, particularly if internationalization is a desirable goal. Typically, labels are specified in a application's app-defaults file. Fonts may also be specified in the app-defaults file, or left as a user preference.

This program's class name is "Editor", as specified by the second argument to `XtApp-Initialize()` on line 19, so the app-defaults file would normally be installed in the file /usr/lib/X11/app-defaults/Editor. The editor program's app-defaults file might look like this:

```
1    !!!!!!!!!!!!!!!!!!!!!!!!!!!!!!!!!!!!!!!!!!!!!!!!!!!!!!!!!!!
2    !! Editor: app-defaults file for the editor program
3    !!!!!!!!!!!!!!!!!!!!!!!!!!!!!!!!!!!!!!!!!!!!!!!!!!!!!!!!!!!
4
5    !  Labels for buttons used in editor program
6
7    *options*button1*labelString: Option 1
8    *options*button2*labelString: Option 2
9    *options*button3*labelString: Option 3
10   *commands*button1*labelString: Command One
```

```
11   *commands*button2*labelString: Command Two
12   *commands*button3*labelString: Command Three
13
14   ! Default fonts
15
16   *fontList:   8x13
```

As mentioned previously, colors pose a difficult issue for application developers. For example, a developer may wish to choose colors that make an application attractive. For some applications, colors may even be important to the information the application is trying to convey. However, applications that hard-code colors may not run on systems that do not support color. Color is a limited server resource, and even on color displays, applications may not be able to get the colors they want. Furthermore, users may have different tastes in colors and may wish to coordinate an application's color with those of other applications. Also, a significant portion of the population is color-blind, so an inappropriate choice of colors could make it hard for some users to use an application whose colors are hard-coded.

Several approaches are commonly used. First, many applications simply leave color up to the user. By default, Motif applications appear in a shade of blue. Users can change the colors if they wish, although setting detailed colors for an application may require the user to know the widget hierarchy, and perhaps names of widgets as well. An application's widget hierarchy is seldom something users know, or should need to know.

A simple alternative is to provide colors, chosen to work well with the specific application, in the application's app-defaults file, but keep them well-isolated and provided detailed comments to allow the colors to be changed easily. Some applications suggest colors in comments initially, so that the user or system administrator can decide whether to use these colors when the program is installed. For example, an app-defaults file for the editor program could be written like this:

```
1    !!!!!!!!!!!!!!!!!!!!!!!!!!!!!!!!!!!!!!!!!!!!!!!!!!!!!
2    !! Editor: app-defaults file for the editor program
3    !!!!!!!!!!!!!!!!!!!!!!!!!!!!!!!!!!!!!!!!!!!!!!!!!!!!!
4
5    !   Labels for buttons used in editor program
6
7    *options*button1*labelString: Option 1
8    *options*button2*labelString: Option 2
9    *options*button3*labelString: Option 3
10
11   *commands*button1*labelString: Command One
12   *commands*button2*labelString: Command Two
13   *commands*button3*labelString: Command Three
14
15   ! Default fonts
16
17   !*fontList:   8x13
18
19   ! Color resources. Uncomment the following lines
20   ! if you have a color display
```

```
21
22   !*foreground:                        white
23   !*XmDrawingArea*background:          Turquoise
24   !*options*background:                Blue
25   !*commands*background:               Green
26   !*options*XmPushButton*background:   LightBlue
27   !*commands*XmPushButton*background:  grey50
28
29   ! Monochrome resources. Uncomment the following lines
30   ! if you have a black and white display
31
32   !*foreground: white
33   !*background: black
```

A similar approach is to provide both monochrome and color app-default files and allow the user to choose which one to install.

These options have one serious deficiency. An application may run on one machine (a machine with a color display, for example) and also be displayed on another (a black and white display, for example). In this case, the user may choose the color resource for use locally, and therefore be unable to display the application on a monochrome display remotely. The customization resource (%C) capability of the Xt search path, described on page 58, provides one way to deal with this issue. Two app-defaults files can be installed, one named Editor-color, the other Editor-monochrome. Then, by setting the value of the Customization resource to "-color", or "-monochrome", the appropriate file can be picked up.

Several vendors support more sophisticated mechanisms, often known as "schemes", that allow users to apply various pre-defined color palettes to all applications by setting a single resource. When using monochrome displays, users can specify a monochrome scheme, while on color displays, they may choose from an assortment of color palettes according to their individual taste and needs.

Figure 3.4 shows the widget layout created by this program, when used with this resource file.

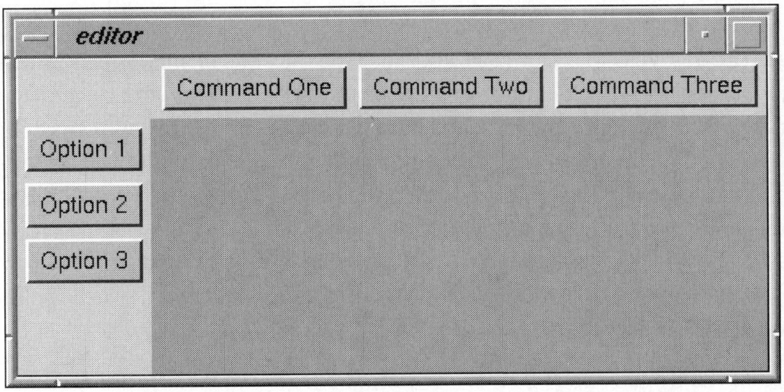

Figure 3.4 The editor program with the given application resources.

3.6   Managing Application Resources

Applications often need to support user-configurable parameters that have nothing to do with widgets and perhaps little to do with the application's user interface. Most UNIX applications accept one or more command-line arguments that affect the way the applications behave. Xt allows applications to use the same resource management mechanism used by widgets to configure application-level customizable parameters. In this way, the resource manager provides programmers with a consistent mechanism for retrieving all options and resources used by applications as well as widgets. This section demonstrates how the Xt resource manager facilities can be used to support customizable application-level resources.

Retrieving Application Resources

Applications can use the resource manager to retrieve the values of application level options and resources, by specifying the resources to be retrieved from the database in an `XtResource` structure. This structure is defined in the header file Intrinsic.h as:

```
typedef struct _XtResource {
   String       resource_name;    /* Resource name             */
   String       resource_class;   /* Resource class            */
   String       resource_type;    /* Desired type              */
   Cardinal     resource_size;    /* Size in bytes             */
   Cardinal     resource_offset;  /* Offset from base          */
   String       default_type;     /* Type of specified default */
   XtPointer    default_addr;     /* Address of default value  */
} XtResource;
```

The `resource_name` member specifies the name of the resource being retrieved. The `resource_class` member indicates the class name used by the resource manager's matching algorithm.

The `resource_type` member is a string that specifies the desired type of the resource. This type can be any valid data type, including any application-defined type. For example, an application might reasonably ask for a color by name (a character string) or ask for an index (of type `Pixel`) that represents the color. In Motif, the file XmStrDefs.h contains definitions of symbols used to represent common types. For example, the resource type for a character string is `XmRString`. The type that corresponds to a Pixel is `XmRPixel`.

The `resource_size` member indicates the size, in bytes, of the resource to be retrieved. The `resource_offset` member of the `XtResource` structure indicates a relative address where the retrieved value should be stored. Xt provides a utility macro:

```
XtOffset ( type *, field )
```

that determines the byte offset of a member of a C structure and provides a convenient way to specify relative addresses.

The last two members of the `XtResource` structure specify a default value for the resource and the type of the default value. The resource manager uses this default if it does not find a match in the user's resource database. This provides a simple way for the application programmer to specify default values for all resources.

For example, the following code segment specifies the names, types, and default values of several resources in an array of type `XtResource`:

```
static XtResource resources[] = {
  { "delay", "Delay", XmRInt, sizeof  ( int ),
    XtOffset ( GlobalOptionsStruct *, delay ),
    XmRImmediate,  ( XtPointer )  2 },

  { "verbose", "Verbose", XmRBoolean, sizeof  ( Boolean ),
    XtOffset ( GlobalOptionsStruct *, verbose ),
    XmRString, "FALSE"},
};
```

This array contains two resource specifications. The first specifies a resource whose name is "delay" and whose class name is "Delay". The type of this resource is expected to be an integer, and therefore the type field of the `XtResource` struct is set to `XmRInt`. The data is to be stored in the `delay` member of a structure of type `GlobalOptionsStruct`. Finally, a default value is supplied. The type of the default value is given as `XmRImmediate`, which means that the default value is to be taken literally. In this case, the default value is the integer value, 2.

The second resource is similar, but represents a Boolean value. Therefore, its type is specified as `XmRBoolean`. The default value for this function is given as a string (type `XmRString`) whose value is "FALSE". Xt will convert this value to an equivalent Boolean value if no other value is present in the resource database.

Applications can use the function:

```
XtGetApplicationResources ( Widget         w,
                            XtPointer      base,
                            XtResourceList resources,
                            Cardinal       nresources,
                            ArgList        args,
                            Cardinal       nargs )
```

to retrieve resources specified in an array of type `XtResource` from the database. The `widget` argument should specify the top-level shell widget that identifies the name and class of the application. The `base` argument specifies the base address of a data structure where the resource manager is to store the retrieved values. If the offsets specified in the `XtResource` array are absolute addresses, rather than offsets within a structure, the `base` argument can be specified as zero. The next argument, `resources`, is an array of type `XtResource`, while `nresources` indicates the number of entries in the `resource` array.

The last arguments, `args` and `nargs`, provide a way for the application to override values in the database. The `args` parameter must be an array of type `Arg` that contains resource names and values, while `nargs` indicates the number of resources in the array.

The following example demonstrates how an application can use this mechanism. A simple test program, named `rmtest`, retrieves and prints the value of two resources, "verbose" and "delay". The program supplies default values for these resources, but the user can also use the resource manager to customize the parameters. The program can be written as follows:

```
1    /*********************************************
2     * rmtest.c: Demo the resource manager
3     *********************************************/
4    #include <Xm/Xm.h>
5    #include <stdio.h>
6
7    typedef struct {
8      int       delay;
9      Boolean   verbose;
10   } GlobalOptionsStruct;
11
12   static XtResource resources[] = {
13     { "delay", "Delay", XtRInt, sizeof ( int ),
14       XtOffset ( GlobalOptionsStruct *, delay ),
15       XmRImmediate, ( XtPointer ) 2 },
16     { "verbose", "Verbose", XtRBoolean, sizeof ( Boolean ),
17       XtOffset ( GlobalOptionsStruct *, verbose ), XmRString, "FALSE" },
18   };
19
20   GlobalOptionsStruct globalData;
21
22   void main ( int argc, char **argv )
23   {
24       Widget          shell;
25       XtAppContext    app;
26
27       /*
28        * Initialize Xt
29        */
30
31       shell = XtAppInitialize ( &app, "Rmtest",  NULL, 0,
32                                 &argc, argv, NULL, NULL, 0 );
33
34       /*
35        * Retrieve the application resources.
36        */
37
38       XtGetApplicationResources ( shell, &globalData,
39                                   resources, XtNumber ( resources ),
40                                   NULL, 0 );
```

```
41      /*
42       * Print the results and exit.
43       */
44
45      printf ( "delay = %d, verbose = %d\n",
46                  globalData.delay, globalData.verbose );
47  }
```

The rmtest example uses XtGetApplicationResources() to retrieve the resources and then prints each value before exiting. Notice that this example specifies the address of the ApplicationData structure, data, as the base address relative to which the function XtGetApplicationResources() is to store the values retrieved from the resource data base.

If a resource in the resources array is not specified in any of the resource files loaded by the application, the resource manager uses the default value provided as part of the XtResource structure. So, if there are no matching entries in any resource file, running rmtest gives the following output:

```
% rmtest
delay = 2, verbose = 0,
```

Notice that the resource manager converts the value of verbose from the string "FALSE" to the Boolean value zero used by convention in C to mean FALSE.

Since the class name of this program is "Rmtest", resources can be specified in an application resource file, /usr/lib/X11/app-defaults/Rmtest. Suppose the rmtest program's application resource file contains the following lines:

```
!!!!!!!!!!!!!!!!!!!!!!!!!!!!!!!!!
!! AppDefaults file for rmtest
!!!!!!!!!!!!!!!!!!!!!!!!!!!!!!!!!
*delay:         10
*verbose:       TRUE
```

Now, running the program rmtest from a shell produces the following output:

```
% rmtest
delay = 10, verbose = 1
```

In this case, the resource manager has obtained the values of delay and verbose from the application resource file rather than from the application-defined defaults.

End users of an application can selectively override any or all resources specified in the application resource file in their own .Xdefaults file. Suppose the following line is placed in the file $HOME/.Xdefaults:

```
*delay:         20
```

Remember that if the root window has a RESOURCE_MANAGER property, the resource manager assumes that this property contains the user's defaults and the .Xdefaults file is not searched. To install the contents of the .Xdefaults file in the RESOURCE_MANAGER property, use the xrdb command:

```
% xrdb -m $HOME/.Xdefaults
```

Now, running this program should produce the following results:

```
% rmtest
  delay = 20, verbose = 1,
```

In this example, the resource manager obtains the value for verbose from the application resource file, and retrieves the value of delay from the resources stored in the user's RESOURCE_MANAGER property.

Retrieving Resources from the Command Line

It is usually more convenient to specify options using resource files than to use the conventional UNIX command-line argument mechanism, because resource files allow defaults to be specified once in a file rather than each time the application is run. Resource files also allow users to specify general defaults to be used by all applications rather than specifying every option to every program on the command line. In addition, in a window-based environment, applications are less likely to be invoked from a UNIX command shell and more likely to be started from a menu or some type of application browser or desktop.

In spite of this, there are many cases where it is convenient or necessary to specify arguments on a command line. One situation in which command-line arguments are necessary is when the user needs to specify options on a per-process basis. For example, a user cannot use a resource file to run one xterm (an X terminal emulator program) with a red foreground and another xterm with a blue foreground. As one way to accomplish this task, Xlib and Xt provide mechanisms for parsing the command-line arguments and placing the contents into the resource database. Placing command-line arguments into the resource database allows applications to use the same retrieval mechanism discussed in the previous section to determine the value of command-line arguments.

Applications can use the options argument to XtAppInitialize() or XtOpen-Display() to define additional command-line arguments. The options argument, which must be an array of type XrmOptionDescList, specifies how additional command-line arguments should be parsed and loaded into the resource database. The XrmOptionDescList structure is defined as:

```
typedef struct {
    char              *option;       /* argv abbreviation */
    char              *specifier;    /* Resource specifier*/
    XrmOptionKind      argKind;      /* Style of option   */
    XPointer           value;        /* Default Value     */
} XrmOptionDescRec, *XrmOptionDescList;
```

The `option` member of this structure is the name by which the resource is recognized on the command line, while the specifier is the name by which the resource is known in the resource database. The `argKind` member specifies the format of the command-line arguments and must be one of the values shown in Figure 3.5.

Argument Style	Meaning
XrmoptionNoArg	Value is specified in `OptionDescRec.value`
XrmoptionIsArg	Value is the option string itself
XrmoptionStickyArg	Value immediately follows the option, with no space
XrmoptionSepArg	Value is next argument in `argv`
XrmoptionResArg	A resource and value are in the next argument in `argv`
XrmoptionSkipArg	Ignore this option and the next argument in `argv`
XrmoptionSkipLine	Ignore this option and the rest of `argv`

Figure 3.5 Command-line parsing options.

Let's see how this works by adding some command-line arguments to the **rmtest** program from the previous section. The command-line arguments provide a way to specify the initial value of the resources supported by the program. The new version of **rmtest** is written as follows:

```
1    /********************************************************
2     * rmtest2.c: Test the use of command-line arguments
3     ********************************************************/
4    #include <Xm/Xm.h>
5    #include <stdio.h>
6
7    typedef struct {
8       int       delay;
9       Boolean   verbose;
10   } GlobalOptionsStruct;
11
12   static XtResource resources[] = {
13   { "delay", "Delay", XmRInt, sizeof  ( int ),
14     XtOffset ( GlobalOptionsStruct *, delay ),
15     XmRImmediate, ( XtPointer ) 2 },
16   { "verbose", "Verbose", XmRBoolean, sizeof ( Boolean ),
17     XtOffset ( GlobalOptionsStruct *, verbose ),
18     XmRString, "FALSE" },
19   };
20
21   XrmOptionDescRec options[] = {
22      { "-verbose", "*verbose", XrmoptionNoArg, "TRUE" },
23      { "-delay",   "*delay",   XrmoptionSepArg, NULL  }
24   };
25
26   GlobalOptionsStruct globalData;
```

```
27
28   void main ( int argc, char **argv )
29   {
30       Widget        shell;
31       XtAppContext app;
32
33       shell = XtAppInitialize ( &app, "Rmtest",
34                                 options, XtNumber ( options ),
35                                 &argc, argv, NULL, NULL, 0 );
36
37       /*
38        * Retrieve the application resources
39        */
40
41       XtGetApplicationResources ( shell, &globalData, resources,
42                                   XtNumber ( resources ), NULL, 0 );
43       /*
44        * Print the results.
45        */
46
47       printf ( "delay = %d, verbose = %d\n",
48                globalData.delay, globalData.verbose );
49   }
```

Now the new command-line options can be used to override the values in all resource files. For example:

```
% rmtest
  delay = 2, verbose = 0
% rmtest2 -delay 15 -verbose
  delay = 15, verbose = 1
```

3.7   Type Conversion

In each of the previous examples, the resource manager automatically converts the requested resources from one data type to another. The resource manager performs these conversions by calling functions known as *type-converters*. The most common type-converters convert from a string to some other data type, because resource files specify resources as strings. However, type-converters can be used to convert between any two data types, including application-defined types. For example, Xt defines type converters that convert between strings and pixels, strings and cursors, strings and fonts, and so on.

Applications can define additional type conversions by writing type-converter functions and registering them with the resource manager. A type converter is a procedure that has the following form:

```
void Converter ( Display    *dpy,
                 XrmValue   *args,
                 Cardinal   *nargs,
                 XrmValue   *fromVal
                 XrmValue   *toVal,
                 XtPointer  *data )
```

Three of the arguments to a type converter function are pointers to structures of type `XrmValue`, which is defined as:

```
typedef struct {
  unsigned int  size;
  XtPointer     *addr;
} XrmValue, *XrmValuePtr;
```

This structure holds a pointer to a value, and the size of the value. The `fromVal` and `toVal` parameters of a type converter provide the original data and a way to return the converted value. The type converter is expected to convert the data in the `fromVal` structure and fill in the `toVal` structure with the result. The `args` parameter is an array of type `XrmValue` that contains any additional data required by the converter. The `data` parameter is data that is passed to a destructor function, which can be used to free any memory allocated by the type converter.

Before the resource manager can use a type converter, the function must be registered with the resource manager. The function:

```
void XtSetTypeConverter ( String          from_type,
                          String          to_type,
                          XtTypeConvert   converter,
                          XtConvertArgList args,
                          Cardinal        nargs,
                          XtCacheType     cache_type,
                          XtDestructor    destructor )
```

registers a type converter with the resource manager. The arguments `from_type` and `to_type` must be strings that indicate the data types involved in the conversion. Whenever appropriate, the standard type macros defined by Motif should be used for consistency. The `converter` argument specifies the address of the type-converter function, while `args` and `nargs` specify any additional arguments that should be passed to the type converter when it is called. The `cache_type` argument indicates how caching should be handled and must be one of the constants:

```
XtCacheNone              XtCacheAll               XtCacheByDisplay
```

Any of the above values may be combined (as a logical OR) with `XtCacheRefCount` which specifies that a reference count will be kept of the cached value. When the reference count equals zero, the `destructor` function specified when the converter was registered is called. The destructor can be useful when the type converter allocates memory or resources that should be freed.

The `args` parameter must be an array of type `XtConvertArgList`, which is defined as:

```
typedef struct {
    XtAddressMode    address_mode;
    XtPointer        address_id;
    Cardinal         size;
} XtConvertArgRec, *XtConvertArgList;
```

The `address_mode` argument indicates the type of data provided and may be one of the constants:

```
XtAddress              XtBaseOffset           XtWindowObjBaseOffset
XtImmediate            XtResourceString       XtResourceQuark
```

The `address_id` member specifies the address of the additional data, while the member indicates the size of the resource in bytes. Many converter functions require no additional data, and `args` is often given as `NULL`, and `nargs` as zero.

An Example Type Converter

A common technique for debugging programs is to use print statements. For some programs, it is useful to leave print statements in all the time, and to turn the debugging output on and off with a flag of some kind. In many cases, it is useful to support multiple levels of debugging information ranging from a few simple debugging statements to a detailed trace of each step the program performs. An enumerated type provides a convenient way to handle different debugging levels within a program, and the Xt resource manager provides a convenient way to indicate the current debugging level. This implies a need for some way to convert a string found in a resource file into an equivalent enumerated type. The task is straightforward and can be handled by registering a custom type converter function.

Let's see how such a function could be written. It is convenient to provide some declarations in a header file and place the implementation of the converter in a separate source file. The header file can provide type declarations, while the implementation file could be placed in a library to allow easy use by multiple programs. The header file dbg.h is written as follows:

```
1  /****************************************************************
2   * dbg.h: Declarations to support a resource to control debug levels
3   ****************************************************************/
4  #ifndef STRINGTODBG_H
5  #define STRINGTODBG_H
6  #include <Xm/Xm.h>
7
8  /*
9   * The type convert function, which must be registered by
10  * any program that uses it.
11  */
```

```
12
13   extern Boolean CvtStringToDebugLevel ( Display      *dpy,
14                                           XrmValue     *args,
15                                           Cardinal     *nargs,
16                                           XrmValue     *fromVal,
17                                           XrmValue     *toVal,
18                                           XtPointer    *data );
19
20   /* Enumerated values used to indicate debugging levels */
21
22   typedef enum { LEVEL0, LEVEL1, LEVEL2, LEVEL3, LEVEL4 } DebugLevel;
23
24   /* Resource macros defined for convenience */
25
26   #define XmNdebugLevel "debugLevel"
27   #define XmCDebugLevel "DebugLevel"
28   #define XmRDebugLevel "DebugLevel"
29   #endif
```

The implementation file contains the type-converter function, written as follows:

```
1    /*******************************************
2     * dbg.c: An example Xt type converter
3     *******************************************/
4    #include "dbg.h"
5
6    Boolean CvtStringToDebugLevel ( Display      *dpy,
7                                    XrmValue     *args,
8                                    Cardinal     *nargs,
9                                    XrmValue     *fromVal,
10                                   XrmValue     *toVal,
11                                   XtPointer    *data )
12   {
13       static DebugLevel result;
14
15       /*
16        * Make sure the number of args is correct.
17        */
18
19       if ( *nargs != 0 )
20           XtWarning ( "String to DebugLevel conversion needs no args" );
21       /*
22        * Convert the string in the fromVal to a DebugLevel
23        */
24
25       if ( !strcasecmp ( fromVal->addr, "LEVEL0" ) )
26           result =  LEVEL0;
27       else if ( !strcasecmp ( fromVal->addr, "LEVEL1" ) )
28           result =  LEVEL1;
```

```
29        else if ( !strcasecmp ( fromVal->addr, "LEVEL2" ) )
30            result =   LEVEL2;
31        else if ( !strcasecmp ( fromVal->addr, "LEVEL3" ) )
32            result =   LEVEL3;
33        else if ( !strcasecmp ( fromVal->addr, "LEVEL4" ) )
34            result =   LEVEL4;
35        else
36        {
37            XtDisplayStringConversionWarning ( dpy,
38                                               fromVal->addr,
39                                               XmRDebugLevel );
40            return FALSE;
41        }
42
43    /*
44     * Make toVal point to the result.
45     */
46
47        toVal->size = sizeof ( DebugLevel );
48        *( ( DebugLevel* ) toVal->addr ) = result;
49
50        return ( TRUE );
51 }
```

This type converter first checks how many `arguments` were given as parameters. Because no additional parameters are needed for `CvtStringToDebugLevel()`, the function uses the utility function:

```
void XtWarning ( String message )
```

to print a warning if the number of arguments is not equal to zero.

The type converter uses `strcasecmp()` to find the matching string. The `toVal` structure is then filled in with the size of a `DebugLevel` type and the address of the variable `result`. If the conversion cannot be performed, the function:

```
void XtDisplayStringConversionWarning ( Display *dpy,
                                        String   from,
                                        String   to );
```

is used to issue a warning. This function takes three arguments that indicate the display and the two data types involved in the conversion.

Notice that the variable `result`, which contains the value returned by the type converter, is declared as static. It is important that `result` be declared as static because otherwise the address of `result` would be invalid after the function returns. Functions that call type converters must copy the returned value immediately, because the type converter reuses the same address each time it is called.

The following short program can be used to test the `CvtStringToDebugLevel()` type converter:

```
1   /****************************************************
2    * rmtest3.c: Test the StringToDebug type converter
3    ****************************************************/
4   #include <Xm/Xm.h>
5   #include <stdio.h>
6   #include "dbg.h"
7
8   unsigned char debugLevel;
9
10  static XtResource resources[] = {
11  { XmNdebugLevel, XmCDebugLevel, XmRDebugLevel, sizeof ( unsigned char ),
12    ( Cardinal ) &debugLevel, XmRImmediate,  ( XtPointer )  LEVEL0 },
13  };
14
15  static XrmOptionDescRec options[] = {
16    { "-debug",   "*debugLevel",  XrmoptionSepArg, NULL }
17  };
18
19  void main ( int argc, char **argv )
20  {
21      Widget       shell;
22      XtAppContext app;
23
24      /*
25       * Initialize Xt
26       */
27
28      shell = XtAppInitialize ( &app, "Rmtest",
29                                options, XtNumber ( options ),
30                                &argc, argv, NULL, NULL, 0 );
31
32      /*
33       * Add the string to debug level type-converter.
34       */
35
36      XtSetTypeConverter ( XmRString, XmRDebugLevel,
37                           CvtStringToDebugLevel,
38                           ( XtConvertArgList )  NULL, 0,
39                           XtCacheAll,  ( XtDestructor )  NULL );
40      /*
41       * Retrieve the resources.
42       */
43
44      XtGetApplicationResources ( shell, 0, resources,
45                                  XtNumber ( resources ), NULL, 0 );
46
```

```
47     /*
48      * Print the result.
49      */
50
51     if ( debugLevel == LEVEL0 )
52         printf ( "Debugging disabled\n" );
53     else
54         printf ( "debugging LEVEL%d enabled\n", debugLevel );
55  }
```

The debug level of this example can now be controlled by specifying a value in a resource file, or by using a command-line argument.

Motif Support for Enumerated Types

Because many applications and widgets use enumerated types like that demonstrated in the previous section, Motif provides an easy way to implement type conversion for these types. The function

```
XmRepTypeId XmRepTypeRegister (  String          repType,
                                 String          *names,
                                 unsigned char   values,
                                 unsigned char   num_values );
```

allows the caller to register an array of strings which correspond to a set of numeric values so Motif can perform the conversion automatically. The first argument is a string that identifies the type. In the example in the previous section, this would be the string "DebugLevel", which was defined as XmRDebugLevel. The second argument must be an array of names to be recognized by the type converter. For example, in the debug example, this array could be specified as

```
char *debugLevelNames[] = {
    "level0", "level1", "level2", "level3", "level4"
};
```

The values argument to XmRepTypeRegister() can be given as NULL if the values in the given array of strings corresponds to a sequence of integer values starting at zero. Otherwise, an array of values can be provided. Finally, the num_values argument must specify the number of entries in the names array.

Once XmRepTypeRegister() is called, the specified type is recognized by the Motif type conversion mechanism and can be used in resource files, and so on. XmRepTypeRegister() returns an identifier that can be used by several other related functions. For example, the function

```
Boolean XmRepTypeValidValue ( XmRepTypeId    id,
                              unsigned char  value,
                              Widget         enableWarning )
```

can be used to test a value to see if it falls within the range specified for the corresponding type. The first argument to this function specifies the type, as returned by XmRepTypeRegister(). The second argument indicates the value to be tested. The third argument serves a dual purpose. If this argument is NULL, no warning message is printed if the value is outside the appropriate range. If a warning is desired, this argument must be a widget, which is used to call a Motif warning function. The type of widget is not important.

The following example program uses these functions to implement the same functionality as the example in the previous section, but without writing a custom type converter.

```
1    /********************************************************
2     * rmtest4.c: Test Motif's enumerated type converter
3     ********************************************************/
4    #include <Xm/Xm.h>
5    #include <Xm/RepType.h>
6    #include <stdio.h>
7
8    typedef enum  { LEVEL0, LEVEL1, LEVEL2, LEVEL3, LEVEL4 } DebugLevel;
9    char *debugLevelNames[] = {
10        "level0", "level1", "level2", "level3", "level4"
11    };
12
13   #define XmNdebugLevel "debugLevel"
14   #define XmCDebugLevel "DebugLevel"
15   #define XmRDebugLevel "DebugLevel"
16   unsigned char debugLevel;
17
18   static XtResource resources[] = {
19   { XmNdebugLevel, XmCDebugLevel, XmRDebugLevel, sizeof ( unsigned char ),
20       ( Cardinal ) &debugLevel, XmRImmediate,  ( XtPointer )  LEVEL0 },
21   };
22
23   static XrmOptionDescRec options[] = {
24     {"-debug", "*debugLevel", XrmoptionSepArg, NULL}
25   };
26
27   void main ( int argc, char **argv )
28   {
29       Widget        shell;
30       XtAppContext app;
31       XmRepTypeId  id;
32
33       /*
34        * Initialize Xt
35        */
36
37       shell = XtAppInitialize ( &app, "Rmtest",
38                                 options, XtNumber ( options  ),
39                                 &argc, argv, NULL, NULL, 0  );
```

```
40      /*
41       *   Add the string to debug level type-converter.
42       */
43
44      id = XmRepTypeRegister ( XmRDebugLevel, debugLevelNames, NULL,
45                               XtNumber ( debugLevelNames ) );
46      /*
47       *  Retrieve the resources.
48       */
49
50      XtGetApplicationResources ( shell, 0, resources,
51                                  XtNumber ( resources  ), NULL, 0 );
52      /*
53       * Print the result. Check the result just to demonstrate
54       * how this function is called. Note that by the time we get here,
55       * the type converter will have assured that the value is within
56       * range, so this check is redundant in this case.
57       */
58
59      if ( XmRepTypeValidValue ( id, debugLevel, shell ) )
60      {
61          if ( debugLevel == LEVEL0  )
62              printf ( "Debugging disabled\n"  );
63          else
64              printf ( "debugging LEVEL%d enabled\n", debugLevel );
65      }
66  }
```

3.8   Summary

The resource manager is a powerful mechanism that allows programmers to create customizable applications easily. Even the simplest Motif program requires the programmer to set, retrieves or manipulate resources. In many ways, resources are as much a part of Motif's applications programmer's interface (API) as the Xt functions discussed in Chapter 2. Every Motif programmer must understand the basic principles of the Xlib resource manager and know how to use the Xt-level resource facilities to manage resources. Used carefully, resources allow programmers to write applications that have predictable behavior, while still allowing users to tailor some aspects of the program to their tastes.

Chapters 1, 2, and 3 describe the general architecture of X, the architecture of Xt, and the resource manager, but do not present realistic examples of complete Motif programs. The following chapters introduce the widgets provided by Motif, and begin to put these pieces together while exploring more complex applications.

C h a p t e r   4

Primitive Motif Widgets

The Motif widget set contains many different types of widgets, including scrollbars, menus, buttons, and so on, that can be combined to create user interfaces. Motif widget classes can be divided into several categories based on the general functionality they offer. For example, some widgets display information while others are designed to group other widgets together in various combinations.

The Motif widget set includes several widget classes that are not used directly, but whose sole purpose is to support subclasses. These classes can also be used as a way of separating the various Motif widgets into related categories. The XmPrimitive widget class is the basis of all Motif widget classes that do not support children. The XmPrimitive widget class is never instantiated, and serves primarily to define a set of basic resources inherited by its subclasses. Widget classes derived from the XmPrimitive widget class are often referred to as "primitive" widgets. These widgets are also sometimes called "display" widgets, because they typically display information. Chapter 2 provides examples that use several primitive widgets, including the XmLabel and XmPushButton widgets. This chapter examines these and other Motif primitive widgets in more detail. Other types of Motif widgets are discussed in later chapters.

Xt implements a form of inheritance that allows widget classes to share the behavior of another class. It is useful, when trying to understand what a particular type of widget does, to know how the various widgets are related. Figure 4.1 shows the inheritance hierarchy of the primitive widgets discussed in this chapter. From this figure, it is clear that the XmPushButton widget class inherits the features of the XmLabel widget class, the XmPrimitive widget class, and the Core widget class.

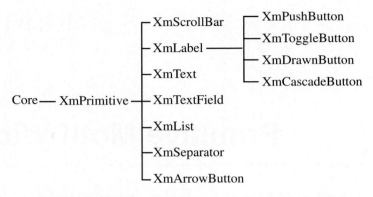

Figure 4.1 Inheritance hierarchy of Motif primitive widgets.

4.1   The Core Widget Class

The Xt Core widget class forms the basis of all Motif widgets. All motif widgets inherit indirectly from the Core widget class and therefore support the resources, callbacks, and other behavior implemented by the Core widget class. The Core widget class defines an `XmNdestroyCallback` list that is inherited by all subclasses. Functions registered with this callback list are invoked whenever a widget is destroyed.

The Core widget class is not intended to be used directly, although it can be instantiated and is occasionally used as an empty window in which to display text or graphics. Normally, Motif applications use the XmDrawingArea widget for this purpose.

Resources

The resources defined by the Core widget class and inherited by all other widget classes include the following:

- `XmNx`, `XmNy`: These resources specify a widget's position. Usually, these values are determined by the widget's parent (see Chapter 5).

- `XmNwidth`, `XmNheight`: The values of these resource determine the width and height of a widget. Each widget class determines its own minimum default value, although a widget's final size is determined by its parent.

- `XmNborderWidth`: The value of this resource determines the width of the border around a widget's window. The default value set by the Core widget class is one pixel.

- `XmNsensitive`: The value of this Boolean resource determines whether a widget can receive input.

- `XmNancestorSensitive`: This read-only resource indicates whether a widget's parent can receive input.
- `XmNcolormap`: The colormap used by this widget's window. See Chapter 9 for more information about colormaps. The value of this resource defaults to the colormap used by the widget's parent.
- `XmNbackground`: The value of this resource determines the background color of a widget. The resource must be set to a pixel value.
- `XmNbackgroundPixmap`: All widgets can have a background pattern, or pixmap. This resource, if set, determines the pixmap whose pattern is displayed in the widget's window.
- `XmNborderColor`: The value of this resource determines the border color of a widget's window.
- `XmNborderPixmap`: Window borders can also have patterns. If set, this resource determines the pixmap used to create the pattern in a widget's window border.
- `XmNmappedWhenManaged`: If the value of this resource is `TRUE`, a widget's window is displayed (mapped) when the widget is managed. If `FALSE`, a widget can be managed by its parent, but not be visible to the user. The default value of this resource is `TRUE`.

4.2   The XmPrimitive Widget Class

The Motif XmPrimitive widget class provides support for all primitive widgets in the Motif widget set. The XmPrimitive class is a subclass of the Xt Core widget class and provides additional key functionality, behavior, resources, and callbacks that are inherited by all subclasses of XmPrimitive. For example, the XmPrimitive class supports the top and bottom shadows displayed by many Motif widgets. The XmPrimitive widget also supports keyboard traversal (see Chapter 5) and implements the support for highlighting a widget's border when it has input focus. The XmPrimitive widget class is never instantiated and the class exists solely to support other Motif widget classes.

Resources

The XmPrimitive widget class inherits all the resources supported by the Core widget class and adds several more of its own. The resources supported by the XmPrimitive widget class, and inherited by all subclasses, include:

- `XmNforeground`: The value of this resource, which must be a pixel value, determines the foreground color used to display text.
- `XmNhighlightOnEnter`: If the value of a widget's `XmNhighlightOnEnter` resource is `TRUE`, the widget displays a border when it has input focus. The default value is `FALSE`.

- **XmNhighlightThickness**: If a widget's **XmNhighlightOnEnter** resource is set to **TRUE**, the value of this resource controls the thickness of the highlight border drawn around the widget. The default thickness is two pixels.
- **XmNhighlightColor**: This resource determines the color of the highlight border that may be drawn around a widget when it receives input focus. The default color is black.
- **XmNshadowThickness**: Most subclasses of the XmPrimitive widget display shadows that produce a three-dimensional effect. The value of the **XmNshadowThickness** resource determines the thickness of that shadow. The default shadow thickness is two pixels.
- **XmNtopShadowColor**: This resource controls the color of a widget's top shadow. If a widget's top shadow color is lighter than its background color, the widget appears to protrude from the screen. If a widget's top shadow color is darker than its background, the widget will appear to be recessed into the screen. By default, the value of a widget's **XmNtopShadow-Color** resource is computed automatically from the widget's background color.
- **XmNbottomShadowColor**: The **XmNbottomShadowColor** resource controls the color of a widget's bottom shadow, which should be chosen to complement the top shadow color. If a widget is to appear to protrude from the screen, the bottom shadow must be darker than the widget's background color. If the widget is to appear to be recessed into the screen, its bottom shadow color must be lighter than it background color. The default bottom shadow color is computed automatically from the widget's background color.
- **XmNuserData**: This resource provides access to an untyped pointer maintained by each Motif widget. Applications can use this resource to associate additional data with a widget.

Callbacks

The XmPrimitive widget inherits the **XmNdestroyCallback** supported by the Xt Core widget class. XmPrimitive also adds a new callback, **XmNhelpCallback**, which supports applications that provide context-sensitive help for users. The **XmNhelpCallback** callback is invoked if a user presses the system help key (usually <F1>). Applications that wish to provide context-sensitive help can register callbacks to handle the user's help request.

4.3   The XmLabel Widget Class

One of the simplest Motif widgets is the XmLabel widget, already demonstrated in Chapter 2. The XmLabel widget simply displays a string or a pixmap in a window. The XmLabel widget does not support any callbacks, other than the **XmNhelpCallback** and **XmNdestroyCallback** lists supported by all Motif widgets. However, the XmLabel widget supports many resources and is a very versatile and commonly used widget. In addition to its many uses when displaying strings and images, the XmLabel widget provides support for several subclasses, including the XmPushButton class.

Resources

Because the XmLabel widget class is a subclass of the XmPrimitive widget class, it inherits the resources supported by the XmPrimitive and Core widget classes. The XmLabel widget class also adds some resources of its own. The resources supported by the XmLabel widget class include the following:

- `XmNalignment`: The value of this resource determines the alignment of the string or image displayed by a label widget. The possible values are `XmALIGNMENT_BEGINNING`, `XmALIGNMENT_CENTER`, or `XmALIGNMENT_END`. For left to right text or images, these values indicate that the contents of the label widget should aligned to the left side, center, or right side of the widget, respectively. The default value is `XmALIGNMENT_CENTER`.

- `XmNlabelType`: The XmLabel widget can display text as well as images in the form of pixmaps. The default value of this resource is `XmSTRING`, which indicates that the widget is to display text. To display a pixmap, this resource must be set to `XmPIXMAP`, and a pixmap must be specified using the `XmNlabelPixmap` resource.

- `XmNmarginHeight`: This resource controls the height of margins along the top and bottom of the label. The default value is two pixels each on the top and bottom.

- `XmNmarginWidth`: This resource controls the width of margins along the left and right sides of a label widget. The default value is two pixels along each side.

- `XmNmarginLeft`: The value of the `XmNmarginLeft` resource determines the amount of space, in addition to the value of the `XmNmarginWidth` resource, along the left side of a label widget. The default value of this resource is zero pixels.

- `XmNmarginRight`: The value of the `XmNmarginRight` resource determines the amount of space, in addition to the value of the `XmNmarginWidth` resource, along the right side of a label widget. The default value of this resource is zero pixels.

- `XmNmarginTop`: This resource specifies the amount of space, in addition to the value of the `XmNmarginHeight` resource, along the top of a label widget. The default value of this resource is zero pixels.

- `XmNmarginBottom`: The value of `XmNmarginBottom` specifies the amount of space, in addition to the value of the `XmNmarginHeight` resource, along the bottom of a label widget. The default value of this resource is zero pixels.

- `XmNfontList`: The value of this resource determines the font, or a list of fonts, with which the string specified by the `XmNlabelString` resource is displayed.

- `XmNlabelPixmap`: If the `XmNlabelType` resource is set to `XmPIXMAP`, the value of this resource indicates the pixmap to be displayed.

- `XmNlabelString`: If the `XmNlabelType` resource is set to `XmSTRING`, this resource specifies the compound string to be displayed by the label. If not set explicitly, the value of the `XmNlabelString` resource defaults to the widget's name.

- `XmNinsensitivePixmap`: Widgets can be sensitive or insensitive to input. Usually, widgets that are insensitive alter their appearance in some way. Motif stipples text automatically, but widgets that display pixmaps can specify an alternate pixmap to be used when the label is insensitive. Because labels are not normally used as input areas, the

XmNinsensitivePixmap resource is seldom directly useful with label widgets. However, this resource is inherited by various button widgets subclassed from the XmLabel widget class.

- XmNrecomputeSize: When widgets are managed by a parent, the parent often needs to know the preferred size of each of its children. If a label widget's XmNrecomputeSize resource is set to TRUE, the label widget will always compute its desired sized based on the size of the string or pixmap displayed by the widget. If this resource value is set to FALSE, the widget will always indicate that its current size is its preferred size, and the widget will not attempt to resize itself if the string or image displayed in the widget changes dynamically.

Many of these resources control spacing within the XmLabel widget. All subclasses of XmLabel also support these resources and spacings.

Using the XmLabel Widget

The following simple program is useful for exploring the behavior and capabilities of the XmLabel widget.

```
1     /******************************************************************
2      * label.c: Simple program for experimenting with label widgets
3      ******************************************************************/
4     #include <Xm/Xm.h>
5     #include <Xm/Label.h>
6
7     void main ( int argc, char **argv )
8     {
9         Widget        shell, label;
10        XtAppContext app;
11
12        shell = XtAppInitialize ( &app, "Label", NULL, 0,
13                                  &argc, argv, NULL, NULL, 0 );
14
15        /*
16         * Create a Motif XmLabel widget
17         */
18
19        label = XtCreateManagedWidget ( "label", xmLabelWidgetClass, shell,
20                                        NULL, 0 );
21
22        /*
23         * Realize the shell and enter an event loop.
24         */
25
26        XtRealizeWidget ( shell );
27        XtAppMainLoop ( app );
28    }
```

This program simply creates a single XmLabel widget. By default, this program displays the name of the widget, the string "label". However, by setting various resources in a resource file, the label can be manipulated in various ways. For example, the following resource specification causes the XmLabel widget in this example to display a multi-line text string:

```
*label.labelString: a multiple line\n\
left-aligned string\n\
displayed in a label widget
```

The newline characters cause this string to be displayed as three lines. By default, these lines will be left-justified, as shown in Figure 4.2, when displayed in a left-to-right language.

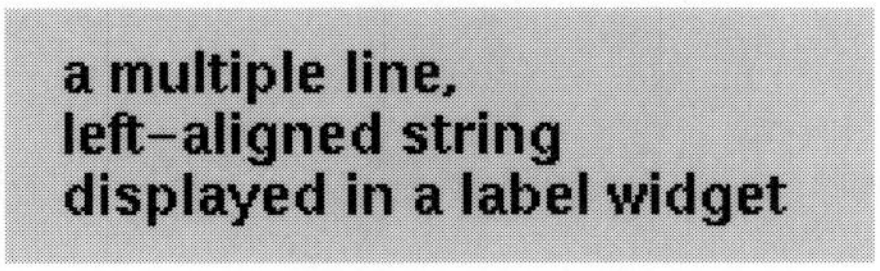

Figure 4.2 A multi-line, left-aligned label.

The `XmNalignment` resource can be used to alter the way the text is displayed. Figure 4.3 shows the result of displaying a multi-line string with the `XmNalignment` resource to `XmALIGNMENT_END`.

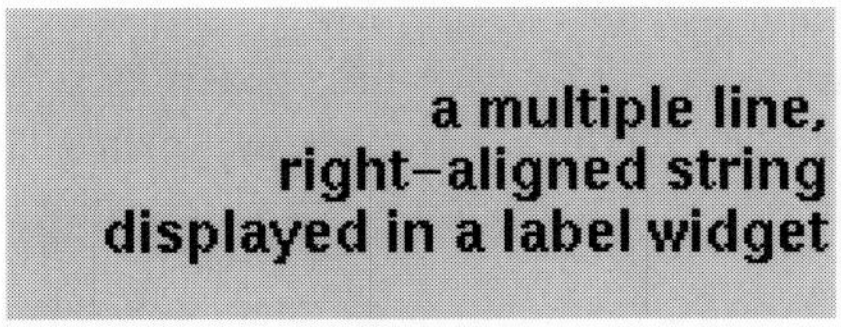

Figure 4.3 A right-aligned multi-line label.

An XmLabel widget can also be used to display an image, in the form of a pixmap. Displaying an image stored in X bitmap format in a file is especially easy. (See Chapter 11 for information about bitmaps and other image formats.) The name of the bitmap file can simply be specified in a resource file as the value of the XmLabel widget's `XmNlabelPixmap` resource. For example, the file /usr/include/X11/bitmaps/xlogo64 contains a 64x64 pixel bitmap of the X logo. The simple program described on page 88 can be used to display this bitmap by setting the following resources in a resource file:

```
*label.labelType: pixmap
*label*labelPixmap: xlogo64
```

With these resource settings, the example program described above creates the image shown in Figure 4.4.

Figure 4.4 An XmLabel widget displaying a pixmap.

4.4   Button Widgets

Several subclasses of XmLabel, such as XmPushButton, XmToggleButton, and XmDrawnButton, act as buttons and allow users to issue commands. These widget classes inherit the features of the XmLabel widget, such as the spacing resources, and the ability to display a string or a pixmap. They also inherit the `XmNhelpCallback` and color-related resources supported by the XmPrimitive widget class. Each of the Motif button widgets adds slightly different behavior to that inherited from its superclasses. The following sections discuss each type of button widget.

The XmPushButton Widget Class

The XmPushButton widget is one of the most commonly used widgets in the Motif widget set. This widget allows users to issue a command by "pushing" the button. When a button is "pushed", its appearance changes, which provides the illusion that the button has been pressed in, as seen in Figure 4.5. When the user releases the button, the widget's colors return to normal.

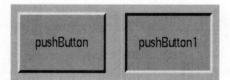

Figure 4.5 The XmPushButton widget, normal state and "pushed in".

Resources

The XmPushButton widget adds several resources to those inherited from the XmLabel, XmPrimitive and Core widget classes. These include

- `XmNarmColor`: This resource indicates the pixel value for the color of a button widget's background when it is *armed* (pushed in). Normally, a widget's arm color is computed automatically based on the background color of the widget, and is usually slightly darker than the background.

- `XmNarmPixmap`: If a button is used to display a pixmap, it may be desirable to have the displayed image change when the button is pressed in, or armed. For example, the image may need to use a different background color to match the arm color specified by the `XmNarmColor` resource. The `XmNarmPixmap` resource can be used to control the pixmap displayed when a button is armed.

- `XmNfillOnArm`: If the value of this resource is `TRUE`, a button widget changes its background color when the user pushes the button. Otherwise, the widget retains the background color displayed when the button is in its normal state. The default value of this resource is `TRUE`.

Callbacks

XmPushButton widgets also support several callbacks in addition to the `XmNhelpCallback` provided by the XmPrimitive widget class. These are:

- `XmNarmCallback`: Functions registered with the `XmNarmCallback` list are called when the button is *armed*. A button is armed when a mouse button is pressed while the pointer is contained in the widget's window. If the resource `XmNfillOnArm` is `TRUE` (the default), the button's colors invert, which creates the illusion of a button being pressed. When this callback list is invoked, the `reason` member of the call data structure is set to `XmCR_ARM`.

- `XmNactivateCallback`: Functions registered with this callback list are invoked when the button is *activated*. Normally a widget is activated when the user releases the mouse button while the pointer is within an armed widget's window. This callback is not invoked if the user releases the mouse button outside of the widget. The `reason` member of the call data structure is set to `XmCR_ACTIVATE` when the `XmNactivateCallback` list is invoked. Buttons can also be activated by typing a <RETURN> key while the button has input focus.

- `XmNdisarmCallback`: Functions registered with a widget's `XmNdisarmCallback` list are called when the widget is *disarmed*. Normally, a widget is disarmed when the user releases the mouse button after arming the button. If the button has been activated, the `XmNactivateCallback` list will be invoked, followed by the `XmNdisarmCallback` list. The `reason` member of the call data structure is set to `XmCR_DISARM`.

All XmPushButton widget callbacks are passed a pointer to a structure of type `XmAnyCallbackStruct` as the `callData` argument. This structure contains a pointer to the X event that caused the callback and a reason. Possible values for the `reason` member are `XmCR_ARM`, `XmCR_DISARM`, and `XmCR_ACTIVATE`.

Using the XmPushButton Widget Class

Let's look at a simple example that uses the XmPushButton widget to see how the XmPushButton callbacks work. The following program creates a single XmPushButton widget and registers the same callback for each of the callback lists discussed above.

```
1    /**************************************************
2     * pushbutton.c: Test the XmPushButton widget.
3     **************************************************/
4    #include <Xm/Xm.h>
5    #include <Xm/PushB.h>
6    #include <stdio.h>
7
8    void ButtonCallback ( Widget    w,
9                          XtPointer clientData,
10                         XtPointer callData );
11
12   void main ( int argc, char **argv )
13   {
14       Widget       shell, button;
15       XtAppContext app;
16
17       /*
18        * Initialize Xt
19        */
20
21       shell = XtAppInitialize ( &app, "Pushbutton", NULL, 0,
22                                 &argc, argv, NULL, NULL, 0 );
23
24       /*
25        * Create the pushbutton widget.
26        */
27
28       button = XtCreateManagedWidget ( "button", xmPushButtonWidgetClass,
29                                        shell, NULL, 0 );
30       /*
31        * Add a callback for each supported callback list.
32        */
33
34       XtAddCallback ( button, XmNactivateCallback,
35                       ButtonCallback, NULL );
36
37       XtAddCallback ( button, XmNarmCallback,
38                       ButtonCallback, NULL );
39
40       XtAddCallback ( button, XmNdisarmCallback,
41                       ButtonCallback, NULL );
42
43       XtRealizeWidget ( shell );
44
45       XtAppMainLoop ( app );
46   }
```

The callback function prints a message that reports the reason indicated in the call data structure when it is invoked.

```
47  void ButtonCallback ( Widget w, XtPointer clientData, XtPointer callData )
48  {
49      XmAnyCallbackStruct *cbs = ( XmAnyCallbackStruct * ) callData;
50
51      switch ( cbs->reason )
52      {
53        case XmCR_ACTIVATE:
54            printf ( "Button activated\n" );
55            break;
56        case XmCR_ARM:
57            printf ( "Button armed\n" );
58            break;
59        case XmCR_DISARM:
60            printf ( "Button disarmed\n" );
61            break;
62      }
63  }
```

Running this program demonstrates how Motif button callbacks work. When the user presses a mouse button while the pointer is in the XmPushButton widget, the widget's appearance changes to indicate that it is "pushed in" and the `ButtonCallback()` function is called with the `reason` member of the call data structure set to `XmCR_ARM`. When the user releases the button, `Button-Callback()` is called with the `reason` field of the `callData` structure set to `XmCR_ACTIVATE`, and then called again with the reason given as `XmCR_DISARM`. As the button is disarmed, it also resumes its normal appearance. If the user moves the pointer out of the button's window before releasing the mouse button, `ButtonCallback()` is called with the `reason` member of the call data structure set to `XmCR_DISARM`. This allows the user to abort a command by moving the pointer out the XmPushButton widget before releasing the mouse button, and also allows the application to know that the user has aborted the operation.

The XmPushButton widget provides a convenient way to issue a command. For example, the `memo` example in Chapter 2 could have used a "quit" button rather than using the window manager's menu. Because many applications need such a quit mechanism, it can be useful to write a simple routine that creates a button that causes an application to exit when the user clicks on the button with the mouse. Such a function is implemented below. This function takes a single argument: the parent widget of the button. The function simply creates an XmPushButton widget labeled "quit" as a child of the given parent and registers several callback functions.

Designing a general-purpose quit button is not quite as simple as it might at first appear. Applications that use a quit button may need to perform other actions before exiting the application. This could be done by registering additional callbacks. However, the order in which the functions on a given callback list are invoked is not defined by Xt. Therefore, it is not sufficient to register an `XmNactivateCallback` function that exits the application, because it is not guaranteed that additional callback functions registered by an application would ever be called.

The three callback lists supported by the XmPushButton widget offer one way to solve this problem, and one solution is shown below. The idea is to use the multiple types of callbacks supported by the Motif XmPushButton widget to guarantee that all functions on the `XmNactivateCallback` list are called before the program exits.

The first callback to be called, the `XmNarmCallback`, initializes a flag to `FALSE`. If the button is activated, an `XmNactivateCallback` function sets this flag to `TRUE`. Finally, if this flag is `TRUE` when the button is disarmed, the `XmNdisarmCallback` function calls `exit()`. Applications that need to perform some cleanup before exiting can add functions to the button's `XmNactivateCallback` list, because all functions registered with the `XmNactivate-Callback` list will now be invoked before the program exits.

```
1     /*******************************************************
2      * quit.c: A utility function that adds a quit button
3      *******************************************************/
4     #include <Xm/Xm.h>
5     #include <Xm/PushB.h>
6
7     /*
8      * Define three callbacks. Make them static - no need
9      * to make them known outside this file.
10     */
11
12    static void ArmCallback ( Widget    w,
13                              XtPointer clientData,
14                              XtPointer callData )
15    {
16        int *flag = ( int * ) clientData;
17
18        *flag = FALSE; /* Initialize a flag when the button is pressed */
19    }
20
21    static void ActivateCallback ( Widget    w,
22                                   XtPointer clientData,
23                                   XtPointer callData )
24    {
25        int *flag = ( int * ) clientData;
26
27        /* Set the flag to indicate that the button
28           has been activated. */
29
30        *flag = TRUE;
31    }
32
33    static void DisarmCallback ( Widget    w,
34                                 XtPointer clientData,
35                                 XtPointer callData )
36    {
37        int * flag = ( int * ) clientData;
38
39        if ( *flag )
40            exit ( 0 );
41    }
```

```
42   /*
43    * Function to add a quit button as a child of any widget.
44    */
45
46   Widget CreateQuitButton ( Widget parent )
47   {
48       Widget      w;
49       static int reallyQuit;
50
51       w = XtCreateManagedWidget ( "quit", xmPushButtonWidgetClass,
52                                    parent, NULL, 0 );
53
54       XtAddCallback ( w, XmNarmCallback,
55                       ArmCallback, ( XtPointer ) &reallyQuit );
56       XtAddCallback ( w, XmNdisarmCallback,
57                       DisarmCallback, ( XtPointer ) &reallyQuit );
58       XtAddCallback ( w, XmNactivateCallback,
59                       ActivateCallback, ( XtPointer ) &reallyQuit );
60       return ( w );
61   }
```

This example is perhaps an uncommon use of the three XmPushButton callbacks, but it demonstrates the flexibility offered by Motif.

The XmArrowButton Widget Class

An XmArrowButton widget is a button that always displays an arrow, as seen in Figure 4.6. Although its behavior is similar to other Motif buttons, the XmArrowButton widget is a direct subclass of XmPrimitive and does not inherit any of the features of XmLabel.

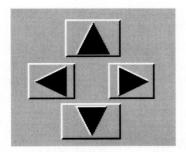

Figure 4.6   XmArrowButton widgets.

The XmArrowButton widget class supports `XmNactivateCallback`, `XmNarm-Callback`, and `XmNdisarmCallback` lists, just like XmPushButton. In addition to those inherited from XmPrimitive, the XmArrowButton widget class recognizes one resource, `XmNarrowDirection`. This resource controls which direction the arrow image is drawn, and may have the values XmARROW_UP, XmARROW_DOWN, XmARROW_LEFT, or XmARROW_RIGHT. Figure 4.6 shows one XmArrowButton widget for each of these values.

The XmDrawnButton Widget Class

The XmDrawnButton is a subclass of the XmLabel widget class designed to support applications that wish to display graphics in a button. The XmDrawnButton widget supports XmNarm-Callback, XmNdisarmCallback, and XmNactivateCallback lists, the same as XmPushButton. In addition to these callback functions, the XmDrawnButton widget class supports an XmNexposeCallback that allows functions to be called when the image displayed in the widget needs to be redrawn, and XmNresizeCallback, which is called when the button changes size.

The XmDrawnButton mimics the visual behavior of a push button if the resource XmNpushButtonEnabled is set to TRUE. The default value is FALSE. The XmDrawnButton also supports several different shadow types, as shown in Figure 4.7. The type of shadow is determined by the XmNshadowType resource, which can be set to one of XmSHADOW_IN, XmSHADOW_OUT, XmSHADOW_ETCHED_IN, or XmSHADOW_ETCHED_OUT.

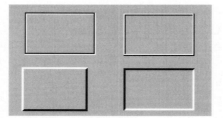

Figure 4.7 XmDrawnButton widgets with different shadow types.

The XmCascadeButton Widget Class

The XmCascadeButton widget class is a subclass of the XmLabel widget class that supports cascading menu panes in menus. The XmCascadeButton widget class offers the same functionality as an XmPushButton widget, but adds the ability to display a cascade indicator and to pop up a menu pane when the button is armed. XmCascadeButton widgets are not expected to be used outside menus, and are discussed in more detail in Chapter 6.

The XmToggleButton Widget Class

The XmToggleButton widget class is a subclass of XmLabel and inherits the resources and behavior of the XmLabel, XmPrimitive, and Core widgets. XmToggleButton widgets display two states and are often used to allow users to select from a set of options. Figure 4.8 shows two sets of XmToggleButton widgets. The set to the right supports N-of-many types of selections. Users can select any or all toggles to choose whether each item is toggled on or off. The buttons to the left are being used to indicate a one-of-many choice, in which users can select only one of the buttons at any one time. The indicator supported by the XmToggleButton widget changes depending on the selection mode for which it is used.

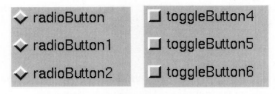

Figure 4.8 XmToggleButton widgets.

Resources

In addition to those resources inherited from the XmLabel widget class, the XmToggleButton class supports several new resources, including the following:

- `XmNvisibleWhenOff`: This resource controls whether the indicator symbol on an XmToggleButton widget is visible when the widget is not selected. If `TRUE` (the default) the indicator changes its appearance when the widget is selected or unselected. If the value of this resource is set to `FALSE`, the indicator simply disappears when the widget is not selected.

- `XmNindicatorSize`: This resource controls the width and height, in pixels, of the indicator.

- `XmNindicatorType`: This resource determines whether the indicator is drawn in the style used to indicate a one-of-many choice or an N-of-many choice. The default value is `XmN_OF_MANY`. The value `XmONE_OF_MANY` is set automatically for XmToggleButton widgets created as a child of a RadioBox widget (see Chapter 5).

- `XmNspacing`: The value of this resource determines the number of pixels between the indicator and the label displayed by an XmToggleButton widget class. The default value is 4 pixels.

- `XmNselectPixmap`: If an XmToggleButton's `XmNlabelType` resource is set to `XmPIXMAP`, the `XmNlabelPixmap` resource controls the pixmap displayed in the label portion of the widget in its normal, unselected state. The `XmNselectPixmap` resource specifies the pixmap to be displayed when the widget has been selected, if `XmNlabelType` is set to `XmPIXMAP`.

- `XmNset`: The value of this resource can be set to `TRUE` to programmatically change an XmToggleButton widget's selected state. The value can also be retrieved at any time to determine the button's current state. The default value is `FALSE`.

- `XmNindicatorOn`: If `TRUE` (the default), an indicator is shown to the left of the label when an XmToggleButton is selected. An indicator may also be shown when a widget is not selected, depending on the value of `XmNvisibleWhenOff`. If the value of `XmNindicatorOn` is set to `FALSE`, the indicator is never shown.

- **XmNfillOnSelect**: If this resource is set to TRUE (the default) the center of a selected XmToggleButton widget's indicator is drawn in the color indicated by the value of the **XmNselectColor** resource.
- **XmNselectColor**: This resource determines the color of the center portion of the XmToggleButton widget's indicator when **XmNfillOnSelect** is TRUE.

Callbacks

The XmToggleButton widget supports several callbacks, in addition to the **XmNhelpCallback** inherited from the XmPrimitive widget class. The callbacks are:

- **XmNvalueChangedCallback**: Callback functions registered with this callback list are invoked whenever an XmToggleButton changes between being "set" and "unset".
- **XmNarmCallback**: Callbacks registered with this callback list are invoked when the button is armed. This callback works the same way as the XmPushButton callback of the same name.
- **XmNdisarmCallback**: Callbacks registered with this callback list are invoked when the button is disarmed. This callback works the same way as the XmPushButton callback of the same name.

XmToggleButton callback functions are passed a pointer to a structure of type **XmToggleButtonCallbackStruct**. This structure is defined as follows:

```
typedef struct {
    int      reason;
    XEvent *event;
    int      set;
} XmToggleButtonCallbackStruct;
```

The **set** member is always non-zero if the XmToggleButton is currently selected and zero if it is not.

Convenience Functions

The XmToggleButton widget class supports several convenience functions. These include:

```
void XmToggleButtonSetState ( Widget w, int newstate, Boolean notify );
Boolean XmToggleButtonGetState ( Widget w );
```

XmToggleButtonSetState() is used to change an XmToggleButton widget's selected state programmatically. (A toggle button's state can also be changed by calling **XtSetValues()** to change the value of the widget's **XmNset** resource.) If the **notify** argument is TRUE, the widget will invoke all **XmNvalueChangedCallback** functions registered with this widget. Changing the state of a toggle button widget by calling **XtSetValues()** does not invoke any **XmNvalueChangedCallback** functions.

XmToggleButtonGetState() returns the current value of the **XmNset** resource, which can also be retrieved using **XtGetValues()**.

Using the XmToggleButton Widget

The following program demonstrates how an XmToggleButton widget works. The program simply creates an XmToggleButton widget, and registers one callback function to be called when the button's state changes.

```
1    /**********************************************************
2     * toggle.c: Demonstrate a Motif toggle button widget
3     **********************************************************/
4    #include <Xm/Xm.h>
5    #include <Xm/ToggleB.h>
6    #include <stdio.h>
7
8    static void ValueChangedCallback ( Widget     w,
9                                       XtPointer clientData,
10                                      XtPointer callData );
11
12   void main ( int argc, char **argv )
13   {
14       Widget        shell, toggle;
15       XtAppContext app;
16
17       /*
18        * Initialize Xt
19        */
20
21       shell = XtAppInitialize ( &app, "Toggle", NULL, 0,
22                                 &argc, argv, NULL, NULL, 0 );
23
24       /*
25        * Create an XmToggleButton widget
26        */
27
28       toggle = XtCreateManagedWidget ( "toggle",
29                                        xmToggleButtonWidgetClass,
30                                        shell, NULL, 0 );
31
32       XtAddCallback ( toggle, XmNvalueChangedCallback,
33                       ValueChangedCallback, NULL );
34
35       /*
36        * Realize the shell and enter the event loop.
37        */
38
39       XtRealizeWidget ( shell );
40       XtAppMainLoop ( app );
41   }
```

ValueChangedCallback() just prints a message when the toggle button changes state:

```
42   static void ValueChangedCallback ( Widget      w,
43                                       XtPointer clientData,
44                                       XtPointer callData )
45   {
46       XmToggleButtonCallbackStruct *cbs =
47                         ( XmToggleButtonCallbackStruct * ) callData;
48       /*
49        * Report the new state of the toggle button for which this
50        * callback function was called.
51        */
52
53       if ( cbs->set )
54           printf ( "button set\n" );
55       else
56           printf ( "button unset\n" );
57   }
```

Although the XmToggleButton widget normally appears as seen in Figure 4.8, the XmToggle-Button widget is quite versatile, and various resources can be combined to achieve different effects. For example, the following resources can be used to make the above example toggle between two bitmapped images, which are assumed to be in an X bitmap file format (see Chapter 11) and found in a standard location for bitmap files. These resources configure the XmToggleButton widget to not display the indicator at all, but to simply toggle between two images when the button is selected by the user.

```
!!!!!!!!!!!!!!!!!!!!!!!!!!!!!!!!!!!!!!!!!!!!!!!!!!!!!!!!!!!!!!!
!! Resources required to use bitmap images instead of
!! indicators to indicate toggle state.
!!!!!!!!!!!!!!!!!!!!!!!!!!!!!!!!!!!!!!!!!!!!!!!!!!!!!!!!!!!!!!!
! No indicator at all

*XmToggleButton*indicatorOn:     FALSE

! Display images

*XmToggleButton*labelType:       pixmap

! not selected image

*XmToggleButton*labelPixmap:     thumbs_down

! image when selected

*XmToggleButton*selectPixmap:    thumbs_up
```

Assuming the specified bitmaps (or some other bitmaps) are available and located on the application's bitmap search path, the above resources alter the toggle demo program to appear as shown in Figure 4.9.

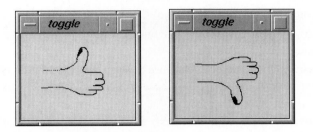

Figure 4.9 Using toggled bitmaps in an XmToggleButton widget.

4.5   The XmText and XmTextField Widget Classes

Motif provides two widgets that allow users to enter and edit text. The XmText widget allows users to edit multiple or single lines of text. In single-line mode, this widget is useful for applications that require a short string. In multi-line mode, the XmText widget functions as a complete text editor. A large number of convenience functions allow programmers to scroll the contents of the XmText widget, set the widget to edit mode or read-only mode, set and retrieve the text displayed, insert text, and so on.

The XmTextField widget is similar to the XmText widget, but supports only a single-line mode. This widget is designed to be more efficient than using the XmText widget for single-line applications, and is primarily used when creating forms with many text entry areas. The XmText and XmTextField widgets support very similar interfaces and similar sets of resources. In fact, most XmText widget convenience functions can be used with either widget, although there are equivalent versions specifically for the XmTextField widget.

Resources

The following are some of the commonly used resources supported by both the XmText and XmTextField widget classes:

- `XmNvalue`: This resource represents the string displayed by a text widget. As of Motif version 1.2, the XmText and XmTextField widgets do not use compound strings, but use simple character strings instead. This resource can be used to specify a character string to be displayed in a text widget, or to retrieve a text widget's current contents.
- `XmNmarginHeight`: This resource controls the vertical margin above and below the text displayed in a text widget. The default value is 5 pixels.
- `XmNmarginWidth`: This resource controls the horizontal margin between the characters displayed in a text widget and the boundaries of the widget. The default value is 5 pixels.

- `XmNcursorPosition`: This resource represents the number of characters between the current insertion point and the beginning of the text widget's buffer.

- `XmNcolumns`: This resource controls the initial width of a text widget in character spaces. The default value is 20 characters.

- `XmNmaxLength`: This resource determines the maximum number of characters than can be added to a text widget. The default value is determined by the value of `MAXINT` on the system.

- `XmNblinkRate`: The rate in milliseconds at which a text widget's insertion cursor blinks can be retrieved or set using this resource. The default is to blink every 500 milliseconds.

- `XmNfontList`: The value of this resource determines the font used to display characters in a text widget.

- `XmNeditable`: If this resource is `TRUE` (the default), users may type into a text widget. If `FALSE`, attempts to enter text will cause a "beep" to sound.

- `XmNcursorPositionVisible`: Normally, a text widget's insertion cursor is visible as an "i-beam" shape at the current insertion point. If this resource is set to `FALSE`, the insertion cursor will no longer be visible.

- `XmNverifyBell`: Various callbacks supported by the text widget classes allow applications to disallow insertion, cursor motion, or other modifications to a widget's text buffer. If this resource is `TRUE` (the default), the text widget will automatically "beep" when such an operation is disallowed. If this resource is set to `FALSE`, no audible warning is made.

Callbacks

The XmText and XmTextField widget classes support several useful callbacks. These include:

- `XmNactivateCallback`: Functions registered with this callback list are called when a user types the <RETURN> key. Typically, this callback is used to accept whatever text has been entered.

- `XmNfocusCallback`: Functions registered with this callback list are invoked before the XmText widget receives input focus.

- `XmNlosingFocusCallback`: Functions on this callback list are called before the XmText widget loses input focus.

- `XmNvalueChangedCallback`: This callback list is invoked whenever the text in an XmText widget is modified via the functions `XtSetValues()`, `XmTextSetString()`, or `XmTextReplace()`.

- `XmNmotionVerifyCallback`: Functions registered with this callback list are called whenever the widget's insertion cursor position changes. Functions registered with this callback list can examine the information in the call data structure to determine if the motion should be permitted. If the motion is to be disallowed, the callback function must set the `doit` member of the call data structure to `FALSE`. This member is initialized to `TRUE` before the function is called, so motion is allowed by default.

- **XmNmodifyVerifyCallback**: Functions registered with this callback list are invoked whenever the text in an XmText or XmTextField widget is modified. Like the **XmNmotionVerifyCallback** callback list, functions registered with the **XmNmodifyVerifyCallback** list can examine the information in the call data structure to determine if the modification should be permitted. If the modification is not allowed, the callback function must set the **doit** member of the **XmTextVerifyCallbackStruct** call data structure to **FALSE**.

The XmText and XmTextField widget classes's **XmNmodifyVerifyCallback**, **XmNmotionVerifyCallback**, and **XmNlosingFocusCallback** lists provide a pointer to a **XmTextVerifyCallbackStruct** structure as call data. This structure is defined as follows:

```
typedef struct {
    int            reason;
    XEvent         *event;
    Boolean        doit;
    XmTextPosition currInsert, newInsert;
    XmTextPosition startPos, endPos;
    XmTextBlock    text;
} XmTextVerifyCallbackStruct;
```

The **XmTextBlock** structure is defined as follows:

```
typedef struct {
    char           *ptr;
    int            length;
    XmTextFormat format;
} XmTextBlockRec, *XmTextBlock;
```

Functions called when a text widget has been modified can examine the information in these structures to determine if the reported modification should be permitted. If the modification is to be disallowed, the callback function should set the **doit** member of the **XmTextVerifyCall-backStruct** to **FALSE**. The **doit** member is initialized to **TRUE** before the callback is invoked, so this field can be ignored if the modification is acceptable. An example that uses this callback structure can be seen on page 111.

Using the XmTextField Widget

The following simple program demonstrates the use of an XmTextField widget to accept some input from a user. The program is split into two files. The first implements a driver program that handles the Xt initialization, event loop, and so on. This driver calls an externally defined function, **CreateInputField()** which returns an XmTextField widget. The driver adds a callback to this widget that prints the contents of the text field when the user types the **<RETURN>** key. This driver program can be written as follows:

```
1     /*****************************************************************
2      * driver.c: Driver program for experimenting with text fields
3      *****************************************************************/
4     #include <Xm/Xm.h>
5     #include <Xm/TextF.h>
6     #include <stdio.h>
7
8     /* Function declarations */
9
10    extern Widget CreateInputField ( Widget parent );
11
12    static void EnterCallback ( Widget    w,
13                                XtPointer clientData,
14                                XtPointer callData);
15
16    void main ( int argc, char **argv )
17    {
18        Widget       shell, text;
19        XtAppContext app;
20
21        /*
22         * Initialize Xt
23         */
24
25        shell = XtAppInitialize ( &app, "Inputtest", NULL, 0,
26                                  &argc, argv, NULL, NULL, 0 );
27
28        /*
29         * Create an input field and register a callback to
30         * be called when the user types a <Return> key
31         */
32
33        text = CreateInputField ( shell );
34
35        XtAddCallback ( text, XmNactivateCallback, EnterCallback, NULL);
36
37        /*
38         * Realize the shell and enter the event loop.
39         */
40
41        XtRealizeWidget ( shell );
42        XtAppMainLoop ( app );
43    }
```

The callback function, `EnterCallback()`, is registered with the text widget as an `XmNactivateCallback` function. This function calls the convenience function, `XmTextFieldGetString()`, to extract the content of the text field and echoes the string to standard output.

```
44   static void EnterCallback ( Widget      w,
45                                XtPointer clientData,
46                                XtPointer callData )
47   {
48       printf ( "text entered = %s\n", XmTextFieldGetString ( w ) );
49   }
```

The second file contains the function `CreateInputField()`. This version of the function simply creates and returns an XmTextField widget. Later examples modify this function to demonstrate additional features of the Motif text widgets. Notice that a Motif convenience function is used to create the XmTextField widget in this example. It does not matter whether convenience functions are used, or if `XtCreateWidget()` is called directly.

```
1    /***********************************************************
2     * inputfield.c: Create and return a simple text input area
3     ***********************************************************/
4    #include <Xm/Xm.h>
5    #include <Xm/TextF.h>
6
7    Widget CreateInputField ( Widget parent )
8    {
9        Widget text = XmCreateTextField ( parent, "input", NULL, 0 );
10
11       XtManageChild ( text );
12
13       return ( text );
14   }
```

To build this example, these two files must be compiled and linked with the Motif and X libraries, as follows:

```
cc -o inputtest driver.c inputfield.c -lXm -lXt -lX11
```

Running this example program displays a one-line editable text field. Typing text into the input field and typing a <RETURN> key causes the program to print the content of the text field to standard output.

Convenience Functions

The XmText widget provides many public functions that can be used to manipulate the contents of the widget, as shown in the following partial list. Each of these functions has an equivalent XmText-Field version. The XmTextField versions have similar names, but with the addition of the word "Field". For example, the XmText widget supports a function named `XmTextGetString()`. The XmTextField widget supports an equivalent function named `XmTextFieldGetString()`.

The functions shown below are just a sample of the convenience functions supported by the XmText and XmTextField widget classes. Each of these functions requires an XmText widget as its first argument. The position parameters (a value of type `XmTextPosition`) accepted or returned by these functions indicate an index into the character buffer maintained by a text widget.

- `XmTextGetString()`: This function returns the contents of the given text widget's text buffer.

```
char * XmTextGetString ( Widget w )
```

- `XmTextGetLastPosition()`: This function returns the length of string in the given text widget's buffer.

```
XmTextPosition XmTextGetLastPosition ( Widget w )
```

- `XmTextSetString()`: This function initializes the contents of the given text widget's buffer to the specified string.

```
void XmTextSetString ( Widget  w,
                       char    *value )
```

- `XmTextReplace()`: This function replaces any text that currently occupies the position between the two given character indexes with the specified string.

```
void XmTextReplace (  Widget          w,
                      XmTextPosition from_pos,
                      XmTextPosition to_pos,
                      char           *value )
```

- `XmTextInsert()`: This function inserts the given string at the specified position.

```
void XmTextInsert ( Widget         w,
                    XmTextPosition position,
                    char           *value )
```

- `XmTextGetInsertionPosition()`: This function returns the position within the text buffer at which text would be inserted if a user typed into the text widget.

```
XmTextPosition XmTextGetInsertionPosition ( Widget w )
```

- `XmTextSetInsertionPosition()`: This function moves the insertion point to the specified position.

```
void XmTextSetInsertionPosition ( Widget         w,
                                  XmTextPosition position )
```

- `XmTextGetSelection()`: This function returns a copy of the text currently selected in a text widget.

```
char *XmTextGetSelection ( Widget w )
```

- **XmTextRemove()**: This function removes all text from a text widget.

```
Boolean XmTextRemove ( Widget w )
```

- **XmTextCopy()**: This function copies any currently selected text to the Motif clipboard. This function returns TRUE if any text was actually copied. The `clip_time` argument should be an X time stamp, ideally retrieved from the most recent event. (See Chapter 14 for more information about the Motif clipboard.)

```
Boolean XmTextCopy ( Widget w,
                     Time    clip_time)
```

- **XmTextCut()**: This function is like **XmTextCopy()**, but **XmTextCut()** deletes the selected portion of text after copying it to the Motif clipboard.

```
Boolean XmTextCut ( Widget w,
                    Time    clip_time)
```

- **XmTextPaste()**: This function pastes the current contents of the Motif clipboard into the given text widget. The text is inserted at the current insertion position.

```
Boolean XmTextPaste ( Widget w )
```

- **XmTextClearSelection()**: This function deselects any selected text within a text widget. The `sel_time` argument is needed to prevent race conditions. (See Chapter 14 for information about time stamps and selections.)

```
void XmTextClearSelection ( Widget w,
                            Time    sel_time )
```

- **XmTextSetSelection()**: This function programmatically selects the text between the two given positions.

```
void XmTextSetSelection ( Widget         w,
                          XmTextPosition first,
                          XmTextPosition last,
                          Time           sel_time )
```

- **XmTextShowPosition()**: This function scrolls the contents of a text widget to display the text at the specified position.

```
void XmTextShowPosition ( Widget         w,
                          XmTextPosition position )
```

A Numeric Input Field Using an XmTextField Widget

One of the more useful features of the Motif text widgets is the ability to examine the characters entered by a user before they are displayed in a text widget, and to perform various tests or operations on these characters. The following variation on the `CreateInputField()` function, originally described on page 105, creates an input field that allows only numeric digits to be entered. This version of `CreateInputField()` creates and returns an XmTextField widget as before, but this time a callback function is registered as well. This callback function is to be called whenever the contents of the text widget are modified.

The creation function can be written as follows:

```
1    /*******************************************************************
2     * numeric.c: Create an input field that allows only numeric input
3     *******************************************************************/
4    #include <Xm/Xm.h>
5    #include <Xm/TextF.h>
6    #include <ctype.h>
7
8    /* Callback declarations */
9
10   static void TextModifiedCallback ( Widget      w,
11                                       XtPointer clientData,
12                                       XtPointer callData );
13
14   Widget CreateInputField ( Widget parent )
15   {
16      /* Create a text field widget */
17
18      Widget text = XmCreateTextField ( parent, "input", NULL, 0 );
19
20      XtManageChild ( text );
21
22      /* Add a callback to ensure that all input consists of digits */
23
24      XtAddCallback ( text, XmNmodifyVerifyCallback,
25                      TextModifiedCallback, NULL );
26
27      return ( text );
28   }
```

The `TextModifiedCallback()` function is called when any text is entered or deleted. This function uses the `callData` argument provided by the XmTextField widget to determine what characters have been entered. Any new characters are contained in the `XmTextBlock` structure nested inside the `XmTextVerifyCallbackStruct`. The `ptr` field of the `XmTextBlock` will be `NULL` if the callback function has been called because text was deleted. If text has been inserted, the `ptr` member will contain the new characters and the `length` member will indicate the number of new characters to be inserted.

The callback function uses the macro `isdigit()` to check that each inserted character is numeric. If this callback has been called because a user has manually typed some new text, the `ptr` field will contain only a single character. However, paste and other similar operations could cause multiple characters to be inserted at once, so each inserted character must be tested. If any character fails the test, the `doit` field of the `callData` structure is set to `FALSE`. Otherwise, the insertion is allowed to proceed.

```
29  static void TextModifiedCallback ( Widget     w,
30                                      XtPointer clientData,
31                                      XtPointer callData )
32  {
33      XmTextVerifyCallbackStruct *cbs =
34                      ( XmTextVerifyCallbackStruct * ) callData;
35
36      /*
37       * Test all characters of any new input to be sure they are
38       * digits only. Set doit to FALSE if any character fails
39       */
40
41      if ( cbs->text->ptr )
42      {
43          char *string = cbs->text->ptr;
44          int i;
45
46          for ( i = 0; i < cbs->text->length; i++ )
47              if ( !isdigit ( string[i] ) )
48                  cbs->doit = FALSE;
49      }
50  }
```

A Password Input Field

In some applications, it is necessary to modify the text entered by a user in some way, The following example program demonstrates the commonly needed password field. This version of `CreateInputField()` returns an XmTextField widget that always echoes an "*" character for each character typed. The real text entered is saved elsewhere for later recall. Besides disguising the input, this function supports a strict entry mode that prevents the user from editing text that has already been entered and limits input to single characters — the user is not allowed to paste passwords.

This version of `CreateInputField()` creates an XmTextField widget and registers two callbacks. The first is called when the text widget is modified in any way, while the second is called when the insertion cursor moves for any reason. In addition to the creation function and callbacks used to implement the password input field, the file password.c defines a static character array used to store the text originally typed by the user.

```
1    /******************************************************************
2     * password.c: An input field suitable for obtaining a password
3     ******************************************************************/
4    #include <Xm/Xm.h>
5    #include <Xm/TextF.h>
6
7    static char *password = NULL; /* Buffer for storing password */
8    static int   index = 0;      /* Position of next character in buffer */
9
10   /* Function declarations */
11
12   static void MotionCallback ( Widget     w,
13                                XtPointer clientData,
14                                XtPointer callData );
15
16   static void TextModifiedCallback ( Widget     w,
17                                      XtPointer clientData,
18                                      XtPointer callData );
19
20   Widget CreateInputField ( Widget parent )
21   {
22      /* Create a text field widget */
23
24      Widget text = XmCreateTextField ( parent, "input", NULL, 0 );
25
26      XtManageChild ( text );
27
28      /* Add callbacks that handle hiding the true input */
29
30      XtAddCallback ( text, XmNmodifyVerifyCallback,
31                      TextModifiedCallback, NULL );
32
33      XtAddCallback ( text, XmNmotionVerifyCallback,
34                      MotionCallback, NULL );
35
36      return ( text );
37   }
```

The driver program described earlier will report a string of "*" characters when it retrieves the string contained by the password field. To test the password field, the driver program must be modified to print the password that has been saved away before the text field was filled with dummy characters. The following access function can be used to retrieve the password typed by the user.

```
38   char *GetPassword()
39   {
40      return ( password );
41   }
```

The `MotionCallback()` function is used to prevent the user from modifying text after it has been entered. This is a reasonable restriction for passwords and also makes the password input field easier to implement. The function simply tests the `newInsert` and `currInsert` members of the call data structure supplied by the XmTextField widget. If the `newInsert` position is less than the current position, the user is attempting to move the insertion point backwards or to backspace. In either case, the edit is disallowed by setting the `doit` member to `FALSE` before returning.

```
42   static void MotionCallback ( Widget      w,
43                                 XtPointer clientData,
44                                 XtPointer callData )
45   {
46       XmTextVerifyCallbackStruct *cbs =
47                           ( XmTextVerifyCallbackStruct * ) callData;
48
49       /*
50        * By disallowing all backward motion, this function disallows
51        * backspaces and also simplifies the password maintenance by
52        * disallowing all editing
53        */
54
55       if ( cbs->newInsert < cbs->currInsert )
56           cbs->doit = FALSE;
57   }
```

The `TextModifiedCallback()` function checks the length of the inserted text and disallows any attempt to insert more than one character at a time. If a single character has been input, the new character is copied into the password buffer so it can be available later. The `ptr` field of the `XmTextBlock` structure supplied by the XmTextField widget is then modified, replacing the text typed by the user with an "*" character. When the function returns, the XmTextField widget inserts the contents of this array, causing the text field to display an "*" instead of the text the user typed.

```
58   static void TextModifiedCallback ( Widget      w,
59                                       XtPointer clientData,
60                                       XtPointer callData )
61   {
62       XmTextVerifyCallbackStruct *cbs =
63                           ( XmTextVerifyCallbackStruct * ) callData;
64
65       /*
66        * Check for invalid operations
67        */
68
69       if  ( cbs->text->ptr == NULL ||        /* Check for NULL text */
70             cbs->text->length > 1 )          /* Don't allow paste    */
71       {
72           cbs->doit = FALSE;
73       }
```

```
74      else /* A new valid character has been entered */
75      {
76          /* Store the entered text in a buffer */
77
78           password = XtRealloc ( password, sizeof ( char ) * index + 2);
79           password [ index++ ] = cbs->text->ptr [ 0 ];
80           password [ index ] = '\0';
81
82          /* Replace the typed character with an '*' character */
83
84           cbs->text->ptr [ 0 ] = '*';
85      }
86  }
```

The XmText and XmTextField widgets are extremely complex and flexible. The examples shown here only begin to demonstrate some of the ways these widgets can be used. Later chapters use these widgets in other examples as well.

4.6   The XmList Widget Class

The XmList widget is a useful widget that displays a list of text items and allows the user to select entries in the list. The items displayed by the XmList widget must be specified as an array of compound strings. The XmList widget supports modes that allow both single and multiple items to be selected from a list at once. Because the number of items on a list may be large, the XmList widget is often used with an XmScrolledWindow widget to support scrollable lists. The easiest way to create a scrollable list is to use the convenience function `XmCreateScrolledList()`. When this function is used, the XmScrolledWindow widget is mostly transparent and scrolling support is automatic.

Resources

The XmList widget supports several resources in addition to those inherited from XmPrimitive and Core. These resources include the following:

- `XmNlistSpacing`: The value of this resource determines the number of pixels between each item on the list. The default spacing is zero pixels.
- `XmNlistMarginWidth`: The value of this resource specifies the size of the margin, in pixels, between the contents of the list and the edges of the XmList widget. The default value is zero pixels.
- `XmNlistMarginHeight`: The value of this resource determines the number of pixels between the top and bottom of the items in a list and the corresponding top and bottom edge of the XmList widget. The default spacing is zero pixels.

- `XmNfontList`: This resource controls the font or fonts used to display items in the list.
- `XmNitems`: The value of this resource is an array of compound strings. Each entry in the array corresponds to one item displayed in the list. The XmList widget makes an internal copy of the items in a list passed to `XtSetValues()`. However, if the value of this resource is retrieved by calling `XtGetValues()`, a direct pointer to the internal data is returned. This data must not be freed by applications. Setting this resource is the most efficient way to display items in a list. If a list is empty, the value of this resource is `NULL`.
- `XmNitemCount`: This resource determines the number of items displayed in a list, which must match the number of items in the compound string array, as specified by the `XmNitems` resource.
- `XmNselectedItems`: This resource always contains an array of compound strings that represent the items in a list that are currently selected. If no items are selected, the value of this resource is `NULL`. Applications that retrieve the value of this resource must not free it, as `XtGetValues()` returns a pointer to internal storage.
- `XmNselectedItemCount`: The value of this resource specifies the number of items currently selected.
- `XmNvisibleItemCount`: This resource controls number of items that can potentially be visible, based on the size of the XmList widget. If the value of this resource is changed, the XmList widget will attempt to resize itself to display the requested number of lines.
- `XmNtopItemPosition`: The value of this resource represents the integer index of the top-most visible item in a list.
- `XmNselectionPolicy`: This resource determines how users can select items on a list. See the discussion of the various policies, below.

Callbacks

The XmList widget supports several selection policies and has different selection callbacks related to each of these policies. The selection policy can be selected by setting the `XmNselection-Policy` resource. The selection policies and corresponding callbacks supported by the XmList widget are:

- `XmSINGLE_SELECT`: When the `XmNselectionPolicy` is set to `XmSINGLE_SELECT`, the `XmNsingleSelectionCallback` list is invoked when the user presses a mouse button over an item. If an item is already selected, and the user selects a second item, the first item is no longer selected.
- `XmMULTIPLE_SELECT`: When the `XmNselectionPolicy` resource is set to `XmMULTIPLE_SELECT`, functions on the `XmNmultipleSelectionCallback` list are invoked when the user selects one or more items from the list. Items are selected by pressing a mouse button while the pointer is over an item. In this mode, selecting additional items does not de-select previous items.
- `XmEXTENDED_SELECT`: When the value of the `XmNselectionPolicy` resource is set to `XmEXTENDED_SELECT`, the `XmNextendedSelectionCallback` list is invoked when the user selects one or more items from the list. In this mode, the user selects an initial

item by pressing the mouse button while the pointer is over the desired item. Then additional items can be selected by dragging the pointer over the desired items. Once all desired items have been selected, the user can end the selection by releasing the mouse button, which invokes the callback.

- XmBROWSE_SELECT: When the XmNselectionPolicy is set to XmBROWSE_SELECT, the XmNbrowseSelectionCallback list is invoked when the user releases a mouse button while an item is selected. The user selects an initial item by pressing the mouse button while the pointer is over an item. Then, while holding the mouse button down, the user can move the selection by dragging the pointer over other items. Only a single item is selected at any one time.

A list widget's selection policy can be specified programmatically or chosen by the user by changing the value of the widget's XmNselectionPolicy resource. The default policy is XmBROWSE_SELECT. Regardless of the chosen selection policy, the XmList widget passes callback functions a pointer to an XmListCallbackStruct as call data. This structure is defined as follows:

```
typedef struct {
    int        reason;         /* The reason this callback was called*/
    XEvent    *event;          /* The event that caused this callback */
    XmString   item;           /* The last item selected when this
                                  callback was called */
    int        item_length;    /* The size, in bytes, of item */
    int        item_position;  /* The position of the string specified
                                  in the item field */
    XmString *selected_items;  /* A list of all selected items */
    int        selected_item_count;     /* Number of items selected */
    int       *selected_item_positions; /* Position indexes of
                                           selected items */
    int        selection_type; /* The type of the current selection.
                                  Can be one of XmINITIAL,
                                             XmMODIFICATION
                                             XmADDITIONAL */
} XmListCallbackStruct;
```

All XmList callbacks set the reason member of the call data structure to one of the following constants, depending on the widget's selection policy:

XmCR_SINGLE_SELECT	XmCR_BROWSE_SELECT
XmCR_MULTIPLE_SELECT	XmCR_EXTENDED_SELECT

The rest of the XmListCallbackStruct structure contains information about selected items. The information in this structure points to temporary internal storage. Applications that need to retain or modify this information should make copies.

Convenience Functions

Most operations on the XmList widget can be performed using the resources supported by the XmList widget class. However, the XmList widget also supports many convenience functions that are useful in some situations. The following are some of the more commonly used functions:

- **XmListAddItem( )**: This function adds a single item to an existing list, at a specified position. Calling this function causes the internal buffer of text items to be reallocated, so this is an extremely inefficient way to construct an entire list. Whenever possible, **XtSetValues( )** should be used to set the **XmNitems** and **XmNitemCount** resources instead of using this convenience function. However, this function is useful when it is necessary to add a single item to a specific position within an existing list.

```
void XmListAddItem ( Widget   w,
                     XmString item,
                     int      pos )
```

- **XmListAddItems( )**: This function takes an array of compound strings and inserts them into a list, starting at a specified position. This function provides a more efficient way to construct a list than calling **XmListAddItem( )** multiple times, but is less efficient than using **XtSetValues( )**. **XmListAddItems( )** should be used only for situations in which it is necessary to add items to an already existing list.

```
void XmListAddItems ( Widget   w,
                      XmString *items,
                      int      item_count,
                      int      pos )
```

- **XmListDeleteItem( )**: This function removes a named item from a list. If all items are to be removed, it is faster to use **XtSetValues( )** to set **XmNitems** to **NULL** and **XmNitemCount** to zero.

```
void XmListDeleteItem ( Widget   w,
                        XmString item )
```

- **XmListDeleteItems( )**: This function removes a set of items from a list. If all items on the list are to be removed it is more efficient to set **XmNitems** to **NULL** and **XmNitem-Count** to zero. Depending on what information the application maintains, it may also be more efficient to just install a new list instead of deleting a small number of items from a list.

```
void XmListDeleteItems ( Widget   w,
                         XmString *items,
                         int      item_count )
```

- `XmListDeletePos()`: This function deletes the single item located at the specified position in the list.

  ```
  void XmListDeletePos ( Widget w, int pos )
  ```

- `XmListDeleteAllItems()`: This function deletes all items from a list. As noted earlier, it is more efficient to use `XtSetValues()` to set the `XmNitems` resource to `NULL`.

  ```
  void XmListDeleteAllItems ( Widget w )
  ```

- `XmListReplaceItems()`: This function replaces the items contained in a list of compound strings with the corresponding items in a second list of compound strings. Both lists must contain the same number of entries.

  ```
  void XmListReplaceItems ( Widget      w,
                            XmString *old_items,
                            int       item_count,
                            XmString *new_items)
  ```

- `XmListSelectItem()`: This function programmatically selects the specified item. If the `notify` argument is `TRUE`, the appropriate selection callback functions are invoked.

  ```
  void XmListSelectItem ( Widget   w,
                          XmString item,
                          Boolean  notify )
  ```

- `XmListDeselectItem()`: This function programmatically de-selects the specified item.

  ```
  void XmListDeselectItem ( Widget   w,
                            XmString item )
  ```

- `XmListItemExists()`: This function returns `TRUE` if the given compound string is an item in the list widget.

  ```
  Boolean XmListItemExists ( Widget   w,
                             XmString item )
  ```

- `XmListItemPos()`: This function returns the integer position of the specified compound string.

  ```
  int XmListItemPos ( Widget   w,
                      XmString item )
  ```

- `XmListGetSelectedPos()`: This function returns an array that indicates the positions of all selected items. If no items are selected, the function returns `FALSE`.

```
Boolean XmListGetSlectedPos ( Widget    w,
                              int      *positions,
                              int       numPositions )
```

Using the XmListWidget

Let's see how the list widget works by writing a simple program, **chooseone**, that places its command-line arguments in a list. The example uses the **XmBROWSE_SELECT** selection policy. When the user selects one of the items in the list, the program prints the selection and exits. This program could be useful in a UNIX shell script as a way to allow the user to select from several alternatives. For example, this program could be used as:

```
cat 'chooseone *.c'
```

resulting in a window similar to that shown in Figure 4.10.

Figure 4.10 An XmList widget.

The main body of the **chooseone** program is written as follows:

```
1   /****************************************************************
2    * chooseone.c: Allow the user to select a command-line argument
3    ****************************************************************/
4   #include <Xm/Xm.h>
5   #include <Xm/List.h>
6   #include <stdio.h>
7   #include <stdlib.h>
8
9   static void BrowseCallback ( Widget widget,
10                               XtPointer clientData,
11                               XtPointer callData );
12
13  const char usageString[] = "Usage: chooseone <non-zero list of choices>";
14
```

```
15  void main ( int argc, char **argv )
16  {
17      Widget        shell, list;
18      int           i;
19      XmString      *xmstr;
20      XtAppContext  app;
21
22      shell = XtAppInitialize ( &app, "Chooseone",  NULL, 0,
23                                &argc, argv, NULL, NULL, 0 );
24
25      if ( argc <= 1 )
26      {
27          fprintf ( stderr, usageString );
28          exit ( -1 );
29      }
30
31      /*
32       * Convert all command-line arguments to an array of
33       * type XmString, ignoring argv[0].
34       */
35
36      xmstr = ( XmString * ) XtMalloc ( sizeof ( XmString ) * argc - 1 );
37
38      for ( i = 1; i < argc; i++ )
39        xmstr [ i - 1 ] = XmStringCreateLtoR ( argv[i],
40                                              XmFONTLIST_DEFAULT_TAG );
41
42      /*
43       * Create the list widget and register a browse callback.
44       */
45
46      list = XmCreateScrolledList ( shell, "list", NULL, 0 );
47      XtManageChild ( list );
48
49      XtVaSetValues ( list,
50                      XmNitems,            xmstr,
51                      XmNitemCount,        argc - 1,
52                      XmNvisibleItemCount, 20,
53                      NULL );
54
55      XtAddCallback ( list, XmNbrowseSelectionCallback,
56                      BrowseCallback, NULL );
57
58      XtRealizeWidget ( shell );
59      XtAppMainLoop ( app );
60  }
```

The callback function `BrowseCallback()` is invoked when the user selects an entry in the list. This function simply extracts a character string from the call data, using the function

`XmStringGetLtoR()` to convert the compound string contained in the call data structure to a character string. (See Chapter 12 for more information about this function and compound strings.) The `BrowseCallback()` function then prints the selected item, and calls `exit()`.

```
61   static void BrowseCallback ( Widget     w,
62                                XtPointer clientData,
63                                XtPointer callData)
64   {
65       XmListCallbackStruct *cbs = ( XmListCallbackStruct * ) callData;
66       Boolean  result;
67       char     *text;
68
69       /*
70        * Retrieve the character data from the compound string
71        */
72
73       if ( ( result = XmStringGetLtoR ( cbs->item,
74                                         XmFONTLIST_DEFAULT_TAG,
75                                         &text ) ) == TRUE )
76       {
77           /*
78            * If some text was retrieved, print it. Normally, this data
79            * should be freed, but the program is going to exit, anyway.
80            */
81
82           printf ( "%s\n", text );
83       }
84
85       exit ( 0 );
86   }
```

4.7   The XmSeparator Widget Class

The XmSeparator widget is useful for visually separating areas of a window. The XmSeparator can have several distinct visual appearances, as shown in Figure 4.11. The XmSeparator widget has no callbacks, but supports several resources. These resources include `XmNseparatorType` and `XmNorientation`. The `XmNorientation` resource defaults to `XmHORIZONTAL`, which produces a horizontal separator. This resource can also be set to `XmVERTICAL`. The `XmNseparatorType` resource can have any one of the following values:

XmNO_LINE	XmDOUBLE_LINE	XmDOUBLE_DASHED_LINE
XmSHADOW_ETCHED_OUT	XmSHADOW_ETCHED_IN	XmSINGLE_LINE
XmSINGLE_DASHED_LINE	XmSHADOW_ETCHED_OUT_DASH	XmSHADOW_ETCHED_IN
XmSHADOW_ETCHED_IN_DASH		

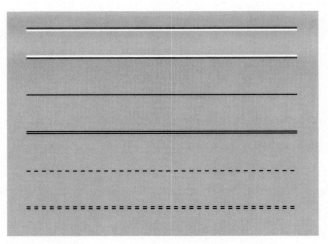

Figure 4.11 Some of the styles supported by the XmSeparator widget.

4.8   The XmScrollBar Widget Class

The XmScrollBar widget allows users to select a value from a range, using a moveable *thumb*, or *slider*, that travels in a *trough*. Figure 4.12 shows a Motif XmScrollBar widget. The XmScrollBar can be oriented vertically or horizontally, and is designed to scroll a large area, such as a text window. Programmers can control the range of the scrollbar, the size of the thumb, the appearance of the arrows at each end, and so on. There are also a variety of callbacks that can be installed.

The XmScrollBar is often created automatically in various widgets. For example, the XmList widget has an associated convenience function, `XmCreateScrolledList()` that automatically arranges for a list to display scrollbars. The XmScrolledWindow widget allows applications to easily create a window layout that combines vertical and horizontal scrollbars with a scrollable work area. Applications can also create instances of the XmScrollBar widget class directly if needed.

Figure 4.12 An XmScrollBar widget.

Resources

In addition to those resources inherited from the XmPrimitive and Core widget classes, the XmScrollBar widget class supports the following resources:

- **XmNtroughColor**: The value of this resource should be a pixel that indicates the color of the trough area of the scrollbar.
- **XmNvalue**: The value of this resource corresponds to the current position of the scrollbar thumb. Setting this resource moves the thumb.
- **XmNminimum**: The value of this resource determines the lowest value represented by the scrollbar. The default value is zero.
- **XmNmaximum**: The value of this resource determines the highest value represented by the scrollbar. The default value is 100.
- **XmNsliderSize**: The value of this resource determines the size of the scrollbar thumb. This value is normally set to show that the thumb size is proportional to the size of the visible part of the scrolled area.
- **XmNshowArrows**: If this resource is set to **TRUE**, the arrows on both ends of the XmScrollBar widget are displayed. The default value is **TRUE**.
- **XmNorientation**: This resource controls the orientation of a scrollbar widget. The default value is **XmVERTICAL**. This resource can also have the value **XmHORIZONTAL**.
- **XmNprocessingDirection**: The value of this resource determines which end of the scrollbar represents the minimum or maximum value. If a scrollbar's orientation is horizontal, this resource may be either **XmMAX_ON_LEFT** or **XmMAX_ON_RIGHT**. The default is **XmMAX_ON_RIGHT**. If the orientation is vertical, the possible values are **XmMAX_ON_TOP** or **XmMAX_ON_BOTTOM**. The default is **XmMAX_ON_TOP**.
- **XmNincrement**: The value of this resource determines how far the thumb should move for one "increment". The default value is 1.
- **XmNpageIncrement**: The value of this resource determines how far the thumb moves when moved by one "page". The default value is 10.

Callbacks

The XmScrollBar widget supports a variety of callback functions. Many applications use only the simplest of these callbacks, **XmNvalueChanged**, and possibly the **XmNdragCallback** list. The remaining callbacks allow applications to be notified when special situations occur, such as moving to the top of a page, or scrolling down by one page or by one line.

All XmScrollBar callbacks pass a pointer to an **XmScrollBarCallbackStruct** structure as the call data argument. This structure is defined as follows:

```
typedef struct {
    int      reason;
    XEvent *event;
    int      value;
    int      pixel;
} XmScrollBarCallbackStruct;
```

The `value` member reports the current position of the thumb in terms of the minimum and maximum range of the scrollbar, while the `pixel` member reports the position of the thumb in pixels.

The callbacks supported by the XmScrollBar widget class include:

- `XmNvalueChangedCallback`: Functions on this callback list are invoked when the thumb has moved to a new value. If the user drags the thumb continuously, this callback is only called when the mouse button is released and the dragging stops.

- `XmNdragCallback`: Functions registered with this callback list are invoked continuously while the user drags the scrollbar thumb.

- `XmNincrementCallback`: This callback list is invoked when the thumb position is increased by a single "increment", usually corresponding to one line in text-based applications. This is normally caused by the user pressing the arrow button at the top of the scrollbar.

- `XmNdecrementCallback`: This callback list is invoked when the thumb position is decreased by a single "increment", which usually corresponds to one line in text-based applications. This is normally caused by the user pressing the arrow button at the bottom of the scrollbar.

- `XmNpageIncrementCallback`: This callback list is invoked when the thumb position is increased by a single "page", which usually corresponds to the visible size of the scrolled region. This is normally caused by the user clicking the left mouse button inside the scrollbar trough, between the thumb and the top arrow button.

- `XmNpageDecrementCallback`: This callback list is invoked when the thumb position is decreased by a single "page", which usually corresponds to the visible size of the scrolled region. This is normally caused by the user clicking the left mouse button inside the scrollbar trough, between the thumb and the bottom arrow button.

- `XmNtoTopCallback`: Functions registered with this callback list are invoked when the scrollbar thumb is moved to the top of the scrollbar range.

- `XmNtoBottomCallback`: This callback list is invoked when the scrollbar thumb is moved to the bottom of the scrollbar range.

4.9 Gadgets

In addition to widgets, Motif provides types of user interface components known as *gadget*s. Gadgets are similar to widgets, except that they have no window of their own. Because they have no windows of their own, gadgets must display text or graphics in a window provided by their parents, and must also rely on their parents for input. Gadgets can support callback functions and have the same appearance as the corresponding widgets. Motif provides gadget versions of most primitive widgets.

The Motif gadget classes include the following:

```
    XmArrowButtonGadget   XmLabelGadget          XmPushButtonGadget
    XmSeparatorGadget     XmToggleButtonGadget   XmCascadeButtonGadget
```

Gadgets can be created the same way as widgets, using `XtCreateWidget()`, by specifying a gadget class pointer as the class argument. For example:

```
XtCreateWidget ( "message", xmLabelGadgetClass, shell, NULL, 0 )
```

Motif also provides convenience functions that can be used to create gadgets. For example, a label gadget can be created by calling the function `XmCreateLabelGadget()`.

From the application programmer's viewpoint, gadgets can be used in much the same way as other display widgets, except for several restrictions. Gadgets cannot support event handlers (see Chapter 8), translations, or popup children (see Chapter 7). In current versions of Motif, each gadget must also have the same background color as its parent, although this may change in the future. Programmers who use gadgets must also be careful when using certain functions. For example, `XtDisplay()` does not return the correct value when used with a gadget. To extract a `Display` pointer from a gadget, one can either call:

```
XtDisplay ( XtParent ( gadget ) )
```

or use the Xt function:

```
XtDisplayOfObject ( gadget )
```

Gadgets were intended to be more efficient than widgets in some situations. Because reducing the number of windows in an application reduces server resources and may also reduce the number of server requests in some situations, using gadgets can make some applications more efficient, particularly with respect to start-up time. Since gadgets were originally designed, the X server has become more efficient at creating and manipulating windows, and the difference in performance between widgets and gadgets has decreased. Many programmers feel that the small performance gain that might be achieved by using gadgets is outweighed by the restrictions associated with gadgets. In some situations, using gadgets may actually be less efficient than using widgets.

The argument has been made that the additional code added to the Motif toolkit to handle gadgets can make an application larger and slower. Managers must track mouse motion and handle focus and input to gadgets manually instead of allowing the server to notify the applications. Managers that have gadget children must request mouse motion events, which leads to increased server traffic. Also, manager widgets must manually check the bounds of each `Expose` event against the bounding box of each gadget child when any `Expose` event is received. Widgets can handle their own `Expose` events, which will be received only if the individual widget needs to be redrawn. When gadgets are used, manager widgets have to perform additional processing beyond that already performed by the X server. All these points are valid, but gadgets are still useful in some situations.

As a rule of thumb, it is probably not worthwhile to use a gadget in a small panel with only a few widgets. Certainly, replacing any individual widget with an equivalent gadget will not produce any noticeable improvement in performance, and may reduce performance due to the larger amount of code and processing involved. However, when large numbers of widgets are needed, for example, hundreds of widgets in a scrolling window, gadgets may produce a noticeable improvement in performance on some systems. Menus are the most effective place to use gadgets in most applications. Menu panes are always displayed at one time (when the menu is popped up), items in a menu are generally all the same color, and applications often have menus with large numbers of entries. In such situations, gadgets will sometimes perform substantially better than widgets, although it is important to consider the characteristics of the system on which the application is expected to run.

4.10 Summary

This chapter explores some of the simple primitive widget classes provided by Motif. These widgets play an important role in any application, because they accept input from users, and display information to users. Primitive widgets are used in menus, dialogs, control panels, and anywhere that user input is required. Most of these widgets are extremely flexible, and, with practice, programmers can use resources and callbacks to configure them to fit the needs of many different applications.

By themselves, these simple display widgets cannot provide a complete interface for most applications. Most real applications combine many primitive widgets to create a complete user interface. The following chapter describes the Motif manager widgets that can be used to combine other widgets to form more complex interfaces.

C h a p t e r 5

Manager Widgets

Most of the examples discussed in earlier chapters create a single widget that occupies the entire top-level window of each application. Because few real applications are this simple, the Motif widget set provides many widgets that can be used to combine other widgets. These widgets allow endless combinations of buttons, scrollbars, text panes, and so on, to be grouped together to form more complex user interfaces. Widgets can be combined by using a *manager* widget, which is a widget that is responsible for determining the position of each of its children.

Widgets that contain children must be subclasses of the Composite widget class implemented by Xt. In the Motif widget set, most widgets that support children are subclasses of the XmManager widget, which is an indirect subclass of the Composite widget class. The XmManager class provides some basic support for subclasses, in much the same way that the XmPrimitive widget class supports simple Motif display widgets. Motif widgets that are subclasses of the XmManager widget class are often referred to as *manager* widgets. Because these widgets are also subclasses of the Xt Composite widget class, they may be referred to as *composite* widgets, as well.

The Motif manager widgets include:

XmDrawingArea	XmFrame	XmMainWindow
XmRowColumn	XmScale	XmScrolledWindow
XmPanedWindow	XmBulletinBoard	XmForm

Motif supports a different approach to window layout than some toolkits. In some window systems and user interface toolkits, applications are responsible for positioning all user interface elements, and implementing the application's behavior when the application's top-level window is resized. Many toolkits also support only a flat model for arranging the elements of an application's interface. In such systems, applications create a single window for each top-level window in its interface and position all user interface elements directly in that window.

Motif works differently in several important ways. First, Motif provides *algorithmic* layout managers. Applications can control how a set of user interface elements are laid out by choosing a manager widget that implements a certain *layout policy*, or algorithm. For example, the Motif XmRowColumn widget arranges its children in rows and columns. Once an application has chosen a particular manager widget, the application has relatively little control over how the children of that widget are positioned or sized. Therefore, in Motif, there is less emphasis on precisely positioning individual widgets, and more emphasis on choosing and configuring a manager widget that provides the type of layout desired. Most Motif manager widgets support variations of their basic layout algorithm. For example, the XmRowColumn widget allows applications to specify the number of rows and columns, and to control some aspects of widget alignment within the rows and columns. The following sections examine each of the Motif manager widgets and discuss their layout policies.

Second, because it is based on Xt, Motif supports hierarchical window layouts. Each top-level window in a Motif application contains one manager widget that arranges its children according to its policy. Each of those widgets in turn may be a manager widget that has still more children, all arranged according to their parent's layout policy. Section 5.11 discusses how to create and take advantage of widget hierarchies.

Like the primitive widgets, the Motif manager widgets inherit various features from other widgets. It is useful to know what widget classes any given widget class inherits from, because each widget class will exhibit the behavior of its superclasses plus any extended behavior it implements. Figure 5.1 shows the inheritance hierarchy of the manager widgets discussed in this chapter.

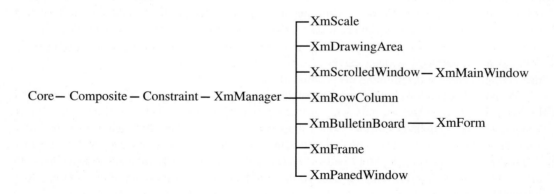

Figure 5.1 Inheritance hierarchy of Motif manager widgets.

5.1   Xt Support for Manager Widgets

Xt provides two abstract widget classes designed to support widget classes that manage children. These classes are the Composite widget class and the Constraint widget class. The Composite widget class provides the basic support for handling multiple children, controlling the size and position of each child, and so on. The Constraint widget class provides support for widgets that need to associate information with each child. This information is normally used to determine how the parent widget positions or sizes each child. The following sections discuss the basic features of each of these widget classes.

The Composite Widget Class

The Composite widget class supports widgets that manage children. To accomplish this, the Composite widget class adds several features to those it inherits from the Core widget class. Each Composite widget maintains a list of children, and also supports mechanisms that allow composite widgets to be notified when children are added or removed, when children are managed or unmanaged, and when children request changes in their geometry. Chapter 16 examines the internal architecture of the Composite widget class in detail.

In addition to the resources inherited from the Core widget class, the Composite widget class supports the following resources:

- `XmNchildren`: This read-only resource points to the list of children maintained by a composite widget. The value of this resource can be retrieved by applications that need to operate on the children of a composite widget. Such access is rarely needed. Applications should take particular care not to modify this list. Children are added to the list automatically when a new child widget is created.

- `XmNnumChildren`: This read-only resource can be used to retrieve the number of children maintained by a composite widget.

The Constraint Widget Class

The Constraint widget class inherits the features of the Core and Composite widget classes and adds some features of its own. The Constraint widget class does not define any additional resources. However, the Constraint widget class implements support for manager widget classes that wish to add *constraint resources* to their children. Constraint resources are resources that are defined by a manager widget, but are set and retrieved as if they belonged to children of the parent widget. When a widget is created as a child of a constraint widget, any constraint resources defined by the parent are added to the set of resources recognized by the child. The XmForm widget, described in Section 5.5, is one of the best known examples of a constraint widget. The XmForm widget adds resources to each child that can be used to specify each child's relative size and position as well as its dynamic behavior when the parent changes size.

5.2   The XmManager Widget Class

The Motif XmManager widget class provides support for all Motif widgets that contain, or manage, other widgets. The XmManager widget is a subclass of the Xt Constraint widget class, and therefore inherits the behavior of the Constraint, Composite and Core widget classes. In Motif, even manager widgets that do not require the features of the Constraint widget class are subclasses of XmManager.

The XmManager widget class is an abstract class that is never used directly in applications. The XmManager widget class provides support for all Motif manager widgets, in much the same way as the XmPrimitive widget class provides support for Motif primitive widget classes. The XmManager widget adds resources and support for Motif's top and bottom shadows, and also supports input focus and keyboard navigation. Resources related to keyboard navigation are discussed in Section 5.13. The remaining resources supported by the XmManager widget class include the following:

- `XmNforeground`: The value of this resource, which must be a Pixel, specifies the foreground color supported by a widget.
- `XmNshadowThickness`: Some subclasses of the XmManager widget draw a shadow that produces a three-dimensional effect. The value of this resource determines the thickness of that shadow. The default shadow thickness is 0 pixels.
- `XmNtopShadowColor`: This resource controls the color of a widget's top shadow. If the top shadow color is lighter than the widget's background color, the widget will appear to be protruding from the screen, while if the color is darker than the background, the widget will appear to be recessed into the screen. By default, the value of the `XmNtopShadowColor` resource is computed automatically from the widget's background color.
- `XmNbottomShadowColor`: The value of this resource controls the color of a widget's bottom shadow. The bottom shadow color should be chosen to complement the top shadow color. If the widget is to appear to protrude from the screen, the bottom shadow must be darker than the widget's background color. If the widget is to appear recessed into the screen, the bottom shadow color should be lighter than the widget's background. The default color is computed automatically from the widget's background color.
- `XmNuserData`: This resource provides access to an untyped pointer maintained by each Motif widget. Applications can use this resource to associate additional data with a widget. The data can be set and retrieved using `XtSetValues()` and `XtGetValues()`.

The XmManager widget class also inherits all the resources supported by the Constraint, Composite and Core widget classes.

All subclasses of the XmManager widget class also support an `XmNhelpCallback`. This callback is invoked if a user presses the system help key (usually <F1>). Applications that wish to provide context-sensitive help can register callbacks to handle the user's help request.

5.3   The XmBulletinBoard Widget Class

Of all the Motif manager widgets, the XmBulletinBoard widget class supports one of the simplest layout strategies. All children of the XmBulletinBoard widget must be explicitly positioned by setting the XmNx and XmNy resources supported by each child. If no position is specified for a child, the XmBulletinBoard widget places it at location *(0, 0)*. The XmBulletinBoard widget will not ordinarily move or resize any child. This simplistic approach to managing children makes the XmBulletinBoard widget class less useful than some of the other Motif manager widgets for many applications. However, the XmBulletinBoard widget class provides resources and services that are used by many subclasses. The XmBulletinBoard class also provides support for Motif dialogs, as discussed in Chapter 7.

Chapter 2 contains an example that uses the XmBulletinBoard widget to manage several children. The XmBulletinBoard widget is occasionally used when an application does not need to support resizable windows or when the application itself needs to control the position and sizes of a collection of widgets. Notice that layouts based on the XmBulletinBoard will not automatically handle layouts that change because labels or fonts change. Labels or fonts are often changed either because of user preferences or because an application is being displayed using a different language than the one for which it was originally written. If an application implements its own layout strategy, based on the XmBulletinBoard widget class, it will have to handle these situations.

Resources

The resources supported by the XmBulletinBoard widget class fall into two categories. The first category affects the behavior of this widget class and other manager subclasses. These resources include the following:

- XmNshadowType: This resource determines the type of shadow drawn around an XmBulletinBoard widget. The bulletin board widget can have shadows of the types XmSHADOW_ETCHED_IN, XmSHADOW_ETCHED_OUT, XmSHADOW_IN, and the default, XmSHADOW_OUT.

- XmNshadowThickness: This resource controls the thickness of the XmBulletinBoard widget's shadow. The default value is zero, so the shadow is not visible.

- XmNfocusCallback: Functions on this callback list are called when the XmBulletinBoard widget or one of its children receive input focus.

- XmNallowOverlap: If this resource is TRUE, children may be positioned so that they overlap. If FALSE, children may not overlap. The default value is TRUE.

- XmNresizePolicy: The value of this resource determines what happens when a child of an XmBulletinBoard widget changes size, or new widgets are added or removed. The possible values are:

    — XmRESIZE_NONE: With this value, the XmBulletinBoard widget will not change its size.

— `XmRESIZE_ANY`: When this value is specified, the XmBulletinBoard widget can shrink or grow, as needed. The widget will attempt to be just large enough to contain its children. This is the default.

— `XmRESIZE_GROW`: When this value is specified, the XmBulletinBoard widget attempts to grow large enough to display all its children. However, the widget does not shrink if the space required by its children is reduced.

- `XmNbuttonFontList`: If this resource is set, its value specifies the font list used for button widgets that are children of the XmBulletinBoard widget.

- `XmNlabelFontList`: The value of this resource indicates the font used by all children that belong to the XmLabel and XmLabelGadget classes.

- `XmNtextFontList`: This resource can be used to specify the font used by all children that belong to the XmText, XmTextField, and XmList widget classes.

- `XmNtextTranslations`: Any translations specified by the value of this resource are added to any text widget children of the XmBulletinBoard widget.

The second category of resources supported by the XmBulletinBoard widget class includes those designed to support Motif dialogs, which are described in Chapter 7.

5.4   The XmRowColumn Widget Class

The XmRowColumn widget class is a subclass of the XmManager widget class that organizes its children as rows and columns. This widget has several uses. Some applications use the XmRow-Column widget to arrange children in rows and columns. The XmRowColumn widget class can also be used as a RadioBox widget that manages XmToggleButton widgets and allows only one button to be selected at once. The XmRowColumn widget class can also be used as both a menubar and a menu pane. The behavior of an XmRowColumn widget can be controlled either by setting appropriate resources or by using one of several convenience functions to create the widget.

This section looks at how the XmRowColumn widget class can be used to organize widgets into rows and columns. Chapter 6 looks at some of the other uses for XmRowColumn widgets.

Resources

In addition to those inherited from its superclasses, the XmRowColumn widget provides several resources that determine how it arranges its children. These resources include the following:

- `XmNorientation`: This resource determines whether the XmRowColumn widget should arrange its children in row major or column major order. This resource may be set to `XmVERTICAL` to select a column major layout, or `XmHORIZONTAL` to specify a row major layout.

- `XmNpacking`: This resource specifies how children of the XmRowColumn widget are sized. The value of this resource may be `XmPACK_TIGHT`, `XmPACK_COLUMN`, or

XmPACK_NONE. If XmPACK_TIGHT is chosen, the XmRowColumn widget allows each child to have its natural width. The XmRowColumn widget packs its children tightly along each row until no more children fit in a given row. At this point a new row is begun. If XmPACK_COLUMN is chosen, each child is resized to the width of the largest child, and the children are placed in aligned rows and columns. The number of rows or columns is determined by the XmNnumColumns resource. The value XmPACK_NONE means that no packing is performed, and no sizes are changed. The widgets are positioned according to their *x,y* positions. When XmNpacking is set to either XmPACK_COLUMN or XmPACK_TIGHT, all children are forced to have the same height.

- XmNnumColumns: If XmNpacking is set to XmPACK_COLUMN, the value of XmNnumColumns determines the maximum number of rows or columns. If the orientation is vertical, this resource indicates the maximum number of columns. Otherwise, it indicates the maximum number of rows.

- XmNadjustLast: If this resource is TRUE, the XmRowColumn widget resizes the last column of children in each row (if XmNorientation is XmVERTICAL) to fill any remaining space. If XmNorientation is XmHORIZONTAL, the bottom widget in each column is extended to fill any remaining space. The default value is TRUE.

- XmNisHomogeneous: If the value of this resource is TRUE, the XmRowColumn widget can manage only children that belong to the widget class indicated by the XmNentryClass resource. The default value is FALSE.

- XmNentryClass: This resource can be used to specify the class of widgets that can be added as children when a row column widget's XmNisHomogeneous resource is set to TRUE.

- XmNisAligned: This resource specifies whether text displayed by each child of the XmRowColumn widget should be aligned. This applies only to children that are subclasses of the XmLabel widget class or the XmLabelGadget class.

- XmNentryAlignment: If XmNisAligned is TRUE, the value of this resource specifies the type of alignment used by all children. The possible values of this resource are XmALIGNMENT_CENTER, XmALIGNMENT_BEGINNING, and XmALIGNMENT_END. The default is XmALIGNMENT_CENTER.

- XmNentryBorder: If non-zero, the value of this resource specifies a border thickness which is imposed on all children. The default value is zero, which disables this behavior.

- XmNresizeWidth: If the value of this resource is TRUE (the default), the XmRowColumn widget attempts to change its width in response to requests from children to change size.

- XmNresizeHeight: If the value of this resource is TRUE (the default), the XmRow-Column widget attempts to change its height in response to requests from children to change size.

- XmNadjustMargin: If the value of this resource is TRUE, the margins of all children are forced to the same size. The default value is TRUE.

- XmNradioBehavior: If the value of this resource is TRUE, the XmRowColumn widget exhibits "radio" behavior. If used to manage a group of toggle buttons (XmToggleButton), the XmRowColumn widget will arrange for at most one toggle button to be set at one time.

Selecting a toggle button forces all other toggles managed by the same widget to be unset. The default value of this resource is FALSE.

- XmNradioAlwaysOne: If XmNradioBehavior is set to TRUE, the value of XmNradioAlwaysOne determines whether one child must always be set, or if it is possible to have no currently set children. The default value of this resource is TRUE.

- XmNentryVerticalAlignment: This resource controls how widgets that display text are aligned when placed in a row within an XmRowColumn widget. The possible values are:

    — XmALIGNMENT_BASELINE_BOTTOM: This value causes the bottom baseline of the text in all widgets in a row to be aligned.

    — XmALIGNMENT_BASELINE_TOP: This value causes the top baseline of the text in all children in a row to be aligned. Note that the difference between XmALIGNMENT_BASELINE_TOP and XmALIGNMENT_BASELINE_BOTTOM is only apparent if children are displaying multiple lines of text.

    — XmALIGNMENT_CONTENTS_BOTTOM: This value causes the bottom of the text or pixmaps displayed by children of an XmRowColumn widget to be aligned.

    — XmALIGNMENT_CENTER: This causes all children in a row to be aligned by their centers. This is the default.

    — XmALIGNMENT_CONTENTS_TOP: This causes all items in a row to be aligned by the top of their contents.

An Example

This section presents a simple example and explores a few of the XmRowColumn widget class's resources. The following example, a program named rctest, creates an XmRowColumn widget that manages six XmPushButton widgets.

```
1   /***************************************************
2    * rctest.c: An example using a row column widget
3    ***************************************************/
4   #include <Xm/Xm.h>
5   #include <Xm/RowColumn.h>
6   #include <Xm/PushB.h>
7
8   char *buttons[] = { "button1", "button2", "button3",
9                       "button4", "button5", "button6" };
10
11  void main ( int argc, char **argv )
12  {
13      Widget        shell, rowcol;
14      XtAppContext  app;
15      int           i;
16
17      shell = XtAppInitialize ( &app, "Rctest", NULL, 0,
18                                &argc, argv, NULL, NULL, 0 );
19
```

```
20
21      /*
22       * Create an XmRowColumn widget.
23       */
24
25      rowcol = XtCreateManagedWidget ( "rowcol", xmRowColumnWidgetClass,
26                                       shell, NULL, 0 );
27
28      /*
29       * Create the children of the XmRowColumn widget.
30       */
31
32      for ( i = 0; i < XtNumber ( buttons ); i++ )
33          XtCreateManagedWidget ( buttons[i], xmPushButtonWidgetClass,
34                                  rowcol, NULL, 0 );
35
36      XtRealizeWidget ( shell );
37      XtAppMainLoop ( app );
38  }
```

Figure 5.2 shows the initial layout produced by building and running this program.

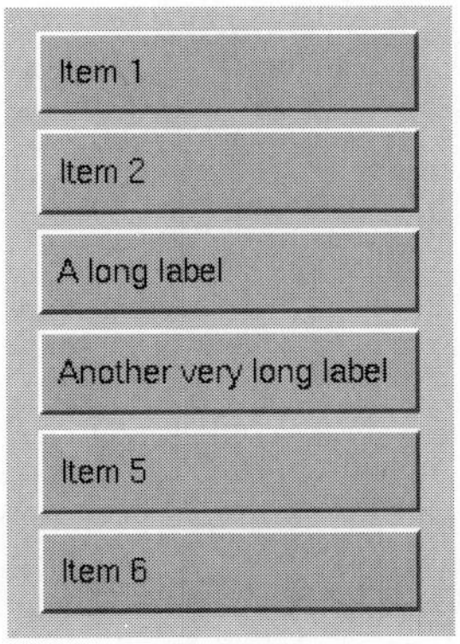

Figure 5.2 Initial layout of the rctest program.

The layout of the XmPushButton widgets in the rctest program can be altered significantly by changing the values of various resources. The following set of resources uses the **XmNnumColumns** resource to arrange the buttons into three columns, as shown in Figure 5.3.

```
!!!!!!!!!!!!!!!!!!!!!!!!!!!!!!!!!!!!!!!!!!!!!!!!!!!
! Rctest: App-defaults file for rctest.c
!!!!!!!!!!!!!!!!!!!!!!!!!!!!!!!!!!!!!!!!!!!!!!!!!!!

! Specify labels for all buttons.
```

```
*Rctest*button1.labelString:       Button One
*Rctest*button2.labelString:       Button Two
*Rctest*button3.labelString:       Button Three
*Rctest*button4.labelString:       Button Four
*Rctest*button5.labelString:       Button Five
*Rctest*button6.labelString:       Button Six With a Long Label

! Request buttons in 3 rows, by setting orientation to
! horizontal and requesting 3 columns  ( minor-dimension )

*Rctest*orientation:               horizontal
*Rctest*rowcol*numColumns:         3
*Rctest*rowcol*packing:            pack_column
```

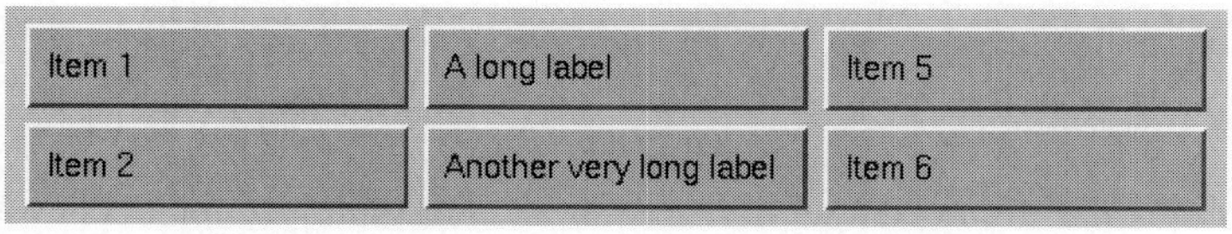

Figure 5.3 An XmRowColumn widget with three columns.

The XmRowColumn widget's layout can be changed so that the children are packed as tightly as possible by changing the resource file to include the line:

```
*Rctest*rowcol*packing:       pack_tight
```

This results in the layout shown in Figure 5.4.

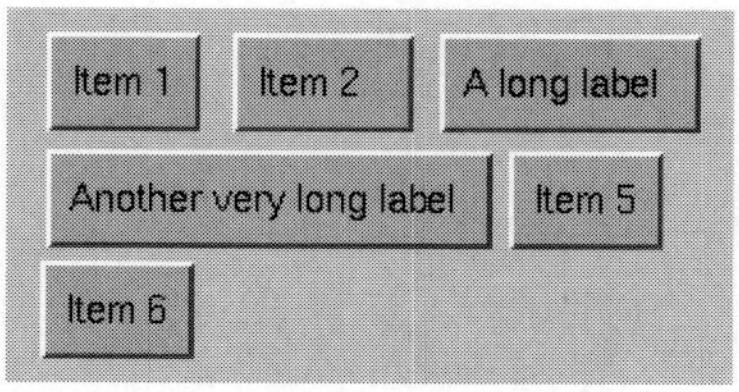

Figure 5.4 A tightly packed XmRowColumn widget.

With the XmNpacking resource set to pack_tight, the XmRowColumn widget puts as many widgets as possible in each row. When there is no more space on a given row, a new row is started. For example, resizing the rctest window to be wider can result in the layout shown in Figure 5.5. This layout changes dynamically as the XmRowColumn widget is resized.

Figure 5.5 A tightly packed XmRowColumn widget, resized.

A RadioBox Example

XmRowColumn widgets are often used to create "radio boxes". When a XmRowColumn widget is used to manage a set of XmToggleButton widgets, and the XmRowColumn widget's `XmNradioBehavior` resource is set to TRUE, only one XmToggleButton widget can be selected at one time. The following example demonstrates this behavior.

```
1    /***********************************************************
2     * radiobox.c: Demonstrate the Motif radio box behavior
3     ***********************************************************/
4    #include <Xm/Xm.h>
5    #include <Xm/RowColumn.h>
6    #include <Xm/ToggleB.h>
7    #include <stdio.h>
8
9    char * buttons[] = { "button1", "button2", "button3",
10                         "button4", "button5", "button6" };
11
12   static void ValueChangedCallback ( Widget      w,
13                                       XtPointer clientData,
14                                       XtPointer callData );
15
16   void main ( int argc, char **argv )
17   {
18       Widget        shell, rowcol;
19       XtAppContext  app;
20       int           i;
21
22       shell = XtAppInitialize ( &app, "Radio", NULL, 0,
23                                 &argc, argv, NULL, NULL, 0 );
24
25
26       /*
27        * Create an XmRowColumn widget configured as a radio box.
28        */
29
30       rowcol = XmCreateRadioBox ( shell, "rowcol", NULL, 0 );
31
```

```
32        XtManageChild ( rowcol );
33
34      /*
35       * Create the children of the XmRowColumn widget.
36       */
37
38      for ( i = 0; i < XtNumber ( buttons ); i++ )
39      {
40          Widget toggle =
41                      XtCreateManagedWidget ( buttons[i],
42                                              xmToggleButtonWidgetClass,
43                                              rowcol, NULL, 0 );
44
45          XtAddCallback ( toggle, XmNvalueChangedCallback,
46                          ValueChangedCallback, NULL );
47      }
48
49      XtRealizeWidget ( shell );
50      XtAppMainLoop ( app );
51  }
```

This program initializes Xt and then uses the Motif convenience function XmCreateRadioBox() to create an XmRowColumn widget configured for radio behavior. The program then creates a collection of XmToggleButton widgets as children of the XmRowColumn widget. Each toggle button widget has a callback registered to be called when the button changes state. This callback simply prints the name of the widget whose state has changed and the current state. This function can be written as follows:

```
52  static void ValueChangedCallback ( Widget    w,
53                                      XtPointer clientData,
54                                      XtPointer callData )
55  {
56      XmToggleButtonCallbackStruct *cbs =
57                      ( XmToggleButtonCallbackStruct * ) callData;
58      /*
59       * Report the state of the button, as indicated by the callData.
60       */
61
62      printf ( "%s: %s\n", XtName ( w ) , cbs->set ? "set" : "unset" );
63  }
```

Running this program provides a demonstration of the radio box behavior of an XmRow-Column widget. Once an initial button is selected, selecting a second button unsets the currently selected button and sets the new button. The callbacks registered with both buttons are called, first to unset the current button, and then to set the newly selected button. The window displayed by this program is shown in Figure 5.6. Notice that the XmToggleButton widgets display their toggle indicators as a diamond to indicate one-of-many selection.

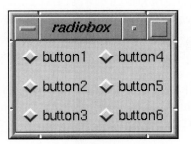

Figure 5.6 A radio box.

5.5   The XmForm Widget Class

The XmForm widget class is a subclass of the XmManager widget class that positions its children based on the values of constraint resources associated with each child. These constraints specify the position of each child relative to another widget, relative to a fractional position within the parent, or relative to the edges of the parent. Each child of an XmForm can have an "attachment" specified for each of its top, bottom, left, and right sides. By carefully specifying the attachments, it is possible to specify how the children of a XmForm widget are positioned, and also how each child's position and size are affected when an XmForm widget is resized.

Although it is often challenging to set up the various constraint resources correctly, the XmForm widget is one of the most flexible, and therefore most widely used of the Motif manager widgets. This widget class is also one of the few that support dynamically resizable widget layouts. Because the XmForm widget is used so extensively, it is worthwhile to spend the time required to learn how to use it.

Resources

The XmForm widget class supports two types of resources. The first affect the behavior of the XmForm widget itself, while the second set of resources affect the way an XmForm widget treats each child. The resources that have an overall effect on the behavior of an XmForm widget include the following:

- XmNrubberPositioning: This resource controls the default attachment for any child that leaves an attachment unspecified (set to XmATTACH_NONE). If this resource is set to TRUE, a child with no attachment in any one direction is assigned a positional attachment based on the initial position of the child. For example, if a child has no XmNleftAttachment, and XmNrubberPositioning is TRUE, the value of the widget's XmNleftAttachment is set to XmATTACH_POSITION, and the value of XmNleftPosition is set to a value proportional to the widget's *x* location divided by the width of the form. If the value of `XmNrubberPositioning` is set to `FALSE`, (the default), widgets with no attachment are given values of `XmATTACH_FORM`, with an offset of zero.

- `XmNresizable`: If the value of this resource is `TRUE` (the default), resize requests from a child are considered by the form widget. If the resource is set to `FALSE`, all requests are denied.

- `XmNfractionBase`: This resource specifies the denominator of a fraction used to calculate relative positions of children whose attachments are set to `XmATTACH_POSITION`. By default, the value of `XmNfractionBase` is 100.

Constraint Resources

The XmForm widget attaches additional resources to each managed child that allow programmers to specify how each widget is positioned within the form. These resources include:

`XmNtopAttachment`, `XmNbottomAttachment`, `XmNleftAttachment`, and `XmNrightAttachment`: These resources specify how and where a child widget is attached. The possible values are:

— `XmATTACH_NONE`: Do not attach this side. (See `XmNrubberPositioning`.)

— `XmATTACH_FORM`: Attach a side of the widget to the corresponding side of the Xm-Form widget. In other words, setting a widget's `XmNbottomAttachment` resource to `XmATTACH_FORM` attaches the bottom of that widget to the bottom of its parent form.

— `XmATTACH_WIDGET`: Attach a side of the child to the opposite side of the reference widget. For example, setting a widget's `XmNbottomAttachment` resource to `XmATTACH_WIDGET` attaches the bottom of that widget to the top of the reference widget specified as the value of the `XmNbottomWidget` resource.

— `XmATTACH_OPPOSITE_WIDGET`: Attach a side of the child to the same side of the reference widget. So, setting a widget's `XmNbottomAttachment` resource to `XmATTACH_OPPOSITE_WIDGET` attaches the bottom of that widget to the bottom of the reference widget specified as the value of the `XmNbottomWidget` resource.

— `XmATTACH_POSITION`: Attach a side of the child to the position given by the `XmNtopPosition`, `XmNbottomPosition`, `XmNleftPosition`, or `XmNrightPosition` resources.

— `XmATTACH_SELF`: Attach the child to the position specified by the value of its `XmNx`, `XmNy`, `XmNwidth`, and/or `XmNheight` resources.

- `XmNtopWidget`, `XmNbottomWidget`, `XmNleftWidget`, and `XmNrightWidget`: These resources specify the reference widget for this child, if the corresponding attachment is `XmATTACH_WIDGET` or `XmATTACH_OPPOSITE_WIDGET`.

`XmNtopPosition`, `XmNbottomPosition`, `XmNleftPosition`, and `XmNright-Position`: These resources specify the attachment position of a widget, if the corresponding attachment resource is set to `XmATTACH_POSITION`. The value is interpreted as a fraction of the corresponding dimension of the XmForm widget. This resource specifies the numerator of the fraction, while the `XmNfractionBase` resource specifies the denominator.

- `XmNtopOffset`, `XmNbottomOffset`, `XmNleftOffset`, and `XmNrightOffset`: These resources specify an offset between the corresponding side of the child and the widget or position to which it is attached.

The XmForm widget retains the specified relationships between children when the form is resized, when new children are added or deleted, or when one or more of the children are resized.

Setting Widget Attachments

The easiest way to understand how to use the XmForm widget is by looking at examples. The following simple program creates an XmForm widget that manages three XmPushButton widgets.

```
1   /****************************************************
2    * formtest.c: demonstrate some XmForm attachments
3    ****************************************************/
4   #include <Xm/Xm.h>
5   #include <Xm/Form.h>
6   #include <Xm/PushB.h>
7
8   void main ( int argc, char ** argv )
9   {
10      Widget        shell, form, button1, button2, button3;
11      XtAppContext app;
12      int          i;
13
14      shell = XtAppInitialize ( &app, "Formtest",  NULL, 0,
15                                &argc, argv, NULL, NULL, 0 );
16
17      /*
18       * Create an XmForm manager widget
19       */
20
21      form = XtCreateManagedWidget ( "form", xmFormWidgetClass,
22                                      shell, NULL, 0 );
23
24      /*
25       * Add three XmPushButton widgets to the Form Widget.
26       * Set constraint resources for each button, setting up
27       * a shape like this:
28       *           button one
29       *           button two
30       *           button three
31       */
32
33      button1 =
34          XtVaCreateManagedWidget ( "button1", xmPushButtonWidgetClass,
```

```
35                                      form,
36                                      XmNtopAttachment,    XmATTACH_FORM,
37                                      XmNbottomAttachment, XmATTACH_NONE,
38                                      XmNleftAttachment,   XmATTACH_FORM,
39                                      XmNrightAttachment,  XmATTACH_FORM,
40                                      149NULL );
41
42      button2 =
43          XtVaCreateManagedWidget ( "button2", xmPushButtonWidgetClass,
44                                      form,
45                                      XmNtopAttachment,    XmATTACH_WIDGET,
46                                      XmNtopWidget,        button1,
47                                      XmNbottomAttachment,XmATTACH_NONE,
48                                      XmNleftAttachment,   XmATTACH_FORM,
49                                      XmNrightAttachment, XmATTACH_FORM,
50                                      NULL );
51
52      button3 =
53          XtVaCreateManagedWidget ( "button3", xmPushButtonWidgetClass,
54                                      form,
55                                      XmNtopAttachment,    XmATTACH_WIDGET,
56                                      XmNtopWidget,        button2,
57                                      XmNbottomAttachment,XmATTACH_FORM,
58                                      XmNleftAttachment,   XmATTACH_FORM,
59                                      XmNrightAttachment, XmATTACH_FORM,
60                                      NULL );
61
62      XtRealizeWidget ( shell );
63      XtAppMainLoop ( app );
64  }
```

The constraints specified in this example attach the left and right sides of all three buttons to the parent XmForm widget. The top of button1 and the bottom of button3 are also attached to the XmForm widget. The top of button2 is attached to the bottom of button1, and the top of button3 is attached to the bottom of button2. Figure 5.7 shows the initial layout produced by these resources, while Figure 5.8 shows the layout after resizing the XmForm widget.

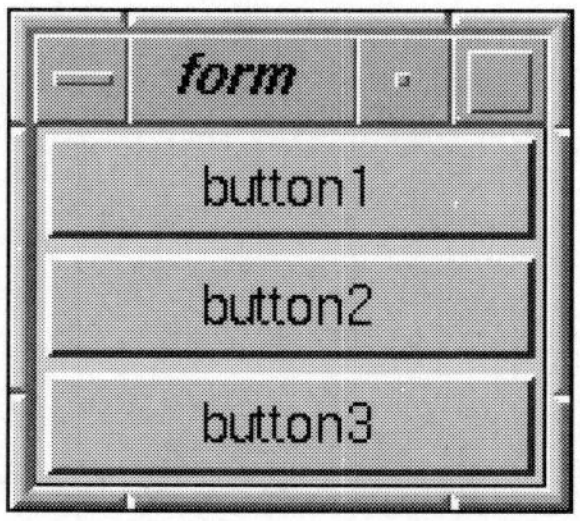

Figure 5.7 An XmForm widget layout.

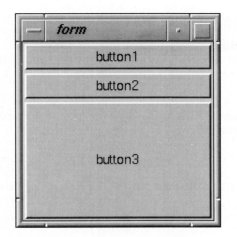

Figure 5.8 Resized version of Figure 5.7.

Using Position Attachments

Although it is often useful to attach widgets to each other, some applications need layouts in which relative sizes are maintained as the application's window is resized. Notice that with the previous constraints, only `button3` grows vertically as the XmForm widget is resized. Position-based attachments can be used to specify that all three buttons should maintain some relative size.

The following example is a version of the `formtest` program that uses position-based attachments. Because this type of attachment does not require references to widgets, all resource values can be specified in a resource file. First, all resource specifications must be removed from the code. The modified program looks like this:

```
1  /*********************************************************
2   * formtest.c: demonstrate position-based attachments
3   *********************************************************/
4  #include <Xm/Xm.h>
5  #include <Xm/Form.h>
6  #include <Xm/PushB.h>
7
8  void main ( int argc, char ** argv )
9  {
10      Widget       shell, form, button1, button2, button3;
11      XtAppContext app;
12      int          i;
13
14      shell = XtAppInitialize ( &app, "Formtest", NULL, 0,
15                                &argc, argv, NULL, NULL, 0 );
16
```

```
17      /*
18       * Create an XmForm manager widget
19       */
20
21      form = XtCreateManagedWidget ( "form", xmFormWidgetClass,
22                                      shell, NULL, 0 );
23
24      /*
25       * Create three children of the form. Attachments are specified
26       * in a resource file.
27       */
28
29      button1 =
30            XtCreateManagedWidget ( "button1",xmPushButtonWidgetClass,
31                                      form, NULL, 0 );
32
33      button2 =
34            XtCreateManagedWidget ( "button2", xmPushButtonWidgetClass,
35                                      form, NULL, 0 );
36
37      button3 =
38          XtCreateManagedWidget ( "button3", xmPushButtonWidgetClass,
39                                    form, NULL, 0 );
40
41      XtRealizeWidget ( shell );
42
43      XtAppMainLoop ( app );
44  }
```

Now, the following resources can be used to specify that each button should occupy 30 percent of the height of the XmForm widget and stretch from 1 to 99 percent of the width.

```
1    !!!!!!!!!!!!!!!!!!!!!!!!!!!!!!!!!!!!!!!!!!!!!!!!!!!!
2    ! Formtest: An app-defaults file for formtest
3    !!!!!!!!!!!!!!!!!!!!!!!!!!!!!!!!!!!!!!!!!!!!!!!!!!!!
4
5    ! Specify all attachments as attach_position
6
7    Formtest*topAttachment:            attach_position
8    Formtest*bottomAttachment:         attach_position
9    Formtest*leftAttachment:           attach_position
10   Formtest*rightAttachment:          attach_position
11
12   ! Set up the buttons to stretch across the entire form
13   ! and each occupy 30 % of the height.
14
15   Formtest*button1.leftPosition:     1
16   Formtest*button1.rightPosition:    99
```

```
17   Formtest*button1.topPosition:        1
18   Formtest*button1.bottomPosition:    31
19
20   Formtest*button2.leftPosition:       1
21   Formtest*button2.rightPosition:     99
22   Formtest*button2.topPosition:       35
23   Formtest*button2.bottomPosition:    65
24
25   Formtest*button3.leftPosition:       1
26   Formtest*button3.rightPosition:     99
27   Formtest*button3.topPosition:       69
28   Formtest*button3.bottomPosition:    99
```

The relative positions and sizes specified in the Formtest app-defaults file are maintained as the XmForm widget is resized, as shown in Figure 5.9 and Figure 5.10.

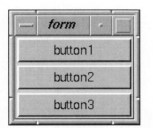

Figure 5.9 Layout based on position attachments.

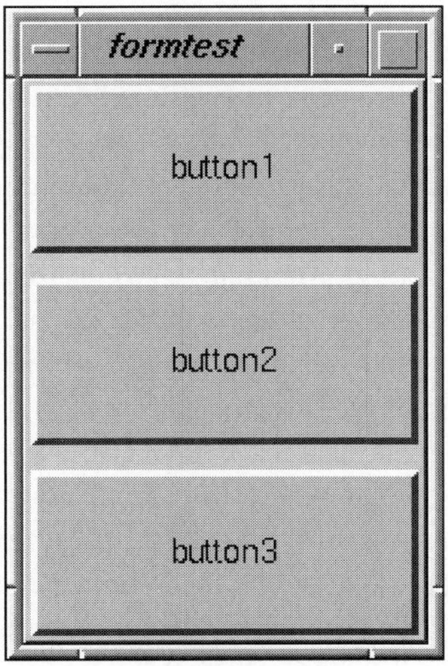

Figure 5.10 Resized version of Figure 5.9.

A Typical XmForm Layout

Let's look at how the XmForm widget might be used to create a typical window layout, as shown in Figure 5.11. This example requires a more complex set of attachments than previous examples. The layout centers around a multi-line text edit area, which has a label above, buttons below, and a set of toggle buttons to the right. When the window is resized, the text area should grow in size, but the other widgets should not.

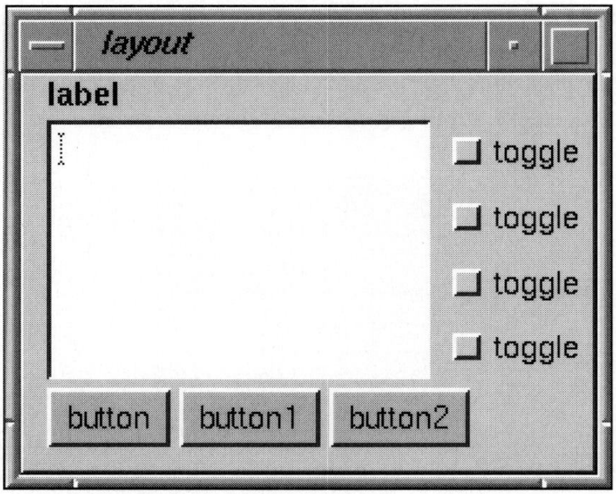

Figure 5.11 A typical XmForm layout.

For this example, the buttons along the bottom of the window should always stay alined with the left side of the text widget, and the group of toggle buttons should always stay aligned with the top of the text widget. The space between each button should not change. These rules are arbitrary, of course, and represent a conscious design decision. One could just as easily decide that the XmPushButton widgets should span the bottom of the window with any extra space interspersed between them, or that the buttons should also change size as the overall window changes size.

Figure 5.12 shows the behavior of the widgets in this layout when the window is resized. Here, the XmText widget has grown, while all other widgets remain their original size. All widgets maintain their relative positions. The goal in such a layout is to resize the widget or widgets that can reveal more information to the user and to keep widgets of lesser importance the same size.

This layout can be implemented by using a single XmForm to contain all of the major elements of the window. The layout of each set of buttons is straight-forward and could be implemented in several ways. For example, the buttons could be positioned using attachments, or they could be placed in XmRowColumn widgets. This example demonstrates both approaches. The toggle buttons are placed in a vertical row column, which is attached to other widgets in the window. However, the XmPushButton widgets along the bottom are individually positioned using form attachments.

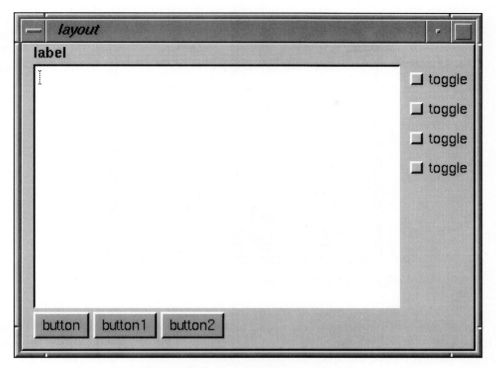

Figure 5.12 Resizing the form layout.

The goal, when laying out the buttons along the bottom, is to align the tops and bottoms of each widget. In this example, all three buttons are forced to be the height of the first button. This can be accomplished by setting the top and bottom attachments of the two widgets on the right to XmATTACH_OPPOSITE_WIDGET, thereby attaching the tops of button1 and button2 to the top of button, and the bottom sides of both widgets to the bottom of button.

Figure 5.13 shows what happens to the height of the buttons if a multi-line label is specified for the first button. In this case, the other buttons grow to match the size of the first button. Notice that these attachments fail to produce the same effect if button2 is made larger than the first button. In all cases, button1 and button2 are tied to the height of button1. There are times when this is the desired effect. If all buttons are expected to always be the same height, the buttons could be placed in an XmRowColumn manager and then attached to the other widgets as a unit. In fact, using an XmRow-Column widget is clearly the easiest way to layout these buttons. This example uses constraints only to demonstrate the power and flexibility of the XmForm widget.

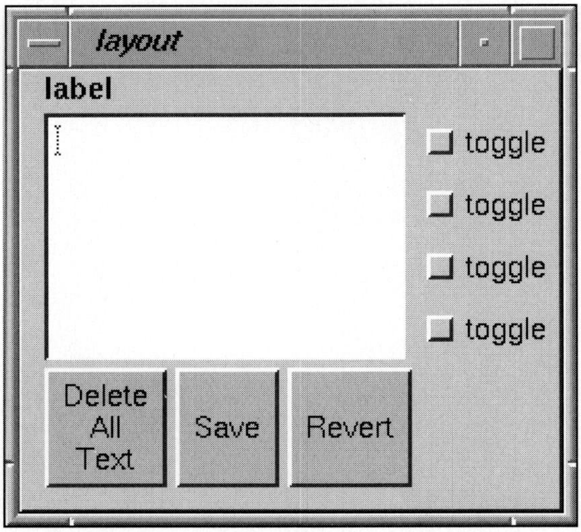

Figure 5.13 Effect of changing the size of the first button.

Figure 5.14 shows the attachments that could be used to produce the layout first shown in Figure 5.11. The label at the top is attached to the left and top of the form and is unattached at the bottom and right. The text widget, which is to be resizable is attached to other widgets on all four sides. The text widget is attached to the label on the top, the form on the left, the first XmPushButton widget on the bottom, and the XmRowColumn widget that contains the toggles on the right.

The row of XmPushButton widgets is created by attaching the first button to the form on the left and then attaching the left side of each button to the right side of the previous widget. The bottom of the first button is attached to the bottom of the form, but is left unattached on the right and top. The tops and bottoms of the remaining button widgets are attached only to the first button and not to the form.

Finally, the set of toggle buttons on the right side, which are all contained in a single XmRow-Column widget are attached to the right side of the form, to the label at the top and the first button on the bottom. This forces the top edge of the toggle buttons to align with bottom of the label, and therefore the top of the text widget. The bottom of the toggles could be left unattached, but that would result in an initial layout in which the bottom of the toggles reached the bottom of the form, possibly overlapping the row of buttons along the bottom. By attaching the bottom of the toggles to the top of the first button at the bottom, the toggles start out above the row of buttons.

Notice the important role of the first button in this layout. Every widget except the label is attached to this widget in one way or another. This is not necessary typical, but it works for this layout. The XmForm widget is extremely flexible and the types of layouts and dynamic behavior that can be achieved is nearly endless. The layout described in this section is just one example.

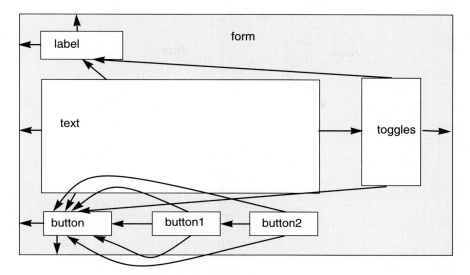

Figure 5.14 Attachments used to produce the layout in Figure 5.11.

Besides the basic attachments shown in Figure 5.14, the `layout` program, which implements the widget layout described in this section, uses some offsets to provide better aesthetics. The layout shown in Figure 5.11 through Figure 5.13 can be implemented as follows.

```
1   /*****************************************************
2    * layout.c: Demonstrate typical XmForm attachments
3    *****************************************************/
4   #include <Xm/Xm.h>
5   #include <Xm/Form.h>
6   #include <Xm/PushB.h>
7   #include <Xm/Label.h>
8   #include <Xm/RowColumn.h>
9   #include <Xm/Text.h>
10  #include <Xm/ToggleB.h>
11
12  void main ( int argc, char ** argv )
13  {
14      Widget       shell, form, button, button1, button2, text,
15                   options, label;
16      XtAppContext app;
17      int          i;
18
19      shell = XtAppInitialize ( &app, "Layout",  NULL, 0,
20                                &argc, argv, NULL, NULL, 0 );
21
```

```
22      /*
23       * Create an XmForm manager widget
24       */
25
26      form = XtCreateManagedWidget ( "form", xmFormWidgetClass,
27                                      shell, NULL, 0 );
28      /*
29       * Create a label, attached to the upper left corner of the form
30       */
31
32      label =
33          XtVaCreateManagedWidget ( "label", xmLabelWidgetClass,
34                                     form,
35                                     XmNalignment, XmALIGNMENT_BEGINNING,
36                                     XmNleftAttachment,   XmATTACH_FORM,
37                                     XmNtopAttachment,    XmATTACH_FORM,
38                                     XmNrightAttachment,  XmATTACH_NONE,
39                                     XmNbottomAttachment, XmATTACH_NONE,
40                                     XmNleftOffset,       10,
41                                     NULL ) ;
42      /*
43       * Create the row of buttons along the bottom. The first button
44       * serves as an anchor, attaching to the bottom left corner
45       * while setting an offset from left and bottom for visual
46       * aesthetics. All other buttons are forced to align top and
47       * bottom with this first button, and are attached in order.
48       */
49
50      button =
51          XtVaCreateManagedWidget ( "button", xmPushButtonWidgetClass,
52                                     form,
53                                     XmNtopAttachment,    XmATTACH_NONE,
54                                     XmNbottomAttachment, XmATTACH_FORM,
55                                     XmNbottomOffset,     10,
56                                     XmNleftAttachment,   XmATTACH_FORM,
57                                     XmNleftOffset,       10,
58                                     XmNrightAttachment,  XmATTACH_NONE,
59                                     NULL );
60      button1 =
61          XtVaCreateManagedWidget ( "button1", xmPushButtonWidgetClass,
62                                   form,
63                          XmNtopAttachment,    XmATTACH_OPPOSITE_WIDGET,
64                          XmNtopWidget,        button,
65                          XmNbottomAttachment, XmATTACH_OPPOSITE_WIDGET,
66                          XmNbottomWidget,     button,
67                          XmNleftAttachment,   XmATTACH_WIDGET,
68                          XmNleftWidget,       button,
69                          XmNrightAttachment,  XmATTACH_NONE,
70                          NULL ) ;
```

```
71      button2 =
72          XtVaCreateManagedWidget ( "button2", xmPushButtonWidgetClass,
73                      form,
74                      XmNtopAttachment,    XmATTACH_OPPOSITE_WIDGET,
75                      XmNtopWidget,        button,
76                      XmNbottomAttachment, XmATTACH_OPPOSITE_WIDGET,
77                      XmNbottomWidget,     button,
78                      XmNleftAttachment,   XmATTACH_WIDGET,
79                      XmNleftWidget,       button1,
80                      XmNrightAttachment,  XmATTACH_NONE,
81                      NULL ) ;
82
83      /*
84       * Create a row column widget to hold a column of toggle buttons.
85       * Make the top of the row column aline with the bottom of the
86       * label, attach the right edge to the form, and let the left
87       * side float. The bottom needs to be attached to the top of the
88       * row of buttons so the two can't overlay each other.
89       */
90
91      options =
92          XtVaCreateManagedWidget ( "options", xmRowColumnWidgetClass,
93                          form,
94                          XmNtopAttachment,    XmATTACH_WIDGET,
95                          XmNtopWidget,        label,
96                          XmNbottomAttachment, XmATTACH_NONE,
97                          XmNleftAttachment,   XmATTACH_NONE,
98                          XmNrightAttachment,  XmATTACH_FORM,
99                          XmNbottomAttachment, XmATTACH_WIDGET,
100                         XmNbottomWidget,     button,
101                         NULL );
102     /*
103      * Add some toggle buttons to the rwo column widget. These
104      * are not involved in the form constraints.
105      */
106
107     for ( i = 0 ; i < 4; i++ )
108         XtCreateManagedWidget ( "toggle", xmToggleButtonWidgetClass,
109                         options, NULL, 0 ) ;
110     /*
111      * Attach the text widget to the label on the top, to the form
112      * on the left, to the option row column on the right, and to
113      * the top of the buttons on the bottom. Becase the text widget is
114      * the only widget attached on all four sides, this widget
115      * stretches when the form is resized.
116      */
117
118     text =
119       XtVaCreateManagedWidget ( "text", xmTextWidgetClass, form,
```

```
120                                        XmNtopAttachment,     XmATTACH_WIDGET,
121                                        XmNtopWidget,         label,
122                                        XmNbottomAttachment, XmATTACH_WIDGET,
123                                        XmNbottomWidget,      button1,
124                                        XmNleftAttachment,    XmATTACH_FORM,
125                                        XmNleftOffset,        10,
126                                        XmNrightAttachment,  XmATTACH_WIDGET,
127                                        XmNrightWidget,       options,
128                                        NULL );
129       XtRealizeWidget ( shell );
130       XtAppMainLoop ( app );
131  }
```

5.6   The XmFrame Widget Class

The XmFrame widget class is a manager class that primarily manages a single widget. The XmFrame can be used to add Motif's 3-dimensional shadows to a widget that does not have one, or it can be used to visually separate a widget or group of widgets from the rest of the user interface. The XmFrame widget is particularly useful for visually grouping a set of widgets, as the example later in this section demonstrates. Besides the child framed by an XmFrame widget, this widget class supports an additional child that can be used as a title for the frame.

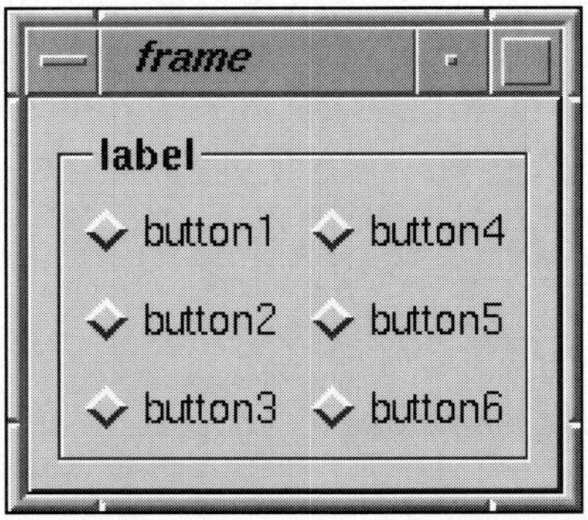

Figure 5.15 An XmFrame widget with a title around a radio box.

Resources

The XmFrame widget class supports several resources that operate directly on the XmFrame widget, and also supports a set of constraint resources that are added to children of an XmFrame widget. The direct resources include:

- `XmNshadowType`: The value of this resource determines the type of shadow displayed by the XmFrame widget. The type of shadow normally used with XmPushButton widgets can be obtained by setting this resource to `XmSHADOW_OUT`. The value `XmSHADOW_IN` is the inverse of `XmSHADOW_OUT`. `XmSHADOW_ETCHED_IN` and `XmSHADOW_ETCHED_OUT` produce the etched look, shown in Figure 4.7 in Chapter 4. If the XmFrame widget's parent is a Shell widget, the default shadow type is `XmSHADOW_OUT`. Otherwise, the default is `XmSHADOW_ETCHED_IN`.
- `XmNshadowThickness`: This resource controls the thickness of the XmFrame shadow. The default is two pixels, unless the XmFrame widget's parent is a Shell widget, in which case the default value is one pixel.

The constraint resources supported by the XmFrame widget are used to control the placement of the optional title widget. This widget is normally expected to be an XmLabel widget or XmLabel-Gadget. The XmFrame constraint resources include:

- `XmNchildType`: The XmFrame widget can have two types of children. The framed widget is the `XmFRAME_WORKAREA_CHILD`, while a child used as the title of the frame is specified as an `XmFRAME_TITLE_CHILD`. If no value is specified for this resource, the XmFrame widget assumes `XmFRAME_WORKAREA_CHILD`.
- `XmNchildHorizontalAlignment`: This resource controls the horizontal positioning of the widget used as the title child. The possible values are `XmALIGNMENT_END`, `XmALIGNMENT_BEGINNING`, and `XmALIGNMENT_CENTER`. The default value is `XmALIGNMENT_BEGINNING`.
- `XmNchildVerticalAlignment`: The value of this resource determines how the title child aligns vertically with the frame shadow. The possible values are:
  - `XmALIGNMENT_BASELINE_BOTTOM`: With this value, the baseline of the last line of text in the title aligns with the top shadow of the frame.
  - `XmALIGNMENT_BASELINE_TOP`: This value causes the baseline of the first line of text in the title widget to align with the frame widget's top shadow.
  - `XmALIGNMENT_WIDGET_TOP`: This value causes the top of the title widget to align with the frame widget's top shadow.
  - `XmALIGNMENT_WIDGET_BOTTOM`: This value causes the bottom of the title widget to align with the frame widget's top shadow.
  - `XmALIGNMENT_CENTER`: This is the default value. When `XmNchildVerticalAlignment` is set to this value, the center of the title child is aligned with the frame widget's top shadow.
- `XmNchildHorizontalSpacing`: This resource specifies the minimum distance between the inner edge of the frame's shadow and the title child.

The following example creates a radio box with a set of toggle buttons, contained in an XmFrame widget.

```
1     /****************************************************
2      * frame.c: Show a typical use of a titled frame.
3      ***************************************************/
4     #include <Xm/Xm.h>
5     #include <Xm/RowColumn.h>
6     #include <Xm/ToggleB.h>
7     #include <Xm/Frame.h>
8     #include <Xm/Label.h>
9     #include <Xm/Form.h>
10
11    char *buttons[] = { "button1", "button2", "button3",
12                        "button4", "button5", "button6" };
13
14    void main ( int argc, char **argv )
15    {
16        Widget        shell, rowcol, frame, label, form;
17        XtAppContext app;
18        int           i;
19
20        shell = XtAppInitialize ( &app, "Frame", NULL, 0,
21                                  &argc, argv, NULL, NULL, 0 );
22
23        /*
24         * Create a form to add a margin around the frame
25         */
26
27        form = XtCreateManagedWidget ( "form", xmFormWidgetClass, shell,
28                                       NULL, 0 );
29
30        /*
31         * Create a frame to hold a labeled radio box
32         */
33
34        frame = XtCreateManagedWidget ( "frame", xmFrameWidgetClass, form,
35                                        NULL, 0 );
36
37        label =
38              XtVaCreateManagedWidget ( "label",  xmLabelWidgetClass,
39                                         frame,
40                                         XmNchildType,XmFRAME_TITLE_CHILD,
41                                         NULL );
42        /*
43         * Create an XmRowColumn widget configured as a radio box.
44         */
45
46        rowcol = XmCreateRadioBox ( frame, "rowcol", NULL, 0 );
47
48        XtManageChild ( rowcol );
49
```

```
50      /*
51       * Create children of the XmRowColumn widget.
52       */
53
54      for ( i = 0; i < XtNumber ( buttons ); i++ )
55      {
56          Widget toggle =
57                      XtCreateManagedWidget ( buttons[i],
58                                              xmToggleButtonWidgetClass,
59                                              rowcol, NULL, 0 );
60      }
61
62      XtRealizeWidget ( shell );
63      XtAppMainLoop ( app );
64  }
```

This program produces the window shown in Figure 5.15. This figure can be produced by running the program with the following set of resources:

```
1   !!!!!!!!!!!!!!!!!!!!!!!!!!!!!!!!!!!!!!!!!!!!!!!!!!!!!!!!!
2   !! Frame: Application resources for the frame example
3   !!!!!!!!!!!!!!!!!!!!!!!!!!!!!!!!!!!!!!!!!!!!!!!!!!!!!!!!!
4   *numColumns:            2
5   *frame.shadowType:      shadow_etched_in
6   *frame*topAttachment:   attach_form
7   *frame*bottomAttachment: attach_form
8   *frame*leftAttachment:  attach_form
9   *frame*rightAttachment: attach_form
10  *Offset:                10
```

5.7   The XmScrolledWindow Widget Class

The XmScrolledWindow widget class is an often-used widget class that can automatically scroll a single child. The XmScrolledWindow widget class provides a layout that includes a scrollable work area, as well as vertical and horizontal scrollbars. Applications can use the XmScrolledWindow widget primarily to handle layout, while creating and controlling the scrollbars explicitly, or the XmScrolledWindow widget can automatically create the scrollbars and handle scrolling by moving the child in the work area as needed.

Figure 5.16 illustrates how the XmScrolledWindow widget provides automatic scrolling. The scrollable child of the XmScrolledWindow widget, known as the "work window", is allowed to be as large as necessary. This work window is clipped by a "clip window", so that only a portion of the work window is visible. The scrollbars allow the position of the work window to be changed to make different portions of the work window visible. Applications can simply treat the work window as if the entire window is visible, updating the contents of the window in response to Expose events, and do not need to be aware of the XmScrolledWindow's behavior. (See Chapter 8 and Chapter 13 for more information on handling `Expose` events.)

The automatic model works well for many applications, but is inadequate for others. For example, if the automatic technique were to be used for a text editor, the work window would need to be large enough to display all the text in an edit buffer at once. This would be fine for small amounts of text, but it would be easy to insert a large text file into the buffer that would require a larger window than X supports. For such applications, the scrolled window widget allows applications to handle scrolling explicitly. In the case of a text editor, the application would normally leave the work window the same size at all times and just change the starting point in the text buffer to be drawn in the window.

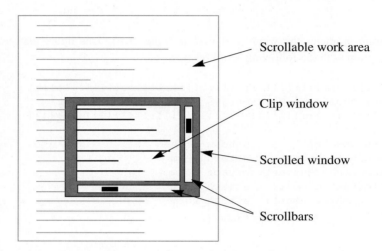

Figure 5.16 Automatic scrolling using the XmScrolledWindow widget.

Resources

The XmScrolledWindow widget class supports several resources, in addition to those inherited from its superclasses, that can be used to modify the widget's behavior. Some of the common resources include:

- `XmNhorizontalScrollBar`: This resource allows applications to retrieve the widget ID of the horizontal scrollbar, or to specify that an application-created scrollbar widget should be used as the horizontal scrollbar.

- `XmNverticalScrollBar`: This resource can be used to retrieve the widget ID of the vertical scrollbar, or to specify that an application-created scrollbar widget should be used as the vertical scrollbar.

- `XmNworkWindow`: This resource specifies the widget being scrolled. Normally, the `XmNworkWindow` resource is set simply by creating a child of the XmScrolledWindow widget.

- `XmNclipWindow`: This read-only resource can be used to retrieve the widget ID of the widget used as a clip window. The clip window only exists if the XmScrolledWindow widget's `XmNvisualPolicy` resource is set to `XmCONSTANT`. The clip window is an XmDrawingArea widget.

- `XmNscrollingPolicy`: When this resource is set to the default value of `XmAPPLICATION_DEFINED`, the XmScrolledWindow widget simply provides the layout for application-provided scrollbars. In this case, the application must handle the scrolling manually by registering callbacks with the scrollbar widgets and managing the contents of the work window. When the value of `XmNscrollingPolicy` is set to `XmAUTOMATIC`, the XmScrolledWindow widget automatically creates vertical and horizontal scrollbars. In this mode, the XmScrolledWindow widget manages the work window, scrolling it by moving the entire window as needed.

- `XmNvisualPolicy`: When this resource is set to `XmVARIABLE`, the XmScrolledWindow attempts to adjust its layout to accommodate the size of the work window. When the value is set to `XmCONSTANT`, the XmScrolledWindow widget allows the work window to grow or shrink as needed, but the clip window does not resize, so that the size of the visible portion of the work window remains constant.

- `XmNscrollBarDisplayPolicy`: When the XmScrolledWindow creates its own scrollbars (when `XmNscrollingPolicy` is set to `XmAUTOMATIC`), this resource determines when the scrollbars are displayed. If the value of `XmNscrollBarDisplayPolicy` is set to `XmAS_NEEDED`, each scrollbar is only displayed when the size of the work window exceeds the size of the clip window in the corresponding dimension. When `XmNscrollBarDisplayPolicy` is set to `XmSTATIC`, both scrollbars are always displayed.

- `XmNscrollBarPlacement`: The XmScrolledWindow widget supports several different layouts. If this resource is set to `XmTOP_LEFT`, the horizontal scrollbar is placed at the top of the window, while the vertical scrollbar is placed on the left. Other possible values are `XmBOTTOM_LEFT`, `XmTOP_RIGHT`, and `XmBOTTOM_RIGHT` (the default).

- `XmNscrolledWindowMarginWidth`: The value of this resource determines the margins on the top and bottom of the XmScrolledWindow widget.

- `XmNscrolledWindowMarginHeight`: The value of this resource determines the margins on the left and right sides of the XmScrolledWindow widget.

- `XmNspacing`: This resource determines the distance between the work window and the scrollbars. The default spacing is 4 pixels.

An Example

The following example demonstrates the simplest way to use the XmScrolledWindow widget class. This program creates an XmLabel widget as a child of an XmScrolledWindow widget. The XmScrolledWindow widget is configured to create scrollbars automatically and to automatically scroll its work window if the work window grows larger than the XmScrolledWindow widget's clip window. The XmScrolledWindow widget is also configured to always display scrollbars regardless of the size of the work window.

```
1    /*******************************************************
2     * scroll.c: Demonstrate an XmScrolledWindow widget
3     *******************************************************/
4    #include <Xm/Xm.h>
5    #include <Xm/Label.h>
6    #include <Xm/ScrolledW.h>
7
8    void main ( int argc, char **argv )
9    {
10       Widget        shell, swindow, label;
11       XtAppContext app;
12
13       /*
14        * Initialize Xt
15        */
16
17       shell = XtAppInitialize ( &app, "Scroll", NULL, 0,
18                                 &argc, argv,
19                                 NULL, NULL, 0 );
20
21       /*
22        * Create a scrolled window, configured to automatically
23        * scroll its child, and to alwasy display scrollbars.
24        */
25
26       swindow =
27          XtVaCreateManagedWidget ( "scrolledWindow",
28                                    xmScrolledWindowWidgetClass, shell,
29                                    XmNscrollingPolicy, XmAUTOMATIC,
30                                    XmNscrollBarDisplayPolicy, XmSTATIC,
31                                    NULL );
32
33       label = XtCreateManagedWidget ( "label",xmLabelWidgetClass,
34                                       swindow, NULL, 0 );
35
36       XtManageChild ( swindow );
37
38       /*
39        * Realize the shell and enter the event loop.
40        */
41
42       XtRealizeWidget ( shell );
43       XtAppMainLoop ( app );
44    }
```

By default, the label widget in this example is unlikely to need to be scrolled. The label can be forced to a larger size by setting some resources to display an image (a pixmap) in the label. One large image can be displayed by setting the following resources in a resource file:

```
*label*labelType:     pixmap
*label*labelPixmap:   escherknot
```

Figure 5.17 shows the appearance of the program described above when these resources are set.

Figure 5.17 An XmScrolledWindow widget.

5.8   The XmMainWindow Widget Class

The XmMainWindow widget class is designed to provide a common layout typically needed by applications' top-level windows. The XmMainWindow widget supports four distinct areas, each of which can be used to display a widget. These areas are the menu bar, the work area, the command window, and the message window. All areas are optional, and the XmMainWindow widget may have children in any or all of these locations. Figure 5.18 shows the default layout supported by the XmMainWindow widget, when all four areas are used.

The XmMainWindow widget is often used in applications that do not need all areas. A typical configuration uses only the work area and a menu bar. The XmMainWindow can automatically scroll the work area, if desired. This is particularly useful when the work area is a simple drawing area. Many applications have more complex interfaces and ignore this feature, but still find the XmMainWindow's layout support convenient.

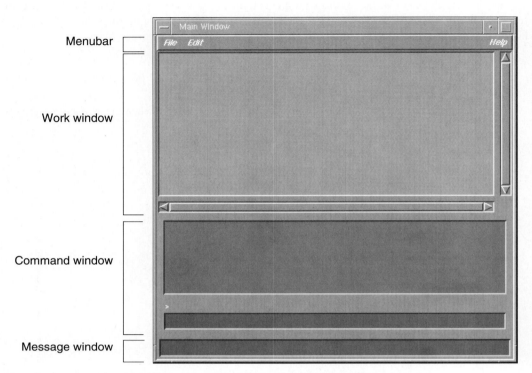

Figure 5.18 A completely configured XmMainWindow widget.

Resources

The XmMainWindow widget supports several resources that determine how the widget manages its children. These include the following:

- XmNcommandWindow: This resource specifies a widget to be used as the command window. The widget must first be created as a child of the XmMainWindow widget. The command window is expected to be an XmCommand widget, which combines an input text field with a scrollable history list. However, few interfaces require this rarely used widget, and any widget can be installed as the command window.

- XmNcommandWindowLocation: The value of this resource determines the position of the command window. Possible values are XmCOMMAND_BELOW_WORKSPACE which places the command window along the bottom of the XmMainWindow widget, and the default value, XmCOMMAND_ABOVE_WORKSPACE, which places the command window at the top of the XmMainWindow widget.

- XmNmenuBar: This resource specifies the widget ID of the widget to be installed as a menu bar. This widget must have been previously created as a child of the XmMainWindow widget.

- **XmNmessageWindow**: This resource specifies the widget to be installed as the message window. This widget must have been previously created as a child of the XmMainWindow widget.

- **XmNshowSeparator**: If the value of this resource is `TRUE`, the XmMainWindow creates and displays separator widgets between each of the major components of the XmMain-Window widget. The default value is `FALSE`.

An Example

The following simple example creates an XmMainWindow widget that contains a menu bar and a framed collection of XmToggleButton widgets. The menu bar is empty in this example because menus have not yet been discussed. Notice that all widgets contained in the XmMainWindow widget are created as children of the XmMainWindow widget. The position of each child is specified by calling `XtVaSetValues()` to set the `XmNmenuBar` and `XmNworkWindow` resources.

```
1     /***********************************************************
2      * mainwindow.c: Demonstrate the XmMainWindow widget
3      ***********************************************************/
4     #include <Xm/Xm.h>
5     #include <Xm/RowColumn.h>
6     #include <Xm/MainW.h>
7     #include <Xm/Frame.h>
8     #include <Xm/Label.h>
9     #include <Xm/ToggleB.h>
10
11    void main ( int argc, char ** argv )
12    {
13        XtAppContext app;
14        Widget       menu, shell, mainwindow, rowcol, frame, label;
15        int          i;
16
17        /*
18         * Initialize Xt
19         */
20
21        shell = XtAppInitialize ( &app, "Mainwindow", NULL, 0,
22                                  &argc, argv, NULL, NULL, 0 );
23
24        mainwindow = XtVaCreateManagedWidget ( "mainwindow",
25                                               xmMainWindowWidgetClass,
26                                               shell, NULL, 0 );
27
28        frame = XtCreateManagedWidget ( "frame", xmFrameWidgetClass,
29                                        mainwindow, NULL, 0 );
30
31        label = XtVaCreateManagedWidget ( "label", xmLabelWidgetClass,
32                                          frame,
```

```
33                                      XmNchildType,XmFRAME_TITLE_CHILD,
34                                      NULL );
35
36      /*
37       * Create an XmRowColumn widget configured as a radio box.
38       */
39
40      rowcol = XmCreateRadioBox ( frame, "rowcol", NULL, 0 );
41      XtManageChild ( rowcol );
42
43      /*
44       * Create children of the XmRowColumn widget.
45       */
46
47      for ( i = 0; i < 4; i++ )
48      {
49          Widget toggle =
50                      XtCreateManagedWidget ( "toggle",
51                                              xmToggleButtonWidgetClass,
52                                              rowcol, NULL, 0 );
53      }
54
55      menu = XmCreateMenuBar ( mainwindow, "menu", NULL, 0 );
56
57      /*
58       * Specify the widgets to be used as a work area and menu bar.
59       */
60
61      XtVaSetValues ( mainwindow,
62                      XmNmenuBar,    menu,
63                      XmNworkWindow, frame,
64                      NULL );
65
66      XtRealizeWidget ( shell );
67      XtAppMainLoop ( app );
68  }
```

5.9   The XmScale Widget Class

The XmScale widget class is similar to the XmScrollBar widget, but has no arrow buttons. Unlike the XmScrollBar widget, the XmScale widget supports a label and can display a numeric value beside the thumb. Also, while the XmScrollBar is a primitive widget, the XmScale widget is a manager widget that can support children. The XmScale widget is often used to allow users to choose a numeric value within a range, or to display a value. Figure 5.19 shows the XmScale widget as it typically appears. Any children added to the XmScale widget are added above the numeric display, and are evenly spaced in a row, when the XmScale widget is horizontal. When the XmScale widget is vertically oriented, children are added to the left of the optional numeric display and are evenly spaced in a column.

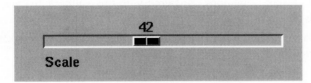

Figure 5.19 The XmScale widget.

Resources

The XmScale widget class provides resources to control the range of values covered by the scale, the current value, the title of the scale, and so on. These resources include the following:

- `XmNvalue`: The value of this resource indicates the current value of the scale, as indicated by the slider position.
- `XmNmaximum`: This resource specifies the maximum value of the scale. The default value is 100.
- `XmNminimum`: This resource specifies the minimum value of the scale. The default value is zero.
- `XmNorientation`: This resource determines whether the scale is displayed vertically (`XmVERTICAL`) or horizontally (`XmHORIZONTAL`). The default value is `XmVERTICAL`.
- `XmNprocessingDirection`: The value of this resource determines whether the maximum value is on the left or right (when the value of `XmNorientation` is `XmHORIZONTAL`) or top or bottom (when the value of `XmNorientation` is `XmVERTICAL`). The possible values are `XmMAX_ON_TOP`, `XmMAX_ON_BOTTOM`, `XmMAX_ON_RIGHT`, and `XmMAX_ON_LEFT`. The default values are `XmMAX_ON_TOP` when the scale is vertical and `XmMAX_ON_RIGHT` when the scale is horizontal.
- `XmNtitleString`: This resource allows applications to specify a compound string to be displayed as a title for the scale.
- `XmNshowValue`: If this resource is `TRUE`, the current value of the scale is shown floating above or next to the slider.
- `XmNdecimalPoints`: The value of this resource determines how many places to shift the slider value when it is displayed. For example, if the value of the `XmNvalue` resource is 1234 and the value of `XmNdecimalPoints` is 3, the number is displayed as 1.234.
- `XmNscaleWidth`: The value of this resource specifies the width of the slider area.
- `XmNscaleHeight`: The value of this resource specifies the height of the slider area.

Callbacks

Unlike the XmScrollBar widget, the XmScale widget supports only two callbacks:

- XmNvalueChangedCallback: This callback is invoked when the value of the XmScale widget changes.
- XmNdragCallback: Functions registered with this callback list are invoked as the user slides the scale thumb.

Both callbacks pass a pointer to a structure of type XmScaleCallbackStruct as call data. This structure is defined as:

```
typedef struct {
   int      reason;
   XEvent *event;
   int      value;
} XmScaleCallbackStruct;
```

The value member of this structure reports the current position of the slider.

An Example

The following example exercises the XmScale widget. In this example, an XmScale allows users to select a value between zero and 100. However, the program only allows values that are multiples of 10 to be selected. Tick marks are displayed for the values 0, 10, 20, 30,and so on. If the user tries to drag the XmScale widget's thumb, the thumb "clicks" to the nearest tick mark.

Figure 5.20 shows an XmScale widget as configured by this program.

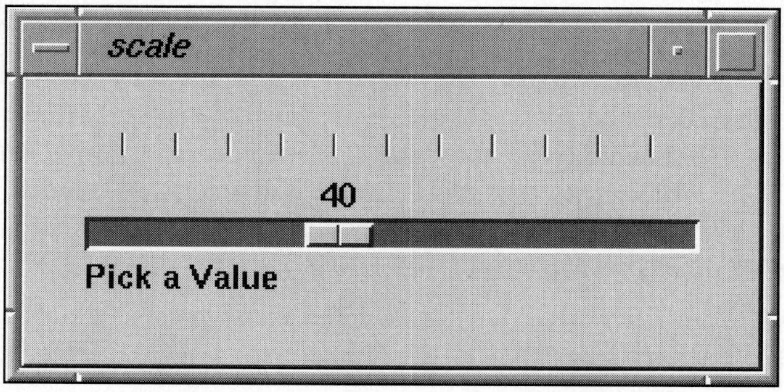

Figure 5.20 An XmScale widget with children that form tick marks.

This example can be written as follows:

```
1    /***********************************************
2     * scale.c: Demonstrate an XmScale widget
3     **********************************************/
4    #include <Xm/Xm.h>
5    #include <Xm/Scale.h>
6    #include <Xm/Separator.h>
7    #include <Xm/Form.h>
8    #include <stdio.h>
9
10   static void ReportValueCallback ( Widget    w,
11                                     XtPointer clientData,
12                                     XtPointer callData );
13   static void ClickCallback ( Widget    w,
14                               XtPointer clientData,
15                               XtPointer callData );
16
17   void main ( int argc, char **argv )
18   {
19       Widget       shell, scale, form;
20       XtAppContext app;
21       int          i;
22
23       /*
24        * Initialize Xt and create a form to hold a scale
25        */
26
27       shell = XtAppInitialize ( &app, "Scale", NULL, 0,
28                                 &argc, argv, NULL, NULL, 0 );
29
30       form = XtCreateManagedWidget ( "form", xmFormWidgetClass,
31                                      shell, NULL, 0 );
32
33       /*
34        * Create a scale with min = 0, max = 100, and display
35        * the current value.
36        */
37
38       scale = XtVaCreateManagedWidget ( "scale", xmScaleWidgetClass,
39                                         form,
40                                         XmNshowValue,   TRUE,
41                                         XmNminimum,        0,
42                                         XmNmaximum,      100,
43                                         XmNscaleHeight, 300,
44                                         NULL );
45       /*
46        * Add one callback to report the value when the slider
47        * moves, and another to force the thumb to click to
48        * intervals of 10 when dragged.
49        */
```

```
50
51        XtAddCallback ( scale, XmNvalueChangedCallback,
52                          ReportValueCallback, NULL );
53
54        XtAddCallback ( scale, XmNdragCallback, ClickCallback, NULL );
55
56        /*
57         * Add tick marks.
58         */
59
60        for ( i = 0; i < 11; i++ )
61            XtCreateManagedWidget ( "sep",xmSeparatorWidgetClass,
62                                     scale, NULL, 0 );
63
64        /*
65         * Realize the shell and enter the event loop.
66         */
67
68        XtRealizeWidget ( shell );
69
70        XtAppMainLoop ( app );
71    }
```

This program creates a scale widget that displays a value from zero to 100. The callback functions registered on lines 51 through 54 are used to demonstrate how to access the value of the scale and also to implement the click-to-tick mark behavior. Lines 60 through 62 create children of the XmScale. These children will be evenly spaced, so it is possible to create tick marks in increments that correspond to the value 10 by managing eleven separator widgets. If the XmScale widget is to be display horizontally, the separators should be oriented vertically, and vice-versa.The orientation of the XmScale and the XmSeparator widgets is controlled by resources in a resource file.

The function ReportValueCallback() is registered as an XmNvalueChanged-Callback function with the XmScale widget in this example. This function demonstrates how the current value of an XmScale widget can be determined. The call data provided by the scale includes the current value represented by the slider position. In this example, the function only reports values that are even multiples of 10.

```
72    static void ReportValueCallback ( Widget     w,
73                                       XtPointer clientData,
74                                       XtPointer callData )
75    {
76        XmScaleCallbackStruct *cbs = ( XmScaleCallbackStruct * ) callData;
77
78        printf ( "value = %d\n", cbs->value );
79    }
```

Functions registered with an XmScale widget's XmNdragCallback list are called whenever a user moves the scale widget's slider. The value member of the XmScaleCallbackStruct passed as call data indicates the new position of the XmScale widget's slider. To force the scale to click to the tick marks used in this example, a callback function can round this value to the nearest multiple of 10 and call the convenience function `XmScaleSetValue()` to move the slider. Changing the slider's position programmatically does not call functions on the `XmNdrag-Callback` list, so this function will not be called recursively. However, when the slider is moved, functions registered with the `XmNvalueChanged` callback list will be invoked, so `ReportValueCallback()` will be called.

The `ClickCallback()` function can be written as follows:

```
80   static void ClickCallback ( Widget      w,
81                                XtPointer clientData,
82                                XtPointer callData )
83   {
84       XmScaleCallbackStruct *cbs = ( XmScaleCallbackStruct * ) callData;
85
86       /* Round the value to the nearest multiple of 10 */
87
88       int value = ( ( cbs->value + 5 )  / 10 )  * 10;
89
90       /* Move the slider to the rounded value. */
91
92       XmScaleSetValue ( w, value );
93   }
```

The following application resource file specifies the resources needed to produce the window shown in Figure 5.21. When the orientation is horizontal, the value for the separator widget's `XmNheight` resource must be removed, and the `XmNwidth` resource set instead.

```
1    !!!!!!!!!!!!!!!!!!!!!!!!!!!!!!!!!!!!!!!!!!!!!!!!!!!!!
2    ! Scale: Application resources for scale example
3    !!!!!!!!!!!!!!!!!!!!!!!!!!!!!!!!!!!!!!!!!!!!!!!!!!!!!
4
5    *topAttachment:         attach_form
6    *bottomAttachment:      attach_form
7    *Offset:                25
8    *leftAttachment:        attach_form
9    *rightAttachment:       attach_form
10
11   *titleString:           Pick a Value
12
13   *XmScale.orientation:   horizontal
14   *XmScale*orientation:   vertical
15   *XmSeparator*height:    10
```

Figure 5.21 shows the scale example when the orientation is vertical.

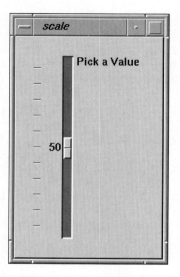

Figure 5.21 A vertical XmScale widget.

5.10 The XmPanedWindow Widget Class

The XmPanedWindow widget class manages all children in adjustable, vertical panes. Figure 5.22 shows an XmPanedWindow widget that manages three XmPushButton widgets. Each widget is separated by an XmSeparator widget. At the right side of each separator is a special widget known as a *sash*. Users can drag this sash using the mouse to adjust the size of each pane in the window. The right side of Figure 5.22 shows how the sash can be used to change the heights of the XmPaned-Window widget's children.

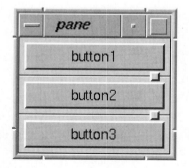

Figure 5.22 An XmPanedWindow widget.

Resources

The XmPanedWindow widget class supports several new direct resources, and also adds constraint resources to its children. The resources that affect the XmPanedWindow widget include the following:

- `XmNrefigureMode`: If this resource is set to `TRUE` (the default), the size and position of each pane is recomputed when any change is made to the XmPanedWindow widget. Setting this resource to `FALSE` prevents the XmPanedWindow widget from attempting to update its layout.
- `XmNseparatorOn`: If the value of this resource is `TRUE`, the XmPanedWindow widget displays a separator between panes. The default value is `TRUE`.
- `XmNsashIndent`: This resource controls the number of pixels by which the sash widget is indented. The default value is 10 pixels.
- `XmNsashWidth`: This resource determines the width of the sash. The default width is 10 pixels.
- `XmNsashHeight`: The value of this resource determines the height of the sash widget. The default height is 10 pixels.
- `XmNsashShadowThickness`: This resource controls the shadow thickness of the sash. The default shadow thickness is two pixels.

The XmPanedWindow widget also supports several constraint resources, which are added to the set of resources recognized by all children of an XmPanedWindow widget. These resources include the following:

- `XmNallowResize`: If the value of this resource is `TRUE`, the XmPanedWindow widget will attempt to honor resize requests from a child. The default value is `FALSE`.
- `XmNpaneMinimum`: This resource controls the minimum height of this pane. The default minimum is one pixel.
- `XmNpaneMaximum`: This resource controls the maximum size of this pane. The default maximum is 1000 pixels. If a pane's minimum size is equal to its maximum, the pane cannot be resized.

An Example

The following program demonstrates the XmPanedWindow widget and creates the window shown in Figure 5.22. The program creates an XmPanedWindow widget and adds three children, all XmPushButton widgets.

```
1    /******************************************************
2     * pane.c: demonstrate an XmPanedWindow widget.
3     ******************************************************/
4    #include <Xm/Xm.h>
5    #include <Xm/PanedW.h>
6    #include <Xm/PushB.h>
```

```
7
8   void main ( int argc, char **argv )
9   {
10      Widget shell, button1, button2, button3, pane;
11      XtAppContext app;
12
13      shell = XtAppInitialize ( &app, "Pane", NULL, 0,
14                                &argc, argv, NULL, NULL, 0 );
15
16      /*
17       * Create a paned window widget with three children.
18       */
19
20      pane =  XtCreateManagedWidget ( "pane", xmPanedWindowWidgetClass,
21                                      shell, NULL, 0 );
22
23      button1 =  XtCreateManagedWidget ( "button1",
24                                         xmPushButtonWidgetClass,
25                                         pane, NULL, 0 );
26      button2 =  XtCreateManagedWidget ( "button2",
27                                         xmPushButtonWidgetClass,
28                                         pane, NULL, 0 );
29      button3 =  XtCreateManagedWidget ( "button3",
30                                         xmPushButtonWidgetClass,
31                                         pane, NULL, 0 );
32
33      XtRealizeWidget ( shell );
34      XtAppMainLoop ( app );
35  }
```

5.11 Designing Widget Hierarchies

Most of the examples discussed so far use a single manager widget to demonstrate a simple layout. However, most real applications have more complex interfaces than those described so far. Often the layout needed for a particular application does not fit neatly into rows and columns, or stacked panes. It is even common for developers to start developing an application based on a user interface design created by a graphics artist, who may not know about the types of layouts supported by Motif. Often, such drawings are difficult to implement because the designer may not consciously think in terms of rows and columns, form attachments, and so on, when creating the layout. In such cases, different kinds of Motif manager widgets can be combined to create the desired effect.

Most applications have user interfaces that are made up of a hierarchy of widgets. Each window starts with a shell widget at the top of the hierarchy. The shell widget contains a single child, most likely an XmForm widget or an XmMainWindow widget. This widget may contain many children. Some of the children may be primitive widgets, but others may be manager widgets, which may, in turn, contain more primitive or manager widgets. The task of implementing a particular layout involves choosing the appropriate manager widgets to create each small part of the application's user interface and then combining these managers to create the overall layout.

Let's look at a simple example. Figure 5.23 shows a typical user interface for a small stopwatch program. Although the interface is very simple, it is difficult to achieve exactly this layout using any single Motif manager widget. The layout is somewhat like that provided by an XmRowColumn widget, but the various primitive widgets do not line up evenly in rows and columns. The buttons at the bottom seem to hang on to the right edge of the window, which cannot be done with an XmRow-Column widget.

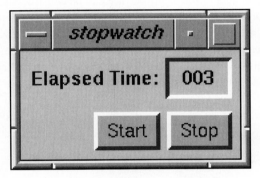

Figure 5.23 A stopwatch user interface.

The layout could be handled by using a single XmForm widget, but the attachments begin to get rather complex and error-prone even with this simple layout. An easier way to create the layout is to break the interface down into smaller pieces that are more easily implemented.

Figure 5.24 shows just the small area that displays elapsed time in the stopwatch interface. This appearance could be created in several ways. This output area could simply be a single XmTextField widget. It is possible to configure the XmTextField to be read-only, and to not show any insertion cursor. Alternately, this appearance could be produced by managing an XmLabel widget inside an XmFrame widget. This widget hierarchy is shown beside the interface in Figure 5.24.

XmFrame
|
XmLabel

Figure 5.24 The digital output area.

Once this small widget hierarchy has been created, the output area can be created by combining the XmFrame widget (and its child) with another XmLabel widget. This layout, shown in Figure 5.25, can be created easily using an XmRowColumn widget, with `XmNorientation` set to `XmHORIZONTAL` and `XmNpacking` set to `XmPACK_TIGHT`.

Figure 5.25 The "face" of the stopwatch.

Next, the control button area of the user interface can be constructed. The easiest way to create a layout that allows the buttons to float along the right side of a window is to use an XmForm widget. The stop button can be attached to the right, top, and bottom sides of the XmForm widget, while the stop button can be attached to the top and bottom of the XmForm widget, and to the left side of the stop button. A few carefully chosen values for `XmNtopOffset`, `XmNbottomOffset`, and `XmNrightOffset` produce the desired spacing.

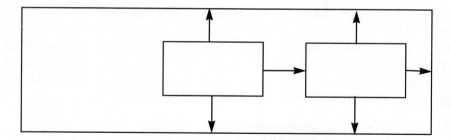

Figure 5.26 The control panel area of the stopwatch.

Figure 5.27 shows the attachments required to produce the layout shown in Figure 5.26.

Figure 5.27 Attachments for the control panel area.

Finally, the control panel area (XmForm) can be combined with the face area (XmRowColumn) to complete the layout. Several widgets could be used to create the simple vertical stacking required to combine these two widgets, but it is easiest to use an XmRowColumn widget, with the `XmNori-entation` resource set to `XmVERTICAL`. `XmNpacking` set to `XmPACK_COLUMN`, and `XmNnumColumns` set to 2.

Figure 5.28 shows the complete widget hierarchy created by this example.

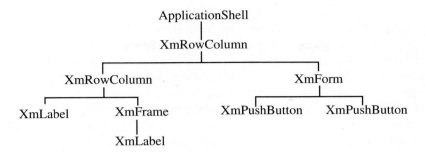

Figure 5.28 Complete nested widget hierarchy used to create layout in Figure 5.23.

Although still simpler than most real applications, this example demonstrates how different Motif manager widgets can be combined to create layouts that are more complex than those supported by any one widget class. Identifying appropriate manager widgets to produce a specific layout requires experience and practice using and configuring the various Motif manager widgets. The Motif manager widgets are extremely flexible and be combined in nearly endless ways. Even the layout described in this section could be achieved in a variety of ways. The widget hierarchy demonstrated here is only one possibility.

5.12 Shell Widgets

A Shell widget is a special type of composite widget that serves as an interface between an application and the window manager. There are many types of shell widgets, each of which serve a specific purpose. All shell classes are implemented by Xt, with the exception of the VendorShell. Most applications use the ApplicationShell and TopLevelShell classes. Dialogs may be based on the TransientShell widget class, although Motif applications generally use the XmDialogShell widget class, which is a subclass of TransientShell. Menus in Motif are supported by the XmMenuShell class, which is a subclass of the OverrideShell widget class.

This section describes the most common Shell classes, and discusses common ways they are used. Figure 5.29 show the inheritance hierarchy of the various Shell widget classes.

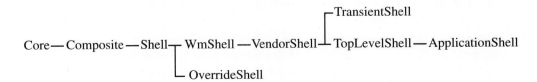

Figure 5.29 Inheritance hierarchy of common shell widgets.

Shell

The Shell widget class is a subclass of the Composite widget class. The Shell widget class is not used directly. It simply provides resources that are inherited by subclasses of Shell. Unlike other composite widgets, shell widgets can support only a single child. Typically, applications create an XmForm or XmMainWindow widget as a child of a shell widget. The more complex Motif manager widgets can then be used to position multiple children in a window.

The Shell widget class provides support for all subclasses, including several resources used by all shell classes. Of course, the Shell widget class inherits all the resources of Core and Composite in addition to those it adds. The commonly used resources added by the Shell widget class include:

- `XmNallowShellResize`: If the value of this resource is `TRUE`, the shell widget attempts to resize itself in response to resize requests from its child. The default value is `FALSE`.
- `XmNgeometry`: This resource can be used to set the initial size of a shell. The resource only takes effect if set before the shell is realized.

The Shell widget class also supports two callback lists that can be used by applications that wish to be notified when a window pops up or down. These callback lists are:

- `XmNpopupCallback`: Callbacks registered with this callback list are called when a shell widget is popped up using the Xt function `XtPopup()`.
- `XmNpopdownCallback`: Callbacks registered with this callback list are called when a shell widget is popped down using the Xt function `XtPopdown()`.

WmShell

The WmShell widget class is a subclass of Shell that adds additional support for interacting with a window manager. The WmShell widget class allows applications to set up window manager hints, as specified by the ICCCM, by setting resources on a WMShell widget. The resources added by the WmShell widget class include the following:

- `XmNbaseHeight, XmNbaseWidth`: The values of these resources specify a base size for a window. These values are combined with the values of the `XmNheightInc` and `XmNwidthInc` resources to specify preferred sizes for the window when the user attempts to resize the window. For example, if `XmNbaseHeight` is set to 200 and `XmNheightInc` is set to 25, then the application would prefer to have heights that are multiples of 25, starting at 200.
- `XmNheightInc, XmNwidthInc`: The values of these resources specify an application's preferred resize increments, which are used in conjunction with the `XmNbaseHeight` and `XmNbaseWidth` resources.
- `XmNinitialState`: This resource can be used to specify how a shell window is initially displayed. If the value of `XmNinitialState` is `NormalState`, the window manager is requested to display this window normally upon startup. If the value is `IconicState`, the window manager should show the icon window associated with this shell. This resource is only effective when set before the shell is realized.

- `XmNtitle`: The value of this resource specifies the string to be displayed by the window manager as the name of the window. If this resource is not set explicitly, the value defaults to the icon name of the window, or to the name of the application if no icon name is given.

- `XmNminWidth, XmNminHeight, XmNmaxWidth, XmNmaxHeight`: These resources can be used to specify the minimum and maximum sizes a window should be allowed to have.

- `XmNiconPixmap`: The resource can be used to provide a pixmap to be displayed in the icon associated with this shell. See Chapter 14 for more information.

- `XmNiconWindow`: This resource can be used to specify a window that should be used as the icon for this shell. Normally, most window managers create an icon window automatically, but some applications would like to have more control over the icon window. See Chapter 14 for more information.

VendorShell

The VendorShell widget class provided by Xt is an empty shell class that is meant to be re-implemented by a vendor or a specific toolkit to introduce vendor or toolkit-specific functionality that can be inherited by all subclasses. Motif implements a VendorShell class that adds some Motif-specific functionality to all shell subclasses. Most of these resources involve window manager interaction. See Chapter 14 for more information about interacting and communicating with the window manager. Some of the more useful resources added by the Motif VendorShell include the following:

- `XmNdeleteResponse`: The value of this resource determines what action the shell takes when the user closes the window using the window manager. The ICCCM specifies that window managers can send applications a `WM_DELETE_WINDOW` message to close a window. The VendorShell can perform three possible actions in response to such a message. If the value of `XmNdeleteResponse` is `XmDESTROY`, the window is destroyed, along with all its children. If the value of `XmNdeleteResponse` is `XmUNMAP`, the shell is simply unmapped and disappears from the screen. If `XmNdeleteResponse` is set to `XmDO_NOTHING`, the window manager message is ignored. The default value is `XmDESTROY`. See Chapter 14 for more information.

- `XmNkeyBoardFocusPolicy`: If the value of this resource is `XmEXPLICIT`, the application has a click-to-type input policy. Input is always directed to a specific widget regardless of the position of the pointer. Focus can be changed by clicking on the area (widget) to which input focus should be directed. If the value of this resource is set to `XmPOINTER`, the input focus moves with the pointer. The default value is `XmEXPLICIT`. See Section 5.13 for more information.

- `XmNmwmDecorations, XmNmwmFunctions, XmNmwmMenu`: These resources allow applications to determine what window manager decorations and menu items the window manager attaches to a given window. See Chapter 14 for more details.

TransientShell

The TransientShell widget class is used for windows that are expected to appear for only a short time, such as dialogs. Motif applications normally use the XmDialogShell widget for such tasks.

TopLevelShell

The TopLevelShell widget class is used for most normal top-level windows when applications need more than one top-level window. Applications that need only one window generally use the ApplicationShell class for that window. The TopLevelShell widget class adds the following resource to those inherited from its superclasses:

- `XmNiconic`: If the value of this resource is set to `TRUE` before the shell is realized, the window is displayed in an iconic state. If `TRUE`, the value of this resource overrides the value of the `XmNinitialState` resource inherited from the WmShell widget class.
- `XmNiconName`: This resource can be used to specify a name to be displayed in the associated icon. If no value is specified for this resource, the window manager uses the name of the window for the icon name. However, window names are sometimes rather lengthy, and an abbreviated name is often used as the name displayed by an icon.

ApplicationShell

The ApplicationShell widget class is intended to be used as the main top-level window of an application. Normally, an application has only one ApplicationShell. `XtAppInitialize()` returns an ApplicationShell, which is typically used as an application's main window.

Using Popup Shells

Some applications may need to display multiple top-level windows. There are several recommended ways to do this. The first way is to create an ApplicationShell as the main window of the application, and to create all other shells as *popup* children of this shell. The second approach is to create a single ApplicationShell that is never realized, and then to create all other windows as popup shells of this shell. Recall that a shell can have only one child. However, a shell can have as many popup children as needed.

A popup shell is a shell created with the function:

```
Widget XtCreatePopupShell ( String      name,
                            WidgetClass widgetclass,
                            Widget      parent,
                            ArgList     args,
                            Cardinal    numArgs )
```

This function is similar to `XtCreateWidget()`, but adds the newly created widget to the list of popup shells supported by its parent, rather than to the parent's children list.

Widgets created using `XtCreatePopupShell()` are not managed or realized. Instead, they are displayed by calling the function:

```
void XtPopup ( Widget shell, XtGrabKind grabKind )
```

This function realizes the widget, if necessary, and displays the widget. The grabKind parameter determines how input focus is handled while the shell is popped up. If the value is XtGrabNone, events can be directed to any window in the application, as it normally would be. If the value is XtGrabNonexclusive, all input is directed to this window and the chain of widgets from which this shell was popped up. If the value of grabKind is set to XtGrabExclusive, only this shell can receive input. When used to display a normal popup window, the value of this parameter should be given as XtGrabNone. Normally, in Motif, the other input modes are handled by setting resources on dialog widgets.

A window that has been popped up by calling XtPopup() can be hidden by calling the function

```
void XtPopdown ( Widget shell )
```

An Example

The following simple program demonstrates the second approach mentioned above for using multiple shells. The example creates a single, invisible ApplicationShell widget class and then creates two popup shells from the hidden shell. Each popup shell contains a Motif XmMainWindow widget, which can be used to manage other widgets as needed.

```
1    /**************************************************
2     * twoshells.c: Demonstrate use of shells in a
3     *              multi-window program
4     **************************************************/
5    #include <Xm/Xm.h>
6    #include <Xm/MainW.h>
7
8    void main ( int argc, char **argv )
9    {
10       Widget       hiddenShell, shell1, shell2;
11       XtAppContext app;
12
13       /*
14        * Initialize Xt
15        */
16
17       hiddenShell = XtVaAppInitialize ( &app, "Twoshells", NULL, 0,
18                                         &argc, argv, NULL,
19                                         XmNmappedWhenManaged, FALSE,
20                                         NULL );
21
22       XtRealizeWidget ( hiddenShell );
23
24       /*
25        * Create two TopLevelShell widgets as popups.
26        */
27
```

```
28        shell1= XtCreatePopupShell ( "shell1", topLevelShellWidgetClass,
29                                     hiddenShell, NULL, 0 );
30
31        shell2 = XtCreatePopupShell ( "shell2", topLevelShellWidgetClass,
32                                     hiddenShell, NULL, 0 );
33
34     /*
35      * Create children of each shell.
36      */
37
38        XtCreateManagedWidget ( "Widget", xmMainWindowWidgetClass,
39                                shell1, NULL, 0 );
40
41        XtCreateManagedWidget ( "Widget2", xmMainWindowWidgetClass,
42                                shell2, NULL, 0 );
43
44     /*
45      * Popup the shells to display them.
46      */
47
48        XtPopup ( shell1, XtGrabNone );
49        XtPopup ( shell2, XtGrabNone );
50
51     XtAppMainLoop ( app );
52  }
```

5.13 Managing Keyboard Focus

One important responsibility of all Motif manager widgets is directing input focus to its children. Motif supports two different keyboard focus models:

- **pointer**: When using this model, the widget that contains the pointer always receives keyboard events.
- **explicit**: When using this model, the user must click on a widget to specify that the widget is to receive keyboard events. Once the focus is explicitly set, the focus widget continues to receive keyboard input, even if the user moves the pointer out of the focus window. The widget can lose the focus if the window manager takes the focus completely away from the application.

The focus model used by an application is determined by the `XmNkeyboardFocusPolicy` resource, which can be set to either `XmPOINTER` or `XmEXPLICIT`. Only display widgets (subclasses of XmPrimitive) and gadgets can have the keyboard focus. Container widgets control which children receive the focus. The process of moving the focus from one widget to another is referred to as "traversal". An `XmNtraversalOn` resource supported by all primitive Motif widgets determines whether or not the widget accepts the focus from a manager widget when the application is operating in explicit focus mode. By default, `XmNtraversalOn` is `FALSE`, which indicates that the widget cannot accept focus. When a Motif widget has the keyboard focus, it has a highlighted border, as determined by the `XmNhighlightColor` and `XmNhighlightThickness` resources.

Depending on the setting of the `XmNkeyboardFocusPolicy` resource, Motif allows the user to change the focus widget in several ways. If the pointer focus model is used, the focus changes as the pointer moves between primitive widgets. The focus is always determined by the widget that contains the pointer.

When using the explicit model, the user can set the focus using the mouse, by clicking mouse button one in a widget to set the focus, or by using the `<TAB>` and arrow keys to move the focus from widget to widget. The manner in which these keys allow the user to traverse a set of widgets depends on the order in which widgets are created and by the way in which the widgets are organized into *tab groups*.

A tab group is a manager widget that allows the user to use arrow keys to traverse its children. The user can move between different tab groups using the `<TAB>` key. By default, most Motif manager widgets act as tab groups. The `XmNnavigationType` resource allows applications to control the behavior of a tab group. This resource, which is supported by all Motif manager widgets, can have several possible values:

— `XmNONE`: If a manager widget's `XmNnavigationType` is set to `XmNONE`, it is not treated as a tab group.

— `XmTAB_GROUP`: This value indicates that a widget acts as a tab group. This is the default value.

— `XmEXCLUSIVE_TAB_GROUP`: This value forces a widget to be a tab group, and causes the traversal mechanism to ignore any other widgets in the widget hierarchy that are set to `XmTAB_GROUP`.

— `XmSTICKY_TAB_GROUP`: This value forces a widget to act as a tab group, even if another widget in the hierarchy is set to `XmEXCLUSIVE_TAB_GROUP`.

When explicit mode is used, applications can also set the `XmNinitialFocus` resource to indicate a widget that should initially receive focus when its parent receives focus. For example, a dialog used to request a password from the user might set the initial focus to the XmTextField in which the password is to be entered.

An Example

Let's see how tab groups work with a simple example. This example creates two XmRowColumn widgets, each of which automatically becomes a tab group. Each XmRowColumn manages three XmPushButton widgets.

```
1     /****************************************************************
2      * traverse.c: simple example for experimenting with keyboard
3      *             traversal between tab groups
4      ****************************************************************/
5     #include <Xm/Xm.h>
6     #include <Xm/RowColumn.h>
7     #include <Xm/PushB.h>
8
9     char *buttons_one[] = { "button1", "button2", "button3" };
10    char *buttons_two[] = { "button4", "button5", "button6" };
11
12    void main ( int argc, char **argv )
13    {
14        Widget        shell, rowcol, box1, box2;
15        int           i;
16        XtAppContext app;
17
18        shell = XtAppInitialize ( &app, "Traverse",   NULL, 0,
19                                  &argc, argv, NULL, NULL, 0 );
20
21        /*
22         * Create an XmRowColumn widget with two children, each
23         * of which are XmRowColumn widgets as well. Each widget
24         * will be in its own tab group.
25         */
26
27        rowcol = XtCreateManagedWidget ( "rowcol", xmRowColumnWidgetClass,
28                                         shell, NULL, 0 );
29        box1 = XtCreateManagedWidget ( "box1", xmRowColumnWidgetClass,
30                                       rowcol, NULL, 0 );
31        box2 = XtCreateManagedWidget ( "box2", xmRowColumnWidgetClass,
32                                       rowcol, NULL, 0 );
33        /*
34         * Create three children of each XmRowColumn widget.
35         */
36
37        for ( i = 0;i < XtNumber ( buttons_one ); i++ )
38            XtCreateManagedWidget ( buttons_one[i],
39                                    xmPushButtonWidgetClass,
40                                    box1, NULL, 0 );
41
42        for ( i = 0;i < XtNumber ( buttons_two ); i++ )
43            XtCreateManagedWidget ( buttons_one[i],
44                                    xmPushButtonWidgetClass,
45                                    box2, NULL, 0 );
46
47        XtRealizeWidget ( shell );
48        XtAppMainLoop ( app );
49    }
```

Now this program can be used to experiment with the Motif's keyboard traversal. To see this, set the `XmNtraversalOn` resource to `TRUE`, give a non-zero value for `XmNhighlight-Thickness`, and choose a color for the `XmNhighlightColor` resource. For example, you could put the following resource in a resource file:

```
*traversalOn:           TRUE
*highlightColor:        Red
*highlightThickness:    5
```

To use the pointer focus model, also add the resources:

```
*keyboardFocusPolicy: pointer
*highlightOnEnter:      TRUE
```

Now, as the pointer moves across each of the XmPushButton widgets in this example, the button is highlighted while the pointer remains in the widget. To experiment with the explicit focus model, change the focus policy by specifying:

```
*keyboardFocusPolicy: explicit
```

In this mode, this example allows the user to move sequentially from `button1` to `button2` to `button3`, and back again to `button1` using the arrow keys. The `<TAB>` key moves the focus to the second tab group. Within this second tab group, users can use the arrow keys to move between `button4`, `button5`, and `button6`.

Figure 5.30 shows the window created by this example.

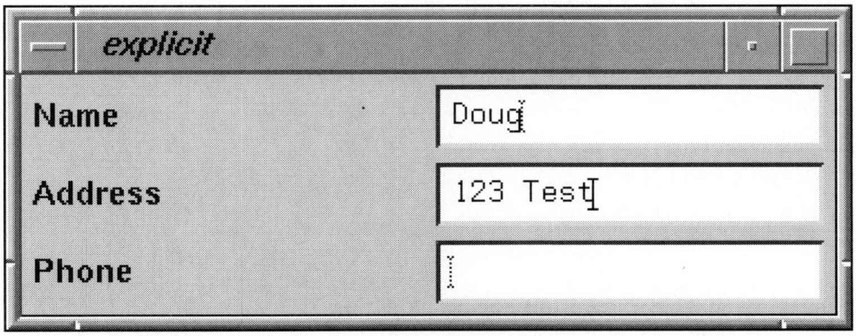

Figure 5.30 A typical use of explicit keyboard focus.

Programmatically Controlling Input Focus

Often, applications need to be able to control which widget receives input focus programmatically. For example, an application might display a window that supports multiple input fields into which the user is expected to enter information somewhat sequentially. For example, a program might need the user to enter a name, address, phone, and so on. It can be tedious for a user to position the mouse in one input field, enter the data, move the mouse to a second input field to enter that data, and so on. Such applications typically allow users to type a <RETURN> to enter the data in one field and advance to the next.

Motif provides a function:

```
Boolean XmProcessTraversal ( Widget w, char direction )
```

that can be used to control which widget has the input focus. This function requires a widget, typically the widget that currently has input focus, and a parameter that indicates the direction with respect to the given widget in which the focus should be moved. The possible directions are:

XmTRAVERSE_CURRENT	XmTRAVERSE_NEXT
XmTRAVERSE_PREV	XmTRAVERSE_HOME
XmTRAVERSE_NEXT_TAB_GROUP	XmTRAVERSE_PREV_TAB_GROUP
XmTRAVERSE_UP	XmTRAVERSE_DOWN
XmTRAVERSE_LEFT	XmTRAVERSE_RIGHT

XmProcessTraversal() returns TRUE if the function succeeds in fulfilling the request. It returns FALSE if the keyboard focus policy is not set to XmEXPLICIT for the shell parent in this hierarchy, if there are no widgets to traverse, or if the parameters are invalid.

The following example program demonstrates a typical use of XmProcessTraversal(). This program presents the user with a sequence of text fields to be filled in. When the user completes one field, and types a <RETURN> key, the input focus automatically moves to the next field. To accomplish this, the program simply installs an XmNactivateCallback function for each text field which calls XmProcessTraversal() with a value of XmTRAVERSE_NEXT_TAB_-GROUP. XmText and XmTextField widgets are always in their own tab group.

```
1    /*****************************************************
2     * explicit.c: Demo programmatic tab group control
3     *****************************************************/
4    #include <Xm/Xm.h>
5    #include <Xm/Label.h>
6    #include <Xm/RowColumn.h>
7    #include <Xm/TextF.h>
8
9    static void traverseNextCallback ( Widget     w,
10                                       XtPointer clientData,
11                                       XtPointer callData )
12   {
13       /*
14        * Move to the next widget in the tab group.
15        */
16
17       XmProcessTraversal ( w,  XmTRAVERSE_NEXT_TAB_GROUP );
18   }
19
20   static char *fields[] = { "Name", "Address", "Phone" };
```

```
21  void main ( int argc, char **argv )
22  {
23      XtAppContext app;
24      Widget       shell, rc, *editors, *labels;
25      int          numFields = XtNumber ( fields );
26      int          i;
27
28      /*
29       * Initialize Xt
30       */
31
32      shell = XtAppInitialize ( &app, "Explicit", NULL, 0,
33                                &argc, argv, NULL, NULL, 0 );
34
35      rc = XtVaCreateManagedWidget ( "rc", xmRowColumnWidgetClass, shell,
36                                     XmNnumColumns,  2,
37                                     XmNpacking,     XmPACK_COLUMN,
38                                     XmNorientation, XmVERTICAL,
39                                     NULL );
40
41      for ( i = 0; i < numFields; i++ )
42      {
43          Widget label = XtCreateManagedWidget ( fields[i],
44                                                 xmLabelWidgetClass,
45                                                 rc, NULL, 0 );
46      }
47
48      for ( i = 0; i < numFields; i++ )
49      {
50          Widget editor =
51                  XtCreateManagedWidget ( fields[i],
52                                          xmTextFieldWidgetClass,
53                                          rc, NULL, 0 );
54          if ( i == 0 )
55              XtVaSetValues ( rc, XmNinitialFocus, editor, NULL );
56
57          XtAddCallback ( editor, XmNactivateCallback,
58                          traverseNextCallback, NULL );
59      }
60
61      XtRealizeWidget ( shell );
62      XtAppMainLoop ( app );
63  }
```

To demonstrate this example, it is necessary to set XmNtraversalOn to TRUE, give a non-zero value for XmNhighlightThickness, and choose a color for the XmNhighlightColor resource. The XmNkeyBoardFocusPolicy resource must also be set to TRUE. For example, the following resources could be set in a resource file:

```
*traversalOn:         TRUE
*highlightColor:      Red
*highlightThickness:  5
*keyboardFocusPolicy: explicit
```

With these resources set, the program allows the user to type into the name input field without moving the mouse. When the user types the <RETURN> key, focus automatically moves to the second text field, and finally to the third input field.

5.14 Summary

Choosing and configuring manager widgets is one of the most important activities when creating a user interface. Achieving a desired layout takes practice, patience, and a working knowledge of the capabilities of the various manager widgets. Creating a layout for an application's user interface consists of choosing the right manager widgets and configuring them until the desired effect is achieved. Motif provides an assortment of manager widgets that support a wide range of layout styles. The remaining chapters in this book continue to demonstrate the use of manager widgets to produce common layouts, even when the primary focus is on other aspects of programming with X and Motif.

C h a p t e r   6

Menus

Motif supports several types of menus, including popup, pulldown, and option menus. Popup menus are menu panes that "pop up" when the user presses a mouse button. Pulldown menus are menu panes that cascade off an already existing menu structure, which could be a popup menu pane, a menu bar, or another pulldown menu. Option menus allow users to select one item from a list of choices. The option menu is always displayed, and shows the currently selected option.

Motif provides an assortment of widgets from which to create popup and pulldown menus. A menu pane consists of a popup shell widget which manages an XmRowColumn widget that contains buttons, labels, and occasionally other types of widgets. The buttons are the selectable entries in the menu. An action can be associated with each menu entry by registering a callback function with the corresponding button in the menu. By combining different types of widgets, the programmer can create many different types of menus: pulldowns, popups, cascading pulldowns, and so on.

This chapter examines each of the menu types supported by Motif and explores ways to create and use menus in typical applications.

6.1   The Elements of a Menu

Motif does not have specific menu widgets. Instead, menus are constructed from various widgets. Before looking at how to construct a menu, let's look briefly at each of the components of a Motif menu:

- The XmRowColumn widget class is used as both a pulldown menu bar and a popup menu pane. When used as a popup or pulldown, the XmRowColumn widget must be created as a child of an XmMenuShell widget. Motif provides convenience functions to create both a popup shell widget (XmMenuShell) and the XmRowColumn widget with the proper resources already set. These convenience functions are:

```
Widget XmCreatePopupMenu ( Widget parent, String name,
                          ArgList args, Cardinal nargs )

Widget XmCreatePulldownMenu ( Widget parent, String  name,
                             ArgList args, Cardinal nargs )
```

- An XmPushButton widget is commonly used as a menu entry. It is used exactly as it has been used in examples in previous chapters. Callback functions registered for the `XmNactivateCallback`, `XmNarmCallback`, and `XmNdisarmCallback` lists are called when the menu button is activated, armed, and disarmed, respectively.
- An XmToggleButton widget is often used in menus to represent an item that has an on/off state. Callbacks registered for the `XmNvalueChangedCallback` list are called when the menu item is selected or de-selected.
- The XmCascadeButton widget class is used to pop up a submenu. An XmCascadeButton widget is managed by an XmRowColumn widget and looks much like an XmPushButton widget. However, the XmCascadeButton widget can have a pulldown menu associated with it, which appears when the XmCascadeButton is armed. When a menu is associated with an XmCascadeButton widget, the button displays an arrow to the right of its label.
- The XmLabel widget class is often used to display non-selectable text, such as a menu title or subtitle.
- An XmSeparator widget displays a line. This widget can be used to delineate different sections of the menu, for example, to set the title off from the menu selections.

Motif menu items can be widgets or gadget equivalents. Menus are one place that can often benefit from gadgets, and it is common to use the XmPushButtonGadget, XmLabelGadget, XmSeparatorGadget, and XmCascadeButtonGadget classes instead of the corresponding widget versions.

6.2 Popup Menus

Most Motif menus are created in approximately the same way. This first example demonstrates a popup menu. Creating a popup menu requires only three basic steps.

1. Create the popup menu pane by calling `XmCreatePopupMenu()`.
2. Create the items in the menu. These can be XmLabel widgets, XmPushButton widgets,

XmToggleButton widgets, XmSeparator widgets, XmCascadeButton widgets, or the corresponding gadgets.

3.   Register callbacks for each XmPushButton or XmToggleButton widget.

The following example demonstrates a simple popup menu. The main body of the program simply creates a widget and calls another function to create a popup menu that will appear when the user presses mouse button three over the application's window.

```
1   /******************************************************
2    * popupmenu.c: Demonstrate how to create a popup
3    ******************************************************/
4   #include <Xm/Xm.h>
5   #include <Xm/Label.h>
6   #include <Xm/RowColumn.h>
7   #include <Xm/PushB.h>
8   #include <Xm/Separator.h>
9   #include <Xm/BulletinB.h>
10  #include <Xm/CascadeB.h>
11  #include <stdio.h>
12
13  /*
14   * Event handlers and callback functions used in the menu.
15   */
16
17  static void PostMenu ( Widget    w,  XtPointer clientData,
18                         XEvent   *event,  Boolean  *flag );
19
20  static void SampleCallback ( Widget    w,
21                               XtPointer clientData,
22                               XtPointer callData );
23
24  void CreatePopupMenu ( Widget parent ); /* Utility function */
25
26  void main ( int argc, char ** argv )
27  {
28      Widget       shell, bboard;
29      XtAppContext app;
30
31      /*
32       * Initialize Xt and create a widget
33       */
34
35      shell = XtAppInitialize (  &app, "Popupmenu", NULL, 0,
36                                 &argc, argv, NULL, NULL, 0 );
37
38      bboard = XtCreateManagedWidget ( "bboard",
39                                       xmBulletinBoardWidgetClass,
40                                       shell, NULL, 0 );
```

```
41      /*
42       * Create the popup menu, to be popped up from the bulletin board
43       */
44
45      CreatePopupMenu ( bboard );
46
47      XtRealizeWidget ( shell );
48      XtAppMainLoop ( app );
49  }
```

The function `CreatePopupMenu()` creates a popup menu that automatically pops up when the user presses mouse button three over the given widget. `CreatePopupMenu()` calls `XmCreatePopupMenu()` to create the popup menu pane and adds an event handler to the given parent, passing the menu pane as client data. This function will be responsible for popping up the menu. Next, buttons, labels, and separators are added as children of the popup pane. An example callback function, `SampleCallback()`, is registered with each button widget.

```
50  void CreatePopupMenu ( Widget parent )
51  {
52      Widget menu, button1, button2, button3;
53
54      /*
55       * Step 1. Create a popup menu. Add an event handler
56       * to the given widget to pop up the menu when
57       * a mouse button is pressed.
58       */
59
60      menu = XmCreatePopupMenu ( parent, "menu", NULL, 0 );
61
62      XtAddEventHandler ( parent, ButtonPressMask, FALSE,
63                          PostMenu, menu );
64
65      /*
66       * Step 2. Add buttons, labels, and separators to the pane.
67       * Step 3. Register callbacks to define the action
68       *         associated with each menu entry.
69       */
70
71      XtCreateManagedWidget ( "Title", xmLabelWidgetClass, menu,
72                              NULL, 0 );
73
74      XtCreateManagedWidget ( "separator", xmSeparatorWidgetClass,
75                              menu, NULL, 0 );
76
77      button1 = XtCreateManagedWidget ( "Item1",
78                                xmPushButtonWidgetClass,
79                                menu, NULL, 0 );
80
```

```
81        XtAddCallback ( button1, XmNactivateCallback,
82                        SampleCallback, NULL );
83
84        button2 = XtCreateManagedWidget ( "Item2",
85                                          xmPushButtonWidgetClass,
86                                          menu, NULL, 0 );
87
88        XtAddCallback ( button2, XmNactivateCallback,
89                        SampleCallback, NULL );
90
91        button3 = XtCreateManagedWidget ( "Item3",
92                                          xmPushButtonWidgetClass,
93                                          menu, NULL, 0 );
94
95        XtAddCallback ( button3, XmNactivateCallback,
96                        SampleCallback, NULL );
97  }
```

Usually, each selectable entry in a menu has a unique callback function. In this example, because the menu items don't really do anything, the same example callback is added to all menu entries. This callback simply prints the name of the widget the user selected from the menu, using the Xt function `XtName()` to extract the name of the widget passed to the callback.

```
98  static void SampleCallback ( Widget     w,
99                               XtPointer clientData,
100                              XtPointer callData )
101  {
102      printf ( "%s selected\n",  XtName ( w ) );
103  }
```

The function `createPopupMenu()` registers an event handler, `PostMenu()`, which is called when a button press event occurs in the parent of the popup menu. This event handler is responsible for popping up the menu pane. The function must check that the correct mouse button was pressed, and then call the Motif function:

```
    void XmMenuPosition ( Widget menu, XButtonPressedEvent *event )
```

to position the menu under the mouse. After the menu has been positioned, `PostMenu()` calls `XtManageChild()` to display the menu.

```
104  static void PostMenu (  Widget w, XtPointer clientData,
105                          XEvent *event, Boolean *flag )
106  {
107      Widget  menu = ( Widget ) clientData;
108
109      if ( event->xbutton.button == Button3 )
110      {
```

```
111
112          /*
113           * Position the menu over the pointer and post the menu
114           */
115
116          XmMenuPosition ( menu, ( XButtonPressedEvent * ) event );
117          XtManageChild ( menu );
118     }
119  }
```

Figure 6.1 shows the popup menu created by this example.

Figure 6.1 A popup menu.

Cascading Menu Panes

Sometimes an application may need to provide more choices to the user than can reasonably fit into a single menu pane. If the choices can be organized into a hierarchy of related operations, it may be useful to create a cascading menu pane to contain some of the choices. Figure 6.2 shows a popup menu with a cascading menu pane.

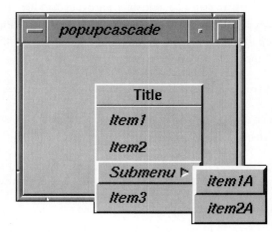

Figure 6.2 A popup menu with a cascading menu pane.

The menu in Figure 6.2 can be created by slightly modifying the `CreatePopupMenu()` function used in the previous example. The version shown below creates the same menu items as the earlier version, but also calls a function `CreateCascadingMenu()` to add a cascading pane to the popup menu.

```
void CreatePopupMenu ( Widget parent )
{
    Widget menu, button1, button2, button3;

  /*
   * Create a popup menu. Add an event handler to the given
   * widget to pop up the menu when a mouse button is pressed.
   */

    menu = XmCreatePopupMenu ( parent, "menu", NULL, 0 );

    XtAddEventHandler ( parent, ButtonPressMask,  FALSE,
                        PostMenu, menu );
  /*
   * Add buttons, labels, and separators to the pane. Register
   * callbacks to define the action associated with each menu entry.
   */

    XtCreateManagedWidget ( "Title", xmLabelWidgetClass, menu,
                            NULL, 0 );

    XtCreateManagedWidget ( "separator",  xmSeparatorWidgetClass,
                            menu, NULL, 0 );

    button1 = XtCreateManagedWidget ( "Item1",xmPushButtonWidgetClass,
                                      menu, NULL, 0 );

    XtAddCallback ( button1, XmNactivateCallback,
                    SampleCallback, NULL );

    button2 = XtCreateManagedWidget ( "Item2",xmPushButtonWidgetClass,
                                      menu, NULL, 0 );

    XtAddCallback ( button2, XmNactivateCallback,
                    SampleCallback, NULL );

    CreateCascadingPane ( menu );

    button3 = XtCreateManagedWidget ( "Item3",xmPushButtonWidgetClass,
                                      menu, NULL, 0 );
    XtAddCallback ( button3, XmNactivateCallback,
                    SampleCallback, NULL );
}
```

To create a cascading pane, a separate pulldown menu must be created, using the function XmCreatePulldownMenu(). This pulldown menu must be created as a child of the menu pane, and must be associated with an XmCascadeButton widget by setting the XmCascadeButton widget's XmNsubMenuId resource. The XmCascadeButton widget must also be a child of the menu pane from which the pane is to cascade. The function CreateCascadingMenu() can be written like this:

```
void CreateCascadingPane ( Widget parent )
{
    Widget cascade, submenu, button1, button2;

    /*
     * Create a pulldown menu pane as a child of the given widget
     */

    submenu = XmCreatePulldownMenu ( parent, "submenu", NULL, 0 );

    /*
     * Create a cascade button widget as a sibling of the submenu.
     * Attach the menu pane to the cascade button so it will
     * automatically post when the button is selected.
     */

    cascade = XtVaCreateManagedWidget ( "Submenu",
                                xmCascadeButtonWidgetClass,
                                parent,
                                XmNsubMenuId, submenu,
                                NULL);
    /*
     * Add buttons and other items to the cascading menu pane.
     */

    button1 = XtCreateManagedWidget ( "item1A",
                                xmPushButtonWidgetClass,
                                submenu, NULL, 0 );

    XtAddCallback ( button1, XmNactivateCallback,
                    SampleCallback, NULL );

    button2 = XtCreateManagedWidget ( "item2A",
                                xmPushButtonWidgetClass,
                                submenu, NULL, 0 );

    XtAddCallback ( button2, XmNactivateCallback,
                    SampleCallback, NULL );
}
```

6.3   Menu Bars

A menu bar is essentially a horizontal menu pane that is always visible on the screen. Each pane in a menu bar is a cascading menu, created the same way as the cascading menu pane in the previous section. Motif uses an XmRowColumn widget as a menu bar. The XmRowColumn widget can be created and configured for use as a menu bar by calling the convenience function `XmCreate-MenuBar()`.

The steps for creating a menu bar with pulldown menu panes are:

1. Use the `XmCreateMenuBar()` convenience function to create an XmRowColumn widget configured as a menu bar.

2. Use the `XmCreatePulldownMenu()` convenience function to create pulldown menu panes as children of the menu bar widget.

3. For each pulldown pane, create an XmCascadeButton widget as a child of the menu bar widget.

4. Attach each menu pane to its corresponding XmCascadeButton widget, by specifying a menu pane as the value of each XmCascadeButton widget's `XmNsubMenuId` resource.

5. Create the menu entries in each pane, as desired.

The following example program creates a menu bar with several menu panes. Motif programs typically use an XmMainWindow widget to manage layout when menu bars are used. This example demonstrates a typical layout and a typical menu structure, but the items in the menus do not perform any actions. The actions the various menu items would perform are represented by empty callback functions. In this example, the process of creating a menu bar and the various menu panes is broken down into individual functions that create the menu bar itself and each pane.

```
1    /*****************************************************
2     * menubar.c: demonstrate a typical menu bar
3     *****************************************************/
4    #include <Xm/Xm.h>
5    #include <Xm/RowColumn.h>
6    #include <Xm/MainW.h>
7    #include <Xm/PushB.h>
8    #include <Xm/BulletinB.h>
9    #include <Xm/CascadeB.h>
10   #include <Xm/Text.h>
11
12   /* Declarations of convenience functions */
13
14   Widget CreateMenuBar ( Widget parent );
15   void   CreateFilePane ( Widget parent );
16   void   CreateEditPane ( Widget parent );
17   void   CreateHelpPane ( Widget parent );
```

```
18
19   /*
20    * Stub callback functions. If implemented, these would perform
21    * an action when the corresponding menu item is selected.
22    */
23
24   void PasteCallback ( Widget w, XtPointer clientData, XtPointer callData )
25   {
26        /* Empty Stub Function */
27   }
28
29   void CutCallback ( Widget w, XtPointer clientData, XtPointer callData )
30   {
31        /* Empty Stub Function */
32   }
33
34   void OpenCallback ( Widget w, XtPointer clientData, XtPointer callData )
35   {
36        /* Empty Stub Function */
37   }
38
39   void CloseCallback ( Widget w, XtPointer clientData, XtPointer callData )
40   {
41        /* Empty Stub Function */
42   }
43
44   void HelpCallback ( Widget w, XtPointer clientData, XtPointer callData )
45   {
46        /* Empty Stub Function */
47   }
48
49
50   void main ( int argc, char ** argv )
51   {
52       XtAppContext app;
53       Widget       menu, shell, mainwindow, text;
54
55       /*
56        * Initialize Xt and create an XmMainWindow widget to handle layout
57        */
58
59       shell = XtAppInitialize ( &app, "Mainwindow", NULL, 0,
60                                 &argc, argv, NULL, NULL, 0 );
61
62       mainwindow = XtCreateManagedWidget ( "mainwindow",
63                                            xmMainWindowWidgetClass,
64                                            shell, NULL, 0 );
65
66       text = XmCreateScrolledText ( mainwindow, "text", NULL, 0 );
```

```
67        XtManageChild ( text );
68
69        /* Create the menu bar */
70
71         menu = CreateMenuBar ( mainwindow );
72
73        /*
74         * Specify the widgets to be used as a work area and menu bar.
75         * Because XmCreateScrolledText() returns a grandchild of
76         * its parent, XtParent() must be called to get the true child
77         * to be set as the work area.
78         */
79
80        XtVaSetValues ( mainwindow,
81                        XmNmenuBar,     menu,
82                        XmNworkWindow, XtParent ( text ),
83                        NULL );
84
85        XtRealizeWidget ( shell );
86        XtAppMainLoop ( app );
87  }
```

The function `CreateMenuBar()` just calls `XmCreateMenuBar()` and then calls three convenience functions to create an application pane, an edit pane, and a help menu pane.

```
88  Widget CreateMenuBar ( Widget parent )
89  {
90      Widget menu;
91
92      /*
93       *  Create a menu bar and then call additional
94       *  menu panes before returning the menu widget.
95       */
96
97      menu = XmCreateMenuBar ( parent, "menu", NULL, 0 );
98
99      CreateFilePane ( menu );
100     CreateEditPane ( menu );
101     CreateHelpPane ( menu );
102
103     XtManageChild ( menu );
104
105     return ( menu );
106 }
```

The function `CreateFilePane()` creates an XmCascadeButton widget to be placed in the menu bar, and then creates a pulldown menu pane with two selectable items in the pane.

```
107   void CreateFilePane ( Widget parent )
108   {
109       Widget cascade, submenu, button1, button2;
110
111       /*
112        * Create the cascading submenu pane that is popped up when
113        * the user clicks on the File cascade button.
114        */
115
116       submenu = XmCreatePulldownMenu ( parent, "fileSubmenu",
117                                         NULL, 0 );
118       /*
119        * Create a cascade button named "File". This is the
120        * label seen in the menu bar.
121        * Attach the menu pane to the cascade button.
122        */
123
124       cascade = XtVaCreateManagedWidget ( "File",
125                                           xmCascadeButtonWidgetClass,
126                                           parent,
127                                           XmNsubMenuId, submenu,
128                                           NULL  );
129       /*
130        * Add the content of the menu pane.
131        */
132
133       button1 = XtCreateManagedWidget ( "Open",
134                                         xmPushButtonWidgetClass,
135                                         submenu, NULL, 0 );
136       XtAddCallback ( button1, XmNactivateCallback,
137                       OpenCallback, NULL );
138
139       button2 = XtCreateManagedWidget ( "Close",
140                                         xmPushButtonWidgetClass,
141                                         submenu, NULL, 0 );
142       XtAddCallback ( button2, XmNactivateCallback,
143                       CloseCallback, NULL );
144   }
```

The second menu pane is created in the same way, although this pane has different commands and different callbacks associated with it.

```
145   void CreateEditPane ( Widget parent )
146   {
147       Widget cascade, submenu, button1, button2;
148
149       submenu = XmCreatePulldownMenu ( parent, "editSubmenu", NULL, 0 );
150
```

```
151        cascade = XtVaCreateManagedWidget ( "Edit",
152                                            xmCascadeButtonWidgetClass,
153                                            parent,
154                                            XmNsubMenuId, submenu,
155                                            NULL );
156
157        button1 = XtCreateManagedWidget ( "Cut", xmPushButtonWidgetClass,
158                                          submenu, NULL, 0 );
159        XtAddCallback ( button1, XmNactivateCallback,
160                        CutCallback, NULL );
161
162        button2 = XtCreateManagedWidget ( "Paste",
163                                          xmPushButtonWidgetClass,
164                                          submenu, NULL, 0 );
165        XtAddCallback ( button2, XmNactivateCallback,
166                        PasteCallback, NULL );
167    }
```

The function `CreateHelpPane()` adds a help menu pane to the menu bar. The *Motif Style Guide* calls for the help menu pane to be positioned at the right side of the menu bar. The Motif menu bar supports this style with a resource, `XmNmenuHelpWidget`, which can be set on the menu bar widget. The value of this resource should be the XmCascadeButton widget associated with the help pane. Once this resource is set, the menubar automatically positions the help pane on the right side of the menubar.

The following function creates a typical help pane:

```
168  void CreateHelpPane ( Widget parent )
169  {
170      Widget cascade, submenu, button1;
171
172      /*
173       * Create the pulldown pane
174       */
175
176      submenu = XmCreatePulldownMenu ( parent, "helpSubmenu", NULL, 0 );
177
178      /*
179       * Create the cascade button from which to pull down the
180       * help menu pane.
181       */
182
183      cascade = XtVaCreateManagedWidget ( "Help",
184                                          xmCascadeButtonWidgetClass,
185                                          parent,
186                                          XmNsubMenuId, submenu,
187                                          NULL );
188      /*
189       * Establish this widget as the help menu widget for
```

```
190        * this menu bar.
191        */
192
193        XtVaSetValues ( parent, XmNmenuHelpWidget, cascade, NULL );
194
195        /*
196         * Create the help menu items.
197         */
198
199        button1 = XtCreateManagedWidget ( "Help", xmPushButtonWidgetClass,
200                                             submenu, NULL, 0 );
201        XtAddCallback ( button1, XmNactivateCallback,
202                        HelpCallback, NULL );
203    }
```

Figure 6.4 shows the window layout and menus created by this program.

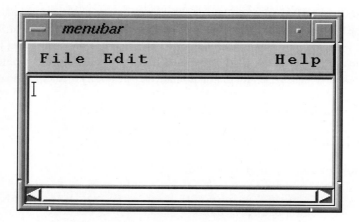

Figure 6.3 An XmMainWindow widget with a menu bar.

Creating Tear-Off Menu Panes

Beginning with version 1.2 of Motif, pulldown menu panes can be "torn off" from the cascade button from which they are posted. Once "torn off", a menu pane remains on the screen, which allows users to select items from the menu without having to pull it down. Such menus are convenient for often-used operations, where the action of pulling the menu down each time becomes tedious for users.

Figure 6.4 shows a tear-off menu pane as it appears before it is torn off. A dashed line appears as the first item in a tear-off pane. Selecting this dashed menu item causes the pane to detach itself from the menu and remain on the screen. A dashed line appears as the first item in a tear-off pane. Figure 6.4 shows the tear-off menu pane as it appears after it is torn off. The tear-off menu can be returned to the menu from which it came by using the window manager to close the tear-off window.

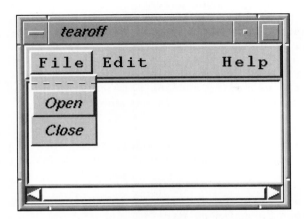

Figure 6.4 A tear-off menu pane before tearing off the pane.

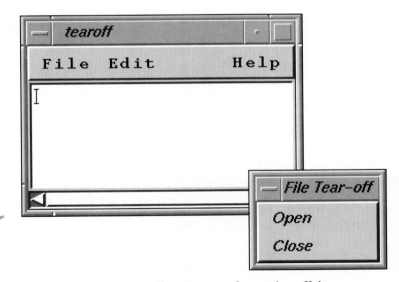

Figure 6.5 A tear-off menu pane after tearing off the pane.

It is easy to create a tear-off menu pane. The XmRowColumn widget supports a resource, `XmNtearOffModel`, that determines whether or not a menu pane can be torn off. If the value of this resource is set to `XmTEAR_OFF_ENABLED`, the menu can be torn off. If the value is `XmTEAR_OFF_DISABLED`, the menu cannot be torn off. The default value is `XmTEAR_OFF_DISABLED`. The following code segment shows the `CreateFilePane()` function described in the previous example, but this time the function creates a tear-off menu pane.

```
void CreateFilePane ( Widget parent )
{
    Widget cascade, submenu, button1, button2;
    Arg args[1];

    /*
     * Create the cascading submenu pane that is popped up when
     * the user clicks on the File cascade button.
     */

    XtSetArg (args[0], XmNtearOffModel, XmTEAR_OFF_ENABLED);
    submenu = XmCreatePulldownMenu ( parent, "applicationSubmenu",
                                     args, 1 );
    /*
     * Create a cascade button named "File". This is the
     * label seen in the menu bar.
     */

    cascade = XtVaCreateManagedWidget ( "File",
                                        xmCascadeButtonWidgetClass,
                                        parent,
                                        XmNsubMenuId, submenu,
                                        NULL );
    /*
     * Add the content of the menu pane
     */

    button1 = XtCreateManagedWidget ( "Open", xmPushButtonWidgetClass,
                                      submenu, NULL, 0 );
    XtAddCallback ( button1, XmNactivateCallback,
                    OpenCallback, NULL );

    button2 = XtCreateManagedWidget ( "Close", mPushButtonWidgetClass,
                                      submenu, NULL, 0 );
    XtAddCallback ( button2, XmNactivateCallback,
                    CloseCallback, NULL );
}
```

By default, Motif does not install a type converter for the XmNtearOffModel resource, so tear-offs cannot be controlled within a resource file. However, Motif provides a convenience function that installs a type converter. Applications that wish to allow users to activate or deactivate tear-off menus can call the following function somewhere in their program before the first menu pane is created:

```
XmRepTypeInstallTearOffModelConverter();
```

Once this function has been called, tear-off menus can be controlled by specifying resources in resource files.

6.4   Accelerators and Mnemonics

The examples in the previous sections assume that user will use the mouse to display menus and select items in a menu. Although this is generally the case, Motif also provides support for selecting and activating menus using the keyboard. Motif supports two different mechanisms, accelerators and mnemonics. These two mechanisms address slightly different needs, but both allow users to execute commands in a menu without using the mouse. The following sections describe each of these facilities.

Accelerators

Many applications support commands that are used frequently, or repetitively. For example, users often delete, paste, or move text when using a text editor. Typically, applications provide commonly needed operations on a menu to allow novice users to access these operations. However, moving to a menu bar, pulling down a menu and selecting an item over and over quickly becomes tedious. Once users have learned the application, they would often like to be able to perform common operations more quickly. To address this need, Motif support accelerators on all menu items.

Accelerators are key bindings that can be used to activate an item on a menu without posting the menu. An accelerator can be assigned to a particular menu item by setting the XmNaccelerator resource supported by all subclasses of the XmLabel widget. Accelerators can be set programmatically, but are normally set in a resource file. Hard coding an accelerator is poor practice because users may customize the labels displayed by the menu items and may wish to change the accelerators as well. An application that hard-codes the accelerator binding does not support internationalization.

When set in a resource file, the accelerator resource uses the syntax as the Xt translation manager syntax. For example, the example in the previous section has an Edit menu pane that contains a Cut command. An accelerator could be installed for this command by setting the following resource in a resource file:

```
*Cut*accelerator:   Ctrl<Key>X
```

With this resource set, if the user types Ctrl-X, the CutCallback() function will be invoked. The menu pane will not be posted and there will be no visible sign that the menu item has been selected, other than the action taken by the callback.

When accelerators are installed, it is good practice to indicate the accelerator on the menu item so users know that this feature is available. Motif button widgets also support an XmNacceleratorText resource that can be set to display the accelerator beside the button label. The contents of the accelerator text is completely arbitrary, although the Motif Style Guide recommends a specific style. According to the Motif Style Guide, the accelerator text for the Cut menu item described above should be "Ctrl+X". This resource could be set like this:

```
*Cut*acceleratorText: Ctrl+X
```

Figure 6.6 shows the menubar example program implemented in Section 6.3 with accelerators installed for the File menu pane. This figure was produced by providing the following application resource file:

```
1    !!!!!!!!!!!!!!!!!!!!!!!!!!!!!!!!!!!!!!!!!!!!!!!!!!!!!!!!!!!!!!!!!!!!!!!!
2    !! Menubar: accelerator resources for the menubar example program
3    !!!!!!!!!!!!!!!!!!!!!!!!!!!!!!!!!!!!!!!!!!!!!!!!!!!!!!!!!!!!!!!!!!!!!!!!
4
5    *Cut*accelerator:        Ctrl<Key>X
6    *Cut*acceleratorText:    Ctrl+X
7    *Paste*accelerator:      Ctrl<Key>V
8    *Paste*acceleratorText:  Ctrl+V
9    *Open*accelerator:       Ctrl<Key>O
10   *Open*acceleratorText:   Ctrl+O
11   *Close*accelerator:      Ctrl<Key>C
12   *Close*acceleratorText:  Ctrl+C
```

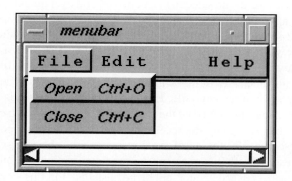

Figure 6.6 The menubar example with accelerators installed.

Accelerators should be used carefully and somewhat sparingly. Users are unlikely to remember accelerators for every item on a menu. Accelerators are best used for a few key commands that are used frequently. Many people also try to avoid accelerators on potentially dangerous commands, or accelerators that could be confusing for users. For example, programmers who use the emacs editor are used to typing Ctrl-E to go to the end of a line of text. Such programmers might easily make mistakes when using an application that installs Ctrl-E as an accelerator for an "Exit" command.

Mnemonics

Mnemonics also allow menu items to be selected without using the mouse, although the way they work is somewhat different. Mnemonics are intended primarily for systems that do not have a mouse, or for users who would prefer to navigate through the menu hierarchy using the keyboard. When using mnemonics, each selectable item in a menu, including the menu panes of a menu bar, has one of the characters in its label designated as a mnemonic. Users can post a pane in a menu bar by typing the <Alt> key and the mnemonic associated with the menu pane. (The key that functions as the <Alt> key varies from system to system. Sometimes it is called "Meta", for example.) Once a menu pane is posted, the user can move to other menu panes by simply typing the mnemonic associated with the desired pane. While a pane is posted, any item in the menu pane can be selected or activated by typing the mnemonic associated with the item.

Mnemonics can be set using the `XmNmnemonic` resource supported by all XmLabel and XmLabelGadget subclasses. The value of this resource is expected to be a single character, which must be one of the characters in the label displayed by the item. Typically, the first character is used, but in case of conflicts any character in the label can be used. When processing a mnemonic, Motif searches a menu hierarchy depth-first. In case of duplicate entries, the first match wins. The same letter can be used multiple times, as long as there is a unique path for each sequence of mnemonics.

For example, the character 'C' could be assigned as a mnemonic for both the Close and Cut commands in the menubar example in Section 6.3, as long as the File and Edit menus had unique mnemonics. Assuming the letters 'F' and 'E' were used for these items, respectively, a user could perform the cut operation by typing <Alt>-F, C and perform the Close operation by typing <Alt>-E, C.

Like accelerators, mnemonics can be set programmatically, but this should rarely be done. To all applications to be localized, the labels in a menu must be able to be changed. Therefore, the mnemonics associated with an item must be changeable as well. Mnemonics should always be set in a resource file.

Figure 6.6 shows the menubar example from Section 6.3 with both mnemonics and accelerators installed. This figure is the result of setting the following resources in the application's resource file:

```
1   !!!!!!!!!!!!!!!!!!!!!!!!!!!!!!!!!!!!!!!!!!!!!!!!!!!!!!!!!!!!!!!!!!!
2   !! Menubar: accelerators and mnemonics for the menubar example
3   !!!!!!!!!!!!!!!!!!!!!!!!!!!!!!!!!!!!!!!!!!!!!!!!!!!!!!!!!!!!!!!!!!!
4
5   *Cut*accelerator:        Ctrl<Key>X
6   *Cut*acceleratorText:    Ctrl+X
7   *Paste*accelerator:      Ctrl<Key>V
8   *Paste*acceleratorText:  Ctrl+V
9   *Open*accelerator:       Ctrl<Key>O
10  *Open*acceleratorText:   Ctrl+O
11  *Close*accelerator:      Ctrl<Key>C
12  *Close*acceleratorText:  Ctrl+C
13
14  ! mnemonics
15
16  *File*mnemonic:          F
17  *Edit*mnemonic:          E
18  *Cut*mnemonic:           C
19  *Paste*mnemonic:         P
20  *Open*mnemonic:          O
21  *Close*mnemonic:         C
22  *Help*mnemonic:          H
```

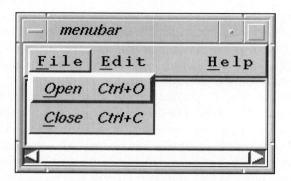

Figure 6.7 The menubar example with mnemonics installed.

6.5   Option Menus

An option menu allows users to select from a list of items, while always displaying the most recently selected option. Figure 6.8 shows two option menus. The menu on the left shows the normal state of an option menu. The menu displays a label on the left side. The button-like area on the right side of the menu shows the most recent selection. The image on the right side of Figure 6.8 shows how an option menu appears when a selection is being made.

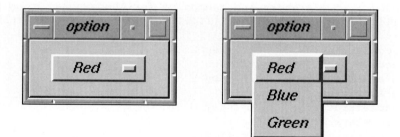

Figure 6.8 Option menus showing a recent selection, and a selection in progress.

Option menus are created in much the same way as menu bars, except that an option menu is created with the following convenience function:

```
Widget XmCreateOptionMenu ( Widget   parent,
                            String   name,
                            ArgList  args,
                            Cardinal nargs )
```

After creating the option menu itself, an application must add a pulldown menu pane to the option menu and attach the pane by setting the option menu's `XmNsubMenuId` to indicate the menu pane. The following example illustrates this process. The first part of the program is a simple driver, similar to those used in earlier sections of this chapter. The program creates an XmBulletinBoard widget and calls another function, `CreateOptionMenu()`, to create and display an option menu as a child of the XmBulletinBoard widget.

```
1    /***********************************************
2     * option.c: Demonstrate an option menu
3     ***********************************************/
4    #include <Xm/Xm.h>
5    #include <Xm/Label.h>
6    #include <Xm/RowColumn.h>
7    #include <Xm/PushB.h>
8    #include <Xm/Separator.h>
9    #include <Xm/BulletinB.h>
10   #include <Xm/CascadeB.h>
11   #include <stdio.h>
12
13   void CreateOptionMenu ( Widget parent );
14   static void OptionChanged ( Widget      w,
15                               XtPointer clientData,
16                               XtPointer callData );
17
18   void main ( int argc, char ** argv )
19   {
20       Widget        shell, bboard;
21       XtAppContext app;
22
23       /*
24        * Initialize Xt
25        */
26
27       shell = XtAppInitialize (  &app, "Option", NULL, 0,
28                                  &argc, argv, NULL, NULL, 0 );
29
30       bboard = XtCreateManagedWidget ( "bboard",
31                                        xmBulletinBoardWidgetClass,
32                                        shell, NULL, 0 );
33
34       CreateOptionMenu ( bboard );
35
36       XtRealizeWidget ( shell );
37       XtAppMainLoop ( app );
38   }
```

The function `CreateOptionMenu()` demonstrates the steps necessary to create an option menu. First, an XmRowColumn widget, configured as an option menu, is created using the convenience function `XmCreateOptionMenu()`. Next, a pulldown menu pane is created using the function `XmCreatePulldownMenu()`. The pulldown pane is specified as the value of the option menu's `XmNsubMenuId` resource. Finally, children are added to the menu pane to represent each option in the menu. In this example, each button has a callback registered to be called when the button is selected.

```
39   void CreateOptionMenu ( Widget parent )
40   {
41       Widget menu, pane, button1, button2, button3;
42
43       /*
44        * Create an option menu
45        */
46
47       menu = XmCreateOptionMenu ( parent, "menu", NULL, 0 );
48
49       /*
50        * Create a pulldown pane and attach it to the option menu
51        */
52
53       pane = XmCreatePulldownMenu ( parent, "pane", NULL, 0 );
54       XtVaSetValues ( menu, XmNsubMenuId, pane, NULL );
55
56       XtManageChild ( menu );
57
58       /*
59        * Add buttons to the pane and register callbacks
60        * to define the action associated with each menu entry.
61        */
62
63       button1 = XtCreateManagedWidget ( "Red", xmPushButtonWidgetClass,
64                                           pane, NULL, 0 );
65       XtAddCallback ( button1, XmNactivateCallback,
66                       OptionChanged, NULL );
67
68       button2 = XtCreateManagedWidget ( "Blue", xmPushButtonWidgetClass,
69                                           pane, NULL, 0 );
70
71       XtAddCallback ( button2, XmNactivateCallback,
72                       OptionChanged, NULL );
73
74       button3 = XtCreateManagedWidget ( "Green",
75                                           xmPushButtonWidgetClass,
76                                           pane, NULL, 0 );
77
78       XtAddCallback ( button3, XmNactivateCallback,
79                       OptionChanged, NULL );
80   }
```

The callback registered in this example simply prints the currently selected widget.

```
81   static void OptionChanged ( Widget      w,
82                                XtPointer clientData,
83                                XtPointer callData )
84   {
85       printf ( "%s selected\n", XtName ( w ) );
86   }
```

It is often inconvenient to register a callback for each item in a menu. Dealing with individual callbacks seems particularly unnecessary when using option menus, because it would be more convenient to think of the option menu as a single widget that allows the user to choose from various options. In such cases, it is easier to use a single callback. Motif supports this style of option menu with the XmRowColumn widget's **XmNentryCallback**. If a function is registered with this callback list for a menu pane, the callback is automatically registered with each button in the menu pane. For example, using this feature, **CreateOptionMenu()** could be written as follows:

```
void CreateOptionMenu ( Widget parent )
{
    Widget menu, pane, button1, button2, button3;

   /*
    *   Create an option menu
    */

    menu = XmCreateOptionMenu ( parent, "menu", NULL, 0 );

   /*
    * Create a pulldown pane and attach it to the option menu
    */

    pane = XmCreatePulldownMenu ( parent, "pane", NULL, 0 );

    XtVaSetValues ( menu, XmNsubMenuId, pane, NULL );

    XtManageChild ( menu );

   /*
    * Add a callback to be called when any button in this
    * menu pane is selected.
    */

    XtAddCallback ( pane, XmNentryCallback,
                    OptionChanged, NULL );

   /*
    * Add buttons to the pane
    */
```

```
    button1 = XtCreateManagedWidget ( "Red",
                                      xmPushButtonWidgetClass,
                                      pane, NULL, 0 );

    button2 = XtCreateManagedWidget ( "Green",
                                      xmPushButtonWidgetClass,
                                      pane, NULL, 0 );

    button3 = XtCreateManagedWidget ( "Blue",
                                      xmPushButtonWidgetClass,
                                      pane, NULL, 0 );
}
```

When this callback function `OptionChanged()` is called, the widget passed as the first parameter is the menu pane, an XmRowColumn widget. The widget that actually triggered the callback is passed in the `widget` member of the XmRowColumn widget's call data structure. Therefore, the `OptionChanged()` function must be rewritten as follows:

```
static void OptionChanged ( Widget    w,
                            XtPointer clientData,
                            XtPointer callData )
{
    XmRowColumnCallbackStruct *cbs =
                        ( XmRowColumnCallbackStruct * )  callData;

    printf ( "%s selected\n", XtName ( cbs->widget ) );
}
```

6.6   A Menu Convenience Package

Some applications have many large menus, and creating each menu as shown in the earlier examples quickly becomes tedious. Creating each item in each menu allows maximum flexibility in configuring menus and setting the resources of each individual pane and menu button. However, it is often easier to wrap the steps of the menu creation in some higher-level functions. This section describes one way to make the process of creating a menu a little clearer and easier by defining a higher-level interface to the Motif menu facilities.

The menu creation can be reduced to two simple steps. First, the menu must be described using a simple static structure. Then, the application can call a function that uses the menu description to create the menu entries, assign callbacks, and so on.

First, let's look at a structure that can be used to describe any Motif menu. The following header file provides all the definitions needed by a program that uses this facility.

```
1    /***********************************************************
2     * MenuSupport.h: Definitions for a simple menu package.
3     ***********************************************************/
4    #ifndef MENUSUPPORT_H
5    #define MENUSUPPORT_H
6    #include <Xm/Xm.h>
7
8    /*
9     * Declare some symbols that can be used to identify
10    * the logical elements of a menu.
11    */
12
13   typedef enum _menu_type { END,
14                             POPUP,
15                             MENUBAR,
16                             OPTION,
17                             PULLDOWN,
18                             RADIOPULLDOWN,
19                             HELPPANE,
20                             BUTTON,
21                             LABEL,
22                             TOGGLE,
23                             SEPARATOR } MenuType;
24
25   /*
26    * Declare a data structure that contains the information
27    * required to describe a menu hierarchy.
28    */
29
30   typedef struct _menu_desc {
31      MenuType            type;
32      char*               name;     /* name of the button */
33      XtCallbackProc      func;      /* Callback to be invoked */
34      XtPointer           data;      /* Data for the callback */
35      struct _menu_desc   *subMenu; /* data for submenu of this menu  */
36   } MenuDescription;
37
38   /*
39    * A function that creates a menu from a MenuDescription structure.
40    */
41
42   Widget CreateMenu ( MenuType          menuType,
43                       char             *name,
44                       Widget            parent,
45                       MenuDescription *desc,
46                       XtPointer         defaultClientData );
47
48   void ContextHelpCallback ( Widget, XtPointer, XtPointer );
49   #endif
```

The `MenuDescription` structure allows applications to specify the type of each menu entry, the name of each menu entry, a callback function to be invoked when an item is selected, and any additional data to be passed to that callback. In addition, if an entry has a submenu attached to it, the structure contains a pointer to the description of the submenu. Therefore, a `MenuDescription` structure defines a tree of menus and submenus.

Before describing the function that creates menu entries from this structure, consider how a menu description can be used within an application. The following example re-implements the cascading menu example from Section 6.2, using a `MenuDescription` structure to describe the menu.

```
1     /***************************************************
2      * popupmenu.c: Demonstrate how to create a popup
3      ***************************************************/
4     #include <Xm/Xm.h>
5     #include <Xm/BulletinB.h>
6     #include "MenuSupport.h"
7
8     static void SampleCallback ( Widget    w,
9                                  XtPointer clientData,
10                                 XtPointer callData )
11    /*
12     * Setup the menu structure for the cascading menu pane,
13     * and then the popup menu pane.
14     */
15
16    static MenuDescription submenu[] = {
17    { LABEL,     "Title" }.
18    { SEPARATOR          },
19    { BUTTON,    "Item1A", SampleCallback },
20    { BUTTON,    "Item2A", SampleCallback },
21      END
22    };
23
24    static MenuDescription pane[] = {
25    { LABEL,     "Title" }.
26    { SEPARATOR          },
27    { BUTTON,    "Item1", SampleCallback },
28    { BUTTON,    "Item2", SampleCallback },
29    { PULLDOWN,  "menu",  NULL, NULL, submenu },
30    { BUTTON,    "Item3", SampleCallback },
31      END
32    };
33
34    void main ( int argc, char ** argv )
35    {
36        Widget        shell, bboard;
37        XtAppContext app;
38
```

```
39        shell = XtAppInitialize (  &app, "Popupmenu", NULL, 0,
40                                    &argc, argv, NULL, NULL, 0 );
41
42        bboard = XtCreateManagedWidget ( "bboard",
43                                           xmBulletinBoardWidgetClass,
44                                           shell, NULL, 0 );
45    /*
46     * Create a popup menu, to be popped up from the bulletin board
47     */
48
49        CreateMenu ( POPUP, "popup", bboard, pane, NULL );
50
51        XtRealizeWidget ( shell );
52
53        XtAppMainLoop ( app );
54  }
```

This example is shorter than the earlier version and it is also easier to add new entries to a menu. Rather than having to read the code and trying to decipher the menu structure, the menu structure is clearly defined by the MenuDescription arrays. Adding a new entry requires only that the programmer define a callback function and add an entry to the array that describes the menu.

It is also easy to define different types of menus. For example, the menu bar structure created in Section 6.3 can be defined as follows:

```
static MenuDescription fileDesc[] = {
  { BUTTON, "Open",  OpenCallback   },
  { BUTTON, "Close", CloseCallback  },
    END
};

static MenuDescription editDesc[] = {
  { BUTTON, "Cut",   CutCallback   },
  { BUTTON, "Paste", PasteCallback },
    END
};

static MenuDescription menuBarDesc[] = {
  { PULLDOWN, "File", NULL, NULL, fileDesc },
  { PULLDOWN, "Edit", NULL, NULL, editDesc },
    END
};
```

This menu bar could be created by calling CreateMenu ( ), as follows:

```
    CreateMenu ( MENUBAR, "menubar", parent, menuBarDesc, NULL );
```

The option menu from Section 6.5 could be described as follows:

```
    static MenuDescription optionDesc[] = {
     { BUTTON, "Red",   OptionChanged  },
     { BUTTON, "Green", OptionChanged  },
     { BUTTON, "Blue",  OoptionChanged },
        END
    };
```

This menu structure could be used to create an option menu by calling `CreateMenu()`, like this:

```
    CreateMenu ( OPTION, "optionMenu", parent, optionDesc, NULL );
```

Now let's look at the `CreateMenu()` function. This function provides the single interface to a collection of functions that use the menu description and the information in a `MenuDescription` structure to create the appropriate widgets for each entry and each type of menu. `CreateMenu()` creates the option menu, popup menu, or menu bar, as specified by the first argument. The menu is created as a child of the given parent, and in the case of popup menus, the function arranges for the menu to be popped up from the given parent.

The last argument to `CreateMenu()` allows some default client data to be specified. The `MenuDescription` structure allows applications to specify client data for the callback associated with each item in the menu. However, applications must be able to specify this client data statically, which may not always be possible. The final argument to `CreateMenu()` allows an application to provide some data to be passed as client data for any menu item that does not already specify client data. This parameter allows applications to pass client data that must be dynamically allocated, and also allows applications to provide a single piece of data to all items in a menu.

```
1    /*********************************************************
2     * MenuSupport.c: Convenience functions that make it
3     *                easier to create Motif menus
4     *********************************************************/
5    #include <Xm/Xm.h>
6    #include <Xm/Separator.h>
7    #include <Xm/PushB.h>
8    #include <Xm/CascadeB.h>
9    #include <Xm/RowColumn.h>
10   #include <Xm/Label.h>
11   #include <Xm/ToggleB.h>
12   #include "MenuSupport.h"
13
14   /*
15    * Declarations of internal functions used in this package.
16    */
17
18   static void PostMenuHandler ( Widget    w,
19                                 XtPointer clientData,
20                                 XEvent    *event,
21                                 Boolean   *flag );
```

```
22
23   static void AttachPopup ( Widget parent, Widget menu );
24
25   static void CreateMenuChildren ( Widget           parent,
26                                    MenuDescription *desc,
27                                    XtPointer        defaultClientData );
28   /*
29    * External interface function, called by applications
30    * to create option menus, popup menus, or menubars.
31    */
32
33   Widget CreateMenu ( MenuType         menuType,
34                       char            *name,
35                       Widget           parent,
36                       MenuDescription *desc,
37                       XtPointer        defaultClientData )
38   {
39       Widget w;
40
41       /*
42        * Create the basic menu widget, based on the type of
43        * menu requested. Do any special setup required
44        * and then call CreateMenuChildren() to populate the menu.
45        */
46
47       switch ( menuType )
48       {
49         case POPUP:
50
51           /*
52            * Popups must have an event handler registered with the
53            * parent to display the menu when button 3 is pressed.
54            */
55
56           w = XmCreatePopupMenu ( parent, name, NULL, 0 );
57
58           AttachPopup ( parent, w );
59
60           CreateMenuChildren ( w, desc, defaultClientData );
61
62           return ( w );
63
64         case MENUBAR:
65
66           /*
67            * For menu bars, just create the menu bar, and then
68            * add children. All direct children are expected
69            * to be pulldown menus.
70            */
```

```
 71
 72            w = XmCreateMenuBar ( parent, name, NULL, 0 );
 73
 74            CreateMenuChildren ( w, desc, defaultClientData );
 75
 76            XtManageChild ( w );
 77
 78            return ( w );
 79
 80        case OPTION:
 81        {
 82
 83          /*
 84           * All option menus have a pulldown, but it is nicer to hide
 85           * this, allowing the programmer to just specify the contents
 86           * of the pane. So, create the option menu, create and attach
 87           * a pulldown pane, and then call CreateMenuChildren() to
 88           * populate the pulldown menu pane.
 89           */
 90
 91          Widget option = XmCreateOptionMenu ( parent, name,
 92                                               NULL, 0 );
 93
 94          w = XmCreatePulldownMenu ( parent, name, NULL, 0 );
 95
 96          XtVaSetValues ( option, XmNsubMenuId, w, NULL );
 97
 98          CreateMenuChildren ( w, desc, defaultClientData );
 99
100          XtManageChild ( option );
101
102          return ( option );
103        }
104
105        default:
106
107          XtError ( "Invalid Menu Type" );
108          return ( NULL );
109      }
110  }
```

The function `CreateMenuChildren()` is called by `CreateMenu()` to add buttons, labels, separators, and submenus, based on a static menu description. This function simply loops through each item in a description and creates the corresponding widgets, registers callbacks, and so on. If an entry is a pulldown cascading menu, `CreateMenuChildren()` sets up the pulldown pane and then calls itself recursively to add children to the pane. The function is fairly long, but straightforward.

```
111   static void CreateMenuChildren ( Widget             parent,
112                                     MenuDescription *desc,
113                                     XtPointer          defaultClientData )
114   {
115       Widget   w;
116       int      i;
117
118       /*
119        * Create an entry for each item in the menu.
120        */
121
122       for ( i=0; desc[i].type != END; i++ )
123       {
124           switch ( desc[i].type )
125           {
126             case LABEL:
127
128               w = XtCreateManagedWidget ( desc[i].name,
129                                           xmLabelWidgetClass,
130                                           parent, NULL, 0 );
131
132               break;
133
134             case BUTTON:
135
136               /*
137                * Create a button, and add the specified callback.
138                * If the item-specific client data is NULL, add
139                * the default client data passed to this function.
140                */
141
142               w = XtCreateManagedWidget ( desc[i].name,
143                                           xmPushButtonWidgetClass,
144                                           parent, NULL, 0 );
145               XtAddCallback ( w,
146                               XmNactivateCallback,
147                               desc[i].func,
148                               desc[i].data ?
149                                       desc[i].data :
150                                       defaultClientData );
151               break;
152
153             case TOGGLE:
154
155               /*
156                * Toggles are handled just like buttons, except for
157                * the name of the callback list.
158                */
159
```

```
160                     w = XtCreateManagedWidget ( desc[i].name,
161                                             xmToggleButtonWidgetClass,
162                                             parent, NULL, 0 );
163                 XtAddCallback ( w,
164                             XmNvalueChangedCallback,
165                             desc[i].func,
166                             desc[i].data ?
167                                     desc[i].data :
168                                     defaultClientData );
169                 break;
170
171             case SEPARATOR:
172
173                 XtCreateManagedWidget ( "separator",
174                                     xmSeparatorWidgetClass,
175                                     parent, NULL, 0 );
176                 break;
177
178             case PULLDOWN:
179             {
180                 Widget pulldown;
181
182                 /*
183                  * A pulldown requires the creation of a pulldown
184                  * menu pane and a cascade button. Children are added to
185                  * the pane by calling this function recursively.
186                  */
187
188                 pulldown = XmCreatePulldownMenu ( parent,
189                                                 desc[i].name,
190                                                 NULL, 0 );
191
192                 w = XtVaCreateManagedWidget ( desc[i].name,
193                                             xmCascadeButtonWidgetClass,
194                                             parent,
195                                             XmNsubMenuId, pulldown,
196                                             NULL );
197
198                 CreateMenuChildren ( pulldown, desc[i].subMenu,
199                                     defaultClientData );
200                 break;
201             }
202
203             case HELPPANE:
204             {
205                 Widget pulldown;
206
207                 /*
208                  * A help pane can be handled just like the pulldown case,
```

```
209                 * but the cascade button is used as the value of
210                 * the menubar's XmNmenuHelpWidget resource.
211                 */
212
213                 pulldown = XmCreatePulldownMenu ( parent, desc[i].name,
214                                                   NULL, 0 );
215
216                 w = XtVaCreateManagedWidget ( desc[i].name,
217                                               xmCascadeButtonWidgetClass,
218                                               parent,
219                                               XmNsubMenuId, pulldown,
220                                               NULL );
221
222                 XtVaSetValues ( parent, XmNmenuHelpWidget, w, NULL );
223
224                 CreateMenuChildren ( pulldown, desc[i].subMenu,
225                                      defaultClientData );
226
227                 break;
228             }
229
230         case RADIOPULLDOWN:
231             {
232                 Widget pulldown;
233
234                 /*
235                  * A radio pulldown is handled just like a pulldown,
236                  * but the menu pane is set to exhibit radio behavior.
237                  * Items added to this pane are expected to be toggles.
238                  */
239
240                 pulldown = XmCreatePulldownMenu ( parent, desc[i].name,
241                                                   NULL, 0 );
242
243                 XtVaSetValues ( pulldown, XmNradioBehavior, TRUE, NULL );
244
245                 w = XtVaCreateManagedWidget ( desc[i].name,
246                                               xmCascadeButtonWidgetClass,
247                                               parent,
248                                               XmNsubMenuId, pulldown,
249                                               NULL );
250
251                 CreateMenuChildren ( pulldown, desc[i].subMenu,
252                                      defaultClientData );
253                 break;
254             }
255         }
256     }
257 }
```

The menu package is completed with two simple auxiliary functions. The first simply installs an event handler to pop up a popup menu when the appropriate event occurs. The second is the event handler, which handles the mouse button event and displays a popup menu.

```
258    static void AttachPopup ( Widget parent, Widget menu )
259    {
260        XtAddEventHandler ( parent, ButtonPressMask, FALSE,
261                            PostMenuHandler, menu );
262    }

263    static void PostMenuHandler ( Widget w, XtPointer clientData,
264                                  XEvent *event, Boolean *flag )
265    {
266        int button;
267        Widget menu = ( Widget )  clientData;
268
269        if ( event->type == ButtonPress &&
270             event->xbutton.button == Button3 )
271        {
272            /*
273             * Position the menu over the pointer and post the menu.
274             */
275
276            XmMenuPosition ( menu, ( XButtonPressedEvent * )  event );
277            XtManageChild ( menu );
278        }
279    }
```

The techniques used in this menu package can greatly simplify many applications' use of menus. The functions used here could be extended in several ways for applications that need more power or flexibility. For example, tear-off menu panes could be added to this package by adding a flag to the MenuDescription structure or by creating a new type, TEAROFF, to be recognized by the CreateMenuChildren() function.

There are a few limitations to the approach demonstrated in this section. For example, because menus are created from a static description, it is more difficult to add or remove items dynamically. It is also more difficult to customize certain aspects of each item in the menu. However, for most applications, this technique provides the functionality required to build menus in a more organized fashion.

6.7 Supporting Context-Sensitive Help

The *Motif Style Guide* recommends that all applications provide context-sensitive help. There are two ways the user can request context-sensitive help for an application. The first is to press the help key while the pointer is over an item on which help is needed. By default, on most systems, the help key is <F1>. All Motif widgets support an `XmNhelpCallback` that allows applications to register help callbacks. If <F1> is pressed over a widget that does not have an `XmNhelpCallback`, Motif searches up the widget hierarchy for a widget that does have a help callback, and invokes the callback relative to that widget. This approach allows applications to provide help for an entire panel by registering a single callback, instead of registering a callback for every widget in a program.

The second recommended way for a user to request context-sensitive help is to select a menu item from a Help menu pane that allows the user to select a widget within the application. Once the menu item is selected, the application is expected to display a question mark cursor (or something similar) to prompt the user to click on a widget. Once the user has selected a widget, the application is expected to provide help on the role that widget plays in the program.

Motif provides a simple function that handles the process of selecting a widget for context-sensitive help. `XmTrackingEvent()` grabs the pointer and displays a cursor until the user clicks a mouse button. At that point, `XmTrackingEvent()` returns the selected widget or gadget. If no widget has been selected, `XmTrackingEvent()` returns NULL. `XmTrackingEvent()` is declared as follows:

```
Widget XmTrackingEvent ( Widget    widget,
                         Cursor    cursor,
                         Boolean   confineTo,
                         XEvent    *event );
```

The `widget` argument is expected to be the root of a widget hierarchy within which a widget is to be selected. Normally, this would be a shell widget. The `cursor` argument allows the caller to specify a cursor to be displayed during the time the pointer is grabbed. If the `confineTo` argument is TRUE, the pointer is confined to the bounds of the specified widget. The last argument, `event`, returns the `ButtonPress` event that ended the operation.

Using this function, it is relatively easy to implement a callback function that can be used to provide a simple, but generic context-sensitive help facility. The `ContextHelpCallback()` function, shown below, can be registered as an `XmNhelpCallback` callback with any Motif widget. Typically, it would be registered with the root of a widget hierarchy, because the implementation makes it unnecessary to register the callback with each individual widget. The same function can also be registered as a callback for a menu item used to invoked context-sensitive help. When used as a callback in a help menu, this function expects to receive a widget as client data. This widget should be the top of the widget hierarchy in which help is needed.

The `ContextHelpCallback()` function is written as follows:

```
1    /**********************************************************
2     * help.c: A utility callback function that supports
3     *         context-sensitive help
4     **********************************************************/
5    #include <Xm/Xm.h>
6    #include <Xm/MessageB.h>
7    #include <X11/cursorfont.h>
8
9    static char *GetHelpText ( Widget w );
```

```
10   void ContextHelpCallback ( Widget     w,
11                              XtPointer clientData,
12                              XtPointer callData )
13   {
14       XmAnyCallbackStruct *cbs  =  ( XmAnyCallbackStruct * ) callData;
15       Widget       selectedWidget = NULL;
16       char        *helpString;
17       Widget       dialog;
18       static Cursor cursor = NULL;
19       XEvent        event;
20       Widget       parent = XtParent ( w ); /* In case w is a gadget */
21       Widget       mainWindow = ( Widget ) clientData;
22
23       /*
24        * If called from an XmNhelpCallback (invoked with <F1>))
25        * the reason will be XmCR_HELP. Extract the smallest
26        * window in which the help request occurred, and find
27        * the corresponding widget.
28        */
29
30       if ( cbs->reason == XmCR_HELP )
31       {
32           if ( cbs->event && cbs->event->xany.window )
33               selectedWidget =
34                       XtWindowToWidget ( XtDisplay ( parent ),
35                                          cbs->event->xany.window );
36       }
37       else
38       {
39           /*
40            * if the reason is not XmCR_HELP, this callback must have been
41            * invoked from somewhere else, probably a help menu item.
42            * Allow the user to interactively select a widget on which
43            * help is required.
44            */
45
46           if ( !cursor )
47               cursor = XCreateFontCursor ( XtDisplay ( parent ),
48                                            XC_question_arrow );
49           selectedWidget = XmTrackingEvent ( mainWindow, cursor,
50                                              FALSE,  &event );
51       }
52
53       /*
54        * Check for a valid widget
55        */
56
57       if ( !selectedWidget )
58           return;
```

```
59      /*
60       * Retrieve the text of a help message from the resource
61       * database to the selected widget.
62       */
63
64      helpString =  GetHelpText ( selectedWidget );
65
66      /*
67       * If some help text has been found, create a dialog to
68       * display the information.
69       */
70
71      if ( helpString )
72      {
73          dialog = XmCreateInformationDialog ( mainWindow, "helpdialog",
74                                                 NULL, 0 );
75
76          XtUnmanageChild ( XmMessageBoxGetChild ( dialog,
77                                                    XmDIALOG_HELP_BUTTON ) );
78          XtUnmanageChild ( XmMessageBoxGetChild ( dialog,
79                                                    XmDIALOG_CANCEL_BUTTON ) );
80
81          XtVaSetValues ( dialog,
82                          XtVaTypedArg, XmNmessageString, XmRString,
83                          helpString, strlen ( helpString ) + 1,
84                          NULL );
85
86          XtManageChild ( dialog );
87      }
88  }
```

As implemented, the key to this function is the ability to retrieve some help text based on a given widget. This task is handled by an auxiliary function named GetHelpText(). GetHelpText() could be implemented in any number of ways. One simple implementation uses the given widget to retrieve a resource from the application's resource database. Xt supports a function, XtGetSubresources(), that can be used for this purpose. This function is defined as:

```
XtGetSubresources ( Widget         w,
                    XtPointer      base,
                    String         name,
                    String         class,
                    XtResourceList resources,
                    Cardinal       numResources,
                    ArgList        args,
                    Cardinal       numArgs )
```

This function is similar to the function XtGetApplicationResources(), described in Chapter 3. However, XtGetSubresources() is intended to be used to retrieve a subresource of the given widget. A subresource is simply a named category that can be treated as a subpart of a widget. The name and class of the subpart are specified in the `name` and `class` arguments. Resources that are part of this subpart can be specified in the `XtResourceList` array. `XtGet-Subresources()` can retrieve such a resource from a resource database even if the resource is not defined by the widget.

For example, assume that an application creates an XmMainWindow widget named "mainWindow" as a child of a shell. We can define some help text for this widget using a resource specification that can be retrieved by `XtGetSubresources()`. The resource specification could be written like this:

```
*mainWindow*help*text:   Some help text
```

Here, `mainWindow` is the name of the widget, "help" is the name of a subpart, and "text" is a subresource within the "help" subpart. All of the resource manager's matching algorithms can be used as well. For example, an application might provide a global help message that would match any widget, while providing more specific help on other widgets. Using this approach, a typical application defaults file might contain lines such as the following:

```
*help*text:              Sorry, no help available on this topic.
*mainWindow*help*text: This is the main window of this application
```

Using `XtGetSubresources()`, `GetHelpText()` can be written as follows:

```
89   static char *GetHelpText ( Widget w )
90   {
91        static char *returnValue = NULL;
92        XtResource    requestResources;
93
94        /*
95         * Request the value of a "text" resource in the "help"
96         * subpart of the given widget.
97         */
98
99        requestResources.resource_name   = "text";
100       requestResources.resource_class  = "Text";
101       requestResources.resource_type   = XmRString;
102       requestResources.resource_size   = sizeof ( char * );
103       requestResources.default_type    = XmRImmediate;
104       requestResources.resource_offset = 0;
105       requestResources.default_addr    = ( XtPointer ) NULL;
106
107       XtGetSubresources ( w,  ( XtPointer ) &returnValue,
108                           "help", "Help",
109                           &requestResources, 1, NULL, 0 );
110
111       return ( returnValue );
112   }
```

With these functions, an application can add context-sensitive help easily. The following example program creates an XmMainWindow widget that manages an XmPushButton widget in its work area. A menu bar supports a help pane that contains an item that allows the user to request context-sensitive help, using the `ContextHelpCallback()` function described above. In addition, the program installs this same callback as the XmMainWindow widget's `XmNhelp-Callback` function. This callback supports user's requests made by pressing <F1> within the XmMainWindow widget or any children.

```
1   /*****************************************************
2    * helpdemo.c: Demonstrate context-sensitive help
3    *****************************************************/
4   #include <Xm/Xm.h>
5   #include <Xm/MainW.h>
6   #include <Xm/PushB.h>
7   #include "MenuSupport.h"
8
9   static MenuDescription helpPane[] = {
10  { BUTTON,    "HelpOnContext", ContextHelpCallback },
11    END
12  };
13
14  static MenuDescription menuBar[] = {
15  { HELPPANE, "Help",  NULL, NULL, helpPane },
16    END
17  };
18
19  void main ( int argc, char ** argv )
20  {
21      Widget        shell, mainWindow, button, help, menu;
22      XtAppContext app;
23
24      shell = XtAppInitialize (  &app, "Helpdemo", NULL, 0,
25                                 &argc, argv, NULL, NULL, 0 );
26
27      mainWindow = XtCreateManagedWidget ( "mainWindow",
28                                           xmMainWindowWidgetClass,
29                                           shell, NULL, 0 );
30
31      XtAddCallback ( mainWindow, XmNhelpCallback,
32                      ContextHelpCallback, NULL );
33      /*
34       * Create a menubar. Specify the bulletion board as default
35       * client data for the help menu callback.
36       */
37
38      menu =  CreateMenu ( MENUBAR, "menubar",
39                           mainWindow, menuBar, mainWindow );
40
```

```
41      button = XtCreateManagedWidget ( "button", xmPushButtonWidgetClass,
42                                        mainWindow, NULL, 0 );
43
44      XtVaSetValues ( mainWindow, XmNmenuBar,     menu,
45                                  XmNworkWindow, button,
46                                  NULL );
47
48      XtRealizeWidget ( shell );
49      XtAppMainLoop ( app );
50  }
```

An application defaults file that tests the `ContextHelpCallback()` function as used by this program could be written as follows:

```
!!!!!!!!!!!!!!!!!!!!!!!!!!!!!!!!!!!!!!!!!!!!!!!!!!!!!!!!!!!!!!
!! Sample app-defaults file used to test helpdemo program
!!!!!!!!!!!!!!!!!!!!!!!!!!!!!!!!!!!!!!!!!!!!!!!!!!!!!!!!!!!!!!

*help*text:                Sorry, no help available on this topic
*mainWindow*help*text:     Help text for XmMainWindow widget
*mainWindow*button*help*text: Help text for button
```

6.8 Summary

Most Motif applications use many menus. This chapter explores popup menus, pulldown menus, menu bars, and option menus. Menus can be constructed from various individual Motif widgets, which offer great flexibility. It is also possible to create convenience functions that make is easier to create the most common types of menus, with the loss of some flexibility. Examples in later chapters in this book continue to demonstrate the use of menus, and to use the menu convenience package described in Section 6.6.

C h a p t e r 7

Dialogs

Most applications need, at various times, to display messages to the user, or to ask the user to answer a question. Although it is possible to provide areas in an application's main window to display such messages, it is often useful to create and display additional windows in which to display such messages. Such windows are often displayed for a relatively short amount of time, and the user is expected to dismiss these windows when they are no longer needed. Such windows are known as dialogs. Motif provides many commonly needed types of dialogs and also allows applications to create their own custom dialogs. This chapter explores the predefined dialogs supported by Motif, discusses how such dialogs are typically used, and demonstrates how to create custom dialogs when needed.

7.1   Xt Support for Dialogs

Xt supports dialogs in several basic ways. First, Xt provides a TransientShell widget class, which is used as the basis of all Motif dialogs. All TransientShell dialogs are automatically configured so that the window manager treats them as temporary windows. A TransientShell widget is always associated with a specific, more permanent, window (such as an application's main window). The window manager always keeps a TransientShell widget raised above its associated permanent window. By default, each TransientShell widget is positioned in the center of its associated window. If the permanent window is iconified, the window manager removes any associated TransientShell widget from the screen. TransientShell widgets are never independently iconified.

Xt also provides the functions `XtPopup()` and `XtPopDown()`, which are used to display and remove a TransientShell. These functions are described in Chapter 5. An application that pops up an TransientShell widget can specify how input is to be handled by specifying the type of grab that should take effect. Some dialogs have no effect on the input behavior of an application. For other dialogs, it is useful to dictate that all input be directed to the dialog until the user dismisses the window.

Motif applications do not normally use the Xt support for dialogs directly. Motif dialogs are based on the XmDialogShell widget class, which is a subclass of TransientShell. The Motif dialog interface hides all calls to `XtPopup()` and `XtPopDown()`. And finally, Motif provides its own style of dialog modality which builds on the Xt grab mechanism to control input while dialogs are displayed.

Motif Dialogs

Motif provides a wide range of support for applications that need to use dialogs, including an assortment of ready-made dialogs. Many applications find that the pre-defined dialog types supported by Motif provide all the functionality they need. For applications with additional requirements, it is easy to modify the existing dialogs to provide nearly any type of dialog required. In addition, many of the Motif manager widgets can be combined with the Motif XmDialogShell widget to create completely custom dialogs. Many Motif widget classes, such as the XmBulletin-Board and XmForm widget classes, provide convenience functions that create dialog versions of these managers.

Using Pre-Defined Motif Dialogs

The most common types of dialog supported by Motif are those based on the XmMessageBox widget class. These dialogs generally display an iconic symbol, a application-specified message, and one to three buttons. The iconic symbol indicates the type of dialog. For example, a question dialog will display a question mark, while a warning has an exclamation mark symbol. The buttons provided by these dialog include an OK button, a Cancel button, and a Help button. The actions associated with these buttons can be defined by the application.

The types of basic dialogs support by Motif include the following:

Error   Information   Warning   Working   Question

Figure 7.1 shows several of these common Motif dialogs.

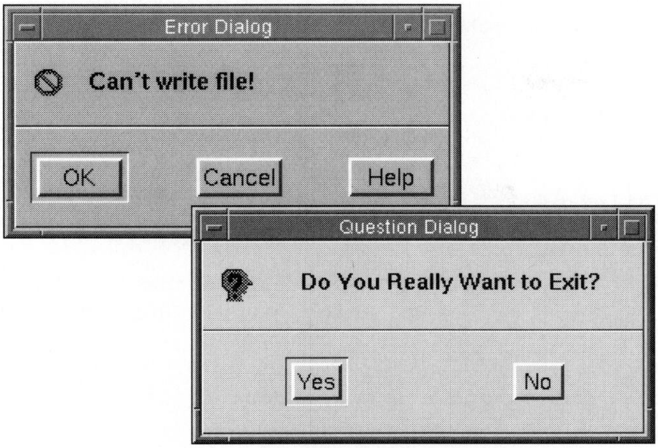

Figure 7.1 Typical Motif dialogs.

The easiest way to create one of these dialogs is to use the Motif convenience function that corresponds to the desired dialog type. For example, an application can create an error dialog by calling `XmCreateErrorDialog()`, or a question dialog by calling `XmCreateQuestion-Dialog()`. There is no difference in behavior between the various dialog types. The convenience functions simply configure the icon symbol to be displayed by the dialog.

The following simple example demonstrates how a dialog can be created and displayed. The example creates a push button widget labeled "Quit". When the user activates the push button, the program posts a dialog asking, "Do you really want to quit?" If the user selects the "OK" button, the program exits. Otherwise, the dialog is dismissed and the application continues running. The body of the program creates an XmPushButton widget and registers a callback to be invoked when the button is activated.

```
1   /***********************************************************
2    * dialogdemo.c: Demonstrate a simple Motif dialog widget
3    ***********************************************************/
4   #include <Xm/Xm.h>
5   #include <Xm/MessageB.h>
6   #include <Xm/PushB.h>
7   #include <stdlib.h>
8
9   /* Declarations of callback functions */
10
11  void QuitCallback ( Widget     w,
12                      XtPointer clientData,
13                      XtPointer callData );
14  void ReallyQuitCallback ( Widget     w,
15                            XtPointer clientData,
16                            XtPointer callData );
```

```
17
18  void main ( int argc, char **argv )
19  {
20      Widget       shell, button;
21      XtAppContext app;
22
23      /*
24       * Initialize Xt
25       */
26
27      shell = XtAppInitialize ( &app, "Dialogdemo", NULL, 0,
28                                &argc, argv, NULL, NULL, 0 );
29
30
31      /* Create a button and add a callback to launch a dialog */
32
33      button = XtCreateManagedWidget ( "Quit",
34                                       xmPushButtonWidgetClass,
35                                       shell, NULL, 0 );
36
37      XtAddCallback ( button, XmNactivateCallback,
38                      QuitCallback, NULL );
39
40      /*
41       * Realize the shell and enter the event loop
42       */
43
44      XtRealizeWidget ( shell );
45
46      XtAppMainLoop ( app );
47  }
```

The `QuitCallback()` function, listed below, creates a dialog by calling `XmCreateQuestionDialog()`. All of the Motif convenience functions for creating the basic dialog types are declared in the file MessageB.h, included at the top of this file. Once the dialog is created, `XtVaSetValues()` is used to set the `XmNmessageString` resource, which controls the string to be displayed by the dialog.

`QuitCallback()` adds a callback for the dialog's `XmNokCallback` callback list, which is invoked when the user selects the OK button on the dialog. `ReallyQuitCallback()` is the function that will really exit, if the user confirms the action by selecting the OK button on the dialog. By default, Motif dialogs are dismissed automatically when any button is selected, so it is not necessary to install a callback for the Cancel button. If the user selects the Cancel button, the dialog will simply be dismissed and no callbacks will be called.

Finally, on line 68, the dialog is managed. In Motif, dialogs are not displayed by calling `XtPopup()`. Instead, managing a dialog pops up the dialog automatically. A dialog can be popped down by unmanaging it.

```
48   #define QUITMESSAGE "Do you really want to quit?"
49
50   void QuitCallback ( Widget     w,
51                       XtPointer clientData,
52                       XtPointer callData )
53   {
54       static Widget dialog = NULL;
55
56       if ( !dialog )
57       {
58           dialog = XmCreateQuestionDialog ( w, "dialog", NULL, 0 );
59
60           XtVaSetValues ( dialog,
61                           XtVaTypedArg, XmNmessageString, XmRString,
62                           QUITMESSAGE, strlen ( QUITMESSAGE )+1,
63                           NULL );
64           XtAddCallback ( dialog, XmNokCallback,
65                           ReallyQuitCallback, NULL );
66       }
67
68       XtManageChild ( dialog );
69   }
```

The `ReallyQuitCallback()` function is invoked when the user selects the OK button on the question dialog. This function just calls `exit()` to terminate the program.

```
70   void ReallyQuitCallback ( Widget     w,
71                             XtPointer clientData,
72                             XtPointer callData )
73   {
74       exit ( 0 );
75   }
```

Modal Dialogs

The previous example uses a completely non-modal dialog. The question dialog pops up to display a message, but in no way restrains the user from continuing to interact with the rest of the program. It is even possible for the user to push the button that posts the dialog a second time while the dialog is still displayed. Posting the dialog a second time causes no harm in this example, but it is often desirable to limit the user's ability to interact with other parts of a program until the user has acknowledged the dialog. One way to limit a user's ability to interact with other windows is to use a modal dialog.

Motif dialogs have four levels of modality:

- Non-modal: Non-modal dialogs do not affect the user's ability to interact with other windows in any way.

- Primary application modal: When a dialog is set to primary application modal, all input to the window that launched the dialog is locked out. The user can interact with the dialog, and other windows in the application, but not with the window from which the dialog was launched.

- Full application modal: When a dialog is set to this mode, input to the application that displayed the dialog is locked out. The user can interact with the dialog, but cannot interact with any other windows in the application. Windows that belong to other programs running on the system are unaffected.

- Full system modal: When a dialog is set to full system modal, all input is directed to the dialog. The user cannot interact with any other window on the system.

Full system modal is seldom needed and should be used with great care. There is seldom any reason for an application to prevent input from the entire system. The choices between the other modal styles depends on the context in which the dialog is used. For example, the example in the previous section would be best implemented as full application modal, so that the user must exit the application or cancel the action before making any changes to the application.

Dialog modality can be controlled by setting an XmNdialogStyle resource supported by all Motif dialogs. The possible values for this resource are:

```
XmDIALOG_SYSTEM_MODAL                XmDIALOG_PRIMARY_APPLICATION_MODAL
XmDIALOG_FULL_APPLICATION_MODAL      XmDIALOG_MODELESS.
```

To change the dialog in the previous example to full application modal, the function QuitCallback() could be rewritten as follows:

```
void QuitCallback ( Widget w, XtPointer clientData, XtPointer callData )
{
    static Widget dialog = NULL;

    if ( !dialog )
    {
        dialog = XmCreateQuestionDialog ( w, "dialog",NULL, 0 );

        XtVaSetValues ( dialog,
                        XmNdialogStyle,
                                XmDIALOG_FULL_APPLICATION_MODAL,
                        XtVaTypedArg, XmNmessageString, XmRString,
                        QUITMESSAGE, strlen ( QUITMESSAGE )+1,
                        NULL );

        XtAddCallback ( dialog, XmNokCallback,
                        ReallyQuitCallback, NULL );
    }

    XtManageChild ( dialog );
}
```

Blocking Dialogs

In general, the model applications use when dealing with dialogs closely follows the examples discussed earlier in this chapter. Applications usually post a dialog and return to the event loop as quickly as possible to allow the application to continue to handle events. If an application requires the user to answer a question, the application registers callbacks for the XmNokCallback and XmNcancelCallback lists. Generally, whatever action is to be taken in response to the user's selection is performed in those callbacks.

Often, the code structure that results from using callbacks to determine a user's response to a dialog is rather inconvenient. Programmers sometimes wish they could write code in a more linear fashion. For example, sometimes it would be simpler to write a code segment like this:

```
if ( AskQuestion ( "Do you want to save files before exiting?" ) )
{
    /* Save files, etc. */
}

 exit ( 0 );
```

Unlike applications that use standard I/O for input and output, it is not possible to completely block while waiting for user input in any Motif application. The application must process events to even allow the user to select a button on a dialog. However, it is possible to simulate blocking behavior, such as that demonstrated above, by creating a secondary event loop. For example, the function AskQuestion(), demonstrated above, could create and post a dialog and then enter a loop that handles events until the user dismisses the dialog. At that point the function could return a Boolean value, depending on what button the user activated to dismiss the dialog.

One implementation of the function AskQuestion() is shown below. Notice that AskQuestion() requires a widget to be used as the parent of the dialog.

```
1   /*****************************************************************
2    * AskQuestion.c: A function that posts a question dialog and
3    *                does not return until the user has responded.
4    *****************************************************************/
5   #include <Xm/Xm.h>
6   #include <Xm/MessageB.h>
7
8   static void YesCallback ( Widget     w,
9                             XtPointer clientData,
10                            XtPointer callData );
11
12   Boolean AskQuestion ( Widget parent, char *str )
13   {
14       static int result;
15       Widget dialog;
16
17       dialog = XmCreateQuestionDialog ( parent, "question", NULL, 0 );
18
```

```
19        XtVaSetValues ( dialog,
20                        XmNdialogStyle, XmDIALOG_FULL_APPLICATION_MODAL,
21                        XtVaTypedArg, XmNmessageString,
22                        XmRString, str, strlen ( str ) + 1,
23                        NULL );
24
25     /*
26      * Register a callback to be called if the user answers OK.
27      * Pass a pointer to the variable "result".
28      */
29
30        XtAddCallback ( dialog, XmNokCallback,
31                        YesCallback, ( XtPointer ) &result );
32
33     /*
34      * Initialize the result to FALSE. If the user dismisses the dialog
35      * in any way other than activating the OK button, the result will
36      * be FALSE.
37      */
38
39        result = FALSE;
40
41     /*
42      * Manage the dialog to display it.
43      */
44
45        XtManageChild ( dialog );
46
47     /*
48      * Enter an event loop that lasts as long as the dialog is managed.
49      * The event loop will be exited when the user dismisses the dialog
50      * in any way.
51      */
52
53        while ( XtIsManaged ( dialog ) )
54        {
55            XEvent event;
56
57            XtAppNextEvent ( XtWidgetToApplicationContext ( dialog ),
58                             &event );
59
60            XtDispatchEvent ( &event );
61        }
62
63     /*
64      * Destroy the dialog because it is no longer needed.
65      */
66
67        XtDestroyWidget ( dialog );
```

```
68        /*
69         * Return the value of result, which may have been set by the
70         * YesCallback function.
71         */
72
73        return ( result );
74    }
```

The `YesCallback()` function retrieves the pointer passed in as client data and sets the value to `TRUE`, which causes `AskQuestion()` to return `TRUE` once the function leaves the event loop.

```
75   static void YesCallback ( Widget     w,
76                             XtPointer clientData,
77                             XtPointer callData )
78   {
79        int *result = ( int * ) clientData;
80
81        *result = TRUE;
82   }
```

This technique should be used with caution and with a good understanding of what is really happening while waiting for the user to respond. Used properly, secondary event loops can make posting dialogs simpler and can lead to cleaner code structure. However, programmers must be aware that the application is not really blocked while waiting for the user to respond. The secondary event loop will dispatch *all* events received by the application, not just those associated with the dialog. Programmers should be sure that the user cannot perform actions that would lead to problems with re-entrance. Notice, for example, that the function `AskQuestion()` is not re-entrant because of the static `result` variable. For safety, all dialogs used with secondary event loops should be configured as full application modal.

7.2   XmBulletinBoard Support for Dialogs

Motif dialogs consist of an XmDialogShell widget combined with a Motif manager widget, usually an XmBulletinBoard widget or a subclass of XmBulletinBoard. For example, the simple pre-defined dialogs discussed earlier in this chapter are composed of an XmDialogShell widget and an XmMessageBox dialog. The XmMessageBox widget class is a subclass of the XmBulletinBoard widget class. The XmDialogShell widget is nearly always transparent to applications that use Motif dialogs. An application simply interacts with a dialog by manipulating the child of the dialog shell. For example, Motif dialogs are not popped up by calling `XtPopup()`. Instead, they are displayed by managing the child of the dialog shell. Arguments passed to a Motif convenience function such as `XmCreateWarningDialog()` are passed to the child of the dialog shell, as well as the XmDialogShell widget.

Chapter 5 discusses some of the resources supported by the XmBulletinBoard widget class. These resources can also be useful with dialogs based on the XmBulletinBoard widget class. However, the XmBulletinBoard widget class also supports some additional resources intended specifically to support dialogs. The XmBulletinBoard resources that support dialogs include the following:

- **XmNautoUnmanage**: If the value of this resource is TRUE, and the XmBulletinBoard widget is a child of an XmDialogShell widget, dialogs based on the XmBulletinBoard widget class will automatically be removed from the screen when any button managed by the dialog is activated. The default value is TRUE.

- **XmNcancelButton**: This resource can be used to specify a widget that acts as the cancel button on a dialog.

- **XmNdefaultButton**: This resource can be used to specify a button widget that is activated by default when the user types a <RETURN> key.

- **XmNdefaultPosition**: If this resource is set to TRUE, dialogs are centered over their parent. If FALSE, dialogs are not automatically centered. The default value is TRUE.

- **XmNdialogStyle**: This resource specifies how input is handled when a dialog is displayed. The possible values are

  — **XmDIALOG_SYSTEM_MODAL**: When the value of a dialog widget's XmNdialogStyle resource is XmDIALOG_SYSTEM_MODAL, all input to windows other than the dialog is locked out.

  — **XmDIALOG_PRIMARY_APPLICATION_MODAL**: When a dialog is posted using this style, all input to the window that launched the dialog is locked out.

  — **XmDIALOG_FULL_APPLICATION_MODAL**: When a dialog whose style is full application modal is posted, input to the application that displayed the dialog is locked out.

  — **XmDIALOG_MODELESS**: When a dialog's XmNdialogStyle resource is set to XmDIALOG_MODELESS, an application's ability to handle input is unaffected. All windows continue to receive input normally.

- **XmNdialogTitle**: This resource can be used to specify a title for a dialog. The value of the resource must be a compound string.

- **XmNnoResize**: If the value of this resource is TRUE, the dialog's window manager frame will have a resize control. The default is FALSE.

As a manager widget, the XmBulletinBoard widget does not support many callbacks. However, when used to support dialogs, the XmBulletinBoard widget provides two callbacks that can be used to notify applications when a dialog appears and disappears from the screen. These callbacks are:

- **XmNmapCallback**: Functions registered with this callback list are invoked when an XmBulletinBoard widget whose parent is an XmDialogShell widget is mapped.

- **XmNunmapCallback**: Functions registered with this callback list are invoked when an XmBulletinBoard widget whose parent is an XmDialogShell widget is unmapped.

7.3   The XmMessageBox Widget Class

The simple Motif pre-defined dialogs are all based on the XmMessageBox widget class. Each XmMessageBox widget creates several children, including two labels, one for a message string and the other for a pixmap that indicates the dialog type. Each XmMessageBox widget also creates three buttons and a separator. The XmMessageBox widget class is a subclass of the XmBulletinBoard widget class and inherits the resources supported by that widget class. It also adds some new resources that can be used to modify the appearance and behavior of the standard Motif dialogs.

Resources

The following resources are supported by the XmMessageBox class and can be used with all dialogs based on the XmMessageBox widget class. The XmMessageBox widget is actually a composite of several widgets, including several labels, a separator, and various buttons. The resources for these sub-components are typically set using the resources defined by the XmMessageBox widget class.

- `XmNmessageString`: The value of this resource determines the text of the message displayed by the dialog. The resource must be a compound string.
- `XmNsymbolPixmap`: The value of this resource determines the pixmap displayed by the dialog. When the Motif convenience functions are used, the appropriate pixmap is installed automatically, based on the type of dialog. Applications can also override the default to display a custom symbol.
- `XmNokLabelString`: The value of this resource determines the label displayed on the OK button.
- `XmNcancelLabelString`: The value of this resource determines the label displayed on the Cancel button.
- `XmNhelpLabelString`. The value of this resource determines the label displayed on a dialog's Help button.
- `XmNdialogType`: This resource specifies the type of a dialog. Possible values are `XmDIALOG_MESSAGE`, `XmDIALOG_ERROR`, `XmDIALOG_QUESTION`, and so on. Normally, this resource is set by a corresponding Motif convenience function, `XmCreateErrorDialog()`, `XmCreateWarningDialog()`, and so on.
- `XmNdefaultButtonType`: Most dialogs have a button that is automatically activated when the user types the <Return> key. The value of this resource determines which button is activated by default. By default, this resource is set to `XmDIALOG_OK_BUTTON`. Other possible values include `XmDIALOG_CANCEL_BUTTON`, `XmDIALOG_HELP_BUTTON`, and `XmDIALOG_NONE`.
- `XmNmessageAlignment`: The value of this resource determines the alignment of the string displayed in the dialog. The default value is `XmALIGNMENT_BEGINNING`.

XmMessageBox Callbacks

The XmMessageBox class creates several button widgets to handle the OK, Cancel and Help functions of a dialog. Although applications could install `XmNactivateCallback` functions for these widgets, the XmMessageBox defines its own callback lists specifically for this purpose. The callbacks support by an XmMessageBox widget are:

- `XmNokCallback`: Functions registered with this callback list are invoked when the user activates the OK button on an XmMessageBox widget.

- `XmNcancelCallback`: Functions registered with this callback list are invoked when the user activates the Cancel button on an XmMessageBox widget.

- `XmNhelpCallback`: Callbacks registered with this list are invoked when the user activates the Help button on an XmMessageBox widget.

An XmMessageBox Example

The XmMessageBox widget can be used as a dialog or as a normal widget. For example, using the XmMessageBox widget, it is easy to implement the `xecute` example first presented in Chapter 2. The XmMessageBox widget class provides a much improved layout and is simpler to use than handling the layout within the application. Using the XmMessageBox widget, the example can be written as follows:

```
1     /*******************************************************
2      * xecute.c: Execute a command if the user confirms
3      *******************************************************/
4     #include <Xm/Xm.h>
5     #include <Xm/MessageB.h>
6     #include <stdio.h>
7     #include <stdlib.h>
8
9     /* Declarations of callback functions */
10
11    void YesCallback ( Widget w, XtPointer clientData, XtPointer callData );
12    void NoCallback ( Widget w, XtPointer clientData, XtPointer callData );
13
14    void main ( int argc, char **argv )
15    {
16        Widget        shell, mb;
17        XtAppContext  app;
18        XmString      xmstr;
19        Dimension     height;
20
21        shell = XtAppInitialize ( &app, "Xecute", NULL, 0,
22                                  &argc, argv, NULL, NULL, 0 );
23
24        if ( argc != 3 ) /* Make sure there are exactly two arguments */
25        {
```

```
26              fprintf (stderr, "Usage:  xecute message-string command\n" );
27              exit ( 1 );
28         }
29
30      /* Create a simple manager widget to hold the other widgets */
31
32      mb = XtVaCreateManagedWidget ( "bboard", xmMessageBoxWidgetClass,
33                                      shell,
34                                      XtVaTypedArg, XmNmessageString,
35                                      XmRString,
36                                      argv[1], strlen ( argv[1] ) + 1,
37                                      XmNdialogType, XmDIALOG_QUESTION,
38                                      NULL );
39      /*
40       * Add a callback to each button, for "yes" and "no"
41       * Pass the command to be executed as client data
42       */
43
44      XtAddCallback ( mb, XmNokCallback,
45                      YesCallback, ( XtPointer ) argv[2] );
46
47      XtAddCallback ( mb, XmNcancelCallback,
48                      NoCallback, NULL );
49
50      /*
51       * Realize the shell and enter the event loop.
52       */
53
54      XtRealizeWidget ( shell );
55      XtAppMainLoop ( app );
56  }
```

The `YesCallback()` function is responsible for executing the command specified on the command line. This function casts its `clientData` argument to a string, calls `system()` (a UNIX function that executes a program by name) to execute the program named by this string, and then exits.

```
57  void YesCallback ( Widget w, XtPointer clientData, XtPointer callData )
58  {
59      /* Cast the clientdata to the expected command string */
60
61      char * cmd = (char *) clientData;
62
63      if ( cmd )
64          system ( cmd ); /* Execute the command */
65
66      exit ( 0 );
67  }
```

The `NoCallback()` function simply calls `exit()` to terminate the program with no further actions.

```
68   void NoCallback ( Widget w, XtPointer clientData, XtPointer callData)
69   {
70       /* No action is necessary, just exit. */
71
72       exit ( 0 );
73   }
```

7.4   The File Selection Dialog

The Motif XmFileSelectionDialog widget class allows users to select a file or directory and to navigate through the file system. The dialog displays lists of files and directories, which can be selected by the user. The user can also type into a text entry area to enter a file name directly. Figure 7.2 shows how the XmFileSelectionDialog appears on the screen.

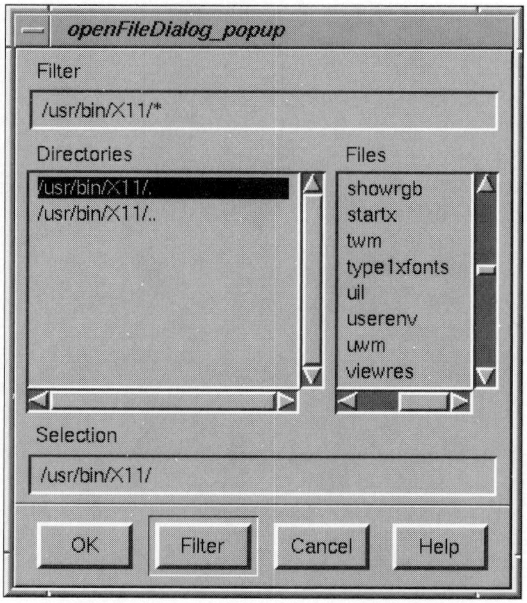

Figure 7.2 The XmFileSelectionDialog widget.

The XmFileSelectionDialog consists of an XmDialogShell and an XmFileSelectionBox widget. The XmFileSelectionBox widget is a composite widget that manages two scrollable lists for files and directories, an XmTextField widget in which file names can be displayed and entered, and another XmTextField widget that displays a filter that controls what files are displayed in the list of files. The XmFileSelectionBox widget also supports four button widgets, labeled OK, Filter, Cancel, and Help. The XmFileSelectionBox widget can also support a single application-defined child, which allows applications to add additional controls.

The XmFileSelectionBox widget is very complex and supports many resources. Most applications need very few of these, however. The following resources are most commonly needed:

- **XmNdirectory**: This resource specifies the base directory from which to display files and subdirectories. By default, this resource is set to the current working directory.

- **XmNdirSpec**: This resource specifies the full path name of a selected file.

- **XmNpattern**: This resource can be used to specify a pattern that determines what files are displayed. The default value is "*", which displays all files.

The XmFileSelectionBox widget supports callbacks for each button. The Filter button normally just applies the filter specified by the **XmNpattern** resource to the currently browsed directory. The other callbacks are similar to those supported by other Motif dialogs. The XmFileSelectionBox widget supports **XmNokCallback**, **XmNcancelCallback**, and **XmNhelpCallback** lists.

All XmFileSelectionBox callbacks are passed a pointer to an **XmFileSelectionBox-CallbackStruct** structure as call data. This structure is defined as follows:

```
typedef struct
{
    int        reason;
    XEvent    *event;
    XmString   value;
    int        length;
    XmString   mask;
    int        mask_length;
    XmString   dir;
    int        dir_length;
    XmString   pattern;
    int        pattern_length;
} XmFileSelectionBoxCallbackStruct;
```

This callback structure provides several useful pieces of information. In particular, the **value** member reports the current value of the **XmNdirSpec** resource, which is the complete path name of the currently selected file. The **dir** member reports the current base directory. The **pattern** member specifies the currently applied pattern.

An Example

The following example program demonstrates how a program can allow users to select a file and how to retrieve the selected file name for further action by the program. The example has a simple driver that just displays a button. Pressing the button calls a callback function that creates and displays an XmFileSelectionBox dialog.

```
1    /*************************************************
2     * filedemo.c: Get a file name from the user
3     *************************************************/
4    #include <Xm/Xm.h>
5    #include <Xm/PushB.h>
6    #include <Xm/FileSB.h>
7    #include <stdio.h>
8
9    /* Forward declarations of callback functions */
10
11   void SelectFileCallback ( Widget     w,
12                             XtPointer clientData,
13                             XtPointer callData );
14   void CancelCallback ( Widget     w,
15                         XtPointer clientData,
16                         XtPointer callData );
17
18   void OKCallback ( Widget     w,
19                     XtPointer clientData,
20                     XtPointer callData );
21
22   void main ( int argc, char **argv )
23   {
24       Widget        shell, button;
25       XtAppContext app;
26
27       /*
28        * Initialize Xt
29        */
30
31       shell = XtAppInitialize ( &app, "Filedemo", NULL, 0,
32                                 &argc, argv, NULL, NULL, 0 );
33
34
35       /* Create a button and add a callback to launch a dialog */
36
37       button = XtCreateManagedWidget ( "pushme", xmPushButtonWidgetClass,
38                                        shell, NULL, 0 );
39
40       XtAddCallback ( button, XmNactivateCallback,
41                       SelectFileCallback, ( XtPointer ) argv[2] );
42
43       /*
44        * Realize the shell and enter the event loop.
45        */
46
47       XtRealizeWidget ( shell );
48       XtAppMainLoop ( app );
49   }
```

`SelectFileCallback()` is invoked when the user clicks on the button in this example. This callback creates an XmFileSelectionDialog the first time it is called. Callbacks are installed for the `XmNokCallback` and the `XmNcancelCallback`.

```
50  void SelectFileCallback ( Widget     w,
51                            XtPointer clientData,
52                            XtPointer callData)
53  {
54      Widget text = (Widget) clientData;
55      static Widget dialog = NULL;
56
57      if ( !dialog )
58      {
59          dialog = XmCreateFileSelectionDialog ( w, "openFileDialog",
60                                                 NULL, 0 );
61
62          XtAddCallback ( dialog, XmNokCallback,
63                          OKCallback, NULL );
64          XtAddCallback ( dialog, XmNcancelCallback,
65                          CancelCallback, NULL );
66      }
67
68      XtManageChild ( dialog );
69  }
```

When the user selects a file and clicks on the XmFileSelectionBox widget's OK button, or double clicks on a file in the scrolled list of file names, the `OKCallback()` function is called. This function removes the dialog from the screen by calling `XtUnmanageChild()`. It is necessary to explicitly unmanage the dialog because the XmFileSelectionDialog does not set `XmNautoUnmanage` to TRUE by default. Setting the `XmNautoUnmanage` resource to TRUE would mean that the dialog would be dismissed if the user clicked on the Filter button, which would not normally be the desired behavior. The callback function then retrieves a text string from the `value` member of the call data structure and prints the resulting file name. Normally, an application would open the selected file, or use the file name in some other way.

```
70  void OKCallback ( Widget w, XtPointer clientData, XtPointer callData )
71  {
72      XmFileSelectionBoxCallbackStruct *cbs =
73                      ( XmFileSelectionBoxCallbackStruct * ) callData;
74      char *fileName;
75
76      /*
77       * Remove the widget from the screen.
78       */
79
80      XtUnmanageChild ( w );
81
```

```
82      /*
83       * Retrieve the character string from the compound string format.
84       */
85
86      XmStringGetLtoR ( cbs->value, XmFONTLIST_DEFAULT_TAG, &fileName );
87
88      /*
89       * For this demo, just echo the selected string to standard out.
90       */
91
92      printf ( "Selected file = %s\n", fileName );
93  }
```

Because the XmFileSelectionBox widget does not automatically dismiss itself when a button is selected, the application must handle removing the widget from the screen when the cancel button is selected. The `CancelCallback()` function just calls `XtUnmanageChild()` to hide the dialog.

```
94  void CancelCallback ( Widget     w,
95                        XtPointer clientData,
96                        XtPointer callData )
97  {
98      XtUnmanageChild ( w );
99  }
```

7.5 Creating Custom Dialogs

Although many applications make extensive use of the ready-made Motif dialogs, some applications require dialogs that are very different from those provided by Motif. In such cases, applications can create custom dialogs that match their needs. There are several possible ways to create custom dialogs. For example, an application could create a manager widget as a child of an XmDialogShell widget and create any layout desired. Many of the Motif manager widgets have convenience functions that will automatically create the manager as a child of an XmDialogShell. For example, the function `XmCreateFormDialog()` creates an XmForm widget as a child of an XmDialog-Shell.

However, it is seldom necessary to create a dialog completely from scratch, and it is usually easier to modify one of the ready-made dialogs. Dialogs based on the XmMessageBox widget class can be extensively modified. Children can be removed from the dialogs and others can be added. For example, an application can destroy or simply unmanage the XmLabel used to display a pixmap, to completely remove the iconic symbol from a question dialog. The various children of an XmMessageBox widget can be accessed using the function:

```
Widget XmMessageBoxGetChild ( Widget messagebox, unsigned char child )
```

This function takes an XmMessageBox widget as the first argument and one of the following symbols as the second argument:

```
XmDIALOG_OK_BUTTON              XmDIALOG_CANCEL_BUTTON
XmDIALOG_HELP_BUTTON            XmDIALOG_SEPARATOR
XmDIALOG_SYMBOL_LABEL           XmDIALOG_MESSAGE_LABEL
```

So, for example, the following code segment removes the help button from a dialog:

```
XtUnmanageChild ( XmMessageBoxGetChild ( dialog, XmDIALOG_HELP_BUTTON ) );
```

Widgets can also be added to the XmMessageBox widget. If an XmPushButton widget or gadget is created as a child of an XmMessageBox widget, the message box automatically adds the child to the button area and handles all layout. The application must handle callbacks for these new buttons directly, however. If a menu bar is added to the message box, the menu is placed at the top of the dialog, as a menu bar should be handled. If any other widget type is added, the XmMessageBox widget assumes the widget is to be placed in the work area, where the label and pixmap normally are located. One typical approach to creating custom dialogs is to remove the label and pixmap label from the dialog and to add a manager, such as an XmForm widget as a work area. This manager can then handle the layout of any number of children. The XmMessageBox continues to handle the buttons, and generally performs as any other dialog.

An Example Custom Dialog

The following example program shows how to create a simple custom dialog. The dialog displays a list of text entry fields and labels, as shown in Figure 7.3. The dialog behaves as any simple Motif dialog. Users can select the OK or Cancel buttons, but can also interact with the text fields in the top part of the dialog window.

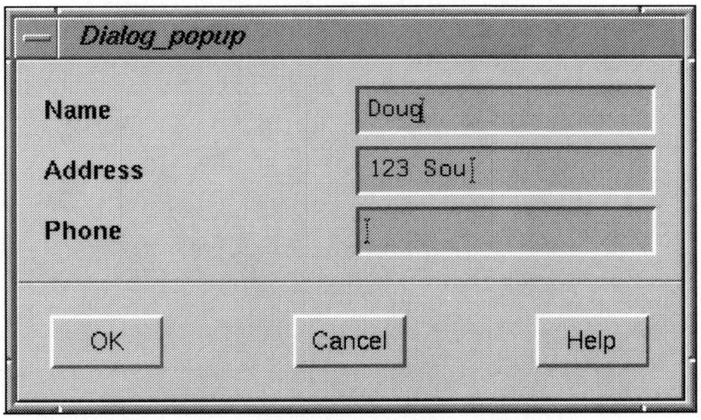

Figure 7.3 A custom dialog.

The body of this example just creates an XmPushButton widget. Pushing on the button invokes a callback that displays the dialog. The function `CreateDialog()` creates the custom dialog widget.

```
1    /**************************************************
2     * customdialog.c: Demonstrate a custom dialog
3     **************************************************/
4    #include <Xm/Xm.h>
5    #include <Xm/Label.h>
6    #include <Xm/RowColumn.h>
7    #include <Xm/TextF.h>
8    #include <Xm/PushB.h>
9    #include <Xm/MessageB.h>
10
11   Widget CreateDialog ( Widget parent, char *name );
12
13   static void ShowDialogCallback ( Widget     w,
14                                    XtPointer clientData,
15                                    XtPointer callData )
16   {
17       Widget     dialog = ( Widget ) clientData;
18
19       XtManageChild ( dialog );
20   }
21
22   void main ( int argc, char **argv )
23   {
24       Widget       shell, button, dialog;
25       XtAppContext app;
26
27       /*
28        * Initialize Xt
29        */
30
31       shell = XtAppInitialize ( &app, "Customdialog", NULL, 0,
32                               &argc, argv, NULL, NULL, 0 );
33
34       button = XtCreateManagedWidget ( "button", xmPushButtonWidgetClass,
35                                        shell, NULL, 0);
36
37       /*
38        * Create a popup dialog and a register a callback
39        * function to display the dialog when the button is activated.
40        */
41
42       dialog = CreateDialog ( button, "Dialog" );
43
44       XtAddCallback ( button, XmNactivateCallback,
45                       ShowDialogCallback, dialog );
46
47       XtRealizeWidget ( shell );
48       XtAppMainLoop ( app );
49   }
```

The function `CreateDialog()` begins by creating a message dialog. The function then removes the label and pixmap areas of the message dialog and adds an XmRowColumn widget as a work area widget. The XmRowColumn widget manages a series of labels and XmTextField widgets.

```
50   const char *fields[] = {"Name", "Address", "Phone"};
51
52   Widget CreateDialog ( Widget parent, char *name )
53   {
54       Widget dialog, rc;
55       int    numFields = XtNumber ( fields );
56       int    i;
57
58       /*
59        * Create the dialog widget.
60        */
61
62       dialog = XmCreateMessageDialog ( parent, name, NULL, 0 );
63
64       /*
65        * Remove unnneeded children.
66        */
67
68       XtUnmanageChild ( XmMessageBoxGetChild ( dialog,
69                                             XmDIALOG_SYMBOL_LABEL ) );
70       XtUnmanageChild ( XmMessageBoxGetChild ( dialog,
71                                             XmDIALOG_MESSAGE_LABEL ) );
72       /*
73        * Create a manager widget as a child of the dialog, to be used
74        * as the work area of the dialog, replacing the label and icon.
75        */
76
77       rc = XtVaCreateManagedWidget ( "rc", xmRowColumnWidgetClass,dialog,
78                                     XmNnumColumns,  2,
79                                     XmNpacking,     XmPACK_COLUMN,
80                                     XmNorientation, XmVERTICAL,
81                                     NULL );
82       /*
83        * Create children of the manager.
84        */
85
86       for ( i=0; i < numFields; i++ )
87          XtCreateManagedWidget ( fields [i], xmLabelWidgetClass,
88                                 rc, NULL, 0 );
89       for ( i=0; i < numFields; i++ )
90          XtCreateManagedWidget ( fields [i], xmTextFieldWidgetClass,
91                                 rc, NULL, 0);
92       return ( dialog );
93   }
```

Notice that this example does not provide any way to access the widgets added to the dialog. For example, an application would most likely need to access the various text fields to retrieve any text entered by the user. Individual applications will need to design some way to retrieve the text, according to their needs. One possible approach is to store the widgets in a structure which is passed as client data to the callbacks.

For example, the following variation of `CreateDialog()` stores the XmTextField widgets in a structure passed to the callbacks registered with the dialog. In this example, the function `CreateDialog()` allows OK, Cancel, and Apply callbacks to be specified. Because the message dialog does not support an apply button, one is added.

```
typedef struct {
    Widget name, addr, phone;
} DialogWidgets;

Widget CreateDialog ( Widget parent, char *name,
                      XtCallbackProc OkCallback,
                      XtCallbackProc ApplyCallback,
                      XtCallbackProc CancelCallback )
{
    Widget dialog, rc, apply;
    int    i;
    DialogWidgets *widgets;

    widgets = ( DialogWidgets * ) XtMalloc ( sizeof ( DialogWidgets ) );


   /*
    * Create a standard message dialog
    */

    dialog = XmCreateMessageDialog ( parent, name, NULL, 0 );

   /*
    * Remove unwanted children
    */

    XtUnmanageChild ( XmMessageBoxGetChild ( dialog,
                                          XmDIALOG_SYMBOL_LABEL ) );
    XtUnmanageChild ( XmMessageBoxGetChild ( dialog,
                                          XmDIALOG_MESSAGE_LABEL ) );

   /*
    * Add an apply button if there is a callback
    */

    if ( ApplyCallback )
      apply = XtCreateManagedWidget ( "apply", xmPushButtonWidgetClass,
                                      dialog, NULL, 0 );
```

```
    /*
     * Add callbacks. Note different treatment of apply button
     */

    if ( OkCallback )
        XtAddCallback ( dialog, XmNokCallback,
                        OkCallback, widgets );
    if ( CancelCallback )
        XtAddCallback ( dialog, XmNokCallback,
                        CancelCallback,widgets );
    if ( ApplyCallback )
        XtAddCallback ( apply, XmNactivateCallback,
                        ApplyCallback, widgets );

    /*
     * Create a manager widget to handle the dialog layout
     */

    rc = XtVaCreateManagedWidget ( "rc", xmRowColumnWidgetClass, dialog,
                                   XmNnumColumns,  2,
                                   XmNpacking,     XmPACK_COLUMN,
                                   XmNorientation, XmVERTICAL,
                                   NULL );
    /*
     * Create the labels
     */

    XtCreateManagedWidget ( "Name", xmLabelWidgetClass, rc, NULL, 0 );
    XtCreateManagedWidget ( "Address", xmLabelWidgetClass,
                            rc, NULL, 0 );
    XtCreateManagedWidget ( "Phone", xmLabelWidgetClass,
                            rc, NULL, 0 );

    /*
     * Create the text input field
     */

    widgets->name = XtCreateManagedWidget ( "name",
                                            xmTextFieldWidgetClass,
                                            rc, NULL, 0);
    widgets->addr = XtCreateManagedWidget ( "addr",
                                            xmTextFieldWidgetClass,
                                            rc, NULL, 0);
    widgets->phone = XtCreateManagedWidget ( "phone",
                                             xmTextFieldWidgetClass,
                                             rc, NULL, 0);

    return ( dialog );
}
```

Template Dialogs

An XmMessageBox widget can be configured in several ways. In addition to the standard message, error, and warning styles, an XmMessageBox widget can be configured as a template that is intended to support custom dialogs. The easiest way to create a template dialog is to call the convenience creation function XmCreateTemplateDialog(). This function creates an XmMessageBox dialog that has no children other than the separator between the button area and the work area. Applications can add their own children. Normally, the children that most applications need to create are placed in the work area of the dialog, although button widgets can also be created. Any child other than an XmPushButton or menu bar is treated as a work area widget. For most applications, this widget will be a manager widget that can contain other widgets as needed.

A template dialog supports the standard Motif dialog buttons if the application sets label resources for these buttons. So all that is required to have an OK button appear in a template dialog is to set a resource in a resource file, as follows:

```
*customDialog*okLabelString: OK
```

The template dialog resources could also be set programmatically.

Setting the XmNsymbolPixmap resource displays a pixmap in the usual location, and setting the XmNmessageString resource displays a label widget in the work area. So by setting several resources, the template dialog can be made to function just like a message dialog. However, it is normally used as an alternative to the custom dialog approach described in the previous section.

The following variation of the CreateDialog() function uses an XmCreateTemplate-Dialog() to create the same custom dialog described in the previous section.

```
Widget CreateDialog ( Widget parent, char *name,
                      XtCallbackProc OkCallback,
                      XtCallbackProc ApplyCallback,
                      XtCallbackProc CancelCallback )
{
    Widget          dialog, rc, apply;
    DialogWidgets *widgets;
    int             i;

    widgets = ( DialogWidgets * ) XtMalloc ( sizeof ( DialogWidgets ) );

    /*
     * Create the template dialog.
     */

    dialog = XmCreateTemplateDialog ( parent, name, NULL, 0 );

    /*
     * Add an apply button if there is a callback
     */

    if ( ApplyCallback )
```

```
        apply = XtCreateManagedWidget ( "apply",
                                         xmPushButtonWidgetClass,
                                         dialog, NULL, 0 );
/*
 * Add callbacks. Note different treatment of apply button
 */

    if ( OkCallback )
        XtAddCallback ( dialog, XmNokCallback, OkCallback, widgets );
    if ( CancelCallback )
        XtAddCallback ( dialog, XmNokCallback,
                        CancelCallback, widgets );
    if ( ApplyCallback )
        XtAddCallback ( apply, XmNactivateCallback,
                        ApplyCallback, widgets );
/*
 * Create a manager widget to handle the dialog layout
 */

    rc = XtVaCreateManagedWidget ( "rc", xmRowColumnWidgetClass,dialog,
                                   XmNnumColumns,  2,
                                   XmNpacking,      XmPACK_COLUMN,
                                   XmNorientation, XmVERTICAL,
                                   NULL );
/*
 * Create the labels
 */

    XtCreateManagedWidget ( "Name", xmLabelWidgetClass, rc, NULL, 0 );
    XtCreateManagedWidget ( "Address", xmLabelWidgetClass,
                            rc, NULL, 0 );
    XtCreateManagedWidget ( "Phone", xmLabelWidgetClass,
                            rc, NULL, 0 );
/*
 * Create the text input field
 */

    widgets->name = XtCreateManagedWidget ( "name",
                                            xmTextFieldWidgetClass,
                                            rc, NULL, 0);
    widgets->addr = XtCreateManagedWidget ( "addr",
                                            xmTextFieldWidgetClass,
                                            rc, NULL, 0);
    widgets->phone = XtCreateManagedWidget ( "phone",
                                             xmTextFieldWidgetClass,
                                             rc, NULL, 0);

    return ( dialog );
}
```

To display the standard buttons for this dialog, the label resources must also be set. For example, the following resources cause the OK and Cancel buttons to appear.

```
*okLabelString:     OK
*cancelLabelString: Cancel
```

7.6 Summary

This chapter demonstrates some basic ways to use Motif dialogs. Most large applications use dialogs as a way to present additional information that is not needed at all times. Applications also use dialogs to communicate important information, such as error conditions, and may also use dialogs to request information from the user. Motif provides a core set of basic dialogs that are ready to use. Applications that need custom dialogs can usually customize an existing dialog class by adding or removing items.

Dialogs can be a useful part of an application's user interface, but they can also be misused or overused. Applications that continually pop up dialogs to report non-critical situations can quickly become tiresome. Dialogs should generally be limited to critical situations that require a user's attention, or that require the user to acknowledge the situation before continuing.

Chapter 8

Events
and
Other Input Techniques

The X server communicates with clients by sending *events*. When using Xt or Motif, individual widgets normally handle most common events automatically, and some applications may not even need to handle the events generated by the X server directly. For example, most widgets handle the `Expose` events sent by the server when the contents of a widget's window must be refreshed, and also handle configuration events generated by the server when a window is resized. In addition, most widgets use the translation manager to handle keyboard and mouse input. Programmers are usually notified of such input via callbacks. In spite of this, most programmers still find occasions when they must handle events directly, even when using Motif. Having a good understanding of the events generated by the X server also helps the programmer understand and use widgets more effectively.

This chapter examines the types of events that can be sent to an application and provides examples that use features of Xt to handle events. The chapter first examines the events and event structures provided by X and Xlib and then looks at the event-handling mechanisms built on top of Xlib by Xt. This chapter also examines some applications that depend on input from sources other than X events.

8.1 What Is an Event?

An *event* is a notification, sent by the X server to a client, that something has happened or that some condition has changed. The X server generates events as a result of user input, or as a side effect of a request to the X server. The server sends each event to all interested clients, who determine what kind of event has occurred by looking at the *type* of each event. Applications do not receive events automatically. They must specifically request the X server to send the types of events in which they are interested. Of course, Motif requests many types of events automatically, so Motif programmers may not be aware of the events their applications (or the widgets used by their applications) have requested.

Events always occur relative to a window, known as the *source window* of the event. If no client has requested a given type of event for the source window, the server propagates the event up the X window hierarchy until it finds a window for which some client has requested the event, or it finds a window that prohibits the event propagation. If the server reaches the root of the window tree without finding a client interested in the event, the event is discarded. The window to which the server finally reports the event is known as the *event window*. The server only propagates *device events* generated as a result of a key, mouse button, or pointer motion. Other events, such as configuration events and exposure events, are not propagated.

The X server places all events in an event queue. Motif applications usually remove events from the event queue using the Xt function, `XtAppNextEvent()`. This function fills in an `XEvent` structure allocated by the application. Each event type is defined as a C structure. The `XEvent` structure is a C union of all event types.

All events contain a core set of basic information, contained in the first five members of every event structure. For each event, these members indicate:

- The type of the event.
- The display where the event occurred.
- The event window.
- The serial number of the last request processed by the server.
- Whether this event was generated by the server or whether the event was sent by another client. The send_event member of the event structure is set to `TRUE` if the event was sent by another client, and `FALSE` if the event was sent by the server.

The structure `XAnyEvent` is defined to allow access to those members that are common to all event types. Clients can access this basic information in any event using the `xany` member of the `XEvent` union. For example, the event window can be retrieved from any event, as follows:

```
event.xany.window
```

The type of every event can also be accessed directly using:

```
event.type
```

Each event structure contains additional information, specific to the type of the event, that must be accessed using the member of the union that corresponds to that event type. For example, the width of a window can be extracted from an `XConfigureNotify` event with:

```
event.xconfigure.width
```

8.2   Event Masks

When using Xlib, an X application must request the event types it wishes the server to report for each window by passing an *event mask* to the Xlib function `XSelectInput()`. For example, the statement:

```
XSelectInput ( display, window,
               ButtonPressMask | ButtonReleaseMask );
```

requests the server to generate events when a mouse button is pressed or released in the given window. Xt and Motif applications rarely use `XSelectInput()` directly. Instead, Motif applications request events by registering an *event handler* for a widget using the Xt function `XtAddEventHandler()`. (See Section 8.4 for a discussion of event handlers.)

Figure 8.1 shows the X event masks defined in X.h. There is not always a direct correlation between a mask used to request an event and the types of events reported by the server. For example, a client that selects events with `ExposureMask` may be sent `Expose`, `GraphicsExpose`, and `NoExpose` events. On the other hand, clients that requests events using `PointerMotionMask` or `ButtonMotionMask` receive a `MotionNotify` event when either situation occurs.

NoEventMask	KeyPressMask
KeyReleaseMask	ButtonPressMask
ButtonReleaseMask	EnterWindowMask
LeaveWindowMask	PointerMotionMask
PointerMotionHintMask	Button1MotionMask
Button2MotionMask	Button3MotionMask
Button4MotionMask	Button5MotionMask
ButtonMotionMask	KeymapStateMask
ExposureMask	VisibilityChangeMask
StructureNotifyMask	ResizeRedirectMask
SubstructureNotifyMask	SubstructureRedirectMask
FocusChangeMask	PropertyChangeMask
ColormapChangeMask	OwnerGrabButtonMask

Figure 8.1 Event masks used to select X events.

8.3   Event Types

The events supported by X can be grouped into several general categories. The following sections discuss each event category and examine the information contained in these events.

Keyboard Events

The server generates a `KeyPress` event whenever a key is pressed, and generates a `KeyRelease` event when the key is released. All keys, including modifier keys (the `<SHIFT>` key, for example), generate events. A client can request `KeyPress` events using the `KeyPressMask` as the event mask. Clients request `KeyRelease` events using `KeyReleaseMask`.

The server reports both `KeyRelease` and `KeyPress` events using an `XKeyEvent` structure. In addition to the members common to all X events, the `XKeyEvent` structure contains some additional information:

```
Window          root;
Window          subwindow;
Time            time;
int             x, y;
int             x_root, y_root;
unsigned int    state;
unsigned int    keycode;
Bool            same_screen;
```

The `root` member reports the ID of the root window of the screen where the event occurred. If the source window is a descendent of the event window, the `subwindow` member indicates the ID of the immediate child of the event window that lies between the event window and the source window.

For example, assume that a window named BaseWindow has a child named ScrollBar, and that ScrollBar has a child named Slider, as shown in Figure 8.2 and Figure 8.3. Also assume that only BaseWindow has selected `KeyPress` events. If a `KeyPress` event occurs in Slider, the event propagates to BaseWindow. The source window is Slider. The event received by BaseWindow indicates BaseWindow as the event window. The `subwindow` member of the event contains the ID of the ScrollBar window.

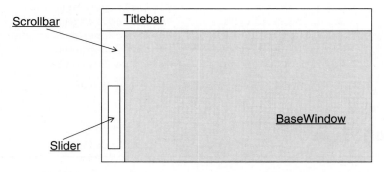

Figure 8.2 A complex window composed of multiple X windows.

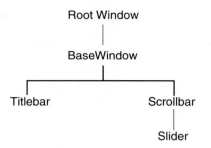

Figure 8.3 Window tree for Figure 8.2.

The `time` member of an `XKeyPressedEvent` structure indicates the time in milliseconds since the server last reset. This information can be used to help prevent race conditions that can arise because the X server and its clients run asynchronously with respect to each other.

The `XKeyEvent` structure also contains the coordinates of the pointer relative to both the event window and the root window, as long as the event window is on the same screen as the root window. If this is not the case, the event reports the coordinates of the pointer as *(0, 0)*, relative to the root window.

The `XKeyEvent` structure contains a keycode that uniquely identifies the key that caused the event. Applications can use the Xlib function `XLookupString()` to map this keycode to the character it represents.

The `state` member of the event contains a mask that indicates which, if any, modifier keys were depressed when this key was pressed. X supports many modifier keys, including `<SHIFT>`, `<SHIFTLOCK>`, `<CONTROL>`, as well as up to five additional system-dependent modifier keys.

Pointer Events

The server generates `ButtonPress`, `ButtonRelease`, and `MotionNotify` events when a user presses or releases a mouse button or moves the pointer. The source window for pointer events is always the smallest window that contains the pointer, unless some client has *grabbed* the pointer. When the pointer is grabbed, the server reports all pointer events with respect to a window designated by the application that initiates the grab.

The server reports `ButtonPress` and `ButtonRelease` events using an `XButtonEvent` structure. This event structure is similar to the `KeyPress` event structure, but instead of a key code, the `XButtonEvent` structure contains a `button` member which indicates which mouse button was pressed or released. X supports up to five mouse buttons, defined in the file X.h as `Button1`, `Button2`, `Button3`, `Button4`, and `Button5`. The mouse buttons can also be combined with a modifier key, such as the `<SHIFT>` or `<META>` key. The state of all modifier keys at the time the event occurred is indicated by the `state` member.

The server reports pointer motion events using an `XMotionEvent` structure. Clients can request the server to generate motion events whenever the user moves the pointer, or to generate events only when the user moves the pointer while holding down a particular button or combination of buttons. However, the server reports all motion events as type `MotionNotify`, using the `XMotionEvent` structure. Clients can determine the state of the mouse buttons (which buttons are up and which are down) by looking at the `state` member of the event.

By default, the server reports motion events continuously as the pointer moves. Clients can also request the server to *compress* motion events and generate events only when the pointer starts or stops moving. Most applications do not need continuous motion events and should request the server to compress pointer motion events into *hints*, by requesting motion events with `PointerMotionHintMask`. The `is_hint` member of the `XMotionEvent` structure indicates whether an event indicates continuous motion or a hint. Other members of the event structure report the *x, y* position of the pointer relative to both the event window and the root window. The members of the `XMotionEvent` event structure include:

```
Window          root;
Window          subwindow;
Time            time;
int             x, y;
int             x_root, y_root;
unsigned int    state;
char            is_hint;
Bool            same_screen;
```

Crossing Events

The server generates crossing events whenever the pointer crosses the boundary of a window. The server reports an `EnterNotify` event when the pointer enters a window and a `LeaveNotify` event when the pointer leaves a window. The server also generates crossing events when the pointer enters a window because of a change in the window hierarchy.

For example, if a window that contains the pointer is lowered to the bottom of the window stack in such a way that the pointer is now in another window, the first window receives a `LeaveNotify` event and the second window receives a `EnterNotify` event. Clients must request `EnterNotify` events using `EnterWindowMask` and `LeaveNotify` events using the mask `LeaveWindowMask`. Both crossing events are reported in the `XCrossingEvent` structure, which includes the members:

```
Window          root;
Window          subwindow;
Time            time;
int             x, y;
int             x_root, y_root;
int             mode;
int             detail;
Bool            same_screen;
Bool            focus;
unsigned int    state;
```

The `XCrossingEvent` structure always contains the final *(x, y)* coordinate of the pointer relative to both the event window and the root window. The `state` member of the event structure indicates the state of the mouse buttons immediately preceding the event.

Applications often need to determine the hierarchical relationship of the windows involved in a crossing event. For example, consider a program that changes the appearance of a window whenever the window contains the pointer. Switching states whenever the client receives an `EnterNotify` or `LeaveNotify` event for that window works correctly, unless the window has subwindows. When the pointer is moved into a subwindow, the client receives a `LeaveNotify` event for the parent window, even thought the pointer is still contained by the parent window. In addition, if the application has not requested `EnterNotify` events for the subwindow, the server propagates the event to the parent window, which causes further complications.

To handle such events correctly, an application must inspect the `detail` member of the event structure. The server sets this member to one of the constants `NotifyAncestor`, `NotifyVirtual`, `NotifyInferior`, `NotifyNonlinear`, or `NotifyNonlinear-Virtual`, to indicate which of the different types of window crossings has occurred.

Figure 8.4 through Figure 8.7 show the root window, and two children, Window A and Window B. Window A and Window B have subwindows Window C and Window D respectively. The vector in each figure represents a pointer movement starting in one window and ending in the window that contains the arrow head. The widget hierarchy included in each figure also shows the pointer motion. The text at the beginning and end of each line indicates the type of event generated in that window, with the value of the `detail` member of the event structure shown in parenthesis.

Figure 8.4 illustrates the pointer moving from the root window into a child, Window B. The root window receives a `LeaveNotify` event with the `detail` member of the event set to `NotifyInferior`, while Window B receives an `EnterNotify` event, with the `detail` member set to `NotifyAncestor`.

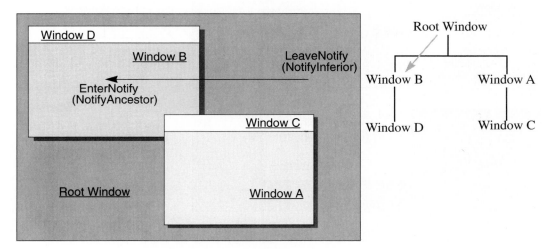

Figure 8.4 Crossing events.

Figure 8.5 illustrates the opposite situation, in which the pointer moves from a window into the window's parent.

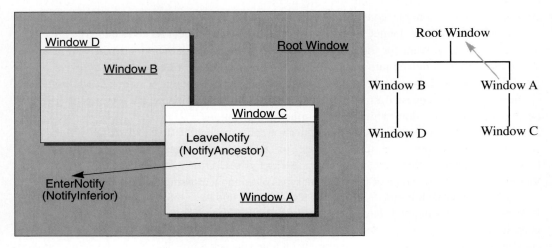

Figure 8.5 Crossing events.

Figure 8.6 illustrates movement of the pointer between two siblings. In this case, the server sets the `detail` member of each event to `NotifyNonlinear`.

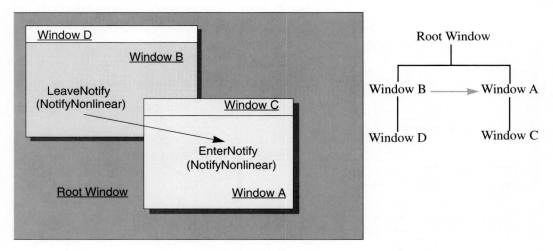

Figure 8.6 Crossing events.

Figure 8.7 shows the most complex situation, in which the pointer moves between two windows that are neither parent and child, nor siblings. In this case, Window C receives a `LeaveNotify` event and Window B receives an `EnterNotify` event. The `detail` member in both events is `NotifyNonlinear`. However, Window A also receives a `LeaveNotify` event, with the `detail` member set to `NotifyNonlinearVirtual`.

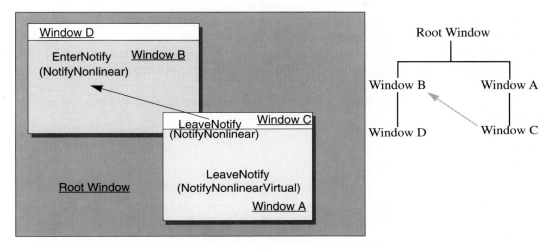

Figure 8.7 Crossing events.

The server also generates crossing events when an application grabs or ungrabs the pointer. When an application grabs the pointer, the server sends the window that contains the pointer a `LeaveNotify` event with the `mode` member set to the constant `NotifyGrab`. When the grabbing application ungrabs the pointer, the server sends the window that contains the pointer an `EnterNotify` event with the `mode` member set to `NotifyUngrab`. If the crossing event is not a result of a grab, the server sets the `mode` member of the event to `NotifyNormal`.

Focus Events

The window to which the X server sends keyboard events is known as the focus window. The server generates `FocusIn` and `FocusOut` events whenever the focus window changes, usually because a window manager explicitly changes the focus window. Applications that wish to receive these events must select them using `FocusChangeMask`. Focus events are similar to `EnterNotify` and `LeaveNotify` events, but are even more complex, because the pointer is not necessarily in any of the windows involved in the change of focus. Most applications that use Xt or Motif do not need to handle focus events directly, because focus is handled by manager widgets.

Exposure Events

The server generates exposure events when a window or a portion of a window becomes visible. Clients must request exposure events using the `ExposureMask` event mask. There are three types of exposure events. The most common type, `Expose`, is generated when the contents of a region of a window are lost for any reason. The server sends the second type, `GraphicsExpose`, when a client attempts to use `XCopyArea()` to copy an obscured region of a window. The final type of expose event, `NoExpose`, can also be generated when copying an area between drawables. The server generates a `NoExpose` event when an application requests `GraphicsExpose` events, but no `GraphicsExpose` events are generated during a copy. GraphicsExpose and NoExpose events are only received if an application sets the graphics-expose attribute of the graphics context used to perform the copy (see Chapter 10).

The server reports `Expose` events using an `XExposeEvent` structure, which includes the following members:

```
int    x, y;
int    width, height;
int    count;
```

The `XExposeEvent` structure contains the *x* and *y* coordinates relative to the upper left corner of the window and the width and height of the rectangular region of the window that has been exposed. The event also contains a `count` member which indicates how many `Expose` events are still pending. If `count` is zero, there are no more `Expose` events pending for this window. However, if the `count` member is non-zero, then *at least* this many events are still pending. Multiple `Expose` events occur primarily when an exposed region consists of more than one rectangular region. Applications that are not capable of redrawing arbitrary regions of windows can ignore `Expose` events with a non-zero `count` member, and redraw the entire contents of the window when the server generates an event whose `count` member is zero.

Xt allows widgets to request that multiple exposure events be *compressed* into a single `Expose` event. Xt automatically accumulates all `Expose` events until an event with `count` set to zero is received. Xt then replaces the coordinates in this last `Expose` event with the bounding box of the areas in all previous `Expose` events and invokes the widget's `Expose` event handler with the single `Expose` event. The ability to compress events is an internal feature of Xt that is available within a widget. Applications cannot control whether an existing widget compresses events.

`GraphicsExpose` events are reported in an `XGraphicsExposeEvent` structure and `NoExpose` events are reported in an `XNoExposeEvent` structure. Both event structures contain a `drawable` member instead of the `window` member supported by other event types. In addition, both event types include the following members:

```
int x, y;
int width, height;
int count;
int major_code;
```

The `drawable` member is set to the destination of the copy operation. The `major_code` member indicates whether the expose was a result of a call to `XCopyArea()` or `XCopyPlane()`.

Structure Control

The server reports structure control events to clients that ask for requests to be *redirected*. Window managers generally use event redirection to exercise control over an application's windows. For example, if a window manager requests events using the mask `ResizeRedirectMask`, the X server ignores all requests from other applications to resize windows and instead sends a `ResizeRequest` event to the window manager. The window manager then has the opportunity to act on the request according to its screen management policy.

Requests that circulate a window's position in the stacking order, configure the window in any way, or map the window can also be redirected. If a window manager requests events with the mask `SubstructureRedirectMask`, the X server sends `MapRequest`, `CirculateRequest`, and `ConfigureRequest` events to the window manager, instead of acting directly on these requests. Only one application can request the server to redirect events at any one time.

State Notification

Some applications need to be informed when its windows are reconfigured in any way. Clients can use the `StructureNotifyMask` event mask to request events when a window's configuration changes, or `SubstructureNotifyMask` to request notification of changes to a window's subwindows.

Clients that request `StructureNotify` events can receive many different types of events, depending on what changes occur. When a window's position in the stacking order changes due to a call to the Xlib functions `XCirculateSubwindows()`, `XCirculateSubwindowsUp()`, or `XCirculateSubwindowsDown()`, the server generates a `CirculateNotify` event, which is reported in an `XCirculateEvent` structure. This structure includes the members:

```
Window  event;
Window  window;
int     place;
```

The `event` member of this structure indicates the event window. The `window` member is set to the ID of the window that was restacked. This window is not necessarily the same as the event window. The server also sets the `place` member of this event to the constant `PlaceOnBottom`, which indicates that the window is below all siblings, or the constant `PlaceOnTop`, which indicates that the window is above all siblings.

The server generates `ConfigureNotify` events whenever a window's size, position, or border width changes. The server reports this event using an `XConfigureEvent` structure. `ConfigureNotify` events are also generated when a window's position in the stacking order changes because of a call to the Xlib functions `XLowerWindow()`, `XRaiseWindow()`, `XRestackWindow()`, or `XRestackWindows()`. The members in the `XConfigureEvent` structure include:

```
Window   event;
Window   window;
int      x, y;
int      width, height;
int      border_width;
Window   above;
Bool     override_redirect;
```

The `event` member of the `XConfigureEvent` structure indicates the event window while the `window` member indicates the window that has changed. The `above` member contains the ID of the sibling window just below the window whose position in the stacking order has changed. If the window is on the bottom of the stacking order, the `above` member of the `XConfigureNotify` event is set to `None`.

The server generates `CreateNotify` and `DestroyNotify` events whenever a window is created or destroyed, respectively. Clients that wish to receive these events must request events for the window's parent using `SubstructureNotifyMask`. The event structure used to report `CreateNotify` events contains the IDs of both the new window and the parent of the new window, and also the size and location of the window. The `DestroyNotify` event structure contains only the event window and the ID of the destroyed window.

Other types of structure notification events include `GravityNotify`, `MapNotify`, `MappingNotify`, `ReparentNotify`, `UnmapNotify`, and `VisibilityNotify`. Application programmers seldom need to deal with these events directly, because Xt and Motif normally handle them automatically.

Colormap Notification

Applications that need to know when a new color map is installed can request `ColormapNotify` events using the mask `ColormapChangeMask`. Color maps determine the colors available to an application, and are discussed in Chapter 9. The server reports `ColormapNotify` events using an `XColormapEvent` structure that contains the ID of the colormap, a Boolean value that indicates whether the colormap is new, and a `state` member set to one of the constants `ColormapInstalled` or `ColormapUninstalled`. The members of the `XColormapEvent` structure include:

```
Colormap colormap;
Bool     new;
int      state;
```

Communication Events

X also supports events that allow direct communication between applications, and events that provide a mechanism for exchanging and sharing data between applications. `ClientMessage` events can be used by applications to act as additional event types that can be sent between applications using the Xlib function:

```
XSendEvent ( Display          display,
             Window           window,
             Boolean          propagate,
             unsigned long    mask,
             XEvent           *event )
```

Applications cannot specifically request `ClientMessage` events. The server always sends `ClientMessage` events to the destination window. Chapter 14 discusses `ClientMessage` events and shows some examples of direct interclient communication.

The server generates `PropertyNotify` events when the value of a window *property* is modified. Applications interested in receiving `PropertyNotify` events must select the event by specifying `PropertyChangeMask` as part of the mask argument to `XSelectInput()` or `XtAddEventHandler()`. Properties and `PropertyNotify` events are discussed in Chapter 14.

`SelectionClear`, `SelectionNotify`, and `SelectionRequest` events are used by the X selection mechanism for exchanging data between applications. Like `ClientMessage` events, selection events cannot be specifically selected by an application. Selections are also discussed in Chapter 14.

8.4   Handling Events in Motif Applications

Xt and Motif hide many of the details of handing events from the programmer and allow widgets to handle many of the common X events automatically. As a result, many applications built using Motif do not need to deal directly with events at all. However, Xt does provide facilities that allow Motif applications to handle events directly if needed. Applications can request a specific type of event by defining an *event handler* for that event. The following sections explore some ways to use events and event handlers.

Event Handlers

An event handler is a function, registered with Xt, that can be called when an event is received by an application for the window that corresponds to a specific widget. Event handlers are registered by calling the function:

```
XtAddEventHandler ( Widget          widget,
                    EventMask       mask,
                    Boolean         nonMaskable,
                    XtEventHandler  handler
                    XtPointer       clientData )
```

The first argument to this function is the widget for which events are to be handled. The second argument indicates the event mask for the events to be handled. This event mask can indicate a single event type, or can specify a combination of events by providing the logical OR of one or more event masks.

Some events have no event mask. Such events, which are always sent to an application whether it has requested them or not, are called non-maskable events. To register an event handler for a non-maskable event, the `nonMaskable` argument to `XtAddEventHandler()` must be set to `TRUE`. The next argument specifies the function to be called when one of the specified events occurs in the given widget's window. Finally, the `clientData` argument allows applications to provide some data that is passed to the event handler when it is called.

The form of every event handler must be:

```
void EventHandler ( Widget      w,
                    XtPointer   clientData,
                    XEvent      *event,
                    Boolean     *continueToDispatch )
```

Here, the first argument specifies the widget in whose window the event occurred. The second argument supplies any client data provided when the event handler was registered. The `event` argument provides a pointer to the event that caused this function to be called. The fourth argument is a pointer to a Boolean value. If the event handler sets this value to `FALSE`, any additional event handlers registered for this same event will not be called. Since it is not possible to know what other event handlers are registered for any given event, and the order in which event handlers is called is undetermined, this feature should rarely be used, and applications normally ignore it.

Using Event Handlers

This section examines two programs that use event handlers to handle `MotionNotify` events, `ButtonPress` events, and crossing events. These examples demonstrate how to access and use the information in the event structures.

The first example implements a function that tracks and reports the position of the pointer in an arbitrary widget. This facility is referred to a *mouse tracker*. For purposes of demonstration, the mouse tracker displays the current position of the pointer in an XmLabel widget, but it could be used in other ways. Let's first examine the body of a simple driver program to test the mouse tracker, named `mousetracks`.

```
1    /***********************************************************
2     * mousetracks.c: Driver to test the mouse tracker module
3     ***********************************************************/
4    #include <Xm/Xm.h>
5    #include <Xm/MainW.h>
6    #include <Xm/DrawingA.h>
7
8    extern Widget CreateMouseTracker ( Widget parent, Widget target );
9
10   void main ( int argc, char **argv )
11   {
12       Widget          shell, mainWindow, target, tracker;
```

```
13          XtAppContext app;
14
15      /*
16       * Initialize Xt.
17       */
18
19          shell = XtAppInitialize ( &app, "Mousetracks",  NULL,  0,
20                                      &argc, argv,   NULL,  NULL, 0 );
21
22
23      /*
24       * Create a main window widget, to hold
25       * all the other widgets.
26       */
27
28          mainWindow = XtCreateManagedWidget ( "mainW",
29                                               xmMainWindowWidgetClass,
30                                               shell, NULL, 0 );
31      /*
32       *  Create the widget in which to track the
33       *  motion of the pointer.
34       */
35
36          target = XtCreateManagedWidget ( "target",
37                                           xmDrawingAreaWidgetClass,
38                                           mainWindow, NULL, 0 );
39
40      /*
41       * Create the mouse tracker.
42       */
43
44          tracker = CreateMouseTracker ( mainWindow, target );
45
46          XtVaSetValues ( mainWindow, XmNworkWindow, target,
47                                      XmNmessageWindow, tracker,
48                                      NULL );
49
50          XtRealizeWidget ( shell );
51          XtAppMainLoop ( app );
52  }
```

This test driver initializes Xt and then creates an XmMainWindow widget that manages two children, an XmDrawingArea widget in whose window the pointer's location is tracked, and the tracker widget itself. Figure 8.8 shows the widget tree formed by the widgets in this example.

The function CreateMouseTracker() creates the mouse tracker widget, and takes two arguments. The first indicates a parent widget that manages the XmLabel widget created by the mouse tracker. The second specifies the target widget in which the pointer position is to be tracked. The mouse tracker only reports the pointer position when the pointer is in the target widget.

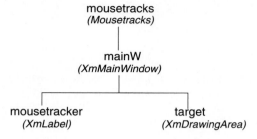

Figure 8.8 The mousetracks widget tree.

The function `CreateMouseTracker()` can be written as follows:

```
1   /*************************************************
2    * mousetracker.c: The mouse tracker facility
3    *************************************************/
4   #include <Xm/Xm.h>
5   #include <Xm/Label.h>
6
7   static void TrackMousePosition ( Widget w, XtPointer clientData,
8                                     XEvent *event, Boolean  *flag );
9   static void ClearTracker ( Widget w, XtPointer clientData,
10                             XEvent *event, Boolean  *flag );
11  extern void wprintf ( Widget w, const char * format, ...);
12
13  Widget CreateMouseTracker ( Widget parent, Widget target )
14  {
15      Widget        tracker;
16
17      /*
18       * Create the tracker widget and register event
19       * handlers for the target widget.
20       */
21
22      tracker = XtCreateManagedWidget ( "mousetracker",
23                                         xmLabelWidgetClass,
24                                         parent, NULL, 0 );
25      wprintf ( tracker, " " );
26
27      XtAddEventHandler ( target, LeaveWindowMask, FALSE,
28                          ClearTracker, ( XtPointer ) tracker );
29      XtAddEventHandler ( target, PointerMotionMask, FALSE,
30                          TrackMousePosition, ( XtPointer ) tracker );
31
32      return ( tracker );
33  }
```

This function creates an XmLabel widget, `tracker`, as a child of the given parent widget and then registers two event handlers for the specified `target` widget. The first event handler handles `PointerMotion` events while the other handles `LeaveNotify` events. The `tracker` widget is specified as client data for both event handlers.

The function `wprintf()` is a simple routine that displays text in a widget using the same syntax as `printf()`. This function is described after the description of the tracker module.

Xt invokes the event handler `TrackMouseMotion()` whenever the user moves the pointer within the `target` window. This function extracts the current pointer location from the event structure and displays it in the `tracker` widget. This event handler is defined as:

```
34  static void TrackMousePosition ( Widget       w,
35                                    XtPointer   clientData,
36                                    XEvent      *event,
37                                    Boolean     *flag )
38  {
39      Widget  tracker = ( Widget ) clientData;
40
41      /*
42       * Extract the position of the pointer from the event
43       * and display it in the tracker widget.
44       */
45
46      wprintf ( tracker, "X: %04d, Y: %04d",
47                event->xmotion.x, event->xmotion.y );
48  }
```

It is usually a bad idea to display status information when it is no longer valid, such as when the pointer is no longer contained by the target window. The `ClearTracker()` event handler clears the information displayed by the `tracker` widget when the pointer is moved out of the `target` widget's window.

```
49  static void ClearTracker ( Widget       w,
50                             XtPointer   clientData,
51                             XEvent      *event,
52                             Boolean     *flag )
53  {
54      Widget  tracker = ( Widget ) clientData;
55
56      /*
57       * Display an empty string in the tracker widget.
58       */
59
60      wprintf ( tracker, " " );
61  }
```

The mouse tracker could be added to nearly any application without interfering with the normal operation of the program. Xt allows applications to define multiple event handlers for each event, so the event handlers added by `CreateMouseTracker()` are invoked in addition to any other handlers registered with the target widget for the same events.

The wprintf() Function

The function `wprintf()` is a useful function that uses `XtSetValues()` to change the string displayed in any subclass of the XmLabel widget class. This function has a form similar to the `stdio` library function `fprintf()`, except that it displays its output in a widget. The function uses the utility macros found in the UNIX header file /usr/include/varargs.h in combination with `vsprintf()` to handle a variable number of arguments.

```
1     /********************************************************
2      * wprintf.c: A convenient function that displays text
3      *            in a label or button, providing the same
4      *            syntax as printf()
5      ********************************************************/
6     #include <varargs.h>
7     #include <stdio.h>
8     #include <Xm/Xm.h>
9     #include <Xm/Label.h>
10
11    void wprintf ( va_alist )
12      va_dcl
13    {
14        Widget      w;
15        char        *format;
16        va_list     args;
17        char        str[1000];   /* DANGER: Fixed buffer size */
18        Arg         wargs[1];
19        XmString    xmstr;
20
21        /*
22         * Init the variable length args list.
23         */
24
25        va_start ( args );
26
27        /*
28         * Extract the destination widget.
29         * Make sure it is a subclass of XmLabel.
30         */
31
32        w = va_arg ( args, Widget );
33
34        if ( !XtIsSubclass ( w, xmLabelWidgetClass ) )
35            XtError ( "wprintf () requires a Label Widget" );
36
37
```

```
38      /*
39       * Extract the format to be used.
40       */
41
42      format = va_arg ( args, char * );
43
44      /*
45       * Use vsprintf to format the string to be displayed in the
46       * XmLabel widget, then convert it to a compound string
47       */
48
49      vsprintf ( str, format, args );
50
51      xmstr =  XmStringCreateLtoR ( str, XmFONTLIST_DEFAULT_TAG );
52      XtVaSetValues ( w, XmNlabelString, xmstr, NULL );
53      XmStringFree ( xmstr );
54
55      va_end ( args );
56  }
```

Not all systems support varargs, and not all system support `vsprintf()`. For systems that do not support varargs, this function can be replaced by code that calls `sprintf()` to format the arguments into an intermediate buffer, which can then be converted to a compound string and displayed in a widget.

A Variation

The previous example uses event handlers in a very straightforward way, but there are many other techniques that could be explored. For example, the mouse tracker facility could be modified to report the position of the pointer only while a mouse button is pressed. To support this behavior, `CreateMouseTracker()` and its associated functions must be reimplemented. In this example, lines of code that are changed from the previous version are shown in bold.

```
1      /********************************************************
2       * mousetracker2.c: Track the position of the pointer
3       *                  while the mouse button is held down
4       ********************************************************/
5      #include <Xm/Xm.h>
6      #include <Xm/Label.h>
7
8      static void ShowMousePosition ( Widget     w,
9                                      XtPointer  clientData,
10                                     XEvent     *event,
11                                     Boolean    *flag );
12     static void TrackMousePosition ( Widget     w,
13                                      XtPointer clientData,
14                                      XEvent     *event,
15                                      Boolean    *flag );
```

```
16   static void ClearTracker ( Widget      w,
17                               XtPointer  clientData,
18                               XEvent     *event,
19                               Boolean    *flag );
20   extern void wprintf ( Widget w, const char * format, ...);
21
22   Widget CreateMouseTracker ( Widget parent, Widget target )
23   {
24       Widget          tracker;
25
26       /*
27        * Create the tracker widget and register event
28        * handlers for the target widget.
29        */
30
31       tracker = XtCreateManagedWidget ( "mousetracker",
32                                         xmLabelWidgetClass,
33                                         parent, NULL, 0 );
34       wprintf ( tracker, " " );
35
36       XtAddEventHandler ( target, ButtonPressMask, FALSE,
37                           ShowMousePosition, ( XtPointer ) tracker );
38
39       XtAddEventHandler ( target, ButtonMotionMask, FALSE,
40                           TrackMousePosition, ( XtPointer ) tracker );
41
42       XtAddEventHandler ( target,
43                           ButtonReleaseMask | LeaveWindowMask,
44                           FALSE, ClearTracker, ( XtPointer ) tracker );
45
46       return ( tracker );
47   }
```

This variation registers three event handlers for the `target` widget. The function `TrackMousePosition()` (implemented exactly as described earlier) is registered for `MotionNotify` events using the `ButtonMotionMask` instead of the `PointerMotionMask` event mask. This function is only invoked if the user moves the pointer while holding down a mouse button.

This version of the mouse tracker registers a new event handler for `ButtonPress` events. This function, `ShowMousePosition()`, is implemented as follows:

```
48   static void ShowMousePosition ( Widget      w,
49                                    XtPointer  clientData,
50                                    XEvent     *event,
51                                    Boolean    *flag )
52   {
53       Widget  tracker = ( Widget ) clientData;
54
```

```
55      /*
56       * Extract the position of the pointer from the event
57       * and display it in the tracker widget.
58       */
59
60      wprintf ( tracker, "X: %04d, Y: %04d",
61                 event->xbutton.x, event->xbutton.y );
62  }
```

This function is nearly the same as `TrackMousePosition()`, except that it extracts the position of the pointer from the `XButtonPressedEvent` structure, using the `xbutton` member of the `XEvent` union rather than `xmotion`. The same function could be used to handle both of these events, because the definition of the `XButtonEvent` and `XMotionEvent` event structures are identical, except for the names. The expressions:

```
event->xbutton.x
```

and:

```
event->xmotion.x
```

both access the same member in the event structure. However, it is not good programming practice to rely on such implementation-dependent details.

The function `TrackMousePosition()` is unchanged:

```
63  static void TrackMousePosition ( Widget      w,
64                                    XtPointer   clientData,
65                                    XEvent      *event,
66                                    Boolean     *flag )
67  {
68      Widget  tracker = ( Widget ) clientData;
69
70      /*
71       * Extract the position of the pointer from the event
72       * and display it in the tracker widget.
73       */
74
75      wprintf ( tracker, "X: %04d, Y: %04d",
76                 event->xmotion.x, event->xmotion.y );
77  }
```

In this version of the mouse tracker facility, the function `ClearTracker()` (also implemented exactly as in the earlier version) is registered as an event handler for both `LeaveNotify` and `ButtonRelease` events by passing the inclusive-OR of both event masks to `XtAddEventHandler()`. When a single function handles multiple types of events, the event handler can check the `type` member of the event to determine the event type. In this example,

`ClearTracker()` performs the same action in either case. This function is implemented as follows:

```
78   static void ClearTracker ( Widget      w,
79                              XtPointer  clientData,
80                              XEvent     *event,
81                              Boolean    *flag )
82   {
83       Widget  tracker = ( Widget ) clientData;
84
85       /*
86        * Display an empty string in the tracker widget.
87        */
88
89       wprintf ( tracker, " " );
90   }
```

8.5   Managing the Event Queue

Most applications use the function `XtAppMainLoop()` to remove events from the event queue and dispatch them to the appropriate widgets. However, occasionally an application needs to have more control over this process. Xlib provides many functions that can be used to examine and manipulate the event queue. These are seldom needed by applications that use Xt and Motif, although they can be used if needed. Xt provides its own versions of the most common functions for examining the event queue:

```
    XtInputMask XtAppPending ( XtAppContext app )
```

and:

```
    Boolean XtAppPeekEvent ( XtAppContext app, XEvent *event )
```

`XtAppPeekEvent()` copies the event at the top of the event queue into the application-supplied event structure, but does not remove the event from the event queue. `XtAppPending()` returns a mask of type `XtInputMask` that indicates the type of input available or zero if the event queue is empty. The possible return values include `XtIMXEvent`, `XtIMTimer`, `XtIMAlternateInput`, and `XtIMAll`.

A return value of `XtIMXEvent` indicates that an X event is pending, while a return value of `XtIMTimer` indicates that an Xt timeout event is waiting to be handled. (See Section 8.6.) If `XtIMAlternateInput` is returned, there is input available from an input source, registered using `XtAppAddInput()`. (See Section 8.8.) A return value of `XtIMAll` indicates that all types of events are pending. For example, `XtAppPending()` could be used to allow an application to perform other tasks whenever there are no events in the event queue. For example, a custom event loop might be written as follows:

```
while ( !done )
    if ( XtAppPending ( app ) )
    {
        XtAppNextEvent ( app, &event );
        XtDispatchEvent ( &event )
    }
    else
    {
        /* Do something else for a while */
        /* When completely done, set done = TRUE */
    }
```

This approach should be used with care, because an event loop like this never blocks and therefore can consume all of the available CPU cycles. Section 8.6 and Section 8.7 describe two better techniques for performing other tasks in between handling events.

Another use of `XtAppPending()` is to allow an application to handle all pending events before proceeding. For example, the following function handles all pending events and then returns:

```
void HandlePendingEvents ( XtAppContext app )
{
    XEvent event;

    while ( XtAppPending ( app ) )
    {
        XtAppNextEvent ( app, &event );
        XtDispatchEvent ( &event )
    }
}
```

A function like this can be useful when an application is unable to return to the main event loop, but needs to handle events to keep the user interface alive. Motif provides a similar function:

```
void XmUpdateDisplay ( Display *display )
```

which can be useful at times. `XmUpdateDisplay()` only processes `Expose` events, which is often a useful restriction. The `HandlePendingEvents()` function shown above receives and dispatches all events, regardless of their type. In some cases, it might also be useful to write custom event loops that examine the return value of XtAppPending() and treat timer events, input events, and so, differently. However, because all X applications are so dependent on events, it is important to be careful when writing custom event loops. It is easy to inadvertently introduce problems with such event loops that can be very difficult to detect and debug.

8.6   Using Timeouts

Although many useful X applications only respond to user input, some applications need to perform other tasks as well. The next few sections explore facilities provided by Xt that extend Xlib's notion of events to allow applications to use Xt's event dispatching mechanism to perform these tasks. One such feature, described in this section, allows applications to register a callback function to be invoked by Xt when a specified length of time has passed.

Applications can use the function:

```
XtIntervalId XtAppAddTimeOut ( XtAppContext    app,
                               int             interval,
                               XtTimerCallback proc,
                               XtPointer       clientData )
```

to register a timeout callback and specify the time delay before it is invoked. `XtAppAddTimeOut()` returns an ID of type `XtIntervalId` that uniquely identifies this timeout event. Following the obligatory application context, the second argument to `XtAppAddTimeOut()` specifies the length of time, in milliseconds, until Xt should invoke the specified callback function. The `clientData` parameter allows applications to specify some client data to be passed to the timeout callback function when it is called.

The form of a timeout callback must be:

```
void TimeoutCallback ( XtPointer clientData, XtIntervalId *id )
```

where `clientData` is the client data specified in the call to `XtAppAddTimeOut()` and `id` is a pointer to the `XtIntervalId` identifier of the timeout event. When a timeout event occurs, Xt invokes the corresponding callback and then automatically removes the callback. Therefore, timeout events are only invoked once.

Applications can use the function:

```
XtRemoveTimeOut ( XtIntervalId id )
```

to remove a timeout callback before the timeout occurs. The argument, `id`, must be the `XtIntervalId` of the timer event to be removed.

Cyclic Timeouts

Applications often need to perform some action repeatedly at regular intervals. Although Xt automatically removes timeout callbacks when the timeout event occurs, applications can arrange for timeout callbacks to be invoked repeatedly by designing the callback to re-install itself each time it is called. An obvious application of this technique is a clock. A digital clock can be written easily using an XmLabel widget and a single timeout callback. The body of the clock program is:

```
1    /*******************************************************
2     * xclock: Demonstrate the use of timeout callbacks
3     *******************************************************/
4    #include <Xm/Xm.h>
5    #include <Xm/Label.h>
6    #include <time.h>
7
8    extern void wprintf ( Widget w, const char * format, ... );
9    static void UpdateTime ( XtPointer    clientData,
10                            XtIntervalId id );
11
12   void main ( int argc, char **argv )
13   {
14       Widget        shell, face;
15       XtAppContext app ;
16
17       shell = XtAppInitialize ( &app, "XClock",  NULL, 0,
18                                 &argc, argv, NULL, NULL, 0 );
19
20       face = XtCreateManagedWidget ( "face", xmLabelWidgetClass,
21                                      shell, NULL, 0 );
22       /*
23        * Get the initial time.
24        */
25
26       UpdateTime ( ( XtPointer ) face, NULL );
27
28       XtRealizeWidget ( shell );
29       XtAppMainLoop ( app );
30   }
```

Before entering the main loop, this program calls the function `UpdateTime()` to display the initial time in the widget. The `UpdateTime()` function can be implemented as follows. Notice that this function uses the `wprintf()` function described on page 266.

```
31   static void UpdateTime ( XtPointer clientData, XtIntervalId id )
32   {
33       Widget w = ( Widget ) clientData;
34       long   tloc, rounded_tloc, next_minute;
35
36       /*
37        * Get the system time.
38        */
39
40       time ( &tloc );
41
42       /*
43        * Convert the time to a string and display it,
```

```
44           * after rounding it down to the last minute.
45           */
46
47           rounded_tloc = tloc / 60 * 60;
48
49           wprintf ( w, "%s", ctime ( &rounded_tloc ) );
50
51       /*
52        * Adjust the time to reflect the time until
53        * the next round minute.
54        */
55
56           next_minute = ( 60 - tloc % 60 ) * 1000;
57
58       /*
59        * Xt removes timeouts when they occur,
60        * so re-register the function.
61        */
62
63           XtAppAddTimeOut ( XtWidgetToApplicationContext ( w ),
64                             next_minute, UpdateTime, ( XtPointer ) w );
65   }
```

This function uses the UNIX system call `time()` to determine the current time in seconds since 00:00:00 GMT (Greenwich Mean Time), Jan 1, 1970. After rounding the time to the nearest minute, the function calls the UNIX library routine `ctime()` to convert this value to a string representing the current time and date. After displaying the string in the XmLabel widget, `UpdateTime()` registers itself as a timeout callback. Each time the callback is invoked, it re-registers itself.

The delay until the next timeout event is calculated to occur on the next full minute, to keep the clock reasonably accurate in spite of any variations in the timeouts. The correction is necessary because the Xt timeout callbacks can only be called when the application is in the event loop. It is possible, therefore, for timeout callbacks to miss their intended interval by large amounts. It is also important to understand that timeout callbacks are not interrupt-driven. They are simply called from the Xt main event loop as part of the event dispatching procedure. If an application does not return to the event loop, any registered timeout callbacks will not be called.

Figure 8.9 shows the digital clock created by this example.

Figure 8.9 xclock: A digital clock.

8.7   Work Procedures

Xt supports still another type of callback function known as a *work procedure* that provides a limited form of background processing. A work procedure is a callback function invoked by Xt whenever there are no events pending in the application's event queue. A work procedure takes only a single argument, which is client-defined data. The procedure is expected to return TRUE if the callback should be removed after it is called, and FALSE otherwise. Applications can register a work procedure using the function:

```
XtWorkProcId XtAppAddWorkProc ( XtAppContext app,
                                XtWorkProc   proc,
                                XtPointer    clientDdata )
```

This function returns an ID that identifies the work procedure. The `clientData` argument specifies some application-defined data to be passed to the work procedure.

Work procedures can be removed by calling the function:

```
void XtRemoveWorkProc ( XtWorkProcId id )
```

where `id` is the identifier returned by `XtAddWorkProc()`.

Work procedures can be used to simulate background processing. When used in this manner, the work procedure must perform a small task and return quickly to allow the application to continue to be responsive to the user. If a task involves regular, periodic operations, an Xt timeout callback may be more appropriate. However, a work procedure can be used effectively when a function simply needs to be called as often as possible until a task is completed.

Work procedures are sometimes used to perform a series of actions upon startup after the application's user interface has appeared. For example, imagine a text editor that sometimes loads a large file and displays the file's contents in an XmText widget upon startup. The user's perception of the application's startup time may be improved by reading and displaying reasonably sized pieces of the file each time a work procedure is called. When using this approach, an application's user interface may appear on the screen more rapidly, and the application can begin to handle events, thereby handling the exposure events necessary to draw the widgets in the user interface. The work procedures begin to load the file once all initial events have been processed.

Work procedures are also used as a convenient way to specify that a function should be executed once control is returned to the application's main event loop. For example, an application might display a busy cursor, register a work procedure that restores the normal cursor when it is called, and then start a long operation. The busy cursor will be displayed as long as the application does not return to the event loop. Once the application does return to the event loop, any pending events are processed, and then the work procedure will be called to restore the original cursor.

The following example demonstrates this technique:

```
1    /**********************************************************
2     * busy.c: Demonstrate the use of a work procedure
3     *           to unset a busy cursor
4     **********************************************************/
5    #include <Xm/Xm.h>
6    #include <Xm/PushB.h>
7    #include <X11/cursorfont.h>
8    #include <unistd.h>
9
10   static void DoTask ( Widget     w,
11                        XtPointer clientData,
12                        XtPointer callData );
13   static void DisplayBusyCursor ( Widget w );
14   static Boolean RemoveBusyCursor ( XtPointer clientData );
15
16   void main ( int argc, char **argv )
17   {
18       Widget   shell, button;
19
20       XtAppContext app;
21
22       /*
23        * Initialize Xt and create a button that starts a long task
24        */
25
26       shell = XtAppInitialize ( &app, "Busy", NULL,  0,
27                                 &argc, argv, NULL, NULL, 0 );
28
29       button = XtCreateManagedWidget ( "pushme", xmPushButtonWidgetClass,
30                                        shell, NULL, 0 );
31
32       XtAddCallback ( button, XmNactivateCallback,
33                       DoTask, NULL );
34
35       XtRealizeWidget ( shell );
36       XtAppMainLoop ( app );
37   }
```

The body of this program creates a button that executes a function named doTask() when it is pushed. The function doTask() simulates a lengthy task. This function simply calls DisplayBusyCursor() and then sleeps for five seconds.

```
38   static void DoTask ( Widget w, XtPointer clientData, XtPointer callData )
39   {
40       DisplayBusyCursor ( w );
41
42       sleep ( 5 ); /* simulate a long activity */
43   }
```

The function `DisplayBusyCursor()` creates a busy cursor using the Xlib function `XCreateFontCursor()`. This function takes a `Display` pointer and an index, defined in the X header file cursorfont.h, that represents a busy cursor. The Xlib function `XDefineCursor()` causes a cursor to be displayed in a window. The call to `XFlush()` causes all pending requests not yet processed by the X server to be handled immediately. Without this call, the X server might not handle the request to display the cursor until later. Finally, `DisplayBusyCursor()` installs a work procedure to be called when the application returns to its event loop.

```
44  void DisplayBusyCursor ( Widget w )
45  {
46      static cursor = NULL;
47
48      if ( !cursor )
49          cursor = XCreateFontCursor ( XtDisplay ( w ), XC_watch );
50
51      XDefineCursor ( XtDisplay ( w ), XtWindow ( w ), cursor );
52
53      XFlush ( XtDisplay ( w ) );
54
55      XtAppAddWorkProc ( XtWidgetToApplicationContext ( w ),
56                         RemoveBusyCursor, ( XtPointer ) w );
57  }
```

The function `RemoveBusyCursor()` is installed as a work procedure before the application enters its busy stage and called when the application returns to the event loop. `RemoveBusyCursor()` just calls the Xlib function, `XUndefineCursor()`, to revert the given window to its original cursor.

```
58  Boolean RemoveBusyCursor ( XtPointer clientData )
59  {
60      Widget w = ( Widget ) clientData;
61
62      XUndefineCursor ( XtDisplay ( w ), XtWindow ( w ) );
63
64      return ( TRUE );
65  }
```

8.8   Handling Other Input Sources

Many X applications must accept input from sources other than the X event queue. Xt provides a simple way to handle additional input sources, by allowing applications to define callbacks to be invoked when input is available from a file descriptor. The function:

```
XtInputId XtAppAddInput ( XtAppContext             app,
                          int                      source,
                          XtPointer                condition,
                          XtInputCallbackProc      proc,
                          XtPointer                clientData )
```

registers an input callback with Xt. `XtAppAddInput()` returns an identifier of type `XtInputId` that uniquely identifies this input source. The `source` argument must be a UNIX file number, while `condition` indicates under what circumstances the input callback should be invoked. The `condition` must be one of the constants:

```
XtInputNoneMask          XtInputReadMask
XtInputWriteMask         XtInputExceptMask
```

When the given condition occurs, Xt invokes the callback function specified by `proc`. The `clientData` parameter allows the application to provide some data to be passed to the callback function when it is called.

Input callback functions must have the form:

```
void inputCallback ( XtPointer clientData, int *fd, XtInputId *id )
```

When Xt invokes an input callback, it passes the client data provided by the application along with a pointer to the file number of the source responsible for the callback. It also provides a pointer to the `XtInputId` associated with this callback.

Input callbacks that are no longer needed can be removed using the function:

```
XtRemoveInput ( XtInputId id )
```

The argument, `id`, must be the `XtInputId` identifier for the input callback to be removed.

Using Input Callbacks

This section presents an example that uses an input callback to read from a UNIX *pipe*. Pipes provide a way to connect the output of one UNIX program to the input of another. This example uses pipes to add a mouse-driven interface to a standard UNIX utility without modifying the code of the original application in any way. The example builds a simple interface for the UNIX calculator program `bc` that allows the user to input commands using the mouse and displays the results in a window. The resulting "desktop calculator," named `xbc`, communicates with `bc` using UNIX pipes. To keep this example simple, `xbc` provides only a few basic arithmetic functions, although it could easily be extended to take advantage of more advanced features of `bc`. Figure 8.10 shows the window-based interface to `bc`.

Figure 8.10 xbc: A mouse-driven calculator.

The body of the calculator program initializes Xt and calls the application-defined function `CreateCalculator()` to create the main interface for xbc.

```
1    /******************************************
2     * xbc:An X interface to bc
3     ******************************************/
4    #include <Xm/Xm.h>
5    extern Widget  CreateCalculator ( Widget parent );
6
7    void main ( int argc, char **argv )
8    {
9        Widget        shell;
10       XtAppContext app;
11
12       /*
13        * Initialize Xt
14        */
15
16       shell = XtAppInitialize ( &app, "XBc", NULL,  0,
17                                 &argc, argv, NULL,  NULL, 0 );
18       /*
19        * Create the UI for xbc
20        */
21
```

```
22        CreateCalculator ( shell );
23
24        /*
25         *  Realize the shell and enter the event loop
26         */
27
28        XtRealizeWidget ( shell );
29        XtAppMainLoop ( app );
30  }
```

The calculator interface is implemented in a separate file that contains the `CreateCalculator()` function as well as other supporting functions. This file begins with the following include statements and function prototype declarations:

```
1     /**************************************************
2      * calc.c: The CreateCalculator() function and
3      *          other supporting functions.
4      **************************************************/
5     #include <stdio.h>
6     #include <ctype.h>
7     #include <stdlib.h>
8     #include <unistd.h>
9     #include <Xm/Xm.h>
10    #include <Xm/PushB.h>
11    #include <Xm/PanedW.h>
12    #include <Xm/RowColumn.h>
13    #include <Xm/TextF.h>
14
15    /* Declarations of private functions */
16
17    static Widget CreateButton ( char *name, Widget parent );
18    static void QuitCallback ( Widget     w,
19                               XtPointer clientData,
20                               XtPointer callData );
21    static void SendToBc ( Widget      w,
22                           XtPointer clientData,
23                           XtPointer callData );
24    static void  GetFromBc ( XtPointer  clientData,
25                             int        *fid,
26                             XtInputId *id );
27
28    /* Calculator output display and related function */
29
30    static Widget  displayWidget;
31    static void    AppendToDisplay ( char *buf );
32    static void    ClearDisplay ( void );
33    static char    *DisplayedString ( void );
34
```

```
35  /* Declare the function used to setup communication with bc */
36
37  extern void SetUpTwoWayPipe ( char *cmd );
```

The function `CreateCalculator()` creates the widgets in the xbc user interface. The main layout is handled by an XmPanedWindow widget. This paned window contains two children. The upper child is a XmTextField widget used to display data as it is entered as well as results of a calculation. The lower pane is an XmRowColumn widget used to manage the calculator buttons. The function can be written as follows:

```
38  Widget CreateCalculator ( Widget parent )
39  {
40      Widget panel, keyboard, qbutton;
41
42      /*
43       * Create a vertical paned widget as a base for the
44       * rest of the calculator.
45       */
46
47      panel = XtCreateManagedWidget ( "panel", xmPanedWindowWidgetClass,
48                                      parent, NULL, 0 );
49      /*
50       * Create the calculator display widget.
51       */
52
53      displayWidget =
54              XtVaCreateManagedWidget ( "display",
55                                        xmTextFieldWidgetClass,
56                                        panel,
57                                        XmNeditable, FALSE,
58                                        XmNcursorPositionVisible, FALSE,
59                                        NULL );
60      /*
61       * Make the keyboard, which manages 5 rows of buttons
62       */
63
64      keyboard = XtVaCreateManagedWidget ( "keyboard",
65                                           xmRowColumnWidgetClass,
66                                           panel,
67                                           XmNorientation, XmHORIZONTAL,
68                                           XmNnumColumns,  5,
69                                           XmNadjustLast,  False,
70                                           XmNpacking,     XmPACK_COLUMN,
71                                           NULL );
72      /*
73       * Create the keyboard buttons. This order makes it
74       * look like a typical desktop calculator.
75       */
```

```
76        CreateButton ( "1", keyboard );
77        CreateButton ( "2", keyboard );
78        CreateButton ( "3", keyboard );
79        CreateButton ( "+", keyboard );
80        CreateButton ( "4", keyboard );
81        CreateButton ( "5", keyboard );
82        CreateButton ( "6", keyboard );
83        CreateButton ( "-", keyboard );
84        CreateButton ( "7", keyboard );
85        CreateButton ( "8", keyboard );
86        CreateButton ( "9", keyboard );
87        CreateButton ( "*", keyboard );
88        CreateButton ( "0", keyboard );
89        CreateButton ( ".", keyboard );
90        CreateButton ( "=", keyboard );
91        CreateButton ( "/", keyboard );
92
93      /*
94       *   Create a quit button and add a callback to
95       *   handle exiting bc.
96       */
97
98      qbutton = XtCreateManagedWidget ( "quit",
99                                        xmPushButtonWidgetClass,
100                                       keyboard, NULL, 0 );
101     XtAddCallback ( qbutton, XmNactivateCallback, QuitCallback, NULL );
102
103     /*
104      * Add callback GetFromBc () --  invoked when input
105      * is available from stdin.
106      */
107
108     XtAppAddInput ( XtWidgetToApplicationContext ( parent ),
109                     fileno ( stdin ), ( XtPointer ) XtInputReadMask,
110                     GetFromBc, NULL );
111
112     /*
113      * Exec the program "bc" and set up pipes
114      * between it and and the calculator process.
115      */
116
117     SetUpTwoWayPipe ( "bc" );
118     return ( panel );
119   }
```

After creating the user interface, `CreateCalculator()` uses `XtAppAddInput()` to register a callback to be called when there is any input on `stdin`. Output from the calculator keyboard will be written to `stdout`. The function `SetUpTwoWayPipe()` runs the `bc` process and arranges for the program to be connected to **xbc**'s standard input and standard output. This is discussed in more detail later.

Figure 8.11 shows the widget tree created by **xbc**. The calculator consists of a display area (an XmText widget) and a keyboard area (an XmRowColumn widget). Both of these widgets are managed by an XmPanedWindow widget. The XmRowColumn widget manages five rows of buttons used for input to the calculator.

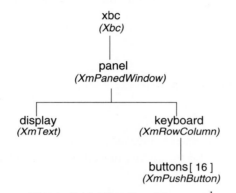

Figure 8.11 The xbc widget tree.[1]

As a convenience, the function `CreateCalculator()` calls another application-defined function, `CreateButton()` to create each widget in the keyboard. The function `CreateButton()` takes two arguments, a label for the calculator key and widget that serves as a parent for the new button. This function creates a single XmPushButton widget and adds the callback `SendToBc()` to the widget's `XmNactivateCallback` list. The name of the widget is also specified as client data, to be used as a string that is sent to **bc** when the user activates the button.

The `CreateButton()` function is implemented as follows:

```
120   static Widget CreateButton ( char *name, Widget parent )
121   {
122       Widget        button;
123
124       /*
125        * Create a single button and attach an activate callback.
126        */
127
128       button = XtCreateManagedWidget ( name, xmPushButtonWidgetClass,
129                                         parent, NULL, 0 );
130       XtAddCallback ( button, XmNactivateCallback, SendToBc, name );
131
132       return ( button );
133   }
```

---

[1] The array-style brackets after "buttons" indicate many, in this case 16, widgets.

CreateCalculator() creates a quit button, and registers a callback function to allow the user to exit the application. This callback sends the string "quit" to the bc process when the user activates the button, causing the bc process to exit.

```
134   static void QuitCallback ( Widget      w,
135                             XtPointer clientData,
136                             XtPointer callData )
137   {
138       /*
139        * Tell bc to quit, then exit.
140        */
141
142       fprintf ( stdout, "quit\n" );
143       exit ( 0 );
144   }
```

The callback function SendToBc(), invoked each time a button on the calculator's keyboard is activated, sends a command to bc by printing to stdout. As a first pass, this function could be written something like this:

```
/* INCOMPLETE VERSION */

void SendToBc ( Widget     w,
                XtPointer clientData,
                XtPointer callData )
{
    char *buffer = ( char * ) clientData;

    fprintf ( stdout, "%s", buffer );  /* Not Good Enough! */
    AppendToDisplay ( buffer );
}
```

This overly simplified function prints the characters given as client data to stdout (now attached to the input of bc) and calls AppendToDisplay(), a yet-to-be-defined function that appends a string to the current contents of the display widget. Although this function illustrates the general idea, a slightly more complex function is needed to make xbc act like a real calculator and also send correct input to bc. The complete SendToBc() function is written as follows:

```
145   static void SendToBc ( Widget      w,
146                          XtPointer clientData,
147                          XtPointer callData )
148   {
149       char      *buffer = ( char * ) clientData;
150       XmAnyCallbackStruct *cb;
151
152       static int  startNewEntry = TRUE;
153
```

```
154      /*
155       * If this is the beginning of a new operand,
156       * clear the display.
157       */
158
159      if ( startNewEntry )
160      {
161          ClearDisplay ();
162          startNewEntry = FALSE;
163      }
164
165      switch ( buffer[0] )
166      {
167        case '=':
168
169          /*
170           * If the user entered and '=', send bc a newline, clear
171           * the display, and get ready for a new operand.
172           */
173
174          fprintf ( stdout, "%s", DisplayedString () );
175          fprintf ( stdout, "\n" );
176          ClearDisplay ();
177          startNewEntry = TRUE;
178          break;
179
180        case '-':
181        case '+':
182        case '/':
183        case '*':
184        case '^':
185
186          /*
187           * If this is an operator, get the previous operand
188           * from the display buffer, and send it to bc before
189           * sending the operand.
190           */
191
192          fprintf ( stdout, "%s", DisplayedString () );
193          fprintf ( stdout, "%s", buffer );
194          ClearDisplay ();
195          break;
196
197        default:
198
199          /*
200           * Anything else must be a digit, so append it to the
201           * display buffer.
202           */
```

```
203
204            AppendToDisplay ( buffer );
205      }
206
207      fflush ( stdout );
208  }
```

SendToBc() creates an interface between the input bc expects and the behavior expected from a desktop calculator. A flag, startNewEntry, indicates when one calculation sequence has been completed and another one is beginning. If startNewEntry is TRUE, the calculator display is cleared and reset using the auxiliary function ClearDisplay().

Normally, a calculator displays the results of a calculation when the user presses the "=" key. However, bc evaluates an expression when a newline character is entered. The first case ("=") in the switch statement uses the auxiliary function DisplayedString() to retrieve the contents of the display widget, sends it to bc by printing it to stdout, and then prints a newline character to get bc to evaluate the expression. It also sets the flag startNewEntry to TRUE to signal the end of a calculation sequence, and calls ClearDisplay() to clear the display widget.

Calculators display numbers as they are entered, but do not usually display math operators. Therefore, all operators are sent to bc, but not displayed. When an operator is selected, SendToBc() prints the current contents of the display widget, followed by the operator. It then clears the display widget to prepare for the next operand.

The default case handles all digits and calls AppendToDisplay() to insert the digit at the current position in the display widget. The digit is not sent to bc until the user presses an operator, the "=" button, or any operand.

The display widget is not accessed directly in this example, but instead is manipulated by a set of simple convenience functions. The function AppendToDisplay() simply inserts text at the last position of the display widget.

```
209  static void AppendToDisplay ( char *buf )
210  {
211      XmTextFieldInsert ( displayWidget,
212                          XmTextFieldGetLastPosition ( displayWidget ),
213                          buf );
214  }
```

The DisplayedString() function is just a convenience function that retrieves the text from the XmTextField display widget.

```
215  static char *DisplayedString ()
216  {
217      return ( XmTextFieldGetString ( displayWidget ) );
218  }
```

The ClearDisplay() function displays an empty string in the display widget and resets the insertion position to zero.

```
219  static void ClearDisplay ()
220  {
221
222      /*
223       * Clear the text buffer and go to position 1.
224       */
225
226      XmTextFieldSetString ( displayWidget, "" );
227      XmTextFieldSetInsertionPosition ( displayWidget, 0 );
228  }
```

The XmTextField widget used to display values could be used directly throughout the xbc program, but using these simple access functions simplifies the code.

The input callback GetFromBc() handles output from bc. This function reads from standard input, and, after adding a NULL to the end of the buffer to NULL-terminate the string, calls AppendToDisplay() to display the string.

```
229  static void GetFromBc ( XtPointer clientData, int *fid, XtInputId *id )
230  {
231      char        buf[BUFSIZ];
232      int         nbytes, i;
233
234      /*
235       * Get all pending input and append it to the display
236       * widget. Discard lines that begin with a newline.
237       */
238
239      nbytes = read ( *fid, buf, BUFSIZ );
240
241      if ( nbytes && buf[0] != '\n' )
242      {
243
244          /*
245           * Null terminate the string at the first newline,
246           * or at the end of the bytes read.
247           */
248
249          for ( i=0;i<nbytes;i++ )
250              if ( buf[i] == '\n' )
251                  buf[i] = '\0';
252
253          buf[nbytes] = '\0';
254
255          AppendToDisplay ( buf );
256      }
257  }
```

The only complication here is that this function must handle the newline characters that bc prints after each result, by ignoring the data if the first character is a newline character and by stripping off any other newlines that appear in the input.

The SetUpTwoWayPipe() Function

The function SetUpTwoWayPipe() executes one program from another and arranges for output from the first process to be connected to the input of the second, and vice versa. Although used here to connect the xbc interface to the bc calculator program, this function could be used to establish similar pipes between any two programs. Initially, SetUpTwoWayPipe() creates two pipes and *forks* a new process. The fork() function is a UNIX system call that creates a duplicate of the calling process, and returns the process ID of the newly created process to the parent. Both processes have access to the pipes created earlier. The calling process closes its stdin and stdout file descriptors and replaces them, using the dup() system call, with one end of each pipe. Similarly, the forked process closes its input and output files and replaces them by the other end of the same pipes. Finally, the forked process is overlaid by the given executable by calling execlp().

This function is a bit oversimplified in that it performs no error checking, and does not handle various situations, such as the death of the child, that should normally be handled when using UNIX subprocesses. The function can be written as follows:

```
1   /*************************************************
2    * pipe.c: connect input and out of two programs
3    *************************************************/
4   #include         <stdio.h>
5
6   void SetUpTwoWayPipe ( const char *cmd )
7   {
8      int to_child[2];   /* pipe descriptors from parent->child */
9      int to_parent[2]; /* pipe descriptors from child->parent */
10     int   pid;
11
12     pipe ( to_child );
13     pipe ( to_parent );
14
15     if ( pid = fork (), pid == 0 )      /* in the child   */
16     {
17         close ( 0 );                    /* redirect stdin */
18         dup ( to_child[0] );
19         close ( 1 );                    /* redirect stdout*/
20         dup ( to_parent[1] );
21
22         close ( to_child[0] );          /* close pipes    */
23         close ( to_child[1] );
24         close ( to_parent[0] );
25         close ( to_parent[1] );
26
27         execlp ( cmd, cmd, NULL );       /* exec the new cmd */
28     }
```

```
29      else if ( pid > 0 )                    /* in the parent   */
30      {
31          close ( 0 );                       /* redirect stdin */
32          dup ( to_parent[0] );
33          close ( 1 );                       /* redirect stdout  */
34          dup ( to_child[1] );
35
36          setbuf ( stdout, NULL );           /* no buffered output */
37
38          close ( to_child[0] );             /* close pipes */
39          close ( to_child[1] );
40          close ( to_parent[0] );
41          close ( to_parent[1] );
42      }
43      else                                   /* error!          */
44      {
45          fprintf ( stderr,"Couldn't fork process %s\n", cmd );
46          exit ( 1 );
47      }
48  }
```

The UNIX standard I/O (`stdio`) package normally buffers its output. The function `setbuf()` turns off buffering so that all output from the parent process is sent to the child process immediately. Unfortunately, it is only possible to unbuffer the output in the parent process. To avoid problems, both processes should use unbuffered output, but the parent process does not have access to the child process in this case.

After calling `SetUpTwoWayPipe()`, when `xbc` reads from `stdin`, it is really reading from the pipe connected to the output of `bc`. When `xbc` writes to `stdout`, it is actually writing to a pipe connected to the input of `bc`. Notice that `bc` does not have to be modified in any way. As far as `bc` is concerned, it is reading from `stdin` and writing to `stdout`.

This approach can be used to create window-based interfaces to many UNIX applications. However, writing an interface to existing UNIX commands is not always straightforward, partially. because of variations in the output format of UNIX commands. In spite of UNIX conventions that encourage small applications that can be piped together in various combinations, the output of UNIX applications is often inconsistent. For example, many applications add headers at the top of each page. Others format their output differently depending on the options specified on the command line. The same utility may also behave differently on different vendor's machines. Therefore, one of the difficulties in using existing UNIX applications this way is sending the correct input to the application and parsing the results.

The pipe mechanism itself can also cause other problems. Handling all the exceptions and error conditions that can occur when using two-way pipes can be difficult. For example, this version of `SetUpTwoWayPipe()` neglects the problems that can arise when either process exits unexpectedly, and also does not attempt to handle any signals. Problems can also occur if the maximum buffer size of a pipe is exceeded. The buffer size is usually not a problem for `xbc` because only a few digits cross the pipes at any time.

8.9   Summary

This chapter examines many of the events supported by X and introduces the event-handling mecha-nisms provided by Xt. Xlib reports events whenever any aspect of a window's environment changes. Xt provides a higher level interface to the X event mechanism and also adds the ability to handle input from sources other than the X server using a similar event handling mechanism. Timeout callbacks and work procedures provide simple ways to perform tasks not directly related to user input.

It is possible to write Motif applications that never handle events directly, and that do not use work procedures or timers. In fact, Xt's event handler mechanism was originally intended for internal use by Xt and widgets. However, many large applications do need to handle some events directly, and the mechanisms described in this chapter are available to applications that need them. It is also important to remember that even applications that do not deal directly with events *are* handling events — Xt and Motif simply handle the events transparently.

Chapter 9

Using Color

Previous chapters demonstrate various simple applications using Motif. These programs use widgets to display the information specified by an application, leaving the details of rendering the information to the widgets. The next few chapters focus on Xlib facilities that allow applications to display text and graphics directly in windows. Discussing these facilities provides a better understanding of X and allows programmers to write applications that cannot be built from existing widgets alone.

To use the Xlib text and graphics functions, it is first necessary to understand the color model supported by X. This chapter discusses how X uses color, and presents a simple color palette editor as an example.

9.1 The X Color Model

X uses a flexible color model that provides a common interface to many different types of display hardware. The color model allows a properly designed application to run equally well on a variety of monochrome and color screens.

It is particularly difficult to design a color model for a window system that supports multiple processes, because most color screens support a limited number of colors. For example, a color display with a four-bit *frame buffer* supports only 16 colors at one time. Often, these 16 colors can be chosen from a large palette of available colors. It is typical for modern display hardware to support a palette of over 16 million different colors; however, on a screen with four-bit planes, only 16 of these colors can be displayed at any given time. On a system with an eight-plane frame buffer, only 256 colors can be displayed at once.

This might not be a serious problem for systems where one graphics application controls the entire screen. However, in a multiprocess window-based system, many applications are present on the screen at once, and therefore each application competes for the limited number of colors available. Applications based on Motif, with its top and bottom shadows, select and arm colors, and so on, quickly use a surprisingly large number of colors. Although Motif can be displayed on even a monochrome display, a display with only 16 colors would be quite limiting for the typical Motif application.

To make maximum use of available colors, X uses an approach that allows each application to use as many colors as it needs, but also encourages applications to share colors. The approach used by X is based on an allocation scheme in which an application requests the server to allocate only those colors it needs. If two applications request the same color, the server gives each application a pointer to the same color cell. X also supports a mechanism that allows each application to allocate as many colors as the display supports, even if those colors are different from those needed by other applications.

Colormaps

The central feature of the X color model is a *colormap*. A colormap, sometimes called a color lookup table, is an array of colors. Applications refer to colors using an index into the colormap. The colormap provides a level of indirection between the color index used by an application and the color displayed on the screen. Most displays provide a hardware colormap.

To draw a point on the screen, applications place a value in the appropriate location of the display's *frame buffer*. A frame buffer is a large contiguous area of memory. The frame buffer must contain least one bit for each individual element (pixel) on the screen. The amount of memory that corresponds to one bit for each pixel on the screen is known as a *bit plane*. The number of colors that a screen can display at one time is determined by the number of bit planes in the frame buffer, according to the relation $colors = 2^{planes}$. For example, a frame buffer with three bit planes can support eight different colors.

On most systems, the value in each pixel of the frame buffer is used as an index into the colormap. The value stored in that location of the colormap is then used to determine the color and intensity of the color shown on the screen for that pixel. Figure 9.1 shows how a typical hardware display uses the colormap to convert a value in the frame buffer to a color on the screen. Figure 9.1 illustrates a display with a three-plane frame buffer. The hardware scans each cell, or pixel, in the frame buffer, and uses the combined value of all planes as an index to the colormap. The value stored in this location in the colormap is then converted to an intensity on the screen.

Figure 9.1 shows a four-bit colormap for a monochrome display. A display with a single four-bit colormap and a single color gun can display 16 levels of a single color. Typically, a colormap supports more color intensities by adding more bits to the lookup table. Also, color displays typically divide the colormap into different fields to control each of the red, green, and blue color components.

Each X window has a virtual colormap associated with it. Before the colors in this colormap are reflected on the screen, the colormap must be *installed* into the hardware colormap. Some hardware displays allow multiple colormaps to be installed at once, but many support only one colormap at a time. By convention, X window managers install the colormap of the current focus window, allowing the application that uses this window to be displayed with the correct colors. However, when this approach is used, other applications on the screen may not be displayed in their true colors, because the colors stored in the hardware color map change, but the indexes used by applications do not.

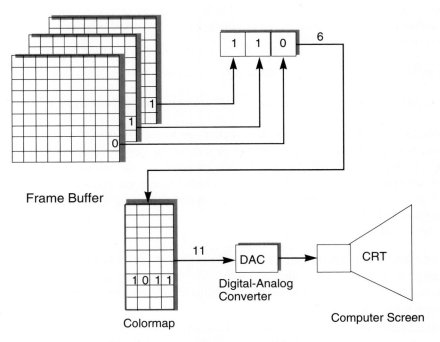

Figure 9.1 A pseudo-color architecture.

Applications can often share the same colormap. By default, windows inherit the colormap of their parent, and most applications can use the default colormap of the root window. Applications can use the macro:

```
Colormap DefaultColormap ( Display *display, int screenNumber )
```

to access the default colormap of any screen. This default colormap is installed by the X server when the server is started. The server normally allocates two colors, black and white, from the default colormap. All other color cells can be allocated by clients.

Applications can also create their own colormaps. A programmer might consider creating a new colormap when an application needs many colors, requires colors to be placed in particular locations in the colormap, or needs to alter the contents of the colormap dynamically.

Applications can use the function:

```
Colormap XCreateColormap ( Display *display,
                           Window   window,
                           Visual  *visual,
                           int      alloc )
```

to create a colormap. `XCreateColormap()` returns a unique ID for a new colormap. `XCreateColormap()` uses the `window` argument only to determine the screen where the colormap is used, so this window does not need to be the window associated with the colormap, but only a window on the same screen as that on which the colormap will be used.

Applications can use the function

```
XFreeColormap ( Display *display, Colormap cmap )
```

to free a colormap when it is no longer needed. The `cmap` argument must specify the colormap to be freed.

`XCreateColormap()` requires the programmer to specify the *visual type* of the screen. Every screen supports one or more visual types. A visual type is represented by a structure, `XVisual`, defined in the header file Xlib.h. This structure contains information about the screen, including how many colormap entries it supports, whether it supports monochrome, color, gray scale only, and so on. It is also possible for a screen to support more than one visual type, and in some case to support multiple visuals at the same time.

The visual types recognized by X are:

- `PseudoColor`: When using a `PseudoColor` visual, pixel values are treated as an index into an array of colors (a colormap) to produce independent, dynamically changeable red, green, and blue values. Most of the discussion in this chapter assumes a `PseudoColor` visual type.

- `StaticColor`: This type is similar to `PseudoColor`, except that the colormap contains predefined (fixed) values.

- `GrayScale`: This visual type is similar to `PseudoColor`, except that only a single hue (often gray) is available.

- `StaticGray`: Screens with a `StaticGray` visual type have a fixed, predetermined monochrome colormap.

- `DirectColor`: Screens that support `DirectColor` decompose pixel values into separate red, green, and blue fields. Each component is then used as an index into a separate color lookup table.

- `TrueColor`: This visual type is similar to `DirectColor` except that the colormap contains pre-defined, fixed values.

The previous discussion of colormaps applies most directly to a screen whose visual type is `PseudoColor`.

The default visual structure for a particular screen can be obtained using the Xlib macro:

```
DefaultVisual ( Display *display, int screenNumber )
```

Some systems support multiple visual types, in which case the default visual type may not be the correct one to use. A valid visual type can also be obtained by calling the Xlib function:

```
Status XMatchVisualInfo ( Displa        *display,
                          int            screenNumber,
                          int            depth,
                          int            class,
                          XVisualInfo *info )
```

This function returns a status of TRUE if it was able to find a visual type to match the specified screen and depth. It fills in the info argument, which is an XVisualInfo struct. This structure contains a variety of information about the visual type. In particular, the visual member of this structure contains a valid visual type. For example, the following code segment can be used to determine if it is possible to use a PseudoColor visual type on a certain screen.

```
Status       result;
Display      *dpy    = XtDisplay ( widget );
int           screen = DefaultScreen ( dpy );
XVisualInfo  info;
Visual       *my_visual;

result = XMatchVisualInfo ( dpy, screen, DefaultDepth ( dpy, screen ),
                            PseudoColor, &info ) )
if ( result )
    my_visual = info.visual;
```

Once a valid visual type has been identified, a colormap can be created. Colormaps contain no colors when first created. Before an application can store colors in a colormap, the application must *allocate* color cells. The last argument to XCreateColormap() specifies how many entries in the colormap should be allocated initially. This argument must be one of the constants AllocNone or AllocAll. The value AllocNone must be used for screens with a static visual type.

Windows and Colormaps

Before an application can display colors defined by a colormap, the colormap must be installed. Colormaps are installed by the window manager, which typically installs the colormap associated with a window when that window receives input focus. It is common for a window to inherit the colormap of its parent. Therefore, by default, most windows use the colormap associated with the root window. Applications whose windows need to use a different colormap can associate a colormap with a window by calling the following function:

```
XSetWindowColormap ( Display *display, Window window, Colormap cmap )
```

Applications that wish to use their own colormap should call this function to set the colormap of their top-level window and rely on the window manager to install it for them.

Some applications need to support multiple colormaps within the same application or even within a window hierarchy. Applications whose windows require a different colormap than the

colormap used by the top-level window must call `XSetWindowColormap()` to associate a
colormap with each affected window. In addition, an application that uses multiple colormaps must
list the windows whose colormaps must be installed in a property on the top-level window, so that
window manager can install the proper colormaps. This list can be provided by calling the function:

```
Status XSetWMColormapWindows ( Display *display,
                               Window   toplevel_window,
                               Window  *colormap_windows;
                               int      count )
```

The arguments to this function must specify the window on which the property is to be stored
(usually an application's top-level shell window), and a list of windows whose colormaps should be
installed when the top-level window gets input focus. The `count` parameter specifies the number
of windows in the list.

The success of using multiple colormaps within the same main window depends on the
colormap support provided by the display on which the application is running. If a display can only
support one colormap at a time, windows that use anything except the currently installed colormap
will not be displayed correctly. On systems that support multiple colormaps at the same time, each
window will be displayed correctly, using its own colormap, as long as the number of colormaps
supported by the hardware is not exceeded.

Standard Colormaps

X supports the concept of *standard colormaps*. Standard colormaps may be stored in a property (see
Chapter 14) in the X server, where they can be retrieved by any application that wishes to use them.
Xlib defines the property names for several standard colormaps, including `RGB_DEFAULT_MAP`,
`RGB_BEST_MAP`, and `RGB_GRAY_MAP`. Notice that only the *names* of these colormaps are
defined. The colormaps, as well as the exact organization of the colormaps, are not precisely defined.
These colormaps exist only if some application (most often a window manager) defines them and
stores them in the server.

A standard colormap can be stored in the server using the Xlib function:

```
XSetStandardColormap ( Display           *display,
                       Window             window,
                       XStandardColormap *cmap,
                       Atom               property )
```

The `XStandardColormap` structure contains a member that is a `Colormap`, but also contains
other information about the colormap. Once a standard colormap has been stored in the server,
applications can use the following Xlib function to retrieve a standard colormap from the server:

```
Status XGetStandardColormap ( Display           *display,
                              Window             window,
                              XStandardColormap *cmap,
                              Atom               property )
```

Programmers who are interested in using standard colormaps should refer to the ICCCM for details on how they are meant to be used.

Allocating Colors

Once an application has access to a colormap for a dynamic visual type, the application can allocate colors and manipulate cells in that colormap. The Xlib functions that allocate colors use an XColor structure. This structure includes the members:

```
unsigned long   pixel;
unsigned short  red, green, blue;
char            flags;
```

The pixel member indicates an index into the colormap, while the red, green, and blue members represent corresponding components of a color. The flags member indicates which of the red, green, and blue members contain valid values. The flags member can be set to the inclusive OR of DoRed, DoGreen, and/or DoBlue.

Colors are specified by the intensity of each of their red, green, and blue (RGB) components. The values of these components can range from 0 to 65535, where 0 corresponds to the lowest intensity of a color component, and 65535 corresponds to the highest intensity. The X server scales these values to the range of color intensities supported by the hardware. For example, an XColor structure that represents bright white can be initialized as follows:

```
XColor color;
color.red   = 65535;
color.green = 65535;
color.blue  = 65535;
```

A color structure can be initialized to represent bright red with:

```
XColor color;
color.red   = 65535;
color.green = 0;
color.blue  = 0;
```

Color cells of a colormap can be *read-only* or *read-write*. The color components in a read-only cell cannot be altered, and therefore can be shared between all applications that use the same colormap. Attempts to change the value of a read-only cell generate an error. A read-write cell cannot be shared between applications, because the application that allocates the cell can change it at any time.

The Xlib function:

```
Status XAllocColor ( Display *display, Colormap cmap, XColor *color )
```

allocates a read-only entry in the specified colormap. This function requires an XColor structure that specifies the RGB components of the color to be allocated. If some other application has already

allocated the same color as a read-only cell, the same cell is reused and the `pixel` member of the
`XColor` structure is set to the value of the existing colormap cell. Otherwise, `XAllocColor()`
attempts to store the given color components in the next available cell of the colormap `cmap`. If
successful, the function fills in the `pixel` member of the `XColor` structure to the newly allocated
color cell and returns a status of `TRUE`.

To see how `XAllocColor()` is used, let's write a function named `GetPixel()` that
allocates a color cell from the default colormap and loads it with a color. The function takes a widget
and the red, green, and blue components of the desired color as input. `GetPixel()` returns a pixel
index that represents the specified color.

```
1      /***********************************************************
2       * getpixel.c: Implement GetPixel(), a function that allocates
3       *             a color to represent the given rgb value
4       ***********************************************************/
5      #include <Xm/Xm.h>
6
7      Pixel GetPixel ( Widget w, short red, short green, short blue )
8      {
9         Display *dpy  = XtDisplay ( w );
10        int      scr  = DefaultScreen ( dpy );
11        Colormap cmap = DefaultColormap ( dpy, scr );
12        XColor   color;
13
14        /*
15         * Fill in the color structure.
16         */
17
18        color.red   = red;
19        color.green = green;
20        color.blue  = blue;
21        color.flags = DoRed | DoGreen | DoBlue;
22
23        /*
24         * Try to allocate the color.
25         */
26
27        if ( XAllocColor ( dpy, cmap, &color ) )
28          return ( color.pixel );
29        else
30        {
31           XtWarning ( "Couldn't allocate requested color" );
32           return ( BlackPixel ( dpy, scr ) );
33        }
34    }
```

Whenever color allocation fails, applications should always be prepared to use one of the
default values, usually black or white, available in all visual types. Applications can use the macros:

```
Pixel BlackPixel ( Display *display, int screen )
Pixel WhitePixel ( Display *display, int screen )
```

to access the default pixels that represent black and white on a particular screen.

Because new colors are allocated in the next available cell of the colormap, applications must not assume that the index that represents a particular color in a shared colormap is the same each time the application runs. The exact index used to refer to a particular color depends on the order in which all applications request the colors.

Applications sometimes need to be able to retrieve the color components associated with any pixel index of a colormap. The function:

```
XQueryColor ( Display display, Colormap cmap, XColor *color )
```

fills in the RGB components of the XColor structure with the values found in the colormap entry indicated by the pixel member of the structure. The function

```
XQueryColors ( Display *display, Colormap cmap,
               XColor *colors, int ncolors )
```

fills in the RGB components of an array of colors.

Sometimes applications need to set up a colormap in a specific way, controlling the colors in each cell. Such applications should first allocate the number of color cells needed, by calling the function:

```
Status XAllocColorCells ( Display      *display,
                          Colormap        cmap,
                          Boolean         contig,
                          unsigned long *planes_mask,
                          unsigned int   nplanes,
                          unsigned long *pixels,
                          unsigned int   ncells )
```

This function allocates $ncells * 2^{nplanes}$ read-write color cells. Applications that do not need to control the bit planes of the screen can specify nplanes as zero.[1]

The function XAllocColorCells() allocates read-write color cells. If the application requires the color cells to be contiguous, it must set the contig argument to TRUE. Otherwise the planes and cells are allocated from wherever they are available. XAllocColorCells() fails and returns a status of FALSE if it cannot allocate the exact number of planes and cells. If the server is able to allocate the requested number of colors, this function returns the allocated color cells in the pixels parameter, which must be an array of Pixel. If the application requests one or more planes,

---

[1] A common mistake is to attempt to allocate all planes and all color cells. This generates more colors than the screen supports. For example, on a screen with four bit-planes (and therefore 16 colors), a request such as

```
XAllocColorCells ( display, cmap, TRUE, planes, 4, cells, 16 );
```

attempts to allocate 16 * 2 4, or 256 colors.

the `planes_mask` argument, which must also be an array of unsigned integers, returns a mask with all bits that correspond to the allocated planes set to one.

Once color cells are allocated, applications can use the function:

```
XStoreColor ( Display *display, Colormap cmap, XColor *color )
```

to alter the values stored in each cell of the colormap. The `color` argument must be an `XColor` structure that contains both the `pixel` value and the `red`, `green`, and `blue` values to store in that cell. Let's see how this works by defining a function, `LoadRgb()`, that loads the colors red, green, and blue into three consecutive color cells of the default colormap. The pixel indexes are assigned to the parameters `red`, `green`, and `blue`.

```
1    /**********************************************************
2     * loadrgb.c: Implement LoadRGB(), a sample function
3     *            that allocates and returns three colors
4     **********************************************************/
5    #include <Xm/Xm.h>
6
7    void LoadRGB ( Widget w, Pixel *red, Pixel *green, Pixel *blue )
8    {
9        Display *dpy  = XtDisplay ( w );
10       int      scr  = DefaultScreen ( dpy );
11       Colormap cmap = DefaultColormap ( dpy, scr );
12       XColor   color;
13       Pixel    cells[3];
14
15       /*
16        * Try to allocate three consecutive color cells.
17        */
18
19       if ( XAllocColorCells ( dpy, cmap, True,
20                               NULL, 0, cells, 3 ) )
21       {
22
23           /*
24            * If successful, create a red color struct, and store
25            * it in the first allocated cell.
26            */
27
28           color.red = 65535;
29           color.green = color.blue = 0;
30           *red = color.pixel = cells[0];
31           XStoreColor ( dpy, cmap, &color );
32
33           /*
34            * Store green in the second cell.
35            */
36
```

```
37                color.green = 65535;
38                color.red   =   color.blue = 0;
39              *green = color.pixel = cells[1];
40                XStoreColor ( dpy, cmap, &color );
41
42          /*
43           * Store blue in the second cell.
44           */
45
46                color.blue = 65535;
47                color.red   = color.green = 0;
48                *blue = color.pixel = cells[2];
49                XStoreColor ( dpy, cmap, &color );
50          }
51      else
52          {
53                XtWarning ( "Couldn't allocate color cells" );
54
55                *blue = *red = *green = BlackPixel ( dpy, scr );
56          }
57  }
```

The function:

```
XStoreColors ( Display  *display,
               Colormap  colormap,
               XColor   *colors,
               int       ncolors )
```

stores values in multiple color cells with a single request. The `colors` argument must be an array of `XColor` structures, and `ncolors` indicates the number of colors in the array.

Xlib also provides functions that allow applications to refer to colors by their symbolic names. Color names are stored in a database along with their RGB components. The location and format of this database is operating-system-dependent. On UNIX systems, the color database files are usually found in the directory /usr/lib/X11/. The file rgb.txt contains a human-readable version of the database.

The color database distributed with X defines many common colors, and users can add additional colors. The function:

```
Status XLookupColor ( Display  *display,
                      Colormap  cmap,
                      char     *name,
                      XColor   *color,
                      XColor   *exact )
```

returns the color components that correspond to a named color in the color database. If the color exists in the database, `XLookupColor()` fills in the `red`, `green`, and `blue` members of the

XColor structures color and exact. The color argument contains the closest color supported by the hardware, while exact indicates the precise value of color components specified in the color database. The cmap argument must specify a colormap ID. XLookupColor() uses this colormap only to determine the visual type of the screen on which the color is used. This function does not allocate or store the color in the colormap.

Applications can allocate colors by name, by calling the function:

```
XAllocNamedColor ( Display  *display,
                   Colormap  cmap,
                   char      *name,
                   XColor    *color,
                   XColor    *exact )
```

XAllocNamedColor() is similar to XAllocColor(), except that the color is specified by name. Let's use XAllocNamedColor() to write an example function called GetPixelByName(). This function is similar to the GetPixel() function described earlier, but it returns a pixel index for a named color.

```
1     /**************************************************************
2      * getpixelbyname.c: Get a Pixel value to represent a named color
3      **************************************************************/
4     #include <Xm/Xm.h>
5
6     Pixel GetPixelByName ( Widget w, char *colorname )
7     {
8         Display *dpy  = XtDisplay ( w );
9         int      scr  = DefaultScreen ( dpy );
10        Colormap cmap = DefaultColormap ( dpy, scr );
11        XColor   color, ignore;
12
13        /*
14         * Allocate the named color.
15         */
16
17        if ( XAllocNamedColor ( dpy, cmap, colorname, &color, &ignore ) )
18            return ( color.pixel );
19        else
20        {
21            XtWarning ( "Couldn't allocate color" );
22
23            return ( BlackPixel ( dpy, scr ) );
24        }
25    }
```

9.2   An Example: A Color Palette Editor

This section demonstrates how the Xlib color functions described in the previous section can be used in a program named `coloredit` that allows the user to select and modify a set of colors interactively. The color editor allocates a group of color cells in a colormap and allows the user to alter the red, green, and blue components stored in each cell.

Figure 9.2 shows the window layout of the `coloredit` program. The rows of widgets near the top of the editor display the color cells available for editing. The user chooses a color cell to be edited by selecting one of these XmToggleButton widgets using the mouse. The selected color can then be edited using the three sliders located below the color pane. Each slider allows the user to set the intensity of one component of the current color. When the user selects a color, each of the three sliders moves to the position that corresponds to the red, green, or blue values of the selected color. An XmDrawnButton widget also shows the current color.

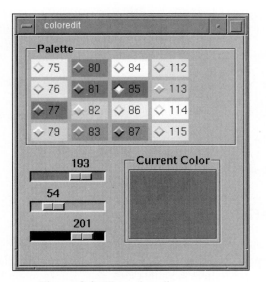

Figure 9.2 The coloredit program.

The Coloredit Program Body

The body of this program simply initializes Xt, creates a shell, and enters the event loop. The externally defined function `CreatePaletteEditor()` is called to create the widget subtree that forms the user interface of the color editor.

```
1    /*******************************************************
2     * coloredit.c: A simple color palette editor
3     *******************************************************/
4    #include <Xm/Xm.h>
5
6    #define NUMCOLORS    16
7
8    extern Widget CreatePaletteEditor ( Widget parent, int ncolors );
9
10   void main ( int argc, char **argv )
11   {
12       XtAppContext app;
13       Widget    shell, colorEditor;
14
15       /*
16        * Initialize Xt
17        */
18
19       shell = XtAppInitialize ( &app, "Coloredit", NULL, 0,
20                                 &argc, argv, NULL, NULL, 0 );
21
22       /* Create the color editor UI */
23
24       colorEditor = CreatePaletteEditor ( shell, NUMCOLORS );
25
26       /* Realize widgets and enter event loop */
27
28       XtRealizeWidget ( shell );
29
30       XtAppMainLoop ( app );
31   }
```

The CreatePaletteEditor () Function

The file paletteEditor.c contains the `CreatePaletteEditor()` function and various supporting functions. Separating the palette editing functionality from the program that uses it allows the palette editor to be designed as a stand-alone module. Other applications might incorporate this functionality by just calling `CreatePaletteEditor()` to create a widget hierarchy within any part of an application's user interface.

The file paletteEditor.c begins by including various Motif header files needed by this module and providing declarations of various functions and callbacks. Notice that all functions in this file are declared to be static except for the `CreatePaletteEditor()` function, which provides the only external interface to this module.

```
1   /**********************************************************
2    * paletteEditor.c: create a palette editor
3    **********************************************************/
4   #include <Xm/Xm.h>
5   #include <Xm/Form.h>
6   #include <Xm/Frame.h>
7   #include <Xm/Scale.h>
8   #include <Xm/RowColumn.h>
9   #include <Xm/DrawnB.h>
10  #include <Xm/ToggleB.h>
11  #include <Xm/Label.h>
12  #include <Xm/MessageB.h>
13  #include <stdio.h>
14
15  /* Widgets globally available within this file. */
16
17  static Widget  swatch, currentToggle = NULL;
18  static Widget  redSlider, blueSlider, greenSlider;
19
20  /* Function declarations and callbacks */
21
22  static Widget  CreateControlArea ( Widget parent );
23  static Widget  MakeSlider ( char          *name,
24                              Widget         parent,
25                              XtCallbackProc callback );
26  static Widget  CreateColorSelector ( Widget parent, int ncolors );
27  static void    RedSliderMoved ( Widget    w,
28                                  XtPointer clientData,
29                                  XtPointer callData );
30  static void    BlueSliderMoved ( Widget    w,
31                                   XtPointer clientData,
32                                   XtPointer callData );
33  static void    GreenSliderMoved ( Widget    w,
34                                    XtPointer clientData,
35                                    XtPointer callData );
36  static void    SelectColorCallback ( Widget     w,
37                                       XtPointer clientData,
38                                       XtPointer callData );
39  static void    WarnUserNoColor ( Widget parent );
40  static void    SetShadowColors ( Widget parent );
```

The function CreatePaletteEditor() creates a widget hierarchy and installs various callbacks used within the palette editor module. This function begins by creating an XmForm widget that contains a control area and a color selector panel. The functions CreateControlArea() and CreateColorSelector() are responsible for the widgets and actions associated with each of these areas. The CreatePaletteEditor() function simply provides the overall layout of the palette editor. The form attachments and offsets are chosen to provide an aesthetically pleasing layout for the user interface.

```
41  Widget CreatePaletteEditor ( Widget parent, int ncolors )
42  {
43      Widget form, colors, controls, separator;
44
45      /*
46       * Create a base to hold everything.
47       */
48
49      form = XtCreateManagedWidget ( "base", xmFormWidgetClass,
50                                        parent, NULL, 0 );
51
52      /*
53       * Create the controls that allow the user to manipulate
54       * the colors in the palette.
55       */
56
57      controls = CreateControlArea ( form );
58
59      XtVaSetValues ( controls,
60                      XmNtopAttachment,    XmATTACH_NONE,
61                      XmNbottomAttachment, XmATTACH_FORM,
62                      XmNleftAttachment,   XmATTACH_FORM,
63                      XmNrightAttachment,  XmATTACH_FORM,
64                      XmNleftOffset,       10,
65                      XmNtopOffset,        10,
66                      XmNbottomOffset,     10,
67                      XmNrightOffset,      10,
68                      NULL );
69
70      /*
71       * Create a grid of buttons, one for each
72       * color in the palette, from which the user can choose.
73       */
74
75      colors = CreateColorSelector ( form, ncolors );
76
77      XtVaSetValues ( colors,
78                      XmNtopAttachment,    XmATTACH_FORM,
79                      XmNbottomAttachment, XmATTACH_WIDGET,
80                      XmNbottomWidget,     controls,
81                      XmNleftAttachment,   XmATTACH_FORM,
82                      XmNrightAttachment,  XmATTACH_FORM,
83                      XmNleftOffset,       10,
84                      XmNtopOffset,        10,
85                      XmNbottomOffset,     10,
86                      XmNrightOffset,      10,
87                      NULL );
88  }
```

The `CreateControlArea()` function creates and positions the widgets that can be used to manipulate colors in the color palette. The function creates a widget tree whose root is an XmForm widget. The form manages a color "swatch" used to display the color currently being edited. The swatch is implemented as an XmDrawnButton and is placed inside a labeled frame to set it off from the rest of the control area. Notice that the swatch widget is declared at the top of the paletteEditor.c file, and can be accessed by all functions in this file.

In addition to the swatch area, `CreateControlArea()` creates and positions three sliders that can be used to alter the red, green, and blue components of the selected color. The scale widgets are created by an auxiliary function, `MakeSlider()`.

```
89   static Widget CreateControlArea ( Widget parent )
90   {
91       Widget form, frame, sliders;
92
93       /*
94        * Create a form widget to manage the overall layout.
95        */
96
97       form = XtCreateManagedWidget ( "controls", xmFormWidgetClass,
98                                       parent, NULL, 0 );
99
100      /*
101       * The swatch displays the color cell currently being edited.
102       * The swatch itself is a drawn button, and is placed inside
103       * a labeled frame for visual effect.
104       */
105
106      frame =
107          XtVaCreateManagedWidget ( "frame", xmFrameWidgetClass, form,
108                                    XmNtopAttachment,    XmATTACH_FORM,
109                                    XmNbottomAttachment, XmATTACH_FORM,
110                                    XmNleftAttachment,   XmATTACH_NONE,
111                                    XmNrightAttachment,  XmATTACH_FORM,
112                                    XmNbottomOffset,     20,
113                                    XmNrightOffset,      20,
114                                    NULL );
115
116      XtVaCreateManagedWidget ( "swatchLabel", xmLabelWidgetClass,
117                                frame,
118                                XmNchildType, XmFRAME_TITLE_CHILD,
119                                NULL );
120
121      swatch = XtVaCreateManagedWidget ( "display",
122                                         xmDrawnButtonWidgetClass,
123                                         frame,
124                                         XmNwidth,      100,
125                                         XmNheight,     100,
126                                         NULL );
```

```
127      /*
128       * Create a row column widget to contain three sliders,
129       * one for each color component.
130       */
131
132      sliders =
133        XtVaCreateManagedWidget ( "sliderpanel",
134                                   xmRowColumnWidgetClass, form,
135                                   XmNtopAttachment,     XmATTACH_FORM,
136                                   XmNbottomAttachment,  XmATTACH_NONE,
137                                   XmNleftAttachment,    XmATTACH_FORM,
138                                   XmNrightAttachment,   XmATTACH_WIDGET,
139                                   XmNrightWidget,       swatch,
140                                   XmNrightOffset,       20,
141                                   NULL );
142
143      redSlider   = MakeSlider ( "redSlider",
144                                 sliders, RedSliderMoved );
145      greenSlider = MakeSlider ( "greenSlider",
146                                 sliders, GreenSliderMoved );
147      blueSlider  = MakeSlider ( "blueSlider",
148                                 sliders, BlueSliderMoved );
149
150      return ( form );
151    }
```

The function `MakeSlider()` creates an XmScale widget used to control one color component and assigns the associated callbacks. The range between the minimum and maximum values of the slider allows the program to map between the position of a slider and the color component controlled by the slider. The minimum value of the slider, zero, corresponds to zero contribution from that color component, while the maximum valuator position (255) corresponds to a one hundred percent contribution from that component. Notice that color components in X range from 0-65535, so these values must be scaled before being used to set color components.

Functions on the scale widget's `XmNvalueChangedCallback` list are invoked when the user clicks the mouse inside the XmScale widget, while functions registered as `XmNdrag-Callback` functions are invoked when the users drags the slider by holding a mouse button down while moving the sprite. The same function, `SliderMoved()`, is registered for both of these callback lists.

```
152 Widget MakeSlider ( char * name, Widget parent, XtCallbackProc callback )
153 {
154      Widget  w;
155
156      /*
157       * Create an XmScale widget.
158       */
159
160      w = XtVaCreateManagedWidget ( name, xmScaleWidgetClass, parent,
```

```
161                                    XmNminimum,     0,
162                                    XmNmaximum,     255,
163                                    XmNshowValue,   TRUE,
164                                    XmNorientation, XmHORIZONTAL,
165                                    NULL );
166
167      /*
168       * Add callbacks to be invoked when the slider moves.
169       */
170
171      XtAddCallback ( w, XmNvalueChangedCallback, callback, NULL );
172      XtAddCallback ( w, XmNdragCallback,         callback, NULL );
173
174      return ( w );
175  }
```

The function `CreateColorSelector()` creates a row of XmToggleButton widgets, one for each color to be edited, managed by an XmRowColumn widget. This function sets the background color of each widget to one of the pixel values allocated for editing. Selecting one of these widgets selects the corresponding color cell for editing.

The color cells to be edited are allocated by calling the Xlib function `XAllocColor-Cells()`. This function attempts to allocate three times the number of colors requested for the palette. The extra colors are needed because Motif's shadow effect uses a top and bottom shadow color for each background color displayed. As a color cell is edited, the top and bottom shadow colors of each XmToggleButton widget must also be changed, as well as the colors of the XmDrawn-Button used as larger color swatch. Unless the top and bottom shadow colors are changed each time a background color is changed, the Motif three dimensional illusion will be broken. To change the shadow colors, we must allocate read-write cells for these colors as well.

```
176  static Widget CreateColorSelector ( Widget parent, int ncolors )
177  {
178      Widget  panel, frame;
179      int     i;
180      Pixel   *pixels;
181
182      /*
183       * Allocate an array of pixels large enough for the palette
184       * plus top and bottom shadow colors for each background.
185       */
186
187      pixels = ( Pixel* ) XtMalloc ( sizeof ( Pixel ) * ncolors * 3 );
188
189      if ( !XAllocColorCells ( XtDisplay ( parent ),
190                      DefaultColormapOfScreen ( XtScreen ( parent ) ),
191                               FALSE, NULL, 0,
192                               pixels, ncolors * 3 ) )
193          XtError ( "Can't allocate color cells" );
194
```

```
195       /*
196        * Put everything inside a labeled frame widget
197        */
198
199       frame = XtCreateManagedWidget ( "frame", xmFrameWidgetClass,
200                                        parent, NULL, 0 );
201
202       XtVaCreateManagedWidget ( "selectorLabel", xmLabelWidgetClass,
203                                  frame,
204                                  XmNchildType, XmFRAME_TITLE_CHILD,
205                                  NULL );
206
207       /*
208        * Place the palette entries in a 4-column radio box.
209        */
210
211       panel = XtVaCreateManagedWidget ( "colorpanel",
212                                          xmRowColumnWidgetClass, frame,
213                                          XmNradioBehavior, TRUE,
214                                          XmNnumColumns,    4,
215                                          XmNpacking,       XmPACK_COLUMN,
216                                          XmNadjustLast,    FALSE,
217                                          NULL );
218
219       /*
220        * Create an XmToggleButton widget for each color in the palette.
221        * Just assign the background color to an allocated pixel. Actual
222        * initial color displayed by each button is random. Also
223        * assign top and bottom shadows to allocated color cells.
224        */
225
226       for ( i = 0; i < ncolors; i++ )
227       {
228           Widget toggle;
229           char   name[10];
230
231           sprintf ( name,"%d", pixels[i] );
232
233           toggle  =
234               XtVaCreateManagedWidget ( name,
235                                          xmToggleButtonWidgetClass, panel,
236                                          XmNbackground, pixels[i],
237                                          XmNtopShadowColor,
238                                                    pixels[i + ncolors],
239                                          XmNbottomShadowColor,
240                                                    pixels[i + 2 * ncolors],
241                                          NULL );
242          /*
243           * Initialize the shadows of each button. The background is
```

```
244              * random, but at least the shadows should look right.
245              */
246
247             SetShadowColors ( toggle );
248
249         /*
250          * Callback to set the currently editable color cell.
251          */
252
253             XtAddCallback ( toggle, XmNvalueChangedCallback,
254                             SelectColorCallback, ( XtPointer ) NULL );
255     }
256
257     XtFree ( (char *) pixels );
258
259     return ( frame );
260 }
```

At this point, the widget hierarchy is complete. Figure 9.3 shows the widget tree created by the `coloredit` program.

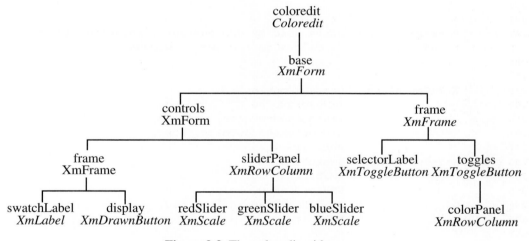

Figure 9.3 The coloredit widget tree.

The function `SelectColorCallback()` is invoked when the user selects a toggle button from the palette display. This function's purpose is to install the selected color cell as the cell currently being edited. The function displays the currently selected color in the swatch widget and moves each red, green, and blue color slider to the value corresponding to its respective color component within the selected color.

```
261    static void SelectColorCallback ( Widget      w,
262                                       XtPointer clientData,
263                                       XtPointer callData )
264    {
265        XColor color;
266        Pixel bg, tsc, bsc;
267        XmToggleButtonCallbackStruct *cbs =
268                            ( XmToggleButtonCallbackStruct* ) callData;
269        /*
270         * Ignore calls that result from a button being unset.
271         */
272
273        if ( cbs->set == FALSE )
274            return;
275
276        /*
277         * Register the selected toggle button as the
278         * currently selected widget
279         */
280
281        currentToggle = w;
282
283        /*
284         * Retrieve the colors used by the currently selected widget,
285         * and assign these colors to the swatch widget.
286         */
287
288        XtVaGetValues ( currentToggle,
289                        XmNbackground,          &bg,
290                        XmNtopShadowColor,      &tsc,
291                        XmNbottomShadowColor, &bsc,
292                        NULL );
293        XtVaSetValues ( swatch,
294                        XmNbackground,          bg,
295                        XmNtopShadowColor,      tsc,
296                        XmNbottomShadowColor, bsc,
297                        NULL );
298        /*
299         * Get the color components (rgb) of the selected color cell.
300         */
301
302        color.flags = DoRed | DoGreen | DoBlue;
303        color.pixel = bg;
304
305        XQueryColor ( XtDisplay ( w ),
306                      DefaultColormapOfScreen ( XtScreen ( w ) ),
307                      &color );
308        /*
309         * Use each color component value to determine the
```

```
310        * new position of the corresponding slider.
311        */
312
313        XtVaSetValues ( redSlider,   XmNvalue, color.red   / 256,   NULL );
314        XtVaSetValues ( greenSlider, XmNvalue, color.green / 256,   NULL );
315        XtVaSetValues ( blueSlider,  XmNvalue, color.blue  / 256,   NULL );
316    }
```

Whenever the user moves a slider, that slider's callback function is invoked. Each slider has a callback function that controls the red, green, or blue components of the currently selected color. Each slider's callback sets the corresponding member of a XColor structure to the value indicated by the current position of the slider, extracted from the XmScale widget's call data. The flags member of the XColor structure allows each callback function to only affect the corresponding color component of the cell being edited.

The callback function registered with the red slider is written as follows:

```
317    static void RedSliderMoved ( Widget      w,
318                                 XtPointer clientData,
319                                 XtPointer callData )
320    {
321        XColor color;
322        Pixel pixel;
323        XmScaleCallbackStruct *cb = ( XmScaleCallbackStruct * ) callData;
324
325        /*
326         * Make sure there is a color to edit.
327         */
328
329        if ( !currentToggle )
330        {
331            WarnUserNoColor ( w );
332            return;
333        }
334
335        /*
336         * Retrieve the background pixel of the swatch widget
337         * and change the red component of the color according to
338         * the new value of the red slider.
339         */
340
341        XtVaGetValues ( swatch, XmNbackground, &pixel, NULL );
342
343        color.red   =  cb->value * 256;
344        color.pixel =  pixel;
345        color.flags =  DoRed;
346        XStoreColor ( XtDisplay ( w ),
347                      DefaultColormapOfScreen ( XtScreen ( w ) ),
348                      &color );
```

```
349        /*
350         * Correct the shadow colors.
351         */
352
353        SetShadowColors ( currentToggle );
354   }
```

The blue slider's callback function is the same, except that only the blue component of the color cell is updated.

```
355   static void BlueSliderMoved ( Widget    w,
356                                 XtPointer clientData,
357                                 XtPointer callData )
358   {
359       XColor color;
360       Pixel pixel;
361       XmScaleCallbackStruct *cb = ( XmScaleCallbackStruct * ) callData;
362
363       /*
364        * Make sure there is a color to edit.
365        */
366
367       if ( !currentToggle )
368       {
369           WarnUserNoColor ( w );
370           return;
371       }
372
373       /*
374        * Retrieve the background pixel of the swatch widget
375        * and change the blue component of the color according to
376        * the new value of the blue slider.
377        */
378
379       XtVaGetValues ( swatch, XmNbackground, &pixel, NULL );
380       color.blue  =  cb->value * 256;
381       color.pixel =  pixel;
382       color.flags =  DoBlue;
383
384       XStoreColor ( XtDisplay ( w ),
385                     DefaultColormapOfScreen ( XtScreen ( w ) ),
386                     &color );
387       /*
388        * Correct the shadow colors.
389        */
390
391        SetShadowColors ( currentToggle );
392   }
```

The green slider's callback function is also similar, but modifies the value of the green component of the current color.

```
393   static void GreenSliderMoved ( Widget    w,
394                                   XtPointer clientData,
395                                   XtPointer callData )
396   {
397       XColor color;
398       Pixel  pixel;
399       XmScaleCallbackStruct *cb = ( XmScaleCallbackStruct * ) callData;
400
401       /*
402        * Make sure there is a color to edit.
403        */
404
405       if ( !currentToggle )
406       {
407         WarnUserNoColor ( w );
408         return;
409       }
410
411       /*
412        * Retrieve the background pixel of the swatch widget
413        * and change the greem component of the color according to
414        * the new value of the green slider.
415        */
416
417       XtVaGetValues ( swatch, XmNbackground, &pixel, NULL );
418       color.green =  cb->value * 256;
419       color.pixel =  pixel;
420       color.flags =  DoGreen;
421
422       XStoreColor ( XtDisplay ( w ),
423                     DefaultColormapOfScreen ( XtScreen ( w ) ),
424                     &color );
425       /*
426        * Correct the shadow colors.
427        */
428
429       SetShadowColors ( currentToggle );
430   }
```

The function `WarnUserNoColor()` is called from the scale callbacks if the user moves a scale before selecting any color in the palette. This function simply creates and posts a warning dialog. The message displayed by the dialog never changes and is set in the coloredit program's app-defaults file.

```
431  static void WarnUserNoColor ( Widget parent )
432  {
433      static Widget dialog = NULL;
434
435      if ( !dialog )
436          dialog = XmCreateWarningDialog ( parent,
437                                           "noColorWarningDialog",
438                                           NULL, 0 );
439      XtManageChild ( dialog );
440  }
```

The function `SetShadowColors()` improves the visual effect of editing the palette by changing the top and bottom shadow colors of the currently selected toggle button and the swatch widget to match the displayed background. Because both the swatch and the current toggle widget share the same color cells, both can be corrected at once. The heart of this function involves a Motif function that can be used to calculate top and bottom shadow colors for any given background color. Motif provides a function, `XmGetColors()` that can be called directly to determine the top and bottom shadow colors for any given background. This function has the form:

```
void XmGetColors ( Screen   *screen,
                   Colormap cmap,
                   Pixel    background,
                   Pixel    *foreground,
                   Pixel    *topShadow,
                   Pixel    *bottomShadow,
                   Pixel    *selectColor )
```

Given a background pixel, this function provides pixels that represent the other colors used by the shadows in Motif widgets. The function also returns a suitable select (or arm) color for use with toggle buttons and push buttons. In addition, this function computes a contrasting foreground color for the given background. If the background is light, the foreground will typically be black, while if the background is dark, the foreground is specified as white.

Another useful function is:

```
void XmChangeColor ( Widget w, Pixel background )
```

This function calls `XmGetColors()` and then installs the result in the given widget.

Although these functions are convenient for many applications, they are unsuitable for use in the palette editor. These functions cannot be used because `XmGetColors()` caches pixel values. Although caching is generally desirable, in this case it gets in the way. To correct the shadow colors of a color cell whose color components have been altered, we must compute a color based on the contents of the color cell, not just return a cached pixel index that matched contents of a cell at some time in the past.

Fortunately, Motif provides access to a lower level color calculation function. The function `XmGetColorCalculation()` returns a pointer to a function that takes an XColor structure and returns XColor structures for each of the calculated colors. The form of this type of function is:

```
void ColorProc ( XColor *bg,
                 XColor *fg,
                 XColor *selectColor,
                 XColor *topShadow,
                 XColor *bottomShadow )
```

Although this facility is more difficult to use than the convenience functions provided by Motif, it does not cache, which makes it more flexible.

Using this function, we can write `SetShadowColors()` as follows:

```
441  static void SetShadowColors ( Widget w )
442  {
443      XColor         select, fg, bs, ts, bg;
444      XmColorProc  proc = XmGetColorCalculation();
445
446      bg.flags = DoRed | DoBlue | DoGreen;
447      ts.flags = DoRed | DoBlue | DoGreen;
448      bs.flags = DoRed | DoBlue | DoGreen;
449
450      /*
451       * Get the top, bottom, and background pixels of the
452       * given widget and determine the color components
453       * of the background color.
454       */
455
456      XtVaGetValues ( w,
457                      XmNbackground,          &bg.pixel,
458                      XmNtopShadowColor,      &ts.pixel,
459                      XmNbottomShadowColor, &bs.pixel,
460                      NULL );
461
462      XQueryColor ( XtDisplay ( w ),
463                    DefaultColormapOfScreen ( XtScreen ( w ) ), &bg );
464
465      /*
466       * Call the currently installed Motif color calculation function
467       * to fill in the rgb components of the top and bottom shadow
468       * colors that match the given background.
469       */
470
471      ( *proc ) ( &bg, &fg, &select, &ts, &bs );
472
473      /*
474       * The calculation function fills in the color structures. Now we
475       * have to store the colors in the corresponding color cells to
476       * display these colors.
477       */
478
```

```
479      XStoreColor ( XtDisplay ( w ),
480                    DefaultColormapOfScreen ( XtScreen ( w ) ),
481                    &ts );
482      XStoreColor ( XtDisplay ( w ),
483                    DefaultColormapOfScreen ( XtScreen ( w ) ),
484                    &bs );
485  }
```

The Coloredit App-Defaults File

The coloredit program relies on several resources for proper operation and best appearance. These resources can be specified in an application resource file, Coloredit. The application's resource file corresponding to the layout shown in Figure 9.2 contains the following resources:

```
1    !!!!!!!!!!!!!!!!!!!!!!!!!!!!!!!!!!!!!!!!!!!!!!!!!!!!!!!!!!!!!
2    ! Coloredit: Resources for the coloredit program
3    !!!!!!!!!!!!!!!!!!!!!!!!!!!!!!!!!!!!!!!!!!!!!!!!!!!!!!!!!!!!!
4
5    ! Labels
6    *selectorLabel*labelString: Palette
7    *swatchLabel*labelString:   Current Color
8
9    ! Colors for the color sliders
10   coloredit*redSlider*troughColor:    red
11   coloredit*blueSlider*troughColor:   blue
12   coloredit*greenSlider*troughColor: green
13
14   ! Message to be displayed if user tries to move the sliders
15   ! without selecting a color to edit
16   *noColorWarningDialog*messageString: You must select a color \n\
17    from the palette first.
```

9.3   Summary

This chapter introduces the use of color in the X Window System. X supports a color model that supports the design of applications that are portable across many types of displays, from monochrome to "true color" displays. Although Motif allocates colors for all widgets automatically, many applications need to allocate and manipulate color directly, as well. It is important for programmers to use color correctly so that their applications function properly on as many display types as possible. At one time color displays were found only on a few very high-priced systems and color was considered to be a luxury. Increasingly, color workstations and terminals are becoming more common, and color is becoming an important part of a complete user interface.

Chapter 10

Graphics Contexts

All graphics operations use a set of attributes that determine the width of lines, foreground and background colors, fill patterns, fonts to be used when displaying text, and so on. X stores these attributes in an internal data structure known as a *graphics context*, often abbreviated as GC. This chapter discusses the attributes of GCs as well as the Xlib and Xt functions that create and manipulate them. Later chapters show how to use graphics contexts with the X text and graphics functions.

10.1 Creating Graphics Contexts

The Xlib function:

```
GC XCreateGC ( Display       *display,
               Drawable       drawable,
               unsigned long mask,
               XGCVGalue     *values )
```

creates a graphics context and returns a resource identifier that applications can use to refer to the GC. The X server maintains the data associated with the graphics context, and all clients must reference the graphics context by its ID. Graphics contexts are associated with a specific drawable, but can be used with any drawable of the same depth on a screen with the same visual type.

Applications can specify the initial value of each component of a graphics context in the `values` argument when calling `XCreateGC()`. This argument must be an `XGCValues` structure, which includes the following members:

```
int             function;    /* logical operation        */
unsigned long plane_mask;    /* plane mask               */
unsigned long foreground;    /* foreground pixel         */
unsigned long background;    /* background pixel         */
int             line_width;  /* line width (in pixels)   */
int             line_style;  /* LineSolid,
                                LineOnOffDash, or
                                LineDoubleDash            */
int             cap_style;   /* CapNotLast, CapButt,
                                CapRound, CapProjecting   */
int             join_style;  /* JoinMiter, JoinRound,
                                or JoinBevel              */
int             fill_style;  /* FillSolid, FillTiled,
                                FillStippled,
                                or FillOpaqueStippled     */
int             fill_rule;   /* EvenOddRule, WindingRule  */
int             arc_mode;    /* ArcChord, ArcPieSlice     */
Pixmap          tile;        /* tile pixmap for tiling    */
Pixmap          stipple;     /* stipple 1 plane pixmap    */
int             ts_x_origin; /* tile and stipple offset   */
int             ts_y_origin;
Font            font;        /* default text font         */
int     subwindow_mode;      /* ClipByChildren, or
                                IncludeInferiors          */
Bool    graphics_exposures;  /* report graphics exposures?*/
int     clip_x_origin;       /* clipping origin           */
int     clip_y_origin;
Pixmap clip_mask;            /* bitmap clipping           */
int     dash_offset;         /* line information          */
char    dashes;
```

The `mask` argument to `XCreateGC()` specifies which members of the `XGCValues` structure contain valid information. If this mask is zero, the GC will be created with default values for all attributes. To override the default value for a particular field, the mask must include a constant that corresponds to that field. Figure 10.1 lists the GC attribute masks, along with the default values of each attribute.

Mask	Default Value of GC
GCFunction	GXCopy
GCPlaneMask	AllPlanes
GCForeground	0
GCBackground	1
GCLineWidth	0
GCLineStyle	LineSolid
GCCapStyle	CapButt
GCJoinStyle	JoinMiter
GCFillStyle	FillSolid
GCFillRule	EvenOddRule
GCTile	Foreground
GCStipple	0
GCTileStipXOrigin	0
GCTileStipYOrigin	1
GCFont	Implementation-Dependent
GCSubwindowMode	ClipByChildren
GCGraphicsExposures	TRUE
GCClipXOrigin	0
GCClipYOrigin	0
GCClipMask	None
GCDashOffset	0
GCDashList	4
GCArcMode	ArcPieSlice

Figure 10.1 Masks used with graphics contexts.

For example, the following code segment creates a graphics context that specifies the foreground pixel, background pixel, and line style:

```
XGCValues gcv;
GC        gc;
gcv.foreground = 1;
gcv.background = 2;
gcv.line_style = LineOnOffDash;
gc = XCreateGC ( display, window,
                GCForeground | GCBackground | GCLineStyle, &gcv);
```

Xt also provides a function that can be used to create graphics contexts:

```
GC XtGetGC ( Widget widget, XtGCMask mask, XGCValues *values)
```

This function caches graphics contexts to allow GCs to be shared within an application. Therefore, applications must not modify GCs created with XGetGC().

Xt also supports modifiable shared graphics contexts. The following function can be used to create a graphics context:

```
GC XtAllocateGC ( Widget      widget,
                  Cardinal    depth,
                  XtGCMask    valueMask,
                  XGCValues *values,
                  XtGCMask    modifiableMask,
                  XtGCMask    unusedMask )
```

This function allows the caller to specify that some attributes of a GC are shareable, that some may be modified, and that some others are unused. This information allows Xt to provide a more intelligent caching behavior. The `depth` argument may be used to specify the depth of the visual on which this GC will be used, or the depth can be specified as zero. If the depth is given as zero, `XtAllocateGC()` uses the depth of the widget provided as the first argument.

10.2 Manipulating Graphics Contexts

After a GC is created, applications can use the function:

```
XChangeGC ( Display        *display,
            GC             gc,
            unsigned long  mask,
            XGCValues      *values )
```

to modify any attributes of the given graphics context. The `mask` and `values` arguments serve the same function here as they do in `XCreateGC()`. Xlib also provides many convenience functions that can be used to modify individual GC attributes. The following sections introduce many of these functions and discuss the purpose of each of the attributes of a graphics context. It is important to remember that none of these functions should be used to alter a shared GC created with `XtGetGC()`.

Display Functions

A graphics context's `GCFunction` attribute specifies a logical display function that determines how each pixel of a new image is combined with the current contents of a destination drawable. The new image, referred to as the *source*, could be copied from another drawable, or be generated by a graphics request. For example, when this attribute is set to `GXcopy`, the source image completely replaces the current contents of the affected region of the drawable. On the other hand, if the same figure is drawn using the `GXor` display function, the bits of the affected region of the drawable are set to the logical OR of the source and the previous contents of the destination.

Figure 10.2 shows the display functions defined in Xlib.h, along with their corresponding logical operations. The `src` parameter represents the bits being written and the `dst` parameter represents the current state of the bits in the drawable.

Mask	Display Function
GXclear	0
GXand	src AND dst
GXandReverse	src AND NOT dst
GXcopy	src
GXandInverted	(NOT src) AND dst
GXnoop	dst
GXxor	src XOR dst
GXor	src OR dst
GXnor	NOT (src OR dst)
GXequiv	(NOT src) XOR dst
GXinvert	NOT dst
GXorReverse	src OR (NOT dst)
GXcopyInverted	NOT src
GXorInverted	(NOT src) OR dst
GXnand	NOT (src AND dst)
GXset	1

Figure 10.2 Display functions.

When used with color visual types, these logical operations are performed bit-wise on each pixel within the affected area. For example, consider a line drawn using the GXand drawing function and a pixel index of 3 for the foreground color. If the line is rendered in a drawable whose background color is pixel 10 on a display with four bit planes, the resulting line color is represented by pixel 2. This is easier to see by examining the binary representation of these numbers:

$$3_{10} \text{ AND } 10_{10} = 2_{10}$$
$$0011_2 \text{ AND } 1010_2 = 0010_2$$

The *exclusive-OR* (XOR) function, specified by the constant GXxor, is a commonly used display function. The XOR function has the interesting property that drawing a figure twice in XOR mode restores the screen to its original state. Therefore, an image drawn in XOR mode can be erased simply by drawing it a second time. Contrast this approach with erasing an object on the screen by drawing the object in the background color of the window. In the latter case, the application must redraw the previous contents, if any, of the window. When an image is redrawn in XOR mode, the previous contents of the window are restored, as long as nothing else on the screen has changed.

The most common use of the XOR display function is for *rubber banding* operations, where an object on the screen, often a line or rectangle, is moved and stretched in response to mouse motion. The XOR mode allows the rubber band object to move across other objects on the screen without disturbing them. Chapter 13 presents an example that demonstrates rubber banding.

The function:

```
XSetFunction ( Display *display, GC gc, int function )
```

provides an easy way for applications to alter a graphics context's display function. The default value is GXcopy.

Plane Mask

The value of the GCPlaneMask attribute determines which bit planes of a drawable are affected by a graphics operation. The plane mask contains a one in each bit that can be modified. The function:

```
XSetPlaneMask ( Display *display, GC gc, unsigned long mask )
```

sets the plane mask of a graphics context. For example, a line drawn with foreground pixel 6 would normally affect bit planes 2 and 3 ($6_{10} = 0110_2$). However, if the plane mask of the graphics context is set to 5_{10} (0101_2), drawing a line with a foreground pixel 6 affects only plane 3, and the resulting line is displayed in the color indicated by the pixel index 4. Applications can use a macro:

```
AllPlanes
```

to indicate all planes supported by a screen. The default value of the GCPlaneMask attribute is AllPlanes.

Foreground and Background

The GCForeground and GCBackground attributes of a graphics context indicate the pixels used as foreground and background colors for graphics operations. The pixel index must be an integer between zero and $n - 1$, where n is the number of colors supported by the display. This index is usually obtained using the color allocation functions discussed in Chapter 9. The function:

```
XSetForeground ( Display *display, GC gc, Pixel pixel )
```

sets the GCForeground attribute of a GC. The function:

```
XSetBackground ( Display *display, GC gc, Pixel pixel )
```

sets the GCBackground attribute of a GC. The default value of GCForeground is zero and the default value of GCBackground is one.

Line Attributes

Several GC attributes determine how a line is drawn. The GCLineWidth controls the width, in pixels, of the line. The default width is zero. The server draws zero-width lines one pixel wide using an implementation-dependent algorithm. On displays that have hardware support for line drawing, using zero-width lines is often the fastest way to draw lines. The GCLineStyle attribute can be one of the constants:

LineSolid   LineOnOffDash   LineDoubleDash

Figure 10.3 shows each of these styles. The default value is LineSolid.

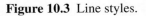

Figure 10.3 Line styles.

Graphics contexts also control how the server draws the ends of wide lines. The `GCCapStyle` of a line can be one of the constants:

> `CapNotLast`   `CapButt`   `CapRound`   `CapProjecting`

The default value is `CapButt`. Figure 10.4 shows how X would draw each of these styles for a line four pixels wide.

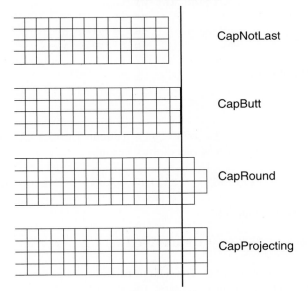

Figure 10.4 Line cap styles.

The graphics context also determines how the server draws connected lines. The style is determined by the `GCJoinStyle` attribute and can be one of the constants:

`JoinMiter`   `JoinRound`   `JoinBevel`

Figure 10.5 illustrates each of these styles. The default style is `JoinMiter`.

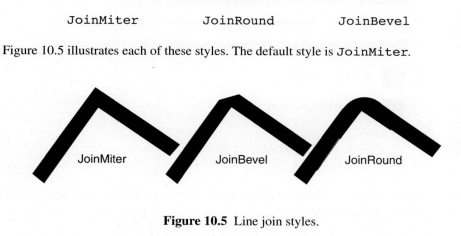

Figure 10.5 Line join styles.

The function:

```
XSetLineAttributes ( Display        *display,
                     GC              gc,
                     unsigned int    width,
                     int             style,
                     int             cap_style,
                     int             join_style )
```

sets each of a GC's line attributes.

Fill Styles

X allows graphics figures to be *filled* by some color or pattern. The `GCFillStyle` attribute determines how figures are filled and must be one of the constants:

`FillSolid`   `FillTiled`   `FillStippled`   `FillOpaqueStippled`

Applications can use the function:

```
XSetFillStyle ( Display *display, GC gc, int style )
```

to set the fill style of a graphics context. The default fill style, `FillSolid`, specifies that figures are to be filled with the current foreground color. The `FillTiled` style indicates that figures are to be filled with the pixmap pattern specified in the `tile` attribute. This pixmap must have the same depth as the drawable with which the graphics context is used. See Chapter 11 for more information about pixmaps.

The function:

```
XSetTile ( Display *display, GC gc, Pixamp tile )
```

sets a graphics context's `GCTile` attribute. Setting the `GCFillStyle` to `FillStippled` or `FillOpaqueStippled` specifies that regions be filled with a *stipple*. A stipple is a repeating pattern produced by using a bitmap (a pixmap of depth one) as a mask in the drawing operation. When `FillStippled` is specified, graphics operations only operate on those bits of the stipple pattern that are set to one. When `FillOpaqueStippled` is specified, bits in the stipple pattern that contain a one are drawn using the foreground color of the graphics context and those that contain a zero are drawn using the background color.

The function:

```
XSetStipple ( Display *display, GC gc, Pixamp stipple )
```

sets a GC's stipple pattern.

Graphics contexts also use a fill rule attribute, `GCFillRule`, to determine the algorithm used to fill a region. The fill rule must be one of the constants `EvenOddRule` or `WindingRule`. The function:

```
XSetFillRule ( Display *display, GC gc, int rule )
```

sets the fill rule for a graphics context.

Figure 10.6 shows how the fill rule affects the appearance of a filled polygon. If `EvenOddRule` is specified, the server sets a pixel at a particular point if an imaginary line drawn between the point and the outside of the figure crosses the figure an odd number of times. If `WindingRule` is specified, the server determines whether a point should be filled using an imaginary line between the point and a vertex of the figure. The line is rotated about the point so that it touches each vertex of the figure, in order, until it returns to the original position. If the line makes one or more complete rotations, the point is considered to be inside the figure, and the point is filled.

Unfilled Figure   WindingRule   EvenOddRule

Figure 10.6 Comparison of EvenOddRule and WindingRule.

Fonts

The `GCFont` attribute of a graphics context determines the font used for all text operations. The function:

```
XSetFont ( Display *display, GC gc, Font font_id )
```

sets a graphics context's font attribute. The default font is implementation-dependent. Chapter 12 discusses fonts and how they are used to display text in a window.

Clip Masks

The `GCClipMask` attribute specifies a bitmap as a clip mask for all drawing operations. If a graphics context has a clip mask, drawing operations affect only those pixels in the drawable that correspond to a 1 in the clip mask.

The function:

```
XSetClipMask ( Display *display, GC gc, Pixmap clipmask )
```

sets the pixmap used as a clip mask. The default value is `None`, in which case no clipping is performed. The function:

```
XSetClipOrigon ( Display *display, GC gc, int x, int y )
```

alters the location of the clipmask relative to the origin of the drawable. A clipping region can also be specified as a list of rectangular areas, using the function:

```
XSetClipRectangles ( Display     *display,
                      GC           gc,
                      int          xoffset,
                      int          yoffset,
                      XRectangles *rect,
                      int          nrect,
                      int          ordering )
```

The arguments `xoffset` and `yoffset` indicate an offset to be added to the origin of all rectangles. The `rect` argument must be an array of `XRectangle` structures. This structure has the members:

```
short          x, y;
unsigned short width, height;
```

If the list of rectangles is given as `None`, no clipping is performed. Some X servers can perform clipping more efficiently if they know the order of the rectangles. The `order` argument must specify one of the constants `Unsorted`, `YSorted`, `YXSorted`, or `YXBanded` to indicate the order of the rectangles within the array.

10.3 Graphics Exposures

The server generates `GraphicsExpose` events when an `XCopyArea()` or `XCopyPlane()` function is unable to copy an area because the area is occluded by a window. The function:

```
XSetGraphicsExposures ( Display *display, GC gc, Boolean flag )
```

enables or disables generation of these events for graphics operations that use the graphics context. `GraphicsExpose` events are enabled when `flag` is set to `TRUE`. The default value is `TRUE`.

10.4 Regions

X provides a set of utility routines that can be used to represent and manipulate non-rectangular areas. For example, applications often need to determine whether an exposed area intersects with the area occupied by a particular object on the screen. To deal with such situations, X provides an opaque data structure, `Region`, and a set of functions that operate on regions. Internally, a region consists of an array of rectangles. Applications cannot access the region data structure directly, but must use functions provided by Xlib to manipulate `Region`s. Functions that manipulate regions do not make requests to the server; all calculations are done locally in the client. Applications that use regions must include the header file Xutil.h.

Some widgets use regions when handling exposure events. Widgets that request Xt to compress exposure events are passed a `Region` that defines the sum of all exposed areas after all expose events are received. Some widgets choose to pass the region on to the application in callbacks.

The function:

```
Region XCreateRegion()
```

creates and returns a new, empty `Region`.

The function:

```
Region XPolygonRegion ( XPoint *points_array, int npoints, int fill_rule )
```

creates a `Region` that represents the polygonal area defined by an array of `XPoint` structures. This structure contains the members:

```
        short x, y;
```

The `fill_rule` argument to `XPolygonRegion()` determines the algorithm used to convert the polygon to a region and may be one of the constants `EvenOddRule` or `WindingRule`.

The function:

```
XDestroyRegion ( Region region )
```

destroys a `Region` and frees the memory used by the `Region`.
The function:

```
Boolean XEqualRegion ( Region r1, region r2 )
```

compares two regions and returns TRUE if they are equal, or FALSE if they are not.
The function:

```
 Boolean XEmptyRegion ( Region region )
```

returns TRUE if the given `Region` is empty. A new `Region` defined by the intersection of two `Regions` can obtained using the function:

```
XIntersectRegion ( Region region1, Region region2,  Region result )
```

For example, `XIntersectRegion()` can be used to write a simple function that determines if two regions intersect:

```
1   /***********************************************************
2    * intersect.c: Demonstrate simple use of Region functions.
3    *              Determine whether two Regions intersect.
4    ***********************************************************/
5   #include <X11/Xlib.h>
6   #include <X11/Xutil.h> /* Contains Region declarations */
7
8
9   int DoesIntersect ( Region region1, Region region2 )
10  {
11      int    is_empty;
12      Region intersection;
13
14      /*
15       * Create the empty intersection region.
16       */
17
18      intersection = XCreateRegion();
19
20      /*
21       * Get the intersection of the two regions.
22       */
23
24      XIntersectRegion ( region1, region2, intersection );
25
```

```
26      /*
27       * Check whether the result is an empty region.
28       */
29
30      is_empty = XEmptyRegion ( intersection );
31
32      /*
33       * Free the region before returning the result.
34       */
35
36      XDestroyRegion ( intersection );
37
38      return ( !is_empty );
39  }
```

The function:

```
Boolean XPointInRegion ( Region region, int x, int y )
```

returns TRUE if the given *x,y* point lies within the bounds of the region, while the function:

```
Boolean XRectInRegion ( Region       region,
                        int          x,
                        int          y,
                        unsigned int width,
                        unsigned int height )
```

determines whether a rectangular area intersects a region. XRectInRegion() returns the constant RectangleIn if the rectangle is totally contained within the region, RectangleOut if the rectangle lies completely outside the region, and RectanglePart if the rectangle partially intersects the given region.

The smallest enclosing rectangle of a region can be obtained by calling the function:

```
XClipBox ( Region region, XRectangle *rect )
```

When this function returns, the XRectangle structure rect contains the bounding box of the specified region.

Applications can also use a Region as a clip mask in a graphics context. The function:

```
XSetRegion ( Display * display, GC gc, Region region )
```

sets the clip mask of a graphics context to the given region.

Xlib also includes many other useful functions that operate on regions. These include functions that find the union of two regions, subtract regions, move regions, and so on. Xt also provides a function that can be used to convert the area reported in an Expose event to a region. The function:

```
void XtAddExposureToRegion ( XEvent *event, Region region )
```

computes the union of the region and the rectangle contained in the `Expose` event and stores the result in the region.

10.5 Summary

Graphics contexts control color, style and other attributes used by the Xlib text and graphics primitives. Applications that only create and manipulate widgets are unlikely to need graphics contexts. However, applications that need to draw images, display text in ways that go beyond the capabilities of the XmLabel and XmText widgets, or applications that require custom widgets will need to use graphics contexts.

This chapter also discusses regions, which are often used by graphics applications to define clipping areas. Regions allow rectangular or non-rectangular areas to be represented, compared, and manipulated. Regions are also important when writing new widget classes, as discussed in Chapters 15 through 17.

Chapter 11

Bitmaps, Pixmaps, and Images

X provides many functions for creating and manipulating images stored in off-screen memory in addition to those displayed on the screen. These images fall into three categories: *pixmaps, bitmaps,* and *images*. Pixmaps and bitmaps are often used to display *icons*. Window managers often provide icons that can represent the entire application, and applications may also use iconic images as part of the application's user interface. This chapter introduces the Xlib functions for creating and manipulating these images and briefly describes how they are used, with an emphasis on how these images can be used in Motif applications.

11.1 Pixmaps

A pixmap is a chunk of memory similar to a rectangular region of the screen, except that pixmaps are stored in *off-screen memory* and therefore are not visible to the user. Pixmaps have a depth, which is often, but not necessarily, the same as the depth of the screen with which it is associated. The function:

```
Pixmap XCreatePixmap ( Display      *display,
                       Drawable      drawable,
                       unsigned int  width,
                       unsigned int  height,
                       unsigned int  depth )
```

creates a pixmap `width` by `height` pixels in size. Each pixel contains `depth` bits. The new pixmap is associated with the same screen as the specified `drawable`. The pixmap can be used only on screen with which it is associated, or on a screen with the same visual type.

Applications can deallocate pixmaps when they are no longer needed using the Xlib function:

```
XFreePixmap ( Display *display, Pixmap pixmap )
```

Pixmaps are drawables and can be used as destinations for text and graphics operations in the same way as windows. Because data can also be copied between drawables, pixmaps can be used to store off-screen representations of windows. Pixmaps can be used to specify clipping regions for graphics operations and can also be combined with other graphics operations to create patterns used by many Xlib graphics primitives.

Pixmaps are sometimes referred to as *tiles*, because they are often used as a repeating background or fill pattern. A pixmap used as a tile is usually small (16 by 16 pixels), to facilitate rapid duplication.

11.2 Bitmaps

A pixmap with a depth of one is referred to as a *bitmap*. Applications can create a bitmap by specifying a depth of one when calling the function `XCreatePixmap()`. However, Xlib also provides functions used specifically to create bitmaps. The function:

```
Pixmap XCreateBitmapFromData ( Display       *display,
                               Drawable       drawable,
                               char          *data,
                               unsigned int width,
                               unsigned int height )
```

creates a bitmap of `width` by `height` from the specified `data`, which must be a series of bits that represent the value of each pixel in the bitmap.

One easy way to generate the data for a bitmap is to create it interactively using the `bitmap` program, usually distributed with X. The bitmap program creates a file that can be included directly in a program.

The directory:

```
/usr/include/X11/bitmaps/
```

also contains some predefined bitmap files. For example, the file:

```
/usr/include/X11/bitmaps/xlogo64
```

defines the data for a bitmap of the X logo shown in Figure 11.1.

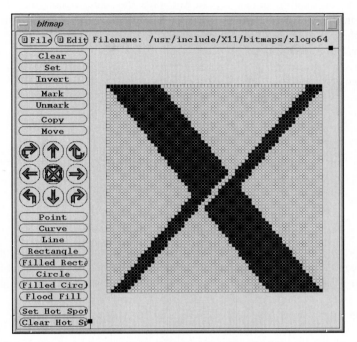

Figure 11.1 A bitmap of the X logo, edited by the bitmap program.

11.3 Copying Between Drawables

The contents of a drawable (a window or a pixmap) may be copied to any other drawable that has the same depth by calling the function:

```
XCopyArea ( Display       *display,
            Drawable      source,
            Drawable      destination,
            GC            gc,
            int           src_x,
            int           src_y,
            unsigned int  width,
            unsigned int  height,
            int           dest_x,
            int           dest_y )
```

XCopyArea() copies the rectangular region whose size is `width` by `height`, starting at coordinate *src_x,src_y* in the `source` drawable, to *dest_x,dest_y* in the `destination` drawable.

If the source and destination drawables do not have the same depth, the server generates a `BadMatch` error. The graphics context, `gc`, controls how the bits from the source drawable are combined with the bits in the destination drawable.

Applications can use the function:

```
XCopyPlane (  Display         *display,
              Drawable         source,
              Drawable         destination,
              GC               gc,
              int              src_x,
              int              src_y,
              unsigned int     width,
              unsigned int     height,
              int              dest_x,
              int              dest_y,
              unsigned long plane )
```

to copy data between drawables of different depths. `XCopyPlane()` copies the contents of a single plane of the specified region in the source drawable to the destination drawable. The graphics context determines the foreground and background color of the pattern in the destination drawable.

An Example

This section demonstrates a simple program named `xlogo` that uses bitmaps, pixmaps, and some of the functions described so far to display the X logo shown in Figure 11.1. The program begins by including several Motif header files, the Xlib header X11/Xutil.h, and the xlogo64 bitmap file. The program also declares a global pixmap and a graphics context used by several different functions in this program. The beginning of the file also declares several functions used later in the program.

The body of the program creates an XmDrawingArea widget in which to display the pixmap and then calls the function `InstallPixmap()` to create a pixmap that contains the X logo. This function also registers callbacks to redisplay the pixmap when the XmDrawingArea widget is resized or needs to be redrawn.

```
1    /****************************************************************
2     * xlogo.c: First example of manipulating and displaying pixmaps
3     ****************************************************************/
4    #include <Xm/Xm.h>
5    #include <Xm/DrawingA.h>
6    #include <X11/Xutil.h>
7    #include <X11/bitmaps/xlogo64>
8
9    static void RedisplayCallback ( Widget, XtPointer, XtPointer );
10   static void ResizeCallback ( Widget, XtPointer, XtPointer  );
11   static void InstallPixmap ( Widget w );
12
13   Pixmap xlogoPixmap;
14   GC     gc;
```

```
15  void main ( int argc, char **argv )
16  {
17      Widget        shell, canvas;
18      XtAppContext app;
19
20      shell = XtAppInitialize ( &app, "Xlogo", NULL, 0,
21                                &argc, argv, NULL, NULL, 0  );
22
23      /*
24       * Create a widget in which display the logo.
25       */
26
27      canvas = XtCreateManagedWidget ( "canvas",
28                                       xmDrawingAreaWidgetClass,
29                                       shell, NULL, 0 );
30      InstallPixmap ( canvas );
31
32      XtRealizeWidget ( shell );
33
34      XtAppMainLoop ( app );
35  }
```

The function `InstallPixmap()` creates a pixmap that contains the bit pattern defined in the file xlogo64. The function begins by retrieving the foreground and background colors of the XmDrawingArea widget provided as an argument. These values are retrieved and stored directly into the appropriate members of an `XGCValues` structure. A GC is then created using the retrieved colors.

Next, `XCreateBitmapFromData()` creates a bitmap from the data in xlogo64. `XCreateBitmapFromData()` creates a bitmap, a one-plane version of the xlogo64 image. However, the goal of this program is to display a pixmap using the foreground and background colors of the XmDrawingArea widget. One way to do that is to create a pixmap version of this bitmap. To do this, `InstallPixmap()` must create a pixmap of the same size and copy the single plane of the bitmap to the pixmap.

`XCreatePixmap()` creates a pixmap of the same width and height as the bitmap, but with the same depth as the XmDrawingArea widget. Then, `XCopyPlane()` copies the contents of the bitmap from the single plane of the bitmap to the pixmap. The graphics context determines the foreground and background colors of the pixmap. If a bit on the copied plane is set to one, it is copied to the pixmap as the foreground color indicated by the graphics context. If a bit is a zero, the bit is copied to the pixmap as the background color. Once the image is copied to the pixmap, the bitmap is no longer needed and it can be freed using `XFreePixmap()`.

So far, `InstallPixmap()` has created a color pixmap, but it has not been displayed anywhere. The callback functions `ResizeCallback()` and `RedisplayCallback()` are responsible for positioning and displaying the pixmap in the XmDrawingArea widget. `InstallPixmap()` registers these functions as `XmNresizeCallback` and `XmNexpose-Callback` functions, respectively.

```
36   static void InstallPixmap ( Widget w )
37   {
38       XGCValues   values;
39       Pixmap      bitmap;
40       int         depth;
41
42       /*
43        * Use the foreground and background colors
44        * of the canvas to create a graphics context.
45        */
46
47       XtVaGetValues ( w,   XmNforeground, &values.foreground,
48                            XmNbackground, &values.background,
49                            XmNdepth,        &depth,
50                            NULL  );
51       gc = XtGetGC ( w, GCForeground | GCBackground, &values );
52
53       /*
54        * Create a bitmap of the X logo, and then an empty
55        * pixmap of the same size.
56        */
57
58       bitmap =
59           XCreateBitmapFromData ( XtDisplay ( w ),
60                                   RootWindowOfScreen ( XtScreen ( w ) ),
61                                   xlogo64_bits, xlogo64_width,
62                                   xlogo64_height );
63       xlogoPixmap =
64               XCreatePixmap ( XtDisplay ( w ),
65                               RootWindowOfScreen ( XtScreen ( w ) ),
66                               xlogo64_width, xlogo64_height, depth );
67       /*
68        * Copy the contents of plane 1 of the bitmap to the
69        * pixmap, using the widget's foreground and background colors.
70        */
71
72       XCopyPlane ( XtDisplay ( w ), bitmap, xlogoPixmap, gc, 0, 0,
73                    xlogo64_width, xlogo64_height, 0, 0, 1 );
74
75       XFreePixmap ( XtDisplay ( w ), bitmap );
76
77       /*
78        * Register callbacks to display the pixmap and keep it
79        * centered in the XmDrawingArea widget.
80        */
81
82       XtAddCallback ( w, XmNexposeCallback, RedisplayCallback,  NULL );
83       XtAddCallback ( w, XmNresizeCallback, ResizeCallback,     NULL );
84   }
```

The function `RedisplayCallback()` is registered as an `XmNexposeCallback` function. The XmDrawingArea widget calls all callback functions on this list when the widget's window needs to be redrawn. The `RedisplayCallback()` callback function checks the current width and height of the widget and then uses `XCopyArea()` to transfer the contents of the xlogo pixmap to the center of the XmDrawingArea widget's window.

```
85   static void RedisplayCallback  ( Widget     w,
86                                     XtPointer clientData,
87                                     XtPointer callData )
88   {
89       Dimension width, height;
90
91       /*
92        * Get the current size of the widget window.
93        */
94
95       XtVaGetValues ( w,
96                       XmNwidth,  &width,
97                       XmNheight, &height,
98                       NULL  );
99       /*
100       * Copy the pixmap to the center of the window
101       */
102
103      XCopyArea ( XtDisplay ( w ), xlogoPixmap, XtWindow ( w ),
104                  gc, 0, 0, xlogo64_width, xlogo64_height,
105                  ( width - xlogo64_width ) / 2,
106                  ( height - xlogo64_height ) / 2 );
107  }
```

The `ResizeCallback()` callback simply clears the XmDrawingArea widget's window, if the widget is realized. It is important to check whether or not the widget is realized, because functions on the `XmNresizeCallback` list can be called when the widget is resized, even if the window does not yet exist. This callback uses the Xlib function:

```
XClearArea (  Display       *display,
              Window        window,
              int           x,
              int           y,
              unsigned int  width,
              unsigned int  height,
              Boolean       exposures )
```

to clear the window. `XClearArea()` clears a rectangular area in a window. If the `width` is given as zero, it is replaced by the width of the window minus `x`. Similarly, if the `height` is given as zero, it is replaced by the height of the window minus `y`. The `exposures` parameter indicates whether or not exposure events should be generated for the cleared area.

Because of the way the XmDrawingArea widget is implemented, the Redisplay-Callback() function will not be invoked when the XmDrawingArea widget is made smaller. However, by calling XClearArea() with exposures set to TRUE, ResizeCallback() can trigger an Expose event for the entire window every time the window is resized. It is important to trigger a redisplay because RedisplayCallback() centers the pixmap in the window.

The ResizeCallback() function is written as follows:

```
108   static void ResizeCallback ( Widget      w,
109                                 XtPointer clientData,
110                                 XtPointer callData )
111   {
112       if ( XtIsRealized ( w ) )
113           XClearArea ( XtDisplay ( w ),
114                        XtWindow ( w ),
115                        0, 0, 0, 0, TRUE );
116   }
```

Figure 11.2 shows how this program appears on the screen.

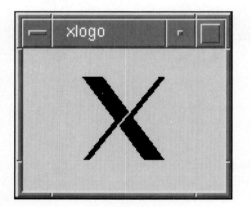

Figure 11.2 The X logo pixmap.

A Variation

The xlogo example program illustrates many of the Xlib functions that create and initialize bitmaps and pixmaps, and also shows how data can be transferred between bitmaps, pixmaps, and windows. However, you may have noticed that one step in this example is unnecessary. The RedisplayCallback() function could use XCopyPlane() to copy directly between a *bitmap* and the widget window, which completely eliminates the need for the pixmap.

Using this approach, InstallPixmap() can be rewritten to be slightly shorter and to create less pixmaps. In the following functions, changes from the previous implementation are shown in bold.

```
static void InstallPixmap ( Widget w )
{
    XGCValues     values;

    /*
     * Use the foreground and background colors
     * of the canvas to create a graphics context.
     */

    XtVaGetValues ( w,
                    XmNforeground, &values.foreground,
                    XmNbackground, &values.background,
                    NULL );

    gc = XtGetGC ( w, GCForeground | GCBackground, &values );

    /*
     * Create the bitmap of the X logo.
     */

    xlogoPixmap =
            XCreateBitmapFromData ( XtDisplay ( w ),
                                    RootWindowOfScreen ( XtScreen (w)),
                                    xlogo64_bits,
                                    xlogo64_width,
                                    xlogo64_height );
    /*
     * Register callbacks to display the pixmap and keep it
     * centered in the XmDrawingArea widget.
     */

    XtAddCallback ( w, XmNexposeCallback, RedisplayCallback, NULL );
    XtAddCallback ( w, XmNresizeCallback, ResizeCallback,    NULL );
}
```

The RedisplayCallback() function must also be changed. The new version of RedisplayCallback() displays the xlogo in the XmDrawingArea widget by copying a plane of the bitmap directly to the XmDrawingArea widget, as follows:

```
static void RedisplayCallback ( Widget w,
                                XtPointer clientData,
                                XtPointer callData )
{
    Dimension width, height;

    /*
     * Get the current size of the widget window.
     */
```

```
XtVaGetValues ( w,
                XmNwidth,  &width,
                XmNheight, &height,
                NULL  );

/*
 * Copy plane 1 of the bitmap to the center
 * of the window, using the widget's foreground
 * and background color.
 */

XCopyPlane ( XtDisplay ( w ), xlogoPixmap, XtWindow ( w ),
             gc, 0, 0,  xlogo64_width, xlogo64_height,
             ( width - xlogo64_width ) / 2,
             ( height - xlogo64_height ) / 2, 1 );
}
```

Another slight improvement in this example would be to have `ResizeCallback()` detect changes in the width and height of the widget. This would be a more efficient way to handle changes to the widget's size, because it would eliminate the need to retrieve the widget's width and height every time the widget's window is exposed. However, to do this, `ResizeCallback()` would need to store the size information somewhere and make it available to the `Redisplay-Callback()` function.

Also, it is important to realize that the purpose of the examples in this section is to demonstrate pixmaps and their related functions and not necessarily to show the easiest way to display the X logo. The easiest way to display a pixmap such as the X logo, is to use an XmLabel widget, with the `XmNlabelType` resource set to `XmPIXMAP` to display the pixmap. An example that uses this approach is discussed in Section 11.5.

11.4 Images

X provides a way to transfer images between applications and the server using an `XImage` data structure. This structure stores data in a device-dependent format; therefore, applications are not expected to access the data directly. The server handles byte-swapping and other data transformations that are sometimes necessary when exchanging images between applications running on different machines. The `XImage` data structure contains the pixel data that represents the image as well as information about the format of the image.

Creating Images

Applications can create an `XImage` using the function:

```
XImage *XCreateImage ( Display        *display,
                       Visual         *visual,
                       unsigned int depth,
                       int            format,
                       int            offset,
                       char           *data,
                       unsigned int width,
                       unsigned int height,
                       int            bitmap_pad,
                       int            bytes_per_line )
```

In addition to the usual `Display` pointer, this function requires a pointer to a `Visual` structure that represents a visual type with which the image is to be used. The `data` argument must specify an array of bits that represent the image. The size of this data is specified by the `width`, `height` and `depth`. The `format` specifies the byte order of the data and must be one of the constants `XYPixmap`, `XYBitmap`, or `ZPixmap`. In `XYPixmap` format, each byte of data specifies values for one plane of eight consecutive pixels, and each bit of the data contributes to one pixel. `ZPixmap` format specifies the image *depth-first*. For example, in `ZPixmap` format, on a display with eight bit planes, each byte of data represents one pixel. For an image whose depth is 24 bits, each set of three bytes represents one pixel. The argument `bytes_per_line` specifies the number of bytes in one line and must be a multiple of 8, 16, or 32 bits.

Images may also be extracted from a drawable using the function:

```
XImage *XGetImage ( Display        *display,
                    Drawable       drawable,
                    int            x,
                    int            y,
                    unsigned int   width,
                    unsigned int   height,
                    unsigned long  plane_mask,
                    int            format )
```

`XGetImage()` creates an `XImage` structure, copies a rectangular region of a drawable into the image, and returns a pointer to the `XImage` structure. The argument `plane_mask` determines which planes in the drawable are included in the image, while the `format` argument determines whether the image is created in `XYPixmap` or `ZPixmap` format.

X also provides several other functions for manipulating images:

• `XSubImage()` creates a new image and copies the contents of a rectangular sub-region of an old image into the new image. The form of this function is:

```
XImage *XSubImage ( XImage         *image,
                    int            x,
                    int            y,
                    unsigned int width,
                    unsigned int height );
```

- `XDestroyImage()` frees an image. This function has the form:

```
XDestroyImage ( XImage *image )
```

- `XPutPixel()` sets the pixel value of an *x,y* location in an `XImage`.

```
XPutPixel ( XImage *image, int x, int y, unsigned long pixel );
```

- `XGetPixel()` retrieves the value of a pixel at a particular *x,y* location with an `XImage`.

```
unsigned long XGetPixel ( XImage *image, int x, int y )
```

- `XPutImage()` transfers an image to a drawable.

```
XPutImage ( Display        *display,
            Drawable       drawable,
            GC             gc,
            XImage         *image,
            int            src_x,
            int            src_y,
            int            dest_x,
            int            dest_y,
            unsigned int   width,
            unsigned int   height )
```

11.5 Caching Pixmaps

Motif includes a pixmap caching facility that can be used to store and retrieve commonly used pixmaps. Motif caches a number of built-in pixmaps, and applications can also store additional patterns. The function

```
Pixmap XmGetPixmap ( Screen *screen,
                     char   *name,
                     Pixel   foreground,
                     Pixel   background )
```

returns a named pixmap with the depth of the specified screen, using the given foreground and background colors. The name must be one of the built-in pixmaps, the name of a file on a bitmap search path, or an image previously registered by the application.

The pre-defined patterns provided by Motif include:

```
"background"          "25_foreground"       "50_foreground"
"75_foreground"       "horizontal"          "vertical"
"slant_right"         "slant_left"          "menu_cascade"
"menu_checkmark"
```

Because these pixmaps are cached and may be used in more than one place, applications should treat them as read-only.

XmGetPixmap() can also create a pixmap from a bitmap file. In this case, the given name must identify the name of a file on a bitmap search path. This search path looks first in the directory /usr/include/X11/bitmaps and then the user's home directory for a named file.

For example, the following program uses XmGetPixmap() to display the xlogo64 image used earlier in this chapter. This program simply creates an XmLabel widget and calls XmGetPixmap() to create a pixmap of the X logo using the colors of the XmLabel widget. The pixmap is displayed by setting the XmLabel widget's XmNlabelType resource to XmPIXMAP and specifying the xlogo pixmap as the value of the XmNlabelPixmap resource.

```
1     /***********************************************
2      * xlogo.c: Display a pixmap on the screen
3      ***********************************************/
4     #include <Xm/Xm.h>
5     #include <Xm/Label.h>
6
7     void main ( int argc, char **argv  )
8     {
9         Widget        shell, label;
10        XtAppContext  app;
11        Pixel         fg, bg;
12        Pixmap        pix;
13
14        shell = XtAppInitialize ( &app, "Xlogo", NULL, 0,
15                                  &argc, argv, NULL, NULL, 0  );
16
17        /*
18         * Create an XmLabel widget
19         */
20
21        label = XtCreateManagedWidget ( "label", xmLabelWidgetClass,
22                                        shell, NULL, 0 );
23
24        /* Get the label's foreground and background colors */
25
26        XtVaGetValues ( label,
27                        XmNforeground, &fg,
28                        XmNbackground, &bg,
29                        NULL );
```

```
30      /*
31       * Create a pixmap, using the bitmap file
32       * found in /usr/include/X11/bitmaps
33       */
34
35      pix =  XmGetPixmap ( XtScreen ( shell ), "xlogo64", fg, bg );
36
37      /* Display the pixmap in the label */
38
39      XtVaSetValues ( label, XmNlabelType, XmPIXMAP,
40                             XmNlabelPixmap, pix,
41                             NULL );
42      /*
43       * Realize the shell and enter the event loop.
44       */
45
46      XtRealizeWidget ( shell );
47      XtAppMainLoop ( app );
48  }
```

This example is functionally equivalent to the xlogo example in Chapter 4. The Chapter 4 example specifies the pixmap by setting the `XmNlabelType` and `XmNlabelPixmap` in a resource file, which causes the XmLabel widget to load and convert the named file. This example handles the pixmap explicitly in the program. Both techniques are useful.

Sometimes applications need to define new patterns. Programs can cache additional pixmaps by registering an `XImage` that represents the desired pattern. Images can be added to the cache by calling the function:

```
Boolean XmInstallImage ( XImage *image, char *name )
```

The specified image must be in `XYBitmap` format and have a depth of one. `XmGetPixmap()` can generate pixmaps for any color combination from the registered monochrome image.

The following function shows how to use this approach to cache a new pattern that can be retrieved as a pixmap using `XmGetPixmap()`. `RegisterBitmap()` can be used to register any bit pattern, like that found in the xlogo bitmap file. The function simply creates an `XImage` from the bits and then uses `XmInstallImage()` to register the image.

```
void RegisterBitmap ( Widget w, char *name, char *bits,
                      int width, int height )
{
    XImage *image =
            XCreateImage ( XtDisplay ( w ),
                           DefaultVisualOfScreen ( XtScreen ( w ) ),
                           1, XYBitmap, 0,
                           bits, width, height, 8, 2 );
    XmInstallImage ( image, name );
}
```

A Pixmap Browser

This section demonstrates a simple pixmap browser that uses some of the functions discussed in the previous section. The browser allows the user to select from a list of patterns displayed in a dialog. This example displays some of the Motif built-in images as well as an additional image registered by the browser, a "foreground" pixmap. Motif does not provide a "foreground" pixmap pattern, which is useful in some cases. The bit pattern for a foreground pixmap is just a 16 by 16 bit array of ones.

The example is broken into two parts: a general purpose pixmap browser and an example program that uses the browser. The browser consists of several functions, some publicly accessible and some private. All the code for the browser can be placed in one file. The browser simply takes a list of named patterns and displays the corresponding pixmaps. It is the caller's responsibility to ensure that all the names provided have been previously registered with the Motif pixmap caching facility. The names can also correspond to bitmap files found in /usr/include/X11/bitmaps, or the user's home directory. The caller can also provide a callback function to be called when the user has selected a pixmap pattern.

The main interface to the pixmap browser is the function `CreatePixmapBrowser()`, which is written as follows:

```
1   /***********************************************************
2    * pixmapBrowser.c  Display a selectable set of patterns
3    ***********************************************************/
4   #include <Xm/Xm.h>
5   #include <Xm/ToggleB.h>
6   #include <Xm/RowColumn.h>
7   #include <Xm/MessageB.h>
8
9   static void SelectPixmapCallback ( Widget    w,
10                                     XtPointer clientData,
11                                     XtPointer callData);
12  static void OkCallback ( Widget    w,
13                           XtPointer clientData,
14                           XtPointer callData );
15
16  Widget CreatePixmapBrowser ( Widget          parent,
17                               char            **patterns,
18                               int             numPatterns,
19                               XtCallbackProc  callback )
20  {
21      Widget      browser, dialog;
22      int         i;
23
24      dialog = XmCreateTemplateDialog ( parent, "pixmapBrowser",
25                                        NULL, 0 );
26      /*
27       * Create a "RadioBox" RowColumn widget.
28       */
```

```
29        browser = XmCreateRadioBox ( dialog, "pixmapBrowser", NULL, 0 );
30
31        XtManageChild ( browser );
32
33     /*
34      * Create a button for each pixmap.
35      */
36
37        for ( i = 0; i < numPatterns; i++ )
38        {
39            Pixmap  pixmap;
40            Pixel   fg, bg;
41            Widget  button;
42
43            button = XtCreateManagedWidget ( patterns[i],
44                                             xmToggleButtonWidgetClass,
45                                             browser, NULL, 0 );
46         /*
47          * Retrieve the colors used by this button
48          */
49
50            XtVaGetValues ( button,
51                            XtNforeground, &fg,
52                            XtNbackground, &bg,
53                            NULL );
54         /*
55          * Get the pattern using the colors of the toggle
56          */
57
58            pixmap = XmGetPixmap  ( XtScreen ( button ),
59                                    patterns[i], fg, bg );
60
61         /*
62          * Install the pixmap in the toggle button.
63          */
64
65            XtVaSetValues ( button,
66                            XmNlabelType,   XmPIXMAP,
67                            XmNlabelPixmap, pixmap,
68                            XmNuserData,    pixmap,
69                            NULL );
70
71         /*
72          * Register a callback to be invoked when this pixmap
73          * is selected
74          */
75
76            XtAddCallback ( button,
77                            XmNvalueChangedCallback,
```

```
78                          SelectPixmapCallback, dialog );
79       }
80
81       /*
82        * Register a callback to be called when the
83        * user dismisses the dialog. Specify the user-provided
84        * callback as client data.
85        */
86
87       XtAddCallback ( dialog, XmNokCallback,
88                          OkCallback, ( XtPointer ) callback );
89
90       return ( dialog );
91   }
```

CreatePixmapBrowser() must be called with an array of named pixmaps that can be retrieved with XmGetPixmap(). The function creates an XmTemplateDialog whose work area is a radio box. The radio box contains XmToggleButton widgets that each display a single pixmap. The pixmaps are created by XmGetPixmap(), which is used to create a pixmap whose colors match that of the button used to display the pixmap. Each pixmap is displayed in an XmToggleButton by setting the corresponding widget's XmNlabelPixmap resource. The pixmap's resource identifier is also stored in the widget's XmNuserData resource. A callback function is also registered with each XmToggleButton widget, to be invoked when one of the toggles is selected. CreatePixmapBrowser() ends by registering a function with the dialog's XmNokCallback function, and then returning the dialog.

The other public function provided as part of the pixmap browser is RegisterBitmap(), a function discussed earlier in this chapter. This function allows applications to register bitmap patterns with the Motif pixmap caching mechanism, to allow the pattern to be displayed by the pixmap browser.

```
92 void RegisterBitmap ( Widget w, char *name, char *bits, int width, int height )
93   {
94       XImage *image =
95                  XCreateImage ( XtDisplay ( w ),
96                                 DefaultVisualOfScreen ( XtScreen ( w ) ),
97                                 1, XYBitmap, 0,
98                                 bits, width, height, 8, 2 );
99
100      XmInstallImage ( image, name );
101  }
```

When an XmToggleButton in the pixmap browser is selected, the function SelectPixmap-Callback() is invoked. This function checks whether the toggle button that invoked this callback was set, and if so, retrieves the pixmap associated with this widget by getting the value of the widgets XmNuserData resource. This information needs to be available to the application that uses the browser when the users selects the dialog's OK button. There are may ways to do this, but in this example, the selected pixmap is stored as the value of the dialog's XmNuserData resource.

```
102   static void SelectPixmapCallback ( Widget    w,
103                                       XtPointer clientData,
104                                       XtPointer callData )
105   {
106       Widget dialog = ( Widget ) clientData;
107       XmToggleButtonCallbackStruct *cbs =
108                       ( XmToggleButtonCallbackStruct * ) callData;
109       Pixmap pixmap;
110
111       /*
112        * If this widget has been selected, retrieve the
113        * pixmap from the toggle button and store it in the dialog
114        * where it can be retrieved by the caller.
115        */
116
117       if ( !cbs->set )
118           return;
119
120       XtVaGetValues ( w, XmNuserData, &pixmap, NULL );
121       XtVaSetValues ( dialog, XmNuserData, pixmap, NULL );
122   }
```

The function `OkCallback()` is called when the user selects the OK button of the pixmap browser dialog. This function retrieves the currently selected pixmap and then invokes the callback provided by the calling application. The application's callback function is invoked on line 133. The arguments passed to the callback function are the dialog widget, the selected pixmap (as client data) and the call data passed to the OkCallback function.

```
123   static void OkCallback ( Widget    w,
124                            XtPointer clientData,
125                            XtPointer callData )
126   {
127       Pixmap pixmap;
128       XtCallbackProc callback = ( XtCallbackProc ) clientData;
129
130       XtVaGetValues ( w, XmNuserData, &pixmap, NULL );
131
132       if ( callback )
133           ( *callback ) ( w, ( XtPointer ) pixmap, callData );
134   }
```

The second part of this example is a simple program that calls `CreatePixmapBrowser()` and uses it to select from a set of patterns. This program allows the user to select from one of the predefined patterns supported by Motif, and also adds an additional program-defined pattern. The program begins by defining a "foreground" bitmap pattern in which all bits are set, creating an array of named patterns from which the user can choose, and declaring various functions used in the example.

```
1   /**********************************************************
2    * browser.c: a simple test program for the pixmap browser
3    **********************************************************/
4   #include <Xm/Xm.h>
5   #include <Xm/PushB.h>
6
7   static unsigned char fgBitmap[32] = {    /*  foreground */
8       0xff, 0xff, 0xff, 0xff, 0xff, 0xff, 0xff, 0xff,
9       0xff, 0xff, 0xff, 0xff, 0xff, 0xff, 0xff, 0xff,
10      0xff, 0xff, 0xff, 0xff, 0xff, 0xff, 0xff, 0xff,
11      0xff, 0xff, 0xff, 0xff, 0xff, 0xff, 0xff, 0xff
12  };
13
14  #define fgWidth   16
15  #define fgHeight 16
16
17  static char *patterns[] = { "foreground",
18                              "background",
19                              "25_foreground",
20                              "50_foreground",
21                              "75_foreground",
22                              "vertical",
23                              "horizontal",
24                              "slant_right",
25                              "slant_left",
26                            };
27
28  void PostBrowserCallback ( Widget    w,
29                             XtPointer clientData,
30                             XtPointer callData );
31  void PixmapSelectedCallback ( Widget    w,
32                                XtPointer clientData,
33                                XtPointer callData );
34  extern Widget CreatePixmapBrowser ( Widget        w,
35                                      char          **patterns,
36                                      int           numPatterns,
37                                      XtCallbackProc callback );
38  extern void RegisterBitmap ( Widget  w,
39                               char    *name,
40                               char    *bits,
41                               int     width,
42                               int     height );
43  Widget button;
```

The body of this program creates a button, which, when pushed, creates and displays a pixmap browser. The browser is created the first time the `PostBrowserCallback()` is invoked. If the user selects a pixmap from the browser, the pushbutton created by the application is changed to display the pixmap.

```
44   void main ( int argc, char **argv )
45   {
46       Widget       shell;
47       XtAppContext app;
48
49       shell = XtAppInitialize ( &app, "Browser", NULL, 0,
50                                  &argc, argv, NULL, NULL, 0  );
51
52       button = XtCreateManagedWidget ( "pushme",
53                                         xmPushButtonWidgetClass,
54                                         shell, NULL, 0 );
55
56       XtAddCallback ( button, XmNactivateCallback,
57                      PostBrowserCallback, NULL );
58
59       XtRealizeWidget ( shell );
60       XtAppMainLoop ( app );
61   }
```

PostBrowserCallback() calls CreatePixmapBrowser() with the list of patterns from which the user is to select. The foreground pattern, which is not part of the built-in Motif pixmaps patterns, must be registered first by calling RegisterBitmap(). Once the pixmap browser is created, subsequent calls to PostBrowserCallback() just manage the browser dialog.

```
62   void PostBrowserCallback ( Widget    w,
63                              XtPointer clientData,
64                              XtPointer callData )
65   {
66       static Widget pixmapBrowser = NULL;
67
68       /*
69        * Create the pixmap browser dialog the first time this function
70        * is caled, registering the application-defined pattern first.
71        */
72
73       if ( !pixmapBrowser )
74       {
75           RegisterBitmap ( w, "foreground", fgBitmap,
76                           fgWidth, fgHeight );
77
78           pixmapBrowser = CreatePixmapBrowser ( w, patterns,
79                                                  XtNumber (patterns ),
80                                                  PixmapSelectedCallback);
81       }
82
83       XtManageChild ( pixmapBrowser );
84   }
```

The function `PixmapSelectedCallback()` is registered by `PostBrowser-Callback()` when the pixmap browser is created. This function is called when the user selects the OK button on the pixmap browser dialog. `PixmapSelectedCallback()` retrieves the selected pixmap from the client data and displays it in the push button used to launch the pixmap browser.

```
85   void PixmapSelectedCallback ( Widget       w,
86                                 XtPointer clientData,
87                                 XtPointer callData )
88   {
89       Pixmap pixmap = ( Pixmap ) clientData;
90
91       XtVaSetValues ( button,
92                       XmNlabelType,    XmPIXMAP,
93                       XmNlabelPixmap, pixmap,
94                       NULL );
95   }
```

Figure 11.3 shows the pixmap browser created by this example.

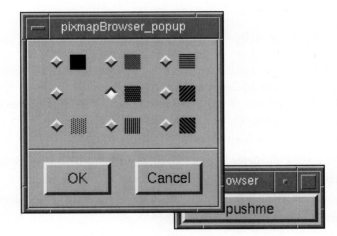

Figure 11.3 The pixmap browser.

11.6 The Xpm Pixmap Format

Although X defines a text-based format for storing bitmaps in a file, it does not define an equivalent format for storing color pixmaps. However, there is a widely available package that does support saving pixmaps in files, reading pixmaps from files, and easily representing multi-color pixmaps. This package is called Xpm (X Pixmap). Xpm is available as part of the contributed software distributed with X. Xpm was developed by Groupe Bull and carries a copyright similar to that used by X itself. Although Xpm is not "public domain", everyone is free to use it.

Xpm was designed to support applications that need to create color icons. The X bitmap format, which consists of a simple array of characters, is too limiting for application that need color pixmaps. The Xpm format is more complex, but still easy to use. An Xpm pixmap description consists of an array of strings, with six different sections. An Xpm description has the form:

```
char *variable_name [] =  {
Values
Colors
Pixels
Extensions
};
```

The Values section is a string that defines the width and height of the pixmap, the number of colors used by the pixmap, the number of characters per pixel, and an optional hotspot coordinate. For example, the following line

```
"16 16 3 1",
```

indicates a three-color pixmap 16 by 16 pixels in size. The description maps one character to one pixel.

The Colors section contains a string for each color used by the pixmap. Each string indicates a key (a character used to indicate this color in the pixels section) followed by a color specification.

A color specification consists of any number of pairs of mode identifiers and colors. The currently supported mode identifiers are:

- m: Indicates a color to be used with a monochrome visual.
- s: Indicates a symbolic name to be replaced by a color provided by the application.
- g4: Indicates a color to be used with a four-level monochrome visual.
- g: Indicates a color to be used with a monochrome visual with more than 4 levels.
- c: Indicates a color to be used with a color visual.

The various modes indicate what colors should be used in different situations and allow an application to set up a pixmap that can work on a number of different displays and visual types. The color names themselves can be given using a color name (as found in the rgb.text database), a hex RGB specification, or an HSV specification.

For example, a pixmap might contain a color specification like this:

```
"X c red m white g4 grey75 g grey 85 s brightColor"
```

This indicates that any pixel marked with an "X" in the pixels section of the pixmap description should be displayed as red on a color display, white on a monochrome display, the color named "grey75" on a four-level grey scale display, and "grey85" on a display with more than 4 levels of grey. In addition, this pixel is assigned a symbolic name of "`brightColor`". This symbolic name allows an application to override the color choice easily.

The Pixels section contains an array of strings whose width is equal to the width of the pixmap. There are as many strings as the height of the pixmap.

For example, the following Xpm pixmap specification represents a three-color X logo. This pixmap is 16 by 16 pixels and uses one character to represent one pixel. The background is represented by the "." character and is set by default to white on both color and monochrome displays. The background color is also associated with a symbolic name of "background". There are two other colors in the pixmap, represented by the characters "a" and "X". On a color display, these colors are red and blue, while on a monochrome display they are both black. Neither of these colors has a symbolic name.

```
static char * xlogo16[] = {
"16 16 3 1",
"a c red m black",
". c white m white s background",
"X c blue m black",
"aaaa..........X",
".aaaa.........X",
"..aaaa........X.",
"...aaaa......X..",
"...aaaa.....X...",
"....aaaa...X....",
".....aaaa..X....",
"......aaa.X.....",
"......aa.X......",
"......a.XXX.....",
".....a..XXXX....",
".....a...XXXX...",
"....a....XXXX...",
"...a......XXXX..",
"..a........XXXX.",
".a..........XXXX" };
```

The Xpm package includes a library that contains a number of functions that allow applications to create and manipulate the Xpm format. For example, a pixmap can be created from the data shown above, using the function:

```
int XpmCreatePixmapFromData ( Display        *display,
                              Drawable       d,
                              char           **data,
                              Pixmap         *pixmap_return,
                              Pixmap         *shapemask_return,
                              XpmAttributes *attributes ) )
```

The first argument to this function must be a pointer to a `Display`, while the second is expected to be a drawable. The third argument is the Xpm description, like the X logo description shown above. The fourth and fifth arguments are used to return a pixmap and a mask corresponding to the given data.

The final argument to this function is a data structure of type `XpmAttributes`, which is used to pass information to the function, and also returns information about pixmaps once they are created.

The `XpmAttributes` structure is defined as follows:

```
typedef struct {
    unsigned long valuemask;        /* Specifies which attributes are
                                        defined */
    Visual *visual;                 /* Specifies the visual to use */
    Colormap colormap;              /* Specifies the colormap to use */
    unsigned int depth;             /* Specifies the depth */
    unsigned int width;             /* Returns the width of the created
                                        pixmap */
    unsigned int height;            /* Returns the height of the created
                                        pixmap */
    unsigned int x_hotspot;         /* Returns the x hotspot's
                                        coordinate */
    unsigned int y_hotspot;         /* Returns the y hotspot's
                                        coordinate */
    unsigned int cpp;               /* Specifies the number of char per
                                        pixel */
    Pixel *pixels;                  /* List of used color pixels */
    unsigned int npixels;           /* Number of pixels */
    XpmColorSymbol *colorsymbols;   /* Array of color symbols to
                                        override */
    unsigned int numsymbols;        /* Number of symbols */
    char *rgb_fname;                /* RGB text file name */
    unsigned int nextensions;       /* number of extensions */
    XpmExtension *extensions;       /* pointer to array of extensions */
    unsigned int ncolors;           /* Number of colors */
    char ***colorTable;             /* Color table pointer */
    char *hints_cmt;                /* Comment of the hints section */
    char *colors_cmt;               /* Comment of the colors section */
    char *pixels_cmt;               /* Comment of the pixels section */
    unsigned int mask_pixel;        /* Transparent pixel's color table
                                        index */
} XpmAttributes;
```

The `XpmAttributes` structure is used with a mask, much like the `XGCValues` structure and its mask. The values that can be used in an `XpmAttributes` mask include:

XpmVisual	XpmColormap	XpmDepth	XpmSize
XpmHotspot	XpmCharsPerPixel	XpmColorSymbols	XpmRgbFilename
XpmInfos	XpmExtensions	XpmReturnPixels	XpmReturnInfos

The values can be combined (using a logical OR) to form a mask that indicates which members of the XpmAttributes structure contain valid information. At a minimum, information about the colormap, the visual type, and desired depth of the pixmap must be provided. For example, the following program creates an XmPushButton widget and installs the X logo pixmap described above. The first part of the program implements a simple driver that handles initialization and the event loop.

```
1   /**************************************************
2    * xpmlogo.c: Display the X Logo using Xpm format
3    **************************************************/
4   #include <Xm/Xm.h>
5   #include <Xm/PushB.h>
6   #include <X11/xpm.h>   /* Non-standard header file */
7
8   static char * xlogo16[] = {
9   "16 16 3 1",
10  "a c red m black",
11  ". c white m white s background",
12  "X c blue m black",
13  "aaaa..........X",
14  ".aaaa.........X",
15  "..aaaa........X.",
16  "...aaaa......X..",
17  "...aaaa.....X...",
18  "....aaaa...X....",
19  ".....aaaa..X....",
20  "......aaa.X.....",
21  "......aa.X......",
22  "......a.XXX.....",
23  ".....a..XXXX....",
24  ".....a...XXXX...",
25  "....a....XXXX...",
26  "...a......XXXX..",
27  "..a........XXXX.",
28  ".a..........XXXX"};
29
30  Widget CreateXlogoButton ( Widget parent );
31
32  void main ( int argc, char **argv )
33  {
34      Widget        shell, button;
35      XtAppContext app;
36
37      shell = XtAppInitialize ( &app, "XPmlogo", NULL, 0,
38                                &argc, argv, NULL, NULL, 0  );
39
40      button = CreateXlogoButton ( shell );
```

```
41        XtRealizeWidget ( shell );
42        XtAppMainLoop ( app );
43   }
```

The function `CreateXlogoButton()` creates and returns an XmPushButton widget after creating the Xlogo pixmap and setting the appropriate resource to display it in the button

```
44   Widget CreateXlogoButton ( Widget parent )
45   {
46       Widget           button;
47       Pixmap           pix, mask;
48       XpmAttributes    attributes;
49       int              status;
50       Display          *dpy = XtDisplay ( parent );
51
52       /*
53        * Create a button widget
54        */
55
56       button = XtCreateManagedWidget ( "button",
57                                        xmPushButtonWidgetClass,
58                                        parent, NULL, 0 );
59       /*
60        * Retrieve the depth and colormap used by this widget
61        * and store the results in the corresponding field
62        * of an XpmAttributes structure.
63        */
64
65       XtVaGetValues ( button,
66                       XmNdepth,     &attributes.depth,
67                       XmNcolormap, &attributes.colormap,
68                       NULL);
69
70       /*
71        * Specify the visual to be used and set the XpmAttributes mask.
72        */
73
74       attributes.visual = DefaultVisual ( dpy, DefaultScreen ( dpy ) );
75       attributes.valuemask = XpmDepth | XpmColormap | XpmVisual;
76
77       /*
78        * Create the pixmap
79        */
80
81       status = XpmCreatePixmapFromData ( dpy,
82                                          DefaultRootWindow ( dpy ),
83                                          xlogo16, &pix, &mask,
84                                          &attributes );
```

```
85        /*
86         * The mask isn't used, so free it if one was created.
87         */
88
89        if ( mask )
90            XFreePixmap( dpy, mask );
91
92        /*
93         * Install the pixmap in the button
94         */
95
96        if ( status == XpmSuccess )
97            XtVaSetValues ( button, XmNlabelType, XmPIXMAP,
98                                    XmNlabelPixmap, pix,
99                                    NULL );
100
101       return ( button );
102   }
```

Figure 11.4 shows the image created by this program.

Figure 11.4 X logo created by Xpm example.

One complication when installing multi-color pixmaps in Motif buttons or labels is that the colors may not work well with the colors of the widgets. Usually, button and label backgrounds can be customized by the end user, so it is difficult to match the background of an iconic image with that of the button or label. Xpm provides a feature that makes this easy. The optional symbolic name that can be assigned to a color can be associated with a specific color at run time. Symbolic colors are associated with actual colors using an `XpmColorSymbol` structure, which can be passed to `XpmCreatePixmapFromData()` as an attribute.

The `XpmColorSymbol` structure has the following members:

```
char *name;
char *value;
Pixel pixel;
```

To associate a symbolic color with a real color, a programmer simply specifies the symbolic color as the `name` member, and provides either a named color in the `value` member, or sets the `value` member to `NULL` and provides a specific pixel value in the `pixel` member. An array of such structures can then be passed as an attribute when creating the pixmap.

Let's look at an example. In the `CreateXlogoButton()` function described earlier, the pixmap has a white background, which may look bad on a button whose background color has been chosen to be something else (See Figure 11.4). The background color used by the pixmap can be made to match the widget's background by making just a few small changes.

Recall that the xlogo16 pixmap description on page 357 specifies a symbolic color name for the pixel used as the pixmap background. The symbolic name can be any arbitrary string, but in this case, the descriptive name "background" is used. The following variation of `CreateXlogoButton()` uses an `XpmColorSymbol` array to replace this symbolic name with the background color of the widget in which the pixmap is displayed. Changes from the previous implementation are shown in bold.

```
Widget CreateXlogoButton ( Widget parent )
{
    Widget          button;
    Pixmap          pix, mask;
    XpmAttributes   attributes;
    int             status;
    Display         *dpy = XtDisplay ( parent );
    XpmColorSymbol  symbols[1];
    Pixel           bg;

    /*
     * Create a button widget
     */

    button = XtCreateManagedWidget ( "button",
                                     xmPushButtonWidgetClass,
                                     parent, NULL, 0 );
    /*
     * Retrieve the depth and colormap used by this widget
     * and store the results in the corresponding field
     * of an XpmAttributes structure. Also retrieve the
     * background color of the button widget.
     */

    XtVaGetValues ( button,
                    XmNdepth,      &attributes.depth,
                    XmNcolormap,   &attributes.colormap,
                    XmNbackground, &bg,
                    NULL);
    /*
     * Set up the XpmColorSymbol array, binding the name "background"
     * to the actual background color of the widget.
```

```
        */

        symbols[0].name = "background";
        symbols[0].value = NULL;
        symbols[0].pixel = bg;

    /*
     * Set the resulting information in the attributes structure
     */

        attributes.colorsymbols = symbols;
        attributes.numsymbols = 1;

    /*
     * Specify the visual to be used and set the XpmAttributes mask.
     */

        attributes.visual = DefaultVisual ( dpy, DefaultScreen ( dpy ) );
        attributes.valuemask = XpmColorSymbols | XpmDepth |
                               XpmColormap | XpmVisual;
    /*
     * Create the pixmap
     */

        status = XpmCreatePixmapFromData ( dpy,
                                           DefaultRootWindow ( dpy ),
                                           xlogo16, &pix, &mask,
                                           &attributes );
    /*
     * The mask isn't used, so free it if one was created.
     */

        if ( mask )
            XFreePixmap ( dpy, mask );

    /*
     * Install the pixmap in the button
     */

        if ( status == XpmSuccess )
            XtVaSetValues ( button, XmNlabelType, XmPIXMAP,
                            XmNlabelPixmap, pix,
                            NULL );
        return ( button );
}
```

Figure 11.4 shows the image created by this program. Notice that the pixmap background now blends with the background color of the widget.

Figure 11.5 X logo created by Xpm example.

There are many other Xpm functions, including functions that can be used to read an Xpm pixmap description from a file, or write a pixmap in the form of an Xpm description. These functions have the same form as `XpmCreatePixmapFromData()`, and are defined as follows:

```
int XpmReadFileToPixmap ( Display        *display,
                          Drawable        d,
                          char           *filename,
                          Pixmap         *pixmap_return,
                          Pixmap         *shapemask_return,
                          XpmAttributes  *attributes)

int XpmWriteFileFromPixmap ( Display        *display,
                             char           *filename,
                             Pixmap          pixmap,
                             Pixmap          shapemask,
                             XpmAttributes  *attributes)
```

11.7 Summary

This chapter introduces various types of images and the Xlib functions that manipulate them. X supports several image formats, including bitmaps, pixmaps, and `XImage` structures. Pixmaps and are stored in off-screen memory, which allows programs to store and manipulate images without displaying them on the screen. Xlib provides functions for manipulating pixmaps and bitmaps. The Xpm library contains additional facilities for using color pixmaps. Pixmaps and bitmaps play an important role in applications that provide iconic interfaces. Used appropriately, pixmaps and bitmaps can enhance an application's interface by providing a more graphical appearance.

Chapter 12

Text and Fonts

Xlib provides a set of primitive functions for drawing text in a window or pixmap. X draws characters on the screen using bitmaps that represent each character. A *font* is a collection of bitmapped characters. This chapter discusses fonts and presents the Xlib functions that draw text in a window. The chapter also presents examples that combine the elements of the last few chapters with the Xlib text-drawing functions.

Although it is useful to understand the X support for fonts and text, Motif does not directly use the font and text rendering functions provided by Xlib. Instead, Motif builds on the Xlib mechanisms to provide an abstraction known as a *compound string* that represents text in a language-independent manner. This chapter describes compound strings and also discusses the functions provided by Motif for creating, manipulating, and drawing compound strings.

12.1 Fonts

A font is a collection of *glyphs*, which are rectangular bitmaps that represent an image. Although a glyph may contain any bit pattern, fonts usually contain text characters. Each glyph represents on character.

Before an application can use a font, it must load the font into the server. The function:

```
Font XLoadFont ( Display *display, char *font_name )
```

finds and loads the named font, and returns a resource ID that refers to the font.

The function:

```
XFontStruct *XQueryFont ( Display * display, Font font_ID )
```

returns an XFontStruct structure that contains detailed information about a font. The function:

```
XFontStruct *XLoadQueryFont ( Display *display, char *name )
```

performs the equivalent of an XLoadFont() followed by an XQueryFont() and returns the XFontStruct information with a single server request. The members of the XFontStruct structure includes:

- fid: The resource ID used to refer to the font.
- direction: A flag that indicates whether the characters in the font are defined left to right or right to left. X supports only horizontally drawn text.
- min_bounds: An XCharStruct structure that contains the bounding box of the smallest character in the font.
- max_bounds: An XCharStruct structure that contains the bounding box of the largest character in the font.
- ascent: An integer that indicates how far the font extends above the baseline.
- descent: An integer that indicates how far the font extends below the baseline.
- per_char: An array of XCharStruct structures for each character in the font. X fonts can be *mono-spaced* (having the same width) or *proportional* (varying widths among characters).

The XCharStruct structure is defined in Xlib.h and contains the following information:

```
short           lbearing;
short           rbearing;
short           width;
short           ascent;
short           descent;
unsigned short  attributes;
```

This structure contains information about the size and location of a single character relative to the origin, as shown in Figure 12.1.

Xlib provides functions that calculate the size, in pixels, of character strings based on the font used. The function:

```
int XTextWidth ( XFontStruct *fontstruct, char *string, int length )
```

calculates the pixel length of a character string for a particular font.

The function:

```
XTextExtents ( XFontStruct  *font,
               char         *string,
               int           nchars,
               int          *direction,
               int          *fontAscent,
               int          *fontDescent,
               XCharSet     *overall )
```

provides additional information. This function returns the direction, ascent, and descent for the entire string, and also returns an `XCharStruct` that contains the width, left bearing, and right bearing of the entire string.

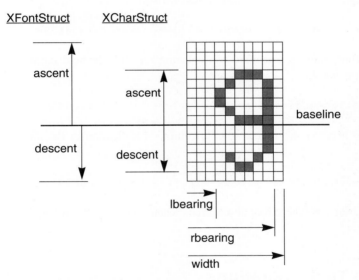

Figure 12.1 Bounding box of a character.

Specifying Fonts in Resource Files

X allows fonts to be specified in resource files using a format known as the X Logical Font Description, or XLFD. The `XLFD` consists of two parts, a font name and a list of font properties. Most programmers and users are only concerned with the font name. Font names have the following form:

```
-*-helvetica-medium-r-normal-*-12-*-*-*-*-*-iso8859-1
```

This string consists of a sequence of fields, separated by dashes. Each field represents some characteristic of a font. The asterisks are used as wildcards to indicate that a particular characteristic is not important, and that any available font that matches the non-wildcard fields is acceptable. For example, the first field, shown here as an "*", is the foundry field is generally identifies the producer of the font. For example, if a programmer specifically wishes to use fonts supplied by Adobe, this field could be given as the string "adobe". Typically, this field is given as a wildcard.

The most commonly used fields are the family name field, the weight name field, the slant field, the setwidth name field, and the point size field. The family name field indicates a general typeface, such as Helvetica, Times Roman, Courier, and so on. The weight field indicates the "blackness" of the font, and is usually one of medium, bold, or demibold. The fourth field is known as the "slant" field, and can have the values "r" for roman, "i" for italic, "o" for oblique, "ri" for reverse italic, "ro" for reverse oblique, and so on. The setwidth name field is typically set to "normal", but could have other values, including "condensed" or "narrow".

So, the above string specifies a twelve point, medium font that belongs to the Helvetica family. The font has a normal widget and has a roman slant. An oblique version of this font could be specified by replacing the "r" in the fourth field with an "o" for "oblique":

```
-*-helvetica-medium-o-normal-*-12-*-*-*-*-*-iso8859-1
```

A larger font could be specified by replacing the "12" in field number seven with another number, 18 for example:

```
-*-helvetica-medium-o-normal-*-12-*-*-*-*-*-iso8859-1
```

To specify a bold font, replace the "medium" specification in the third field with the word "bold":

```
-*-helvetica-bold-o-normal-*-12-*-*-*-*-*-iso8859-1
```

Motif programs use these font descriptions when specifying a fontlist, as described later in this chapter.

12.2 Xlib Text Operations

X displays text in a drawable by performing a fill operation on a region using the text font as a mask. Xlib provides two simple functions for displaying strings:

```
XDrawString ( Display *display,
              Drawable d,
              GC       gc,
              int      x,
              int      y,
              char     *str,
              int      nchars )
```

and:

```
XDrawImageString ( Display *display,
                   Drawable d,
                   GC       gc,
                   int      x,
                   int      y,
                   char     *str,
                   int      nchars )
```

Both functions display a string in a drawable starting at the given position. The graphics context determines the foreground color, background color, the display function, the font, and the fill style. The graphics context also determines any stipple or tile pattern and clipping region used. `XDrawString()` draws only the foreground component of the text, while `XDrawImageString()` also fills the background region within each character's bounding box.

12.3 Compound Strings

Unlike Xlib, Motif does not use character strings. Instead, Motif represents text using an abstraction known as a *compound string*. The purpose of a compound string is to allow textual data to be encoded in a way that is independent of the underlying assumptions often made about strings. It is often assumed that strings represent ASCII characters, which need not always be the case.

Compound strings break text into several components:

- A *font list tag* which is used in conjunction with a font list to determine how the string is to be displayed.

- A *direction* component that defines the relationship between the keystroke entry order and the order in which the characters in a string are seen on the screen. In English this display order goes from left to right, but in languages such as Hebrew the direction is right to left. The default direction is left-to-right.

- A *text* component which represents the actual data and is not interpreted.

Compound strings can consist of a single text component and its attributes, or a list of compound strings. A special type of compound string, a separator, is just a compound string with no value which is used to separate other segments.

Fontlists

Motif supports the concept of a *fontlist*, a list of fonts identified by a *tag*. A tag is just an identifier. Motif widgets uses an `XmNfontList` resource to determine the font with which text is to be displayed. All Motif widgets recognize the `XmNfontList` resource instead of Xt's `XtNfont` resource. The font used to display a compound string is selected by matching a tag associated with the compound string with the same tag associated with a fontlist.

The function:

```
XmFontList XmFontListAppendEntry ( XmFontList      *fontList,
                                   XmFontListEntry entry )
```

adds a font list *entry* to an existing fontlist. If the given `fontlist` argument is NULL, this function creates and returns a new fontlist that contains the single new entry.

   A font list entry is a data structure that contains a font and a tag that can be used to match the font with a fontlist tag associated with a compound string. A new font list entry can be created programmatically using the function:

```
XmFontListEntry XmFontListEntryCreate  ( char      *tag.
                                         XmFontType type,
                                         XtPointer  font );
```

The `tag` argument to this function may be an arbitrary, NULL-terminated string. If the string represented by the symbol `XmFONTLIST_DEFAULT_TAG` is specified as the tag, this font list entry will be used as the default font in a fontlist. The `font` argument may be either a pointer to an `XFontStruct`, or an `XmFontList`. The `type` argument must be set to `XmFONT_IS_FONT`, or `XmFONT_IS_FONTLIST` to indicate the `type` of the `font` argument.

   Although it is common to simply use a font list that contains a single font, whose tag is `XmFONTLIST_DEFAULT_TAG`, it is possible to construct compound strings that use multiple fonts by creating fontlists that have multiple font entries, each with a unique tag.

   Programs can also create a fontlist by loading one or more fonts. The following function loads a list of fonts and creates a font list entry:

```
XmFontListEntry XmFontListEntryLoad ( Display    *display,
                                      char       *font,
                                      XmFontType type,
                                      char       *tag )
```

Specifying Fontlists in Resource Files

Although fontlists can be created programmatically, it is more common to specify fontlists in resource files. The simplest fontlist consists of just a single font, and can be specified as follows:

```
*fontList:-*-helvetica-medium-r-normal-*-12-*-*-*-*-*-iso8859-1
```

This resource specification describes a list that contains only one, untagged font. Multiple fonts can be specified by separating entries in the list with commas. For example,

```
*fontList: -*-helvetica-medium-r-normal-*-12-*-*-*-*-*-iso8859-1,\
-*-helvetica-medium-o-normal-*-12-*-*-*-*-*-iso8859-1=italic,\
-*-helvetica-bold-r-normal-*-12-*-*-*-*-*-iso8859-1=bold
```

The "=" character followed by a string after a font specifies a tag that can be used within a program to refer to a specific entry in the fontlist. So, this fontlist contains three fonts. The first, which is the default is a normal, medium weight twelve point Helvetica font. The second font is tagged "italic" and is an oblique version of the first font. The third font is tagged "bold" and is a bold version of the same font. The tag can be used to indicate which font in the list is to be used by a specific compound string, as discussed in the following section.

Creating and Manipulating Compound Strings

Motif represents a compound string with an opaque data structure, `XmString`. A compound string can be created by calling the function:

```
XmString XmStringCreate ( char *text, char * tag )
```

This function takes a character string and a character set and returns an equivalent compound string that can be displayed using a font identified by the specified tag. As a convenience, the function:

```
XmString XmStringCreateLocalized ( char * text )
```

creates a compound string whose tag is set to `XmFONTLIST_DEFAULT_TAG`. The `text` argument should be a `NULL`-terminated string that is encoded in the current locale.

The function:

```
XmString XmStringCreateLtoR ( char *text, char *tag )
```

is similar to `XmStringCreate()` except that it searches for newline characters in the character string. All text up to the point where a newline is encountered is placed in a compound string segment. Successive segments are separated by separator components.

Compound strings should be freed when they are no longer needed. Compound strings should always be freed by calling the function:

```
XmStringFree ( XmString string )
```

When passing a compound string to a widget as a resource value, all Motif widgets make a copy of the string. Therefore, the original string should be freed if it is no longer needed. Also, any time a compound string is retrieved as a resource from a Motif widget, a copy is made. The copy can be safely freed once it is no longer needed.

Motif provides several functions that allow the programmer to determine if two compound strings are equal, make copies of compound strings, append one string to another, and so on.

The function:

```
Boolean XmStringByteCompare ( XmString s1, XmString s2 )
```

returns `TRUE` if the two given compound strings are identical, based on a byte-by-byte comparison of the information in the two compound strings. Because a string may be stored in a compiled internal form, the byte-by-byte comparison of two seemingly identical strings may not succeed.

The function:

```
    Boolean XmStringCompare ( XmString s1, XmString s2 )
```

can be used to determine whether or not two compound strings are semantically, but not necessarily byte-for-byte, equivalent. Two strings are semantically equivalent if they have the same text components, the same directions, and the same font list tags. If the strings contain separator components, these must be the same, as well.

The function:

```
    Boolean XmStringEmpty ( XmString s1 )
```

returns TRUE if there are no non-zero-length segments in the given compound string.

The function:

```
    XmString XmStringConcat ( XmString s1, XmString s2 )
```

appends s2 to the end of s1 and returns a new compound string. The original strings are unchanged.

The function:

```
    void XmStringExtent ( XmFontList fl,
                          XmString   string,
                          Dimension *width,
                          Dimension *height )
```

returns the width and height, in pixels, of the rectangular area that would enclose a compound string if it were displayed.

Compound Strings and Fontlists

Fontlists can be used in conjunction with compound strings to display multi-font, and even multi-language text in a single widget. Each compound string can refer to a specific tagged font in a fontlist to designate a specific font with which the string is to be displayed. For example, a complex compound string can be created by calling XmStringConcat() to concatenate several individual strings, each with its own fontlist tag.

Another more common use is to display items in a Motif XmList widget that use different fonts. The XmList widget displays an array of compound strings using a single fontlist. Although all compound strings may use the same font within the fontlist, it is also possible, and sometimes useful to display some items using an alternate font. The following example program shows how this can be done. The program displays four items in a list. The first and last items are displayed using the default font tag, but the second and third items indicate that they should use fonts tagged "bold" and "italic" respectively. This example assumes that the following fontlist is specified in a resource file:

```
    list*fontList: -*-helvetica-medium-r-normal-*-12-*-*-*-*-*-iso8859-1,\
    -*-helvetica-medium-o-normal-*-12-*-*-*-*-*-iso8859-1=italic,\
    -*-helvetica-bold-r-normal-*-12-*-*-*-*-*-iso8859-1=bold
```

The program simply creates an XmList widget by calling `XmCreateScrolledList()`. The compound strings are specified as an array and installed as the value of the XmList widget's `XmNitems` resource.

```
1    /*************************************************
2     * list.c: Use different fonts in a list widget
3     *************************************************/
4    #include <Xm/Xm.h>
5    #include <Xm/List.h>
6
7    void main ( int argc, char **argv )
8    {
9        Widget       shell, list;
10       XmString     xmstr[4];
11       XtAppContext app;
12
13       shell = XtAppInitialize ( &app, "List",  NULL, 0,
14                                 &argc, argv, NULL, NULL, 0 );
15       /*
16        * Create an array of compound strings to be displayed in the
17        * list widget. Each item can have its own font tag.
18        */
19
20       xmstr[0] = XmStringCreateLtoR ("Normal", XmFONTLIST_DEFAULT_TAG );
21       xmstr[1] = XmStringCreateLtoR ("bold",   "bold" );
22       xmstr[2] = XmStringCreateLtoR ("italic", "italic" );
23       xmstr[3] = XmStringCreateLtoR ("Normal", XmFONTLIST_DEFAULT_TAG );
24
25       /*
26        * Create the list widget.
27        */
28
29       list = XmCreateScrolledList ( shell, "list", NULL, 0 );
30       XtManageChild ( list );
31
32       XtVaSetValues ( list,
33                       XmNitems,              xmstr,
34                       XmNitemCount,          4,
35                       XmNvisibleItemCount,   4,
36                       NULL );
37
38       XtRealizeWidget ( shell );
39
40       XtAppMainLoop ( app );
41   }
```

Figure 12.2 shows the resulting window, with different fonts for the various items in the list.

Figure 12.2 Displaying multiple fonts in a single widget.

Drawing Compound Strings

Motif provides several functions that can be used to display compound strings in a drawable. These functions are nearly identical to the corresponding Xlib text drawing functions. One important difference is that the (*x, y*) position specifies the top left corner of the bounding box that contains the string, rather than the lower left corner used by the Xlib drawing functions.

The function:

```
void XmStringDraw ( Display        *display,
                    Window         w,
                    XmFontList     fontlist,
                    XmString       string,
                    GC             gc,
                    Position       x,
                    Position       y,
                    Dimension      width,
                    unsigend char  alignment,
                    unsigned char  layout_direction,
                    XRectangle     *clip );
```

draws a compound string in a window using an appropriate font found in the given fontlist. The **x**, **y**, and **width** arguments specify a region that will contain the string. The **alignment** parameter specifies how the string is aligned within that region. Possible values are **XmALIGNMENT_BEGINNING**, **XmALIGNMENT_CENTER**, and **XmALIGNMENT_END**. The **layout_direction** argument specifies the direction in which the segments of the compound string are drawn, and also determines the meaning of the **alignment** argument. The **clip** argument allows the calling application to define a clipping rectangle that constrains the area in which text is drawn. If this argument is **NULL**, no clipping is performed.

The graphics context passed to this function is used to determine the foreground color with which the string is drawn. The font attribute of the GC is also modified as a side effect of the rendering process. Therefore, the GC passed to this function should not be a shared GC created with **XtGetGC()**.

The function:

```
void XmStringDrawImage ( Display       *display,
                         Window        w,
                         XmFontList    fontlist,
                         XmString      string,
                         GC            gc,
                         Position      x,
                         Position      y,
                         Dimension     width,
                         unsigend char alignment,
                         unsigned char layout_direction,
                         XRectangle    *clip )
```

is similar to `XmStringDraw()`, except that it corresponds semantically to `XDrawImage-String()`. Both the foreground and background of the text are drawn.

Retrieving Information from Compound Strings

Sometimes it is necessary to extract the contents of a compound string. Motif provides several functions for retrieving segments and components of segments. In the simplest case, the function:

```
Boolean XmStringGetLtoR ( XmString        string,
                          XmStringCharSet tag,
                          char            **text )
```

can be used to search a text segment in the given compound string that matches the given tag. The compound string segments are searched from left to right, as the name suggests. If a compound string consists of only a single segment and the given tag matches that of the string, the text of the string is returned. For example, consider the following code segment, which retrieves the label displayed by an XmLabel widget and extracts the text component of the string:

```
char *GetTextOfLabel ( Widget w )
{
    static char *text;
    XmString     xmstr;

    XtVaGetValues ( w, XmNlabelString, &xmstr, NULL );

    if ( XmStringGetLtoR ( xmstr, XmFONTLIST_DEFAULT_TAG, &text ) )
        return text;
}
```

It is also possible to retrieve the text of a compound string that consists of multiple segments. To retrieve subsequent segments of a compound string, it is useful to have a simple means of remembering the state of the string. The functions that retrieve components from a compound string use a *context* variable of type `XmStringContext` to maintain this state.

Before using these functions, a context must be initialized using the function:

```
Boolean XmStringInitContext ( XmStringContext *context,
                              XmString        string )
```

When a context is no longer needed, it should be freed using the function:

```
void XmStringFreeContext ( XmStringContext context )
```

Successive segments of a string may be retrieved using the function:

```
Boolean XmStringGetNextSegment ( XmStringContext   context,
                                 char              **text,
                                 XmStringCharSet   tag,
                                 XmStringDirection *direction,
                                 Boolean           *separator )
```

Each time this function is called, it returns the text, character set, and direction components of the next segment of a compound string. The Boolean value **separator** is TRUE if the next component is a separator. The function returns FALSE if there are no more segments in the compound string.

This function can be used to write a routine that retrieves the character string from a complex compound string. The function **GetTextFromXmString()** initializes a context and then calls **XmStringGetNextSegment()** repeatedly until there are no more segments in the string. The retrieved text is appended to a buffer after enlarging the buffer with **XtRealloc()**. When all segments have been processed, **GetTextFromXmString()** frees the context and returns the buffered text.

```
1   /*************************************************************
2    * TextFromXmString.c: Retrieve the text components
3    *                     from a multi-segment compound string
4    *                     Treat separators as newlines
5    *************************************************************/
6   #include <Xm/Xm.h>
7
8   char *GetTextFromXmString ( XmString xmstr )
9   {
10      XmStringContext   context;
11      char              *text;
12      XmStringCharSet   tag;
13      XmStringDirection dir;
14      Boolean           separator;
15      char              *buf = NULL;
16      int               length;
17
18      XmStringInitContext ( &context, xmstr );
19
20      length = 0;
21      while ( XmStringGetNextSegment ( context, &text, &tag,
22                                       &dir, &separator ) )
```

```
23   {
24         /* Allocate room for the text and copy the retrieved text
25          * into the buffer
26          */
27
28         if ( text )
29         {
30             buf = XtRealloc ( buf, length + strlen ( text ) + 1 );
31
32             if ( length == 0 )
33                 strcpy ( buf, text );
34             else
35                 strcat ( buf, text );
36
37             length += strlen ( text );
38             XtFree ( text );
39         }
40
41         /*
42          * If the next segment is a separator, append a newline
43          */
44
45         if ( separator )
46         {
47             buf = XtRealloc ( buf, length + 2 );
48             strcat ( buf, "\n" );
49             length += 2;
50         }
51     }
52
53     XmStringFreeContext ( context );
54
55     return ( buf );
56 }
```

Using Compound Strings

Most of the time, applications use Motif widgets to display text and do not need to be concerned with the details described in this chapter. However, there are times when it is necessary to retrieve the text segment from a compound string, or to render a compound string directly in an application. For example, the XmList example program described in Chapter 4 requires the application to extract the text segment of a compound string in order to print it to standard output.

The following example exercises the XmString drawing functions, fonts, and fontlists to implement a function that allows a both a pixmap and a label to be displayed simultaneously in a Motif button widget. Normally, Motif XmLabel and XmPushButton widgets support a label or a pixmap, but not both. However, it is straightforward to create a pixmap, draw the label into the pixmap, and then install the combined image in a widget.

The essence of this program is a function, `InstallLabeledPixmap()`, which takes a Motif XmLabel widget, or subclass, and an Xpm color pixmap description. The function extracts the value of the widget's `XmNlabelString` resource and draws both the string and the given pixmap into another pixmap that is large enough to contain both the label and the image. Then the combined pixmap is installed as the value of the `XmNlabelPixmap` resource.

The Xpm pixmap description should specify a single symbolic color, "background", for the color used as the background of the pixmap, if the pixmap background is to blend in with the color of the widget in which it is displayed.

The only function used in this program that has not been discussed previously is `XGetGeometry()`. This function retrieves the size and other geometry information from any drawable, including a pixmap. This function is defined as follows:

```
Status XGetGeometry ( Display       *display,
                      Drawable       drawable,
                      Window        *root_return,
                      int           *x_return,
                      int           *y_return,
                      unsigned int  *width_return,
                      unsigned int  *height_return,
                      unsigned int  *borderWidth_return,
                      unsigned int  *depth_return )
```

This function returns the *x,y* position, `width`, `height`, border width and `depth` of any drawable. The `root` parameter returns the root window ID of the screen with which the given `drawable` is associated.

The `pixlabel` program begins by implementing the function `InstallLabeled-Pixmap()`, which performs the steps to make a widget display a pixmap and a label at the same time.

```
1    /****************************************************
2     * pixlabel.c: Display both a pixmap and a label
3     ****************************************************/
4    #include <Xm/Xm.h>
5    #include <Xm/PushB.h>
6    #include <X11/xpm.h>
7
8    #define MAX(a,b) (a>b ? a : b)
9    #define PAD 2
10
11   InstallLabeledPixmap ( Widget w, char **xpmDescription )
12   {
13       XmString       label;
14       XmFontList     fontlist;
15       GC             gc;
16       GC             inverseGc;
17       Dimension      width, height;
18       unsigned int   pixmapWidth, pixmapHeight;
```

```
19      XGCValues          values;
20      int                junk, depth;
21      Display            *display = XtDisplay ( w );
22      unsigned char      alignment;
23      XpmAttributes      attributes;
24      XpmColorSymbol symbols[5];
25      int                totalWidth, totalHeight;
26      int                status;
27      Pixmap             labelPixmap,
28                         xpmPixmap;
29      Colormap           cmap;
30
31      /* Retrieve the values used by the given widget  */
32
33      XtVaGetValues ( w,
34                      XmNlabelString, &label,
35                      XmNfontList,    &fontlist,
36                      XmNforeground,  &values.foreground,
37                      XmNbackground,  &values.background,
38                      XmNdepth,       &depth,
39                      XmNalignment,   &alignment,
40                      XmNcolormap,    &cmap,
41                      NULL );
42      /*
43       * Create two GCs, one to draw the text and copy the pixmaps
44       * and another that can be used to erase a pixmap by filling
45       * it with the background color of the label widget. Because
46       * the normal GC is used by XmStringDraw, which modifies
47       * the font attribute of the GC, allocate this GC using
48       * XtAllocateGC() and specify GCFont as modifiable.
49       */
50
51      gc = XtAllocateGC ( w, depth,
52                          GCForeground | GCBackground,
53                          &values, GCFont, 0 );
54
55      values.foreground = values.background;
56
57      inverseGc = XtGetGC ( w,
58                            GCForeground | GCBackground,
59                            &values );
60      /*
61       * Set up the XpmColorSymbol array, binding the name "background"
62       * to the actual background color of the widget.
63       */
64
65      symbols[0].name  = "background";
66      symbols[0].value = NULL;
67      symbols[0].pixel = values.background;
```

```
68
69      /*
70       * Set the resulting information in the attributes structure
71       */
72
73      attributes.colorsymbols = symbols;
74      attributes.numsymbols   = 1;
75
76      /*
77       * Specify the visual, colormap and depth
78       * to be used and set the XpmAttributes mask.
79       */
80
81      attributes.colormap = cmap;
82      attributes.depth    = depth;
83      attributes.visual   = DefaultVisual ( display,
84                                            DefaultScreen ( display ) );
85
86      attributes.valuemask = XpmColorSymbols | XpmDepth |
87                             XpmColormap | XpmVisual;
88
89      /*
90       * Create the pixmap of the given image
91       */
92
93      status = XpmCreatePixmapFromData ( display,
94                                         DefaultRootWindow ( display ),
95                                         xpmDescription,  &xpmPixmap,
96                                         NULL, &attributes );
97
98      /*
99       * Compute the size of the label string and the given pixmap
100      */
101
102     XmStringExtent ( fontlist, label, &width, &height );
103
104     XGetGeometry ( display, xpmPixmap, ( Window * ) &junk,
105                    (int *) &junk, (int *) &junk,
106                    &pixmapWidth, &pixmapHeight,
107                    ( unsigned int *) &junk, ( unsigned int *) &junk );
108
109     /*
110      * Compute the sum of the label and pixmap sizes.
111      */
112
113     totalWidth = MAX ( pixmapWidth, width );
114     totalHeight = pixmapHeight + height + PAD;
115
```

```
116     /*
117      * Create the final pixmap using the combined size and
118      * fill the pixmap with the background color of the widget
119      */
120
121     labelPixmap =
122                 XCreatePixmap ( display,
123                                 RootWindowOfScreen ( XtScreen ( w ) ),
124                                 totalWidth, totalHeight, depth );
125
126     XFillRectangle ( display, labelPixmap,
127                      inverseGc, 0, 0,
128                      totalWidth, totalHeight );
129
130     /*
131      * Copy the Xpm-created pixmap into the larger pixmap and
132      * then draw the string below the pixmap.
133      */
134
135     XCopyArea ( XtDisplay ( w ), xpmPixmap, labelPixmap,
136                 gc, 0, 0, pixmapWidth, pixmapHeight,
137                 ( totalWidth - pixmapWidth ) / 2,
138                 0 );
139
140     XmStringDraw ( display, labelPixmap, fontlist, label,
141                    gc, 0, pixmapHeight + PAD, totalWidth,
142                    alignment, XmSTRING_DIRECTION_L_TO_R, NULL );
143
144     /*
145      * Install the final pixmap in the widget.
146      */
147
148     XtVaSetValues ( w,
149                     XmNlabelPixmap, labelPixmap,
150                     XmNlabelType,   XmPIXMAP,
151                     NULL );
152
153     /*
154      * Free the GCs, the initial pixmap, and the string retrieved
155      * from the label widget.
156      */
157
158     XFreePixmap ( display, xpmPixmap );
159
160     XtReleaseGC ( w, gc);
161     XtReleaseGC ( w, inverseGc );
162     XmStringFree ( label );
163 }
```

The driver for this example defines an Xpm pixmap. The program simply creates an XmPush-Button widget and calls `InstallLabeledPixmap()` to display this image above the normal label displayed by the button.

```
164    static char * xlogo16[] = {
165    "16 16 3 1",
166    "a c red m black",
167    ". c white m white s background",
168    "X c blue m black",
169    "aaaa..........X",
170    ".aaaa..........X",
171    "..aaaa........X.",
172    "...aaaa......X..",
173    "...aaaa.....X...",
174    "....aaaa...X....",
175    ".....aaaa..X....",
176    "......aaa.X.....",
177    "......aa.X......",
178    "......a.XXX.....",
179    ".....a..XXXX....",
180    ".....a...XXXX...",
181    "....a....XXXX...",
182    "...a......XXXX..",
183    "..a.........XXXX.",
184    ".a..........XXXX" };
185
186    void main ( int argc, char **argv )
187    {
188        Widget        shell, button;
189        XtAppContext app;
190
191        shell = XtAppInitialize ( &app, "Pixlabel", NULL, 0,
192                                   &argc, argv, NULL, NULL, 0 );
193
194        button =  XtCreateManagedWidget ( "xlogobutton",
195                                           xmPushButtonWidgetClass,
196                                           shell, NULL, 0 );
197        InstallLabeledPixmap ( button, xlogo16 );
198
199        XtRealizeWidget ( shell );
200        XtAppMainLoop ( app );
201    }
```

In spite of the installed pixmap, the label to be displayed on the XmLabel or XmPushButton widget is still determined by the `XmNlabelString` resource, and can be set in a resource file. For example, Figure 12.3 shows the pixlabel program with the `XmNlabelString` resource set as:

```
*xlogobutton*labelString: The X Logo
```

Figure 12.3 A labeled pixmap in a button.

12.4 Compound Text

X provides support for a text representation known as *compound text*. The compound text format supports text that potentially contains multiple character sets, or multiple languages. Compound text is designed as an interchange format that can be used to exchange data between applications and is not expected to be used as an internal representation. Chapter 14 demonstrates how applications can use compound text to transfer data between applications.

Motif provides functions that can be used to convert between compound text and Motif's compound string format. The function

```
XmString XmCvtCTToXmString ( char *text )
```

converts data in the form of compound text to a compound string.

The function

```
char *XmCvtXmStringToCT ( XmString string )
```

converts a compound string to the compound text format.

12.5 Summary

This chapter discusses functions that can be used to display text in a window, as well as the fonts X uses to represent characters. Few Motif applications need to draw text directly, and most applications use ready-made widgets like XmLabel to display text. However, in special situations, some applications may use the Xlib functions or the Motif text drawing functions to render their own text.

Chapter 13

Using Xlib Graphics

This chapter presents the graphics primitives provided by Xlib and demonstrates how to use these functions within a Motif application. Xlib provides a set of simple two-dimensional graphics functions for drawing points, lines, arcs, and rectangles. These drawing functions use the same integer coordinate system as the functions that operate on windows. Applications that require more complex graphics functions for zooming, scaling, or three-dimensional graphics must usually implement these as a layer above the Xlib graphics functions. Some systems support PEX (Phigs Extension to X), or OpenGL, which both provide the ability to display three dimensional graphics.

All Xlib graphics functions must operate on a drawable, which can be either a window or a pixmap. Therefore, several precautions must be taken when mixing Xlib graphics functions with Motif widgets. Widgets do not have an associated window until they are realized. Any widget can be used to display Xlib graphics once the widget is realized, by using the function `XtWindow()` to retrieve the window ID associated with the widget. Applications should always check that a widget is realized by calling `XtIsRealized()` before passing a widget's window to any Xlib function. Alternately, an application can check that `XtWindow()` returns a non-zero value.

In general, applications are expected to draw into a window only in response to an `Expose` event. Exposure events can only occur once a widget has been realized, so applications that draw only in response to events should have no difficulty.

Although, in theory, any widget can be used to display graphics, many widgets already draw into their windows, which makes it difficult to coordinate the widget's rendering and application-specific needs. Manager widgets such as the XmForm widget or XmBulletinBoard widget can be used to display graphics, because these widgets do not display any graphics of their own. However, Motif provides a special widget class, the XmDrawingArea widget class, specifically for this purpose.

The XmDrawingArea widget class supports three callbacks, `XmNresize-Callback`,`XmNexposeCallback`, and `XmNinputCallback`. Functions registered with these callback lists are invoked when the widget is resized, has pending exposure events, or has pending input. Functions registered with these callback lists are passed a pointer to an `XmDrawingAreaCallbackStruct` as call data. This structure reports the reason for the callback, the event that caused the callback function to be invoked, and the window ID in which the event occurred.

The examples in this chapter use the XmDrawingArea widget to display graphics using Xlib functions.

13.1 Drawing Points

The simplest Xlib graphics function displays a single point in a drawable. The function:

```
XDrawPoint ( Display *display,
             Drawable drawable,
             GC       gc,
             int      x,
             int      y )
```

sets a single pixel at location *x,y* according to the foreground and background colors defined by the specified GC.

It is often more efficient to draw multiple points at once using the following function:

```
XDrawPoints ( Display *display,
              Drawable drawable,
              GC       gc,
              XPoint   *points,
              int       npoints,
              int       mode )
```

This function draws `npoints` points with a single server request. The `points` argument must be an array of `XPoint` structures. The `mode` argument determines how the server interprets the coordinates in this array and must be one of the constants `CoordModeOrigin` or `CoordModePrevious`. If `CoordModeOrigin` is specified, the server interprets each coordinate relative to the origin of the drawable. The constant `CoordModePrevious` specifies that each coordinate should be interpreted relative to the preceding point. The server always interprets the first point relative to the drawable's origin.

Several attributes of the graphics context affect how points are drawn. These are:

```
GCFunction          GCPlaneMask          GCForeground
GCClipYOrigin       GCSubwindowMode      GCClipMask
GCBackground        GCClipXOrigin
```

An Example

This section examines a simple example program that uses `XDrawPoint()` to illustrate the basic use of graphics functions in X. The program computes and displays a *fractal* image. Fractals are patterns produced by iteratively evaluating mathematical expressions based on complex numbers.

This example program displays a fractal image generated by repeatedly evaluating the expression:

$$z = z^2 + k$$

where both z and k are complex numbers. The value of z is initially set to *(0, 0)*, while k is initialized to the value of each x,y position in the image. After evaluating the expression some number of times for each point, the value of z is tested to see how far it has moved from the (x, y) plane. If it is within some predetermined distance of the plane, the pixel is said to be part of the *Mandelbrot Set* and the color of the pixel is set to the same color as all other pixels in the Mandelbrot Set. Otherwise, some other color is chosen for the pixel.

Figure 13.1 shows the main window of the example program, displaying the generated fractal image.

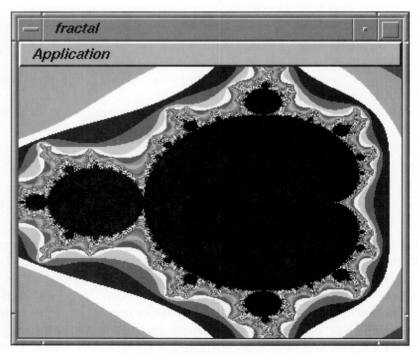

Figure 13.1 The fractal program.

The fractal program consists of three files, one file that implements the main window and the fractal drawing functions, a file that implements a preference panel, and a header file that contains definitions that must be shared between the other two modules. The header file of this program defines several data structures. The fractal program defines a `ComplexNumber` structure to represent complex numbers, and also defines an `ImageData` structure to store a graphics context, a pixmap (used to save the image once it is drawn), and some auxiliary data needed for the image calculation.

```
1    /*************************************************************
2     * fractal.h: Type declarations used in the fractal program
3     *************************************************************/
4    #include <Xm/Xm.h>
5
6    typedef struct {
7        double   real, imag;
8    } ComplexNumber;
9
10   typedef enum { DISTANCE,  ITERATIONS } ColorationType;
11
12   /*
13    * Assorted information needed to generate and draw the image.
14    */
15
16   typedef struct {
17       Widget          canvas;
18       Pixmap          pixmap;
19       GC              gc;
20       Dimension       width, height;
21       int             depth, ncolors;
22       double          range, maxDistance;
23       ComplexNumber   origin;
24       ColorationType  coloration;
25   } ImageData;
```

Several of the members of the `ImageData` structure are used to control how the fractal image is displayed. The `depth` member determines how many times the fractal expression is evaluated for each pixel, while the `origin` member allows the image to be *panned* to view different parts of the image. The `range` parameter determines the width and height of the real coordinates of the image, and can be altered to zoom the image in and out, while the `max_distance` parameter controls the z distance considered to be "close" to the x,y plane.

The main body of the program creates an XmMainWindow widget that manages a menu bar and an XmDrawingArea widget used as a drawing canvas. The menu bar is created using the MenuSupport package described in Chapter 6. The menu bar has a single menu pane, which contains one entry to allow the user to exit the application and another to allow the user to display a preference panel. The preference pane, described later in this chapter, allows the user to manipulate the values stored in the `ImageData` structure to alter the way the fractal is displayed. Before entering the main event loop, the program adds callbacks to handle `Exposure` and resize events in the XmDrawingArea widget.

```
1    /****************************************************************
2     * fractal.c: Main window and rendering code for fractal example
3     ****************************************************************/
4    #include <Xm/Xm.h>
5    #include <Xm/DrawingA.h>
6    #include <Xm/MainW.h>
7    #include <stdlib.h>
8    #include "MenuSupport.h"
9    #include "fractal.h"
10
11   extern ShowPreferences ( Widget parent, ImageData *data );
12
13   static void InitData ( ImageData *data );
14   static void ResizeCallback ( Widget    w,
15                                XtPointer clientData,
16                                XtPointer callData );
17   static void RedisplayCallback ( Widget    w,
18                                   XtPointer clientData,
19                                   XtPointer callData );
20   static void ShowPreferencesCallback ( Widget    w,
21                                         XtPointer clientData,
22                                         XtPointer callData );
23   static void QuitCallback ( Widget    w,
24                              XtPointer clientData,
25                              XtPointer callData );
26   /*
27    * Functions that can be called from preference module
28    */
29
30   void CreateImage ( ImageData *data );
31   void SetupColorMap ( Widget shell, ImageData *data, Boolean ramp );
32
33   /*
34    * Menu descriptions used by this program.
35    */
36
37   static MenuDescription appPaneDesc[] = {
38     { BUTTON,   "Preferences", ShowPreferencesCallback },
39     { BUTTON,   "Quit",        QuitCallback },
40     { NULL }
41   };
42
43   static MenuDescription menuBarDesc[] = {
44     { PULLDOWN,   "Application", NULL, NULL, appPaneDesc },
45     { NULL }
46   };
```

```
47   void main ( int argc, char **argv )
48   {
49       Widget       shell, canvas, mainWindow, menu;
50       XtAppContext app;
51       ImageData    data;
52
53       /*
54        * Initialize Xt
55        */
56
57       shell = XtAppInitialize ( &app, "Fractal", NULL, 0,
58                                 &argc, argv, NULL, NULL, 0 );
59
60       mainWindow = XtCreateManagedWidget ( "mainWindow",
61                                            xmMainWindowWidgetClass,
62                                            shell, NULL, 0 );
63       /*
64        * Create the widget in which to display the fractal
65        */
66
67       canvas = XtCreateManagedWidget ( "canvas",
68                                        xmDrawingAreaWidgetClass,
69                                        mainWindow, NULL, 0 );
70       /*
71        * Create the GCs needed by the fractal program.
72        */
73
74       InitData ( canvas, &data );
75
76       /*
77        * Create the menu bar and set up the window layout.
78        */
79
80       menu = CreateMenu ( MENUBAR, "menuBar",
81                           mainWindow, menuBarDesc, &data );
82
83       XtVaSetValues ( mainWindow,
84                       XmNmenuBar,    menu,
85                       XmNworkWindow, canvas,
86                       NULL );
87       /*
88        * Add callbacks to handle resize and exposures.
89        */
90
91       XtAddCallback ( canvas, XmNexposeCallback,
92                       RedisplayCallback, ( XtPointer ) &data );
93       XtAddCallback ( canvas, XmNresizeCallback,
94                       ResizeCallback, ( XtPointer )  &data );
95
```

```
96        XtRealizeWidget ( shell );
97
98     /*
99      * Once all widgets are realized, call an auxiliary function to
100     * install a colormap in the canvas window, so the fractal can
101     * be displayed with a full range of colors.
102     */
103
104      SetupColorMap ( shell, &data, FALSE );
105
106      XtAppMainLoop ( app );
107
108   }
```

The menu bar in this example contains a single pulldown menu pane, named "Application", that contains only two entries. The first menu entry invokes the callback function `ShowPreferencesCallback()`, which calls an external function, `ShowPreferences()`. This function creates and displays a preference panel that allows the user to manipulate the variables that control the appearance of the fractal image. Notice that the client data provided to `ShowPreferencesCallback()` is a pointer to the `ImageData` structure used throughout the program to maintain the parameters used to display the image.

```
109   static void ShowPreferencesCallback ( Widget    w,
110                                          XtPointer clientData,
111                                          XtPointer callData )
112   {
113       ImageData *data = ( ImageData * ) clientData;
114
115      /* Call external function to display pereference panel. */
116
117       ShowPreferences ( XtParent ( w ), data );
118   }
```

The second menu item simply allows the user to exit the application.

```
119   static void QuitCallback ( Widget    w,
120                              XtPointer clientData,
121                              XtPointer callData )
122   {
123       exit ( 0 );
124   }
```

The function `InitData()` initializes the `ImageData` structure that determines how the fractal is displayed. The members of this structure are initialized to useful values that produce a reasonable image. This function also creates a graphics context, determines how many colors are supported by the display, and initializes the `pixmap` member of the `ImageData` structure to NULL.

```
125   static void InitData ( Widget w, ImageData *data )
126   {
127        /*
128         * Get the size of the drawing area.
129         */
130
131        XtVaGetValues ( w,
132                            XmNwidth,  &data->width,
133                            XmNheight, &data->height,
134                            NULL );
135
136        data->canvas      = w;
137        data->depth       = 20;
138        data->origin.real = -1.4;
139        data->origin.imag = 1.0;
140        data->range       = 2.0;
141        data->maxDistance = 4.0;
142        data->coloration  = ITERATIONS;
143
144        /*
145         * Find out how many colors we have to work with, and
146         * create a default, writable, graphics context.
147         */
148
149        data->ncolors =
150                    XDisplayCells ( XtDisplay ( w ),
151                                    XDefaultScreen ( XtDisplay ( w ) ) );
152
153        data->gc = XCreateGC ( XtDisplay ( w ),
154                               DefaultRootWindow ( XtDisplay ( w ) ),
155                               NULL, NULL );
156        /*
157         *  Initialize the pixmap to NULL.
158         */
159
160        data->pixmap = NULL;
161   }
```

The function `CreateImage()` generates the fractal image. This function uses three nested `for` loops to evaluate the fractal expression. For each *(x, y)* coordinate, `CreateImage()` calculates the value of the expression repeatedly until either the maximum number of iterations are performed or until the *z* distance from the *(x, y)* plane exceeds the specified limit. If the point is still on the plane when all iterations are calculated, no point is drawn (which is equivalent to drawing the window's background color). If a point moves away from the plane before all iterations are calculated, the function draws a point on the screen.

There are many ways to choose the color of each pixel. This example demonstrates two methods that achieve interesting results on color displays. If the `coloration` member of the `ImageData` structure is set to `DISTANCE`, the foreground color of the graphics context is determined by the *z* distance from the plane modulo the number of colors available. If this member is set to ITERATIONS, the color is set to a pixel index equal to the number of iterations performed so far, modulo the number of colors. By default, the fractal program bases the colors on the number of iterations.

Once a pixel location and a color are determined, CreateImage() calls XDrawPoint() to draw a single pixel of the fractal image. Notice that CreateImage() draws each point twice: once in the XmDrawingArea widget and once in a pixmap. This creates a duplicate of the image in off-screen memory. Depending on the size of the window, this image can take considerable time to draw. Storing the image in off-screen memory allows programs to use XCopyArea() to restore the image rather than recalculating the entire image each time the window is exposed. However, the program must take care to draw the point in the window only if the widget has been realized. This is because CreateImage() is called when the canvas widget is resized, which can occur before the widget is realized.

```
162  void CreateImage ( ImageData *data )
163  {
164      Widget w = data->canvas;
165      int  x, y, iteration;
166
167      /*
168       * If the canvas is realized, erase it.
169       */
170
171      if ( XtIsRealized ( w ) )
172          XClearArea ( XtDisplay ( w ), XtWindow ( w ),
173                       0, 0, 0, 0, TRUE );
174
175      /*
176       * Erase the pixmap by filling it with black.
177       */
178
179      XSetForeground ( XtDisplay ( w ), data->gc,
180                       BlackPixelOfScreen ( XtScreen ( w ) ) );
181
182      XFillRectangle ( XtDisplay ( w ), data->pixmap, data->gc, 0, 0,
183                       data->width,  data->height );
184
185      /*
186       * For each pixel on the window....
187       */
188
189      for ( y = 0; y < data->height; y++ )
190      {
191          ComplexNumber z, k;
192
193          for ( x = 0; x < data->width; x++ )
194          {
195
```

```
196              /*
197               * Initialize K to the normalized, floating coordinate
198               * in the x, y plane. Init Z to ( 0.0, 0.0 ) .
199               */
200
201              z.real =  z.imag = 0.0;
202
203              k.real =  data->origin.real +
204                  ( double ) x / ( double ) data->width * data->range;
205              k.imag =  data->origin.imag -
206                  ( double ) y / ( double ) data->height * data->range;
207
208          /*
209           * Calculate z =  z * z + k over and over.
210           */
211
212              for ( iteration = 0; iteration < data->depth; iteration++)
213              {
214                  double    real;
215                  int       distance;
216
217                  real  = z.real;
218                  z.real = z.real * z.real - z.imag * z.imag + k.real;
219                  z.imag = 2 * real * z.imag + k.imag;
220
221                  distance = ( int ) ( z.real * z.real +
222                                       z.imag * z.imag );
223                  /*
224                   * If the z point has moved off the plane, set the
225                   * current foreground color to the distance (cast to
226                   * an int and modulo the number of colors available),
227                   * and draw a point in the window and the pixmap.
228                   */
229
230                  if ( distance  >= data->maxDistance )
231                  {
232                      Pixel color;
233
234                      if ( data->coloration == DISTANCE )
235                        color = ( Pixel ) ( distance % data->ncolors );
236                      else if ( data->coloration == ITERATIONS )
237                          color = ( Pixel ) iteration % data->ncolors;
238
239                      XSetForeground ( XtDisplay ( w ),
240                                          data->gc, color );
241
242                      XDrawPoint ( XtDisplay ( w ),
243                                     data->pixmap,
244                                     data->gc, x, y );
```

```
245                        if ( XtIsRealized ( w ) )
246                            XDrawPoint ( XtDisplay ( w ),
247                                         XtWindow ( w ),
248                                         data->gc,x,y );
249                        break;
250                }
251            }
252        }
253    }
254 }
```

The callback function `RedisplayCallback()` handles `Expose` events by copying the image from a region in the pixmap to the window. `RedisplayCallback()` uses `XCopyArea()` to copy the rectangular area defined by the `Expose` event in the call data from the pixmap to the window. Copying the image between a pixmap and a window is almost always much faster than recomputing the image. This program is a good example of an application that could benefit from a server that provides backing store to automatically maintain a window's contents. However, using a pixmap to maintain the image works even with X servers that do not support this feature, as long as there is sufficient off-screen memory to support the pixmap.

```
255 static void RedisplayCallback ( Widget      w,
256                                 XtPointer clientData,
257                                 XtPointer callData )
258 {
259     ImageData                    *data = ( ImageData * ) clientData;
260     XmDrawingAreaCallbackStruct *cb =
261                             ( XmDrawingAreaCallbackStruct * ) callData;
262
263     XExposeEvent  *event = ( XExposeEvent * ) cb->event;
264
265     /*
266      * Extract the exposed area from the event and copy
267      * from the saved pixmap to the window.
268      */
269
270     XCopyArea ( XtDisplay ( w ), data->pixmap,
271                 XtWindow ( w ), data->gc,
272                 event->x, event->y, event->width, event->height,
273                 event->x, event->y );
274 }
```

The remaining function to be discussed is the `XmNresizeCallback` function, `ResizeCallback()`. This function frees the current pixmap, which no longer corresponds to the size of the window, and creates a new pixmap the same size as the window. The pixmap is cleared by calling `XFillRectangle()` with the default black pixel of the screen. `Redisplay-Callback()` then calls `CreateImage()` to generate a new fractal scaled to the new size of the window.

```
275   static void ResizeCallback ( Widget    w,
276                                 XtPointer clientData,
277                                 XtPointer callData )
278   {
279       ImageData      *data = ( ImageData * ) clientData;
280
281       /*
282        * Get the new window size.
283        */
284
285       XtVaGetValues ( w,
286                       XmNwidth,  &data->width,
287                       XmNheight, &data->height,
288                       NULL );
289       /*
290        * Clear the window, forcing an Expose event to be generated
291        */
292
293       if ( XtIsRealized ( w ) )
294         XClearArea ( XtDisplay ( w ), XtWindow ( w ), 0, 0, 0, 0, TRUE );
295
296       /*
297        * Free the old pixmap and create a new pixmap
298        * the same size as the window.
299        */
300
301       if ( data->pixmap )
302           XFreePixmap ( XtDisplay ( w ), data->pixmap );
303
304       data->pixmap =
305               XCreatePixmap ( XtDisplay ( w ),
306                               DefaultRootWindow ( XtDisplay ( w ) ),
307                               data->width, data->height,
308                               DefaultDepthOfScreen ( XtScreen ( w ) ) );
309
310       XSetForeground ( XtDisplay ( w ), data->gc,
311                        BlackPixelOfScreen ( XtScreen ( w ) ) );
312
313       XFillRectangle ( XtDisplay ( w ), data->pixmap, data->gc, 0, 0,
314                        data->width,  data->height );
315
316       /*
317        * Generate a new image.
318        */
319
320       CreateImage ( data );
321   }
```

An important aspect of any fractal program involves the colors used to display the fractal image. The function `CreateImage()` supports two different ways to color the image, based on the number of iterations or on the distance of a specific point from the z plane. However, the choice of colors also affects the appearance of the fractal. To allow the fractal to be displayed using as many colors as possible, while still allowing the program to manipulate the colormap, it is convenient to install a unique colormap for the `canvas` widget's window. The function `SetupColorMap()`, called on line 104 of main, serves a duel purpose. It creates and installs the colormaps used by the fractal program, and also allows the program to change the contents of the colormap used by the `canvas` widget's window to achieve different effects.

The colormaps installed by `SetupColorMap()` work best with a hardware display that supports multiple colormaps at one time. On such systems, it is possible to install a colormap that is associated with the canvas window, while simultaneously using another colormap for the other widgets in the program. This allows the fractal application to use a normal set of colors for its menus, sliders, and buttons, and to use another colormap that can display and manipulate all available colors for the fractal image. See Chapter 9 for more information about installing and manipulating colormaps.

`SetupColorMap()` allows the program to switch between two colormaps. The first is a ramp that displays a range of colors, which go in a straight line between red and yellow, in an RGB color space. The second color map just uses whatever random colors happen to be in the default colormap when the program is run. Other colormaps are possible, of course, but these two generally produce interesting results.

```
322    void SetupColorMap ( Widget shell, ImageData *data, Boolean ramp )
323    {
324        int              red, green, blue, i;
325        Display         *dpy = XtDisplay ( shell );
326        XColor          *Colors;
327        static Colormap  cmap = NULL;
328        Window           windows [ 2 ];
329
330        /*
331         * The first time, create a colormap and install it in the
332         * canvas widget's window. Also set up the window manager
333         * colormap windows list so both colormaps get installed,
334         * if the system is capable of handling multiple colormaps.
335         */
336
337        if ( !cmap )
338        {
339            cmap =
340                XCreateColormap ( dpy, XtWindow(data->canvas),
341                                  DefaultVisual(dpy, DefaultScreen(dpy)),
342                                  AllocAll );
343
344            XSetWindowColormap ( dpy, XtWindow ( data->canvas ), cmap );
345            windows[0] = XtWindow ( shell );
346            windows[1] = XtWindow ( data->canvas );
```

```
347            XSetWMColormapWindows ( dpy, XtWindow ( shell ), windows, 2 );
348        }
349
350    if ( ramp )
351    {
352        /*
353         * If a ramp is to be set up, allocate enough colors
354         * cells. Then fill in the cells with some computed colors.
355         * This ramp runs from yellow to red.
356         */
357
358        Colors = ( XColor* ) XtMalloc ( sizeof ( XColor ) *
359                                        data->ncolors );
360
361        Colors[0].pixel = 0;
362        Colors[0].flags = DoRed|DoGreen|DoBlue;
363        Colors[0].red   = Colors[0].blue = Colors[0].green =  0;
364        green = 65535;
365
366        for ( i = 1; i < data->ncolors; i++ )
367        {
368            Colors[i].pixel = i;
369            Colors[i].flags = DoRed|DoGreen|DoBlue;
370            Colors[i].red   = 65535;
371            Colors[i].blue  = 0;
372            Colors[i].green = green ;
373            green           -= green / 8;
374        }
375
376        /*
377         * install the color ramp in the canvas's colormap.
378         */
379
380        XStoreColors ( dpy, cmap, Colors, data->ncolors );
381
382        XtFree ( ( char * ) Colors );
383    }
384    else
385    {
386        Colormap def;
387
388        /*
389         * If no ramp is chosen, just use whatever randomw colors
390         * are in the default map. Copy the contents of the default
391         * colormap to the canvas widget's colormap.
392         */
393
394        Colors = ( XColor* ) XtMalloc ( sizeof ( XColor ) *
395                                        data->ncolors );
```

```
396              def = DefaultColormap ( dpy, DefaultScreen ( dpy ) );
397
398              for ( i = 0; i < data->ncolors; i++ )
399              {
400                  Colors[i].pixel = i;
401                  Colors[i].flags = DoRed|DoGreen|DoBlue;
402              }
403
404              XQueryColors ( dpy, def, Colors, data->ncolors );
405
406              XStoreColors ( dpy, cmap, Colors, data->ncolors );
407
408              XtFree ( ( char * ) Colors );
409          }
410  }
```

The Preference Panel

The fractal image generated by this example can be affected by several different parameters. All of these parameters are maintained as part of the `ImageData` structure declared in the main program. It can be useful to write a simple preference panel that allows the user to manipulate these parameters while the program is running to see how they affect the generated image.

Figure 13.2 shows the fractal program, along with the preference panel, which is implemented as a custom dialog. The dialog allows the user to control the origin, range, depth, and color style used to create the image.

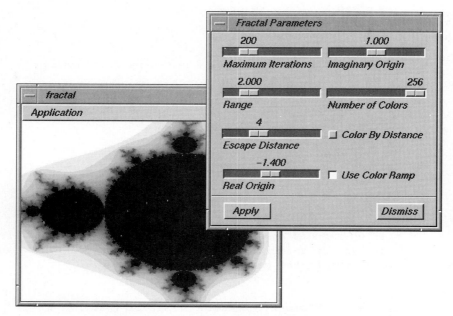

Figure 13.2 Fractal program, with preference panel.

The preference panel is implemented in a separate file as an independent module. The module consists of a function that creates and displays the preference dialog, and several callbacks. The file preference.c begins with some declarations required by the module.

```
1    /*******************************************************
2     * preference.c: Implement a preference dialog to allow
3     *               customization of the fractal image.
4     *******************************************************/
5    #include <Xm/Xm.h>
6    #include <Xm/Scale.h>
7    #include <Xm/ToggleB.h>
8    #include <Xm/MessageB.h>
9    #include <Xm/RowColumn.h>
10   #include <math.h>
11   #include "fractal.h"
12
13   typedef struct   {
14     char      *name;
15     float     multiplier;
16     Widget    w;
17     int       value;
18   } SliderData;
19
20   static void OkCallback ( Widget    w,
21                            XtPointer clientData,
22                            XtPointer callData );
23   static void CancelCallback ( Widget    w,
24                                XtPointer clientData,
25                                XtPointer callData );
26   extern void CreateImage ( ImageData *data );
27   extern void SetupColorMap ( Widget    shell,
28                               ImageData *data,
29                               Boolean   ramp );
30   void  UpdatePreferences ( ImageData *data );
31   typedef enum { DEPTH, RANGE, DIST, REAL, IMAG, NCOLORS } PreferenceTypes;
32
33   static SliderData sliders [] = {
34     { "depth"      },
35     { "range"      },
36     { "distance"   },
37     { "realOrigin" },
38     { "imagOrigin" }
39   };
40
41   static Widget          toggle;
42   static Widget          colorMapToggle;
43   static Widget          dialog = NULL;
44   static ColorationType  currentColoration;
```

The `ShowPreferences()` function modifies an XmMessageBox dialog to create a custom preference dialog. Once the dialog is created, this function simply manages the dialog to display it. An XmRowColumn widget, used as the work area of the dialog, manages five XmScale widgets and two XmToggleButton widgets. The XmScale widgets allow the user to choose a value within a range for each of the parameters that control the appearance of the fractal image. The widget ID of each XmScale widget is kept in an array of structures to allow easy retrieval of each value. The array of structures is initialized at the top on the file, starting on line 33. The name of each parameter is provided, but the other values are left unspecified for now.

Before the dialog is displayed, the `value` member of each entry in this array is initialized to the current value of the corresponding parameter in the `ImageData` structure. This value is then used to initialize the position of the scale when the dialog is first displayed. As each XmScale widget is created, its widget ID is stored in a `SliderData` structure as well.

```
45   void ShowPreferences ( Widget parent, ImageData *data )
46   {
47       Widget rowColumn;
48       int    i;
49
50       /*
51        * If this is the first time this function has been called
52        * create the preference dialog.
53        */
54
55       if ( !dialog )
56       {
57           Arg args[1];
58
59           /*
60            * Use a message box dialog widget, and remove the symbol
61            * and label areas. This dialog is designed to allow the user
62            * to apply data or to dismiss the dialog, so XmNautoUnmanage
63            * is also set to FALSE.
64            */
65
66           XtSetArg ( args[0], XmNautoUnmanage, FALSE );
67           dialog = XmCreateMessageDialog ( parent, "preferences",
68                                            args, 1 );
69           XtUnmanageChild (  XmMessageBoxGetChild ( dialog,
70                                           XmDIALOG_SYMBOL_LABEL ) );
71           XtUnmanageChild ( XmMessageBoxGetChild ( dialog,
72                                           XmDIALOG_MESSAGE_LABEL ) );
73
74           /* Create the work area */
75
76           rowColumn =
77                   XtVaCreateManagedWidget ( "rowColumn",
78                                              xmRowColumnWidgetClass,
79                                              dialog,
```

```
80                                          XmNorientation,XmVERTICAL,
81                                          XmNpacking, XmPACK_COLUMN,
82                                          XmNnumColumns,  2,
83                                          NULL );
84
85       /* Create sliders to control variable values */
86
87        for ( i = 0; i < XtNumber ( sliders ); i++ )
88        {
89            short decimalPoints;
90
91            sliders[i].w = XtVaCreateManagedWidget ( sliders[i].name,
92                                              xmScaleWidgetClass,
93                                              rowColumn,
94                                              NULL );
95          /*
96           * Because the range of each slider can be specified in
97           * a resource file, the program must determine the number
98           * of decimal points to be used when evaluating a slider
99           * position. Get the value, and convert to a power of ten.
100          */
101
102           XtVaGetValues ( sliders[i].w,
103                       XmNdecimalPoints, &decimalPoints,
104                       NULL );
105           sliders[i].multiplier = powf ( 10.0,
106                                       ( double ) decimalPoints );
107
108        }
109
110      /* Create toggles to control coloring style */
111
112       toggle = XtCreateManagedWidget ( "colorStyle",
113                                         xmToggleButtonWidgetClass,
114                                         rowColumn,
115                                         NULL, 0 );
116       colorMapToggle =
117               XtCreateManagedWidget ( "colorMap",
118                                         xmToggleButtonWidgetClass,
119                                         rowColumn,
120                                         NULL, 0 );
121
122      /*
123       * Add callbacks to apply new values and to dismiss the
124       * dialog without applying changes.
125       */
126
127       XtAddCallback ( dialog, XmNokCallback,
128                   OkCallback, ( XtPointer ) data );
```

```
129              XtAddCallback ( dialog, XmNcancelCallback,
130                              CancelCallback, ( XtPointer ) data );
131      }
132
133      /*
134       * Post the dialog, first setting all sliders to the
135       * current values of the corresponding data.
136       */
137
138      UpdatePreferences ( data );
139
140      /*
141       * Set the initial value of the coloring toggle
142       */
143
144      XtVaSetValues ( toggle, XmNvalue,
145                      data->coloration == DISTANCE ? TRUE : FALSE,
146                      NULL );
147      XtManageChild ( dialog );
148  }
```

UpdatePreferences() sets the initial value of each slider and toggle button in the preference panel by multiplying the corresponding value in the ImageData structure by the multiplier for each scale.

```
149  void UpdatePreferences ( ImageData *data )
150  {
151      int i;
152
153      /*
154       * Don't try to update if the dialog doesn't exist yet.
155       */
156
157      if ( !dialog )
158          return;
159      /*
160       * Multiply each value by the multiplier for each scale to
161       * get the correct integer value for each scale.
162       */
163
164      sliders[DEPTH].value  = data->depth * sliders[DEPTH].multiplier;
165      sliders[REAL].value   = data->origin.real *
166                                          sliders[REAL].multiplier;
167      sliders[IMAG].value   = data->origin.imag *
168                                          sliders[IMAG].multiplier;
169      sliders[RANGE].value  = data->range * sliders[RANGE].multiplier;
170      sliders[DIST].value   = data->maxDistance *
171                                          sliders[DIST].multiplier;
```

```
172        sliders[NCOLORS].value    = data->ncolors;
173
174     /*
175      * Move each scale to the correct position.
176      */
177
178     for ( i = 0; i < XtNumber ( sliders ); i++ )
179         XtVaSetValues ( sliders[i].w,
180                         XmNvalue, sliders[i].value,
181                         NULL );
182
183  }
```

The OkCallback() function is called when the user activates the OK button on the dialog. This function loops through XmScale widgets, retrieving the current value represented by each slider. This value is then assigned to a member of the ImageData structure that controls the fractal image.

This approach allows the position of an XmScale to be changed without any immediate effect on the image. The results are only visible when the user selects the OK button. For the fractal program, this approach is more useful than changing the image each time an XmScale widget is moved, because the image takes a substantial amount of time to redraw. One side effect of this model is that it is simple for the user to cancel the dialog without having any changes to slider positions affect the image. Because the slider positions are set each time the dialog is posted, any sliders that have changed before the user cancels the operation will be reset the next time the preference panel is displayed.

Once all values have been established, OkCallback() calls CreateImage() to recompute and redisplay the image.

```
184  static void OkCallback ( Widget    w,
185                           XtPointer clientData,
186                           XtPointer callData )
187  {
188      int i;
189      ImageData *data = ( ImageData * ) clientData;
190
191      /*
192       * Retrieve the current values from all sliders and
193       * store in the ImageData structure.
194       */
195
196      for ( i = 0; i < XtNumber ( sliders ); i++ )
197          XtVaGetValues ( sliders[i].w,
198                          XmNvalue, &( sliders[i].value ),
199                          NULL );
200
201      data->depth       = sliders[DEPTH].value /
202                                      sliders[DEPTH].multiplier;
```

```
203        data->origin.real = sliders[REAL].value  /
204                                         sliders[REAL].multiplier;
205        data->origin.imag = sliders[IMAG].value  /
206                                         sliders[IMAG].multiplier;
207        data->range       = sliders[RANGE].value /
208                                         sliders[RANGE].multiplier;
209        data->maxDistance = sliders[DIST].value /
210                                         sliders[DIST].multiplier;
211        data->ncolors     = sliders[NCOLORS].value;
212
213     /*
214      * Update the color style according to the toggle setting
215      */
216
217        if ( XmToggleButtonGetState ( toggle ) )
218            data->coloration = DISTANCE;
219        else
220            data->coloration = ITERATIONS;
221
222        SetupColorMap ( data->canvas, data,
223                        XmToggleButtonGetState ( colorMapToggle ) );
224     /*
225      * Recompute and redisplay the fractal.
226      */
227
228        CreateImage ( data );
229    }
```

The function `CancelCallback()` simply unmanages the dialog without regard to any changes that have been made to the sliders. The correct values of current parameters will be restored, and the XmScale widget values reset, the next time the dialog is posted.

```
230    static void CancelCallback ( Widget    w,
231                                 XtPointer clientData,
232                                 XtPointer callData )
233    {
234        /*
235         * Just unmanage the dialog without updating any values.
236         */
237
238        XtUnmanageChild ( w );
239    }
```

Application Resources

Like most Motif applications, the fractal program depends on several resources for correct operation. The fractal program's app-defaults file defines the text in the menus and the exact titles of displayed with each scale and button on the preference panel. The fractal program also allows resources to be set in the application defaults file to determine the range of values each slider can have, as well as the initial value of each parameter.

```
 1    !!!!!!!!!!!!!!!!!!!!!!!!!!!!!!!!!!!!!!!!!!!!!!!!!!!!!!!!!!
 2    ! Fractal: Application resources for fractal program
 3    !!!!!!!!!!!!!!!!!!!!!!!!!!!!!!!!!!!!!!!!!!!!!!!!!!!!!!!!!!
 4
 5    ! Set labels for menu items
 6    *Preferences.labelString:               Preferences...
 7
 8    ! Set labels, ranges, and default values for all preference controls
 9    *autoUnmanage:                          False
10    *preferences.dialogTitle:               Fractal Parameters
11    *preferences.okLabelString:             Apply
12    *preferences.cancelLabelString:         Dismiss
13
14    ! All scales should be horizontal and show the numeric value
15    *preferences*XmScale.orientation:        horizontal
16    *preferences*XmScale.showValue:          True
17
18    ! Ranges, default values, and labels for individual controls
19    *preferences*depth.titleString:          Maximum Iterations
20    *preferences*depth.minimum:              1
21    *preferences*depth.maximum:             1000
22    *preferences*depth.decimalPoints:          0
23    *preferences*depth.value:               200
24
25    *preferences*range.titleString:           Range
26    *preferences*range.minimum:              1
27    *preferences*range.maximum:            10000
28    *preferences*range.decimalPoints:          3
29    *preferences*range.value:              2000
30
31    *preferences*distance.titleString:        Escape Distance
32    *preferences*distance.minimum:           1
33    *preferences*distance.maximum:          10
34    *preferences*distance.decimalPoints:       0
35    *preferences*distance.value:             4
36
37    *preferences*realOrigin.titleString:       Real Origin
38    *preferences*realOrigin.minimum:        -3000
39    *preferences*realOrigin.maximum:         300
40    *preferences*realOrigin.decimalPoints:     3
41    *preferences*realOrigin.value:          -1400
42
43    *preferences*imagOrigin.titleString:       Imaginary Origin
44    *preferences*imagOrigin.minimum:        -1000
45    *preferences*imagOrigin.maximum:        3000
46    *preferences*imagOrigin.decimalPoints:     3
```

```
47  *preferences*imagOrigin.value:          1000
48
49  *preferences*numColors.titleString:     Number of Colors
50  *preferences*numColors.minimum:         1
51  *preferences*numColors.maximum:         256
52
53  *preferences*colorMap.labelString:      Use Color Ramp
54  *preferences*colorStyle*labelString:    Color By Distance
```

13.2 Drawing Lines

Xlib provides support for drawing lines in much the same as it supports drawing points. The Xlib function:

```
XDrawLine ( Display *display,
            Drawable d,
            GC        gc,
            int       x1,
            int       y1,
            int       x2,
            int       y2 )
```

draws a single line between two points. The way in which XDrawLine() draws lines is determined by the following attributes of the graphics context:

```
        GCFunction        GCPlaneMask       GCLineWidth
        GCLineStyle       GCCapStyle        GCFillStyle
        GCSubwindowMode   GCClipXOrigin     GCClipYOrigin
        GCClipMask
```

The function:

```
XDrawSegments ( Display  *display,
                Drawable  d,
                GC        gc,
                XSegment *segments,
                int       nsegments )
```

draws multiple, discontiguous line segments with a single request. The line segments are specified by an array of type XSegment, which includes the members:

```
short x1, y1, x2, y2;
```

Although the line segments do not need to be connected, XDrawSegments() draws all segments using the same graphics context. This function uses the same graphics context attributes as XDrawLine().

The function:

```
XDrawLines ( Display *display,
             Drawable d,
             GC       gc,
             XPoint  *points,
             int      npoints,
             int      mode )
```

draws multiple connected lines. This function draws (npoints − 1) lines between the points in the points array. XDrawLines() draws all lines in the order in which the points appear in the array. The mode argument determines whether the points are interpreted relative to the origin of the drawable or relative to the last point drawn, and must be one of CoordModeOrigin or Coord-ModePrevious. XDrawLines() uses the GCJoinStyle attribute of the graphics context, in addition to the graphics context members used by XDrawLine().

We can demonstrate XDrawLine() in a simple program that uses a technique known as *rubber banding*. A rubber band line is usually drawn interactively by the user. The user first sets an initial endpoint, usually by pressing a mouse button. A line is then drawn between this endpoint and the current position of the pointer. As the user moves the pointer, the line appears to stretch as if it were a rubber band connected between the pointer and the initial position. The rubber banding ends in response to some user action, typically when the mouse button is released. This technique is commonly used to allow the user to define a beginning and ending coordinate for drawing lines or other figures interactively.

The following program, named rubberband, allows the user to draw rubber band lines in the window of an XmDrawingArea widget.

```
1   /************************************************
2    * rubberband.c: rubberband line example
3    ************************************************/
4   #include <Xm/Xm.h>
5   #include <X11/cursorfont.h>
6   #include <Xm/DrawingA.h>
7
8   static int startX, startY, lastX, lastY;
9   static GC  gc;
10
11  static void StartRubberBand ( Widget      w,
12                                XtPointer clientData,
13                                XEvent    *event,
14                                Boolean   *flag );
15  static void EndRubberBand ( Widget      w,
16                              XtPointer clientData,
17                              XEvent    *event,
18                              Boolean   *flag );
```

```
19    static void TrackRubberBand ( Widget    w,
20                                   XtPointer clientData,
21                                   XEvent    *event,
22                                   Boolean   *flag );
```

The body of the program simply creates an XmDrawingArea widget and adds event handlers for `ButtonPress`, `ButtonRelease`, and pointer motion events which work together to implement the rubber banding.

```
23    void main ( int argc, char **argv )
24    {
25        Widget        shell, canvas;
26        XtAppContext app;
27        XGCValues     values;
28
29        shell = XtAppInitialize ( &app, "Rubberband", NULL, 0,
30                                  &argc, argv, NULL, NULL, 0 );
31     /*
32      * Create a drawing surface, and add event handlers for
33      * ButtonPress, ButtonRelease and MotionNotify events.
34      */
35
36        canvas = XtCreateManagedWidget ( "canvas",
37                                         xmDrawingAreaWidgetClass,
38                                         shell, NULL, 0 );
39        XtAddEventHandler ( canvas, ButtonPressMask, FALSE,
40                            StartRubberBand, NULL );
41        XtAddEventHandler ( canvas, ButtonMotionMask, FALSE,
42                            TrackRubberBand, NULL );
43        XtAddEventHandler ( canvas, ButtonReleaseMask,
44                            FALSE, EndRubberBand, NULL );
45
46        XtRealizeWidget ( shell );
47
48     /*
49      * Establish a passive grab, for any button press.
50      * Force the mouse cursor to stay within the canvas window,
51      * and change the mouse cursor to a cross_hair.
52      */
53
54        XGrabButton ( XtDisplay ( canvas ), AnyButton, AnyModifier,
55                      XtWindow ( canvas ), TRUE,
56                      ButtonPressMask | ButtonMotionMask |
57                      ButtonReleaseMask,
58                      GrabModeAsync, GrabModeAsync,
59                      XtWindow ( canvas ),
60                      XCreateFontCursor ( XtDisplay ( canvas ),
61                                          XC_crosshair ) );
```

```
62      /*
63       * Create the GC used by the rubber banding functions.
64       */
65
66      XtVaGetValues ( canvas,
67                      XmNforeground, &values.foreground,
68                      XmNbackground, &values.background,
69                      NULL );
70
71      /*
72       * Set the foreground color to the XOR of the foreground
73       * and background colors, so that if an image is drawn
74       * on the background using this GC, it will be displayed as
75       * the foreground color, and vice-versa.
76       */
77
78      values.foreground = values.foreground ^ values.background;
79
80      /*
81       * Set the rubber band gc to use XOR mode and draw
82       * a dashed line.
83       */
84
85      values.line_style = LineOnOffDash;
86      values.function   = GXxor;
87
88      gc = XtGetGC ( canvas, GCForeground | GCBackground |
89                             GCFunction | GCLineStyle,
90                             &values );
91
92      XtAppMainLoop ( app );
93  }
```

This example introduces some new Xlib functions. The function:

```
XGrabButton ( Display        *display,
              unsigned int   button,
              unsigned int   modifiers,
              Window         grab_window,
              Boolean        owner_events,
              unsigned int   event_mask,
              int            pointer_mode,
              int            keyboard_mode,
              Window         confine_to,
              Cursor         cursor )
```

establishes a *passive grab* on the specified mouse button. A passive grab takes effect automatically when the user presses the specified mouse button. Once the pointer is grabbed, the server reports all mouse events to the grabbing client, even if the pointer leaves the window. This allows the server to track pointer motion more efficiently. `XGrabButton()` also allows the program to constrain the pointer to stay within a particular window while the grab is in effect. In this example, the pointer is constrained to the `canvas` window as long as the grab is in effect. `XGrabButton()` also allows the programmer to specify the shape of the mouse cursor while the grab is in effect. In this example, the mouse cursor changes to a crosshair shape when the pointer is grabbed.

The function

```
XCreateFontCursor ( Display display, int cursor_index )
```

retrieves a mouse cursor from a font. The file cursorfont.h defines a set of constants used as indexes into the cursor font. When the user releases the mouse button, the grab automatically terminates and the mouse cursor returns to its previous shape.

The task of drawing the rubber band line is performed by three cooperating event handlers. When the user presses a mouse button, Xt invokes the first event handler, `StartRubberBand()`. This function stores the position of the pointer when the `ButtonPress` event occurs as the initial position of the line, and also sets the last position of the line to the same point. The function `XDrawLine()` is called to draw the initial line, which is simply a point, because the start and end points are the same.

```
94   static void StartRubberBand ( Widget    w,
95                                  XtPointer clientData,
96                                  XEvent    *event,
97                                  Boolean   *flag )
98   {
99       lastX = startX = event->xbutton.x;
100      lastY = startY = event->xbutton.y;
101
102      XDrawLine ( XtDisplay ( w ), XtWindow ( w ),
103                  gc, startX, startY, lastX, lastY );
104  }
```

The function `TrackRubberBand()` is called each time the pointer moves. This function draws a line between the initial position at which the user pressed the mouse button and the last recorded position of the pointer. Because the line is drawn in XOR mode, this erases the current line and restores the previous contents of the screen. The end points of the line are then updated to reflect the new pointer position and the line is drawn again.

```
105  static void TrackRubberBand ( Widget    w,
106                                XtPointer clientData,
107                                XEvent    *event,
108                                Boolean   *flag )
109  {
110      /*
111       * Draw once to clear the previous line.
112       */
```

```
113
114        XDrawLine ( XtDisplay ( w ), XtWindow ( w ), gc,
115                    startX,startY,
116                    lastX, lastY );
117
118     /*
119      * Update the endpoints.
120      */
121
122        lastX  =  event->xbutton.x;
123        lastY  =  event->xbutton.y;
124
125     /*
126      * Draw the new line.
127      */
128
129        XDrawLine ( XtDisplay ( w ), XtWindow ( w ), gc,
130                    startX, startY,
131                    lastX, lastY );
132
133   }
```

When the user releases the mouse button, the event handler `EndRubberBand()` is invoked. This function draws the line one last time in XOR mode to erase the line. The function also stores the current position of the pointer in the client data structure where any interested routine can retrieve it.

```
134   static void EndRubberBand ( Widget     w,
135                               XtPointer clientData,
136                               XEvent    *event,
137                               Boolean   *flag )
138   {
139     /*
140      * Clear the current line and update the endpoint info.
141      */
142
143        XDrawLine ( XtDisplay ( w ), XtWindow ( w ), gc,
144                    startX, startY,
145                    lastX, lastY );
146
147        lastX  =  event->xbutton.x;
148        lastY  =  event->xbutton.y;
149
150   }
```

Notice that `EndRubberBand()` erases the final line, so that nothing is visible when the final drawing operation is completed. Typically, a program that uses rubberbanding techniques uses the final coordinates to perform the next step. The next step could be drawing a line if the application is a drawing editor, but could be any operation that requires the endpoints of a user-defined line.

13.3 Rectangles, Polygons, and Arcs

In addition to points and lines, Xlib also provides functions for drawing more complex figures, including filled and unfilled polygons, arcs, and circles. This section describes some of these functions.

The function:

```
XDrawRectangle ( Display       *display,
                 Drawable      d,
                 GC            gc,
                 int           x,
                 int           y,
                 unsigned int width,
                 unsigned int height )
```

draws the outline of a rectangle, while the function:

```
XDrawRectangles ( Display       *display,
                  Drawable      d,
                  GC            gc,
                  XRectangle *rectangles,
                  int           nrectangles )
```

draws multiple rectangles. The argument `rectangles` must be an array of type `XRectangle`, which includes the members:

```
short         x, y;
unsigned short width, height;
```

An arc can be drawn using the function:

```
XDrawArc ( Display       *display,
           Drawable      d,
           GC            gc,
           int           x,
           int           y,
           unsigned int width,
           unsigned int height,
           int           angle1,
           int           angle2 )
```

This function draws an arc starting from `angle1`, relative to a three o'clock position, to `angle2`, within the bounding rectangle specified by the parameters `x`, `y`, `width`, `height`, as shown in Figure 13.3. The angles are specified in units of *(degrees * 64)*. For example, `XDrawArc()` can be used to draw a circle or ellipse by specifying a starting angle of zero degrees and an ending angle of (*64 * 360)* degrees. Angles greater than (*64 * 360)* degrees are truncated.

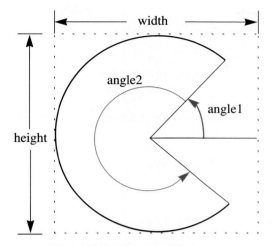

Figure 13.3 Dimensions of an arc.

The function:

```
XDrawArcs ( Display *display,
            Drawable d,
            GC       gc,
            XArc     *arcs,
            int      narcs )
```

draws multiple arcs with a single server request and uses an array of type **XArc** to define the parameters of each arc. The **XArc** structure contains the following members:

```
short            x, y;
unsigned short   width, height;
short            angle1, angle2;
```

Xlib also provides functions for drawing polygons, rectangles, and arcs filled with a solid color or pattern. The function:

```
XFillRectangle ( Display       *display,
                 Drawable      d,
                 GC            gc,
                 int           x,
                 int           y,
                 unsigned int  width,
                 unsigned int  height )
```

draws a single rectangle filled as specified by the `GCForeground`, `GCBackground`, `GCTile`, and `GCStipple` attributes of the graphics context.

The function:

```
XFillRectangles ( Display    *display,
                  Drawable    d,
                  GC          gc,
                  XRectangle *rectangles,
                  int         nrectangles )
```

draws multiple filled rectangles using an array of `XRectangle` structures.

The function:

```
XFillPolygon ( Display *display,
               Drawable d,
               GC       gc,
               XPoint  *points,
               int      npoints,
               int      shape,
               int      mode )
```

draws a single polygon specified by an array of `XPoint` structures. If the figure specified by these points is not closed, `XFillPolygon()` automatically closes the figure before filling the area enclosed by the points. The `shape` parameter can be one of the constants `Complex`, `Convex`, or `Nonconvex`. The server can use this information to select the optimal drawing algorithm. The `mode` argument determines how the points are interpreted and must be one of the constants `CoordModeOrigin` or `CoordModePrevious`. If `CoordModeOrigin` is given, all points are considered to be absolute coordinates. Specifying `CoordModePrevious` means that each point indicates a relative distance from the previous point.

The functions:

```
XFillArc ( Display      *display,
           Drawable      d,
           GC            gc,
           int           x,
           int           y,
           unsigned int width,
           unsigned int height,
           int           angle1,
           int           angle2 )
```

and:

```
XFillArcs ( Display *display,
            Drawable d,
            GC       gc,
            XArc    *arcs,
            int      narcs )
```

draw single and multiple filled arcs, respectively.

In each case, the arguments to a fill function are the same as those to the corresponding non-filled version.

Rubberbanding Rectangles

The previous section demonstrated how lines can be drawn interactively using a simple technique known as rubber banding. Any type of figure can be rubberbanded, using the same XOR technique described in the previous section. Rubberbanded rectangles can be particularly useful when selecting a region of an image for some operation.

For example, the fractal program described in Section 13.1 allows users to move sliders in a preference panel to zoom and pan the image. The primary reason for doing so is to view a specific region of the fractal image. However, selecting parameters on the various scales is a somewhat awkward way to select a specific portion of the fractal image. An easier, more direct way is to sweep out the region to be inspected using a rubber banded rectangle. The following code segments show the changes to the fractal program necessary to add this feature. Only new functions and parts of the program that need to be modified are shown. Code that must be added to the fractal program is shown in bold.

First, the definition of the `ImageData` structure in fractal.h must be modified to add an `xorGC` member:

```
1    /*************************************************************
2     * fractal.h: Type declarations used in the fractal program
3     *************************************************************/
4    #include <Xm/Xm.h>
5
6    typedef struct {
7        double   real, imag;
8    } ComplexNumber;
9
10   typedef enum { DISTANCE, ITERATIONS } ColorationType;
11
12   /*
13    * Assorted information needed to generate and draw the image.
14    */
15
16   typedef struct {
17       Widget           canvas;
18       Pixmap           pixmap;
19       GC               gc;
20       GC               xorGC;
21       Dimension        width, height;
22       int              depth, ncolors;
23       double           range, maxDistance;
24       ComplexNumber    origin;
25       ColorationType   coloration;
26   } ImageData;
```

The beginning of the file fractal.c contains definitions of functions needed throughout the program. Three new functions are needed, StartRubberBand( ), TrackRubberBand( ), and EndRubberBand( ). These functions behave much the same as the functions by the same name described in the previous section, but are slightly different to handle the rectangle. In addition to these event handlers, the rubberbanding facility needs four variables, startX, startY, lastX, and lastY, which are also declared at the top of fractal.c.

```
1    /******************************************************************
2     * fractal.c: main window and rendering code for a version of the
3     *            fractal program that allows the user to select
4     *            a region for closer viewing using rubberbanding
5     ******************************************************************/
6    #include <Xm/Xm.h>
7    #include <Xm/DrawingA.h>
8    #include <Xm/MainW.h>
9    #include <stdlib.h>
10   #include "MenuSupport.h"
11   #include "fractal.h"
12
13   extern ShowPreferences ( Widget parent, ImageData *data );
14
15   static void InitData ( Widget w, ImageData *data );
16
17   static void ResizeCallback ( Widget     w,
18                                XtPointer clientData,
19                                XtPointer callData );
20   static void RedisplayCallback ( Widget     w,
21                                   XtPointer clientData,
22                                   XtPointer callData );
23   static void ShowPreferencesCallback ( Widget     w,
24                                         XtPointer clientData,
25                                         XtPointer callData );
26   static void QuitCallback ( Widget     w,
27                              XtPointer clientData,
28                              XtPointer callData );
29
30   /*
31    * Functions that can be called from preference module
32    */
33
34   void CreateImage ( ImageData *data );
35   void SetupColorMap ( Widget shell, ImageData *data, Boolean ramp );
36
37   /*
38    * Menu descriptions used by this program.
39    */
40
```

```
41  static MenuDescription appPaneDesc[] = {
42    { BUTTON,    "Preferences", ShowPreferencesCallback },
43    { BUTTON,    "Quit",        QuitCallback },
44    { NULL }
45  };
46
47  static MenuDescription menuBarDesc[] = {
48    { PULLDOWN,   "Application", NULL, NULL, appPaneDesc },
49    { NULL }
50  };
51
52  static void StartRubberBand ( Widget     w,
53                                XtPointer clientData,
54                                XEvent    *event,
55                                Boolean   *flag );
56
57  static void TrackRubberBand ( Widget     w,
58                                XtPointer clientData,
59                                XEvent    *event,
60                                Boolean   *flag );
61
62  static void EndRubberBand ( Widget      w,
63                              XtPointer clientData,
64                              XEvent    *event,
65                              Boolean   *flag );
66
67  static int startX, startY, lastX, lastY;
```

The body of the fractal program is the same as the earlier version, except that three event handlers must be added to the `canvas` widget. The event handlers implement the rubberbanding facilities that allows the user to select a region of the fractal image.

```
68  void main ( int argc, char **argv )
69  {
70      Widget       shell, canvas, mainWindow, menu;
71      XtAppContext app;
72      ImageData    data;
73
74      /*
75       * Initialize Xt
76       */
77
78      shell = XtAppInitialize ( &app, "Fractal", NULL, 0,
79                                &argc, argv, NULL, NULL, 0 );
80
81      mainWindow = XtCreateManagedWidget ( "mainWindow",
82                                           xmMainWindowWidgetClass,
83                                           shell, NULL, 0 );
```

```
 84     /*
 85      * Create the widget in which to display the fractal
 86      */
 87
 88      canvas = XtCreateManagedWidget ( "canvas",
 89                                       xmDrawingAreaWidgetClass,
 90                                       mainWindow, NULL, 0 );
 91     /*
 92      * Create the GCs needed by the fractal program.
 93      */
 94
 95      InitData ( canvas, &data );
 96
 97     /*
 98      * Create the menu bar and set up the window layout.
 99      */
100
101      menu = CreateMenu ( MENUBAR, "menuBar",
102                          mainWindow, menuBarDesc, &data );
103
104      XtVaSetValues ( mainWindow,
105                      XmNmenuBar,     menu,
106                      XmNworkWindow, canvas,
107                      NULL );
108     /*
109      * Add callbacks to handle resize and exposures.
110      */
111
112      XtAddCallback ( canvas, XmNexposeCallback,
113                      RedisplayCallback, ( XtPointer ) &data );
114      XtAddCallback ( canvas, XmNresizeCallback,
115                      ResizeCallback, ( XtPointer )  &data );
116     /*
117      * Add event handlers to track the mouse and allow
118      * the user to select a region with rubberband rectangle.
119      */
120
121      XtAddEventHandler ( canvas, ButtonPressMask, FALSE,
122                          StartRubberBand, &data );
123      XtAddEventHandler ( canvas, ButtonMotionMask, FALSE,
124                          TrackRubberBand, &data );
125      XtAddEventHandler ( canvas, ButtonReleaseMask, FALSE,
126                          EndRubberBand, &data );
127
128      XtRealizeWidget ( shell );
129
130     /*
131      * Once all widgets are realized, call an auxiliary function to
132      * install a colormap in the canvas window, so the fractal can
```

```
133      * be displayed with a full range of colors.
134      */
135
136     SetupColorMap( shell, &data, FALSE );
137     XtAppMainLoop ( app );
138 }
```

The `InitData()` function must be modified to create an XOR graphics context that can be used to draw the rubberbanded rectangle. The new version can be written as follows:

```
139 static void InitData ( Widget w, ImageData *data )
140 {
141     XGCValues values;
142
143     /*
144      * Get the size of the drawing area.
145      */
146
147     XtVaGetValues ( w,
148                     XmNwidth,  &data->width,
149                     XmNheight, &data->height,
150                     XmNbackground, &values.foreground,
151                     NULL );
152
153     data->canvas      = w;
154     data->depth       = 20;
155     data->origin.real = -1.4;
156     data->origin.imag = 1.0;
157     data->range       = 2.0;
158     data->maxDistance = 4.0;
159     data->coloration  = ITERATIONS;
160
161     /*
162      * Find out how many colors we have to work with, and
163      * create a default, writable, graphics context.
164      */
165
166     data->ncolors =
167               XDisplayCells ( XtDisplay ( w ),
168                               XDefaultScreen ( XtDisplay ( w ) ) );
169
170     data->gc = XCreateGC ( XtDisplay ( w ),
171                           DefaultRootWindow ( XtDisplay ( w ) ),
172                           NULL, NULL );
173     /*
174      * Create a second GC set to XOR mode to use in the rubberbanding
175      * functions that select a region into which to zoom.
176      */
```

```
177
178        values.function = GXxor;
179
180        data->xorGC = XtGetGC ( w,
181                                GCForeground | GCFunction,
182                                &values );
183
184        /*
185         *  Initialize the pixmap to NULL.
186         */
187
188        data->pixmap = NULL;
189
190    }
```

The `StartRubberBand()` function initializes the variables used to track the pointer position. This function is nearly the same as the one described in the previous section, except that this version does not draw a rectangle, because the width and height of the rectangle would be zero.

```
191    static void StartRubberBand ( Widget     w,
192                                  XtPointer clientData,
193                                  XEvent    *event,
194                                  Boolean   *flag )
195    {
196        lastX = startX = event->xbutton.x;
197
198        lastY = startY = event->xbutton.y;
199    }
```

The function `TrackRubberBand()` handles all the pointer motion while the mouse button is held down. If a rectangle is currently displayed, this function erases it by redrawing a rectangle using the last stored points. The fractal program is a good example of why the XOR technique is important. Using XOR mode, `TrackRubberBand()` is able to draw and erase a figure without disturbing the fractal image. If the fractal had to be recomputed and redrawn to restore the image to undo the damage caused by the rectangle, interactively displaying a rectangle while sweeping out a region would not be practical.

The `TrackRubberBand()` function differs in several ways from the version used in the rubber band line example. Here, `TrackRubberBand()` is being used to select a region into which the fractal program is to zoom. It is useful to limit the user to selecting regions that fit the window in which the fractal is displayed. This implementation arbitrarily accepts the width of the rectangular region defined by the user, but forces the height of the region to a value that matches the aspect ratio of the canvas window.

```
200   static void TrackRubberBand ( Widget     w,
201                                  XtPointer clientData,
202                                  XEvent    *event,
203                                  Boolean   *flag )
204   {
205       int height;
206       ImageData *data = ( ImageData* ) clientData;
207
208       /*
209        * If a non-zero sized rectangle has been previously drawn,
210        * erase it by drawing again in XOR mode.
211        */
212
213       if ( lastX - startX > 0 || lastY - startY > 0 )
214           XDrawRectangle ( XtDisplay ( w ), XtWindow ( w ), data->xorGC,
215                            startX, startY,
216                            lastX - startX, lastY - startY );
217       /*
218        * Update the last point. Force an aspect ratio that
219        * matches the shape of the window
220        */
221
222       lastX  =  event->xmotion.x;
223
224       height = data->height * ( lastX - startX ) / data->width;
225
226       lastY  =  startY + height;
227
228       if ( lastX < startX )
229           lastX = startX;
230
231       if ( lastY < startY )
232           lastY = startY;
233       /*
234        * Draw the new rectangle in XOR mode so it can easily be erased.
235        */
236
237       XDrawRectangle ( XtDisplay ( w ), XtWindow ( w ), data->xorGC,
238                        startX, startY,
239                        lastX - startX, lastY - startY );
240   }
```

The function EndRubberBand() erases the last figure, completely removing the rectangle from the fractal image. Then, if a rectangular region with a non-zero, positive width and height has been selected, this function converts the final coordinates from the pixel-based values reported by the X events to the floating point values used by the fractal. Finally, the function CreateImage() is called to recompute and display a new fractal based on a new range and origin that will display the selected portion of the fractal in the full window.

```
241    static void EndRubberBand ( Widget      w,
242                                 XtPointer clientData,
243                                 XEvent    *event,
244                                 Boolean   *flag )
245    {
246       int height;
247       ImageData *data = ( ImageData* ) clientData;
248
249       /*
250        * If a non-zero sized rectangle has been previously drawn,
251        * erase it by drawing again in XOR mode.
252        */
253
254       if ( lastX - startX > 0 || lastY - startY > 0 )
255           XDrawRectangle ( XtDisplay ( w ), XtWindow ( w ),
256                         data->xorGC, startX, startY,
257                         lastX - startX, lastY - startY );
258
259       /*
260        * Update the last point. Force an aspect ratio that
261        * matches the shape of the window
262        */
263
264       lastX  = event->xmotion.x;
265       height = data->height * ( lastX - startX ) / data->width;
266
267       lastY  =  startY + height;
268
269       /*
270        * Unless a non-zero sized region was selected, just return.
271        */
272
273       if ( lastX <= startX || lastY <= startY )
274           return;
275
276       /*
277        * Convert the pixel-based corrdinates to the real coordinates
278        * used to compute the fractal image.
279        */
280
281       data->origin.real += data->range *
282                           ( double ) startX / ( double ) data->width;
283
284       data->origin.imag -= data->range *
285                           ( double )  startY / ( double ) data->height;
286
287       data->range = data->range *
288               ( double ) ( lastX - startX ) / ( double ) data->width;
289
```

```
290     /*
291      * Create a new image, based on the newly selected range and
292      * origin. Also update the preference panel so it stays in sync.
293      */
294
295         CreateImage ( data );
296         UpdatePreferences ( data );
297     }
```

Figure 13.4 shows the rubberband-based zooming functionality in action. One the left, the user selects a region to be displayed in more detail. On the right, the selected region is displayed in full size. This process can be repeated indefinitely, limited only by the precision of the computation.

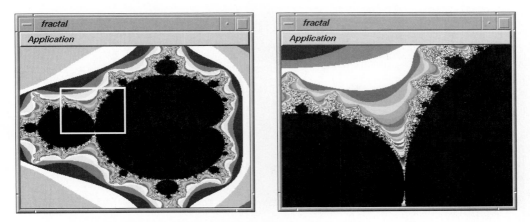

Figure 13.4 Selecting a region in the fractal, before and after.

13.4 Example: A Simple Drawing Program

This section concludes the discussion of Xlib graphics functions by examining a relatively simple drawing program that uses many of the techniques and functions discussed in this chapter, as well as in the previous chapters. The `draw` program shown in Figure 13.5 allows users to select from several possible shapes, and position and size them using the rubber banding techniques discussed in Section 13.2. Users can also select from a palette of colors with which to draw each figure. Drawings can also be saved to a file and reloaded.

Besides demonstrating the use of the various Xlib drawing functions, this program exercises dialogs and menus as well as graphics contexts, and assorted other Motif and X features. The editor allows users to draw simple lines, circles, and rectangles in a window. Users can select the color of each item, and can select and move items as needed.

The `draw` program is the largest example described so far, and is broken into three source files and one header. The file main.c contains a driver that initializes Xt and handles the event loop. A second file, editor.c, sets up the user interface for the draw program. This file creates the widgets, installs callbacks for commands, and so on. The third file, graphics.c, implements a simple display list as well as various functions used to display and manipulate graphics objects stored in the list. The following sections describe the modules represented by each file.

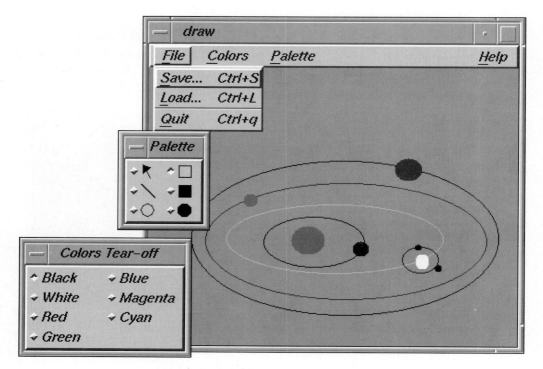

Figure 13.5   Using draw: a simple drawing program.

The Draw Program Body

The main body of the draw program simply initializes Xt and enters the event loop. Before entering the event loop, the program calls an external function, `CreateEditor()`, to set up the user interface and other details of the graphics editor. `CreateEditor()` requires a single argument, a window in which to place the drawing editor. In this case, the shell created by `XtApp-Initialize()` is passed to `CreateEditor()` as the editor's parent.

```
1   /*********************************************************
2    * main.c: Driver for drawing program
3    *********************************************************/
4   #include <Xm/Xm.h>
5
6   extern Widget CreateDrawingEditor ( Widget parent );
7
8   void main ( int argc, char **argv )
9   {
10      Widget         shell;
11      XtAppContext app;
12
13      /*
14       * Initialize Xt, creating an application shell.
15       * Call an external function to create the drawing
16       * editor as a child of the shell.
17       */
18
19      shell = XtAppInitialize ( &app, "Draw", NULL, 0,
20                                &argc, argv, NULL, NULL, 0 );
21
22      CreateDrawingEditor ( shell );
23
24      XtRealizeWidget ( shell );
25      XtAppMainLoop ( app );
26  }
```

Draw.h

The two remaining files need to agree on a common set of symbols to represent the various graphics figures that can be drawn. The user interface is designed to be relatively independent of the drawing module, so these symbols are useful for communicating between the modules.

```
1   /*********************************************************
2    * draw.h: Definitions used thoughout the drawing program
3    *********************************************************/
4   #define NONE           1
5   #define LINE           2
6   #define CIRCLE         3
7   #define RECTANGLE      4
8   #define FILLEDCIRCLE   5
9   #define FILLEDRECTANGLE 6
```

Setting Up the User Interface

The file editor.c contains the user interface for the draw program. This file contains the function CreateDrawingEditor(), which creates the widget hierarchy, as well as various callback functions that allow the user to control the editor. The widget hierarchy consists of an XmMain-

Window widget that manages a menu bar and an XmDrawingArea widget in which figures can be displayed. The menu is created using the `CreateMenu()` convenience function described in Chapter 6.

The file editor.c begins by including various header files, declaring callback functions, and setting up a menu description. The menu bar has four menu panes, a File menu, a Colors menu, a DrawingCommands menu, and a Help menu. The File menu contains entries for saving to a file and reading from a file. The Colors menu allows the user to select a color with which to draw, while the DrawingCommands menu allows the user to select from the types of figures supported by the editor. The Help menu supports context-sensitive help, using the `ContextHelpCallback()` function described in Chapter 6.

```
1    /*****************************************************
2     * editor.c: Drawing editor user interface module
3     *****************************************************/
4    #include <Xm/Xm.h>
5    #include <Xm/MainW.h>
6    #include <Xm/DrawingA.h>
7    #include <Xm/MessageB.h>
8    #include <Xm/Protocols.h>
9    #include <X11/cursorfont.h>
10   #include <stdlib.h>
11   #include "MenuSupport.h"
12   #include "draw.h"
13
14   /*
15    * Callbacks used by menu items.
16    */
17
18   static void QuitCallback ( Widget    w,
19                              XtPointer clientData,
20                              XtPointer callData );
21   static void SaveCallback ( Widget    w,
22                              XtPointer clientData,
23                              XtPointer callData );
24   static void LoadCallback ( Widget    w,
25                              XtPointer clientData,
26                              XtPointer callData );
27
28   static void SetFigureCallback ( Widget    w,
29                                   XtPointer clientData,
30                                   XtPointer callData );
31   static void SetColorCallback ( Widget    w,
32                                  XtPointer clientData,
33                                  XtPointer callData );
34
35   /*
36    * Declare external functions called from this module
37    */
```

```
38
39   extern void XmRepTypeInstallTearOffModelConverter ( void );
40   extern void SetDrawingFunction ( int type );
41   extern void SetCurrentColor ( Pixel pixel );
42   extern void LoadData ( void );
43   extern void SaveData ( void );
44   extern InitGraphics ( Widget w );
45
46   /*
47    * Descriptions of contents of the menu bar. See Chapter 6
48    */
49
50   static MenuDescription drawingCommandsDesc[] = {
51     { TOGGLE,    "None",         SetFigureCallback, ( XtPointer ) NONE   },
52     { TOGGLE,    "Line",         SetFigureCallback, ( XtPointer ) LINE   },
53     { TOGGLE,    "Circle",       SetFigureCallback, ( XtPointer ) CIRCLE },
54     { TOGGLE,    "Rectangle",
55                                  SetFigureCallback, ( XtPointer ) RECTANGLE },
56     { TOGGLE,    "FilledRectangle",
57                         SetFigureCallback, ( XtPointer ) FILLEDRECTANGLE },
58     { TOGGLE,    "FilledCircle",
59                         SetFigureCallback, ( XtPointer ) FILLEDCIRCLE },
60     { NULL }
61   };
62
63   static MenuDescription colorDesc[] = {
64     { TOGGLE,    "Black",   SetColorCallback },
65     { TOGGLE,    "White",   SetColorCallback },
66     { TOGGLE,    "Red",     SetColorCallback },
67     { TOGGLE,    "Green",   SetColorCallback },
68     { TOGGLE,    "Blue",    SetColorCallback },
69     { TOGGLE,    "Magenta", SetColorCallback },
70     { TOGGLE,    "Cyan",    SetColorCallback },
71     { NULL }
72   };
73
74   static MenuDescription filePaneDesc[] = {
75     { BUTTON,    "Save",             SaveCallback },
76     { BUTTON,    "Load",             LoadCallback },
77     { SEPARATOR                                   },
78     { BUTTON,    "Quit",             QuitCallback },
79     { NULL }
80   };
81
82   static MenuDescription helpPaneDesc[] = {
83     { BUTTON,    "HelpOnContext",   ContextHelpCallback },
84     { NULL }
85   };
86
```

```
87   static MenuDescription menuBarDesc[] = {
88     { PULLDOWN,        "File",   NULL, NULL, filePaneDesc },
89     { RADIOPULLDOWN,   "Colors", NULL, NULL, colorDesc    },
90     { RADIOPULLDOWN,   "DrawingCommands",
91                                  NULL, NULL, drawingCommandsDesc },
92     { HELPPANE,        "Help",   NULL, NULL, helpPaneDesc },
93     { NULL }
94   };
```

The function `CreateDrawingEditor()` sets up a widget hierarchy whose root is a child of the given parent widget. `CreateDrawingEditor()` installs a type converter to allow the use of tear-off menus to be controlled in a resource file, and then creates an XmMainWindow widget. The function `CreateMenu()` adds a menu bar to the XmMainWindow widget, and an XmDrawingArea widget is added as the main window widget's work area. The function `InitGraphics()` is defined in the graphics.c module, and sets up the XmDrawingArea widget to display the figures supported by the draw program.

```
95   Widget CreateDrawingEditor ( Widget parent )
96   {
97       Widget canvas, mainWindow;
98
99       /*
100       * Install the tear-off type converter to allow
101       * the tear-off model to be set in a resource file.
102       */
103
104       XmRepTypeInstallTearOffModelConverter();
105
106       /*
107       * Create a main window widget to handle the layout
108       * for the drawing editor.
109       */
110
111       mainWindow = XtCreateManagedWidget ( "mainWindow",
112                                            xmMainWindowWidgetClass,
113                                            parent, NULL, 0 );
114       /*
115       * Add a menu bar to the window. Pass the main window widget
116       * as the default client, needed primarily by the help callback.
117       */
118
119       CreateMenu ( MENUBAR, "menuBar", mainWindow,
120                    menuBarDesc, ( XtPointer ) mainWindow );
121
122       /*
123       * Create the widget used as a drawing surface
124       */
125
```

```
126        canvas = XtCreateManagedWidget ( "canvas",
127                                          xmDrawingAreaWidgetClass,
128                                          mainWindow, NULL, 0 );
129     /*
130      * Initialize the display list and other related functions.
131      */
132
133        InitGraphics ( canvas );
134
135        return mainWindow;
136    }
```

The `QuitCallback()` function simply exits the application. This function is registered as a callback for a menu item on the File menu pane.

```
137  static void QuitCallback ( Widget    w,
138                             XtPointer clientData,
139                             XtPointer callData )
140  {
141      exit ( 0 );
142  }
```

The function `SaveCallback()` is called when the "Save" item is chosen from the File menu pane. This function just calls a function defined in the graphics module to save the current contents of the display list to a file.

```
143  static void SaveCallback ( Widget    w,
144                             XtPointer clientData,
145                             XtPointer callData )
146  {
147      SaveData();
148  }
```

`LoadDataCallback()` just calls the function `LoadData()`, defined in the graphics module, to load a file and display its contents.

```
149  static void LoadCallback ( Widget    w,
150                             XtPointer clientData,
151                             XtPointer callData )
152  {
153      LoadData();
154  }
```

The colors supported by the draw program are taken from the names of the menu items in the Colors menu pane. Each item in this menu uses the same callback. When this function, `SetColorCallback()`, is called a new color is allocated based on the name of the widget that invoked the callback. The menu items in the Colors menu pane are XmToggleButton widgets, so

`SetColorCallback()` must check to see if it has been called because a button has been set or because it has been unset. A color is allocated only if the button has been currently selected. Once a color has been allocated, the function `SetCurrentColor()` is called to designate the color to be used for future drawing operations. `SetCurrentColor()` is defined as part of the graphics.c module.

```
155  static void SetColorCallback ( Widget       w,
156                                  XtPointer clientData,
157                                  XtPointer callData )
158  {
159      Widget      widget = XtParent ( w );
160      Display    *dpy    = XtDisplay (w );
161      int         scr    = DefaultScreen ( dpy );
162      Colormap    cmap   = DefaultColormap ( dpy, scr );
163      XColor      color, ignore;
164      XmToggleButtonCallbackStruct *cbs =
165                      ( XmToggleButtonCallbackStruct * ) callData;
166      /*
167       * Allocate the color named by the name of the widget that
168       * invoked this callback and call SetCurrentColor to install
169       * the resulting pixel and the current color.
170       */
171
172      if ( cbs->set &&
173           XAllocNamedColor ( dpy, cmap, XtName ( w ),
174                              &color, &ignore ) )
175          SetCurrentColor ( color.pixel );
176  }
```

`SetFigureCallback()` is called when an XmToggleButton widget in the DrawingCommands menu pane is selected. If the menu item was set, this function retrieves the corresponding figure type from the client data and calls `SetDrawingFunction()` to establish the type of figure to be drawn next.

```
177  static void SetFigureCallback ( Widget       w,
178                                  XtPointer clientData,
179                                  XtPointer callData )
180  {
181      unsigned char command = ( unsigned char ) clientData;
182      XmToggleButtonCallbackStruct *cbs =
183                      ( XmToggleButtonCallbackStruct * ) callData;
184      /*
185       * Set the current command from the parameter passed as clientData
186       */
187
188      if ( cbs->set )
189          SetDrawingFunction ( command );
190  }
```

The Display List and Drawing Operations

The functional part of the draw program is implemented in the file graphics.c. This module includes a simple display list that stores descriptions of figures to be drawn, along with various functions used to display and manipulate objects in the display list. This file begins by defining some variables needed by multiple functions in the module, defining some data structure to represent graphics objects, and declaring various callback functions and event handlers.

The heart of the graphics module is the display list. The display list is simply an array of structures that represent each figure drawn in the editor. A structure of type **GraphicsObject** stores all the information required to draw a single figure. This information includes the position and size of the figure, the color of the figure, and a pointer to a function that can draw the specific type of figure. The remainder of the file consists largely of functions that allow the application to add new **GraphicsObject** items to the display buffer, redraw the contents of the display buffer, and otherwise manipulate the images drawn into the XmDrawingArea widget created in the editor module.

```
1    /************************************************************
2     * graphics.c: A display list that holds graphics objects
3     *             and associated functions needed to
4     *             display objects in a drawing area widget
5     ************************************************************/
6    #include <Xm/Xm.h>
7    #include <Xm/FileSB.h>
8    #include <stdio.h>
9    #include "draw.h"
10
11   #define MAXOBJECTS 1000 /* The most objects the displayList can hold */
12
13   /*
14    * Define a standard for for all drawing function used in this module
15    * to allow all operation to be invoked with the same API.
16    */
17
18   typedef void ( *DrawingFunction ) ( Window, GC, int, int, int, int );
19
20   /*
21    * Define a data structure that describes a single visible
22    * object in the display list.
23    */
24
25   typedef struct{
26       int             x1, y1, x2, y2;
27       DrawingFunction func;
28       int             figureType;
29       Pixel           foreground;
30       GC              gc;
31   } GraphicsObject;
```

```
32   /*
33    * The display list is just an array of GraphicsObjects
34    */
35
36   GraphicsObject displayList[MAXOBJECTS];
37
38   /*
39    * Various variables used within this module. All are global to
40    * functions in this file, but static, so as to be hidden from
41    * functions in other parts of the program.
42    */
43
44   static int            nextSlot       = 0;    /* Next free spot
45                                                    in displayList */
46   static GraphicsObject *currentObject  = NULL;/* Pointer to currently
47                                                    selected object */
48   static DrawingFunction currentFunction = NULL; /* Function that draws
49                                                    current figure type */
50   static int            currentFigureType = 0; /* Current figure type
51                                                    being drawn. */
52   static Display        *display        = NULL;
53   static Colormap        colormap;
54   static GC              currentGC      = NULL;
55   static GC              xorGC          = NULL;
56   static Pixel           currentForeground = 0;
57   static Pixel           background     = 0;
58   static Widget          canvas         = NULL;
59   static Position startX = 0, startY = 0, lastX = 0, lastY = 0;
60
61   /*
62    * Functions that draw each figure type using the same arguments
63    */
64
65   static void  DrawLine ( Window, GC, int, int, int, int );
66   static void  DrawCircle ( Window, GC, int, int, int, int );
67   static void  DrawRectangle ( Window, GC, int, int, int, int );
68   static void  DrawFilledCircle ( Window, GC, int, int, int, int );
69   static void  DrawFilledRectangle ( Window, GC, int, int, int, int );
70   void FixDataOrdering ( int *x, int *y, int *x2, int *y2 );
71
72   /*
73    * Functions for "flattening" and "unflattening" an object
74    */
75
76   static GraphicsObject *Unpack ( char *str );
77   static char           *Pack ( GraphicsObject *object );
78   /*
79    * Callback functions
80    */
```

```
81    static void Redisplay ( Widget     w,
82                                 XtPointer clientData,
83                                 XtPointer callData );
84
85    static void StartRubberBand ( Widget     w,
86                                 XtPointer  clientData,
87                                 XEvent    *event,
88                                 Boolean   *flag );
89    static void TrackRubberBand ( Widget     w,
90                                 XtPointer  clientData,
91                                 XEvent    *event,
92                                 Boolean   *flag );
93    static void EndRubberBand ( Widget     w,
94                                 XtPointer  clientData,
95                                 XEvent    *event,
96                                 Boolean   *flag );
97    static void LoadDataCallback ( Widget     w,
98                                 XtPointer  clientData,
99                                 XtPointer  callData );
100   static void CancelDialogCallback ( Widget     w,
101                                 XtPointer  clientData,
102                                 XtPointer  callData );
103   static void SaveDataCallback ( Widget     w,
104                                 XtPointer  clientData,
105                                 XtPointer  callData );
106
107   /*
108    * Functions for storing, removing, moving and picking objects
109    * in the display list.
110    */
111
112   static void AddObject ( GraphicsObject *object );
113   static void StoreObject ( void );
114   static void MoveObject ( GraphicsObject *object, int x, int y );
115   static GraphicsObject *PickObject ( int x, int y );
```

Initializing the Graphics Buffer

The function InitGraphics() performs the initialization required to attach the display list and
its various functions to a given XmDrawingArea widget. This function registers an XmNexpose-
Callback function with the XmDrawingArea widget to allow the contents of the display list to be
redrawn as needed. InitGraphics() also installs three event handlers to allow users to draw
new figures. These event handlers are similar to those described in Section 13.2, but are slightly
more complex, because they must deal with the larger assortment of figures supported by this
program. InitGraphics() also allocates a graphics context for use by other functions, and
initializes several variables used throughout this module. These include a Display pointer, the
widget ID of the XmDrawingArea widget in which the display list is to be drawn, and the foreground
and background color used by the XmDrawingArea widget.

```
116   void InitGraphics ( Widget w )
117   {
118       XGCValues values;
119
120       /*
121        * Remember the given widget for use by other functions.
122        * Retrieve the display and colormap for later use.
123        */
124
125       canvas  = w;
126       display = XtDisplay ( canvas );
127       XtVaGetValues ( canvas, XmNcolormap, &colormap, NULL );
128
129       /*
130        * Register a callback to redraw the display list when the
131        * window is exposed, and event handlers to handle adding
132        * new objects to the display list interactively
133        */
134
135       XtAddCallback ( canvas, XmNexposeCallback, Redisplay, NULL );
136       XtAddEventHandler ( canvas, ButtonPressMask, FALSE,
137                           StartRubberBand, NULL );
138       XtAddEventHandler ( canvas, ButtonMotionMask, FALSE,
139                           TrackRubberBand, NULL );
140       XtAddEventHandler ( canvas, ButtonReleaseMask, FALSE,
141                           EndRubberBand, NULL );
142       /*
143        * Get the colors of the canvas.
144        */
145
146       XtVaGetValues ( canvas,
147                       XmNforeground, &currentForeground,
148                       XmNbackground, &background,
149                       NULL );
150       /*
151        * Fill in the values structure
152        */
153
154       values.foreground = currentForeground ^ background;
155       values.function   = GXxor;
156
157       /*
158        * Set the rubber band gc to use XOR mode.
159        */
160
161       xorGC =  XtGetGC ( canvas,
162                         GCForeground | GCFunction,
163                         &values );
164   }
```

Drawing Operations

To make the drawing editor as simple as possible, it is useful to be able to draw all figures supported by the editor in the same way. If the program can simply draw any item represented as a `GraphicsObject` with the same function call, the task of redrawing the display list will be easier. The task of writing a set of functions that allow users to position and size figures can also be simplified if all figures can be displayed in the same way. However, each of the various Xlib drawing function has a slightly different interface.

Fortunately, it is easy to define a set of drawing functions that require the same parameters. Each of the following functions takes a window, a graphics context, and a pair of x,y points. Although all functions have the same form, each interprets its arguments slightly differently, drawing a line in one case, a circle in another, and so on.

For example, the function `DrawLine()` draws a line between two points. This function can be written as follows.

```
165  static void DrawLine ( Window w, GC gc, int x, int y, int x2, int y2 )
166  {
167      XDrawLine ( display,   w, gc, x, y, x2, y2 );
168  }
```

The DrawLine function has nearly the same form as `XDrawLine()`, expect for the additional `Display` argument required by `XDrawLine()`. In this case, the two pairs of points are treated as the end-points of the line.

The functions `DrawRectangle()` and `DrawFilledRectangle()` draw rectangles using the given points as the upper left and lower right corners of the rectangle. Notice that the arguments to `DrawRectangle()` specify the bounding box of the rectangle in absolute coordinates, while `XDrawRectangle()` uses relative coordinates for the final two arguments.

```
169  void DrawRectangle ( Window w, GC gc, int x, int y, int x2, int y2 )
170  {
171      FixDataOrdering ( &x, &y, &x2, &y2 );
172
173      XDrawRectangle ( display, w , gc,  x, y, x2 - x, y2 - y );
174  }
```

```
175  void DrawFilledRectangle ( Window w, GC gc, int x, int y, int x2, int y2 )
176  {
177      FixDataOrdering ( &x, &y, &x2, &y2 );
178
179      XFillRectangle ( display,   w, gc, x, y, x2 - x, y2 - y );
180  }
```

The functions `DrawCircle()` and `DrawFilledCircle()` use the two points as the upper left and lower right corners of the bounding box of a circle. The function `XDrawArc()` is a more general function that can draw arcs that are less than a full circle. `DrawCircle()` always uses the given bounding box and draws a complete circle. These functions are defined as follows:

```
181  static void DrawCircle ( Window w, GC gc, int x, int y, int x2, int y2 )
182  {
183       FixDataOrdering ( &x, &y, &x2, &y2 );
184
185       XDrawArc ( display,  w, gc, x, y,
186                  x2 - x, y2 - y, 0, 64 * 360 );
187  }

188  static void DrawFilledCircle ( Window w, GC gc, int x, int y, int x2, int y2 )
189  {
190       FixDataOrdering ( &x, &y, &x2, &y2 );
191
192       XFillArc ( display,  w, gc, x, y,
193                  x2 - x, y2 - y, 0, 64 * 360 );
194  }
```

The Xlib functions used to display figures in the drawing editor expect the data provided to represent a bounding box with a non-negative width and height. If the first point passed to the `DrawRectangle()` or `DrawCircle()` functions represents the upper left corner of the figure, the data provided to the Xlib function will be correct. However, because of the way the functions in the draw program are used, it is possible for the corners of the figures to be reversed. The function `FixDataOrdering()` corrects the ordering of the points to ensure that *x* and *y* in the first point are always less than the corresponding *x* and *y* values in the second point.

```
195  void FixDataOrdering ( int *x, int *y, int *x2, int *y2 )
196  {
197      /*
198       * Swap the given points so that x2 is greater than x
199       * and y2 is greater than y.
200       */
201
202      if ( *x2 < *x )
203      {
204          int tmp = *x;
205          *x      = *x2;
206          *x2     = tmp;
207      }
208
209      if ( *y2 < *y )
210      {
211          int tmp = *y;
212          *y      = *y2;
213          *y2     = tmp;
214      }
215  }
```

The functions used to display figures in the drawing editor are private to the file graphics.c. However, the interface that allows users to specify the figure to be drawn is defined in the editor.c file along with the rest of the user interface. The user interface specifies the current drawing function in terms of the symbols defined in the file draw.h. This makes it necessary to be able to convert between a symbol and an equivalent drawing function. This is handled quite simply by a switch statement in the function `TypeToFunction()`.

```
216  static DrawingFunction TypeToFunction ( int type )
217  {
218
219      /*
220       * Return a pointer to a function that can draw the
221       * given type of figure.
222       */
223
224      switch ( type )
225      {
226        case NONE:
227          return ( NULL );
228        case LINE:
229          return ( DrawLine );
230        case CIRCLE:
231          return ( DrawCircle );
232        case RECTANGLE:
233          return ( DrawRectangle );
234        case FILLEDCIRCLE:
235          return ( DrawFilledCircle );
236        case FILLEDRECTANGLE:
237          return ( DrawFilledRectangle );
238      }
239  }
```

The function `SetDrawingFunction()` is called from the file editor.c when the user selects a new type of figure from the DrawingCommands menu pane. This function simply sets the global variables `currentFigureType` and `currentFunction`.

```
240  void SetDrawingFunction ( int type )
241  {
242      /*
243       * Set both the current type and the current function
244       */
245
246      currentFigureType = type;
247
248      currentFunction = TypeToFunction ( type );
249  }
```

The function `SetCurrentColor()` is called from the file editor.c when the user selects a color from the Colors menu pane. This function simply sets the global variable `currentForeground`.

```
250   SetCurrentColor ( Pixel fg )
251   {
252       currentForeground = fg;
253   }
```

Manipulating Objects in the Display List

The draw program's display list is just an array of `GraphicsObject` structures that represent the figures displayed in the XmDrawingArea widget. Each `GraphicsObject` structure has its position and size information, color information, and a pointer to the function that can be used to display the object. To redisplay any item, it is sufficient to call the associated function, using the remaining data in the structure.

The function `Redisplay()` is called when the XmDrawingArea widget needs to be redrawn. This function just loops through all objects in the display list and redraws each item. `Redisplay()` is very simple because all drawing functions have the same form and take the same arguments.

```
254   static void Redisplay ( Widget      w,
255                           XtPointer clientData,
256                           XtPointer callData )
257   {
258
259       int i;
260
261       /*
262        * Loop though all objects in the display list, drawing
263        * each one in sequence.
264        */
265
266       for ( i = 0; i < nextSlot; i++ )
267             ( *( displayList[i].func ) ) ( XtWindow ( w ),
268                                           displayList[i].gc,
269                                           displayList[i].x1,
270                                           displayList[i].y1,
271                                           displayList[i].x2,
272                                           displayList[i].y2 );
273
274   }
```

For some operations, it is useful to allow the user to select an object after it has been drawn. Because each item in the display list has a bounding box associated with it, is straightforward to write a simple function that returns a `GraphicsObject` structure given an *x,y* position. The function `PickObject()` returns the first object that completely encloses a given point. Because objects can overlap in the drawing editor, `PickObject()` searches the list backwards, which corresponds to searching for the most recently drawn item first.

```
275  GraphicsObject *PickObject ( int x, int y )
276  {
277      int i;
278
279      /*
280       * Search the display list for an object that encloses
281       * the given point. Loop backwards so that the objects
282       * on top are found first.
283       */
284
285      for ( i = nextSlot - 1; i >= 0; i-- )
286      {
287          if ( displayList[i].x1 <= x && displayList[i].x2 >= x &&
288               displayList[i].y1 <= y && displayList[i].y2 >= y )
289          {
290              return ( &displayList[i] );
291          }
292      }
293
294      return ( NULL );
295  }
```

PickObject() is adequate for picking most figures, but is less accurate than it could be. Picking a figure based on its bounding box is completely adequate if the figures are all rectangles, and fairly accurate for circles. However, picking a line based on its bounding box can produce surprising results, as it is possible to pick a line when the mouse cursor appears to the user to be quite far away from the line. For lines, as well as more complex figures, the bounding box test should be used as a first test only. More sophisticated tests should be applied to figures that are chosen based on their bounding box, to ensure that the correct figure is chosen. PickObject() simply uses the bounding box test and does not apply more complex tests.

It is also useful to be able to change object's positions on the screen. The function MoveObject() moves a given object by an *x,y* delta. The figure is first erased from its previous location. The position of the figure is then updated by changing the fields stored in the Graphic-sObject structure, and the newly positioned object is redrawn.

```
296  void MoveObject ( GraphicsObject *object, int dx, int dy )
297  {
298      /*
299       * Move an object by erasing it in its current position,
300       * updating the position information, and then drawing
301       * the figure in its new position.
302       */
303
304      ( *( object->func ) ) ( XtWindow ( canvas ), xorGC,
305                                  object->x1,
306                                  object->y1,
307                                  object->x2,
308                                  object->y2 );
```

```
309          object->x1 += dx;
310          object->y1 += dy;
311          object->x2 += dx;
312          object->y2 += dy;
313
314          ( *( object->func ) ) ( XtWindow ( canvas ), object->gc,
315                                      object->x1,
316                                      object->y1,
317                                      object->x2,
318                                      object->y2 );
319      }
```

When the draw program begins, its display list is initially empty. New figures are added to the display list by calling `AddObject()`. `AddObject()` takes a `GraphicsObject` structure and copies it to the display list. Because the display list in the draw program has a fixed size, the information in the given `GraphicsObject` structure is simply copied to the next available location in the display list. The `GraphicsObject` to be added must be complete with all information except for two members. The graphics context is determined by the foreground color of the object. The function pointer used to draw the object is also determined from the value of the `figureType` field.

```
320  static void AddObject (  GraphicsObject *object )
321  {
322      DrawingFunction  temp;
323
324      XGCValues values;
325
326      /*
327       * Check for space.
328       */
329
330      if ( nextSlot >= MAXOBJECTS )
331      {
332          fprintf ( stderr, "Warning: Display List is full\n" );
333          return;
334      }
335
336      /*
337       * Copy the information into the next available slot
338       * in the display list.
339       */
340
341      displayList[nextSlot].x1         = object->x1;
342      displayList[nextSlot].y1         = object->y1;
343      displayList[nextSlot].x2         = object->x2;
344      displayList[nextSlot].y2         = object->y2;
345      displayList[nextSlot].figureType = object->figureType;
346      displayList[nextSlot].foreground = object->foreground;
```

```
347      /*
348       * Get a GC for this color. Using XtGetGC() ensures that
349       * only as many GC's will be created as there are colors.
350       * Objects with the same color will share a GC.
351       */
352
353      values.foreground = object->foreground;
354      values.background = background;
355
356      displayList[nextSlot].gc = XtGetGC ( canvas,
357                                           GCBackground | GCForeground,
358                                           &values );
359
360     displayList[nextSlot].func = TypeToFunction ( object->figureType );
361
362      /*
363       * For all figures expect a line, permantly correct the bounding
364       * box to allowing easy picking. For a line, the coordinates
365       * canot be changed wihtout changing the appearance of the figure.
366       */
367
368      if (object->figureType != LINE )
369          FixDataOrdering ( &displayList[nextSlot].x1,
370                            &displayList[nextSlot].y1,
371                            &displayList[nextSlot].x2,
372                            &displayList[nextSlot].y2 );
373      /*
374       * Increment the next position index.
375       */
376
377      nextSlot++;
378  }
```

When a user interactively adds a new figure to a drawing, `StoreObject()` is called to fill out the information in a `GraphicsObject` structure. The size and position of the new object are taken from the values of the global variables `startX`, `startY`, `lastX`, and `lastY`. The type of object being added is determined by the value of `currentFigureType`, while the color of the object is determined by the value of the global `currentForeground` variable. Both `current-Foreground` and `currentFigureType` are global to this file, and are set by the user through the menus defined in the file editor.c.

```
379  static void StoreObject()
380  {
381      GraphicsObject object;
382
383      /*
384       * Don't store zero-sized figures.
385       */
```

```
386        if ( startX == lastX && startY == lastY )
387            return;
388
389        /*
390         * Save the current values of all global variables
391         * in a GraphicsObject structure.
392         */
393
394        object.x1        = startX;
395        object.y1        = startY;
396        object.x2        = lastX;
397        object.y2        = lastY;
398        object.figureType = currentFigureType;
399        object.foreground = currentForeground;
400
401        /*
402         * Add the object to the display list.
403         */
404
405        AddObject ( &object );
406    }
```

Interactively Adding Objects

Users can add a new figure to the display list by interactively positioning and sizing a new shape. The functions `StartRubberBand()`, `TrackRubberBand()`, and `EndRubberBand()` handle the actions of fixing the initial placement of a new figure, selecting a size, and then adding the final figure to the display list. These functions work much the same as the equivalent functions in the rubber band example in Section 13.2, but the draw program requires functions that can handle multiple types of figures. All three functions use the function pointer stored in the `current-Function` variable to draw any of figures supported by the draw program. In addition, these functions allow users to drag existing objects to new locations, if `currentFunction` is set to `NULL`.

`StartRubberBand()` is an event handler that is called when the user presses a mouse button within the XmDrawingArea widget. The function checks to see if a current drawing function has been selected from the DrawingCommands menu. If so, a new graphics context is obtained for the currently selected foreground color. This GC is obtained using `XtGetGC()`, so it is shared among all figures that use the same color. Next, the global variables `startX`, `lastX`, `startY`, and `lastY` are initialized to the position of the mouse cursor, as reported in the `ButtonPress` event. Finally, the current figure type is drawn at the selected location, by invoking the current drawing function through the `currentFunction` pointer.

If no current drawing function has been selected, `StartRubberBand()` prepares to allow an object to be dragged by moving the mouse. In this case, the drag does not use Motif's drag and drop facility (see Chapter 14), but simply uses straightforward XOR techniques to move a figure. (Notice that dragging with mouse button one is not Motif Style Guide compliant.) `StartRubberBand()` calls `PickObject()` to see if the mouse button was pressed while the cursor was over an existing graphics object. If so, a new XOR GC is created, using the colors of the selected object. The variables lastX, startX, lastY, and startY are also initialized to the coordinates of the Button-Press event.

```
407   static void StartRubberBand ( Widget     w,
408                                  XtPointer clientData,
409                                  XEvent    *event,
410                                  Boolean   *flag )
411   {
412
413       /*
414        * Ignore any events other than a button press for
415        * mouse button one.
416        */
417
418       if ( event->xbutton.button != Button1 )
419           return;
420
421       if ( currentFunction )
422       {
423
424           /*
425            * If there is a current drawing function, call it to
426            * start positioning the new figure.
427            */
428
429           XGCValues values;
430
431           /*
432            * Get a GC for the current colors
433            */
434
435           values.foreground = currentForeground;
436           values.background = background;
437
438           currentGC = XtGetGC ( w,
439                                 GCBackground | GCForeground,
440                                 &values );
441
442           /*
443            * Store the starting point and draw the initial figure.
444            */
445
446           lastX = startX = event->xbutton.x;
447           lastY = startY = event->xbutton.y;
448
449           ( *( currentFunction ) ) ( XtWindow ( w ), xorGC,
450                                      startX, startY,
451                                      lastX, lastY );
452       }
```

```
453         else if ( !currentFunction && event->xbutton.button == Button1 )
454         {
455            /*
456             * If there is no current function, treat Button1
457             * as a pointer and find the graphics object the mouse
458             * cursor is pointing to.
459             */
460
461            lastX = startX = event->xbutton.x;
462            lastY = startY = event->xbutton.y;
463
464            currentObject = PickObject ( event->xbutton.x,
465                                         event->xbutton.y );
466            if ( currentObject )
467            {
468               /*
469                * If an object was found, any mouse motion will move
470                * the object. Get a new graphics context whose colors
471                * match the colors of the current object.
472                */
473
474               XGCValues values;
475
476               XtReleaseGC ( w, xorGC );
477               values.foreground = currentObject->foreground ^
478                                   background;
479               values.function   = GXxor;
480
481               /*
482                * Change the color of the rubber band gc
483                */
484
485               xorGC =  XtGetGC ( w,  GCForeground | GCFunction,
486                                      &values );
487            }
488         }
489  }
```

TrackRubberBand() is called in response to mouse motion while mouse button one remains pressed. StartRubberBand() is always called before TrackRubberBand(), so the rubber band action (or the process of dragging an existing object) has already begun. If a drawing function has been selected, TrackRubberBand() draws the current figure once, using XOR mode, or erase the previous drawn figure. The variables lastX and lastY are then updated and the figure is drawn again in the new coordinates. When creating a new figure, TrackRubberBand() allows the user to set the size of the figure.

If no drawing function has been selected and the variable currentObject, which was initialized by StartRubberBand(), is non-NULL, TrackRubberBand() moves the current object to match the mouse motion reported in the MouseMotion event.

```
490    static void TrackRubberBand ( Widget     w,
491                                   XtPointer clientData,
492                                   XEvent    *event,
493                                   Boolean   *flag )
494    {
495        /*
496         * If there is a current drawing function, handle the
497         * rubberbanding of the new figure. Otherwise, if there
498         * is a currently selected object, move it, tracking the
499         * cursor position.
500         */
501
502        if ( currentFunction &&
503             ( event->xmotion.state & Button1Mask ) )
504        {
505            /*
506             * Erase the previous figure.
507             */
508
509            ( *( currentFunction ) ) ( XtWindow ( w ), xorGC,
510                                       startX, startY,
511                                       lastX, lastY );
512            /*
513             * Update the last point.
514             */
515
516            lastX  =  event->xmotion.x;
517            lastY  =  event->xmotion.y;
518
519            /*
520             * Draw the figure in the new position.
521             */
522
523             ( *( currentFunction ) ) ( XtWindow ( w ), xorGC,
524                                        startX, startY,
525                                        lastX, lastY );
526        }
527        else if ( currentObject    &&
528                  !currentFunction &&
529                  event->xmotion.state & Button1Mask )
530        {
531            MoveObject ( currentObject,
532                         event->xmotion.x - lastX,
533                         event->xmotion.y - lastY );
534
535            lastX  =  event->xmotion.x;
536            lastY  =  event->xmotion.y;
537        }
538    }
```

EndRubberBand() is called when the user releases the mouse button in the XmDrawingArea widget. If a drawing function has been installed, EndRubberBand() erases the last figure drawn by TrackRubberBand() and draws the new figure in its final position, using the current normal graphics context. The function then adds the object to the display list by calling StoreObject() and calls PickObject() to select the newly created object as the currently selected object. Although the currently selected object is not used in this example, it can be useful when extending the drawing editor. A typical drawing editor allows the user to perform various operations on the currently selected object.

If there is no current drawing function, but there is a currently selected object, EndRubberBand() moves the current object to its final location and forces a redraw to clean up the display.

```
539   static void EndRubberBand ( Widget      w,
540                               XtPointer clientData,
541                               XEvent    *event,
542                               Boolean   *flag )
543   {
544
545       /*
546        * Finalize the operation begun with StartRubberBand(). If there
547        * a current drawing function, clear the last XOR image and draw
548        * the final figure.
549        */
550
551       if ( currentFunction &&
552            event->xbutton.button == Button1 )
553       {
554           /*
555            * Erase the XOR image.
556            */
557
558           ( *( currentFunction ) ) ( XtWindow ( w ), xorGC,
559                                       startX, startY,
560                                       lastX,  lastY );
561
562           /*
563            * Draw the figure using the normal GC.
564            */
565
566           ( *( currentFunction ) ) ( XtWindow ( w ), currentGC,
567                                       startX, startY,
568                                       event->xbutton.x,
569                                       event->xbutton.y );
570
571           /*
572            * Update the data, and store the object in
573            * the display list.
574            */
```

```
575
576              lastX = event->xbutton.x;
577              lastY = event->xbutton.y;
578
579              StoreObject();
580
581              currentObject = PickObject ( event->xbutton.x,
582                                            event->xbutton.y );
583
584      }
585      else if ( currentObject     &&
586                !currentFunction &&
587                event->xbutton.button == Button1 )
588      {
589
590          /*
591           * If the operation was a drag, move the figure
592           * to its final position.
593           */
594
595          MoveObject ( currentObject,
596                       event->xbutton.x - lastX,
597                       event->xbutton.y - lastY );
598
599          /*
600           * Force a complete redraw.
601           */
602
603          XClearArea ( display, XtWindow ( w ), 0, 0, 0, 0, TRUE );
604      }
605 }
```

Saving and Loading Files

It is useful to be able to save drawings to files and to reload saved drawings. The draw program provides a simple mechanism for saving and loading files. Each graphics object can be represented in a file by the name of the figure type, the bounding box, and the color with which the figure is drawn.

To support reading from and writing to files, the draw program implements a function that packs an object into a string, and another that reads a string and creates an equivalent `GraphicsObject` structure. These simple functions just use `sprintf()` and `scanf()` to convert between types. Notice that the foreground color cannot be saved as simply a pixel index. The pixel index would only be correct if the colormap did not change between the time an object is saved and the time is reloaded. The `Pack()` function determines and writes out the RGB values that correspond to the given pixel when saving an object. The `Unpack()` function reads the RGB values and obtains the correct pixel index with which to refer to that color.

```
606   char *Pack ( GraphicsObject *object )
607   {
608
609       /*
610        * Convert an object to a string.
611        */
612
613       static char buf[1000];
614       XColor      color;
615
616       color.pixel = object->foreground;
617       XQueryColor ( display, colormap, &color );
618
619       sprintf ( buf, "%d %d %d %d %d %d %d %d",
620                 object->x1, object->y1,
621                 object->x2, object->y2,
622                 object->figureType,
623                 color.red, color.green, color.blue );
624
625       return ( buf );
626
627   }

628   GraphicsObject *Unpack ( char *str )
629   {
630
631       /*
632        * Convert a string to an object
633        */
634
635       static GraphicsObject object;
636       XColor                color;
637
638       sscanf ( str, "%d %d %d %d %d %hd %hd %hd",
639                &object.x1, &object.y1,
640                &object.x2, &object.y2,
641                &object.figureType,
642                &color.red, &color.green, &color.blue );
643
644       /*
645        * Get the pixel that corresponds to the given color.
646        */
647
648       XAllocColor ( display, colormap, &color );
649       object.foreground = color.pixel;
650
651       return ( &object );
652
653   }
```

The function `SaveData()` is called from the editor.c module, from a callback function registered with the Save menu item. `SaveData()` creates an XmFileSelection dialog to allow the user to select a file name in which to save the figures in the display list. Once the dialog is displayed, the function `SaveDataCallback()` is invoked if the user selects the OK button on the dialog, while `CancelDialogCallback()` is called if the user dismisses the dialog with the Cancel button.

```
654   void SaveData()
655   {
656       FILE  *fp;
657       static Widget dialog = NULL;
658
659       /*
660        * Create the dialog if it doesn't already exist. Install
661        * callbacks for OK and Cancel actions.
662        */
663
664       if ( !dialog )
665       {
666           dialog = XmCreateFileSelectionDialog ( canvas, "saveDialog",
667                                                   NULL, 0 );
668
669           XtAddCallback ( dialog, XmNokCallback,
670                           SaveDataCallback, ( XtPointer ) NULL );
671           XtAddCallback ( dialog, XmNcancelCallback,
672                           CancelDialogCallback, ( XtPointer ) NULL );
673       }
674
675       XtManageChild ( dialog );
676
677   }
```

If the user dismisses the file selection dialog with the Cancel button, `CancelDialog-Callback()` is called. This function just unmanages the file selection dialog to remove it from the screen.

```
678   void CancelDialogCallback ( Widget    w,
679                               XtPointer clientData,
680                               XtPointer callData )
681   {
682       XtUnmanageChild ( w );
683   }
```

The function `SaveDataCallback()` is invoked if the user selects the OK button on the file selection dialog. This function unmanages the dialog to remove it from the screen, and retrieves the complete path name of the selected file. If no file was chosen, `SaveDataCallback()` just returns. Otherwise, it retrieves the text associated with the compound string that represents the file name, opens the file, and prints out the packed version of each object in the display list.

```
684   void SaveDataCallback ( Widget     w,
685                           XtPointer clientData,
686                           XtPointer callData )
687   {
688       FILE     *fp;
689       char     *fileName;
690       XmString xmstr;
691       int      i;
692
693       /*
694        * Remove the dialog from the screen.
695        */
696
697       XtUnmanageChild ( w );
698
699       /*
700        * Retrieve the currently selected file.
701        */
702
703       XtVaGetValues (  w,
704                        XmNdirSpec, &xmstr,
705                        NULL );
706
707       /*
708        * Make sure a file was selected.
709        */
710
711       if ( !xmstr )
712          return;
713
714       /*
715        * Retrieve the name of the file as ASCII.
716        */
717
718       XmStringGetLtoR (  xmstr, XmFONTLIST_DEFAULT_TAG, &fileName );
719
720       /*
721        * Try to open thefile for writing
722        */
723
724       if ( ( fp = fopen ( fileName, "w" ) ) == NULL )
725          return;
726
727       /*
728        * Loop though the display list, writing each object to the
729        * newly opened file.
730        */
731
732
```

```
733          for ( i = 0; i < nextSlot; i++ )
734          {
735              GraphicsObject *object = &( displayList[i] );
736
737              fprintf ( fp, "%s\n", Pack ( object ) );
738          }
739
740          fclose ( fp );
741      }
```

Loading data from a file is just the inverse operation of saving a file. An XmFileSelection dialog widget is created, and callbacks are registered to load data from a selected file. LoadData() simply displays the dialog and returns. If the user dismisses this dialog by choosing the Cancel button, the previously defined CancelDialogCallback() is invoked to remove the dialog from the screen.

```
742  void LoadData()
743  {
744      static Widget dialog = NULL;
745
746      /*
747       * Create a file selection dialog if it doesn't already exist
748       */
749
750      if ( !dialog )
751      {
752          dialog = XmCreateFileSelectionDialog (  canvas,
753                                                  "loadDialog",
754                                                  NULL, 0 );
755          XtAddCallback ( dialog, XmNokCallback,
756                          LoadDataCallback, ( XtPointer ) NULL );
757          XtAddCallback ( dialog, XmNcancelCallback,
758                          CancelDialogCallback, ( XtPointer ) NULL );
759      }
760
761      /*
762       * Display the dialog
763       */
764
765      XtManageChild ( dialog );
766  }
```

The callback function LoadDataCallback() is invoked once the user selects a file to be loaded and activates the OK button on the file selection dialog. This function unmanages the dialog to remove it from the screen and retrieves the full path name of the selected file as a compound string. LoadDataCallback() uses the text equivalent of this compound string as the name of a file to open, and uses scanf() to read each line in the file into a GraphicsObject structure to be added to the display list.

```
767 void LoadDataCallback ( Widget w, XtPointer clientData, XtPointer callData )
768 {
769     /*
770      * This function is called if a user selects a file to load.
771      * Extract the selected file name and read the data.
772      */
773
774     FILE            *fp;
775     char            *fileName;
776     XmString         xmstr;
777     int              results;
778     GraphicsObject object;
779     XColor          color;
780
781     /*
782      * Remove the dialog from the screen.
783      */
784
785     XtUnmanageChild ( w );
786
787     /*
788      * Retrieve the selected file
789      */
790
791     XtVaGetValues (  w,
792                      XmNdirSpec, &xmstr,
793                      NULL );
794     /*
795      * Confirm that a file was selected
796      */
797
798     if ( !xmstr )
799        return;
800
801     /*
802      * Retrieve an ASCII string from the compound string.
803      */
804
805     XmStringGetLtoR ( xmstr, XmFONTLIST_DEFAULT_TAG, &fileName );
806
807     if ( ( fp = fopen ( fileName, "r" ) ) == NULL )
808        return;
809
810     nextSlot = 0;
811
812     /*
813      * Read each object into the displayList
814      */
815
```

```
816        while ( ( results = fscanf ( fp, "%d %d %d %d %d %d %d",
817                                      &object.x1, &object.y1,
818                                      &object.x2, &object.y2,
819                                      &object.figureType,
820                                      &color.red, &color.green,
821                                      &color.blue ) ) != EOF )
822        {
823            /*
824             * Get the pixel that corresponds to the given color.
825             */
826
827            XAllocColor ( display, colormap, &color );
828            object.foreground = color.pixel;
829            AddObject ( &object );
830        }
831
832        /*
833         * Force a redraw.
834         */
835
836        XClearArea ( display, XtWindow ( canvas ), 0, 0, 0, 0, TRUE );
837
838        fclose ( fp );
839    }
```

Draw Application Resources

Most applications require certain resources to operate as intended. The draw program, as the most complex example described so far in this book, uses many resources. Setting certain resources appropriately can improve the appearance and usability of the program. Figure 13.6 shows the draw program as it appears with no resources, while Figure 13.5 shows the same program after some carefully chosen resources have been added to an app-defaults file.

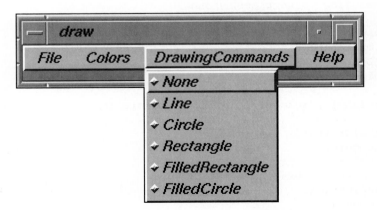

Figure 13.6 An un-configured draw program.

In Figure 13.5, on page 422, the draw interface is shown with a set of tear-off menu panes. The names of all menu panes and menu items have been changed slightly. For example, the labels on menu items that launch a dialog have been changed to add an ellipsis, as recommended by the *Motif Style Guide*. Accelerators and mnemonics have also been added to all menu items. The default window size has been set to a reasonable initial size. In addition, the toggle buttons used for the Colors and DrawingCommands menu panes have been customized to create multi-column menu panes. The items in the DrawingCommands pane have been customized to display iconic images instead of text. Finally, several simple help strings have been added to support context-sensitive help. All of these features can bed by providing an application resource file.

The app-defaults file for the draw program is written as follows:

```
1    !!!!!!!!!!!!!!!!!!!!!!!!!!!!!!!!!!!!!!!!!!!!
2    ! App-defaults file for draw program
3    !!!!!!!!!!!!!!!!!!!!!!!!!!!!!!!!!!!!!!!!!!!!
4
5    ! Initialize the radio button menus to default to no drawing function,
6    ! initial color is black, and ensure that one item is always selected.
7
8    *None*set:         TRUE
9    *radioAlwaysOne:   TRUE
10   *Black*set:        TRUE
11
12   ! Choose a reasonable default size for the drawing area.
13
14   *canvas.width:   400
15   *canvas.height: 350
16
17   ! Activate tear-off menus for the commands and colors panes
18
19   *Colors*tearOffModel:          tear_off_enabled
20   *DrawingCommands*tearOffModel: tear_off_enabled
21
22   ! Add mnemonics to post menu panes
23
24   *File.mnemonic:             F
25   *Colors.mnemonic:           C
26   *DrawingCommands.mnemonic:  P
27   *Help.mnemonic:             H
28
29   ! Set up labels, mnemonics and accelerators for all File items
30
31   *Save*labelString:      Save...
32   *Save*mnemonic:         S
33   *Save.accelerator:      Ctrl<Key>S
34   *Save.acceleratorText:  Ctrl+S
35   *Load*labelString:      Load...
36   *Load*mnemonic:         L
37   *Load.accelerator:      Ctrl<Key>L
```

```
38   *Load.acceleratorText:    Ctrl+L
39
40   *Quit.mnemonic:           Q
41   *Quit.accelerator:        Ctrl<Key>q
42   *Quit.acceleratorText:    Ctrl+q
43
44   ! Configure the DrawingCommands menu as follows:
45   !       Shut off the indicator on all items
46   !       Rename the menu "Palette"
47   !       Configure the menu to have two evenly sized columns
48
49   *DrawingCommands*XmToggleButton*indicatorOn: FALSE
50   *DrawingCommands.labelString: Palette
51   *DrawingCommands*numColumns:  2
52   *DrawingCommands*packing:     pack_column
53   *DrawingCommands*orientation: vertical
54
55   ! Make all entries in the DrawingCommands pane display an icon
56   ! instead of text. Pixmaps are bitmap files that must be on
57   ! the bitmap search path.
58
59   *DrawingCommands*XmToggleButton*labelType:    pixmap
60   *Line.labelPixmap:            line
61   *Rectangle.labelPixmap:       rectangle
62   *Circle.labelPixmap:          circle
63   *FilledRectangle.labelPixmap: filledrect
64   *FilledCircle.labelPixmap:    filledcircle
65   *None.labelPixmap:            pointer
66
67   ! Set up the Colors menu to have two columns
68
69   *Colors*numColumns:  2
70   *Colors*packing:     pack_column
71   *Colors*orientation: vertical
72
73   ! Add nice titles for the dialogs
74
75   *saveDialog_popup*title: Save To File
76   *loadDialog_popup*title: Load From File
77
78   ! Set labels for help menu
79
80   *HelpOnContext.labelString:   Click For Help
81   *HelpOnContext.mnemonic:      C
82
83   ! Provide help strings
84
85   *help.text: Choose a color and a a shape from the\n\
86   palette to draw a figure.
```

13.5 Summary

This chapter explores the graphics facilities provided by Xlib, and demonstrates how they can be used with Xt and Motif widgets. X provides simple two-dimensional graphics primitives, although extensions like PEX and OpenGL provide more sophisticated three-dimensional capabilities. The draw program demonstrates most of the Xlib drawing primitives and also ties together many other topics to produce a fairly realistic and complex program.

Chapter 14

Interclient Communication

X provides many facilities that allow applications to communicate with each other and to exchange and share data. Interclient communication involves the use of *atoms*, *properties*, and *client messages*. These facilities are supported by Xlib and are employed in many different ways. The most common uses for these mechanisms include:

- Communication between window managers and applications.
- Transferring data between applications using *cut and paste.*
- Transferring data between applications using *drag and drop* techniques.

The basis for all X-based inter-application communication is the set of policies defined by the *InterClient Communications Conventions Manual* (ICCCM). Programmers who plan to make extensive use of atoms, selections, and properties should become familiar with the ICCCM. This chapter focuses on the toolkit-level support provided by Xt and Motif. These functions hide many of the details of the ICCCM protocols.

This chapter begins by describing the Xlib support for atoms, properties and client messages. Section 14.4 discusses the basic Xlib support for data transfer using *selections*, and then discusses higher-level facilities provided by Xt to make selections easier for applications to use. Next, Section 14.5 discusses an alternate data transfer mechanism supported by Motif that allows applications to transfer data to a persistent clipboard. Section 14.6 introduces some commonly used techniques for communicating between window managers and applications, and finally, Section 14.7 discusses Motif's support for drag and drop data exchange.

14.1 Atoms

An atom is a unique resource identifier that represents a string. The relationship between the identifier and the string it represents is stored in the X server so that all clients connected to that server share the same ID for any particular string. Atoms are primarily used for efficiency; it is faster to compare two atoms (using ==) than to compare two strings (using `strcmp()`). Atoms can also be passed between applications and used in event structures easily without requiring the space for an entire string.

Creating an atom is referred to as *interning*. The Xlib function:

```
Atom XInternAtom ( Display *dpy, char *name, Boolean only_if_exists )
```

returns a unique atom that corresponds to the given string. When the Boolean argument `only_if_exists` is TRUE, XInternAtom() returns an atom identifier only if the atom already exists. If the atom does not exist, the function returns the constant `None`. When `only_if_exists` is FALSE, XInternAtom() always returns an atom identifier, creating a new atom if necessary. All applications that request an atom for the same string from the same server receive the same identifier. The string must match exactly, including the case.

Applications can create new atoms to represent any arbitrary string. For example, the statement:

```
Atom NEWATOM = XInternAtom ( display, "A New Atom", FALSE );
```

creates an atom, NEWATOM, that represents the string "A New Atom". Once an atom is interned, it exists until the server is restarted, even if the client that created the atom exits.

It is sometimes useful to retrieve the string represented by a particular atom. The function:

```
char *XGetAtomName ( Display *display, Atom atom )
```

returns the string that corresponds to `atom`.

Atoms are useful in any situation that requires a unique identifier that must be shared and recognized by multiple applications. For example, atoms are used to identify the type of data stored in a property. X predefines a small set of atoms to identify common data types such as `Drawable`, `XPoint`, `Integer`, `Font`, and `Pixmap`. The symbols for all predefined atoms are defined as all capital letters, and preceded by the letters "XA_" to avoid name clashes between client-defined atoms. For example, `XA_INTEGER` is the atom that identifies the type `Integer`. X also predefines atoms intended for other uses, including selection types, property names, and font properties. Applications that use these predefined atoms must include the header file Xatom.h.

14.2 Properties

A property is a collection of named, typed data. Every property is associated with a window, and the data stored in a property is maintained by the X server, where it can be accessed or altered by any client that has the window's ID and the name of the property. Properties are named and typed using atoms.

The X server predefines some atoms commonly used as property names, including:

```
XA_WM_HINTS          XA_RESOURCE_MANAGER    XA_WM_ICON_NAME
XA_WM_ICON_SIZE      XA_WM_NAME             XA_WM_NORMAL_HINT
XA_WM_COMMAND        XA_WM_CLASS            XA_WM_TRANSIENT_FOR
```

Although these atoms are predefined by the server, the corresponding properties do not automatically exist, nor do they necessarily contain any data. Xlib predefines property names as a convenience so clients can use these properties without explicitly interning the atoms. Like all predefined atoms, predefined property names begin with the letters XA_. The data associated with a property is simply stored as a stream of bytes, and a second atom associated with the property identifies the type of the data. The server also predefines atoms that can be used to represent some common X data types, including:

```
XA_ARC           XA_ATOM        XA_BITMAP
XA_CARDINAL      XA_COLORMAP    XA_CURSOR
XA_DRAWABLE      XA_FONT        XA_INTEGER
XA_PIXMAP        XA_POINT       XA_WINDOW
XA_RECTANGLE     XA_STRING      XA_VISUALID
```

Applications can create new atoms to represent any data type, including client-defined structures. The server attaches no particular meaning to any atom.

The function:

```
XChangeProperty ( Display       *display,
                  Window        window,
                  Atom          name,
                  Atom          type,
                  int           format,
                  int           mode,
                  unsigned char *data,
                  int           nelements )
```

stores some data in a property associated with the specified window. The third and fourth arguments to XChangeProperty() must be atoms that specify the name of the property and the type of the data stored in the property. The format argument specifies whether the data consists of multiples of 8, 16, or 32 bits. This information allows the server to do byte swapping, if necessary, when data is transferred between clients running on machines with different architectures. The `mode` argument indicates whether the data is to replace any data already stored in the property or be added to the beginning or the end of any existing contents, and must be one of the constants `PropModeReplace`, `PropModePrepend`, or `PropModeAppend`. The `data` argument provides the address of the data to be stored while `nelements` specifies the length of the data in multiples of the unit given by the `format` argument.

Window properties are normally used to share information with other clients. For example, most X window managers expect some basic properties to be stored in properties on every application's top level window. Programmers who use Motif do not usually need to be aware of these properties, because Motif sets them automatically.

One of these window manager properties, `XA_WM_NAME`, is expected to contain the name of the window. The window manager typically displays this string in the window's title bar. Xlib provides a convenience function:

```
XStoreName ( Display *display, Window window, char *name )
```

which stores a string, specified by the `name` argument, in the `XA_WM_NAME` property of the given window. This Xlib function provides an easy-to-use interface to the function `XChangeProperty()`. If Xlib didn't provide `XStoreName()`, the function could be written like this:

```
XStoreName ( Display *dpy, Window w, char *name )
{
    XChangeProperty ( dpy, w, XA_WM_NAME, XA_STRING,
                      8, PropModeReplace,
                      ( unsigned char * ) name,
                      name ? strlen ( name ) : 0 );
}
```

Many other Xlib functions, including `XSetStandardProperties()` and `XSetWM-Hints()`, are implemented similarly.

A property exists until the window with which it is associated is destroyed, or until a client explicitly deletes the property. The lifetime of a property is not determined by the lifetime of the client that stores the property.

The function:

```
XDeleteProperty ( Display *display, Window window, Atom property )
```

deletes a property from a window's property list.

Clients can retrieve the data stored in a property by calling the Xlib function:

```
int XGetWindowProperty ( Display     *display,
                         Window      window,
                         Atom        property,
                         long        offset,
                         long        length,
```

```
Boolean         delete,
Atom            requested_type,
Atom            *actual_type,
int             *actual_format,
unsigned long *nitems,
unsigned long   bytes_left,
unsigned char **data );
```

This function returns the constant `Success`, defined in Xlib.h, if no error condition is encountered while executing the function. A return value of `Success` does not imply that the property was found, or that any data was retrieved. The `name` argument must be an atom that identifies the property that contains the desired data. The `offset` argument specifies the starting point within the data stored in the property from which data should be returned. The offset is measured in 32-bit quantities from the beginning of the stored data. The `length` argument specifies how many 32-bit multiples of the data should be returned. The Boolean argument, `delete`, indicates whether or not the server should delete the data after it is retrieved. The `requested_type` argument must be either an atom identifying the desired type of the data or the constant `AnyPropertyType`.

When `XGetWindowProperty()` returns, the argument `actual_type` is set to an atom that represents the type of the data stored in the property, while `actual_format` contains the format of the stored data. If the property does not exist for the specified window, `actual_type` is set to `None`, and the `actual_format` is set to zero. The arguments `nitems` and `bytes_left` indicate the number of bytes retrieved and how many remaining bytes are stored in the property. Applications can use this information to retrieve large amounts of data by repeated calls to `XGetWindowProperty()`. If the function returns successfully, the `data` argument points to the bytes retrieved from the property. X allocates this data using `Xmalloc()`, and applications should free the data using `Xfree()` when the data is no longer needed.

As an example of how `XGetWindowProperty()` is used, consider the Xlib function:

```
Status XFetchName ( Display *display, Window window, char **name )
```

This function uses `XGetProperty()` to retrieve the name of a window, stored in the `XA_WM_NAME` property. This function is the counterpart to `XStoreName()`. If Xlib did not already provide this function, it could be implemented as follows:

```
Status XFetchName ( Display *dpy, Window w, char **name )
{
    Atom            actual_type;
    int             actual_format;
    unsigned long   nitems;
    unsigned long   leftover;
    unsigned char  *data = NULL;

    if ( XGetWindowProperty ( dpy, w, XA_WM_NAME, 0L, ( long ) BUFSIZ,
                    FALSE, XA_STRING, &actual_type,
                    &actual_format, &nitems,
                    &leftover, &data ) != Success )
```

```
        {
            *name = NULL;
            return ( FALSE );
        }

        if (  ( actual_type == XA_STRING ) && ( actual_format == 8 ) )
        {
            *name =  ( char * ) data;
             return  ( TRUE );
        }

        if ( data )
            Xfree (  ( char * ) data );

        *name = NULL;

        return ( FALSE );
    }
```

If the call to XGetWindowProperty() is unsuccessful, XFetchName() returns FALSE, with name set to NULL. If the call is successful, XGetWindowProperty() returns Success, and XFetchName() checks whether the property type matches the requested type and also checks the format to ensure that the data is in eight bit format. If these conditions are met, XFetchName() sets name to point to the retrieved data and returns TRUE. If the type and format of the data are incorrect, the function frees the retrieved data, using Xfree(), and returns FALSE.

Property Events

The X server notifies interested clients when any change occurs in a window's property list. The server generates a PropertyNotify event when the data stored in a property changes, when a property is initially created, or when a property is deleted. Clients must request PropertyNotify events using the event mask PropertyChangeMask. The server reports PropertyNotify events using an XPropertyEvent structure.

In addition to the basic members included in all events, the XPropertyEvent structure contains the following members:

```
    Atom        atom;
    Time        time;
    int         state;
```

The atom member of this event structure contains the name of the modified property. The state member is set to the constant NewValue if the value of property has changed, or to Deleted if the property has been deleted. The time member is set to the server time when the property was modified.

14.3 Client Messages

Normally, events are generated by the X server and sent to applications that request them. However, X also allows applications to send events to any window. This feature can be used to forward events from one application to another, or to create and send new events.

The function

```
Status XSendEvent ( Display      *display,
                     Window        window,
                     Boolean       propagate,
                     long          mask,
                     XEVent       *event )
```

sends an event to clients that have selected any of the event types indicated by the `mask` argument for the specified window. `XSendEvent()` can be used to send any valid X event type. The `window` argument must be either a valid window ID on the given display, or the constant `PointerWindow`, in which case the event is sent to the window currently containing the pointer. The `window` argument can also be the constant `InputFocus`, which requests that the event be sent to the window that currently has input focus. If `InputFocus` is specified and the pointer is contained within the focus window, the event is sent to the smallest window or subwindow of the focus window that contains the pointer. The Boolean flag, `propagate`, determines whether the server should propagate the event to ancestors if the specified window has not selected the event type.

`XSendEvent()` returns a non-zero value if the function executes correctly. Successful execution does not imply that the intended window received the event, only that no error condition occurred during the process of sending the event.

Client Message Events

One common use of `XSendEvent()` is to send client messages. `ClientMessage` events are never generated by the server. They are used by applications to communicate with each other. `ClientMessage` events have no corresponding event mask and cannot be specifically selected. They are always received by the client that owns the window to which the event is sent.

The `XClientMessageEvent` structure is defined in Xlib.h as:

```
typedef struct {
    int             type;
    unsigned long   serial;
    Bool            send_event;
    Display        *display;
    Window          window;
    Atom            message_type;
    int             format;
```

```
        union {
            char      b[20];
            short     s[10];
            long      l[5];
        } data;
    } XClientMessageEvent;
```

In addition to the first five members, which are common to all event types, the `XClientMessage` event structure contains a `message_type` field that allows an application to specify a type for the event. The type is indicated by an atom whose meaning must be recognized by both the sending and the receiving applications. The X server does not interpret the field. The `format` member specifies the data format of the bytes in the `data` field, and must be one of 8, 16, or 32. The `data` field consists of 20 bytes, declared as a union of bytes, shorts, and longs. Clients are free to use this data field for any purpose.

Motif applications generally handle `XClientMessage` events by registering an event handler. Because `XClientMessage` events are *non-maskable* events, applications should specify `NoEventMask` (or 0) as the event mask when registering event handlers for `XClientMessage` events and must also specify that the handler is being registered for non-maskable events. For example, a function named `MessageHandler()` can be registered as an event handler for a widget with the following statement:

```
    XtAddEventHandler ( w, NoEventMask, TRUE, MessageHandler, NULL );
```

The third argument to `XtAddEventHandler()` indicates whether the function should be called for non-maskable events. Because this argument is `TRUE` in this case, `MessageHandler()` will be called for any non-maskable events. Because client messages are not the only type of non-maskable events, the event handlers must check the type of the event before processing the end.

14.4 Selections: Cut and Paste

Most window systems support some mechanism for transferring information between windows. Interactive data transfer is often referred to as "cut and paste" (or sometimes "copy and paste") because the user removes ("cuts") or copies an object or section of text from one window and transfers ("pastes") it into another window. Because all X applications in the user's environment do not necessarily run on the same machine, X implements cut and paste via an interclient communication mechanism, using the X server as a central communications point.

X provides several events and functions that work together to implement a flexible "copy and paste" mechanism. This section first discusses the basic concepts of this mechanism as provided by Xlib, and then demonstrates the concepts with a simple example that uses some higher level functions provided by Xt. Following this discussion, Section 14.5 presents the Motif clipboard facility, a higher level cut/copy and paste mechanism that offers a slightly different model.

Basic Selection Concepts

Most Motif applications use the facilities supported by Xt to handle copy and paste. However, these mechanisms are based on lower-level facilities supported by Xlib and the X server. This section describes the basic, low level facilities upon which Xt and Motif build to aid in understanding the process.

X supports a quick-transfer type of data exchange between applications through the *selection* mechanism. A selection is a named piece of data that can be transferred between applications. The name of a selection is specified as an atom. The exchange process begins when an application declares *ownership* of a selection. The application into which the user wishes to paste the data can then request the selection owner to transfer the data associated with the selection. Some applications may choose to generate the data represented by a selection only when another application requests a copy of the selection.

Multiple selections can exist at once, each uniquely identified by different atoms. X predefines two selection atoms: `XA_PRIMARY` and `XA_SECONDARY`; applications can also define additional selection atoms.

Any application can claim ownership of a selection by calling the Xlib function:

```
XSetSelectionOwner ( Display *display,
                     Atom     atom,
                     Window   window,
                     Time     time )
```

`XSetSelectionOwner()` informs the X server that the specified window claims ownership of the selection named by the given `atom`. The `time` argument is required to eliminate potential race conditions and should be set to the current server time. Applications can obtain the current server time from many X events. Since most applications grab ownership in response to a user action, the timestamp in the corresponding event can be used to set the time. Xt-based applications that do not have access to the last event can call the Xt function `XtLastTimeStampProcessed()` to retrieve the current timestamp. When an application claims ownership of a selection, the X server automatically sends a `SelectionClear` event to the previous owner to notify it that it has lost the selection.

Any application can ask for the ID of the window that currently owns a selection. The function:

```
Window XGetSelectionOwner ( Display *display, Atom atom )
```

returns the window ID of the current owner of the selection named by `atom`. Applications should call `XGetSelectionOwner()` after they request ownership of the selection to determine if the request has succeeded, because of the potential for race conditions to occur. Once ownership of the selection is confirmed, most applications visually highlight the data that corresponds to the selection in some way.

The function:

```
XConvertSelection ( Display display,
                     Atom    selection,
                     Atom    target,
                     Atom    property,
                     Window  requestor,
                     Time    time )
```

allows applications to request the data that corresponds to a selection. This function requests that the selection identified by the argument `atom` be stored in a property specified by the `target_atom` on the given `window`. In addition, the `type` argument is an atom that specifies the desired form of the selection. For example, one application might request a selection as a string, while another might request the bitmap image of the region containing the selection.

Selection Events

X supports the selection process by sending several different types of events to the applications involved in a data transfer. When `XConvertSelection()` is called, the X server sends a `SelectionRequest` event to the current owner of the selection. The owner of the selection is responsible for converting the contents of the selection to the requested type, and storing the result in the given property of the requestor's window. Afterwards, the selection owner is expected to send a `SelectionNotify` event to the requesting application to inform it that the data has been stored. The requestor is expected to retrieve the data and then delete the property.

The server reports `SelectionRequest` events using an `XSelectionRequestEvent` structure. In addition to the information included in all events, an `XSelectionRequestEvent` structure includes the following members:

```
Window          owner;
Window          requestor;
Atom            selection;
Atom            target;
Atom            property;
Time            time;
```

An `XSelectionRequestEvent` structure reports the window ID of the owner of the selection and also the window ID of the requestor. Three members of the event structure are atoms. The first, `selection`, identifies the name of the requested selection, while the second, `target`, specifies the data type desired by the requestor. The `property` atom indicates the name of a property on the requestor's window where the data is to be stored.

After the owner of the selection converts the selection to the requested type and stores it on the given property of the requestor window, the selection owner is expected to use `XSendEvent()` to send a `SelectionNotify` event to the requestor. This event uses an `XSelectionEvent` structure, which includes the members:

```
Window          requestor;
Atom            selection;
Atom            target;
Atom            property;
Time            time;
```

If the selection owner is able to provide the requested type of data, the owner sets the `target` atom to the requested data type. Otherwise the owner sets the atom to the constant `None`. The `selection` member indicates the name of the selection and the `property` specifies the name of the property in which the selection is stored.

When a client requests ownership of a selection, the X server sends the current owner a `SelectionClear` event to notify the application that it has lost the selection. This event uses the `XSelectionClearEvent` event structure, which includes the members:

```
Atom          selection;
Time          time;
```

The `selection` atom indicates the name of the selection that has been lost, while `time` indicates the server time at which the event occurred.

The Selection Handshake

The X selection process can be summarized by looking at the sequence of steps that occur in a typical exchange. Assume there are two applications, *A* and *B*, and that one of the windows in application *A* currently owns a selection. If *B* requests the value of that selection, the following sequence of events takes place.

1. *B* calls `XConvertSelection()` to ask for the data associated with the current selection.

2. The X server sends *A* a `SelectionRequest` event, because *A* owns the window that currently owns the selection.

3. *A* converts the data associated with the selection to the type requested by *B*.

4. *A* stores the converted data on a property of a window owned by *B*.

5. *A* sends a `SelectionNotify` event to *B*.

6. *B* receives the `SelectionNotify` event.

7. *B* retrieves the data from the property specified by *A*.

8. *B* deletes the property once it has finished retrieving the data.

Now let's assume that B claims ownership of the selection, which is still owned by A. The following sequence of events should occur when B calls `XSetSelectionOwner()` to establish its ownership of the selection.

1. *B* calls `XSetSelectionOwner()` to grab ownership of the selection.

2. *A* receives a `SelectionClear` event.

3. *A* unhighlights its selection.

4. *B* calls `XGetSelectionOwner()` to verify that is actually owns the selection.

5. *B* highlights the selection if it can confirm that it is the new owner of the selection.

Xt Selection Support

The discussion in the previous section is a bit simplistic and ignores several issues. For example, to transfer large amounts of data efficiently, applications must break up any large amount of data into several smaller pieces to allow the data to be transferred easily though the X server. The complete selection protocol is defined by the *InterClient Communications Conventions Manual* (ICCCM). Implementing the selection mechanism as described in this manual can be quite complex.

Fortunately, Xt provides several functions that handle most of the details and allow applications to use a much simpler interface. In addition to being simpler to use, the Xt implementation allows applications to view all selection transfers as being atomic. Xt breaks up large data transfers into smaller ones automatically and transparently. Applications based on Xt or Motif do not normally use any of the Xlib functions described in the previous section, but use higher-level Xt functions instead.

Owning a Selection

Xt provides three basic selection functions. The first of these is used to claim ownership of a selection, and has the form:

```
Boolean XtOwnSelection ( Widget                  widget,
                         Atom                    selection,
                         Time                    time
                         XtConvertSelectionProc  convert,
                         XtLoseSelectionProc     lose,
                         XtSelectionDoneProc     done )
```

XtOwnSelection() returns TRUE if the caller has successfully gained ownership of the selection. The first argument to this function indicates the widget that claims ownership of the atom. The second argument must be an atom that identifies the selection to be owned. For copy-and-paste operations, this atom is usually XA_PRIMARY. The third argument is the current server time, which should be obtained from the most recent event.

The last three arguments to XtOwnSelection() allow the calling application to register callback functions to handle various parts of the data transfer. Xt invokes the first callback when another application requests the data associated with the selection. The second callback is called if the application loses ownership of the selection. The third callback function is called when a requesting application has actually received the data from a request. This procedure is optional and can be given as NULL.

The convert callback function is expected to convert the selection to the type requested, if possible. This callback must have the form:

```
Boolean ConvertCallback ( Widget         widget,
                          Atom           *selection,
                          Atom           *target,
                          Atom           *type,
                          XtPointer      *value,
                          unsigned long  *length,
                          int            *format )
```

All the parameters to a convert callback function except the first are pointers. The `selection` argument is a pointer to the atom that identifies the requested selection (`XA_PRIMARY`, for example). The `target` argument is a pointer to an atom that specifies the requested type, while `type` is a pointer to the type of the data actually supplied by this callback. The `value` parameter is a pointer to the data returned by this function, while `length` and `format` indicate the size of the data pointed to by `value`. The last four arguments are return values that should be supplied by the callback function.

The convert callback function must return `TRUE` if it successfully converts the selection and `FALSE` if it can not fulfill the request.

The `lose` callback must have the form:

```
void LoseCallback ( Widget widget, Atom *selection )
```

Here, the `widget` argument indicates the widget that has lost the selection, and `selection` points to an atom that specifies the selection that was lost.

If an application registers a `done` callback function when the application claims ownership of a selection, the application owns any data associated with the selection. If the application does not register a `done` callback, the convert callback must allocate space for the data to be transferred by calling `XtMalloc()`. If there is no done callback, Xt will free the data automatically when the selection has been transferred.

The done callback function must have the form:

```
void DoneCallback ( Widget widget, Atom *selection, Atom *target )
```

The `widget` argument indicates the widget that owns the selection. The `selection` argument points to an atom that identifies the selection, and `target` points to an atom that indicates the type of the transferred selection.

Requesting the Value of a Selection

To request the data associated with a selection, a Motif application can call the function:

```
XtGetSelectionValue ( Widget                   widget,
                      Atom                     selection,
                      Atom                     target,
                      XtSelectionCallbackProc  callback,
                      XtPointer                client_data,
                      Time                     time )
```

The `widget` argument to this function specifies the widget that has requested the selection value. The `selection` argument must be an atom that indicates the selection name, and `target` must be an atom that indicates the requested type of the data (for example, `XA_STRING`). The `callback` argument can be used to specify a function to be called when the requested data has been transferred. The `clientData` argument allows the caller to provide some data that will be passed to the `callback` function when it is called.

The form of the selection callback function must be:

```
void SelectionCallback ( Widget          widget,
                         XtPointer       clientDdata,
                         Atom            *selection,
                         Atom            *type,
                         XtPointer       value,
                         unsigned long   *length,
                         int             *format )
```

The `widget` argument to this callback function indicates the widget that requested the selection value. The `clientData` parameter contains the client data specified by the application when it registered the callback. The other parameters correspond to the data transferred by the selection owner. The `selection` argument points to an atom that identifies the name of the selection (`XA_PRIMARY`, for example), while the `type` argument points to an atom that identifies the type of the selection (`XA_STRING`, for example). If there is no selection owner, Xt sets the value of `type` to `XT_CONVERT_FAIL`. If the selection owner cannot convert the selection, the value of `type` is set to `None`. The `value` parameter is a pointer to the selection data. This data is owned by the client, and should be freed when it is no longer needed. The `length` argument specifies the number of elements in the transferred data, while `format` specifies the size of each element, in bits (8, 16, or 32).

Disowning the Selection

When an application no longer wishes to own the selection, it can call the function:

```
void XtDisownSelection ( Widget w, Atom selection, Time time )
```

The arguments to this function must specify the `widget` that is relinquishing the selection, the `selection` being given up, and the current `time`.

A Selection Example

This section describes a simple example program named `selectiondemo` that copies and displays the value of the current `XA_PRIMARY` selection upon request. This program allows the user to request the value of the current selection as a character string or as compound text. The program can also request a list of types supported by the owner of the selection. The transferred data is displayed in a window. The user can also have the `selectiondemo` program declare ownership of the selection. The program can transfer data to other applications as a character string or compound text, and can also provide the list of supported types.

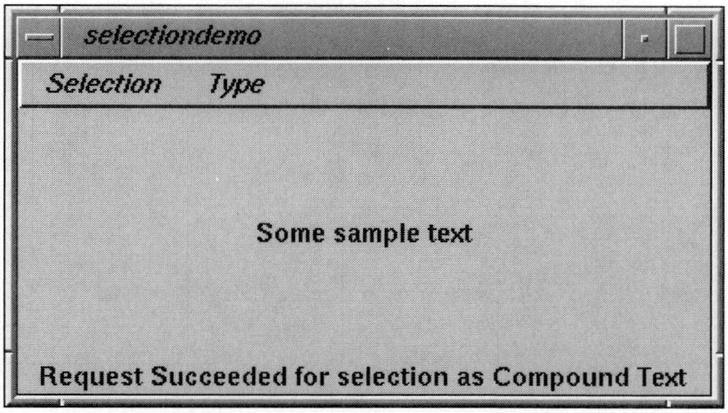

Figure 14.1 The selectiondemo program.

The program begins by declaring various functions and variables needed by the example.

```
1    /**********************************************************
2     * selectiondemo.c: A simple demo of X selection functions
3     **********************************************************/
4    #include <Xm/Xm.h>
5    #include <Xm/Label.h>
6    #include <Xm/MainW.h>
7    #include "MenuSupport.h"
8    #include <X11/Xatom.h>
9    #include <stdio.h>
10
11   Widget      msg, selectionLabel;
12   Atom        TARGETS, DELETE;
13   Atom        COMPOUND_TEXT;
14   Atom        current_type = XA_STRING;
15   char *GetTextFromXmstring ( XmString string ) ;
16   extern void wprintf ( Widget w, const char *format, ... );
17   static void  SetStringType ( Widget     w,
18                                XtPointer clientData,
19                                XtPointer callData );
20
21   static void  SetCTType ( Widget      w,
22                            XtPointer clientData,
23                            XtPointer callData );
24   static void SetTargetType ( Widget      w,
25                               XtPointer clientData,
26                               XtPointer callData );
27
28   static void LoseSelection ( Widget w, Atom *selection );
```

```
29   static Boolean ConvertSelection ( Widget          w,
30                                      Atom            *selection,
31                                      Atom            *target,
32                                      Atom            *type,
33                                      XtPointer       *value,
34                                      unsigned long   *length,
35                                      int             *format );
36
37   static void ToggleType ( Widget    w,
38                            XtPointer clientData,
39                            XtPointer callData );
40   static void ShowSelection ( Widget          w,
41                               XtPointer       clientData,
42                               Atom            *selection,
43                               Atom            *type,
44                               XtPointer       value,
45                               unsigned long   *length,
46                               int             *format );
47   static void RequestSelection ( Widget    w,
48                                  XtPointer clientData,
49                                  XtPointer callData );
50   static void OwnSelection ( Widget    w,
51                              XtPointer clientData,
52                              XtPointer callData );
```

Next, the program uses the MenuSupport facility described in Chapter 6 to create a menu bar that contains two panes. The Selection menu pane allows the application to own the selection and request the value of the selection. The Type menu pane allows users to select the type of data requested.

```
53   static MenuDescription selectionPaneDesc[] = {
54     { BUTTON,    "OwnSelection",        OwnSelection     },
55     { BUTTON,    "RequestSelection",    RequestSelection },
56     { NULL }
57   };
58
59   static MenuDescription typePaneDesc[] = {
60     { TOGGLE,    "String",          SetStringType },
61     { TOGGLE,    "CompoundText",    SetCTType     },
62     { TOGGLE,    "Targets",         SetTargetType },
63     { NULL }
64   };
65
66   static MenuDescription menuBarDesc[] = {
67     { PULLDOWN,         "Selection",   NULL, NULL, selectionPaneDesc },
68     { RADIOPULLDOWN,    "Type",        NULL, NULL, typePaneDesc },
69     { NULL }
70   };
```

The body of the `selectiondemo` program creates the atoms needed to support the selection process and creates the widgets used for the application's window. The interface consists of an XmMainWindow widget that contains a label used to display the value of the data currently maintained by the `selectiondemo` program, and another label that is used to report the current state of the program. The first label widget is displayed as the XmMainWindow widget's work area, while the other is installed in the message area.

```
71  void main ( int argc, char **argv )
72  {
73      Widget    shell, mainWindow;
74      XtAppContext app;
75
76      /*
77       * Initialize Xt
78       */
79
80      shell = XtAppInitialize ( &app, "Clipboard", NULL, 0,
81                                &argc, argv, NULL, NULL, 0 );
82      /*
83       * Intern atoms used to identify data types and
84       * selection targets.
85       */
86
87      COMPOUND_TEXT = XInternAtom ( XtDisplay ( shell ),
88                                    "COMPOUND_TEXT", FALSE );
89      TARGETS = XInternAtom ( XtDisplay ( shell ),
90                              "TARGETS", FALSE );
91      DELETE = XInternAtom ( XtDisplay  ( shell ),
92                             "DELETE", FALSE );
93      /*
94       * Create window layout. A main window widget holds a menu bar,
95       * a label to display the value of the selection, and another
96       * another used to display status.
97       */
98
99      mainWindow = XtCreateManagedWidget ( "mainWindow",
100                                           xmMainWindowWidgetClass,
101                                           shell, NULL, 0 );
102
103     CreateMenu ( MENUBAR, "menuBar", mainWindow, menuBarDesc, NULL );
104
105     selectionLabel = XtCreateManagedWidget ( "label",
106                                              xmLabelWidgetClass,
107                                              mainWindow, NULL, 0 );
108
109     msg = XtCreateManagedWidget ( "msgArea",
110                                   xmLabelWidgetClass,
111                                   mainWindow, NULL, 0 );
```

```
112
113        XtVaSetValues ( mainWindow, XmNmessageWindow, msg, NULL );
114
115        XtRealizeWidget ( shell );
116
117        XtAppMainLoop ( app );
118
119  }
```

The remainder of the program consists of the callbacks registered with the various menu items. `RequestSelection()` is called when the user chooses the RequestSelection item in the Selection menu pane, This function calls `XtGetSelectionValue()` to retrieve the current value of the `XA_PRIMARY` selection. The function `ShowSelection()` is registered to be called when Xt has obtained the value of the `XA_PRIMARY` selection and completed the transfer. Notice that the `time` parameter required by `XtGetSelectionValue()` is obtained from the event reported in the `callData` structure.

```
120  static void RequestSelection ( Widget     w,
121                                 XtPointer clientData,
122                                 XtPointer callData )
123  {
124        XmAnyCallbackStruct *cb = ( XmAnyCallbackStruct* ) callData;
125
126        XtGetSelectionValue ( selectionLabel,
127                              XA_PRIMARY,
128                              current_type,
129                              ShowSelection,
130                              clientData,
131                              cb->event->xbutton.time );
132
133  }
```

`ShowSelection()` is called when Xt obtains the value of the requested selection. This function checks the type of the data received. If the received data type is compound text, `ShowSelection()` converts the compound text to a compound string and calls `XtVaSetValues()` to display the string in the `selectionLabel` widget. `ShowSelection()` also uses `wprintf()` (described in Chapter 6) to display a message in the `msg` widget to announce the successful transfer. If the type of the transferred data is a character string, `ShowSelection()` uses `wprintf()` to display the transferred data in the selectionLabel widget.

If the type of the data transferred is `TARGETS`, the transferred data is an array of atoms that indicates the types of data available from the current selection owner. This could happen if the user has selected the Targets item from the Type menu pane and requested the value of the selection. In this case, `ShowSelection()` extracts the list of available types from the selection data and displays them in the `selectionLabel` widget. If a transfer does not succeed, Xt returns the type as `XT_CONVERT_FAILED`, or `None`. In either case, `ShowSelection()` clears the data displayed by the selectiondemo and announces the failure.

```
134   static void ShowSelection ( Widget        w,
135                               XtPointer     clientData,
136                               Atom          *selection,
137                               Atom          *type,
138                               XtPointer     value,
139                               unsigned long *length,
140                               int           *format )
141   {
142      /*
143       * Check the type of the transfer and handle each accordingly.
144       */
145
146      if ( *type == COMPOUND_TEXT )
147      {
148          XtVaSetValues ( selectionLabel,
149                          XmNlabelString, XmCvtCTToXmString ( value ),
150                          NULL );
151          wprintf ( msg,
152                  "Request Succeeded for selection as Compound Text" );
153      }
154      else if ( *type == XA_STRING )
155      {
156          wprintf ( selectionLabel, "%s", value );
157          wprintf ( msg, "Request Succeeded for selection as String" );
158      }
159      else if ( *type == TARGETS )
160      {
161          int i;
162          char buf [ 1000 ]; /* Danger: Fixed size array */
163
164          sprintf ( buf,"Length = %d\0", length );
165
166          for ( i=0; i < *length; i++ )
167          {
168              char *s = XGetAtomName ( XtDisplay ( selectionLabel ),
169                                       ( ( Atom* ) value ) [ i ] );
170
171              sprintf ( buf + strlen ( buf ), "\n ( %d ) %s", i, s );
172          }
173
174          wprintf ( selectionLabel, "%s", buf );
175          wprintf ( msg, "Current Targets listed" );
176      }
177      else if ( *type == XT_CONVERT_FAIL || *type == None)
178      {
179          wprintf ( selectionLabel, " " );
180          wprintf ( msg, "Request Failed" );
181      }
182   }
```

The type of data requested by the selectiondemo program depends on the value the user selects from the Type menu. Each item in this menu pane calls a function to designate the desired type. The callback function `SetStringType()` is called when the user selects the String item in the Type menu pane. This function sets the global variable `current_type` to the value `XA_STRING`. The value of `current_type` determines the type of data requested when the application requests the value of a selection.

```
183  static void  SetStringType ( Widget      w,
184                                   XtPointer clientData,
185                                   XtPointer callData )
186  {
187      XmToggleButtonCallbackStruct *cb =
188                          ( XmToggleButtonCallbackStruct* ) callData;
189
190      if ( cb->set )
191      {
192          current_type = XA_STRING;
193      }
194  }
```

`SetCTType()` is similar to `SetStringType()`, but sets `current_type` to the type `COMPOUND_TEXT`. This function is called when the user selects the Compound Text item in the Type menu pane.

```
195  static void  SetCTType ( Widget      w,
196                               XtPointer clientData,
197                               XtPointer callData )
198  {
199      XmToggleButtonCallbackStruct *cb =
200                          ( XmToggleButtonCallbackStruct* ) callData;
201
202      if ( cb->set )
203      {
204          current_type = COMPOUND_TEXT;
205      }
206  }
```

`SetTargetType()` is similar to `SetStringType()`, but sets `current_type` to the type `TARGETS`. This function is called when the user selects the Targets item in the Type menu pane.

```
207  static void SetTargetType ( Widget      w,
208                                  XtPointer clientData,
209                                  XtPointer callData )
210  {
211      XmToggleButtonCallbackStruct *cb =
212                          ( XmToggleButtonCallbackStruct* ) callData;
213
```

```
214        if ( cb->set )
215        {
216             current_type = TARGETS;
217        }
218   }
```

The `selectiondemo` program can also attempt to own the selection. The user can select the OwnSelection menu item to establish ownership of the selection. The function `OwnSelection()` calls `XtOwnSelection()`, which handles the details of owning the selection. `OwnSelection()` registers two other callback functions, `ConvertSelection()` and `LoseSelection()`, to handle the details of transferring data and losing the selection. `OwnSelection()` checks the return value of `XtOwnSelection()` and displays a message if the selection has been successfully owned.

```
219   static void OwnSelection ( Widget    w,
220                              XtPointer clientData,
221                              XtPointer callData )
222   {
223       Display *dpy = XtDisplay ( selectionLabel );
224
225       /*
226        * Claim ownership of the PRIMARY selection.
227        */
228
229       if ( XtOwnSelection ( selectionLabel, XA_PRIMARY,
230                             XtLastTimestampProcessed ( dpy ),
231                             ConvertSelection,  /* Handle requests */
232                             LoseSelection,     /* Give up selection*/
233                             NULL ) )
234       {
235           wprintf ( msg, "Selection Owned" );
236       }
237
238   }
```

The callback function `ConvertSelection()` is called if another application requests the value of the selection owned by the `selectiondemo` program. This function checks the type of the requested target and handles the request as needed. If the requestor simply wants a list of the possible types `selectiondemo` can provide, `ConvertSelection()` allocates an array of atoms and uses the array to specify the types of data it can provide. The function then returns `TRUE` to indicate that it could handle the request. Xt can also call `ConvertSelection()` with type set to `DELETE`, in which case `selectiondemo` is expected to delete the current selection. If the selection value is requested as `COMPOUND_TEXT` or `XA_STRING`, `ConvertSelection()` retrieves the value displayed by the `selectionLabel` widget and converts it to the requested type, if necessary. The function `GetTextFromXmString()`, which converts a multi-segment compound string into a multi-line text string, is described in Chapter 12.

```
239    static Boolean ConvertSelection ( Widget          w,
240                                       Atom            *selection,
241                                       Atom            *target,
242                                       Atom            *type,
243                                       XtPointer       *value,
244                                       unsigned long   *length,
245                                       int             *format )
246    {
247        /*
248         * Check the requested type, and handle accordingly
249         */
250
251        if ( *target == TARGETS )
252        {
253            /*
254             * Initialize an array of Atoms to specify the types of data
255             * this program can provide.
256             */
257
258            Atom *targets = ( Atom* ) XtMalloc ( sizeof ( Atom ) * 4 );
259            targets[0] = XA_STRING;
260            targets[1] = COMPOUND_TEXT;
261            targets[2] = TARGETS;
262            targets[3] = DELETE;
263
264            *value = ( XtPointer ) targets;
265            *format = 32;
266            *length = 4 * sizeof(Atom) >> 2;
267            *type   = TARGETS;
268            return ( TRUE );
269        }
270
271        if ( *target == DELETE )
272        {
273            /*
274             * Delete the selection by clearing the label. Also report the
275             * action using wprintf().
276             */
277
278            wprintf ( msg, "Selection Deleted" );
279            wprintf ( selectionLabel, "" );
280
281            *type   = DELETE;
282            *value  = NULL;
283            *length = 0;
284            *format = 8;
285            return ( TRUE );
286        }
287
```

```
288      if ( *target == COMPOUND_TEXT )
289      {
290
291         /*
292          * If the requested type is compound text, convert the
293          * string retrieved from the selectionLabel widget to CT.
294          */
295
296         XmString xmstr;
297
298         XtVaGetValues ( selectionLabel, XmNlabelString,
299                         &xmstr, NULL );
300
301         *type   = COMPOUND_TEXT;
302         *value  = XmCvtXmStringToCT ( xmstr );
303         *length = strlen ( *value );
304         *format = 8;
305         return ( TRUE );
306      }
307
308      if ( *target == XA_STRING )
309      {
310         /*
311          * If the requestor is asking for an ASCII string, get the
312          * compound string from the selectionLabel widget and convert
313          * the results.
314          */
315
316         char     *str;
317         XmString  xmstr;
318
319         XtVaGetValues ( selectionLabel,
320                         XmNlabelString, &xmstr,
321                         NULL );
322
323         *type   = XA_STRING;
324         *value  = GetTextFromXmstring ( xmstr );
325         *length = strlen ( *value );
326         *format = 8;
327         return ( TRUE );
328      }
329
330      /*
331       * If we got here, the requested type was something we could
332       * not handle, so return FALSE.
333       */
334
335      return ( FALSE );
336  }
```

`LoseSelection()` is called when the selectiondemo program loses ownership of the selection. In this case, `LoseSelection()` just updates the message area to show the current status.

```
337   static void LoseSelection ( Widget w, Atom *selection )
338   {
339       wprintf ( msg, "Selection Lost" );
340   }
```

To see how this program works, run the program and at least one other application that supports the ICCCM protocol. An xterm or any Motif program with a text widget will work. Select some text in the other program, select a data type in the selectiondemo, and select the "RequestSelection" menu item. If the other program can supply the specified data type, the data will be transferred to `selectiondemo`. To have `selectiondemo` own the selection, select the OwnSelection menu item. If another program owns the selection at that time, you should see any highlight being used disappear. Pasting into another application should request the current data displayed by `selectiondemo`.

14.5 Using the Motif Clipboard

The X and Xt selection mechanisms described in the previous sections provide a "quick-transfer" type of copy and paste facility, in which the data is transferred directly between an owner and a requestor. This model is often used in X to transfer text. Typically, the user selects some text by sweeping the pointer over the text while holding down the left mouse button. The user clicks the middle mouse button in a window to transfer the text directly to that location. The data in this transaction is transient. If the owner of a selection exits, the selection is lost.

Motif provides an alternate model, in which data is transferred to an intermediate clipboard which is persistent. The Motif clipboard is an unseen location where applications can store and retrieve named, typed data. Applications must explicitly copy and retrieve data to and from the clipboard.

The user model supported by the clipboard is similar to that on most personal computers. In this model, the user selects an object, which may be highlighted in some way. The user then selects a menu item that explicitly copies the item to an intermediate clipboard. To transfer the data to another application, the user selects an insertion point in the other application, and then explicitly selects a menu item that pastes the data from the clipboard to the other application.

The clipboard model was developed out of necessity on personal computers, which normally are not multi-tasking. On UNIX systems, the direct transfer model, which requires two applications to run simultaneously, is more prevalent. However, the clipboard model has several advantages. The most obvious is that the data copied to the clipboard is persistent, and can be stored even after the original application is no longer running. Another advantage is the possibility of supporting smart clipboard programs that allow users to browse the data on the clipboard, and to allow the clipboard to perform complex data conversions without the need for applications to understand the wide variety of data formats that might be used.

The following sections explain a few of the more common functions for interacting with the Motif clipboard and provide a typical example.

Storing Data in the Clipboard

Transferring data to the Motif clipboard requires three steps:

1.   Initialize the clipboard. This step sets up some data structures associated with the clipboard and retrieves an identifier for this transaction.

2.   Specify the data to be copied to the clipboard. Motif supports two types of transfer, immediate and transfer by name. In immediate mode, data is physically transferred to the clipboard. When data is transferred by name, the clipboard is informed that the application has some data to be copied to the clipboard, but no data is actually transferred until another application requests the data from the clipboard.

3.   End the copy. In this step, the data is actually transferred to the clipboard, unless the transfer is being made by name. The clipboard is first locked to prevent any application from accessing the clipboard while the transfer is in progress. Then the data is transferred, and the clipboard unlocked.

Motif provides many functions for dealing with the clipboard, including functions that lock and unlock the clipboard, determine the type and size of the data stored on the clipboard, and so on. However, most applications only need to use a few simple functions that implement the steps described above. The following sections describe the functions used to perform each of these steps.

Starting the Copy

Before copying data to the clipboard, applications must first call the function:

```
XmClipboardStartCopy ( Display        *display,
                       Window          window,
                       XmString        label,
                       Time            time,
                       Widget          widget,
                       XmCutPasteProc  callback,
                       long           *item_id )
```

This function sets up data structures required by the clipboard. The `window` parameter specifies a window ID to be associated with the clipboard data. The `label` specifies a name to be associated with the clipboard. The `time` argument specifies the current server time and should be obtained from the event that triggered the copy.

The `widget` argument indicates a widget that will receive messages requesting data previously passed by name. This widget can be any widget within the application. If the data is not being transferred by name, the widget can be given as `NULL`. The `callback` argument specifies a callback function to be called when data transferred by name is required. If the data is not transferred by name, this function can be given as NULL.

The `item_id` parameter returns an identifier associated with the new transaction. Applications must use this identifier in all subsequent calls to `XmClipboardCopy()`, `XmClipboardEndCopy()`, and `XmClipboardCancelCopy()`.

Providing the Data

Applications provide the data to be copied to the clipboard by calling the following function:

```
XmClipboardCopy ( Display        *display,
                  Window          window,
                  long            item_id,
                  char           *format,
                  XtPointer       buffer,
                  unsigned long   length,
                  long            private,
                  long           *dataid )
```

This function specifies the data to be copied to the clipboard in the `buffer` argument. If `buffer` is given as NULL, the copy is assumed to be by name, and the callback specified in `XmClipboardStartCopy()` will be invoked if the data is needed. If data is provided, the length of the buffer is specified by the `length` argument.

The window ID specified in the call should be the same window ID used for all clipboard functions. The `format` argument specifies the type of the data. This argument is not interpreted by the clipboard. The `item_id` must be the transaction identifier returned by `XmClipboard-StartCopy()`. The `private` parameter allows an application to store a private identifier with the data. If the copy is being made by name, the clipboard assigns an identifier to the data and returns it to the application in the `data_id` parameter.

The data in `buffer` is not actually transferred to the clipboard until the function `XmClipboardEndCopy()` is called. Additional calls to `XmClipboardCopy()` before a call to `XmClipboardEndCopy()` can be used to add additional formats to the data item or append data to an existing format.

`XmClipboardCopy()` returns `ClipboardSuccess` if the function is successful, or `ClipboardLocked` if the clipboard is locked by another application.

Ending the Transaction

To end the clipboard transaction started by `XmClipboardStartCopy()` and actually transfer the data to the clipboard, applications must call the function:

```
XmClipboardEndCopy ( Display *display,
                     Window   window,
                     long     item_id )
```

This function locks the clipboard, transfers the data, and unlocks the clipboard. `XmClipboard-EndCopy()` returns `ClipboardSuccess` if the function is successful, or `ClipboardLocked` if the clipboard is locked by another application.

Transferring by Name

Applications that need to transfer large amounts of data may not want to actually transfer the data to the clipboard until another application wants to retrieve the data from the clipboard. If desired, applications can arrange to transfer the data by name only. In this case, the application provides a callback and a widget in the call to `XmClipboardStartCopy()`, and specifies the data buffer passed to `XmClipboardCopy()` as NULL. Motif calls the given callback when the data is actually required.

The form of an `XmCutPasteProc` callback must be:

```
void CopyByNameCallback ( Widget widget,
                          int    *data_id,
                          int    *private,
                          int    *reason )
```

The `widget` argument specifies the widget given in the previous call to `XmClipboard-StartCopy()`. The `data_id` argument is a pointer to the identifier associated with this data item, while `private` is a pointer to the optional private identifier specified by the application in the function `XmClipboardCopy()`. The `reason` argument indicates why this function was called. This value can be one of the constants, `XmCRClipboardDataDelete` or `XmCRClip-boardDataRequest`. If the reason is `XmCRClipboardDataDelete`, an item passed by name has been deleted from the clipboard and the associated data is no longer needed. If the callback is invoked with the reason given as `XmCRClipboardDataRequest`, the application must transfer the data to the clipboard using the function:

```
XmClipboardCopyByName ( Display       *display,
                        Window        window,
                        long          data_id,
                        XtPointer     buffer,
                        unsigned long length,
                        long          private_id )
```

The `data_id` argument must indicate the identifier for this transaction, as returned by `XmClipBoardStartCopy()`. The `buffer` argument must contain the data to be transferred, while `length` indicates the number of bytes contained in the buffer. The `private` argument specifies an application-defined private ID to be associated with the data on the clipboard.

Retrieving Data from the Clipboard

Applications can retrieve data from the clipboard by calling the function:

```
XmClipboardRetrieve ( Display        *display,
                      Window          window,
                      char           *format,
                      XtPointer       buffer,
                      unsigned long   length,
                      unsigned long  *num_bytes,
                      long           *private_id )
```

This function requests that num_bytes of data be copied into buffer. The size of the buffer, in bytes, is specified by the length argument. If the data is retrieved successfully, XmClipboard-Retrieve() returns the constant ClipboardSuccess. If the clipboard is locked by another application, the function returns ClipboardLocked. If desired, the application can continue to call the function again with the same parameters until the clipboard is no longer locked. If the data in the clipboard is larger than the size of the buffer provided, XmClipboardRetrieve() returns the value ClipboardTruncate, while if the clipboard is empty, XmClipboardRetrieve() returns ClipboardNoData.

Adding Cut and Paste to the Draw Program

This section demonstrates the functions described in the previous sections by adding the ability to transfer objects drawn in the draw program (described in Chapter 13) to and from the clipboard. The user can select an object on the draw program's canvas using the mouse, and then select a Copy or Cut operation from an Edit menu pane. Copy transfers the object to the clipboard, while Cut copies the object to the clipboard and then deletes the local copy. The user can also choose Paste from the Edit menu to paste the current contents of the clipboard into the canvas area of the draw program.

To add this functionality to the draw program, several new functions are needed. The following functions must be added to the declarations at the top of the file editor.c:

```
static void CopyCallback ( Widget    w,
                           XtPointer clientData,
                           XtPointer callData );
static void CutCallback ( Widget    w,
                          XtPointer clientData,
                          XtPointer callData );
static void PasteCallback ( Widget    w,
                            XtPointer clientData,
                            XtPointer callData );
```

In addition, the menu description in editor.c must be augmented to include an Edit menu pane on the menu bar. The following structure describes the Edit pane itself:

```
static MenuDescription editPaneDesc[] = {
  { BUTTON,   "Copy",   CopyCallback  },
  { BUTTON,   "Cut",    CutCallback   },
  { BUTTON,   "Paste",  PasteCallback },
  { NULL }
};
```

The menu bar description must also be modified to add the additional menu pane:

```
static MenuDescription menuBarDesc[] = {
    { PULLDOWN,        "File",   NULL, NULL, filePaneDesc },
    { PULLDOWN,        "Edit",   NULL, NULL, editPaneDesc },
    { RADIOPULLDOWN,   "Colors", NULL, NULL, colorDesc    },
    { RADIOPULLDOWN,   "DrawingCommands",
                                 NULL, NULL, drawingCommandsDesc },
    { HELPPANE,        "Help",   NULL, NULL, helpPaneDesc   },
    { NULL }
};
```

The three callback functions added to editor.c are similar to other callbacks implemented as part of the editor.c module. The functions simply call other functions, defined in graphics.c, which do the real work.

```
static void CopyCallback ( Widget    w,
                           XtPointer clientData,
                           XtPointer callData )
{
    CopySelectedItem();
}

static void CutCallback ( Widget    w,
                          XtPointer clientData,
                          XtPointer callData )
{
    CutSelectedItem();
}

static void PasteCallback ( Widget    w,
                            XtPointer clientData,
                            XtPointer callData )
{
    PasteItem();
}
```

This completes the changes to the editor.c file, which provides the user interface. The remaining changes to the draw program consist of additional functions that must be added to the file graphics.c.

The changes to graphics.c include the functions called from the menu callbacks in editor.c, and also some lower-level functions that actually perform the transfer to and from the clipboard. The function CopyToClipboard() is the first of these lower-level functions. CopyToClip-board() uses XmClipboardStartCopy() to begin a transaction. Once this function succeeds, XmClipboardCopy() specifies the data to be transferred, and finally XmClipboar-dEndCopy() ends the transaction. In this transfer, the data is transferred immediately. Notice that the data is transferred by passing the address of the structure that represents the currently selected graphics object, and specifying the size of the structure to XmClipboardCopy(). Also notice that because this function does not have access to an event, the function `XtLastTimeStampPro-cessed()` is used to obtain a valid value for the `time` parameter.

```
void CopyToClipBoard()
{
    int     result;
    long    itemid, dataid;
    XmString  xmstr;

    xmstr = XmStringCreateLocalized ( "Draw" );


    /*
     * Initalize the clipboard for a transfer by value.
     */

    while ( ( result =
            XmClipboardStartCopy ( display, XtWindow ( canvas ),
                                   xmstr,
                                   XtLastTimestampProcessed ( display ),
                                   NULL, NULL,
                                   &itemid ) ) != ClipboardSuccess )
        ;

    XmStringFree ( xmstr );

    /*
     * Copy the data, which is identified as type "GraphicsObject"
     */

    while ( ( result =
                    XmClipboardCopy ( display,  XtWindow ( canvas ),
                                      itemid,
                                      "GraphicsObject",
                                      ( char * ) currentObject,
                                      sizeof ( GraphicsObject ), 0,
                                      &dataid ) ) != ClipboardSuccess )
        ;

    /*
     * End the transaction.
     */

    while ( ( result =
                    XmClipboardEndCopy ( display, XtWindow ( canvas ),
                                         itemid ) ) != ClipboardSuccess )
        ;
}
```

The function `CopyFromClipboard()` retrieves the current contents of the clipboard and adds the retrieved object to the draw program's display list.

```
void CopyFromClipBoard ()
{
    GraphicsObject    object;
    int               result, pos;
    long              id;
    int               done = FALSE;
    unsigned long     numBytes;

   /*
    * Retrieve the current contents of the clipboard.
    */

    while  ( !done )
    {
        result = XmClipboardRetrieve ( display, XtWindow ( canvas ),
                                       "GraphicsObject", &object,
                                       sizeof ( GraphicsObject ),
                                       &numBytes, &id );
       /*
        * Check the return value. If the clipboard is locked, try
        * again. If data is retrieved successfully, append it
        * to the text buffer. Otherwise abort.
        */

        switch ( result )
        {
          case ClipboardSuccess:

             AddObject ( &object );
             XClearArea ( display, XtWindow ( canvas ),
                          0, 0, 0, 0, TRUE );
             done = TRUE;
             break;

          case ClipboardTruncate:
          case ClipboardNoData:

             done = TRUE;
             break;

          case ClipboardLocked:
             break;
        }
    }
}
```

The function `CutSelectedItem()` provides the top-level interface for cutting an object from the canvas. This function checks whether an object has been selected. If so, `CutSelectedItem()` calls `CopyToClipboard()` to transfer the object to the clipboard, and then calls `RemoveItem()` to delete the current object from the display list.

```c
void CutSelectedItem()
{
    if ( currentObject )
    {
        CopyToClipBoard();

        RemoveItem ( currentObject );
    }
}
```

`CopySelectedItem()` is similar to `CutSelectedItem()` except that the object is not removed from the display list after it has been copied to the clipboard.

```c
void CopySelectedItem()
{
    if ( currentObject )
    {
        CopyToClipBoard();
    }
}
```

`PasteItem()` just calls `CopyFromClipboard()` to obtain the current contents of the clipboard and add the object to the display list.

```c
void PasteItem()
{
    CopyFromClipBoard();
}
```

`CutSelectedItem()` requires the ability to remove an object from the display list, which was not implemented as part of the original draw program. The function `RemoveItem()` finds and removes an object from the display list and then triggers a redraw to erase the visible item.

```c
void RemoveItem ( GraphicsObject *object )
{
    int i;

    for ( i = 0; i < nextSlot; i++ )
    {
        /*
         * Find the specified object
         */
```

```
if ( object ==  &( displayList[i] ) )
{
    int j;

   /*
    * Move all other objects up one slot, leaving out
    * the item to be removed.
    */

    for ( j = i; j < nextSlot - 1; j++ )
    {
        displayList[j].x1    =    displayList[j+1].x1;
        displayList[j].y1    =    displayList[j+1].y1;
        displayList[j].x2    =    displayList[j+1].x2;
        displayList[j].y2    =    displayList[j+1].y2;
        displayList[j].func =    displayList[j+1].func;
        displayList[j].gc   =    displayList[j+1].gc;
        displayList[j].foreground =
                                 displayList[j+1].foreground;
    }

    nextSlot--;

    if ( nextSlot < 0 )
        nextSlot = 0;

   /*
    * Force a redisplay to redraw all remaining objects.
    */

    XClearArea ( display,
                 XtWindow ( canvas ),
                 0, 0, 0, 0, TRUE );

    return;
    }
  }
}
```

With these changes, the draw program can cut, copy, and paste graphics objects to and from the clipboard. Try running two draw programs, for example, and use copy and paste to transfer objects between canvases.

14.6 Interacting with the Motif Window Manager

One of the most common forms of interclient communication in X occurs between applications and the window manager. Most of the time, applications are not directly involved in this communication because it is handled by the X server, Xt, or Motif. Although applications usually do not deal directly with the communication between the client and the window manager, some applications may need to control some aspects of the communication.

The primary areas of interest to application programmers include the following:

- Handling the ICCCM protocol for deleting windows and shutting down applications.
- Specifying minimum and maximum window sizes.
- Determining the current state of an application's windows.
- Controlling the decorations the window manager places around the window's frame.
- Using and controlling window manager menus.
- Specifying the application's window manager icons.

Most of these needs are supported by the ICCCM in a way that is independent of the window manager being used. The mechanisms that allow applications to control the decorations and menus added to the window manager frame by the Motif window manager are Motif-specific, however.

The following sections describe some of the more typical ways applications can interact with the window manager.

Handling the ICCCM Protocol

Most window managers provide some way to close a window. The Motif window manager, by default, supports a menu on the upper left corner of the window manager frame that include a "Quit" item. By default, selecting this menu item on a top-level window causes the application to exit. Selecting this item on the menu attached to a Motif dialog causes the dialog to be unmanaged. For many applications, this is the appropriate behavior. Often, however, applications need to change this behavior or perform additional steps. For example, many applications need to do some cleanup before exiting. Multi-window applications may simply wish to close each individual window.

When the user selects the Quit item on an application's window manager menu, the window manager sends the application a `WM_DELETE_WINDOW` message, using the X client message mechanism. The action automatically performed by Motif upon receipt of this message depends on the value of the `XmNdeleteResponce` resource supported by the shell widget. This resource can be set to one of following values to alter the default response:

- `XmDESTROY`: Destroy the top level window.
- `XmUNMAP`: Unmap the window only.
- `XmDO_NOTHING`: Ignore the message.

In addition, Motif allows applications to register a callback to be invoked when this message is received. Applications that wish to have a chance to clean up before exiting typically set the `XmNdeleteResponce` to `XmDO_NOTHING` and then install a callback to handle the shutdown manually.

For example, the following code segment creates a shell widget by calling `XtVaAppInitialize()`. The arguments to `XtVaAppInitialize()` specify the value of the shell's `XmNdeleteResponce` resource as `XmDO_NOTHING`.

```
shell = XtVaAppInitialize ( &app, "Example",NULL, 0,
                            &argc, argv, NULL,
                            XmNdeleteResponse, XmDO_NOTHING,
                            NULL );
```

The window manager protocol callback function must be registered using an atom that represents the string "WM_DELETE_WINDOW". Applications must obtain this atom by calling `XInternAtom()`.

```
WM_DELETE_WINDOW = XInternAtom ( XtDisplay(shell),
                                 "WM_DELETE_WINDOW", FALSE );
```

Next, a callback can be registered using the Motif function `XmAddWMProtocolCallback()`, as follows:

```
XmAddWMProtocolCallback( shell, WM_DELETE_WINDOW,
                         DeleteWindowCallback, NULL );
```

The callback function registered using `XmAddWMProtocolCallback()` has the same form as all Xt callbacks. This callback will be called when the window manager's `WM_DELETE_WINDOW` message is received. The action taken by the callback is completely application-specific. The application is not required to exit, although the usual action for a single window application would be to clean up and then exit. Multi-window applications might close the window if multiple windows are being displayed, and exit when the last window is closed.

```
void DeleteWindowCallback ( Widget     w,
                            XtPointer clientData,
                            XtPointer callData)
{
     exit(0);
}
```

Specifying Window Sizes

Some applications need to limit the window manager's ability to resize their windows. The window manager looks at various properties on each top-level window that provide hints about how the application's top-level windows should be treated. These properties can be set using

`XChangeProperty()`, but Motif provides an easy-to-use interface for setting these hints. Applications can simply set resources on the top-level shell to specify the minimum acceptable size of the window, the maximum acceptable size, and also specify the increments in which the window should be resized. For example, the following code segment specifies that an application's window should have a minimum size of 150 by 150 pixels, a maximum size of 500 by 500 pixels, and that the window should be resized in increments of 25 pixels.

```
shell = XtVaAppInitialize ( &app, "Example",NULL, 0,
                            &argc, argv, NULL,
                            XmNminWidth,    150,
                            XmNminHeight,   150,
                            XmNmaxHeight,   500,
                            XmNmaxWidth,    500,
                            XmNwidthInc,    25,
                            XmNheightInc,   25,
                            NULL );
```

Window State

Applications sometimes need to control when their windows are in an iconic state and when they are open. Other applications simply need to be notified when a window is iconified or opened. This is easy to do, and can be handled using Xlib functions as defined by the ICCCM.

To specify that a window should be created initially in an iconic state, simply set the value of the `XmNiconic` resource for the corresponding shell widget to `TRUE`. The `XmNiconic` resource is only effective if it is set before the widget is realized. Once a window has been realized, applications can iconify a window by calling the function:

```
Status XIconifyWindow ( Display * display, Window w, int screenNumber )
```

To open an iconified window, an application should call the function

```
XMapWindow ( Display *display, Window window )
```

Applications may wish to call `XMapRaised()` to open the window and raise it to the top with one function call.

Applications that need to keep track of the state of their windows should register an event handler with the shell widget that requests events using the mask `StructureNotifyMask`. An application receives a `MapNotify` event when a window is placed on the screen (uniconified) and an `UnmapNotify` event when a window is iconified.

Controlling Window Manager Decoration

The Motif window manager adds various decorations around all top-level windows that can be used to iconify, resize, or move the window. Some applications need to control the window manager decorations placed in the window manager frame by the Motif window manager. For example, if a window cannot be resized, the application might remove the resize borders.

The window manager decorations can be controlled by setting the value of the shell's XmNmwmDecorations resource. The value of this resource is a mask that specifies what decorations should be shown. The mask must be composed of the following values:

```
MWM_DECOR_ALL          MWM_DECOR_BORDER     MWM_DECOR_RESIZEH
MWM_DECOR_TITLE        MWM_DECOR_MENU       MWM_DECOR_MINIMIZE
MWM_DECOR_MAXIMIZE
```

Including the mask MWM_DECOR_ALL specifies that all window manager decorations should be displayed except for those specified in other bits of the mask. For example, the following code segment creates a shell widget that should be displayed without resize handles and without a maximize control.

```
shell = XtVaAppInitialize ( &app, "Example",NULL, 0,
                            &argc, argv, NULL,
                            XmNmwmDecorations, MWM_DECOR_ALL |
                                               MWM_DECOR_RESIZEH |
                                               MWM_DECOR_MAXIMIZE,
                            NULL );
```

Window Manager Icons

By default, the window manager determines the icon displayed when an application's window is iconified. Mwm allows users to specify an icon using resources that apply to the window manager. This allows users to choose any icons they wish for each application. Some applications, however, may wish to provide a specific icon. Applications that wish to provide an image to be displayed as the application's window manager icon can do so by setting the shell widget's XmNiconPixmap or XmNiconWindow resources. If a simple bitmap is to be provided, the XmNiconPixmap is the simplest resource to use. For example, the following function installs the xlogo_64 bitmap (See Chapter 11) as an application's window manager icon.

```
1   /***************************************************
2    * setupicon.h: Install the xlogo as a window
3    *              manager icon  for a given shell
4    ***************************************************/
5   #include <Xm/Xm.h>
6   #include <X11/bitmaps/xlogo64>
7
8   void SetupIcon ( Widget shell )
9   {
10      Display *dpy = XtDisplay (shell );
11      Window root  = DefaultRootWindow ( dpy );
12      Pixmap bitmap =  XCreateBitmapFromData ( dpy, root, xlogo64_bits,
13                                               xlogo64_width,
14                                               xlogo64_height );
15      XtVaSetValues ( shell, XmNiconPixmap, bitmap, NULL );
16  }
```

Applications can also provide a window to be used as the icon window. Supplying an icon window allows an application to exercise more control over the icon. Applications can provide their own window in which to display a color icon, or might even animate the icon. Applications must not expect to receive input in the icon window, but can receive **Expose** events and use the icon window as the target of draw requests.

The following version of **SetupIcon()** sets up a color window manager icon, using the Xpm functions described in Chapter 11. The function expects a shell widget and an Xpm description as arguments. The window installed as the icon window for the given shell is created as another top-level shell widget whose **XmNmappedWhenManaged** resource is set to **FALSE**. This is necessary because the window manager needs to control when the icon window is visible. The shell widget manages a single child widget, a label in which a color pixmap is displayed.

```
1     /********************************************************
2      * setupicon2.c: Create a window to display an Xpm
3      *               color window manager icon
4      ********************************************************/
5     #include <Xm/Xm.h>
6     #include <Xm/Label.h>
7     #include <X11/xpm.h> /* Non-standard header file */
8
9     void SetupIcon ( Widget shell, char **xpmDesc )
10    {
11        Pixmap          pix;
12        XpmAttributes   attributes;
13        int             status;
14        Display        *dpy = XtDisplay ( shell );
15        Widget          icon_shell, label;
16
17        /*
18         * Create a shell widget, and set mappedWhenManaged to FALSE.
19         * The windowe manager controls when this window is mapped.
20         */
21
22        icon_shell = XtVaAppCreateShell ( "icon_shell", "Icon_shell",
23                                          topLevelShellWidgetClass, dpy,
24                                          XmNmappedWhenManaged, FALSE,
25                                          NULL );
26
27        /*
28         * Create a label to display the pixmap
29         */
30
31        label = XtCreateManagedWidget ( "button",
32                                        xmLabelWidgetClass,
33                                        icon_shell, NULL, 0 );
34
```

```
35      /*
36       * Retrieve the depth and colormap used by this widget
37       * and store the results in the corresponding field
38       * of an XpmAttributes structure.
39       */
40
41      XtVaGetValues ( label,
42                        XmNdepth,     &attributes.depth,
43                        XmNcolormap, &attributes.colormap,
44                        NULL );
45      /*
46       * Specify the visual to be used and set the XpmAttributes mask.
47       */
48
49      attributes.visual = DefaultVisual ( dpy, DefaultScreen ( dpy ) );
50      attributes.valuemask = XpmDepth | XpmColormap | XpmVisual;
51
52      /*
53       * Create the pixmap
54       */
55
56      status = XpmCreatePixmapFromData ( dpy,
57                                          DefaultRootWindow ( dpy ),
58                                          xpmDesc, &pix, NULL,
59                                          &attributes );
60      /*
61       * Install the pixmap in the label
62       */
63
64      if ( status == XpmSuccess )
65         XtVaSetValues ( label,
66                          XmNlabelType,   XmPIXMAP,
67                          XmNlabelPixmap, pix,
68                          NULL );
69      /*
70       * Realize the icon shell to force the shell's window to exist
71       */
72
73      XtRealizeWidget ( icon_shell );
74
75      /*
76       * Install the icon_shell's window as the icon window.
77       */
78
79      XtVaSetValues ( shell, XmNiconWindow,
80                        XtWindow ( icon_shell ), NULL );
81   }
```

14.7 Drag and Drop

Besides supporting data transfer though the Xt selection process and the Motif clipboard, Motif also supports a direct manipulation approach to transferring data that is usually referred to as "drag and drop". For many types of interfaces, drag and drop is a natural way to move data between applications, or even to manipulate data within an application. The technique is most effective when the user interface of the applications involved are based on direct manipulation of objects. For example, the draw program described in Chapter 13 allows the user to select objects and even reposition them within the application's window. With Motif's drag and drop support, these graphical objects could also be dragged between different applications.

When using this technique, the user transfers data from one window to another by selecting an object with the mouse. Then, while holding the mouse button down, the user moves the mouse, which drags the selected item along with the pointer. When the item is over the window to which the user wishes to transfer the data, the user "drops" the item by releasing the mouse button.

Motif's drag and drop mechanism is built on top of the Xt selection facilities, and therefore offers some of the same functionality as the selection mechanism. The primary difference between these facilities is the way in which the user initiates the transfer and the visual effects that occur while setting up the transfer. During the actual transfer, the application in which the drag begins (called the drag *initiator*) is equivalent to the selection owner in the Xt selection model. The application on which the object is dropped (called the *receiver*) is equivalent to the requestor in the Xt selection model. The receiver requests the data as a certain type, and the initiator is expected to convert the data to the requested type and perform the transfer. Motif also allows potential receivers to indicate what types of data they are willing to accept beforehand, and can provide visual feedback about valid drop sites.

With sufficient data conversion facilities, this mechanism can allow drag and drop to be used in a wide variety of situations. For example, consider three very different applications: the draw application, the palette editor described in Chapter 9, and a text editor. Although the data types supported by each of these applications are quite different, drag and drop could still be used to transfer information between these programs. For example, a user could drag a red rectangle out of the draw program and drop it on the text editor. The text editor, which understands only text, might request that the object be transferred as text. In that case, the draw program might provide a text-only description of the object. The user might drag a red rectangle from the drawing editor and drop it over a color item on the color palette editor. The color editor would have no understanding of rectangles, but could ask for the color information associated with the dropped object and could understand "red". On the other hand, dragging a color from the palette editor and dropping it on an object in the draw program could change the color of the object.

Motif supports simple text transfer using drag and drop automatically in many of its widgets. For example, the text in labels, buttons, and text widgets can be dragged. The XmText and XmTextField widgets accept text that is dropped. Items can also be dragged out of the XmList widget. However, other uses of drag and drop are application-specific. The following sections describe the mechanisms provided by Motif to support drag and drop and demonstrates how the draw program from Chapter 13 can be extended to support simple drag and drop.

Protocols

The Motif drag and drop mechanism supports two separate protocols. Applications can support either, both, or none. The two protocols are *preregister* and *dynamic*. Each of the drag initiator and receiver can use either protocol; the actual interaction between the two depends on how the two protocols intersect. In the worst case, no drag effects are provided, but the drag and drop can still take place.

The preregister protocol is intended to be simpler and more efficient than the dynamic protocol. When using the preregister protocol, applications allow Motif to handle all drop site and cursor animation. A drop site preregisters all information about the types of data it is willing to accept. During a drag and drop operation, a drop site that uses the pre-register protocol is not involved in the operation until the drop actually occurs. When using the preregister protocol, the server is grabbed by the initiator, so the drop site cannot manage its own animation effects. This reduces the traffic between the clients and the X server. Some less powerful systems may not perform efficiently enough to handle the dynamic protocol, and may need to support only the preregister protocol.

The dynamic protocol involves more interaction between the drag initiator and receiver to exchange information about the drop site and possible data types. When using the dynamic protocol, the receiver can also choose to handle any animation effects itself, which offers more flexibility. When using the dynamic protocol, the server is not grabbed during the drag, which allows the receiver to make whatever requests are needed.

Which protocol is used depends on the values of two resources for each of the programs involved in the transfer. The resource `XmNdragInitiatorProtocolStyle` controls the protocol used by the initiator, while the value of `XmNdragRecieverProtocolStyle` determines the protocol supported by the receiver. The possible values of these resources are:

- `XmDRAG_NONE`: This value turns off drag and drop support. The client does not participate in drag and drop.

- `XmDRAG_PREREGISTER`: This value specifies that only the preregister protocol should be used.

- `XmDRAG_PREFER_PREREGISTER`: This value specifies that an application should support both protocols, but use the preregister protocol if possible.

- `XmDRAG_PREFER_RECEIVER`: This value applies only to initiators, and specifies that a drag operation should use whatever protocol is supported by the receiver.

- `XmDRAG_PREFER_DYNAMIC`: This value specifies that an application should support both protocols, but use the dynamic protocol if possible.

- `XmDRAG_DYNAMIC`: This value specifies that only the dynamic protocol should be used.

Drop Sites

Before an object can be dropped on a widget, the widget must be registered as a drop site. A drop site must have at least one callback associated with it, which is called when an object is dropped on the drop site. When using the dynamic protocol, drop sites may also register a drag callback that is called continuously as an object is dragged over the drop site. When using the dynamic protocol, the drop site may optionally provide information to the initiator about the validity of the drop site at any time. The drop site may also handle animation effects when using the dynamic protocol. If the preregister protocol is used, Motif handles all effects.

A widget can be registered as a drop site by calling `XmDropSiteRegister()`, which is defined as:

```
void XmDropSiteRegister ( Widget w, ArgList args, Cardinal numArgs )
```

This function accepts many arguments that control how the drop site behaves. These arguments include the following:

- `XmNanimationStyle`: When a dragged object enters a drop site, Motif provides some visual indication that the widget is a valid drop site. The visual effect is controlled by the `XmNanimationStyle` resource. The possible values and corresponding effects are:
  - `XmDRAG_UNDER_HIGHLIGHT`: With a drag under animation style, the drop site is highlighted when an item is dragged over a valid drop site.
  - `XmDRAG_UNDER_SHADOW_OUT`: When this value is specified, the drop site is emphasized with a protruding shadow when an item is dragged over a valid drop site.
  - `XmDRAG_UNDER_SHADOW_IN`: When a drag under shadow animation style is chosen, drop sites emphasized with an inset shadow when an item is dragged over a valid drop site.
  - `XmDRAG_UNDER_PIXMAP`: When this value is specified, the drop site displays the pixmap indicated by the value of the `XmNanimationPixmap`: resource to indicate a valid drop site. The pixmap is drawn starting in the upper left corner of the drop site widget.
  - `XmDRAG_UNDER_NONE`: When a drop site's `XmNanimationStyle` resource is set to `XmDRAG_UNDER_NONE`, no visual effects are provided. Applications that use the dynamic protocol can specify this value and handle their own effects if they wish.
- `XmNanimationPixmap`, `XmNanimationMask`, `XmNanimationPixmapDepth`: These resources allow an application to supply a pixmap and a mask to be displayed when a dragged object enters the drop site, along with the depth of the pixmap. If the depth is one, the colors of the pixmap are taken from the drop site widget. Otherwise, the depth is expected to match the depth of the drop site window.
- `XmNdragProc`: When the dynamic drag and drop protocol is used, applications can register a callback to be called when the dragged object enters, leaves, or moves within the drop site. Applications can use this callback to handle their own animation or other special effects.
- `XmNdropProc`: This resource allows applications to register a callback function to be called when an object is dropped on the drop site.
- `XmNdropRectangles`: Applications can define non-rectangular drop site regions by describing the shape of the drop region as a list of `XRectangle` structures. By default, the value of this resource is `NULL`, in which case the entire widget is used as the drop site.
- `XmNnumRectangles`: The value of this resource must specify the number of `XRectangle` structures in the array given as the `XmNdropRectangles` resource.

- **XmNdropSiteOperations**: This resource specifies the valid operations the drop site is willing to accept. The possible values are:
  - — **XmDROP_COPY**: The data being transferred is to be copied to the drop site.
  - — **XmDROP_MOVE**: The data being transferred is to be moved to the drop site.
  - — **XmDROP_LINK**: The data being transferred is to be linked to the drop site.
  - — **XmDROP_NOOP**: This value effectively disables the drop site; no operations are valid.

  These values can also be combined to allow multiple operations. For example, a value of **XmDROP_COPY | XmDROP_MOVE** allows either copy or move operations.
- **XmNimportTargets**: This resource allows applications to specify an array of atoms that indicate the types of data this drop site can accept.
- **XmNnumImportTargets**: The value of this resource indicates the number of entries in the **XmNimportTargets** array.

The **XmNdropProc** callback function has the same form as other Motif callbacks. This callback function receives a **callData** structure that is defined as follows:

```
typedef struct {
    int           reason;
    XEvent        *event;
    Time          timeStamp;
    Widget        dragContext;
    Position      x;
    Position      y;
    unsigned char dropSiteStatus;
    unsigned char operation;
    unsigned char operations;
    unsigned char dropAction;
} XmDropProcCallbackStruct;
```

The **reason** field of this structure is always set to **XmCR_DROP_MESSAGE**. The **event** member always indicates the event that caused the callback to be called. The **dragContext** member of this structure indicates a widget that is used by Motif to maintain data associated with a drag action. This widget is not visible on the screen; Motif simply uses a widget as a convenient data structure in which to store and manipulate information. The **x** and **y** members indicate the pointer position at the time of the drop.

The **dropSiteStatus** member will be set to **XmDROP_SITE_VALID** if the data types the drop site is prepared to accept are compatible with those the initiator is willing to provide. Otherwise this member is set to **XmDROP_SITE_INVALID**. The drop site callback function may change this member if needed. The **operation** member indicates the operation being performed. The possible values are **XmDROP_MOVE**, **XmDROP_LINK**, **XmDROP_COPY**, and **XmDROP_NOOP**. The **operations** member indicates the possible operations that are available for this transfer. The **dropAction** member indicates the action associated with the drop. The possible values are **XmDROP** and **XmDROP_HELP**. A value of **XmDROP_HELP** means the user has requested help information about this drop site.

The drag callback is passed a call data structure whose type is `XmDragProcCallback-`
`Struct`. This structure is similar to the `XmDropProcCallbackStruct` structure described
above. The only difference is the last member. A Boolean member, `animate`, replaces the
`dropAction` member found in the `XmDropProcCallbackStruct`. This value is to be set by
the callback to indicate whether Motif is to provide animation effects or whether the application will
handle them. If the value of the `animate` member is set to `TRUE`, Motif handles the drag under
effects based on the value of the `XmNanimationStyle` resource.

The `reason` member of the `XmDragProcCallbackStruct` reports the reason the
callback was invoked and can be set to one of the following values:

```
XmCR_DROP_SITE_ENTER_MESSAGE    XmCR_OPERATION_CHANGED_MESSAGE
XmCR_DRAG_MOTION_MESSAGE         XmCR_DROP_SITE_LEAVE_MESSAGE
```

Adding a Drop Site to Draw

To add drag and drop support to the draw program originally described in Chapter 13, several new
functions must be implemented, and some existing functions must be changed. The remainder of this
section demonstrates how the draw program must change to support drag and drop. All changes are
isolated to the file graphics.c. This file must include the header <Xm/DragDrop.h>, which includes
declarations needed by the drag and drop facilities. Next, the declarations at the beginning of the file
must be expanded to include some new functions and several new variables. The file now includes
definitions of several bitmaps that will be used as part of the drag operation. There are also some
new functions that support the drag and drop operations, and some widgets, pixmaps, and atoms that
support the drag and drop process. New code added to support drag and drop is shown in a bold font.

```
1    /*************************************************************
2     * graphics.c: A display list that holds graphics objects
3     *             and associated functions needed to
4     *             display objects in a drawing area widget
5     *************************************************************/
6    #include <Xm/Xm.h>
7    #include <Xm/FileSB.h>
8    #include <stdio.h>
9    #include "draw.h"
10   #include <Xm/CutPaste.h>
11   #include <Xm/DragDrop.h>
12
13   #define MAXOBJECTS 1000 /* The most objects the displayList can hold */
14
15   #define circle_width 16
16   #define circle_height 16
17   static unsigned char circle_bits[] = {
18     0xc0, 0x01, 0x30, 0x06, 0x0c, 0x18, 0x04, 0x10, 0x02, 0x20, 0x02, 0x20,
19     0x01, 0x40, 0x01, 0x40, 0x01, 0x40, 0x02, 0x20, 0x02, 0x20, 0x04, 0x10,
20      0x0c, 0x18, 0x30, 0x06, 0xc0, 0x01, 0x00, 0x00};
21
22   #define filledcircle_width 16
```

```
23  #define filledcircle_height 16
24  static unsigned char filledcircle_bits[] = {
25    0xf0, 0x07, 0xf8, 0x0f, 0xfc, 0x1f, 0xfe, 0x3f, 0xff, 0x7f, 0xff, 0x7f,
26    0xff, 0x7f, 0xff, 0x7f, 0xff, 0x7f, 0xff, 0x7f, 0xff, 0x7f, 0xfe, 0x3f,
27     0xfc, 0x1f, 0xf8, 0x0f, 0xf0, 0x07, 0x00, 0x00};
28
29  #define rectangle_width 16
30  #define rectangle_height 16
31  static unsigned char rectangle_bits[] = {
32    0x00, 0x00, 0xfe, 0x7f, 0x02, 0x40, 0x02, 0x40, 0x02, 0x40, 0x02, 0x40,
33    0x02, 0x40, 0x02, 0x40, 0x02, 0x40, 0x02, 0x40, 0x02, 0x40, 0x02, 0x40,
34     0x02, 0x40, 0x02, 0x40, 0xfe, 0x7f, 0x00, 0x00};
35
36  #define filledrect_width 16
37  #define filledrect_height 16
38  static unsigned char filledrect_bits[] = {
39    0x00, 0x00, 0xfe, 0x7f, 0xfe, 0x7f, 0xfe, 0x7f, 0xfe, 0x7f, 0xfe, 0x7f,
40    0xfe, 0x7f, 0xfe, 0x7f, 0xfe, 0x7f, 0xfe, 0x7f, 0xfe, 0x7f, 0xfe, 0x7f,
41     0xfe, 0x7f, 0xfe, 0x7f, 0xfe, 0x7f, 0x00, 0x00};
42
43  #define line_width 16
44  #define line_height 16
45  static unsigned char line_bits[] = {
46    0x03, 0x00, 0x06, 0x00, 0x0c, 0x00, 0x18, 0x00, 0x30, 0x00, 0x60, 0x00,
47    0xc0, 0x00, 0x80, 0x01, 0x00, 0x03, 0x00, 0x06, 0x00, 0x0c, 0x00, 0x18,
48     0x00, 0x30, 0x00, 0x60, 0x00, 0xc0, 0x00, 0x80};
49
50  Atom    GRAPHICS_OBJECT = NULL;
51  Atom    TARGETS         = NULL;
52  Widget dragIcon;
53  Pixmap dragBitmap;
54
55  static void HandleDrop ( Widget    w,
56                           XtPointer clientData,
57                           XtPointer callData );
58  static void HandleDrag ( Widget    w,
59                           XtPointer clientData,
60                           XtPointer callData );
61  static void StartDrag ( Widget    w,
62                          XtPointer clientData,
63                          XEvent    *event,
64                          Boolean   *continueToDispatch );
65  static void TransferCallback ( Widget            w,
66                          XtPointer         clientData,
67                          Atom              *seltype,
68                          Atom              *type,
69                          XtPointer         value,
70                          unsigned long     *length,
71                          int               *format );
```

```
72  static Boolean ExportObject ( Widget        w,
73                                Atom          *selection,
74                                Atom          *target,
75                                Atom          *type,
76                                XtPointer     *value,
77                                unsigned long *length,
78                                int           *format );
79  static void SetDragIcon ( int type );
80
81  /*
82   * Define a standard type for for all drawing function used in this
83   * module to allow all operation to be invoked with the same API.
84   */
85
86  typedef void ( *DrawingFunction ) ( Window, GC, int, int, int, int );
87
88  /*
89   * Define a data structure that describes a single visible
90   * object in the display list.
91   */
92
93  typedef struct{
94      int            x1, y1, x2, y2;
95      DrawingFunction func;
96      int            figureType;
97      Pixel          foreground;
98      GC             gc;
99  } GraphicsObject;
100
101 /*
102  * The display list is just an array of GraphicsObjects
103  */
104
105 GraphicsObject displayList[MAXOBJECTS];
106
107 /*
108  * Various variables used within this module. All are global to
109  * functions in this file, but static, so as to be hidden from
110  * functions in other parts of the program.
111  */
112
113 static int            nextSlot        = 0;    /* Next free spot
114                                                   in displayList */
115 static GraphicsObject *currentObject  = NULL;/* Pointer to currently
116                                                   selected object */
117 static DrawingFunction currentFunction = NULL; /* Function that draws
118                                                   current figure type */
119 static int            currentFigureType = 0; /* Current figure type
120                                                   being drawn. */
```

```
121  static Display          *display          = NULL;
122  static Colormap          colormap;
123  static GC                currentGC         = NULL;
124  static GC                xorGC             = NULL;
125  static Pixel             currentForeground = 0;
126  static Pixel             background        = 0;
127  static Widget            canvas            = NULL;
128  Position startX = 0, startY = 0, lastX = 0, lastY = 0;
129
130  /*
131   * Functions that draw each figure type using the same arguments
132   */
133
134  static void  DrawLine ( Window, GC, int, int, int, int );
135  static void  DrawCircle ( Window, GC, int, int, int, int );
136  static void  DrawRectangle ( Window, GC, int, int, int, int );
137  static void  DrawFilledCircle ( Window, GC, int, int, int, int );
138  static void  DrawFilledRectangle ( Window, GC, int, int, int, int );
139  void FixDataOrdering ( int *x, int *y, int *x2, int *y2 );
140
141  /*
142   * Functions for "flattening" and "unflattening" an object
143   */
144
145  static GraphicsObject *Unpack ( char *str );
146  static char           *Pack ( GraphicsObject *object );
147
148  /*
149   * Callback functions
150   */
151
152  static void Redisplay ( Widget   w,
153                          XtPointer clientData,
154                          XtPointer callData );
155  static void StartRubberBand ( Widget    w,
156                                XtPointer  clientData,
157                                XEvent    *event,
158                                Boolean   *flag );
159  static void TrackRubberBand ( Widget    w,
160                                XtPointer  clientData,
161                                XEvent    *event,
162                                Boolean   *flag );
163  static void EndRubberBand ( Widget    w,
164                              XtPointer  clientData,
165                              XEvent    *event,
166                              Boolean   *flag );
167  static void LoadDataCallback ( Widget    w,
168                                 XtPointer  clientData,
169                                 XtPointer  callData );
```

```
170   static void CancelDialogCallback ( Widget      w,
171                                       XtPointer   clientData,
172                                       XtPointer   callData );
173   static void SaveDataCallback ( Widget      w,
174                                   XtPointer   clientData,
175                                   XtPointer   callData );
176   /*
177    * Functions for storing, removing, moving and picking objects
178    * in the display list.
179    */
180
181   static void AddObject ( GraphicsObject *object );
182   static void StoreObject ( void );
183   static void MoveObject ( GraphicsObject *object, int x, int y );
184   static GraphicsObject *PickObject ( int x, int y );
185   void CutSelectedItem ( void )
186   void CopySelectedItem ( void )
187   void PasteItem ( void );
188   void RemoveItem ( GraphicsObjects *object );
```

For the rest of this chapter, only new functions and functions that have changed from those described in Chapter 13 are shown. The first function that must be changed is `InitGraphics()`. This function now calls `XmDropSiteRegister()` to register the canvas widget as a drop site. The arguments to this function specify that only copy operations are permitted, and that the only data type supported is identified by the atom `GRAPHICS_OBJECT`. The function `HandleDrop()` is registered as the drop callback, to be called when an object is dropped on the canvas widget. No drag callback is registered for this drop site.

```
189   void InitGraphics ( Widget w )
190   {
191       XGCValues  values;
192       Arg        args[10];
193       Atom       targets[1];
194       int        n;
195
196       /*
197        * Remember the given widget for use by other functions.
198        * Retrieve the display and colormap for later use.
199        */
200
201       canvas = w;
202
203       display = XtDisplay ( canvas );
204       XtVaGetValues ( canvas, XmNcolormap, &colormap, NULL );
205
206       GRAPHICS_OBJECT = XInternAtom ( display, "GraphicsObject",
207                                       FALSE );
208       TARGETS = XInternAtom ( display, "TARGETS", FALSE );
```

```
209
210        targets[0] = GRAPHICS_OBJECT;
211
212        n = 0;
213        XtSetArg ( args[n], XmNdropSiteOperations, XmDROP_COPY ); n++;
214        XtSetArg ( args[n], XmNimportTargets,      targets ); n++;
215        XtSetArg ( args[n], XmNnumImportTargets,   1 ); n++;
216        XtSetArg ( args[n], XmNdropProc,           HandleDrop ); n++;
217        XmDropSiteRegister ( canvas, args, n );
218
219        /*
220         * Register a callback to redraw the display list when the
221         * window is exposed, and event handlers to handle adding
222         * new objects to the display list interactively
223         */
224
225        XtAddCallback ( canvas, XmNexposeCallback, Redisplay, NULL );
226
227        XtAddEventHandler ( canvas, ButtonPressMask, FALSE,
228                            StartRubberBand, NULL );
229        XtAddEventHandler ( canvas, ButtonPressMask, FALSE,
230                            StartDrag, NULL );
231        XtAddEventHandler ( canvas, ButtonMotionMask, FALSE,
232                            TrackRubberBand, NULL );
233        XtAddEventHandler ( canvas, ButtonReleaseMask, FALSE,
234                            EndRubberBand, NULL );
235        /*
236         * Get the colors of the canvas.
237         */
238
239        XtVaGetValues ( canvas,
240                        XmNforeground, &currentForeground,
241                        XmNbackground, &background,
242                        NULL );
243        /*
244         * Fill in the values structure
245         */
246
247        values.foreground = currentForeground ^ background;
248        values.function   = GXxor;
249
250        /*
251         * Set the rubber band gc to use XOR
252         */
253
254        xorGC =  XtGetGC ( canvas,
255                           GCForeground | GCFunction,
256                           &values );
257  }
```

This version of `InitGraphics()` also adds an additional event handler, `StartDrag()`, which handles the process of initiating a drag in the draw program. `StartDrag()` is described on page 511 along with the discussion of the drag process.

Handling the Drop

Once a drop has occurred, the callback specified in the call to `XmDropSiteRegister()` is invoked. This callback function is expected to check the type of the drop, as indicated by the `dropAction` member of the `callData` structure provided to the callback. If the type is `XmDROP_HELP`, the callback should post a help dialog that provides information about the drop site. If the drop site is not valid for any reason, the callback should cancel the operation. Otherwise, the drop callback initiates the transfer by calling `XmDropTransferStart()`. The function `XmDropTransferStart()` is defined as:

```
Widget XmDropTransferStart ( Widget w, ArgList args, Cardinal numArgs )
```

The first argument indicates a drag context widget, which can be obtained from the `callData` passed to the drop callback function.

The arguments that can be passed to `XmDropTransferStart()` include the following:

- `XmNdropTransfers`: This member must be an array of structures of type `XmDrop-TransferEnryRec`, which is defined as:

```
typedef struct {
   XtPointer client_data;
   Atom      target;
} XmDropTransferEntryRec;
```

  This array indicates the types of data the drop site would like to receive and specifies some client data to be passed to the callback that receives the transferred data.

- `XmNnumDropTransfers`: The value of this resource indicates the number of entries in the `XmNdropTransfers` array.

- `XmNtransferProc`: This resource indicates a callback function to be called to receive the transferred data. The type of this function is `XtSelectionCallbackProc`. (See page 468.) As in the Xt selection model, this function is called when data has been transferred and is available for the application to process.

The draw program registers `HandleDrop()` to be called when a drop is made in the draw program's canvas widget. This function checks to see if the drop action is `XmDROP_HELP`. In this example, the draw program does not implement any help and `HandleDrop()` just indicates that the drop is invalid and returns. Next, the function checks to see if the operation includes `XmDROP_COPY`. If not, the function sets the `dropSiteStatus` member of the `callData` structure to `XmINVALID_DROP_SITE`, and also initializes an `ArgList` to indicate that the number of drop operations requested is zero.

If the drop site is valid and the drop operation is `XmDROP_COPY`, `HandleDrop()` uses `XtVaGetValues()` to retrieve the targets exported by the initiator from the drag context widget specified by the call data. If one of the exported types is GRAPHICS_OBJECT, HandleDrop() fills out an XmDropTransferEntryRec structure that indicates the GRAPHICS_OBJECT target type. This structure also stores a pointer to a client data structure that records the location of the drop. HandleDrop() then sets the requested action, as indicated in the dropAction member of the callData structure, to XmDROP_COPY and specifies TransferCallback() as the callback function that will receive the data when it arrives. HandleDrop() finally calls XmDropTransferStart() to begin the transfer.

All functions from this point on are completely new, so these functions are not shown in bold font.

```
258   static void HandleDrop ( Widget      w,
259                                XtPointer clientData,
260                                XtPointer callData )
261   {
262       XmDropProcCallbackStruct *cb =
263                              ( XmDropProcCallbackStruct * ) callData;
264       Arg          args[10];
265       int          n = 0;
266       static XPoint              dropPosition;
267       XmDropTransferEntryRec transfer_entries[2];
268
269       /*
270        * Check to see if the user asked for help. This function should
271        * provide some help information, but for this demo, just indicate
272        * that the drop is invalid and return.
273        */
274
275       if ( cb->dropAction == XmDROP_HELP )
276       {
277           cb->dropSiteStatus = XmINVALID_DROP_SITE;
278           return;
279       }
280
281       /*
282        * Make sure that this is a drop and that the drop action
283        * can be a copy. If not, indicate failure and that no
284        * transfers should be made.
285        */
286
287       if  ( cb->dropAction != XmDROP || cb->operation  != XmDROP_COPY )
288       {
289           n = 0;
290           cb->operation     = XmDROP_NOOP;
291           cb->dropSiteStatus = XmINVALID_DROP_SITE;
292           XtSetArg ( args[n], XmNtransferStatus,
293                             XmTRANSFER_FAILURE ); n++;
294           XtSetArg ( args[n], XmNnumDropTransfers, 0 ); n++;
295       }
```

```
296         else
297         {
298           /*
299            * If this is a valid drop, find out what types of data the
300            * initiator is supporting.
301            */
302
303           Atom *targets;
304           int  numTargets;
305           int  i;
306
307           XtVaGetValues ( cb->dragContext,
308                           XmNexportTargets,    &targets,
309                           XmNnumExportTargets, &numTargets,
310                           NULL );
311           /*
312            * Loop through each exported type, checking to see if there
313            * is type we are interested in. In this case, the only
314            * supported type is GRAPHICS_OBJECT.
315            */
316
317           for ( i = 0; i < numTargets; i++ )
318               if ( targets[i] == GRAPHICS_OBJECT )
319               {
320                 /*
321                  * Fill in a structure that can be used to remember
322                  * the location of the drop so the Transfer callback
323                  * can positon the object in the right place.
324                  */
325
326                 dropPosition.x =  cb->x;
327                 dropPosition.y =  cb->y;
328
329                 /*
330                  * Initialize the transfer information.
331                  */
332
333                 transfer_entries[0].target = GRAPHICS_OBJECT;
334                 transfer_entries[0].client_data = &dropPosition;
335
336                 XtSetArg ( args[n], XmNdropTransfers,
337                                     transfer_entries ); n++;
338                 XtSetArg ( args[n], XmNnumDropTransfers, 1 ); n++;
339
340                 /*
341                  * Specify that TransferCallback should be called
342                  * when the data has actually been transferred.
343                  */
344
```

```
345                    XtSetArg ( args[n], XmNtransferProc,
346                                      TransferCallback ); n++;
347             cb->operation = XmDROP_COPY;
348             break;
349          }
350     }
351
352     /*
353      * Notify the intiator to start the transfer.
354      */
355
356     XmDropTransferStart ( cb->dragContext, args, n );
357  }
```

When the transfer is complete, the function `TransferCallback()` is invoked to handle the data. This function retrieves the data transferred from the initiator, and adds the object to this program's display list. The information passed as client data is used to reposition the graphics object at the position at which the drop occurred.

```
358  static void TransferCallback ( Widget        w,
359                                 XtPointer     clientData,
360                                 Atom          *seltype,
361                                 Atom          *type,
362                                 XtPointer     value,
363                                 unsigned long *length,
364                                 int           *format )
365  {
366      if ( value )
367      {
368          int width, height;
369
370          /*
371           * Get the point at which the drop occurred, and
372           * unpack the transferred data to create a GraphicsObject.
373           */
374
375          XPoint *dropPosition =  ( XPoint * ) clientData;
376          GraphicsObject *object = Unpack ( ( char * ) value );
377
378          /*
379           * Adjust the location of the object to match the
380           * drop site location.
381           */
382
383          width    = object->x2 - object->x1;
384          height   = object->y2 - object->y1;
385
386          object->x1 = dropPosition->x;
```

```
387              object->y1 = dropPosition->y;
388              object->x2 = object->x1 + width;
389              object->y2 = object->y1 + height;
390
391          /*
392           * Add the object to the display list.
393           */
394
395          AddObject ( object );
396      }
397  }
```

This completes the steps needed to make the draw program's canvas widget function as a drop site. Any program that can drop the type GRAPHICS_OBJECT, as defined by the draw program, can drop objects onto the canvas widget. In this example, the features of the dynamic protocol are not exercised. The drop site could register a drag callback and handle animation and other visual feedback itself. Interaction with the other objects in the display list is also possible. For example, the draw program might introduce some constraints on what objects can be dropped on top of other objects. In this case, the dynamic protocol could be used to communicate when the drop site is valid and when it is invalid.

Initiating a Drag

The initiator is responsible for starting the drag operation. In the draw example, the draw program can be both an initiator and a receiver.

To start a drag, a program must call XmDragStart(). This function is defined as:

```
Widget XmDragStart ( Widget widget, XEvent *event,
                     ArgList args, Cardinal numArgs )
```

The widget argument must be the smallest widget that encloses the object being dragged. The event parameter must be the ButtonPress event that triggered the drag. The args parameter allows the application to customize the drag operation by supplying an array of resource values. These resources can be used to alter the behavior of the drag operation. These resources can be separated into several categories. The following resources allow the application to control the appearance of the drag cursor.

- XmNblendModel: By default, the cursor shown during a drag operation consists of three separate sections, blended together to look like one cursor. The three parts are the *source* icon, the *state* icon, and the *operation* icon. The source icon represents the type of data being transferred. The state icon changes dynamically during the drag to show whether the object can be dropped at any particular location. The operation icon can be used to show what operation will take place when the drop occurs (move, copy, or link). Dynamic changes to the drag cursor during the drag operation are known as *drag over effects*. The XmNblendModel resource determines how the three parts of the drag cursor are combined. The possible values are:

— `XmBLEND_ALL`: This is the default value, which shows all three icons in the drag cursor.

— `XmBLEND_STATE_SOURCE`: If this value is specified, only the state and source icons are shown. The operation icon is not shown.

— `XmBLEND_JUST_SOURCE`: When `XmNblendModel` is set to `XmBLEND_JUST_-SOURCE`, only the source icon is shown.

— `XmBLEND_NONE`: This value specifies that none of the standard icons are used. The initiator can use the various callbacks supported when using the dynamic protocol to control the drag over visuals.

- `XmNcursorBackground`: This resource allows the initiator to set the background color of the drag cursor.

- `XmNcursorForeground`: This resource allows the initiator to set the foreground color of the drag cursor when the state icon is not included in the drag cursor.

- `XmNvalidCursorForeground`: The value of this resource determines the color of the drag cursor when the cursor is over a valid drop site.

- `XmNinvalidCursorForeground`: This resource allows the initiator to specify the color of the drag cursor when the state is invalid. This occurs when the drag cursor is over a potential drop site, but the drop site cannot support the data types or operations supplied by the initiator.

- `XmNnoneCursorForeground`: This resource allows the initiator to specify the color of the drag cursor when the state is none. This occurs when the drag cursor is not over a potential drop site.

- `XmNoperationCursorIcon`: This resource allows the initiator to supply a custom icon for the operation part of the drag cursor.

- `XmNsourceCursorIcon`: This resource allows the initiator to supply a custom icon to be used for the source icon when the dynamic protocol is used.

- `XmNsourcePixmapIcon`: When the preregister protocol is used, the source icon can be a pixmap, specified by the value of this resource. If this resource is not set, the cursor specified by `XmNsourceCursorIcon` is used.

- `XmNstateCursorIcon`: This resource allows the initiator to specify an icon for the state portion of the drag cursor.

The following resources allow the initiator to provide information about the nature of the drag to facilitate communication between the initiator and receiver.

- `XmNdragOperations`: This resource indicates the valid operations supported by the initiator. This value should be the inclusive OR of `XmDRAG_COPY`, `XmDRAG_MOVE`, `XmDRAG_LINK`, and/or `XmDRAG_NOOP`.

- `XmNexportTargets`: This resource must be set to a list of atoms that indicates the types the initiator can supply.

- `XmNnumExportTargets`: This resource specifies the number of target atoms specified in the `XmNexportTargets` resource.

The initiator must specify a conversion procedure to be called when the receiver requests data once the drop has taken place. The following resources allow the initiator to specify this function and any associated call data.

- `XmNclientData`: This resource allows the initiator to specify some data to be passed to the function registered using the `XmNconvertProc` resource.
- `XmNconvertProc`: The value of this resource must be a callback function that can convert the data owned by the initiator to the type requested by the receiver when a transfer occurs.

The initiator can also register various callbacks that are called as the drag progresses. The initiator can use these callbacks to handle the drag visuals or provide other effects.

- `XmNtopLevelEnterCallback`: This resource allows the initiator to register a list of callbacks to be invoked when the drag cursor enters a top-level window.
- `XmNtopLevelLeaveCallback`: This resource allows the initiator to register a list of callbacks to be invoked when the drag cursor leaves a top-level window.
- `XmNdragDropFinishCallback`: This resource allows the initiator to register a list of callbacks to be invoked when the drag/drop transaction is finished.
- `XmNdragMotionCallback`: This resource allows the initiator to register a list of callbacks to be called when the drag cursor moves.
- `XmNdropFinishedCallback`: This resource allows the initiator to register a list of callbacks to be called when the drop has been completed.
- `XmNdropStartCallback`: This resource allows the initiator to register a list of callbacks to be called when the drop transaction begins.
- `XmNdropSiteEnterCallback`: This resource allows the initiator to register a list of callbacks to be called when the drag cursor enters a drop site.
- `XmNdropSiteLeaveCallback`: This resource allows the initiator to register a list of callbacks to be called when the drag cursor enters a drop site.
- `XmNoperationChangedCallback`: This resource allows the initiator to register a list of callbacks to be invoked when the user requests that the operation be changed during a drag.

Initiating a Drag in the Draw Program

Changing the draw program to allow dragging of the graphics objects is straightforward. The modified version of `InitGraphics()`, described in the previous section, adds an event handler, `StartDrag()` that is invoked when a `ButtonPress` event occurs. `StartDrag()` finds the object, if any, located under the pointer. Once an object is found, `StartDrag()` calls an auxiliary function, `SetDragIcon()`, to initialize a global pixmap used as part of the drag cursor. `StartDrag()` then initializes an `ArgList`, specifying the function to be called to export the data when a drop occurs, the cursor to be used, the valid operations, and the data types the program can export. Finally, `StartDrag()` passes this information to `XmDragStart()` to initiate the drag operation.

```
398   static void StartDrag ( Widget     w,
399                            XtPointer clientData,
400                            XEvent    *event,
401                            Boolean   *continueToDispatch )
402   {
403
404       Widget drag_context;
405       Arg    args[10];
406       int    n;
407       Atom   targets[1];
408       Pixmap icon;
409       GraphicsObject *item;
410
411       if ( event->xbutton.button != Button2 )
412           return;
413
414       /*
415        * Find the object under the pointer.
416        */
417
418       item = PickObject ( event->xbutton.x,
419                           event->xbutton.y );
420
421       if ( !item )
422           return;
423
424       /*
425        * Set the global variable, dragIcon, to a pixmap that
426        * represents the type of object being dragged.
427        */
428
429       SetDragIcon ( item->figureType );
430
431       /*
432        * Indicate the types of data we can transfer.
433        */
434
435       targets[0] = GRAPHICS_OBJECT;
436
437       /*
438        * Set up the arguments to the drag. Specify a function to
439        * be called to export the object, provide a drag icon,
440        * and specify the supported data types.Also indicate
441        * that a drop will only result in a copy and pass the
442        * object being dragged as client data so that it is available
443        * to ExportObject() when it is called.
444        */
445
```

```
446        n = 0;
447        XtSetArg ( args[n], XmNconvertProc,      ExportObject ); n++;
448        XtSetArg ( args[n], XmNsourceCursorIcon, dragIcon ); n++;
449        XtSetArg ( args[n], XmNexportTargets,    targets ); n++;
450        XtSetArg ( args[n], XmNnumExportTargets, 1 ); n++;
451        XtSetArg ( args[n], XmNclientData,       item ); n++;
452        XtSetArg ( args[n], XmNdragOperations,   XmDROP_COPY ); n++;
453
454        /*
455         * Start the drag.
456         */
457
458        drag_context = XmDragStart ( w, event, args, n );
459    }
```

When the drop occurs, the receiver calls `XmDropTransferStart()`, which results in a call
to the initiator's `XmNconvertProc` function to convert the data to the appropriate type. The draw
program registers the function `ExportObject()` to handle this task. This function works like an
Xt selection callback function. `ExportObject()` first checks to see if the requested type is the
atom `TARGETS`. If so, the function returns an array of types this program can support. The draw
program supports only the `GRAPHICS_OBJECT` type, so an array of length one is provided.

If the request is for an object of type `GRAPHICS_OBJECT`, `ExportObject()` retrieves the
client data from the drag context widget passed to this function. This client data is a pointer to the
currently selected object, as set up in `StartDrag()`. `ExportObject()` calls the `Pack()`
function described in Chapter 13 to pack an object into a string and returns this string as the value
of the transferred data.

Once the data has been exported, the receiver's `XmNtransferProc` callback is invoked to
receive the data.

```
460    static Boolean ExportObject ( Widget        w,
461                                   Atom          *selection,
462                                   Atom          *target,
463                                   Atom          *type,
464                                   XtPointer     *value,
465                                   unsigned long *length,
466                                   int           *format )
467    {
468        GraphicsObject *object;
469        char           *str;
470
471        if ( *target == TARGETS )
472        {
473            static Atom targets[1];
474            targets[0] = GRAPHICS_OBJECT;
475
476            *value = ( XtPointer ) targets;
477            *format = 32;
```

```
478              *length = 1;
479              *type   = TARGETS;
480
481              return ( TRUE );
482          }
483          else if ( *target == GRAPHICS_OBJECT )
484          {
485
486              /*
487               * Retrieve the object stored in the clientData resource
488               * and convert the object to a string format for transmission
489               * to the drop site.
490               */
491
492              XtVaGetValues ( w, XmNclientData, &object, NULL );
493
494              str = Pack ( object );
495
496              *type   = XA_STRING;
497              *format = 8;
498              *value  = str;
499              *length = strlen ( str ) + 1;
500
501              return ( TRUE );
502          }
503
504          return ( FALSE );
505      }
```

Customizing the Drag Cursor

Motif allows the initiator to specify icons to be used as the different parts of the drag cursor. These icons must be created by the function XmCreateDragIcon(), which is defined as:

```
Widget XmCreateDragIcon ( Widget   w,
                          String   name,
                          ArgList  args,
                          Cardinal numArgs )
```

This function returns a widget which is used to represent an icon, and that allows the icon's appearance to be controlled by various resources. These resources include:

- XmNdepth: This resource specifies the depth of the pixmap used by the icon.
- XmNmask: This resource allows a mask to be specified for the given pixmap.
- XmNpixmap: This resource specifies the pixmap to be used in the icon.
- XmNwidth, XmNheight: These resources specify the width and height of the icon.

The draw program sets the source cursor each time an object is dragged, so that the shapes of the source cursor matches the shape of the object being dragged. The images used for these icons are defined as bitmaps at the beginning of the file graphics.c. The function SetDragIcon() takes a figure type and creates an XmDragIcon to display that shape. Only one XmDragIcon is required; once an icon exists, SetDragIcon() uses XtVaSetValues() to customize the icon as needed.

```
506   static void SetDragIcon ( int type )
507   {
508       /*
509        * Create a pixmap for a specified figure type, and install
510        * the result in an XmDragIcon widget. Do lazy evaluation
511        * so pixmaps are not created unless they are needed. Reuse the
512        * same pixmaps once they have been created.
513        */
514
515       static Pixmap lineBitmap = 0;
516       static Pixmap circleBitmap = 0;
517       static Pixmap rectBitmap = 0;
518       static Pixmap filledRectBitmap = 0;
519       static Pixmap filledCircleBitmap = 0;
520       Pixmap pixmap;
521       int    width, height, n;
522       Arg    args[10];
523       Window root = RootWindowOfScreen ( XtScreen ( canvas ) );
524
525       switch ( type )
526       {
527         case LINE:
528
529           if ( !lineBitmap )
530               lineBitmap = XCreateBitmapFromData ( display, root,
531                                                    line_bits,
532                                                    line_width,
533                                                    line_height );
534           width  = line_width;
535           height = line_height;
536           pixmap = lineBitmap;
537           break;
538
539         case CIRCLE:
540
541           if ( !circleBitmap )
542               circleBitmap = XCreateBitmapFromData ( display, root,
543                                                      circle_bits,
544                                                      circle_width,
545                                                      circle_height );
546           width  = circle_width;
547           height = circle_height;
```

```
548                 pixmap = circleBitmap;
549                 break;
550
551             case RECTANGLE:
552
553                 if ( !rectBitmap )
554                     rectBitmap = XCreateBitmapFromData ( display, root,
555                                                          rectangle_bits,
556                                                          rectangle_width,
557                                                          rectangle_height );
558                 width  = rectangle_width;
559                 height = rectangle_height;
560                 pixmap = rectBitmap;
561                 break;
562
563             case FILLEDCIRCLE:
564
565                 if ( !filledCircleBitmap )
566                     filledCircleBitmap =
567                             XCreateBitmapFromData ( display, root,
568                                                     filledcircle_bits,
569                                                     filledcircle_width,
570                                                     filledcircle_height );
571                 width  = filledcircle_width;
572                 height = filledcircle_height;
573                 pixmap = filledCircleBitmap;
574                 break;
575
576             case FILLEDRECTANGLE:
577
578                 if ( !filledRectBitmap )
579                     filledRectBitmap =
580                             XCreateBitmapFromData ( display, root,
581                                                     filledrect_bits,
582                                                     filledrect_width,
583                                                     filledrect_height );
584                 width  = filledrect_width;
585                 height = filledrect_height;
586                 pixmap = filledRectBitmap;
587                 break;
588         }
589
590         if ( !dragIcon )
591         {
592             /*
593              * Create a drag icon the first time this function is called.
594              * Afterwards, just change resources for this icon widget.
595              */
596
```

```
597           n = 0;
598           XtSetArg ( args[n], XmNwidth,      width ); n++;
599           XtSetArg ( args[n], XmNheight,     height ); n++;
600           XtSetArg ( args[n], XmNpixmap,     pixmap ); n++;
601           XtSetArg ( args[n], XmNmask,       pixmap ); n++;
602           dragIcon = XmCreateDragIcon ( canvas, "dragIcon", args, n );
603       }
604       else
605           XtVaSetValues ( dragIcon,
606                           XmNwidth,  width,
607                           XmNheight, height,
608                           XmNpixmap, pixmap,
609                           XmNmask,   pixmap,
610                           NULL );
611   }
```

14.8 Summary

This chapter discusses various facilities that allow X applications to communicate with each other. Atoms provide an efficient way to compare strings and are often used to specify strings that must be recognized by multiple applications. Among other things, atoms can be used to identify properties, property types, and types of client messages.

Properties are collections of data, stored in the server. Every property has a name and also an associated atom that identifies the type of the data stored in the property. The X server does not interpret the data in a property, allowing applications to store and retrieve any series of bytes.

Client messages allow applications to define new event types, which applications use to communicate directly with other applications. Client messages are typed using atoms, and applications that use client messages must agree on the format and meaning of the messages.

X also provides support for exchanging typed data, using selections. Applications can claim ownership of a selection or request the owner to convert the selection to a particular type and transfer it. The server automatically handles notifications between the owner of the selection and applications requesting its contents, or applications seeking to become the owner of the selection.

Motif provides a higher-level model for exchanging data that involves copying data to and from a clipboard. In addition, Motif provides a drag and drop facility that allows direct transfer to be indicated by direct manipulation of objects on the screen.

Chapter 15

Creating New Widget Classes

Chapters 1 through 14 discuss ways to build user interfaces by combining suitable widgets from the Motif widget set, defining a few callbacks and event handlers, and occasionally using Xlib functions. These techniques are adequate for many, and perhaps even most, applications. However, many programmers eventually find that they need a user interface component not supplied by any existing widget set. In this case, the programmer can use the architecture and mechanisms supported by Xt to create a new widget class. After a brief overview of the internal architecture of a typical widget, this chapter presents an example that illustrates how to create a new widget class.

Widgets fall into three major categories. This chapter examines the simplest type of widget: those used primarily to display information. Chapter 16 presents an example of a widget that manages other widgets, and Chapter 17 discusses manager widgets that use *constraints* to control the geometry of their children.

Each example widget presented in this book is implemented as a subclass of a Motif widget class. The simplest widget, described in this chapter, is a subclass of the Motif XmPrimitive widget class. The widgets presented in Chapters 16 and 17 are subclasses of the XmManager widget class.

Writing a widget is a complex and specialized task, and the material in this and the following chapters can only introduce and demonstrate the basic concepts. For more details about the internal architecture of Xt, and the various considerations involved in writing a widget, readers should refer to *The X Window System Toolkit*, by Paul Asente and Ralph Swick. This extensive reference provides detailed information about every aspect of widget writing. However, the Asente/Swick book only describes how to write Xt-based widgets. Motif adds several features to the basic Xt architecture, and requires additional work for programmers who want to create Motif-based widgets. Unfortunately, as this book is being written, there is no official documentation that describes how to write a Motif widget. Such documentation is expected in a future version of Motif.

15.1 The Architecture of a Widget

Applications, such as those described in earlier chapters, treat widgets as "black boxes" that can be manipulated only through functions such as `XtSetValues()`, `XtManageChild()`, and so on. Applications use a well-defined Xt interface to interact with widgets, with no direct access to the internal structure of the widget. The way a programmer writes a new type of widget is dramatically different from the way programmers work with existing widgets to develop applications. Different rules apply, different functions are available, and different issues must be dealt with.

Xt defines the basic internal architecture of a widget. This architecture defines the interface between all widgets and Xt and allows widgets built by different programmers to work together smoothly. Xt defines an object-oriented architecture that organizes widgets into classes. From a widget programmer's viewpoint, a class consists of some private data structures and a set of procedures that operate on that data. Using object-oriented terminology, these procedures are referred to as *methods*.

Every widget consists of two basic elements, a *class part* and an *instance-specific part*. Each of these elements is implemented as a C structure that contains data and pointers to methods. Xt defines the organization of each structure. All widgets that belong to the same class share a single copy of the data and methods in the class part, while each individual widget has its own copy of the data in the instance-specific part.

The structure that contains the class part of a widget is known as the *class record*, while the structure that contains the instance-specific part is referred to as the *instance record*. A widget's class record is usually allocated and initialized statically at compile time, while a unique copy of the instance record is created at run time for each individual widget. The following sections discuss the organization and purpose of each of these widget components.

The Widget Class Record

A widget's class record contains data and methods that are common to all widgets that belong to the class. Since all widgets that belong to the same class share the same class record, the class record must contain only static data that does not relate directly to the state of any individual widget. For example, every widget's class record includes a member that contains the widget's class name. The class record also contains methods that define the appearance and behavior of all widgets in the class. Although most of these methods operate on the data in the widget's instance record, the methods themselves are part of the class record and are shared by all widgets that belong to a class.

All widget classes are subclasses of the Core widget class. This means, among other things, that the members of the Core widget's class record and instance record are included in the corresponding records of all other widget classes. The Core widget's class record is defined as follows:

```
typedef struct {
    CoreClassPart    core_class;
} WidgetClassRec, *WidgetClass;
```

The widget class pointer for Core is declared as a pointer to the Core widget's class record:

```
WidgetClass widgetClass;
```

This is the class pointer that applications use as the `class` argument to `XtCreateWidget()`. For example, an application could create a Core widget as follows:

```
Widget w = XtCreateWidget ( "sample", widgetClass, parent, NULL, 0 );
```

The Core widget's class record contains a single member, `core_class`, which is also a structure, `CoreClassPart`. `CoreClassPart` is a structure that defines the per-class data and methods that belong to the Core widget class. The `CoreClassPart` structure is defined as follows:

```
typedef struct _CoreClassPart {
    WidgetClass       superclass;
    String            class_name;
    Cardinal          widget_size;
    XtProc            class_initialize;
    XtWidgetClassProc class_part_initialize;
    Boolean           class_inited;
    XtInitProc        initialize;
    XtArgsProc        initialize_hook;
    XtRealizeProc     realize;
    XtActionList      actions;
    Cardinal          num_actions;
    XtResourceList    resources;
    Cardinal          num_resources;
    XrmClass          xrm_class;
    Boolean           compress_motion;
    Boolean           compress_exposure;
    Boolean           compress_enterleave;
    Boolean           visible_interest;
    XtWidgetProc      destroy;
    XtWidgetProc      resize;
    XtExposeProc      expose;
    XtSetValuesFunc   set_values;
    XtArgsFunc        set_values_hook;
    XtAlmostProc      set_values_almost;
    XtArgsProc        get_values_hook;
    XtWidgetProc      accept_focus;
    XtVersionType     version;
    _XtOffsetList     *callback_private;
    String            tm_table;
```

```
    XtGeometryHandler  query_geometry;
    XtStringProc       display_accelerator;
    XtPointer          extension;
} CoreClassPart;
```

The members of this structure can be separated into two basic categories: class data and pointers to functions. The data members include:

- **superclass:**. This member is a pointer to the class record defined by the widget's *superclass*. This member is used by Xt to support inheritance among widget classes.

- **class_name:** This member is a string that indicates the name of the class. A widget's class name is used by the resource manager when it retrieves a widget's resources. For the Core widget class, the **class_name** member is initialized to "Core".

- **widget_size:** The **widget_size** member indicates the size of a widget's instance record structure. The value of this member is usually determined by calling **sizeof( )**.

- **class_inited:** This member is a Boolean value that indicates whether this class structure has been initialized. A widget's class structure is initialized only once. Programmers must always initialize this member to **FALSE**. Xt will set it to **TRUE** once the class has been initialized.

- **actions:** This member points to a list of actions supported by the widget class. A widget class's action list is used by the translation manager to associate various functions with user input. See Chapter 2 for more information about translations.

- **num_actions:** This member indicates the length of the **actions** list.

- **resources:** This member is an array of resources used by all widgets that belong to this class. The resource manager uses the **resources** list to initialize each widget's instance record at run time.

- **num_resources:** This member indicates the length of the resource list.

- **xrm_class:** This member is a private data field that contains a compiled representation of the widget's class name. The compiled name is used by the resource manager.

- **compress_motion:** This member is a **Boolean** value that indicates whether Xt should compress mouse motion events for this widget.

- **compress_exposure:** This member indicates whether Xt should compress **Expose** events for instances of this widget class. The possible values include:

  — **XtExposeNoCompress:** If this value is specified, no compression is performed.

  — **XtExposeCompressSeries:** When this value is specified, all **Expose** events in a series are combined into a single event. The event is dispatched when the **count** member of the **Expose** event is zero.

  — **XtExposeCompressMultiple:** When this value is specified, Xt attempts to combine multiple series of events into a single event. In addition to compressing events while the event's **count** field is non-zero, Xt looks at the event queue to examine the next **Expose** event. If the queue is empty, or the next **Expose** event is for a different window, Xt dispatches the event.

— XtExposeCompressMaximal: When this value is given, Xt attempts to combine multiple series of events into a single event. The behavior associated with this value is similar to that associated with XtExposeCompressMultiple, but Xt looks attempts to combine non-contiguous events for the same widget.

- compress_enterleave: This member is a Boolean value that indicates whether EnterNotify and LeaveNotify events should be reported to this widget if there are no other events between them.

- visible_interest: This member is a Boolean value that indicates whether Xt should keep track of when instances of this class are visible.

- version: This member indicates the version of Xt on which this widget is based. This member is usually set to the constant XtVersion. Xt checks this member at run time to ensure that the version of Xt with which the widget was compiled matches the version of Xt with which the application is linked. Widget writers who are sure their widgets will work with multiple versions of Xt can set this field to XtVersionDontCheck.

The remaining members of the Core class record are pointers to functions that determine the behavior of the Core widget class. These members include:

- class_initialize: This member specifies a function to be called when the first instance of a widget class is created. The function is expected to perform any one-time operations that might be required by the class.

- class_part_initialize: This member specifies a function to be called when the first instance of a widget is created. This function is similar to the class_initialize function, except that it is passed a pointer to the widget class record and can operate on the members of this structure.

- initialize: This member points to a function that is called when each instance of a widget class is created. This function is expected to initialize the new widget's instance record.

- initialize_hook: The member is obsolete and is no longer used.

- realize: This member points to a function that is called to create an X window for a widget. Most widget classes inherit this method from the Core widget class.

- destroy: This member points to a function to be called when a widget is destroyed. The function is expected to free any memory allocated by the widget.

- resize: This member indicates a function to be called when the widget is resized.

- expose: This member indicates a function to be called when a widget's window needs to be redrawn.

- set_values: This member specifies a function to be called to process changes in a widget's resources as a result of a call to XtSetValues().

- set_values_hook: This member is obsolete and is no longer used.

- set_values_almost: This member points to a function that can be called if an attempt to change a widget's geometry, via a call to XtSetValues(), fails. Most widgets inherit the set_values_almost method.

- `accept_focus`: This member specifies a function that handles input focus. Motif widgets never use this mechanism and should set this member to `NULL`.

- `query_geometry`: This member points to a function that can be called to determine a widget's preferred size.

Every widget class must define these methods in one way or another. These methods are often inherited from the widget's superclass, and some may also be specified as `NULL` if the widget class does not require the particular method. Section 15.3 discusses each type of method in more detail within the context of an example widget.

The Instance Record

Each individual widget has its own copy of a structure known as an *instance record*. The instance record maintains information about the current state of the specific widget. For example, every widget's instance record contains the window ID of the widget's window, and also the current size and location of the window. The instance record also contains a pointer to the widget's class record. Figure 15.1 illustrates this architecture, showing the relationship between the class record and instance records of several widgets that belong to the Core widget class.

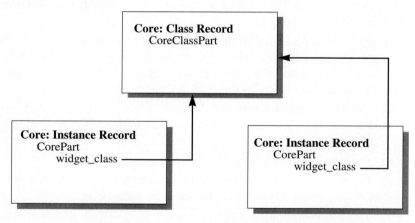

Figure 15.1 Class architecture of a widget.

The Core widget class's instance record is defined as:

```
typedef struct{
    CorePart core;
} WidgetRec, *Widget;
```

From this definition, one might guess that when an application declares a variable of type `Widget`, it is declaring the variable as a pointer to the widget's instance record. This is true, but applications do not have access to this exact definition, because Xt uses data abstraction techniques to hide the definition of the widget structure. The `Widget` type used by applications is declared as a pointer to an undefined structure:

```
typedef struct _WidgetRec *Widget;
```

The function `XtCreateWidget()` returns a pointer to a dynamically allocated copy of the instance record. Xt obtains the size of the instance record from the `widget_size` member of the class record.

The Core widget's instance record contains one member, a structure of type `CorePart`. Every widget contains its own copy of this `CorePart` data structure in its instance record. In addition to general information needed by Xt to manipulate the widget, the `CorePart` structure caches some information about the widget's window, to reduce the need to query the X server for this information.

The information in the `CorePart` structure includes:

- `self`: This member is a pointer to this instance record. The `self` member is of type `Widget`. This pointer is useful for several reasons. One use is to check the validity of a structure. If the `self` member of a widget's instance record is not the same as the widget's address, the widget has probably been destroyed, or corrupted in some way. The Xt function `XtIsObject()` checks to see if the `self` member is valid as part of its heuristics to see if a given pointer is a widget.

- `widget_class`: This member is a pointer to the class record of the widget class to which this widget belongs. Applications can retrieve this pointer using the function `XtClass()`.

- `parent`: This member is a pointer to the instance record of the widget's parent. This is the value returned by the Xt function `XtParent()`.

- `name`: This member stores the name of a widget. Applications can access this value by calling `XtName()`.

- `screen`: This member records the `Screen` structure associated with the display device on which this widget is displayed. The value of this member is accessible by calling `XtScreen()`.

- `colormap`: This member records the ID of the colormap associated with the widget's window. This value can be accessed through the `XmNcolormap` resource.

- `window`: The `window` member contains the ID of the X window used by the widget once the widget is realized. The window ID can be retrieved by calling `XtWindow()`.

- `x, y, width, height`: These members record the position and dimensions of the widget's window. The type of `x` and `y` is `Position`, while the type of `width` and `height` is `Dimension`. The members can be set or retrieved by using `XtSetValues()`/`XtGetValues()` and the `XmNx`, `XmNy`, `XmNwidth`, and `XmNheight` resources.

- `depth`: This member records the depth of the widget's window. This value can be retrieved using the `XmNdepth` resource.

- `border_width`: This member maintains the width of the window's border. This member is declared as type `Dimension`, and can be accessed through the `XmNborderWidth` resource.

- **border_pixel** and **border_pixmap**: These members determine the pixel index and tiling pattern of the window border. Applications can access these values using the **XmNborderColor** and **XmNborderPixmap** resources.

- **background_pixel** and **background_pixmap**: The values of these members determine the pixel index and tiling pattern of the window background.

- **event_table**: This member is a private structure used to maintain the event mask and event handlers used by the widget.

- **constraints**: The **constraints** member is a pointer to a structure supplied by the widget's parent. This field is **NULL** unless the widget is a child of a constraint widget. If so, the contents of the **constraints** structure is defined by the widget's parent. (See Chapter 17 for information about constraint widgets and how they use this member of the instance record.)

- **visible**: If the **visible_interest** member of the widget's class record is set to **TRUE**, this member is guaranteed to be **TRUE** when the widget's window is visible. The member may be **FALSE** if the window is not visible, but this is not guaranteed.

- **sensitive**: If this member is **TRUE**, the widget responds to events (i.e., Xt invokes its event handlers). If a widget's **sensitive** member is **FALSE**, device events are ignored, although **Expose**, **ConfigureNotify**, and some other events are still processed. This member can be set or retrieved using the **XmNsensitive** resource.

- **ancestor_sensitive**: This member is **TRUE** if the widget's parent is sensitive to events. If a widget is insensitive, its children are also insensitive. The value of this resource can be retrieved, but not set.

- **managed**: This member is **TRUE** if the widget is managed by another widget. This value can be retrieved from a widget by calling **XtIsManaged()**.

- **mapped_when_managed**: If this member is set to **TRUE**, Xt automatically maps the widget's window whenever the widget is managed and unmaps it when it is unmanaged. If this value is **FALSE**, managing the widget will not map the widget's window. This value can be set or retrieved using the **XmNmappedWhenManaged** resource.

- **being_destroyed**: Widgets are destroyed in two phases. The first phase sets the **being_destroyed** member to prevent other functions from operating on the widget while it is being destroyed.

- **destroy_callbacks**: This member is a pointer to a list of callbacks to be invoked when the widget is destroyed. Functions can be added to this list by using **XtAddCallback()** to add callbacks for the **XmNdestroyCallback** list.

- **popup_list**: Xt allows popups to be attached to any widget. If a widget has a popup associated with it, the popup widget is listed here.

- **num_popups**: This member records the length of the **popup_list**.

Inheritance

Inheritance is a powerful feature of many object-oriented systems, including that supported by Xt. Inheritance allows new classes to be created that automatically have most or all the characteristics of another class, but with a few additional or different features. Inheritance allows a programmer to create a new widget class without having to program every detail of the new widget. Often, a widget programmer can design a new widget class by specifying only how the new class differs from its superclass.

Many object-oriented languages provide inheritance as part of the language. However, Xt is written in C, which does not directly support object-oriented programming. In Xt, inheritance is implemented by including the components of the class record and the instance record from each of the widget's superclasses in the new widget's class and instance records. Each widget class in the inheritance hierarchy contributes one component to these structures.

For example, consider a hypothetical new widget class whose class name is Basic. Assume that this new Basic widget class is to be identical to the Core widget class except that the Basic widget class should support a foreground pixel and a graphics context, neither of which are provided by the Core widget class. To create this new widget class, the first step is to define a class record for the new widget class.

```
typedef struct{
    CoreClassPart    core_class;
    BasicClassPart   basic_class;
} BasicClassRec, *BasicWidgetClass;
```

The new widget class record contains two members. The first is the same `CoreClassPart` structure defined by the Core widget class. The second is the additional class part for the new widget class. The Basic widget class doesn't require any additional class resources and therefore the structure `BasicClassPart` is defined as an dummy structure:

```
typedef struct{
    int     ignore;
} BasicClassPart;
```

Next, the Basic widget's class pointer can be declared as:

```
BasicWidgetClass basicWidgetClass;
```

The Basic widget's instance record consists of the `CorePart` structure defined by the Core widget class, followed by a structure defined by the Basic widget. The instance record can be declared as:

```
typedef struct{
    CorePart    core;
    BasicPart   basic;
} BasicRec, *BasicWidget;
```

The structure `BasicPart` defines the new instance-specific resources needed by the Basic widget:

```
typedef struct{
   int    foreground;
   GC     gc;
} BasicPart;
```

Internally, the Basic widget's methods can refer to the `foreground` and `gc` members by accessing the `basic` member of the widget's instance record, for example:

```
BasicWidget w;
/* ... */
w->basic.foreground;
```

These methods can also access the members defined by the Core widget class through the `core` member of the instance record, for example:

```
w->core.background_pixel;
```

Figure 15.2 shows the architecture of this hypothetical Basic widget class, including the superclass pointer to the Core widget class.

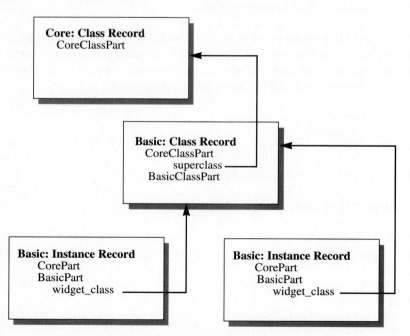

Figure 15.2 Inheriting from the Core widget class.

New widget classes inherit the attributes of their superclass by specifically including the declaration of the superclass structure in the declaration of the new class. However, Xt also provides a mechanism for inheriting the methods defined by a superclass. Inheritance is supported in two ways. The first mechanism is referred to as *chaining*. When a method is chained, Xt invokes the method defined by each of the widget's superclasses first, before invoking the widget's method. Chaining allows a widget class to inherit the behavior of its superclass, and also to extend it. The Core widget methods that are chained are:

```
class_initialize        class_part_initialize
get_values_hook         initialize
set_values              get_values
```

For example, if an application were to create an instance of the Basic widget described in the previous section, Xt would invoke the function pointer listed in the Core widget's `initialize` `member` first, and then the Basic widget's `initialize` method. If needed, the Basic widget's `initialize` method can override any actions taken in the `CorePart` set by the Core widget's `initialize` method. If the Basic widget class requires no initialization beyond that done by the Core `initialize` method, the widget programmer can set the `initialize` member of the subclass record to NULL. In this example, the Basic widget's `initialize` method must create a graphics context based on the foreground color in the `BasicPart` structure and the background color found in the `CorePart` structure.

Xt also provides a mechanism for inheriting methods that are not chained. Special symbols are used to specify the methods in the widget's class record. Each symbol is defined by the superclass that adds the method to the widget's class record. The Core widget class defines the following symbols for its methods:

```
XtInheritTranslations        XtInheritRealize
XtInheritResize              XtInheritExpose
XtInheritSetValuesAlmost     XtInheritAcceptFocus
XtInheritQueryGeometry
```

For example, to specify that a widget should inherit its superclass's translations, the programmer could use the symbol `XtInheritTranslations` as the value of the `transla-` `tions` member of the widget's class record. These symbols can be used by any subclass of the Core widget class.

Classes that contribute new methods to the class record need to define additional symbols for the new methods. For example, the Composite widget class (discussed in Chapter 16) defines symbols for its new methods, including:

```
XtInheritGeometryManager     XtInheritChangeManaged
XtInheritInsertChild         XtInheritDeleteChild
```

When a widget class specifies one of these symbols in the class record, Xt copies the corresponding method used by the widget's superclass into the widget's class structure at class initialization time.

Data Abstraction

Xt uses a data abstraction technique to hide the implementation of a widget from applications that use the widget. This technique involves maintaining both a private, complete definition of each widget structure, and a public, incomplete definition. Applications that use a widget see only the incomplete definition of the widget, and therefore cannot directly access fields in the widget structure. Applications declare all widgets as type `Widget`, which is an *opaque* type. Opaque means the application has a pointer to the widget structure, but does not have access to the real definition of the data that it represents. Therefore it cannot access the contents of the data structure.

To implement this style of data abstraction, the widget programmer must organize the widget implementation into several different files. Typically, each widget implementation consists of one or more private header files, a public header file, and one or more C source files. The private header file contains the real definitions used internally by the widget, while the public header file contains only those definitions required by applications that use the widget. The following sections describe the contents of each of these files.

The Private Header File

Every widget class has at least one private header file that contains the complete definitions of the widget class record and instance record. Most widget classes have only a single private header file whose name, by convention, ends with the letter "P". For example, the name of the Core widget's private header file is CoreP.h. This file contains the definitions of the `CoreClassPart` structure and the `CorePart` structure. Finally, the private header file can contain definitions of any other private data structures or variables used by the widget.

It is customary to enclose widget header files within a set of `#ifdef`/`#endif` statements to prevent problems if the header file is included in a file more than once. In addition, the private header file normally includes the widget class's public header file, as well as the private header file of the widget class's superclass. Using these conventions, the Basic widget's private header file would have the form:

```
#ifndef BASICP_H
#define BASICP_H
#include <CoreP.h>
#include <Basic.h>

/* Declarations go here */

#endif BASICP_H
```

Private header files are not expected to be included by applications. They may not, for example be correctly set up for ANSI C or C++. A widget's private header file is meant for use by that widget class and other widget classes that need access to the internal structure of the widget class.

The Public Header File

The public header file of most widget classes is very simple and declares any public information exported by the widget. At a minimum, a widget's public header file contains an external declaration of a pointer to the widget class record, which is used by applications as an argument to `XtCreateWidget()`. For example, the Core widget class's public file, Core.h, contains the declaration of a pointer to the widget class:

```
extern WidgetClass widgetClass;
```

The public header may also contain definitions of resource strings used by the program, convenience functions supported by the widget class, and so on. Like the private header file, a widget's public header should also be enclosed within **#ifdef/#endif** statements to prevent multiple definitions. By convention, the Basic widget's public header file would have the form:

```
#ifndef BASIC_H
#define BASIC_H

/* Declarations go here */

#endif BASIC_H
```

The public header file defines the external interface to a widget. Many widgets, including all Motif widgets, provide support in the public header file for both ANSI C and non-ANSI C, as well as C++. A widget header that contains function declarations can be set up to accommodate C++ and both styles of C as follows:

```
#ifndef BASIC_H
#define BASIC_H

/* Declarations needed for C++ */
#ifdef __cplusplus
extern "C" {
#endif

/* Declarations go here */
/* Convenience function declarations for ANSI and non-ANSI C. */
#ifdef _NO_PROTO
void SampleFunction();
#else
void SampleFucntion ( Widget w, int parameter );
#endif

/* Closing brace for C++ declarations */
#ifdef __cplusplus
}
#endif
#endif BASIC_H
```

The C++ declarations are needed to allow functions defined by this widget class to be called properly from C++. The `_NO_PROTO` flag can be activated to use traditional C instead of ANSI C.

The Widget Source File

The source files for most widgets have a similar structure. Each file includes the widget class's private header file as well as any other required header files. The file then contains declarations of methods and other internal functions used by the widget, followed by a resource list used by the resource manager to initialize the widget's resources. Next, the file contains a list of the actions used by the translation manager. Next, the widget's class record is statically initialized, and finally the widget's methods are defined. These methods are usually declared as static so that they are not visible to applications.

15.2 The Motif XmPrimitive Widget Class

All simple display widgets included in Motif are subclasses of the XmPrimitive widget class, which is a subclass of Core. The XmPrimitive class adds its own structure to both the instance and class records. To create a new widget class that fits smoothly with other Motif widgets, it is best to create the new widget class as a subclass of XmPrimitive. The following sections describe the additional functionality currently supported by the XmPrimitive widget class.

> *Note*: At the time of this writing, the OSF has not documented how to subclass from Motif widgets. Some details have been known to change from release to release. The exact details of the information provided here are subject to change in future releases of Motif. The various private Motif functions discussed in this and later chapters are almost certain to change without notice. Be prepared to make changes to any widget class that calls any function that begins with `_Xm`. Any direct references to members of Motif widget classes are also suspect. Furthermore, it is difficult to subclass a widget without access to source code. If you do not have access to the Motif source code, be sure to examine the private headers of the various Motif headers carefully for information about how Motif widgets are structured. If you understand the basic concepts, you should be able to adapt to future changes within the Motif widget classes, so long as you create subclasses of only the XmPrimitive and XmManager widget classes.

The XmPrimitive Class Record

The XmPrimitive class record includes the `CoreClassPart` and a new structure for the elements added by the XmPrimitive class. Following the model discussed for the hypothetical Basic widget class, the XmPrimitive class record can be declared as:

```
typedef struct {
    CoreClassPart           core_class;
    XmPrimtiveClassPart     primitive_class;
} XmPrimitiveClassRec, *XmPrimitiveWidgetClass;
```

The `XmPrimitiveClassPart` structure includes several methods supported by all primitive widgets as well as some data members that support additional XmPrimitive features. These include:

- `border_highlight`: This member is a pointer to a function that is called when a widget receives focus and the widget's border should be highlighted. The border is only highlighted if the `XmNhighlightOnEnter` resource is `TRUE`.
- `border_unhighlight`: This member is a pointer to a function that can be called to unhighlight the border.
- `translations`: This member is used to store some translations that control traversal. If traversal is activated, the contents of this translation table are added to the translations defined as part of the `CoreClassPart`. In general, this member can be set to `XtInheritTranslations`.
- `arm_and_activate`: This member supports an action routine that arms and activates a pushbutton or similar widget. This action function supports keyboard traversal and allows button widgets to be activated via the keyboard instead of the mouse.
- `syn_resources`. Some resources may need some processing before they can be set or retrieved using the `XtSetValues()`/`XtGetValues()` interface. Resources installed as synthetic resources are treated differently from other widget resources, in that a function is called to allow the data to be processed or manipulated in some way before being passed to the normal Xt resource mechanism.
- `num_syn_resources`: This member indicates the number of synthetic resources used by the widget.

Most of these members deal with internal details of how Motif widgets interact and new widgets seldom need to be concerned about these items. The `border_highlight` and `border_unhighlight` members can be set to `XmInheritWidgetProc` to inherit the behavior of the Motif superclass.

For the `translations` member, the value `XmInheritTranslations` indicates that the superclass's translations should be used, while the `arm_and_activate` member can be set to `XmInheritArmAndActivate` to inherit the default behavior. If a widget cannot be armed or activated, the `arm_and_activate` member can be set to `NULL`.

The XmPrimitive Instance Record

The XmPrimitive instance record also adds additional members. Following the style used by all widgets, the XmPrimitive instance structure can be declared as:

```
typedef struct {
    CorePart          core;
    XmPrimitivePart   primitive;
} XmPrimitiveRec, *XmPrimitiveWidget;
```

The `XmPrimitivePart` structure contains various items required by instances of subclasses of the XmPrimitive widget class. This data includes:

- `foreground`: This member stores the foreground color of a widget. This value can be set and retrieved using the `XmNforeground` resource.

- `shadow_thickness`: This member indicates the widget's shadow thickness and can be set and retrieved using the `XmNshadowThickness` resource.

- `top_shadow_color`: This member indicates the top shadow color. This value is normally computed automatically from the widget's background and foreground colors, but it can also be set and retrieved using the `XmNtopShadowColor` resource.

- `bottom_shadow_color`: This member indicates the bottom shadow color. This value is normally computed automatically from the widget's background and foreground colors, but it can also be set and retrieved using the `XmNbottomShadowColor` resource.

- `highlighted`: This member is set to `TRUE` of the widget is currently highlighted.

- `highlight_thickness`: This member indicates the widget's highlight thickness. This value can be set and retrieved using the `XmNhighlightThickness` resource.

- `highlight_color`: The `highlight_color` member is a `Pixel` value that indicates the color used to highlight the widget. The color can be set or retrieved using the `XmNhighlightColor` resource.

- `help_callback`: This member contains a callback list of functions to be invoked when the user asks for help.

- `user_data`: The `user_data` member is an untyped pointer than can be used by applications to associate data with a widget. The value of this member can set and retrieved using the `XmNuserData` resource.

- `highlight_GC`: The `highlight_GC` member is a graphics context used to draw a highlight around a widget. This graphics context is created in the XmPrimitive widget's `initialize` method using the value of the `highlight_color` member.

- `top_shadow_GC`: The `top_shadow_GC` member contains a graphics context used to draw a widget's top shadow. This graphics context is created in the XmPrimitive widget's `initialize` method using the value of the `top_shadow_color` member.

- `bottom_shadow_GC`: The `bottom_shadow_GC` member contains a graphics context used to draw a widget's bottom shadow. This graphics context is created in the XmPrimitive widget's `initialize` method using the value of the `bottom_shadow_color` member.

These are just a few of the members added to the instance record by the XmPrimitive widget class. These members can be useful to subclasses that need to display shadows, highlight a widget's border, and so on. Some of these members are used by the example widget in the following section.

Other Primitive Widget Considerations

All Motif primitive widgets follow some guidelines that should be obeyed by new widgets that are expected to work well with other Motif widgets. For example, many Motif primitive widgets have shadows whose width, colors and styles can be customized by applications and users. The XmPrimitive widget class provides graphics contexts and other support for these shadows, but subclasses are responsible for actually drawing the shadows.

Subclasses of XmPrimitive should also be able to highlight themselves when they have focus. This behavior is controlled by the `XmNhighlightOnEnter` resource, which is inherited from XmPrimitive. However, subclasses must handle redrawing the border highlight when the widget is exposed. This can be accomplished by calling the XmPrimitive widget's `border_highlight` method if the value of the highlighted field of the XmPrimitive instance record is `TRUE`, and calling the `border_unhighlight` method if highlighted is `FALSE`.

Subclasses must also be sure that translations are installed correctly to allow the XmPrimitive widget class to handle enter and leave events appropriately. Subclasses that do not define translations can simply specify the symbol `XtInheritTranslations` in the translations filed of their class structure. Widget classes that need to provide additional translations need to add the following bindings to the new list:

```
<EnterWindow>: PrimitiveEnter()
<LeaveWindow>: PrimitiveLeave()
```

Depending on the nature of the new widget class, there may be other considerations as well. For example, new widget classes should conform to the Motif Style Guide, and use the same mouse buttons, keyboard equivalents, and so on as other Motif widgets. Widgets that display text should use Motif's compound strings and compound string rendering functions, and should also recognize the `XmNfontList` resource. Complete Motif-compatible widgets may also need to support drag and drop, the Motif clipboard, Xt selections, and various other features.

15.3 The Dial Widget: An Example

Although at first exposure the widget architecture may seem to be complex and confusing, it is simple to use with some practice. Much of the code for a widget class is "boiler plate," and is quite similar from class to class. This section provides a practical look at the widget architecture by creating a new widget class, the Dial widget class. A Dial widget displays a rotary dial, similar in appearance to an analog clock, that can be used as a gauge or valuator. An indicator, similar to a clock hand, indicates the relative value displayed by the dial. The Dial widget can display information between a range specified by any two integers. The Dial widget defines resources that allow users and applications to control the number of markers between the minimum and maximum values, and also the position of the indicator. The Dial widget also supports a callback list that allows an application to register a function which the widget invokes when the user changes the position of the indicator.

Figure 15.3 shows the physical appearance of a Dial widget. The Dial widget is implemented as a subclass of the Motif XmPrimitive widget class. This widget class serves as a simple example of how to take advantage of various XmPrimitive features, such as shadow colors. As shown in Figure 15.3, the Dial face displays a set of tick marks that are drawn using the top and bottom shadow colors supported by the Motif XmPrimitive widget. The indicator is also drawn as an etched line, using the top and bottom shadow colors supported by Motif. The widget itself also has a shadow that frames the dial.

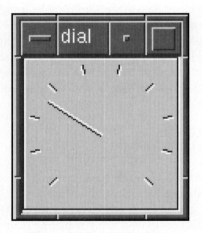

Figure 15.3 A Dial widget.

The widgets described in this and the following chapters are simple examples of typical widgets, designed specifically for this book. They are not part of the Motif widget set nor any vendor's widget set. To avoid confusion, the names of all widgets presented in Chapter 15, 16, and 17 begin with the prefix "Xs", which stands for the "X-Sample" widget set. Otherwise, the naming and capitalization used in the examples follow the conventions normally used by Xt and Motif widgets.

Following widget conventions, names of widget methods have the same names as the corresponding member of the widget class record, except that the method name uses mixed case. For example, the method corresponding to the `set_values` member of a widget's core part is usually named `SetValues()`.

The following sections describe each file involved in the implementation of the Dial widget class in detail, beginning with the private header file, DialP.h.

The Private Header File: DialP.h

The private header file for the Dial widget class is DialP.h. This file begins by including the XmPrimitive widget class's private header file, PrimitiveP.h. The private header file also includes the public header file Dial.h.

```
1    /**********************************************************
2     * DialP.h: Private header file for the Dial widget class
3     **********************************************************/
4    #ifndef DIALP_H
5    #define DIALP_H
6
7    #include <Xm/PrimitiveP.h>
8    #include "Dial.h"
9
10   #define MAXSEGMENTS 200
```

The first step in creating the Dial widget class is to define a structure that contains the Dial widget's contribution to the class record. Even when a widget class has nothing significant to add to the class record, each widget class is expected to add a member to the class record, so the `XsDial-ClassPart` structure contains a single member, which is unused.

```
11   typedef struct _XsDialClassPart{
12          int ignore;
13   } XsDialClassPart;
```

The Dial widget inherits from the XmPrimitive widget class. Therefore, the Dial widget's full class record includes the `CoreClassPart` structure, the `XmPrimitiveClassPart` structure, and then the `XsDialClassPart` structure. The Dial widget class's full class record is defined as follows:

```
14   typedef struct _XsDialClassRec{
15      CoreClassPart          core_class;
16      XmPrimitiveClassPart primitive_class;
17      XsDialClassPart        dial_class;
18   } XsDialClassRec;
19
20   extern XsDialClassRec XsdialClassRec;
```

The Dial widget class's instance record contains various data members that are needed at runtime by each instance of the Dial widget class. The instance record includes contributions from the Core widget class as well as the XmPrimitive widget class. The structure `XsDialPart` declares the resources and other instance data added by the Dial widget.

```
21   typedef struct _XsDialPart {
22      int      minimum;          /* minimum value          */
23      int      maximum;          /* maximum value          */
```

```
24     int         markers;          /* number of marks      */
25     Dimension   marker_length;    /* in pixels            */
26     int         value;            /* indicator position   */
27     Position    indicator_x;      /* x,y position of tip  */
28     Position    indicator_y;      /*    of the indicator  */
29     Position    shadow_delta;
30     Position    center_x;         /* coordinates of the   */
31     Position    center_y;         /*    dial center       */
32     Position    inner_diam;       /* inside of markers    */
33     Position    outer_diam;       /* outside of markers   */
34     GC          inverse_GC;       /* Used to clear indicator*/
35     unsigned    char shadow_type; /* type of frame        */
36     XSegment    segments[MAXSEGMENTS];    /* dark shadow lines */
37     XSegment    highlights[MAXSEGMENTS]; /* light shadow lines */
38     XtCallbackList value_changed;      /* callback list          */
39  } XsDialPart;
```

This structure maintains the current state of each Dial widget, and includes such information as the relative position of the indicator and the number of tick marks (markers) drawn on the face of the dial. Some of the members of this structure (the maximum and minimum dial settings, for example) can be accessed by an application using the Xt functions `XtSetValues()` and `XtGetValues()`. The programmer must define resources in the widget's resource list to allow these functions to be used to set and get the values of corresponding members.

Other fields in the `XsDialPart` are strictly for internal use. The widget's `initialize` method derives the values of some of these members from other resource values. For example, the graphics context is derived from the widget's foreground and background colors.

The `segments` member is an array of points that define the line segments used to draw the face of the dial. The size of this array must be defined earlier in the file. For example, here it is defined as:

```
#define MAXSEGMENTS 200
```

Having defined the `XsDialPart` data structure, the Dial widget's instance record can be created by combining the `CorePart` structure defined by the Core widget class with the `XmPrimitiveClassPart` structure and the newly defined `XsDialPart` structure. The full Dial instance record is declared as follows:

```
40  typedef struct _XsDialRec {
41     CorePart          core;
42     XmPrimitivePart   primitive;
43     XsDialPart        dial;
44  } XsDialRec;
45  #endif /*DIALP_H */
```

This completes the Dial widget class's private header file.

The Public Header File: Dial.h

The Dial widget's public header file declares the Dial widget's class pointer and also defines some strings used to specify resources. Widgets that define new resource names should make these names available to applications by including them in the public header file. The public header file also defines a structure passed as call data for the Dial widget's only callback function, as well as a Motif-style convenience function for creating a Dial widget.

```
1    /**********************************************************
2     * Dial.h: Public header fiel for the Dial widget class
3     **********************************************************/
4    #ifndef  DIAL_H
5    #define  DIAL_H
6    #ifdef __cplusplus
7    extern "C" {
8    #endif
9
10   extern WidgetClass xsDialWidgetClass;
11   typedef struct _XsDialClassRec *XsDialWidgetClass;
12   typedef struct _XsDialRec       *XsDialWidget;
13
14    /* Define resource strings for the Dial widget. */
15
16   #define XmNmarkers         "markers"
17   #define XmNposition        "position"
18   #define XmNmarkerLength    "markerLength"
19   #define XmCMarkers         "Markers"
20   #define XmCMin             "Min"
21   #define XmCMax             "Max"
22
23    /* Structure used for call data argument to Dial callbacks */
24
25   typedef struct {
26       int      reason;
27       XEvent *event;
28       int      value;
29   } XsDialCallbackStruct;
30
31   Widget XsCreateDial ( Widget parent, char *name,
32                         ArgList arglist, Cardinal argcount );
33   #ifdef __cplusplus
34   }
35   #endif
36   #endif
```

Applications can use the class pointer, `xsDialWidgetClass`, as an argument to `XtCreateWidget()` to create a Dial widget.

The Dial Widget Source File: Dial.c

The file Dial.c contains the static initialization of the Dial widget's class record, and also contains the widget's methods. Dial.c begins by including a private Motif header file, XmP.h, as well as the Dial widget class's private header file. In addition, the first part of the file defines several convenient macros used by the widget, and declares the functions that serve as the widget class's methods. Notice that these methods are declared as static, making them private to this file and effectively hiding them from applications that use the widget. In the interest of brevity and clarity, the entire Dial example is written only for ANSI C, and does not include the usual alternative non-ANSI C declarations for all functions.

```
1    /***************************************************
2     * Dial.c: Dial widget methods
3     ***************************************************/
4    #include <Xm/XmP.h>
5    #include "DialP.h"
6    #include <math.h>
7
8    #ifndef M_PI
9    #define M_PI 3.14159265358979323846
10   #endif
11
12   #define   RADIANS( x ) ( M_PI * ( x )  / 180.0 )
13   #define   DEGREES( x ) ( ( x )  / M_PI  * 180.0 )
14   #define   MIN_ANGLE   225.0
15   #define   MAX_ANGLE   270.0
16   #define   MIN( a,b ) ( ( ( a ) < ( b ) )  ? ( a )  : ( b ) )
17
18
19   static void SetIndicatorPosition ( Widget    w,
20                                      XEvent   *event,
21                                      String   *args,
22                                      Cardinal *n_args );
23   static void Initialize ( Widget    req,
24                            Widget    widget,
25                            ArgList   args,
26                            Cardinal *nArgs );
27   static void Redisplay ( Widget  w,
28                           XEvent *event,
29                           Region  region );
30   static void CalculateIndicatorPos ( XsDialWidget w );
31   static void Resize ( Widget w );
32   static void Destroy ( Widget widget );
33   static Boolean SetValues ( Widget    cur,
34                              Widget    req,
35                              Widget    widget,
36                              ArgList   args,
37                              Cardinal *numArgs );
```

```
38   extern void _XmDrawShadows ( Display *display, Window window,
39                                GC top_shadow, GC bottom_shadow,
40                                Position x, Position y,
41                                Dimension width, Dimension height,
42                                Dimension shadow_thickness,
43                                unsigned char shadow_type );
```

The next section of the source file defines an action list and a translations list used by the translation manager to map between a user action and a function to be invoked when the action occurs. These statements specify that, by default, the "set-position()" action is invoked in response to a <Btn1Down> action or a <Btn1Motion> action. Notice that the <EnterWindow> and <LeaveWindow> actions are also specified. The PrimitiveLeave() and PrimitiveEnter() actions are registered by the XmPrimitive class and allow Motif to support keyboard traversal and highlighting of the new widget class. An array of type XtActionsRec maps the "set-position()" action to a function, SetIndicatorPosition(), defined later:

```
44   static char defaultTranslations[] =
45        "<Btn1Down>:     set-position()\n\
46         <Btn1Motion>:   set-position()\n\
47         <EnterWindow>: PrimitiveEnter()\n\
48         <LeaveWindow>: PrimitiveLeave()";
49
50   static XtActionsRec actionsList[] = {
51     { "set-position",   SetIndicatorPosition },
52   };
```

Next, the resource list used by the resource manager to initialize the Dial widget's instance record must be provided. The resource list uses the same format as the application resource mechanism discussed in Chapter 3. The resources are automatically stored in the appropriate fields of the instance record. The Dial widget's resource list is defined as:

```
53   static XtResource resources[] = {
54
55   { XmNmarkers, XmCMarkers, XmRInt, sizeof ( int ),
56       XtOffset ( XsDialWidget, dial.markers ), XmRString, "10"  },
57
58   { XmNminimum, XmCMin, XmRInt, sizeof ( int ),
59       XtOffset ( XsDialWidget, dial.minimum ), XmRString, "0"   },
60
61   { XmNmaximum, XmCMax, XmRInt, sizeof ( int ),
62       XtOffset ( XsDialWidget, dial.maximum ), XmRString, "100" },
63
64   { XmNshadowType, XmCShadowType, XmRShadowType, sizeof ( unsigned char ),
65       XtOffset ( XsDialWidget, dial.shadow_type ),
66       XmRImmediate, ( XtPointer )  XmSHADOW_ETCHED_IN },
67
```

```
68   { XmNvalue, XmCValue, XmRInt, sizeof ( int ),
69     XtOffset ( XsDialWidget, dial.value ), XmRString, "0"   },
70
71   { XmNmarkerLength,XmCLength,XmRDimension,sizeof ( Dimension ),
72     XtOffset ( XsDialWidget, dial.marker_length ),
73     XmRString, "5"                                         },
74
75   { XmNvalueChangedCallback,XmCCallback,XmRCallback,sizeof ( XtPointer ),
76     XtOffset ( XsDialWidget, dial.value_changed ),
77     XmRCallback, NULL                                      },
78   };
```

Notice that only new resources supported by the Dial widget class are included in this list. The Dial widget also inherits the resources defined by the `CorePart` of the widget's instance record from the Core widget class. Resources defined in the `XmPrimitivePart` are inherited from the XmPrimitive widget. The resource manager initializes the resources inherited from the Core widget class and then the XmPrimitive widget class before retrieving the resources defined by the Dial widget class. A widget class can override the default values for resources defined by its superclass if necessary. However, the Dial widget does not need to override any Core or XmPrimitive resources.

The Class Record

The next step is to define the contents of the Dial widget's class record, which is initialized at compile time by declaring the contents of the structure statically in the source code. The following code segment initializes each part of the Dial widget's class record. The first part includes all the members of the `CoreClassPart` structure. The `superclass` member is initialized to point to the XmPrimitive widget's class record. The class name is initialized to a string that identifies the class to which the widget belongs. This string is used by the resource manager for all resources specified by class name. The third member indicates the size of the structure to be allocated when a Dial widget is created. In this case, `XtCreateWidget()` uses this information to allocate a space the size of a `CorePart` plus the size of an `XmPrimitivePart`, plus the size of the `XsDialPart` structure.

In addition to the static initialization of the class record, some classes must be initialized dynamically when the first widget that belongs to the class is created. The `class_initialize` and `class_part_initialize` members allow the widget programmer to define methods to initialize the widget's class record at run time. Because the Dial widget's class record requires no run-time initialization, these members are set to `NULL`. Regardless of whether or not the widget requires dynamic initialization, every widget must initialize the `class_inited` field to `FALSE`.

The `actions` member and the `translations` member of the `CoreClassPart` structure are initialized to the actions and translations tables defined earlier in the file. The `compress_-motion`, `compress_exposure`, and `compress_enterleave` members of the class structure define how the widget wishes to have certain events reported. The Dial widget specifies that Xt should compress all events.

The Dial widget must compute the location of the indicator on the face of the dial and draw the indicator whenever its position changes. It is therefore useful to know if the widget is visible, to avoid redrawing the indicator unnecessarily. Therefore, the Dial class record initializes the `visible_interest` field to TRUE, to request Xt to keep the `visible` member of the Dial widget's instance record up to date.

The members that correspond to methods that are not needed by this widget are set to NULL. The Dial widget installs the `initialize`, `destroy`, `resize`, `expose`, and `set_values` methods, but ignores most others. The `realize` member is set to the value `XtInheritRealize` to inherit the `realize` method used by XmPrimitive. The Dial widget also inherits the values of the `border_highlight` and `border_unhighlight` members as well as the Motif translations. No other Motif members are used.

The Dial widget does not use the `dial` part of the class record and initializes its dummy member to NULL.

```
79  externaldef ( dialclassrec )  XsDialClassRec xsDialClassRec = {
80  {
81    /* CoreClassPart */
82    ( WidgetClass ) &xmPrimitiveClassRec,  /* superclass          */
83    "XsDial",                       /* class_name         */
84    sizeof ( XsDialRec ),           /* widget_size        */
85    NULL,                           /* class_initialize   */
86    NULL,                           /* class_part_initialize */
87    FALSE,                          /* class_inited       */
88    Initialize,                     /* initialize         */
89    NULL,                           /* initialize_hook    */
90    XtInheritRealize,               /* realize            */
91    actionsList,                    /* actions            */
92    XtNumber ( actionsList ),       /* num_actions        */
93    resources,                      /* resources          */
94    XtNumber ( resources ),         /* num_resources      */
95    NULLQUARK,                      /* xrm_class          */
96    TRUE,                           /* compress_motion    */
97    XtExposeCompressMaximal,        /* compress_exposure  */
98    TRUE,                           /* compress_enterleave */
99    TRUE,                           /* visible_interest   */
100   Destroy,                        /* destroy            */
101   Resize,                         /* resize             */
102   Redisplay,                      /* expose             */
103   SetValues,                      /* set_values         */
104   NULL,                           /* set_values_hook    */
105   XtInheritSetValuesAlmost,       /* set_values_almost  */
106   NULL,                           /* get_values_hook    */
107   NULL,                           /* accept_focus       */
108   XtVersion,                      /* version            */
109   NULL,                           /* callback private   */
110   defaultTranslations,            /* tm_table           */
111   NULL,                           /* query_geometry     */
112   NULL,                           /* display_accelerator */
113   NULL,                           /* extension          */
114  },
```

```
115    {
116        /* XmPrimitive          */
117        XmInheritBorderHighlight,        /* border_highlight     */
118        XmInheritBorderUnhighlight,      /* border_unhighlight   */
119        XtInheritTranslations,           /* translations         */
120        NULL,                            /* arm_and_activate      */
121        NULL,                            /* synresources          */
122        0,                               /* num syn_resources     */
123        NULL,                            /* extension             */
124    },
125    {
126        /* Dial class fields */
127        0,                               /* ignore                */
128    }
129    };
130
131    WidgetClass xsDialWidgetClass = ( WidgetClass )  &xsDialClassRec;
```

Class Methods

A widget's methods determine its behavior. All Dial widget methods are private to the Dial widget, and applications can not call them directly. Instead, Xt invokes a widget's methods when events occur or when an application calls the interface functions provided by Xt. For example, applications call `XtCreateWidget()` to create a Dial widget, `XtRealizeWidget()` to realize the widget, `XtManageWidget()` and `XtUnmanageWidget()` to manage and unmanage the widget, and so on. Users can also customize the Dial widget using the resource manager, and applications can use the functions `XtSetValues()` and `XtGetValues()` to set and retrieve the widget's resources. These Xt functions call the appropriate methods based on the class of each particular widget.

Not every widget class defines every method in the class structure. For example, the Dial widget does not define several methods in the class record, including:

```
            class_initialize        class_part_initialize
            get_values_hook         query_geometry
```

The Dial widget initializes the members of the class record that correspond to these unused methods to `NULL`.

The Dial widget class inherits the `realize` and `set_values_almost` methods from its superclass by specifying `XtInheritRealize` and `XtInheritSetValuesAlmost` for these methods. The remaining methods are defined by the Dial widget class. These methods are:

```
            initialize        destroy        set_values
            resize            expose
```

The following sections discuss the methods supported by all primitive display widgets, with an emphasis on those used by the Dial widget.

The class_initialize Method

The `class_initialize` method is called when the first widget of a class is created. Some widget classes have per-class data in the class record that needs to be initialized, or other actions that need to be taken. For example, some widgets may need to install custom type-converter functions. Xt checks the `class_inited` member of the class record when each widget is created. If the `class_inited` member is FALSE, and the class has a `class_initialize` method, this method is called to perform the initialization. The `class_initialize` method is chained, so Xt checks the `class_initialize` member of each class in an inheritance hierarchy, calling each method in turn, starting with the Core class method. Once all methods have been called, Xt sets the `class_inited` member to TRUE.

All `class_initialize` methods have the form:

```
void ClassInitialize();
```

The Dial widget does not need to perform any class initialization and sets the `class_initialize` member to NULL.

The class_part_initialize Method

The `class_initialize` method does not have access to the members of the class with which they are associated. In some cases, widgets need to perform operations on the members of the widget's class structure. To support dynamic initialization of the class record, Xt supports a `class_part_initialize` method. This function has the form:

```
void ClassPartInitialize ( WidgetClass widgetClass )
```

After the `class_initialize` method is called, Xt calls all `class_part_initialize` methods in superclass-to-subclass order. Classes that do not need to perform any additional initialization can set this member to NULL. The Dial widget does not provide a `class_part_initialize` method.

The initialize Method

While the class record of most widgets can be initialized at compile time, the instance record of each widget must be initialized at run time. When a new widget is created, Xt invokes the widget's `initialize` method specified in the widget's class record. Every `initialize` method has the form:

```
void Initialize ( Widget  request, Widget new_w,
                  ArgList args, Cardinal *numArgs )
```

This method requires four parameters. The first two are versions of the widget's instance record. The `new_w` parameter is the real widget, the other is a copy. The third and fourth arguments to the initialize method provide the list of resources passed to `XtCreateWidget()` by the caller.

Each member in the `request` widget's instance record is set to the original value obtained from defaults in the widgets resource list, taken from values specified by the application when creating the widget, or taken from the user's resource files. Initially, the `new_w` structure is also set up the same way, However, by the time this method is called, the `new_w` structure has potentially been modified by each of the widget's superclasses' `initialize` methods. In this example, Xt calls the Core widget class's `initialize` method and then the XmPrimitive widget class's `initialize` method before it calls the Dial widget's `initialize` method. A widget class's `initialize` method may therefore rely on the widget's superclasses to initialize the inherited resources in the instance record. Each widget class needs to initialize only those resources it adds. The `initialize` method can also check any of the resources defined by its superclasses that it cares about and recalculate them if necessary.

The Dial widget's `initialize` method checks the size of the widget and adjusts the values if they are not acceptable. Unless the application or the user sets the size of the widget's window, it will have zero height and width at this point. The X server will generate an error if a widget attempts to create a zero width or height window, so every widget should make sure its window will have acceptable dimensions.

When changing values set by a superclass, the widget may consider both the values in the `new_w` widget structure and the original values provided by the resource manager, found in the `request` parameter. The `request` argument allows the widget to compare the current values with the original values, if desired. All changes must be made to the `new_w` structure.

The Dial widget's `initialize` method is written as follows:

```
132  static void Initialize ( Widget req, Widget widget,
133                              ArgList args, Cardinal *numArgs )
134  {
135      XsDialWidget request = ( XsDialWidget ) req;
136      XsDialWidget dw       = ( XsDialWidget ) widget;
137      XGCValues     values;
138      XtGCMask      valueMask;
139
140      /*
141       * Make sure the window size is not zero. The Core
142       * Initialize() method doesn't do this.
143       */
144
145      if ( request->core.width == 0 )
146          dw->core.width = 100;
147      if ( request->core.height == 0 )
148          dw->core.height = 100;
149      /*
150       * Make sure the min and max dial settings are valid.
151       */
152
153      if ( dw->dial.minimum >= dw->dial.maximum )
154      {
155          XtWarning ( "Maximum must be greater than the Minimum" );
156          dw->dial.minimum = dw->dial.maximum - 1;
157      }
158
```

```
159        if ( dw->dial.value > dw->dial.maximum )
160        {
161            XtWarning ( "Value exceeds the Dial Maximum" );
162            dw->dial.value =  dw->dial.maximum;
163        }
164
165        if ( dw->dial.value < dw->dial.minimum )
166        {
167            XtWarning ( "Value is less than the Dial Minimum" );
168            dw->dial.value =  dw->dial.minimum;
169        }
170
171        /*
172         * Allow only MAXSEGMENTS markers
173         */
174
175        if ( dw->dial.markers > MAXSEGMENTS )
176        {
177            XtWarning ( "Too many markers" );
178            dw->dial.markers = MAXSEGMENTS;
179        }
180
181        /*
182         * Create a graphics contexts used to erase
183         * the indicator.
184         */
185
186        valueMask          = GCForeground | GCBackground;
187        values.foreground  = dw->core.background_pixel;
188        values.background  = dw->core.background_pixel;
189        dw->dial.inverse_GC = XtGetGC ( ( Widget ) dw,
190                                        valueMask, &values );
191
192        /*
193         * Call the widget's resize method through the class
194         * pointer to force certain values to be computed. Use the
195         * class pointer to allow any subclasses to override method.
196         */
197
198        if ( dw->core.widget_class->core_class.resize )
199            (*(dw->core.widget_class->core_class.resize)) ((Widget) dw);
200    }
```

This method begins by checking the size of widget. If the user or the application specifies a size, the resource manager sets the widget size before this method is called. Otherwise, the `initialize` method must ensure that the widget's width and height are greater than zero.

`Initialize()` also checks the value of other parameters, such as the maximum and minimum dial settings, to be sure they are reasonable, and initializes derived data, such as the graphics context used by the widget to erase the dial. The resource manager initializes the widget structure, using the widget's resource list, before the `initialize` method is called. Therefore, the graphics context can be created from the foreground color in the `primitive_part` of the instance record, and the background color in the `core_part` of the instance record. The Dial widget's `initialize` method also calls the widget's `resize` method, which calculates the initial position of the dial markers and indicator.

The realize Method

The function `XtRealizeWidget()` invokes a widget's `realize` method, which is responsible for creating the window used by the widget. Since this method is almost always the same for each widget class, most widget classes inherit their superclass's `realize` method. Unlike the `initialize` method, the `realize` method is not chained. The Dial widget inherits its super-class's `realize` method by specifying the symbol `XtInheritRealize` in the class record. The `realize` member of the widget's class record cannot be set to `NULL` unless the widget class is never realized. Attempting to realize a widget whose `realize` method is `NULL` generates a fatal error.

The destroy Method

Before a widget is destroyed, Xt invokes the widget class's `destroy` method. This method is chained, although the calling order is reversed with respect to other chained methods. The function `XtDestroyWidget()` calls each widget class's `destroy` method before its superclass's `destroy` method. Each widget is expected to free any memory it has allocated and to free any server resources it has created. For example, the Dial widget class creates a graphics context and also defines a callback list that should be removed before the widget is destroyed. A widget class's `destroy` method must not free the widget structure itself; the memory associated with a widget is freed by Xt.

The Dial widget's `destroy` method is implemented as follows:

```
201  static void Destroy ( Widget widget )
202  {
203      XsDialWidget dw = ( XsDialWidget )  widget;
204
205      XtReleaseGC ( ( Widget ) dw, dw->dial.inverse_GC );
206      XtRemoveAllCallbacks ( ( Widget ) dw, XmNvalueChangedCallback );
207  }
```

The resize Method

Xt invokes a widget class's `resize` method whenever the widget's window is reconfigured in any way. The `resize` method should examine the members of the widget structure and recalculate any derived data that is dependent on the configuration of the widget's window.

The Dial widget must recalculate the center of the window, the size of the indicator, and the line segments used to draw the face of the dial. Because the X server generates an `Expose` event if the contents of a window are lost because of a resize, the `resize` method only updates the data needed to allow the `expose` method to redraw the widget correctly and does not actually redraw the window. This method generates a set of line segments that defines the circular face of the dial, centered in the widget window.

The Dial widget's `resize` method is written as follows:

```
208  static void Resize ( Widget w )
209  {
210      XsDialWidget dw = ( XsDialWidget )  w;
211
212      double    angle, cosine, sine, increment;
213      int       i;
214
215      /*
216       * Calculate the center of the widget
217       */
218
219      dw->dial.center_x = dw->core.width / 2;
220      dw->dial.center_y = dw->core.height / 2;
221
222      /*
223       *  Generate the segment array containing the points needed to
224       *  draw the tick marks on the face of the dial.
225       */
226
227      increment = RADIANS ( MAX_ANGLE )  /
228                              ( float ) ( dw->dial.markers -1 );
229      dw->dial.outer_diam =
230                  ( MIN ( dw->core.width, dw->core.height ) -
231                      2 * dw->primitive.shadow_thickness -
232                        2 * dw->primitive.highlight_thickness ) / 2;
233      dw->dial.inner_diam = dw->dial.outer_diam -
234                                      dw->dial.marker_length;
235      angle = RADIANS ( MIN_ANGLE );
236
237      for ( i = 0; i < dw->dial.markers; i++ )
238      {
239          int xdelta;
240
241          cosine = cos ( angle );
242          sine   = sin ( angle );
243
244          dw->dial.segments[i].x1 = dw->dial.center_x +
245                                      dw->dial.outer_diam * sine;
246          dw->dial.segments[i].y1 = dw->dial.center_y -
247                                      dw->dial.outer_diam * cosine;
248          dw->dial.segments[i].x2 = dw->dial.center_x +
249                                      dw->dial.inner_diam * sine;
250          dw->dial.segments[i].y2 = dw->dial.center_y -
251                                      dw->dial.inner_diam * cosine;
```

```
252          /*
253           * Compute a second set of points with which to draw
254           * a top shadow for each mark on the dial. Depending on
255           * the angle of the line, the shadow must be
256           * positioned differently.
257           */
258
259          if ( ( sine < 0 && cosine < 0 )  ||
260                 ( sine > 0 && cosine > 0 ) )
261          {
262              xdelta = 1;
263          }
264          else if ( ( sine < 0 && cosine > 0 )  ||
265                      ( sine > 0 && cosine < 0 ) )
266          {
267              xdelta = -1;
268          }
269
270          dw->dial.highlights[i].x1 = dw->dial.segments[i].x1 + xdelta;
271          dw->dial.highlights[i].x2 = dw->dial.segments[i].x2 + xdelta;
272          dw->dial.highlights[i].y1 = dw->dial.segments[i].y1 + 1;
273          dw->dial.highlights[i].y2 = dw->dial.segments[i].y2 + 1;
274          angle += increment;
275      }
276      CalculateIndicatorPos ( dw );
277  }
```

The auxiliary function `CalculateIndicatorPos()` calculates the coordinates of the end point of the indicator, based on the indicator position and the size of the window. Like `Resize()`, `CalculateIndicatorPosition()` also computes information that can be used to draw the indicator with top and bottom shadows.

```
278  static void CalculateIndicatorPos ( XsDialWidget dw )
279  {
280      double   normalized_pos, angle, sine, cosine;
281      Position indicator_length;
282
283      /*
284       * Make the indicator two pixels shorter than the
285       * inner edge of the markers.
286       */
287
288      indicator_length = dw->dial.outer_diam - dw->dial.marker_length-2;
289
290      /*
291       * Normalize the indicator value to lie between zero
292       * and 1, and then convert it to an angle.
293       */
```

```
294
295        normalized_pos = ( dw->dial.value - dw->dial.minimum ) /
296                     ( float ) ( dw->dial.maximum - dw->dial.minimum );
297        angle = RADIANS ( MIN_ANGLE + MAX_ANGLE  * normalized_pos );
298
299        /*
300         * Find the x,y coordinates of the tip of the indicator.
301         */
302
303        sine = sin ( angle );
304        cosine = cos ( angle );
305
306        if ( ( sine < 0 && cosine < 0 )  ||
307             ( sine > 0 && cosine > 0 ) )
308        {
309            dw->dial.shadow_delta = 1;
310        }
311        else if ( ( sine < 0 && cosine > 0 )  ||
312                ( sine > 0 && cosine < 0 ) )
313        {
314            dw->dial.shadow_delta =  -1;
315        }
316
317        dw->dial.indicator_x = dw->dial.center_x +
318                                    indicator_length * sine;
319
320        dw->dial.indicator_y = dw->dial.center_y -
321                                    indicator_length  * cosine;
322    }
```

The expose Method

A widget's expose method is responsible for redrawing any information in the widget's window when an Expose event occurs. A widget's expose member can be set to NULL if the widget does not need to display anything. The expose method is invoked with three parameters: the widget instance to be redisplayed, a pointer to an Expose event, and a Region. If the compress_exposure member of the widget's class structure is not set to XtExposeNoCompress, the Region contains the sum of the rectangles reported in all Expose events, and the event parameter contains the bounding box of the region. If compress_exposure is FALSE, the region parameter is always NULL.

The Dial widget's expose method, Redisplay(), draws the face of the dial, using the line segments calculated by the resize method, and draws the dial indicator at its current position. The Dial widget requests that Expose events be compressed, so the region argument could be used as a clip mask for the graphics context to eliminate redrawing the dial face unnecessarily. However, this example is so simple that the additional work required to use the region information does not seem necessary. This example redraws the entire face of the dial instead. Notice that expose checks the visible member of the CorePart of the widget's instance record and redraws the dial face only if the widget is visible.

The `Redisplay()` function uses the line segments computed in the `resize` method to draw an etched line for each tick on the face of the dial. The etched look is achieved by drawing two lines, side by side, one using the top shadow color of the widget and the other using the bottom shadow color. The indicator line is also drawn the same way.

```
323   static void Redisplay ( Widget w, XEvent *event, Region region )
324   {
325       XsDialWidget  dw = ( XsDialWidget ) w;
326       XsDialWidgetClass wc = (XsDialWidgetClass) XtClass ( w );
327
328       if ( dw->core.visible && XtIsRealized ( dw ) )
329       {
330           /*
331            * Redraw the correct state of the widget's border.
332            */
333
334           if ( w->primitive.highlighted )
335               (*wc->primitive_class.border_highlight ) ( w );
336           else
337               (*wc->primitive_class.border_unhighlight ) ( w );
338
339           /*
340            * Draw the surrounding shadow
341            */
342
343           _XmDrawShadows ( XtDisplay ( dw ),
344                            XtWindow ( dw ),
345                            dw->primitive.top_shadow_GC,
346                            dw->primitive.bottom_shadow_GC,
347                            0, 0, dw->core.width, dw->core.height,
348                            dw->primitive.shadow_thickness,
349                            dw->dial.shadow_type );
350           /*
351            * Draw the markers used for the dial face.
352            */
353
354           XDrawSegments ( XtDisplay ( dw ), XtWindow ( dw ),
355                           dw->primitive.top_shadow_GC,
356                           dw->dial.highlights, dw->dial.markers );
357
358           XDrawSegments ( XtDisplay ( dw ), XtWindow ( dw ),
359                           dw->primitive.bottom_shadow_GC,
360                           dw->dial.segments, dw->dial.markers );
361
362           /*
363            * Draw the indicator at its current value.
364            */
365
```

```
366            XDrawLine ( XtDisplay ( dw ), XtWindow ( dw ),
367                        dw->primitive.top_shadow_GC,
368                        dw->dial.center_x, dw->dial.center_y,
369                        dw->dial.indicator_x, dw->dial.indicator_y );
370
371            XDrawLine ( XtDisplay ( dw ), XtWindow ( dw ),
372                        dw->primitive.bottom_shadow_GC,
373                        dw->dial.center_x + dw->dial.shadow_delta,
374                        dw->dial.center_y + 1,
375                        dw->dial.indicator_x + dw->dial.shadow_delta,
376                        dw->dial.indicator_y + 1 );
377        }
378    }
```

Notice that `Redisplay()` calls the function `_XmDrawShadows()`, which is an internal Motif function. This function is undocumented and therefore subject to change at any time. In Motif 1.2, this function is declared as follows:

```
void _XmDrawShadows ( Display      *display,
                      Drawable     d,
                      GC           top_gc,
                      GC           bottom_gc,
                      Position     x,
                      Position     y,
                      Dimension    width,
                      Dimension    height
                      Dimension    shadow_thickness,
                      unsigned int shadow_type )
```

`_XmDrawShadows()` draws the Motif style shadow around the given rectangle, based on the information provided. The shadow type can be any one of the supported Motif shadow types, XmSHADOW_IN, XmSHADOW_ETCHED_IN, XmSHADOW_OUT, or XmSHADOW_ETCHED_OUT.

The set_values Method

The `set_values` method allows a widget to be notified when one of its resources is set or changed. A widget's `set_values` method can be called when the resource manager initializes the widget's resources, or when an application calls `XtSetValues()`. The `set_values` methods are chained, and are invoked in superclass-to-subclass order.

The `set_values` method takes three arguments, each a version of the widget's instance record. The form of every `set_values` method is:

```
static Boolean SetValues ( Widget   current,
                           Widget   request,
                           Widget   new_w,
                           ArgList  args,
                           Cardinal *numArgs )
```

The `current` parameter contains the unaltered state of the widget before the request. The `request` parameter contains the values requested for the widget by the application. The `new_w` argument contains the state of the widget after all superclasses' `set_values` methods have been called. Like the `initialize` method, the `set_values` method can examine the other versions of the widget to discover changes made by superclasses and may override any values that it wishes. All changes must be made to the `new_w` widget. Notice that, at this point, Xt has already changed the requested values in the `new_w` widget. The `set_values` method's primary task is to generate any data derived from parameters that have changed and check that all requested values are acceptable.

The `set_values` method returns a `Boolean` value that indicates whether the widget should be redrawn. If this value is `TRUE`, Xt causes an `Expose` event to be generated for the entire window. Because the `set_values` method can be invoked at any time, it must not assume that the widget is realized. Therefore, this method must not perform any graphics operations on the widget's window (which might not exist yet) unless the widget is realized.

The Dial widget's `set_values` method checks the minimum and maximum values of the dial to ensure that they are reasonable, and resets the values if they are out of range. If the foreground or background colors have changed, `set_values` must create a new graphics context.

Last, if the dial position has changed, the `set_values` method calls the auxiliary function `CalculateIndicatorPos()` to compute the new position of the indicator. If only the position of the indicator has changed, and the `redraw` flag is still `FALSE`, the old indicator is erased by drawing it with the inverse GC, and then displayed at the new position by drawing it with the normal graphics contexts. Notice that when erasing the indicator both the old position and the old graphics context are obtained from the `current` widget, in case the indicator moves and changes color at the same time.

The Dial widget's `set_values` method is written as:

```
379    static Boolean SetValues ( Widget    cur,
380                               Widget    req,
381                               Widget    widget,
382                               ArgList   args,
383                               Cardinal  *numArgs )
384    {
385        XsDialWidget current = ( XsDialWidget ) cur;
386        XsDialWidget request = ( XsDialWidget ) req;
387        XsDialWidget dw      = ( XsDialWidget ) widget;
388        XGCValues    values;
389        XtGCMask     valueMask;
390        Boolean      redraw = FALSE;
391        Boolean      redraw_indicator = FALSE;
392
393        /*
394         * Make sure the dial values are reasonable.
395         */
396
397        if ( dw->dial.minimum >= dw->dial.maximum )
398        {
```

```
399          XtWarning ( "Dial Minimum must be less than Maximum" );
400          dw->dial.minimum = 0;
401          dw->dial.maximum = 100;
402      }
403
404      if ( dw->dial.value > dw->dial.maximum )
405      {
406          XtWarning ( "Dial value is greater than the Maximum" );
407          dw->dial.value = dw->dial.maximum;
408      }
409
410      if ( dw->dial.value < dw->dial.minimum )
411      {
412          XtWarning ( "Dial value is less than the Minimum" );
413          dw->dial.value = dw->dial.minimum;
414      }
415
416      /*
417       * If the indicator color or background color
418       * has changed, generate the GC's.
419       */
420
421      if ( dw->core.background_pixel != current->core.background_pixel )
422      {
423          XtReleaseGC ( ( Widget ) current, current->dial.inverse_GC );
424
425          valueMask         = GCForeground | GCBackground;
426          values.foreground = dw->core.background_pixel;
427          values.background = dw->core.background_pixel;
428
429          dw->dial.inverse_GC = XtGetGC ( ( Widget ) dw, valueMask,
430                                          &values );
431
432          redraw_indicator = TRUE;
433      }
434
435      /*
436       * If the indicator value has changed, or if the min/max
437       * values have changed, recompute the indicator coordinates.
438       */
439
440      if ( dw->dial.value   != current->dial.value   ||
441           dw->dial.minimum != current->dial.minimum ||
442           dw->dial.maximum != current->dial.maximum )
443      {
444          CalculateIndicatorPos ( dw );
445          redraw_indicator = TRUE;
446      }
447
```

```
448     /*
449      * If only the indicator needs to be redrawn and
450      * the widget is realized, erase the current indicator
451      * and draw the new one. SetValues functions are not
452      * expected to draw, but this reduces flicker caused
453      * by redrawing the entire widget face. Be sure the
454      * widget is realized.
455      */
456
457     if ( redraw_indicator && !redraw &&
458         XtIsRealized ( dw ) && dw->core.visible )
459     {
460         XDrawLine ( XtDisplay ( dw ), XtWindow ( dw ),
461                     dw->dial.inverse_GC,
462                     current->dial.center_x +
463                                 current->dial.shadow_delta,
464                     current->dial.center_y + 1,
465                     current->dial.indicator_x +
466                                 current->dial.shadow_delta,
467                     current->dial.indicator_y + 1 );
468         XDrawLine ( XtDisplay ( dw ), XtWindow ( dw ),
469                     dw->dial.inverse_GC,
470                     current->dial.center_x, current->dial.center_y,
471                     current->dial.indicator_x,
472                     current->dial.indicator_y );
473
474         XDrawLine ( XtDisplay ( dw ), XtWindow ( dw ),
475                     dw->primitive.top_shadow_GC,
476                     dw->dial.center_x, dw->dial.center_y,
477                     dw->dial.indicator_x, dw->dial.indicator_y );
478         XDrawLine ( XtDisplay ( dw ), XtWindow ( dw ),
479                     dw->primitive.bottom_shadow_GC,
480                     dw->dial.center_x + dw->dial.shadow_delta,
481                     dw->dial.center_y + 1,
482                     dw->dial.indicator_x + dw->dial.shadow_delta,
483                     dw->dial.indicator_y + 1 );
484     }
485     return ( redraw );
486 }
```

The query_geometry Method

It is often useful to be able to determine the preferred size of a widget. Every widget contains a pointer to a `query_geometry` method in its Core class part whose purpose is to supply that information. This method is invoked by the Xt function:

```
XtGeometryResult XtQueryGeometry ( Widget            widget,
                                   XtWidgetGeometry *intended,
                                   XtWidgetGeometry *preferred )
```

A composite widget that intends to change the size or position of one of its children can call this function to determine the child's preferred geometry. The `intended` and `preferred` parameters are structures of type `XtWidgetGeometry`, which contains the members:

```
XtGeometryMask  request_mode;
Position        x, y;
Dimension       width, height, border_width;
Widget          sibling;
int             stack_mode;
```

The `request_mode` member of this structure indicates which members of the structure contain valid information and must be set using the masks:

```
CWX              CWY              CWWidth
CWHeight         CWBorderWidth    CWSibling
CWStackMode
```

Before calling `XtQueryGeometry()`, the parent widget indicates the changes it plans to make in an `XtWidgetGeometry` structure and uses it as the `intended` argument. If the child widget has no `query_geometry` method, `XtQueryGeometry()` fills in the `preferred` geometry structure with the child widget's current geometry. Otherwise it invokes the child's `query_geometry` method. If the proposed changes are acceptable to the child widget, the child's `query_geometry` method should return the constant `XtGeometryYes`. If the changes are unacceptable, or if the child's current geometry is identical to the child's preferred geometry, the method should return `XtGeometryNo`. If some of the proposed changes are acceptable, but others are not, the method can fill in the `preferred` structure with its preferred geometry and return the constant `XtGeometryAlmost`.

A parent widget is under no obligation to a child to maintain any child's preferred geometry, and may choose to ignore the information returned by `XtQueryGeometry()`.

Then Dial widget class does not implement a `query_geometry` method. By setting the `query_geometry` member to `NULL`, the Dial widget indicates that it would prefer to be its current size, whatever that may be.

Defining Action Procedures

The last function supported by the Dial widget is not a method, but is specified in the list of actions defined at the beginning of the file. This list associates an action named "`set-position()`" with a function `SetIndicatorPosition()`. By default, the "`set-position()`" action is bound to the user events `<Btn1Down>` and `<Btn1Motion>`.

The actions provided by a widget are entirely up to the programmer who creates the widget class. The Dial widget assumes that the "`set-position()`" action is the result of a mouse button event, and calculates the position of the indicator based on the coordinates of the mouse cursor, as reported in the event. The position is then used in the `callData` argument to the `XmNvalueChangedCallback`. This callback list is defined in the Dial widget's instance record. The `SetIndicatorPosition()` function uses `XtCallCallbacks()` to invoke any `XmNvalueChangedCallback` functions registered by the application.

The function `SetIndicatorPosition()` is written as:

```
487   static void SetIndicatorPosition ( Widget      w,
488                                       XEvent    *event,
489                                       String    *args,
490                                       Cardinal *n_args )
491   {
492       XsDialWidget    dw = ( XsDialWidget )  w;
493       Position        pos;
494       double          angle;
495       XsDialCallbackStruct cb;
496
497       pos = dw->dial.value;
498
499       if ( event->type == ButtonPress ||
500            event->type == MotionNotify )
501       {
502         /*
503          * Get the angle in radians.
504          */
505
506           angle = atan2 ( ( double ) ( event->xbutton.y -
507                                         dw->dial.center_y ),
508                           ( double ) ( event->xbutton.x -
509                                         dw->dial.center_x ) );
510
511         /*
512          * Convert to degrees from the MIN_ANGLE.
513          */
514
515           angle = DEGREES ( angle )  - ( MIN_ANGLE - 90.0 );
516           if ( angle < 0 )
517               angle = 360.0 + angle;
518
519         /*
520          * Convert the angle to a value.
521          */
522
523           pos = dw->dial.minimum + ( angle /
524                 MAX_ANGLE * ( dw->dial.maximum - dw->dial.minimum ) );
525           if ( pos > dw->dial.maximum || pos < dw->dial.minimum )
526               return;
527       }
528
529     /*
530      * Invoke the callback. Report the value in the call_data
531      * structure
532      */
533
```

```
534        cb.reason = XmCR_VALUE_CHANGED;
535        cb.event  = event;
536        cb.value  = pos;
537
538        XtVaSetValues ( ( Widget )  dw, XmNvalue, pos, NULL );
539
540        XtCallCallbacks ( ( Widget ) dw, XmNvalueChangedCallback, &cb );
541   }
```

Convenience Creation Functions

Most Motif widgets provide a convenience function that can be used to create the widget instead of calling `XtCreateWidget()`. Although not necessary, it is a good idea to provide such a function for new widgets, because programmers familiar with Motif may expect it. The Dial widget's convenience function, `XsCreateDial()` can be implemented as follows:

```
542   Widget XsCreateDial ( Widget   parent,
543                         char     *name,
544                         ArgList  arglist,
545                         Cardinal argcount )
546   {
547       return ( XtCreateWidget ( name, xsDialWidgetClass,
548                                 parent, arglist, argcount ) );
549   }
```

This concludes the implementation of the simple Dial widget. Because the Dial widget uses the architecture and follows the basic conventions of Xt, it can be combined freely with other widgets in Motif applications. The following section looks at an example program that exercises the Dial widget.

Using the Dial Widget

This section examines an application that uses the Dial widget described in the previous section. This simple example creates a single Dial widget and defines a callback that reports the Dial widget's current value when the user clicks or moves the mouse within the Dial window.

Every application that uses the Dial widget must include the Xm.h header file and also the Dial widget's public header file, Dial.h. After initializing Xt, the program creates a Dial widget using `XtCreateManagedWidget()`, and adds a function to the widget's `XmNvalueChanged-Callback` list. After realizing the toplevel widget, the application enters the main event loop. At this point, a single Dial widget, similar to the image in Figure 15.3, should appear on the screen.

```
1   /*********************************************
2    * dialtest.c : Test the Dial widget class
3    *********************************************/
4   #include <Xm/Xm.h>
5   #include "Dial.h"
6   #include <stdio.h>
```

```
7
8   static void ValueChangedCallback ( Widget      w,
9                                      XtPointer clientData,
10                                      XtPointer callData );
11
12  void main ( int argc, char **argv )
13  {
14      Widget        shell, dial;
15      XtAppContext app;
16
17      shell = XtAppInitialize ( &app, "Dial", NULL, 0,
18                                &argc, argv, NULL, NULL, 0 );
19
20      /*
21       * Create a Dial widget and add a select callback.
22       */
23
24      dial = XtCreateManagedWidget ( "dial", xsDialWidgetClass,
25                                     shell, NULL, 0 );
26
27      XtAddCallback ( dial, XmNvalueChangedCallback,
28                      ValueChangedCallback, NULL );
29
30      XtRealizeWidget ( shell );
31      XtAppMainLoop ( app );
32  }
```

The callback function `ValueChangedCallback()` simply reports the current value of the dial, as indicated in the call data structure. The `ValueChangedCallback()` function is implemented as follows:

```
33  static void ValueChangedCallback ( Widget      w,
34                                     XtPointer clientData,
35                                     XtPointer callData )
36  {
37      XsDialCallbackStruct *cbs = ( XsDialCallbackStruct* ) callData;
38
39      printf ( "Position = %d\n", cbs->value );
40  }
```

Compiling the Dial Widget Example

The `dialtest` example can be compiled and linked with the command:

```
cc -o dialtest diatest.c Dialo.c -lXm -lXt -lX11 -lm
```

15.4 Summary

This chapter discusses the architecture of basic Xt and Motif widget classes and creates a simple widget class that inherits from the Motif XmPrimitive widget class. Widgets consist of two basic parts, a class record and an instance record. The class record contains components shared by all widgets of a class, for example, the widget's class name, resource list, and methods. Methods are private functions that operate on the data in the widget's instance record. Each widget has its own copy of the instance record. This structure records the state of the specific widget: the size and position of the widget's window, the colors it uses, and so on.

The implementation of a widget uses a data abstraction technique that uses a private header file that contains the true definition of the widget and a public file that contains an incomplete definition. Applications see only the incomplete definition, and use Xt functions to create and manipulate the widget.

When creating a new widget, programmers can often reuse parts of a similar widget by inheriting from that widget. To inherit the behavior of another class, the programmer includes the superclass's class record and instance record in the new widget's definition. Special symbols also allow the programmer to specify that Xt should copy some of the superclass's methods into the new widget's class record. Other methods are chained, so that the superclass's methods are called first.

Chapter 16

Creating Manager Widget Classes

Chapter 15 describes a simple widget that defines it own appearance and style of interaction. This chapter builds on the information on Chapter 15 and presents a more complex type of widget that can support children. All widget classes that support children are subclasses of the Composite widget class, which is provided by Xt. The Composite widget class is a subclass of the Core widget class described in the previous chapter, and all of the basic characteristics described in Chapter 15 apply to composite widgets as well. The Composite class inherits all the characteristics of the Core widget class, and adds the ability to manage child widgets.

Widgets that belong to subclasses of the Composite widget class are referred to as composite widgets. Composite widgets are used primarily as containers for other widgets and are responsible for managing the geometry of their children. A managed widget is never permitted to resize or move itself directly. Instead, it must request its parent to make the changes. The parent widget considers the request and allows the change, disallows the change, or suggests a compromise, depending on its management policy. Although they do not usually have display semantics, composite widgets are an important part of any widget set because they allow other widgets to be combined to create a complete user interface.

Motif container widget classes never inherit directly from the Composite widget class. Instead, Motif container classes are subclasses of XmManager. The XmManager widget class provides several important features that are used by all Motif container classes. XmManager is actually a subclass of the Constraint widget class, which is a subclass of Composite. This chapter discusses the general architecture and features of the Composite widget class, and then discusses an example widget. The example widget is based on the XmManager widget class, ignoring the features of the

Constraint widget class that lies between the Composite class and the XmManager class. Chapter 17 discusses another manager widget that uses the features added by the Constraint widget class.

16.1 Architecture of a Composite Widget

The Composite widget class, along with Xt, provides the basic mechanism for managing children. Every composite widget's class record contains the methods that implement the widget's management policy. The first two members of every composite widget's class record includes both the Core widget class's `CoreClassPart` structure and a new `CompositeClassPart` structure.

The Composite Class Record

The Composite widget class's class record includes the `CoreClassPart` structure to allow all composite widgets to inherit the behavior of the Core widget class. The Composite widget class's class record also includes a `CompositeClassPart` that adds pointers to additional methods used to manage children. The Composite class record is defined as:

```
typedef struct _CompositeClassRec {
    CoreClassPart       core_class;
    CompositeClassPart  composite_class;
} CompositeClassRec;
```

The `CompositeClassPart` structure contains pointers to the methods that manage children. This structure is defined as:

```
typedef struct _CompositeClassPart {
    XtGeometryHandler   geometry_manager;
    XtWidgetProc        change_managed;
    XtWidgetProc        insert_child;
    XtWidgetProc        delete_child;
    XtPointer           extension;
} CompositeClassPart;
```

Each composite widget class must supply these methods in one way or another. Together, these functions determine how instances of a particular widget class manages children. These members are:

- `geometry_manager`: This member points to a function that is called when a child managed by the composite widget requests a change in size. The `geometry_manager` method can deny the request, allow the request, or suggest a compromise. The `geometry_-`

manager method can also make changes that affect other children, if necessary to accommodate the request.

- **change_managed**: This member is a pointer to a function that is called any time a composite widget's managed set changes. If a child is managed or unmanaged, Xt notifies the parent by calling this function. The parent then has an opportunity to make any adjustments to its layout that might be required.

- **insert_child**: The **insert_child** member is a pointer to a function that is called whenever a widget is created as a child of a composite widget. The **insert_child** method is responsible for adding the widget to the list of children maintained by each composite widget's instance record. This method is normally inherited.

- **delete_child**: The **delete_child** method is the counterpart to the insert_child method. This function is called when any child is destroyed, and is expected to remove the child from its parent's list of children. Most widget classes inherit this method from Composite.

The Composite Instance Record

Each composite widget's instance record includes the **CorePart** structure defined by the Core widget class, followed by a **CompositePart** structure. The Composite widget class's instance record is declared as:

```
typedef struct _CompositeRec {
    CorePart      core;
    CompositePart composite;
} CompositeRec;
```

The **CompositePart** structure is defined in the Composite widget's private header file as:

```
typedef struct _CompositePart {
    WidgetList  children;
    Cardinal    num_children;
    Cardinal    num_slots;
    XtOrderProc insert_position;
} CompositePart;
```

The first member of this structure, **children**, is a list of all widgets managed by the composite widget, while the second member, **num_children**, indicates the number of children on this list. The field **num_slots** is set to the maximum size of the list, and is used by the widget to alter the size of the children list dynamically. The last member of the **CompositePart** structure is a pointer to a method that must return an integer index into the **children** array. This index determines the position in the **children** list where the next child is to be inserted. Most widget classes inherit this method from the Composite widget class, but they can choose to redefine this method to control the order in which widgets are kept on the **children** list.

16.2 The XmManager Widget Class

In Motif, all manager widgets are subclasses of the XmManager widget class, which is an indirect subclass of Composite. To create a new widget class that fits smoothly with other Motif widgets, it is best to create the new manager widget class as a subclass of XmManager. The XmManager widget class is a direct subclass of the Constraint widget class, which is in turn a subclass of Composite. The XmManager class is very similar to the XmPrimitive widget class, in that the XmManager adds resources for Motif's shadows, and support for keyboard traversal. Most of the facilities for managing children, however, are inherited from the Composite widget class. Some, but not all, Motif widgets also use additional capabilities of the Constraint widget class. This chapter discusses only those features that are provided by the Composite widget class. The Constraint widget class will be ignored until Chapter 17.

> *Note*: At the time this book is being written, the OSF has not documented how to subclass from Motif widgets. Many details have been known to change from release to release. The precise details of the information presented here are almost certain to change in future releases of Motif.

The XmManager Class Record

The XmManager class record includes the `CoreClassPart` structure defined by the Core class, the `CompositeClassPart` structure defined by the Composite class, the `Constraint-ClassPart` structure defined by the Constraint class, and a new structure that contains the elements added by the XmManager class. The XmManager class record is declared as:

```
typedef struct {
    CoreClassPart           core_class;
    CompositeClassPart      composite_class;
    ConstraintClassPart     constraint_class;
    XmManagerClassPart      managere_class;
} XmManagerClassRec, *XmManagerWidgetClass;
```

The `XmManagerClassPart` structure includes several methods supported by all manager widgets as well as some data members that support additional XmManager features. These include:

- `translations`: This member is used to store some translations that control traversal. If traversal is activated, the contents of this translation table are added to the translations defined as part of the `CoreClassPart`. Subclasses can often inherit this behavior from XmManager by specifying `XtInheritTranslations` as the value of this member.

- `syn_resources`. Some resources may need some processing before they can be set or retrieved using the `XtSetValues()`/`XtGetValues()` interface. Resources installed as synthetic resources are treated differently from other widget resources, in that a function is called to allow the data to be processed or manipulated in some way before being passed to the normal Xt resource mechanism.

- `num_syn_resources`: This member indicates the number of synthetic resources used by the widget.

- `syn_constraint_resources`. This member serves a similar purpose to that served by the `syn_resources` member, but operates on constraint resources (See Chapter 17.).

- `num_syn_constraint_resources`: This member indicates the number of synthetic constraint resources used by the widget.

- `parent_process`: This member is used by Motif to handle default buttons on dialogs. Subclasses should always specify the value `XmInheritParentProcess` for this field.

The XmManager Instance Record

The XmManager instance record also adds additional members. Following the style used by all widgets, the XmManager instance record can be declared as:

```
typedef struct {
    CorePart          core;
    CompositePart     composite;
    ConstraintPart    constraint;
    XmManagerPart     manager;
} XmManagerRec, *XmManagerWidget;
```

The `XmManagerPart` structure contains various items required by instances of subclasses of the XmManager widget class. The members of this structure include:

- `foreground`: This member stores the foreground color of a widget. This value can be set and retrieved using the `XmNforeground` resource.

- `shadow_thickness`: This member indicates the widget's shadow thickness and can be set and retrieved using the `XmNshadowThickness` resource.

- `top_shadow_color`: This member indicates a widget's top shadow color. This value is normally computed automatically from the widget's background and foreground colors, but it can also be set and retrieved using the `XmNtopShadowColor` resource.

- `bottom_shadow_color`: This member indicates a widget's bottom shadow color. This value is normally computed automatically from the widget's background and foreground colors, but it can also be set and retrieved using the `XmNbottomShadowColor` resource.

- `highlight_color`: The `highlight_color` member is a `Pixel` value that indicates the color used to highlight gadget children of this widget. The color can be set or retrieved using the `XmNhighlightColor` resource.

- `help_callback`: This member contains a callback list. Functions registered with this list are invoked when the user asks for help.

- `user_data`: The `user_data` member is an untyped pointer than can be used by applications to associate data with a widget. The value of this member can set and retrieved using the `XmNuserData` resource.

- `highlight_GC`: The `highlight_GC` member contains a graphics context used to draw a highlight around a widget. This graphics context is created in the XmManager widget's `initialize` method using the value of the `highlight_color` member.

- `background_GC`: The `background_GC` member contains a graphics context that can be used to draw the background of a widget. This graphics context is created in the XmManager widget's `initialize` method using the value of the `background_pixel` member found in the `CorePart` structure.

- `top_shadow_GC`: The `top_shadow_GC` member contains a graphics context used to draw a widget's top shadow. This graphics context is created in the XmManager widget's `initialize` method using the value of the `top_shadow_color` member.

- `bottom_shadow_GC`: The `bottom_shadow_GC` member contains a graphics context used to draw a widget's bottom shadow. This graphics context is created in the XmManager widget's `initialize` method using the value of the `bottom_shadow_color` member.

These are just a few of the members added to the instance record by the XmManager widget class. These members can be useful to subclasses that need to display shadows, and so on. Some of these members are used by the example widgets described in the following section and next chapter.

Other Manager Widget Considerations

Like Motif primitive widgets, all Motif manager widgets follow certain conventions that should also be followed by new subclasses to allow them to work well with other Motif widgets. For example, all manager widgets should be capable of supporting gadgets. Many manager widgets have shadows whose width, colors and styles can be customized by applications and users, just like primitive widgets. Manager widgets are also responsible for keyboard traversal among their children, and must perform some steps to support this facility. The XmManager widget class provides some support a for these features, but subclasses must also cooperate.

Many manager widgets do not implement any translations, in which case, the symbol `XtInheritTranslations` can be specified for the translations member of the Core part of the class record. Manager widgets also install additional translations if the widget's keyboard focus policy is explicit. These translations are installed in the translations member of the XmManager part of the class record. Most subclasses can simply specify `XtInheritTranslations` for this member as well. Classes that do provide additional translations must include the XmManager translations in the new translation table. If you do not have access to the source of the XmManager widget class, the current translations and bindings can be obtained by referring to a current man page for XmManager.

Manager widget must provide support for gadgets by calling an internal Motif function, `_XmRedisplayGadgets()` in the widget's `expose` method, and must also provide some translations to allow gadget children to receive input. If translations are inherited, gadget input can be handled automatically.

When a manager widget's `change_managed` method is invoked, all Motif widgets must call the function `_XmNavigChangeManaged()` to allow Motif to update information about keyboard traversal, which is maintained by the XmManager class.

16.3 A Simple Manager Widget: The Row Widget

This section creates a new manager widget class, the Row widget class. Every manager widget implements its own management policy that determines how its children are positioned. The Row widget's management policy is simple. It places all managed children in a single row, evenly separated by any remaining space. The Row widget determines the position of each child widget; children may not move themselves. The Row widget honors all resize requests from children and attempts to grow to accommodate the request. If a Row widget cannot grow to contain all of its children, the children are clipped, as needed. The Row widget serves only as a container for other widgets and therefore has no display semantics itself.

Figure 16.1 shows a Row widget managing several button widgets. Figure 16.2 shows the same window when the Row widget has been resized.

Figure 16.1 The Row widget.

Figure 16.2 The Row widget's resize behavior.

Like all widgets, manager widgets consist of a private header file, a public header file, and one or more source files. The following sections describe the contents of each of the Row widget's files.

The Private Header File: RowP.h

The Row widget's private header file contains the definitions of the Row widget's class record and the instance record. The Row widget inherits directly from the XmManager widget class. It defines its class record by adding its own class part structure to the class parts defined by the Core, Composite, Constraint, and XmManager widget classes. Because the Row widget uses no additional class data, its class part is a dummy structure.

```
1    /*****************************************************
2     * RowP.h: Private header file for the Row widget.
3     *****************************************************/
4    #ifndef ROWP_H
5    #define ROWP_H
6
7    #include "Row.h"
8    #include <Xm/ManagerP.h>
9
10   typedef struct _XsRowClassPart {
11       int     empty;
12   } XsRowClassPart;
```

The Row widget's complete class record can now be declared by appending the XsRow-ClassPart to the structures provided by the Row widget's superclasses.

```
13   typedef struct _XsRowClassRec {
14       CoreClassPart         core_class;
15       CompositeClassPart    composite_class;
16       ConstraintClassPart   constraint_class;
17       XmManagerClassPart    manager_class;
18       XsRowClassPart        row_class;
19   } XsRowClassRec;
```

The next step in creating a widget is to define the instance record. The Row widget requires no additional data in its instance record, so its contribution to the instance record is also a dummy structure, declared as:

```
20   typedef struct {
21       int empty;
22   } XsRowPart;
```

The Row widget's complete instance record can be declared by adding the XsRowPart structure to those declared by the Row widget's superclasses.

```
23   typedef struct _XsRowRec {
24       CorePart          core;
25       CompositePart     composite;
26       ConstraintPart    constraint;
27       XmManagerPart     manager;
28       XsRowPart         row;
29   } XsRowRec;
30   #endif
```

The Public Header File: Row.h

The Row widget's public header file is similar to most widgets' public header files and consists of only a few public declarations:

```
1    /****************************************************
2     * Row.h: Public header file for the Row widget.
3     ***************************************************/
4    #ifndef ROW_H
5    #define ROW_H
6
7    #ifdef __cplusplus
8    extern "C" {
9    #endif
10
11     extern WidgetClass xsRowWidgetClass;
12     typedef struct _XsRowClassRec *XsRowWidgetClass;
13   typedef struct _XsRowRec       *XsRowWidget;
14
15   #ifdef _NO_PROTO
16   Widget XsCreateRow();
17   #else
18   Widget XsCreateRow ( Widget    parent,
19                        char     *name,
20                        ArgList   arglist,
21                        Cardinal  argcount);
22   #endif
23
24   #ifdef __cplusplus
25   }
26   #endif
27
28   #endif
```

Applications can use the class pointer, `xsRowWidgetClass`, as an argument to `XtCreateWidget()` to create a Row widget.

The Source File: Row.c

The file Row.c contains the static declaration of the Row widget's class record, as well as the Row widget's methods. The source file includes the file XmP.h as well as the private RowP.h header file. The file begins by declaring various functions used by the Row widget class.

```
1    /**********************************************************
2     * Row.c: Methods for the Row widget
3     **********************************************************/
4    #include    <Xm/XmP.h>
5    #include    "RowP.h"
6
7    static void Initialize ( Widget req, Widget new_w,
8                                ArgList args, Cardinal *numArgs );
9    static void Resize ( Widget w );
10   static void ChangeManaged ( Widget w );
11   static void Redisplay ( Widget w, XEvent *event, Region region );
12   static XtGeometryResult GeometryManager ( Widget           w,
13                                             XtWidgetGeometry *request,
14                                             XtWidgetGeometry *reply );
15   static XtGeometryResult QueryGeometry ( Widget           widget,
16                                           XtWidgetGeometry *intended,
17                                           XtWidgetGeometry *reply );
18   static void PreferredSize ( XsRowWidget  rw,
19                               Dimension    *w,
20                               Dimension    *h );
21   static void DoLayout ( XsRowWidget w );
```

The Class Record

The Row widget's class record is initialized entirely at compile time. Because the Row widget has no display semantics of its own and provides no additional actions or resources, it does not use many of the methods defined by the Core class part. For example, there is no need for a `SetValues()` method. However, the Row widget must define several new methods that allow it to manage its children.

The Row widget's class record is initialized as follows:

```
22   XsRowClassRec xsRowClassRec = {
23   {
24       /* core_class members      */
25       ( WidgetClass )  &xmManagerClassRec, /* superclass          */
26       "XsRow",                         /* class_name       */
27       sizeof ( XsRowRec ) ,            /* widget_size      */
28       NULL,                            /* class_initialize */
29       NULL,                            /* class_part_init  */
30       FALSE,                           /* class_inited     */
31       Initialize,                      /* initialize       */
32       NULL,                            /* initialize_hook  */
33       XtInheritRealize,                /* realize          */
34       NULL,                            /* actions          */
35       0,                               /* num_actions      */
36       NULL,                            /* resources        */
37       0,                               /* num_resources    */
38       NULLQUARK,                       /* xrm_class        */
```

```
39        TRUE,                              /* compress_motion      */
40        XtExposeCompressMaximal,           /* compress_exposure    */
41        TRUE,                              /* compress_enterleave*/
42        FALSE,                             /* visible_interest     */
43        NULL,                              /* destroy              */
44        Resize,                            /* resize               */
45        Redisplay,                         /* expose               */
46        NULL,                              /* set_values           */
47        NULL,                              /* set_values_hook      */
48        XtInheritSetValuesAlmost,          /* set_values_almost    */
49        NULL,                              /* get_values_hook      */
50        NULL,                              /* accept_focus         */
51        XtVersion,                         /* version              */
52        NULL,                              /* callback_private     */
53        XtInheritTranslations,             /* tm_table             */
54        QueryGeometry,                     /* query_geometry       */
55        NULL,                              /* display_accelerator*/
56        NULL,                              /* extension            */
57    },
58    {  /* composite_class members */
59        GeometryManager,                   /* geometry_manager     */
60        ChangeManaged,                     /* change_managed       */
61        XtInheritInsertChild,              /* insert_child         */
62        XtInheritDeleteChild,              /* delete_child         */
63        NULL,                              /* extension            */
64    },
65    {  /* constraint_class fields */
66        NULL,                              /* resource list        */
67        0,                                 /* num resources        */
68        0,                                 /* constraint size      */
69        NULL,                              /* init proc            */
70        NULL,                              /* destroy proc         */
71        NULL,                              /* set values proc      */
72        NULL,                              /* extension            */
73    },
74    {  /* manager class       */
75        XtInheritTranslations,             /* translations         */
76        NULL,                              /* syn resources        */
77        0,                                 /* num syn_resources    */
78        NULL,                              /* syn_cont_resources     */
79        0,                                 /* num_syn_cont_resources */
80        XmInheritParentProcess,            /* parent_process       */
81        NULL,                              /* extension            */
82    },
83    {  /* Row class members */
84        0,                                 /* empty                */
85    }
86    };
87    WidgetClass xsRowWidgetClass = ( WidgetClass )  &xsRowClassRec;
```

The `superclass` member of the class record specifies a pointer to `xmManagerClassRec`, the XmManager widget class's class structure. The Row widget requires no run-time initialization of the class structure, so the `class_initialize` and `class_part_initialize` members are set to `NULL`. Because there are no actions or settable resources, the `actions` and `resource` members are also set to `NULL`. The Row widget sets the `visible_interest` member of the class record to `FALSE` because Row widgets do not display anything, and do not care if they are visible.

The Row widget class does not use any features of the Constraint class, and all members of the `ConstraintClassPart` are set to `NULL`. None of the members provided by the XmManager class are used either, and all but the translations member are set to `NULL`. The value of the `translations` member is given as `XtInheritTranslations` to inherit whatever translations are supported by the XmManager superclass. The XmManager translations are needed by all manager widgets, to support traversal.

Methods

The Row widget defines three core part methods similar to those defined by the simple Dial widget in Chapter 15. However, the most interesting aspect of any composite widget class is the way it manages its children. The Row widget defines several methods and auxiliary functions that allow the Row widget to control the geometry of its children and also negotiate the geometry of the Row widget with its parent. The following sections discuss each of the Row widget's methods, beginning with the basic methods that all widget classes must provide before discussing the methods added by the Composite widget class.

The initialize Method

Because the Row widget class defines no additional resources of its own, the Row widget's `Initialize()` method is simple. Every widget's `Initialize()` method should check that the width and height of its window are greater than zero. No other steps are necessary for this widget class.

The `Initialize()` method is defined as:

```
88  static void Initialize ( Widget    request,
89                           Widget    new_w,
90                           ArgList   args,
91                           Cardinal *numArgs )
92  {
93      if ( XtWidth ( new_w )  <= 0 )
94          XtWidth ( new_w )  = 5;
95      if ( XtWidth ( new_w )  <= 0 )
96          XtHeight ( new_w )  = 5;
97  }
```

The realize Method

Like most widgets, the Row widget class inherits the basic method defined by the Core widget class to create its window. The Row widget sets the `realize` member of its class record to the symbol `XtInheritRealize` to inherit the `Realize()` method defined by the Core widget class.

The insert_child Method

Every manager widget must have an `insert_child` method, which is responsible for adding new widgets to the widget's list of children. Xt calls this method when an application creates a widget as a child of a composite widget. Most manager widgets inherit the basic method defined by the Composite widget class by specifying the symbol `XtInheritInsertChild` for the `insert_child` member of the class record. The Composite widget's `insert_child` method adds new children to the `children` list maintained in the widget's instance record, enlarging the list using `XtRealloc()`, if needed.

The default `insert_child` method defined by the Composite widget class calls the widget class's `insert_position` method to determine the next available position in the `children` array. If this method is not defined, the default behavior is to append the child to the end of the list. The list of children contains all widgets created as a child of the manager widget, regardless of whether or not they are currently managed. A manager widget can discover whether a particular child widget is managed by examining the `managed` member of the child's instance record.

The delete_child Method

Every manager widget must provide a method to remove widgets from its list of children. Most widgets, including the Row widget, inherit this method from the Composite class, by setting the `delete_child` member of the widget's class record to the symbol `XtInheritDeleteChild`.

The resize Method

The `resize` method is called when a widget is resized for any reason. The Row widget bases the layout of its children on its own size. The Row widget's `resize` method simply calls an auxiliary function, `DoLayout()`, to recompute the layout of its children when the Row widget's size changes.

```
98   static void Resize ( Widget w )
99   {
100      DoLayout ( ( XsRowWidget ) w );
101  }
```

The function `DoLayout()` determines the position of each managed child. It iterates twice over the children listed in the `children` member of the widget's instance record. On the first pass, `DoLayout()` computes the sum of the widths of all managed children, to determine how much space, if any, it can place between each widget. The second pass positions each managed child, evenly separated, in a single row.

```
102  static void DoLayout ( XsRowWidget rw )
103  {
104      Widget      child;
105      int         i;
106      Dimension   childwidth;
107      Position    xpos;
108      Dimension   pad;
```

```
109        int          numManagedChildren;
110
111     /*
112      * Compute the total width of all managed children
113      */
114
115     childwidth = 0;
116     numManagedChildren = 0;
117
118     for ( i = 0; i < rw->composite.num_children; i++ )
119     {
120         child = rw -> composite.children[i];
121
122         if ( child->core.managed )
123         {
124             childwidth += XtWidth ( child );
125             numManagedChildren++;
126         }
127     }
128
129     /*
130      *  Divide any remaining space by the number
131      *  of spaces between managed children.
132      */
133
134     pad = 0;
135
136     if ( XtWidth ( rw ) > childwidth )
137         pad = ( XtWidth ( rw ) - childwidth ) /
138                                     ( numManagedChildren + 1 );
139
140     /*
141      * Position all managed children.
142      */
143
144     xpos = pad;
145
146     for ( i = 0; i < rw->composite.num_children; i++ )
147     {
148         int verticalPad = 0;
149         child = rw -> composite.children[i];
150
151         if ( child->core.managed )
152         {
153             if ( XtHeight( child) +
154                     2 * XtBorderWidth ( child ) < XtHeight ( rw ) )
155                 verticalPad =  ( XtHeight ( rw )  -
156                                     ( XtHeight ( child )  -
157                                     2 * XtBorderWidth ( child ) ) ) / 2;
```

```
158
159                 _XmConfigureObject ( child, xpos, verticalPad,
160                                 XtWidth ( child ), XtHeight ( child ),
161                                 XtBorderWidth ( child ) );
162             xpos += pad + XtWidth ( child );
163         }
164     }
165 }
```

`DoLayout()` uses an undocumented, internal Motif function to position the Row widget's children. The function `_XmConfigureObject()` is similar to the Xt function `XtConfigureWidget()`. Both functions allow a manager widget to specify the size and position of a child. The Xt function works only with widget children, while the Motif function can be used to configure both widgets and Motif gadgets. The Motif function is declared as follows:

```
void _XmConfigureObject ( Widget    w,
                          Position  x,
                          Position  y,
                          Dimension width,
                          Dimension height,
                          Dimension border_width )
```

Like `XtConfigureWidget()`, this function should only be used by a widget's parent. The function forces the widget to a specific size and position, with no negotiation. Applications should *never* call this function, but must use `XtSetValues()` to set a widget's size or position. When an application calls `XtSetValues()` to set a widget's size, the widget requests its parent to change its size. If an application calls `_XmConfigureObject()` directly, it will bypass the normal geometry management mechanism, possibly causing errors in the layout.

Xt and Motif provide several other functions that are useful to manager widgets when positioning and manipulating children. Xt provides `XtMoveWidget()` and `XtResizeWidget()`, while Motif implements gadget-safe equivalents `_XmMoveObject()` and `_XmResizeObject()`. These functions are defined as:

```
void _XmMoveObject ( Widget w, Position x, Position y );
void _XmResizeObject ( Widget w, Dimension width, Dimension height );
```

All of these functions are for internal use by manager widgets only, and are undocumented, and therefor subject to change at any time.

The expose Method

The Row widget class's `expose` method, `Redisplay()`, is called whenever an `Expose` event occurs within a Row widget's window. The Row widget does not display anything of its own, and all widget children handle their own exposure events. However, if the Row widget manages gadgets, the Row widget must provide support for redrawing the gadgets. Motif provides an internal undocumented function that redisplays all gadget children of a manager widget. This function is defined as:

```
      void _XmRedisplayGadgets ( Widget manager, XEvent *event, Region region )
```

The Row widget's `Redisplay()` method calls `_XmRedisplayGadgets()` to redisplay any gadget children, as needed.

```
166  static void Redisplay ( Widget w, XEvent *event, Region region )
167  {
168      /* Redraw all gadgets.*/
169
170      _XmRedisplayGadgets ( w, event, region );
171  }
```

The query_geometry Method

A widget's `query_geometry` method allows its parent to request the widget's desired size by calling `XtQueryGeometry()`. The Row widget bases its preferred geometry on the maximum height and the total width of its children. The Row widget uses an auxiliary function, `PreferredSize()` to simplify the task of handling geometry requests. `PreferredSize()` returns the Row widget's preferred width and height to its caller. A simple version of this function can be written as follows:

```
172  static void PreferredSize ( XsRowWidget  rw,
173                              Dimension    *w,
174                              Dimension    *h )
175  {
176      int i;
177
178      *w = 0;
179      *h = 0;
180
181      /*
182       * Loop through the list of children, computing the
183       * maximum height and the total width of all managed children.
184       */
185
186      for ( i = 0; i < rw->composite.num_children; i++ )
187      {
188          Widget child = rw->composite.children[i];
189
190          if ( child->core.managed )
191          {
192              *w += XtWidth ( child );
193
194              if ( *h < XtHeight ( child ) )
195                  *h = XtHeight ( child );
196          }
197      }
198  }
```

Notice that, in this function, the preferred size of the Row widget is based on the current size of its children. However, it is possible that a child might have a size that is different than its preferred size. A better way to compute the preferred size of the Row widget would be to ask each child for its preferred size and base the Row widget's computation on the result. A version of `PreferredSize()` that takes this approach could be written as follows:

```
static void PreferredSize ( XsRowWidget   rw,
                            Dimension     *w,
                            Dimension     *h )
{
    int i;

    *w = 0;
    *h = 0;

    /*
     * Loop through the list of children, computing the
     * maximum height and the total width of all children
     * based on their preferred sizes.
     */

    for  ( i = 0; i < rw->composite.num_children; i++ )
    {
        XtWidgetGeometry preferred;
        Widget child = rw->composite.children[i];

        if ( child->core.managed )
        {
            XtQueryGeometry ( child, NULL, &preferred );

            *w += preferred.width;;

            if ( *h < preferred.height )
                *h = preferred.height;
        }
    }
}
```

This version of the function will be less efficient, because each child must be queried, using `XtQueryGeometry()` each time the Row widget's function is called. However, this approach gives a more accurate indication of the Row widget's preferred size.

Using either version of the `PreferredGeometry()` function, the `query_geometry` method can be written as follows:

```
199  static XtGeometryResult QueryGeometry ( Widget                widget,
200                                          XtWidgetGeometry *intended,
201                                          XtWidgetGeometry *reply )
202  {
```

```
203        XsRowWidget rw =  ( XsRowWidget )  widget;
204        Dimension    w, h;
205
206    /*
207     * The Row widget does not care about its position, so
208     * if a query does not involve a change to height or width
209     * just return yes.
210     */
211
212        if ( intended->request_mode & ( ~ ( CWWidth | CWHeight ) ) )
213            return  ( XtGeometryYes );
214
215    /*
216     * Compute the Row widget's preferred size
217     */
218
219        PreferredSize  ( rw, &w, &h );
220
221    /*
222     * If the intended size matches the desired size, return yes.
223     */
224
225        if ( intended->request_mode & CWWidth &&
226             intended->width == w &&
227             intended->request_mode & CWHeight &&
228             intended->height == h )
229           return ( XtGeometryYes );
230
231
232    /*
233     * If the desired size is equal to the current size, return no,
234     * to ask to be left alone.
235     */
236
237        if ( w == XtWidth ( widget ) &&
238             h == XtHeight ( widget ) )
239          return ( XtGeometryNo );
240
241    /*
242     * In all other cases, fill out the reply structure to
243     * indicate the preferred size and reply almost.
244     */
245
246        reply->request_mode = CWWidth | CWHeight;
247        reply->width = w;
248        reply->height = h;
249        return XtGeometryAlmost;
250  }
```

The geometry_manager Method

As mentioned previously, a widget should never attempt to alter its size or location directly, because the geometry of every widget is the responsibility of the widget's parent. Applications must resize widgets by calling `XtSetValues()`, which causes the widget to make a geometry request to its parent. Geometry requests are made using the function:

```
XtGeometryResult XtMakeGeometryRequest ( Widget            widget,
                                         XtWidgetGeometry *request,
                                         XtWidgetGeometry *reply )
```

This function takes an `XtWidgetGeometry` structure as an argument and returns one of the constants:

XtGeometryYes	XtGeometryNo
XtGeometryAlmost	XtGeometryDone

`XtMakeGeometryRequest()` invokes the `geometry_manager` method of the given widget's parent. If the parent allows the request, the parent's `geometry_manager` method should return the constant `XtGeometryYes`. In this case, `XtMakeGeometryRequest()` makes the requested changes. If the parent's `geometry_manager` method fulfills the request itself, it should return `XtGeometryDone`. The parent's `geometry_manager` method can also disallow the request by returning `XtGeometryNo` or suggest a compromise by returning the constant `XtGeometryAlmost`.

Xt also supports a simpler function that can be used instead of `XtMakeGeometryRequest()`, when a widget only wants to change its size. This function is declared as follows:

```
XtGeometryResult XtMakeResizeRequest ( Widget     widget,
                                       Dimension  width,
                                       Dimension  height,
                                       Dimension *repyWidth,
                                       Dimension *replyHeight )
```

This function requests that a widget's width and height be changed to the given dimensions. If the widget's parent returns `XtGeometryAlmost`, the `replyWidth` and `replyHeight` variables return the parent's suggested compromise.

The Row widget's `geometry_manager` method, `GeometryManager()`, begins by checking for and rejecting any changes to the position of a child widget. If the request involves a change in width or height, the method sets the child widget's sizes to those requested. Next, `GeometryManager()` computes the minimum size of the Row widget, based on the child's new size. If the Row widget is not large enough to accommodate the size of its children, `GeometryManager()` calls `XtMakeResizeRequest()` to attempt to grow. This function invokes the `geometry_manager` supported by the Row widget's parent. Once a final size has been established for the Row widget, `GeometryManager()` calls `DoLayout()` to reposition all children before returning `XtGeometryYes` to approve the child's request.

```
251  static XtGeometryResult GeometryManager ( Widget              widget,
252                                             XtWidgetGeometry  *request,
253                                             XtWidgetGeometry  *reply )
254  {
255      XsRowWidget  rw =  ( XsRowWidget )  XtParent ( widget );
256
257      /*
258       * Disallow all motion
259       */
260
261      if  ( request->request_mode &  ( CWX | CWY ) )
262          return  ( XtGeometryNo );
263
264      /*
265       *  Grant all size requests
266       */
267
268      if  ( request->request_mode &  ( CWWidth | CWHeight ) )
269      {
270          Dimension w = 0, h = 0;
271          int i;
272
273          /*
274           * Set the child's size to the requested size.
275           */
276
277          if  ( request->request_mode & CWWidth )
278              XtWidth ( widget )   = request->width;
279          if  ( request->request_mode & CWHeight )
280              XtHeight ( widget )  = request->height;
281
282          /*
283           * Now compute the new minimum size
284           */
285
286          for  ( i = 0; i < rw->composite.num_children; i++ )
287          {
288              Widget child = rw->composite.children[i];
289
290              if ( child->core.managed )
291              {
292                  w += XtWidth ( child );
293
294                  if ( h < XtHeight ( child ) )
295                      h = XtHeight ( child );
296              }
297          }
298
299
```

```
300            /*
301             * if the minimum size required to contain all
302             * children is larger than the current size
303             * of the Row widget, make a request to grow.
304             */
305
306            if ( w > XtWidth ( rw )   ||
307                 h > XtHeight ( rw ) )
308            {
309                XtGeometryResult result;
310
311                Dimension replyWidth, replyHeight;
312
313                /*
314                 * Request a resize
315                 */
316
317                result = XtMakeResizeRequest  ( ( Widget ) rw, w, h,
318                                                 &replyWidth,
319                                                 &replyHeight );
320
321                /*
322                 * If an alternative is proposed, accept it by making
323                 * a second request with the pre-approved values.
324                 */
325
326                if ( result == XtGeometryAlmost )
327                    XtMakeResizeRequest  ( ( Widget ) rw,
328                                             replyWidth, replyHeight,
329                                             NULL, NULL );
330            }
331
332        /*
333         * Recompute the layout based on the new sizes.
334         */
335
336        DoLayout ( rw );
337    }
338
339    return  ( XtGeometryYes );
340 }
```

It is important to understand the basic rules of geometry management, as well as how different manager widgets implement specific policies. The Row widget completely controls the geometry of its children and tries its best to accommodate their preferred sizes. However, the Row widget cannot control its own size; that is controlled by its parent. Each Row widget bases its preferred size on its children's sizes, and attempts to grow if necessary to contain its children.

The change_managed Method

A manager widget's `change_managed` method is invoked whenever one of its children is managed or unmanaged. Manager widgets generally use this method to recalculate the layout of their children when the set of managed widgets changes. The Row widget's `change_managed` method, `ChangeManaged()`, computes the Row widget's preferred size based on the new children, and requests a change in its size if necessary. Once the final size of the Row widget is established, `ChangeManaged()` calls `DoLayout()` to position each managed child.

```
341  static void ChangeManaged ( Widget child )
342  {
343      XsRowWidget rw = ( XsRowWidget ) child;
344      Dimension w, h;
345
346      /*
347       * Call internal Motif function to update translation info.
348       */
349
350      _XmNavigChangeManaged ( child );
351
352      /*
353       * Attempt to establish the Row widget's size.
354       */
355
356      PreferredSize  ( rw, &w, &h );
357
358      if ( w > XtWidth ( rw )  || h > XtHeight ( rw ) )
359      {
360          XtGeometryResult result;
361          Dimension replyWidth, replyHeight;
362
363          result = XtMakeResizeRequest ( ( Widget ) rw, w, h,
364                                     &replyWidth, &replyHeight );
365          if ( result == XtGeometryAlmost )
366              XtMakeResizeRequest ( ( Widget ) rw,
367                                 replyWidth, replyHeight,
368                                 NULL, NULL );
369      }
370
371      /*
372       * Position all children
373       */
374
375      DoLayout ( rw );
376  }
```

Like most Motif widgets, the Row widget provides a convenience function that can be used to create a new Row widget.

```
377   Widget XsCreateRow ( Widget    parent,
378                        char      *name,
379                        ArgList   arglist,
380                        Cardinal  argcount )
381   {
382       return  ( XtCreateWidget ( name, xsRowWidgetClass,
383                                   parent, arglist, argcount ) );
384   }
```

Using the Row Widget

This section describes a simple program, rowtest, that tests the Row widget's management capabilities. The program uses a Row widget to manage four button widgets. Several callbacks allow the buttons to request size changes, and also to add or delete buttons.

```
1     /********************************************
2      * rowtest.c : Demo the Row widget class
3      ********************************************/
4     #include <Xm/Xm.h>
5     #include <Xm/PushB.h>
6     #include "Row.h"
7
8     static void  GrowCallback ( Widget, XtPointer, XtPointer );
9     static void  UnmanageCallback ( Widget, XtPointer, XtPointer );
10    static void  ManageCallback ( Widget, XtPointer, XtPointer );
11
12    void main ( int argc, char **argv )
13    {
14        Widget        shell, row;
15        Widget        button1, button2, button3, button4;
16        XtAppContext  app;
17
18        /*
19         * Initialize Xt.
20         */
21
22        shell = XtAppInitialize ( &app, "RowTest", NULL, 0,
23                                  &argc, argv, NULL, NULL, 0 );
24        /*
25         * Create a Row widget.
26         */
27
28        row = XtCreateManagedWidget ( "row", xsRowWidgetClass,
29                                      shell, NULL, 0 );
30
31        /*
32         * Add children to the Row widget.
33         */
```

```
34
35      button1 = XtCreateManagedWidget ( "button1",
36                                         xmPushButtonWidgetClass,
37                                         row, NULL, 0 );
38
39      button2 = XtCreateManagedWidget ( "button2",
40                                         xmPushButtonWidgetClass,
41                                         row, NULL, 0 );
42
43      button3 = XtCreateManagedWidget ( "button3",
44                                          xmPushButtonWidgetClass,
45                                          row, NULL, 0 );
46
47      button4 = XtCreateManagedWidget ( "button4",
48                                          xmPushButtonWidgetClass,
49                                          row, NULL, 0);
50
51      XtAddCallback ( button1, XmNactivateCallback,
52                      GrowCallback, NULL );
53      XtAddCallback ( button2, XmNactivateCallback,
54                      UnmanageCallback, NULL );
55      XtAddCallback ( button3, XmNactivateCallback,
56                      ManageCallback, ( XtPointer ) button2 );
57      XtAddCallback ( button4, XmNactivateCallback,
58                      GrowCallback, NULL );
59
60      XtRealizeWidget ( shell );
61
62      XtAppMainLoop ( app );
63  }
```

Figure 16.1, on page 566, shows the initial layout of the buttons produced by this program.

The rowtest program defines three callback functions that demonstrate and test the Row widget's geometry manager. The first callback, GrowCallback(), is registered as a XmNactivateCallback function for button1 and button4. Each time the user activates one of these buttons, GrowCallback() requests the Row widget to increase the width and height of the corresponding button by 10 pixels.

```
64  static void GrowCallback ( Widget     w,
65                             XtPointer clientData,
66                             XtPointer callData)
67  {
68      Dimension  width, height;
69
70      /*
71       *  Get the current width and height of the widget.
72       */
73
```

```
74        XtVaGetValues ( w,
75                        XmNwidth,  &width,
76                        XmNheight, &height,
77                        NULL );
78
79    /*
80     * Increment the width and height by 10 pixels before
81     * setting the size.
82     */
83
84        width  +=10;
85        height +=10;
86
87        XtVaSetValues ( w,
88                        XmNwidth,  width,
89                        XmNheight, height,
90                        NULL );
91
92    }
```

Figure 16.3 shows the layout of the rowtest example after this function has been called several times for button1 and button4.

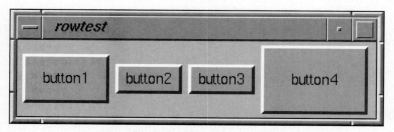

Figure 16.3 Handling resize requests.

A second XmNactivateCallback function is registered for button2. The UnmanageCallback() function calls XtUnmanageChild(), and causes the Row widget's change_managed method to be invoked to recompute the widget layout. This function is defined as:

```
93    void UnmanageCallback ( Widget     w,
94                            XtPointer clientData,
95                            XtPointer callData)
96    {
97        XtUnmanageChild ( w );
98    }
```

The last `XmNactivateCallback` function is registered with `button3`. This function calls `XtManageChild()` to add `button2` back to the Row widget's managed list.

```
99    void ManageCallback ( Widget      w,
100                          XtPointer clientData,
101                          XtPointer callData )
102   {
103       Widget button = ( Widget ) clientData;
104
105       XtManageChild ( button );
106   }
```

Figure 16.4 shows the how the Row widget adjusts the layout when `button2` is unmanaged.

Figure 16.4 Row widget after unmanaging button2.

16.4 Summary

This chapter introduces the architecture of a Motif manager widget, with emphasis on the basic features inherited from the Composite widget class. All manager widgets are subclasses of the Composite widget class. The distinguishing feature of subclasses of Composite is that they can manage other widgets. Manager widgets are primarily responsible for managing the geometry of their children. Widgets can never resize or move themselves directly; instead, they must request their parent to do it for them. The Composite class record defines several methods solely for the purpose of managing children.

The next chapter discusses manager widgets that take advantage of the features supported by the Constraint widget class, a powerful subclass of the Composite widget class.

Chapter 17

Constraint-Based Widget Classes

Chapter 16 demonstrates how to write a manager widget that uses the capabilities of the Composite widget class to manage the layout of other widgets. Widget classes that only use the mechanisms of the Composite widget class apply their management policies uniformly without regard to any special characteristics of their children. However, the Motif XmManager widget class, and therefore all Motif manager widgets, is also based on the Constraint widget class. The Constraint widget class is a subclass of the Composite widget class that supports widget classes that manage children based on additional information associated with each child. The Constraint class name comes from the fact that this information often takes the form of some constraint. For example, one might like to impose the constraint: "The scrollbar widget must always be to the left of the text widget."

Manager classes that use the constraint mechanism have all the responsibilities of composite widget classes, but must also manage the constraints imposed on each widget. This chapter discusses the Constraint widget class and demonstrates a Motif manager widget that uses the features of the Constraint widget class. This widget arranges its children represent nodes of an acyclic hierarchical graph.

17.1 Architecture of Constraint Widgets

The Constraint widget class's architecture is similar to that of the Composite widget class. However, the Constraint widget class adds methods and resources used to handle constraint resources. Every constraint widget class includes the `CoreClassPart` structure, the `CompositeClassPart` structure, and the `ConstraintClassPart` structure as the first components of its class record.

```
typedef struct _ConstraintClassRec {
    CoreClassPart       core_class;
    CompositeClassPart  composite_class;
    ConstraintClassPart constraint_class;
} ConstraintClassRec;
```

The `ConstraintClassPart` structure contains information and methods used by every constraint widget.

```
typedef struct _ConstraintClassPart {
    XtResourceList  resources;
    Cardinal        num_resources;
    Cardinal        constraint_size;
    XtInitProc      initialize;
    XtWidgetProc    destroy;
    XtSetValuesFunc set_values;
    caddr_t         extension;
} ConstraintClassPart;
```

In addition to the basic resource list contained in the Core class part of every widget class, the `ConstraintClassPart` of a constraint widget's class record contains a constraint resource list. The resource manager uses this resource list to initialize the constraints structure attached to each child widget. Every widget has a pointer to a `constraint` structure in the `CorePart` of its instance record (see Chapter 15). This pointer is set to NULL unless the child is managed by a constraint widget. When a widget is managed by a constraint widget, Xt allocates space for a constraint structure, the size of which is determined by the `constraint_size` member of the parent's `ConstraintClassPart` structure. The `ConstraintClassPart` structure also contains pointers to three new methods that initialize and manage the constraints of the widget's children.

The Constraint widget class's instance record is defined as:

```
typedef struct _ConstraintRec {
    CorePart       core;
    CompositePart  composite;
    ConstraintPart constraint;
} ConstraintRec, *ConstraintWidget;
```

The Constraint widget class requires no additional information in its instance record, so `ConstraintPart` is defined as a structure with only one member, which is ignored.

```
typedef struct _ConstraintPart {
    int     ignore;
} ConstraintPart;
```

Each constraint widget must also define the constraint structure attached to each of its children. The contents of this structure are specific to each particular type of constraint widget and the policy it supports. The widget described in the following section provides one example.

The Motif XmManager widget adds its own class record and instance record structures to those supported by the Constraint widget class, as described in Chapter 16.

17.2 A Manager Widget Based on Constraints

The rest of this chapter presents an example of a manager widget that demonstrates the Xt constraint mechanism. The Tree widget class organizes children as a hierarchical graph based on a constraint resource that specifies each child widget's position in the tree. Applications can use the resource manager to specify a constraint for each child when it is created. The following sections describe the public and private header files provided by the Tree widget and then discuss the Tree widget's methods.

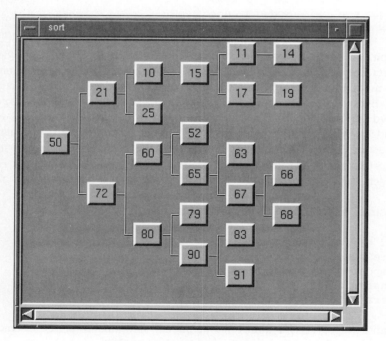

Figure 17.1 The Tree widget.

Figure 17.1 shows the Tree widget, with several children arranged in a hierarchy. Each node in the hierarchy is a widget. The Tree widget positions the widgets and draws connecting lines between them. Like any manager widget, the Tree widget allows any type of widgets as children. Figure 17.1 shows a collection of XmPushButton widgets, but each node can be any type of Motif widget, including a manager widget. The Tree widget positions each child according to a constraint resource associated with each child that specifies the node's relationship to other nodes in the hierarchy.

Because the terms "parent" and "child" are already being used to refer to relationships in a widget hierarchy, this chapter uses the terms *node*, *supernode*, and *subnode* to refer to the hierarchical relationships between children managed by a Tree widget. Every node has a supernode that is positioned higher in the hierarchy, and may also have subnodes that are lower in the hierarchy. As implemented here, the Tree widget allows each node to have only a single supernode. Nodes can have as many subnodes as needed.

The Tree Private Header File: TreeP.h

The Tree widget's private header file defines the class record, the instance record, and the constraint record attached to each widget managed by the Tree widget. The structures defined in this file are similar to that of the widget classes discussed in earlier chapters. The only new feature is the constraint structure.

The file begins by including the public Tree.h header file and the Motif ManagerP.h private header file. The next step is to define the Tree widget class's contribution to the class record. The Tree widget does not define any additional methods, so its contribution to the class record is a dummy structure.

```
1   /***********************************************************
2    * TreeP.h: Private header file for the Tree widget class.
3    ***********************************************************/
4   #ifndef XSTREEP_H
5   #define XSTREEP_H
6
7   #include "Tree.h"
8   #include <Xm/ManagerP.h>
9
10  typedef struct _XsTreeClassPart {
11      int    ignore;
12  } XsTreeClassPart;
```

The Tree widget's complete class record is defined as:

```
13  typedef struct _XsTreeClassRec {
14    CoreClassPart       core_class;
15    CompositeClassPart  composite_class;
16    ConstraintClassPart constraint_class;
17    XmManagerClassPart  manager_class;
18    XsTreeClassPart     tree_class;
19  } XsTreeClassRec;
20  extern XsTreeClassRec xsTreeClassRec;
```

The Tree widget's instance record contains auxiliary information used to position the nodes in the tree and draw connecting lines. This information includes the minimum and maximum spacing between nodes of the tree, and some auxiliary data used by the methods that calculate the position of each widget. The instance record also includes a member that points to a widget used as the root of the tree. The tree widget creates a `tree_root` widget to guarantee that every child widget has a supernode. Forcing all nodes to have a supernode simplifies the tree layout calculations.

The Tree widget also uses an auxiliary structure that maintains an expandable integer array along with the size of the array. This structure, `XsVariableArray` is declared as follows:

```
21    typedef struct {
22        Dimension   *array;
23        int         size;
24    }  XsVariableArray;
```

The `XsTreePart` structure is defined as:

```
25    typedef struct {
26        Dimension         h_min_space;
27        Dimension         v_min_space;
28        XsVariableArray  *horizontal;
29        XsVariableArray  *vertical;
30        Widget            tree_root;
31    } XsTreePart;
```

The Tree widget class's complete instance record can be declared by appending the XsTreePart structure to those defined by the Core, Composite, Constraint, and XmManager widget classes.

```
32    typedef struct _XsTreeRec {
33        CorePart        core;
34        CompositePart   composite;
35        ConstraintPart  constraint;
36        XmManagerPart   manager;
37        XsTreePart      tree;
38    }  XsTreeRec;
```

Widget classes that use constraints must install a constraint structure into the instance record of each widget created as a child. This structure, known as a *constraint record*, follows the same conventions as the class and instance records. Each manager widget defines a constraint part structure, which is appended to the constraint part structures defined by its superclasses to form the complete structure. The Tree widget class defines a structure that contains the information that the widget needs to associate with each child to allow each child to be treated as a node in a graph. This information includes a pointer to the widget that is the child's supernode, a list of the child's subnodes, and a pair of variables in which to record a temporary *x,y* location before the child is actually positioned.

The `XsTreeConstraintPart` structure is declared as follows:

```
39  typedef struct _XsTreeConstraintPart {
40    Widget        super_node;
41    WidgetList    sub_nodes;
42    long          n_sub_nodes;
43    long          max_sub_nodes;
44    Position      x, y;
45  } XsTreeConstraintPart;
```

Core and Composite obviously do not contribute to this structure, because they do not support the constraint mechanisms. The Constraint widget class also does not export a constraint part structure. However, the XmManager widget does provide a constraint part structure. The complete Tree constraint record consists of the XsTreeConstraintPart structure appended to the XmManager-ConstraintPart structure. The **XsTreeConstraintsRec** structure is declared as followed:

```
46  typedef struct _XsTreeConstraintsRec {
47    XmManagerConstraintPart    manager;
48    XsTreeConstraintPart       tree;
49  } XsTreeConstraintsRec, *XsTreeConstraints;
50
51  #endif
```

The Tree Public Header File: Tree.h

The Tree widget's public header file is straightforward and similar to the examples in previous chapters. In addition to the type declarations, the header file defines some additional symbols that represent resources supported by the Tree widget. The file also declares the widget's class pointer and provides several convenience creation functions, as is the custom for Motif widgets.

```
1   /********************************************************
2    * Tree.h: Public header file for the Tree widget class.
3    ********************************************************/
4   #ifndef XSTREE_H
5   #define XSTREE_H
6
7   #ifdef __cplusplus
8   extern "C" {
9   #endif
10
11  extern WidgetClass xsTreeWidgetClass;
12
13  typedef struct _XsTreeClassRec *XsTreeWidgetClass;
14  typedef struct _XsTreeRec       *XsTreeWidget;
15
16  #define XmNhorizontalSpace      "horizontalSpace"
17  #define XmNverticalSpace        "verticalSpace"
18  #define XmCPad                  "Pad"
19  #define XmNsuperNode            "superNode"
```

```
20   #define XmCSuperNode            "SuperNode"
21
22   Widget XsCreateTree ( Widget    parent,
23                         char      *name,
24                         ArgList   arglist,
25                         Cardinal  argcount );
26
27   Widget XsCreateScrolledTree ( Widget    parent,
28                                 char      *name,
29                                 ArgList   arglist,
30                                 Cardinal  argcount );
31
32   #ifdef __cplusplus
33   }
34   #endif
35
36   #endif
```

The Tree Widget Source File: Tree.c

The file Tree.c e initializes the Tree widget class's class record and implements the Tree widget's
private methods. The file begins by including the private Motif header file XmP.h, as well as the Tree
widget header file. Like many Motif widget classes, the Tree widget provides a convenience
function that creates a Tree widget as a child of an XmScrolledWindow widget. Therefore, the
XmScrolledWindow widget class's public header file is included as well.

```
1    /***************************************************
2     * Tree.c: The Tree Widget Source File
3     ***************************************************/
4    #include         <Xm/XmP.h>
5    #include         <Xm/ScrolledW.h>
6    #include         "TreeP.h"
7    #define   MAX(a,b) ((a) > (b) ? (a) : (b))
```

Declarations of the methods and other functions used by the Tree widget come next.

```
8    static void Initialize ( Widget req, Widget new_w,
9                             ArgList args, Cardinal *numArgs );
10   static Boolean ConstraintSetValues ( Widget    current,
11                                        Widget    request,
12                                        Widget    new_w,
13                                        ArgList   args,
14                                        Cardinal  *numArgs );
15   static void ConstraintInitialize ( Widget request, Widget new_w,
16                                      ArgList args, Cardinal *numArgs );
17   static void ConstraintDestroy ( Widget w );
18   static Boolean SetValues ( Widget cur, Widget req, Widget widget,
19                              ArgList args, Cardinal *numArgs );
```

```
20  static XtGeometryResult GeometryManager ( Widget            w,
21                                            XtWidgetGeometry *request,
22                                            XtWidgetGeometry *reply );
23  static void ChangeManaged ( Widget w );
24  static void DeleteNode ( Widget super_node, Widget node );
25  static void Redisplay ( Widget w, XEvent *event, Region region );
26  static XsVariableArray *CreateOffset ( long size );
27  static int ComputePositions ( XsTreeWidget tw,
28                                Widget       w,
29                                long         level );
30  static void SetPositions ( XsTreeWidget tw,
31                             Widget       w,
32                             int     level );
33  static void Reset ( XsVariableArray *offset );
34  static void NewLayout ( XsTreeWidget tw );
35  static void ShiftSubtree ( Widget     w,
36                             Dimension offset );
37  static Position CurrentPosition ( XsVariableArray *offset,
38                                    long             position );
39  static void SetCurrentPosition ( XsVariableArray *offset,
40                                   int             index,
41                                   Dimension       value );
42  static Position SumOfPositions ( XsVariableArray *offset,
43                                   long             index );
44  static void InsertNewNode ( Widget super_node, Widget node );
```

The Tree widget uses the contents of each child's constraint record to position each child. It is convenient to define a macro that allows the constraint record to be accessed easily. Recall that the Core instance record defines the constraint structure as an untyped pointer. The Tree widget class must cast this pointer back to the type of structure actually stored in the `constraints` member. The following macro provides an easy way to retrieve the constraints structure.

```
45  #define TREE_CONSTRAINT( w ) \
46              ( ( XsTreeConstraints ) ( ( w )->core.constraints ) )
```

The Tree widget class supports two resources that affect the overall layout of its children. The Tree widget's additional resources allow applications and users to use the resource manager to control the minimum horizontal and vertical space between nodes. The default is to place a minimum of 20 pixels between each child.

```
47   static XtResource resources[] = {
48
49  { XmNhorizontalSpace,XmCSpace,XmRDimension,sizeof ( Dimension ),
50    XtOffset ( XsTreeWidget, tree.h_min_space ), XtRString,"20" },
51
52  { XmNverticalSpace,XmCSpace, XmRDimension,sizeof ( Dimension ),
53    XtOffset ( XsTreeWidget, tree.v_min_space ), XtRString, "20" },
54  };
```

Widgets that use constraints can specify an additional resource list used by the resource manager to set the values in the constraint structure associated with each child widget. The Tree widget's constraint resource list allows applications to use `XtSetValues()` to specify each widget's supernode.

```
55   static XtResource treeConstraintResources[] = {
56   { XmNsuperNode, XmCSuperNode, XmRPointer, sizeof ( Widget ),
57     XtOffset ( XsTreeConstraints, tree.super_node ),
58     XtRPointer, NULL },
59   };
```

The Class Record

Like each of the widgets discussed in earlier chapters, the Tree widget's class record is initialized entirely at compile time. The Tree widget class inherits the `realize`, `set_values_almost` methods from its superclass. The methods defined by the Tree widget class include the `initialize`, `redisplay`, and `set_values` methods. The Tree widget class also implements a `geometry_manager` method as well as a `change_managed` method.

```
60   XsTreeClassRec xsTreeClassRec = {
61   {
62       /* core_class fields */
63       ( WidgetClass ) &xmManagerClassRec,          /* superclass           */
64       "Tree",                                      /* class_name           */
65       sizeof ( XsTreeRec ),                        /* widget_size          */
66       NULL,                                        /* class_init           */
67       NULL,                                        /* class_part_init      */
68       FALSE,                                       /* class_inited         */
69       Initialize,                                  /* initialize           */
70       NULL,                                        /* initialize_hook      */
71       XtInheritRealize,                            /* realize              */
72       NULL,                                        /* actions              */
73       0,                                           /* num_actions          */
74       resources,                                   /* resources            */
75       XtNumber ( resources ) ,                     /* num_resources        */
76       NULLQUARK,                                   /* xrm_class            */
77       TRUE,                                        /* compress_motion      */
78       XtExposeCompressMaximal,                     /* compress_exposure    */
79       TRUE,                                        /* compress_enterleave  */
80       TRUE,                                        /* visible_interest     */
81       NULL,                                        /* destroy              */
82       NULL,                                        /* resize               */
83       Redisplay,                                   /* expose               */
84       SetValues,                                   /* set_values           */
85       NULL,                                        /* set_values_hook      */
86       XtInheritSetValuesAlmost,                    /* set_values_almost    */
87       NULL,                                        /* get_values_hook      */
88       NULL,                                        /* accept_focus         */
```

```
89      XtVersion,                          /* version              */
90      NULL,                               /* callback_private     */
91      XtInheritTranslations,              /* tm_table             */
92      NULL,                               /* query_geometry       */
93      NULL,                               /* display_accelerator*/
94      NULL,                               /* extension            */
95    },
96    {
97      /* composite_class fields */
98      GeometryManager,                    /* geometry_manager */
99      ChangeManaged,                      /* change_managed */
100     XtInheritInsertChild,               /* insert_child    */
101     XtInheritDeleteChild,               /* delete_child    */
102     NULL,                               /* extension       */
103   },
104   {
105     /* constraint_class fields */
106     treeConstraintResources,            /* subresources       */
107     XtNumber ( treeConstraintResources ),  /* subresource_count */
108     sizeof ( XsTreeConstraintsRec ),    /* constraint_size   */
109     ConstraintInitialize,               /* initialize        */
110     ConstraintDestroy,                  /* destroy           */
111     ConstraintSetValues,                /* set_values        */
112     NULL,                               /* extension         */
113   },
114   {
115     /* manager class */
116     XtInheritTranslations,              /* translations        */
117     NULL,                               /* syn resources       */
118     0,                                  /* num syn_resources   */
119     NULL,                               /* get_cont_resources  */
120     0,                                  /* num_get_cont_resources */
121     XmInheritParentProcess,             /* parent_process      */
122     NULL,                               /* extension           */
123   },
124   {
125     /* Tree class fields */
126     NULL,                               /* ignore              */
127   }
128   };
```

The Tree widget implements several methods for handling children and constraint resources. The `constraint_initialize` and `constraint_destroy` methods initialize and free the constraint records of each child widget. The `constraint_set_values` method is invoked when a child's constraint resource is changed.

The Tree class pointer is declared internally as a pointer to this `xsTreeClassRec` structure.

```
129  WidgetClass xsTreeWidgetClass = ( WidgetClass ) &xsTreeClassRec;
```

Methods

The primary difference between a widget class that uses constraints and one that does not is the addition of several methods that initialize and set the values of the resources in each child's constraint record. The `initialize` and `set_values` methods are used to process the manager widget's resources, while two new methods, `constraint_initialize` and `constraint_set_values` process the constraint resources attached to each child widget.

The following sections describe the implementation of each of the Tree widget class's methods.

The initialize Method

Xt invokes the Tree widget's `initialize` method when the Tree widget is created. The `initialize` method first checks that the width and height of the widget are greater than zero. Next, it creates a widget that serves as the root of the tree. This widget is created, but never managed. It is not visible to the user and only exists to simplify the tree layout calculations. Finally, the `horizontal` and `vertical` members of the Tree widget's instance record are initialized. These members and the function `CreateOffset()` are discussed along with the tree layout algorithm starting on page 607.

```
130   static void Initialize ( Widget req, Widget new_w,
131                            ArgList args, Cardinal *numArgs )
132   {
133       XsTreeWidget tw = ( XsTreeWidget ) new_w;
134       XsTreeWidget request = ( XsTreeWidget ) req;
135
136       /*
137        * Make sure the widget's width and height are
138        * greater than zero.
139        */
140
141       if ( tw->core.width <= 0 )
142           tw->core.width = 100;
143       if ( tw->core.height <= 0 )
144           tw->core.height = 100;
145
146       tw->tree.tree_root = NULL;
147
148       /*
149        * Create the hidden root widget.
150        */
151
152       tw->tree.tree_root =
153               XtVaCreateWidget ( "root", widgetClass, ( Widget ) tw,
154                                  XmNwidth, 1,
155                                  XmNheight, 1,
156                                  XmNmappedWhenManaged, FALSE,
157                                  NULL );
158       /*
```

```
159         * Allocate the tables used by the layout algorithm.
160         */
161
162         tw->tree.horizontal = CreateOffset ( 10 );
163         tw->tree.vertical   = CreateOffset ( 10 );
164    }
```

The constraint_initialize Method

In addition to an `initialize` method, every constraint widget class also needs a `constraint_initialize` method. Xt invokes this method each time a child of the Tree widget is created, to allow the Tree widget to initialize the child's constraint record. The arguments `request` and `new_w` are versions of a child of the Tree widget, not the Tree widget. The `request` parameter is a copy of the child with all resources as originally requested by a combination of command line arguments, the contents of the resource database, and widget defaults. The `new_w` parameter is the widget after it has been processed by all superclasses's `constraint_initialize` methods. The `args` and `numArgs` arguments provide a list of the constraint resources applied to the child.

The Tree widget's `constraint_initialize` method sets the `n_sub_nodes`, `max_sub_nodes`, and `sub_nodes` members of each child's constraint record to zero, zero, and NULL, respectively, and checks to see if the widget has a supernode. If so, the child widget is added to the supernode widget's list of subnodes. Otherwise, the widget is made a subnode of the `tree_root` widget created by the Tree widget. Notice the test to determine whether the `tree_root` widget exists. This test prevents the `tree_root` widget from attempting to add itself recursively to its own list of subnodes when it is created.

```
165    static void ConstraintInitialize ( Widget request, Widget new_w,
166                                       ArgList args, Cardinal *numArgs )
167    {
168        XsTreeConstraints tree_const = TREE_CONSTRAINT ( new_w );
169        XsTreeWidget tw = ( XsTreeWidget ) XtParent ( new_w );
170
171        /*
172         * Initialize the widget to have no sub-nodes.
173         */
174
175        tree_const->tree.n_sub_nodes   = 0;
176        tree_const->tree.max_sub_nodes = 0;
177        tree_const->tree.sub_nodes     = ( WidgetList ) NULL;
178        tree_const->tree.x             = tree_const->tree.y = 0;
179
180        /*
181         * If this widget has a supernode, add it to that
182         * widget's subnodes list. Otherwise make it a subnode of
183         * the tree_root widget.
184         */
185
186        if ( tree_const->tree.super_node )
```

```
187                InsertNewNode ( tree_const->tree.super_node, new_w );
188        else
189            if ( tw->tree.tree_root )
190                InsertNewNode ( tw->tree.tree_root, new_w );
191    }
```

The set_values Method

The Tree widget class's `set_values` method, `SetValues()`, is called when a Tree widget resource is altered. `SetValues()` checks the values of two resources. If either of the horizontal or vertical space resources is modified, `SetValues()` calls the auxiliary functions `NewLayout()` to reposition all children. Finally, `SetValues()` returns the value of the `redraw` flag, which indicates whether or not Xt should force the window to be redrawn.

```
192    static Boolean SetValues ( Widget new_w, Widget old, Widget widget,
193                               ArgList args, Cardinal *numArgs )
194    {
195        XsTreeWidget tw = ( XsTreeWidget ) new_w;
196        XsTreeWidget current = ( XsTreeWidget ) old;
197
198        int redraw = FALSE;
199
200        /*
201         * If the minimum spacing has changed, recalculate the
202         * tree layout. NewLayout() does a redraw, so we don't
203         * need SetValues to do another one. The redraw flag is not
204         * really needed for this simple function, but set it up
205         * to allow for future expansion.
206         */
207
208        if ( tw->tree.v_min_space != current->tree.v_min_space ||
209             tw->tree.h_min_space != current->tree.h_min_space )
210        {
211            NewLayout ( tw );
212            redraw = FALSE;
213        }
214
215        return ( redraw );
216    }
```

The constraint_set_values Method

Xt invokes a widget's `constraint_set_values` method when one or more of a child's constraint resources are altered. The only resource supported by children of the Tree widget is the `XmNsuperNode` resource. If the value of this resource has changed, the Tree widget calls an auxiliary function, `DeleteNode()`, to remove the specified child widget from its current supernode widget's subnode list. Then, the function `InsertNode()` adds the widget to its new supernode widget's list of subnodes.

Notice that the new_w widget is passed to both of these methods. It is important to use the correct widget because each of these methods stores a pointer to the given widget in a list. The new_w widget is the actual widget used, and therefore has the correct address. The other arguments are temporary copies of the widget's instance record, created by Xt before calling the constraint_set_values method. After processing the child's constraint resources, the Tree widget's constraint_set_values method calls the auxiliary function, NewLayout(), to recalculate the position of each child widget.

```
217   static Boolean ConstraintSetValues ( Widget current,
218                                         Widget    request,
219                                         Widget    new_w,
220                                         ArgList   args,
221                                         Cardinal *numArgs )
222   {
223       XsTreeConstraints newconst      = TREE_CONSTRAINT ( new_w );
224       XsTreeConstraints current_const = TREE_CONSTRAINT ( current );
225       XsTreeWidget tw = ( XsTreeWidget ) XtParent ( new_w );
226
227       /*
228        * If the super_node field has changed, remove the widget
229        * from the old widget's sub_nodes list and add it to the
230        * new one.
231        */
232
233       if ( current_const->tree.super_node != newconst->tree.super_node )
234       {
235           if ( current_const->tree.super_node )
236               DeleteNode ( current_const->tree.super_node, new_w );
237
238           if ( newconst->tree.super_node )
239               InsertNewNode ( newconst->tree.super_node, new_w );
240           else
241               if ( tw->tree.tree_root )
242                   InsertNewNode ( tw->tree.tree_root, new_w );
243
244           /*
245            * If the Tree widget has been realized,
246            * compute new layout.
247            */
248
249           if ( XtIsRealized ( tw ) )
250               NewLayout ( tw );
251       }
252
253       return ( FALSE );
254   }
```

Auxiliary Functions

The auxiliary functions InsertNode() and DeleteNode() are responsible for managing the sub_nodes list in each child's constraint record. Each time a new subnode is added, the InsertNode() function checks whether the list is large enough to contain another widget. If not, the list must be enlarged using XtRealloc(). Then the function adds the widget to the end of the list and increments the n_sub_nodes index.

```
255   static void InsertNewNode ( Widget super_node, Widget node )
256   {
257       XsTreeConstraints super_const = TREE_CONSTRAINT ( super_node );
258       XsTreeConstraints node_const  = TREE_CONSTRAINT ( node );
259
260       int index = super_const->tree.n_sub_nodes;
261
262       node_const->tree.super_node = super_node;
263
264       /*
265        * If there is no more room in the sub_nodes array,
266        * allocate additional space.
267        */
268
269       if ( super_const->tree.n_sub_nodes ==
270            super_const->tree.max_sub_nodes )
271       {
272           super_const->tree.max_sub_nodes +=
273                           ( super_const->tree.max_sub_nodes / 2 ) + 2;
274
275           super_const->tree.sub_nodes =
276           (WidgetList) XtRealloc ((char *) super_const->tree.sub_nodes,
277                               ( super_const->tree.max_sub_nodes ) *
278                                       sizeof ( Widget ) );
279       }
280
281       /*
282        * Add the sub_node in the next available slot and
283        * increment the counter.
284        */
285
286       super_const->tree.sub_nodes[index] = node;
287       super_const->tree.n_sub_nodes++;
288   }
```

The function DeleteNode() performs the opposite operation, removing a widget from the list of subnodes, closing any gap in the list caused by the removal of an entry, and decrementing the n_sub_nodes counter.

```
289  static void DeleteNode ( Widget super_node, Widget node )
290  {
291      XsTreeConstraints node_const = TREE_CONSTRAINT ( node );
292      XsTreeConstraints super_const;
293      int pos, i;
294
295      /*
296       * Make sure the super_node exists.
297       */
298      if ( !super_node )
299          return;
300
301      super_const = TREE_CONSTRAINT ( super_node );
302
303      /*
304       * Find the sub_node on its super_node's list.
305       */
306
307      for ( pos = 0; pos < super_const->tree.n_sub_nodes; pos++ )
308          if ( super_const->tree.sub_nodes[pos] == node )
309              break;
310
311      if ( pos == super_const->tree.n_sub_nodes )
312          return;
313      /*
314       * Decrement the number of sub_nodes
315       */
316
317      super_const->tree.n_sub_nodes--;
318
319      /*
320       * Fill in the gap left by the sub_node.
321       * Zero the last slot for good luck.
322       */
323
324      for ( i = pos; i < super_const->tree.n_sub_nodes; i++ )
325          super_const->tree.sub_nodes[i] =
326                                      super_const->tree.sub_nodes[i+1];
327      super_const->tree.sub_nodes[super_const->tree.n_sub_nodes] = 0;
328  }
```

The constraint_destroy Method

The constraint_destroy method is called whenever a child of a constraint widget is destroyed. The constraint_destroy method gives the constraint widget an opportunity to make any adjustments required by the deletion of a child widget. The method is called with only one argument, which indicates the widget being destroyed. In this example, the Tree widget needs to remove any pointers to the widget from other children's constraint records, and relocate any subnodes of the widget being destroyed. The Tree widget simply moves these subnodes to the sub_nodes list of the supernode of the widget being destroyed, and triggers a new layout. The constraint_destroy method must not free the memory used by the constraint record itself; Xt does that automatically.

```
329   static void ConstraintDestroy ( Widget w )
330   {
331       XsTreeConstraints tree_const = TREE_CONSTRAINT ( w );
332       XsTreeWidget parent          = ( XsTreeWidget ) XtParent ( w );
333       int i;
334
335       /*
336        * Remove the widget from its parent's sub-nodes list and
337        * make all this widget's sub-nodes sub-nodes of the parent.
338        */
339
340       if ( tree_const->tree.super_node )
341       {
342           DeleteNode ( tree_const->tree.super_node, w );
343
344           for ( i = 0; i < tree_const->tree.n_sub_nodes; i++ )
345               InsertNewNode ( tree_const->tree.super_node,
346                               tree_const->tree.sub_nodes[i] );
347
348       }
349   }
```

The Constraint Tree

Now that the functions used to initialize and modify the constraint records of the Tree widget's children have been introduced, let's pause and look closer at the structure created by these constraints. The following small code segment creates a Tree widget that manages three children.

```
tree = XtCreateManagedWidget ( "TreeTest", xsTreeWidgetClass,
                               shell, NULL, 0 );
widget1 =  XtCreateManagedWidget ( "One", widgetClass,
                                   tree, NULL, 0 );
widget2 =  XtVaCreateManagedWidget ( "Two", widgetClass, tree,
                                     XmNsuperNode, widget1,
                                     NULL );
widget3 =  XtCreateManagedWidget ( "Three", widgetClass, tree,
                                   XmNsuperNode, widget1,
                                   NULL );
```

Consider the contents of the constraint record of each of these widgets and also the dummy tree_root widget created by the Tree widget at the point after widget3 has been created. The tree_root widget's super_node member is NULL, and its sub_nodes list contains a single widget, widget1. The super_node member of widget2's constraint record contains a pointer to the tree_root widget, and its sub_nodes list contains two widgets, widget2 and `widget3`. The `sub_nodes` members of `widget2` and `widget3` contain a pointer to `widget1`, and their `sub_nodes` list is empty. Figure 17.2 shows how these pointers create a hierarchical graph.

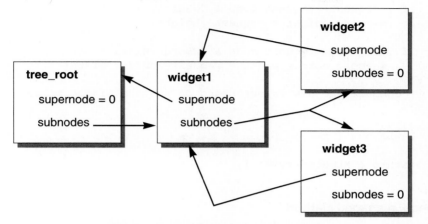

Figure 17.2 A hierarchical constraints structure.

The geometry_manager Method

Xt invokes the Tree widget's `geometry_manager` method, `GeometryManager()`, when a child of the Tree widget makes a geometry request. The Tree widget's management policy does not allow a child to change its position, because the tree layout algorithm determines the position of every widget. However, the geometry manager grants all size requests without question. `GeometryManager()` calls the auxiliary function, `NewLayout()` to recompute and redraw the tree layout before returning `XtGeometryYes`.

```
350  static XtGeometryResult GeometryManager ( Widget            w,
351                                            XtWidgetGeometry *request,
352                                            XtWidgetGeometry *reply )
353  {
354      XsTreeWidget tw = ( XsTreeWidget ) XtParent ( w );
355
356      /*
357       * No position changes allowed!.
358       */
359
360      if ( ( request->request_mode & CWX && request->x != XtX ( w ) ) ||
361           ( request->request_mode & CWY && request->y != XtY ( w ) ) )
362          return ( XtGeometryNo );
363      /*
364       * Allow all resize requests.
365       */
```

```
366
367        if ( request->request_mode & CWWidth )
368            w->core.width = request->width;
369
370        if ( request->request_mode & CWHeight )
371            w->core.height = request->height;
372
373        if ( request->request_mode & CWBorderWidth )
374            w->core.border_width = request->border_width;
375    /*
376     * Compute the new layout based on the new widget sizes;
377     */
378
379        NewLayout ( tw );
380
381        return ( XtGeometryYes );
382  }
```

The change_managed Method

Xt invokes the Tree widget's `ChangeManaged()` method whenever the Tree widget's set of managed children changes. `ChangeManaged()` simply calls `NewLayout()` to calculate the desired position of all children.

```
383  static void ChangeManaged ( Widget w )
384  {
385        XsTreeWidget tw = ( XsTreeWidget ) w;
386        _XmNavigChangeManaged ( w );
387        NewLayout ( tw );
388  }
```

The expose Method

The Tree widget class's `expose` method, `Redisplay()`, is called whenever an `Expose` event occurs within a Tree widget's window. This function loops through each child on the Tree widget's list of children, drawing the connecting lines from the right edge to the left edge of each of the widget's subnodes. The connecting lines are drawn using what is sometimes called a Manhattan style of drawing, in which all lines are horizontal or vertical. Lines are drawn using the top and bottom shadow colors supported by the XmManager widget class, so that all lines have a three dimensional appearance that is consistent with the shadow appearance supported by Motif.

```
389  static void Redisplay ( Widget w, XEvent *event, Region region )
390  {
391        XsTreeWidget       tw = ( XsTreeWidget ) w;
392        int                i, j;
393        XsTreeConstraints  tree_const;
394        Widget             child;
395
```

```
396        /*
397         * If the Tree widget is visible, redraw all lines and gadgets.
398         */
399
400        if ( XtIsRealized ( tw ) && tw->core.visible )
401        {
402            /* Redraw all gadgets. */
403
404            _XmRedisplayGadgets ( w, event, region );
405
406            for ( i = 0; i < tw -> composite.num_children; i++ )
407            {
408                child = tw -> composite.children[i];
409                tree_const = TREE_CONSTRAINT ( child );
410
411              /*
412               * Draw a line between the right edge of each widget
413               * and the left edge of each of its sub_nodes. Don't
414               * draw lines from the fake tree_root. Lines are drawn
415               * "manhattan" style, so that all lines are either
416               * vertical or horizontal, like this:
417               *
418               *                |---- node
419               *                |
420               *     node ----
421               *                |
422               *                |---- node
423               */
424
425                if ( child != tw->tree.tree_root &&
426                      tree_const->tree.n_sub_nodes )
427                {
428                    for ( j = 0; j < tree_const->tree.n_sub_nodes; j++ )
429                    {
430
431                      /*
432                       * Any two given nodes can be connected by
433                       * drawing three line segments. The line
434                       * segments can be described using three x
435                       * values and two y values:
436                       *
437                       *              x1      midX      x2
438                       *               |       |         |
439                       *
440                       *  y1-                   |-------- node
441                       *                        |
442                       *                        |
443                       *  y2-   node -------|
444                       */
```

```
445                        int x1 = XtX ( child ) + XtWidth ( child );
446                        int y1 = XtY ( child ) + XtHeight ( child ) / 2;
447                        int x2 = XtX ( tree_const->tree.sub_nodes[j] );
448                        int y2 = XtY ( tree_const->tree.sub_nodes[j] ) +
449                          XtHeight ( tree_const->tree.sub_nodes[j] ) / 2;
450                        int midX = x1 + ( x2 - x1 ) / 2;
451
452                    /*
453                     *  Draw the first line, once for the bottom
454                     *  shadow and once for the top, one pixel lower.
455                     */
456
457                        XDrawLine ( XtDisplay ( tw ) , XtWindow ( tw ) ,
458                                    tw->manager.top_shadow_GC,
459                                    x1, y1, midX, y1 );
460                        XDrawLine ( XtDisplay ( tw ) , XtWindow ( tw ) ,
461                                    tw->manager.bottom_shadow_GC,
462                                    x1,   y1 + 1,
463                                    midX, y1 + 1 );
464
465                    /*
466                     *  Draw the other horizontal line, both bottom
467                     *  shadow and top shadow.
468                     */
469
470                        XDrawLine ( XtDisplay ( tw ) , XtWindow ( tw ) ,
471                                    tw->manager.top_shadow_GC,
472                                    midX, y2, x2,   y2 );
473                        XDrawLine ( XtDisplay ( tw ) , XtWindow ( tw ) ,
474                                    tw->manager.bottom_shadow_GC,
475                                    midX, y2 +1,
476                                    x2,   y2 + 1 );
477                    /*
478                     *  Because the "etched" lines are not
479                     *  symmetrical, the coordinates of the vertical
480                     *  lines varies with the direction of the line.
481                     */
482
483                        if ( y1 < y2 )
484                        {
485                            XDrawLine ( XtDisplay ( tw ), XtWindow ( tw ),
486                                        tw->manager.top_shadow_GC,
487                                        midX, y1,
488                                        midX, y2 );
489                            XDrawLine ( XtDisplay ( tw ), XtWindow ( tw ),
490                                        tw->manager.bottom_shadow_GC,
491                                        midX + 1, y1,
492                                        midX + 1, y2 - 1 );
493                        }
```

```
494                    else if ( y2 < y1 )
495                    {
496                        XDrawLine ( XtDisplay ( tw ), XtWindow ( tw ),
497                                    tw->manager.top_shadow_GC,
498                                    midX, y1,
499                                    midX, y2 + 1 );
500
501                        XDrawLine ( XtDisplay ( tw ), XtWindow ( tw ),
502                                    tw->manager.bottom_shadow_GC,
503                                    midX + 1, y1,
504                                    midX + 1, y2 + 2 );
505
506                    }
507                }
508            }
509        }
510    }
511 }
```

The Tree Layout Procedures

The previous sections describe each of the Tree widget's methods. The remaining functions are auxiliary functions used to determine the position of each child widget. The layout algorithm uses a few simple rules of thumb, intended to produce an aesthetically pleasing tree layout. The basic rules are:

- The overall tree should be as narrow, top to bottom, as possible.
- Each node should be placed as close as possible to its siblings.
- Each node should be centered to the left of its subnodes.
- Nodes at the same level should begin at the same horizontal position.
- The shape of any given subtree should be independent of its position in the tree.

The concept of the tree layout algorithm is simple. The first node of each level is initially positioned at y coordinate 0, and each successive node on the same level is placed below its neighbor. After the positions of all nodes within a particular branch are determined, the supernode of the branch is centered to the left of its subnodes. If this position is less than the next available position on the supernode's level, the entire subtree must be shifted. The offset necessary to move the supernode to the next available position at its level is calculated and the entire sub-tree is shifted. This operation establishes the y coordinate of each widget. To determine the x position of each widget, the layout functions store the maximum width of all nodes at each level. Once the y position of each widget has been computed, this information is used to determine the final x position of each widget.

The function NewLayout() provides the top-level interface to the layout algorithm. This function resets the auxiliary tables used to store temporary information, then calls other functions to do the real work.

```
512   static void NewLayout ( XsTreeWidget tw )
513   {
514       /*
515        * Reset the auxiliary tables.
516        */
517
518       Reset ( tw->tree.vertical );
519       Reset ( tw->tree.horizontal );
520
521       /*
522        * Compute each widget's x,y position
523        */
524
525       ComputePositions ( tw, tw->tree.tree_root, 0 );
526
527       /*
528        * Move each widget into place.
529        */
530
531       SetPositions ( tw, tw->tree.tree_root, 0 );
532
533       /*
534        *  Trigger a redisplay of the lines connecting nodes.
535        */
536
537       if ( XtIsRealized ( tw ) )
538          XClearArea ( XtDisplay ( tw ), XtWindow ( tw ), 0, 0, 0, 0, TRUE );
539   }
```

The function `Reset()`, which is described later, initializes two data structures that store the next available position in the vertical direction and the maximum width of the widgets on each level in the horizontal direction.

The main portion of the tree layout algorithm is handled by the auxiliary function `ComputePositions()`:

```
540   static int ComputePositions ( XsTreeWidget tw, Widget w, long level )
541   {
542       Position current_hpos, current_vpos;
543       int      i, depth = 0;
544       XsTreeConstraints tree_const = TREE_CONSTRAINT ( w );
545
546       /*
547        * Get the current positions for this level.
548        */
549
550       current_hpos = CurrentPosition ( tw->tree.horizontal, level );
551       current_vpos = CurrentPosition ( tw->tree.vertical, level );
552
```

```
553        /*
554         * Set the current horizontal width to the max widths of all
555         * widgets at this level.
556         */
557
558        SetCurrentPosition ( tw->tree.horizontal, level,
559                             MAX ( current_hpos, XtWidth ( w ) ) );
560
561        /*
562         * If the node has no sub_nodes, just set the vertical
563         * position to the next available space.
564         */
565
566        if ( tree_const->tree.n_sub_nodes == 0 )
567        {
568            tree_const->tree.y = current_vpos;
569        }
570        else
571        {
572            Widget              first_kid, last_kid;
573            XsTreeConstraints   const1, const2;
574            Position            top, bottom;
575
576            /*
577             * If the node has sub_nodes, recursively figure the
578             * positions of each sub_node.
579             */
580
581            for ( i = 0; i < tree_const->tree.n_sub_nodes; i++ )
582                depth = ComputePositions ( tw,
583                                           tree_const->tree.sub_nodes[i],
584                                           level + 1 );
585
586            /*
587             * Now that the vertical positions of all children are
588             * known, find the vertical extent of all sub_nodes.
589             */
590
591            first_kid= tree_const->tree.sub_nodes[0];
592            last_kid =
593              tree_const->tree.sub_nodes[tree_const->tree.n_sub_nodes-1];
594            const1 = TREE_CONSTRAINT ( first_kid );
595            const2 = TREE_CONSTRAINT ( last_kid );
596            top = const1->tree.y + XtHeight ( first_kid ) / 2;
597            bottom = const2->tree.y + XtHeight ( last_kid ) / 2;
598
599            /*
600             * Set the node's position to the center of its sub_nodes.
601             */
```

```
602
603              tree_const->tree.y =( top + bottom ) /2 - (XtHeight ( w ) / 2 );
604
605          /*
606           * If this position is less than the next available
607           * position, correct it to be the next available
608           * position, calculate the amount by which all sub_nodes
609           * must be shifted, and shift the entire sub-tree.
610           */
611
612          if ( tree_const->tree.y < current_vpos )
613          {
614              Dimension offset = current_vpos - tree_const->tree.y;
615
616              for ( i = 0; i < tree_const->tree.n_sub_nodes; i++ )
617                  ShiftSubtree ( tree_const->tree.sub_nodes[i], offset );
618
619           /*
620            * Adjust the next available space at all levels below
621            * the current level.
622            */
623
624              for ( i = level + 1; i <= depth; i++ )
625              {
626                  Position pos = CurrentPosition ( tw->tree.vertical,
627                                                    i );
628
629                  SetCurrentPosition ( tw->tree.vertical, i,
630                                        pos + offset );
631              }
632
633            tree_const->tree.y = current_vpos;
634
635          }
636      }
637
638      /*
639       * Record the current vertical position at this level.
640       */
641
642      SetCurrentPosition ( tw->tree.vertical, level,
643                           tw->tree.v_min_space +
644                           tree_const->tree.y + XtHeight ( w ) );
645
646      return ( MAX ( depth, level ) );
647  }
```

The function **ShiftSubtree( )** moves the given widget's entire subtree by an integer offset.

```
648   static void ShiftSubtree ( Widget w, Dimension offset )
649   {
650       int i;
651       XsTreeConstraints tree_const = TREE_CONSTRAINT ( w );
652
653       /*
654        * Shift the node by the offset.
655        */
656
657       tree_const->tree.y += offset;
658
659       /*
660        * Shift each sub-node into place.
661        */
662
663       for ( i=0; i< tree_const->tree.n_sub_nodes; i++ )
664           ShiftSubtree ( tree_const->tree.sub_nodes[i], offset );
665   }
```

Once the layout of all widgets has been determined, the function `SetPositions()` sets the *x* position of each widget and calls `_XmMoveObject()` to move each widget into place. If all children don't fit in the Tree widget, this function makes a geometry request to the Tree widget's parent to attempt to enlarge the Tree widget.

```
666   static void SetPositions ( XsTreeWidget tw, Widget w, int level )
667   {
668       int i;
669       Dimension         replyWidth = 0, replyHeight = 0;
670       XtGeometryResult result;
671
672       if ( w )
673       {
674           XsTreeConstraints tree_const = TREE_CONSTRAINT ( w );
675
676           /*
677            * Add up the sum of the width's of all nodes to this
678            * depth, and use it as the x position.
679            */
680
681           tree_const->tree.x = ( level * tw->tree.h_min_space ) +
682                           SumOfPositions ( tw->tree.horizontal, level );
683
684           /*
685            * Move the widget into position.
686            */
687
688           _XmMoveObject ( w, tree_const->tree.x, tree_const->tree.y );
689
```

```
690          /*
691           * If the widget position plus its width or height doesn't
692           * fit in the tree, ask if the tree can be resized.
693           */
694
695          if ( XtWidth ( tw ) < tree_const->tree.x + XtWidth ( w ) ||
696              XtHeight ( tw ) < tree_const->tree.y + XtHeight ( w ) )
697          {
698              result =
699                  XtMakeResizeRequest ( ( Widget ) tw,
700                                          MAX ( XtWidth ( tw ),
701                                                tree_const->tree.x +
702                                                    XtWidth ( w ) ),
703                                          MAX ( XtHeight ( tw ) ,
704                                                tree_const->tree.y +
705                                                    XtHeight ( w ) ),
706                                          &replyWidth, &replyHeight );
707
708              /*
709               * Accept any compromise.
710               */
711
712              if ( result == XtGeometryAlmost )
713                  XtMakeResizeRequest ( ( Widget ) tw, replyWidth,
714                                          replyHeight,
715                                          NULL, NULL );
716          }
717
718          /*
719           * Set the positions of all sub_nodes.
720           */
721
722          for ( i = 0; i < tree_const->tree.n_sub_nodes; i++ )
723              SetPositions ( tw,
724                              tree_const->tree.sub_nodes[i], level+1 );
725  }
726  }
```

The remaining functions store and retrieve a value from a dynamically resizable array. The layout functions use these functions to store the next available position and the maximum width of each level. The function CreateOffset() allocates an array of the given size.

```
727  static XsVariableArray  *CreateOffset ( long size )
728  {
729      XsVariableArray  *offset =
730          (XsVariableArray *) XtMalloc ( sizeof ( XsVariableArray ) );
731
732      offset->size = size;
```

```
733
734      offset->array =
735              ( Dimension * ) XtMalloc ( size * sizeof ( Dimension ) );
736
737      Reset ( offset );
738
739      return ( offset );
740  }
```

The Reset ( ) function zeroes all entries in a table.

```
741  static void Reset ( XsVariableArray  *offset )
742  {
743      long i;
744
745      for ( i = 0; i < offset->size; i++ )
746          offset->array[i] = 0;
747  }
```

The function CurrentPosition ( ) returns the value in an given position in a table. If the requested position is greater than the size of the table, the function returns zero.

```
748  static Position CurrentPosition ( XsVariableArray  *offset,
749                                    long             position )
750  {
751      if ( position >= offset->size )
752          return ( 0 );
753      else
754          return ( offset->array [ position ] );
755  }
```

The function SetCurrentPosition ( ) stores a value in a table at a given index position. If the index is larger than the size of the table, the table is enlarged using XtRealloc ( ).

```
756  static void SetCurrentPosition ( XsVariableArray  *offset,
757                                   int              index,
758                                   Dimension        value )
759  {
760
761      if ( index >= offset->size )
762      {
763          int oldSize = offset->size;
764          int i;
765
766          offset->size = index + index / 2;
767          offset->array =
768              ( Dimension * ) XtRealloc ( ( char* ) offset->array,
769                                  offset->size * sizeof ( Dimension ) );
```

```
770
771            for ( i = oldSize; i < offset->size; i++ )
772                offset->array[i] = 0;
773        }
774
775        offset->array[index] = value;
776    }
```

The `SumOfPositions()` function returns the sum of all values in a table up to the given position.

```
777    static Position SumOfPositions ( XsVariableArray  *offset,
778                                       long               index )
779    {
780        int      i;
781        Position sum  = 0;
782        long     stop = index;
783
784        if ( index > offset->size )
785            stop = offset->size;
786
787        for ( i = 0; i < stop; i++ )
788            sum += offset->array[i];
789
790        return ( sum );
791    }
```

Creation Convenience Functions

Like most Motif manager widgets, the Tree widget provides several convenience functions for creating the widget. The first has the standard `XmCreate...` form. `XsCreateTree()` simply calls `XtCreateWidget()`, saving the programmer the need to remember the name of the class pointer.

```
792    Widget XsCreateTree ( Widget parent, char *name,
793                          ArgList arglist, Cardinal argcount )
794    {
795        return ( XtCreateWidget ( name, xsTreeWidgetClass,
796                                  parent, arglist, argcount ) );
797    }
```

Some Motif widgets are often used inside a scrolled window. For such widget classes, Motif usually provides a convenience function that automatically creates an XmScrolledWindow widget as the parent of the widget. For example, Motif provides functions like `XmCreate-ScrolledList()`, `XmCreateScrolledText()`, and so on. The Tree widget may often be used to display hierarchies that are fairly large, so a convenience function `XsCreate-ScrolledTree()` can be useful. Such a function is shown below. This function creates an XmScrolledWindow widget as a child of the specified parent, and sets the XmScrolledWindow widget for automatic scrolling. Any arguments passed to this function are passed on to both the XmScrolledWindow widget and the Tree widget.

   XsCreateScrolledTree() returns the Tree widget, and the XmScrolledWindow widget is invisible to the application, for the most part. The function _XmDestroyParentCallback() is an internal, undocumented Motif callback function that simply destroys the XmScrolledWindow if the Tree widget is destroyed.

```
798   Widget XsCreateScrolledTree ( Widget parent, char *name,
799                                  ArgList arglist, Cardinal argcount )
800   {
801       Widget sw, tw;
802       char   *sw_name;
803       Arg    *args;
804       int    n;
805
806       /*
807        * Generate a name for the scrolled window widget by appending
808        * the letters "SW" to the name of the Tree widget.
809        */
810
811       sw_name = XtMalloc ( strlen ( name ) + 3 );
812       strcpy ( sw_name, name );
813       strcat ( sw_name, "SW" );
814
815       /*
816        * Create an ArgList that can be passed into the scrolled window
817        * widget after appending some additional arguments. Malloc
818        * the list to match the number of arguments passed in, plus
819        * one more. Copy all specified arguments to the new list.
820        */
821
822       args = ( ArgList ) XtMalloc ( ( argcount + 1 ) * sizeof ( Arg ) );
823
824       for ( n = 0; n < argcount; n++ )
825       {
826           args[n].name = arglist[n].name;
827           args[n].value = arglist[n].value;
828       }
829
830       XtSetArg ( args[n], XmNscrollingPolicy, XmAUTOMATIC ); n++;
831
832       /*
833        * Create an XmScrolledWindow widget, passing in all arguments.
834        * The widget will ignore any that don't apply.
835        */
836
837       sw = XtCreateManagedWidget ( sw_name, xmScrolledWindowWidgetClass,
838                                    parent, args, n );
```

```
839        /*
840         * Create the Tree widget as a child of the scrolled window
841         * widget. Pass in the original argument list. Any arguments that
842         * were meant for the scrolled window widget and that are not
843         * recognized by the Tree widget will be ignored.
844         */
845
846        tw = XtCreateWidget ( name, xsTreeWidgetClass,
847                              sw, arglist, argcount );
848        /*
849         * Clean up.
850         */
851
852        XtFree ( ( char * ) args );
853        XtFree ( ( char * ) sw_name );
854
855        /*
856         * The caller gets a pointer to the Tree widget, not the scrolled
857         * window, so if the tree is destroyed, the scrolled window could
858         * be left hanging around. Catch destruction of the Tree widget
859         * and destroy the scrolled window to prevent this.
860         */
861
862        XtAddCallback ( tw, XmNdestroyCallback,
863                        _XmDestroyParentCallback, NULL );
864
865        return ( tw );
866    }
```

This completes the implementation of the Tree widget. The next section discusses an example that uses the Tree widget.

Using the Tree Widget

This section shows how an application can use the Tree widget to display a tree. An example program, named `tree`. This function reads a series of parent/child pairs from standard input, creates widgets for each node and displays the resulting tree. The input has the form:

```
parent parentLabel child childLabel
parent parentLabel child childLabel
```

The parent and child strings must be unique identifiers. The labels can include duplication, although only the first label given for any particular identifier is used. This approach allows multiple nodes in a tree to have the same name. For example, in a directory hierarchy, each identifier could be a full path name, while the label could be just the name of a directory.

The only information the `tree` program requires is the list of parent/child relationships. The program builds the tree from these pairs.

```
1    /*********************************************************************
2     * tree.c: Display tree from parent child pairs read from stdin
3     *********************************************************************/
4    #include <stdio.h>
5    #include <Xm/Xm.h>
6    #include <Xm/DrawnB.h>
7    #include <Xm/ScrolledW.h>
8    #include "Tree.h"
9
10   void main ( int argc, char **argv )
11   {
12       Widget        shell, tree;
13       XtAppContext  app;
14       char          parent[500], parentLabel[500],
15                     child[500], childLabel[500];
16
17       shell = XtAppInitialize ( &app, "Ttree", NULL, 0,
18                                 &argc, argv, NULL, NULL, 0 );
19
20       /*
21        * Create a scrolled tree.
22        */
23
24       tree = XsCreateScrolledTree ( shell, "tree", NULL, 0 );
25       XtManageChild ( tree );
26
27       /*
28        * Read node relationships and labels from stdin.
29        */
30
31       while ( scanf ( "%s %s %s %s", &parent, &parentLabel,
32                                      &child, &childLabel ) != EOF )
33       {
34           Widget p, c;
35
36           /*
37            * If a parent identifier was read, check to see if this name
38            * has already been used as a widget. If so, use the existing
39            * widget as the supernode of the given child.
40            */
41
42           if ( parent )
43               p = XtNameToWidget ( tree, parent );
44
45           if ( !p )
46           {
47               /*
48                * Otherwise, create a new widget for this node.
49                */
```

```
50
51                    p = XtVaCreateManagedWidget ( parent,
52                                                 xmDrawnButtonWidgetClass,
53                                                 tree,
54                                                 XtVaTypedArg, XmNlabelString,
55                                                 XmRString,      parentLabel,
56                                                 strlen ( parentLabel ) + 1,
57                                                 NULL );
58            }
59
60        /*
61         * If a child identifier was read, check to see if this name
62         * has already been used as a widget. If so, use the existing
63         * widget as the subnode of the given parent.
64         */
65
66        if ( child )
67            c = XtNameToWidget ( tree, child );
68
69        if ( !c )
70        {
71
72            /*
73             * Otherwise, create a new widget for this node.
74             */
75
76            c =XtVaCreateManagedWidget ( child,
77                                        xmDrawnButtonWidgetClass,
78                                        tree,
79                                        XmNsuperNode, p,
80                                        XtVaTypedArg, XmNlabelString,
81                                        XmRString,      childLabel,
82                                        strlen ( childLabel ) + 1,
83                                        NULL );
84        }
85    }
86
87    XtRealizeWidget ( shell );
88
89    XtAppMainLoop ( app );
90 }
```

This program can be used in many situations. Because the data an be read from standard input, the tree program can be used to display data gathered by shell scripts and other similar tools. For example, most versions of the **ps** command found on UNIX systems have an option to show the process identifiers of each process as well as the process identifier of each process's parent. This information can be used to display a process tree. The exact format of the ps command varies from system to system, but on the author's system **ps -ef** provides output of the following form:

```
% ps -ef
    UID    PID  PPID  C    STIME TTY        TIME COMD
    root     0    0   0 14:29:51 ?          0:01 sched
    root     1    0   0 14:29:51 ?          0:02 /etc/init
    root     2    0   0 14:29:51 ?          0:12 vhand
    root     3    0   0 14:29:51 ?          0:09 bdflush
```

The PID field provides the process ID of each process, COMD reports the name of the process, and PPID provides the process ID of each command's parent. Given this output, it is easy to manipulate the data into the format expected by the tree program. For example, the following awk command prints each process ID followed by the command name, the parent's process ID, and a place holder. Because each process ID is unique, and each parent ID must have already been seen, the final field in the input to the tree program is unimportant and can be ignored.

Using ps, awk, and the tree program, a process tree can be displayed as follows:

```
ps -ef | awk '{print $3 " " $8 " " $2 " " "ignore"}' | tree
```

Figure 17.3 shows the window produced by this command.

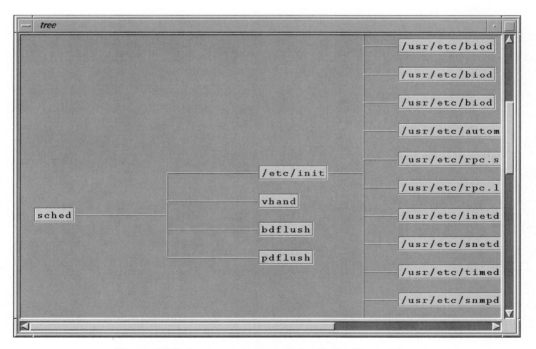

Figure 17.3 A process tree created with the Tree widget.

17.3 Summary

This chapter presented the architecture and construction of a manager widget class that uses the features of the Constraint widget class. The Constraint widget class is a subclass of the Composite widget class that uses additional information attached to its children to determine how the children are managed. Each constraint widget attaches a constraint record to its children to store this additional information, and often provides additional resources for the child widget. The constraint resources allow programmers to specify the corresponding values in the constraint record, and influence the layout of each individual widget. Constraint widgets define additional methods to initialize and manage changes to its children's constraint record.

The Tree widget presented in this chapter provides one example of the type of constraint information that can be attached to a widget. Each widget position is constrained by its hierarchical relationship to other widgets in a tree. The actual positions are determined by heuristics that specify the desirable shape of a tree.

Getting Source Code

The source code for the examples described in this book is available free of charge to anyone with network access. The example source may be downloaded using the ftp command from ftp.prenhall.com or ftp.x.org. You may also find the sources at other ftp sites. On ftp.prenhall.com, the examples can be found under in directory pub/software/doug_young, in a compressed tar file named young.motif2.tar.Z. On ftp.x.org, the file can be found in the contrib directory.

Assuming you have access to the Internet, you can download the software using the following sequence of commands. (Type "ftp" or "anonymous" at the login prompt, provide and your name, email address, or system name as a password, as requested.)

```
% ftp ftp.prenhall.org
> cd pub/software/doug_young
> binary
> get young.motif2.tar.Z
> quit
```

Once you have the compressed tar file, you can unpack the files with the commands:

```
% uncompress young.motif2.tar.Z
% tar xvf young.motif2.tar
```

622

These commands will create a directory named MotifExamples, which contains subdirectories for each chapter in this book, as well as several other files and directories. Look at the README file for additional information about the software, instructions on how to build the examples, and so on.

Ordering Example Source from Prentice Hall

For those without network access, Prentice Hall can provide copies of the software for a small fee. See the reply card in the back of this book for details. Prentice Hall distributes the software on an IBM disk. This software is expected to run on a UNIX system, and should be copied from your PC to a UNIX system. As distributed by Prentice Hall, the software is packed into a single file, known as a "shell archive". The examples are in an ASCII file named examples.shar. To unpack this file, copy examples.shar from your PC to a UNIX system. Then type the following command in a terminal window:

```
% sh examples.shar
```

This command creates the MotifExamples directory as described above. Check the README file for up-to-date information and instructions for building the software.

The Xpm Library

The Xpm library described in this book is distributed with X as contributed software. Some vendors may make this package available on their systems, but others may not, as it is not a standard part of the X Window System. If you do not have it, the sources to Xpm can be downloaded from ftp.x.org.

Index to Example Programs

A

AskQuestion() 229, 229–231
    YesCallback() 231

B

busy 276

C

chooseone 117
    BrowseCallback() 119
coloredit 303–318
    app-defaults file 318
    BlueSliderMoved() 314
    CreateColorSelector() 309
    CreateControlArea() 307
    CreatePaletteEditor() 306
    GreenSliderMoved() 315
    main() 304
    MakeSlider() 308
    RedSliderMoved() 313
    SelectColorCallback() 312
    SetShadowColors() 317
    WarnUserNoColor() 316
ContextHelpCallback() 218
CreateInputField()
    input example() 105
    numeric example() 108
    password example() 110
customdialog 242
    CreateDialog() 244
        template version 246
customedialog
    CreateDialog() 243
CvtStringToDebugLevel() 76–80

D

DeleteWindowCallback() 489
Dial widget...533-559
    CalculateIndicatorPos()................................548
    Destroy() 546
    Initialize()...544
    private header file 535
    public header file 537
    Redisplay()...550
    Resize() 547
    SetIndicatorPosition() 556
    SetValues()...552
    XsCreateDial() 557
dialogdemo 225
dialtest 557
    ValueChangedCallback().............................558
DoesIntersect()..330
draw 422–453
    AddObject() 438
    app-defaults file 452
    CopyCallback()..483
    CopyFromClipBoard()..................................485
    CopySelectedItem() 486
    CopyToClipBoard().......................................484
    CreateDrawingEditor() 426
    CutCallback()...483
    CutSelectedItem() 486
    DrawCircle() 434
    DrawFilledCircle() 434
    DrawFilledRectangle()..................................433
    DrawLine() 433
    DrawRectangle()...433
    EndRubberBand() 444
    ExportObject() 512
    FixDataOrdering()...434
    HandleDrop() 505
    header file 423
    InitGraphics()...432
        modified for drag and drop 502

LoadCallback() 427
LoadData() 449
LoadDataCallback() 450
main() 423
menu description 425
    modified for cut and paste 483
MoveObject() 437
Pack() 446
PasteCallback() 483
PasteItem() 486
PickObject() 437
QuitCallback() 427
Redisplay() 436
RemoveItem() 486
SaveCallback() 427
SaveData() 447
SaveDataCallback() 448
SetColorCallback() 428
SetCurrentColor() 436
SetDragIcon() 514
SetDrawingFunction() 435
SetFigureCallback() 428
StartDrag() 511
StartRubberBand() 441
StoreObject() 439
TrackRubberBand() 443
TransferCallback() 507
TypeToFunction() 435
Unpack() 446
driver
    For XmTextField examples 104

E

editor 63–67
explicit 180

F

filedemo 238
    CancelCallback() 240
    OKCallback() 239
    SelectFileCallback() 239
formtest 139

app-defaults file 142
    layout using position attachments 143
    using position attachments 141
fractal 385–404, 414–421
    app-defaults file 403
    CancelCallback() 402
    CreateImage() 390
    EndRubberBand() 420
    header file 385, 413
    ImageData structure 385, 413
    InitData() 389, 417
    main() 387, 415
    OkCallback() 401
    QuitCallback() 388
    RedisplayCallback() 392
    ResizeCallback() 393
    SetupColorMap() 394
    ShowPreferences() 398
    ShowPreferencesCallback() 388
    StartRubberBand() 418
    TrackRubberBand() 419
frame 152

G

GetHelpText() 220
GetPixel() 298
GetPixelByName() 302
GetTextFromXmString() 374

H

helpdemo 221

I

inputfield 105
InstallLabeledPixmap() 376
InstallPixmap() 341

L

label 88
layout 147–150
list 371
LoadRGB() 300

M

mainwindow 159
memo 24–28
    with added translations 41–42
menubar 191–202
    CreateEditPane()...........................194
    CreateFilePane() 194
    CreateHelpPane().........................195
    CreateMenuBar() 193
MenuSupport
    AttachPopup().............................216
    CreateMenu() 211
    CreateMenuChildren()..................213
    example using 208
    header file 207
    MenuDescription structure 207
    PostMenuHandler() 216
mousetracks..262
    ClearTracker() 265, 270
    CreateMouseTracker()..................268
    ShowMousePosition() 268
    TrackMousePosition() 265, 269

N

numeric 108

O

option 203
    CreateOptionMenu().....................204
        using entryCallbacks 205
    OptionChanged() 205
        using entryCallback 206

P

pane 167
password 110
    CreateInputField() 110
    GetPassword().............................110
    MotionCallback()...........................111
    TextModifiedCallback() 111
popupmenu 185–190
    CreateCascadingPane()..................190
    CreatePopupMenu().......................186
        cascading version 189
    PostMenu()..................................187
    SampleCallback()..........................187
    using MenuSupport functions 208
pushbutton 92

Q

quit 94
    ActivateCallback() 94
    ArmCallback() 94
    CreateQuitButton() 95
    DisarmCallback() 94

R

radiobox 135
    ValueChangedCallback().................136
rctest 132
rmtest 70–72
rmtest2 73–74
rmtest3 79
Row widget 566-585
    ChangeManaged().......................... 581
    DoLayout().................................. 572
    GeometryManager()........................ 579
    Initialize()................................... 571
    PreferredSize() 575, 576
    private header 567
    public header 568
    QueryGeometry()........................... 576
    Redisplay().................................. 575
    Resize().......................................572

rowtest 582
rubberband 405
    EndRubberBand() 409
    main() 406
    StartRubberBand() 408
    TrackRubberBand() 408

S

scale 163–164
    app-defaults file 165
    ClickCallback() 165
    ReportValueCallback() 164
scroll 156
selectiondemo 469–478
    ConvertSelection() 476
    LoseSelection() 478
    main() 471
    OwnSelection() 475
    RequestSelection() 472
    SetCTType() 474
    SetStringType() 474
    SetTargetType() 474
    ShowSelection() 473
SetupIcon 491, 492
stopwatch 169

T

tear-off menus
    CreateFilePane() 198
toggle 99
    ValueChangedCallback() 100
traverse 178
tree 617
Tree widget 589–616
    ChangeManaged() 604
    ComputePositions() 608
    ConstraintDestroy() 602
    ConstraintInitialize() 597
    ConstraintSetValues() 599
    CreateOffset() 612
    CurrentPosition() 613
    DeleteNode() 600

    GeometryManager() 603
    Initialize() 596
    InsertNewNode() 600
    NewLayout() 608
    private header file 589
    public header file 591
    Redisplay() 604
    Reset() 613
    SetCurrentPosition() 613
    SetPositions() 611
    SetValues() 598
    ShiftSubtree() 611
    SumOfPositions() 614
    XsCreateScrolledTree() 615
    XsCreateTree() 614
twoshells 175

W

wprintf() 266

X

xbc 279–289
    AppendToDisplay() 286
    ClearDisplay() 287
    CreateButton() 283
    CreateCalculator() 281
    DisplayedString() 286
    GetFromBc() 287
    main() 279
    QuitCallback() 284
    SendToBc() 284
    SetUpTwoWayPipe() 288
xclock 273
    UpdateTime() 273
xecute 46–50
    NoCallback() 50, 236
    using an XmMessageBox 234
    YesCallback() 49, 235
xlogo ....336, ??–342
    InstallPixmap() 338, 341
    RedisplayCallback() 339, 341
    ResizeCallback() 340

Index

A

accelerators 199
action procedure
      form of 43
actions 40
      registering 41
      setting up a table 41
algorithmic layout management 126
alignment
      in frame widget...................................151
      in XmLabel widgets.............................89
`AllPlanes`.. 324
application context........................... 25, 38
application resource files 30, 65, 66
ApplicationShell widget class 174
arcs... 410
`Arg` 32
`argc`
      Xt modification of 25, 30
`ArgList` 32, 33
`argv`
      Xt modification of 25, 30
atoms... 456
attachments, form 139
      example using 170
      positional 141
      setting in resource files.....................142

B

backing store.. 7
bitmaps.. 333–362
      displaying in XmLabel widgets.....................89
`BlackPixel()` 299
button widgets................................... 90–100

C

callbacks...28, 44-50
      input 277–289
call data 45
`CirculateRequest` 259
class pointer
      Motif naming conventions 21
class record.. 518
      Composite widget class.................................. 561
      Core widget class 518
      Dial widget class 540
      Row widget class 569
      Tree widget class..................................... 594
      XmPrimitive widget class 530
      XmManager widget class........................... 563
client...3
client data 45
`ClientMessage` events 261
client-server...2
clip window 153
clipboard 478
      and XmText widget.............................. 107
      storing data in.................................. 479
      transfer by name................................ 481
`ClipboardLocked`.............................. 480
`ClipboardSuccess` 480
color 291–318
      allocating.. 297
      calculating Motif shadow colors................... 316
      in resource files 66
color cells... 297, 299, 300
colormaps.. 292
`ColormapChangeMask` 251, 260
command-line arguments..............................72–74
Composite widget class.................... 125, 127, 560
      resources 127
compound strings 25, 363, 367–381

compound strings, cont.
    converting between compound text................381
    retrieving text component.............................373
    using fontlists...370
compound text 381, 474
    converting between compound string............381
`ConfigureNotify` 259
`ConfigureRequest` 259
constraint widgets 127
context sensitive help.. 216
Core widget class 84
`CreateNotify` 260
cursors.. 408
custom dialogs 240–248
customization resource 59, 67
cut and paste 462

D

`DefaultColormap()` 293
`DefaultVisual()` 294
`DestroyNotify`.. 260
dialogs............................... 15, 17, 223–248
    blocking 229–231
    custom...241–248
    modal 227
    predefined 224
    template 246
`DirectColor`.. 294
dispatching events.. 39
`Display` structure 39
`DoBlue`.. 297
`DoGreen` 297
`DoRed`.. 297
drag and drop 494–516
    callbacks 510
    cursor 513
    drag over effects 508
    dynamic protocol 495
    initiator..494
    preregister protocol 495
    receiver 494
    starting a drag 508
drawable.. 335
drop sites
    registering 496

E

`EnterNotify` 254
enumerated types
    conversion functions 80
`EvenOddRule` 327, 329
event compression... 520
event handler... 262
event loop.. 40
event masks... 251
event queue 8
event-driven programming.................................. 28
events 249–290
    colormap 260
    communication...260
    crossing 254–257
    dispatching 39
    event handler..261
    exposure 258
    focus 257
    in Motif applications 261–270
    keyboard..252
    loop 40
    pointer 253
    retrieving from event queue 39
    state notification..259
    structure control 259
    timeout 272–274
`ExposureMask`..258

F

fallback resources..30, 59
`FocusChangeMask`...251
fontlists..367
    in resource files 368
fonts..363–365
frame-buffer 291
full application modal 228
full system modal 228
function prototypes 18

G

gadgets 122–124, 574
grabs 407
graphics context 319–332
    modifying attributes 322
`GraphicsExpose` 258, 329
`GravityNotify` 260

H

hotspot 9

I

ICCCM 488
icon, window manager
    name 174
    opening window as 490
    setting image 173
    starting up as 172
`IconicState` 172
icons 333
    color 354
images
    registering with Motif 346
inheritance 524
input focus 176–182
instance record 522

K

`KeyReleaseMask` 251

L

`$LANG` 58, 59
`LeaveNotify` 254
`LeaveWindowMask` 251
libraries
    linking with X and Motif 26

M

manager widget classes 560–585
manager widgets 15
    inheritance hierarchy 126
`MapNotify` 260
`MappingNotify` 260
`MapRequest` 259
menu panes
    cascading 188–190
menus 15, 18, 183–222
    cascading panes 188–190
    convenience package 206–216
    help 216
    option 202
    menu bars 18, 191–196
    tear-off panes 196
methods, widget class
    `accept_focus()` 522
    `change_managed()` 562
        Row widget class 581
        Tree widget class 604
    `class_initialize()` 521
        Dial widget class 543
    `class_part_initialize()` 521
        Dial widget class 543
    `constraint_destroy`
        Tree widget class 601
    `constraint_initialize()`
        Tree widget class 597
    `constraint_set_values()`
        Tree widget class 598
    `delete_child()` 562
        Row widget class 572
    `destroy()` 521
        Dial widget class 546
    `expose()` 521
        Dial widget class 549
        Row widget class 574
        Tree widget class 604
    `geometry_manager()` 561
        Row widget class 578
        Tree widget class 603
    `initialize()` 521
        Dial 543
        Row widget class 571
        Tree widget class 596

methods, widget class, cont.
    `initialize_hook()` 521
    `insert_child()` 562
        Row widget class 572
    `query_geometry()` 522
        Dial widget class.................................. 554
        Row widget class 575
    `realize()` 521
        Dial widget class.................................. 546
        Row widget class 571
    `resize()` 521
        Dial widget class.................................. 546
        Row widget class 572
    `set_values()` 521
        Dial widget class.................................. 551
        Tree widget class................................. 598
    `set_values_almost()` 521
    `set_values_hook()` 521
mnemonics.. 199, 200
Motif, overview 14–18
Motif Style Guide 14
`MotionNotify` 254
multi-line strings.. 89
mwm 14
`MWM_DECOR_ALL` 491

N

`NoEventMask`.. 251
`NoExpose` 258
`NormalState`.. 172

O

Open Software Foundation....................................... 14
option menu 18, 202

P

`PropertyNotify`.. 261
password entry field................................ 109
pipes
    using with `XtAppAddInput()` 288

pixmaps.. 333–362
    copying.. 335
    displaying in labels 87, 157
    Xpm format... 353–362
polygons... 410
popup menus
    creating 184
    posting 187–188
popup shells 174
preregister protocol 495
primary application modal 228
primitive widgets 15, 16, 83
    inheritance hierarchy......................... 84
property... 457
`PropertyChangeMask` 251, 261
`PropertyNotify`....................................... 261
`PseudoColor`... 294, 295

R

radio box 135
realizing... 26, 38
regions... 329–332
`ReparentNotify`....................................... 260
`ResizeRedirectMask` 251, 259
`ResizeRequest` 259
resources
    application.. 68
    conventions for Motif programs 61
    names and classes 52
    name strings 20
    precedence rules................................ 56
    server.. 4, 51
    retrieving.. 36, 47
    widget... 4, 52
    wildcards.. 55
    class strings 20, 21
resource manager
    matching algorithm 55–57
`RESOURCE_MANAGER` property............................60
rubber band line 405

S

SelectionRequest 261
save-unders 8
Screen 39
scrolling 154
search path 58
SelectionClear 261
SelectionNotify 261, 464
selections 462
    and XmText widget 107
    ownership.......................................463
shadow colors 86
shadow types.. 96
shells 25, 171–176
    example using multiple.........................175
    popup 174
    transient 223
siblings.. 5
stacking order 6
StructureNotify 259
StructureNotifyMask......................... 251, 259
SubstructureRedirectMask.............. 251,259
SubstructureNotifyMask 251, 259, 260
subwindows 5

T

tab group 177, 177–179
tear-off menus 196
timeout callbacks 272
title, of window... 173
TopLevelShell widget class.......................... 174
TransientShell............................... 173, 223
translation manager.................... 40, 40–44
translations
    compiling....................................42, 43
    declaring bindings.............................41
    in widget class 555
    merging with existing 44
traversal 176-179
type-converters 74–80
    for enumerated types 80

U

UnmapNotify 260
UIL.. 14

V

vararg functions 33–37
    automatic type conversion 34
VendorShell widget class........................... 173
VisibilityNotify 260
VisibilityChangeMask............................. 251
visual types.. 294

W

WhitePixel() 299
widget classes
    creating new classes 517
    private headers files 528
    public header file............................ 529
    support for C++................................ 529
widget hierarchies 168–171
widget tree.. 26
WidgetList.. 38
widgets
    creating.. 30–32
        with Motif convenience functions 31
        with vararg functions 33
    customizing...................................... 32–37
    destroying...................................... 38
    managing.. 37–38
    mixing with Xlib functions 39
    realizing.. 26
WindingRule 327, 329
windows
    iconifying 490
    mapping... 7
    maximum and minimum sizes 489
    of a widget..................................... 39
    stacking order.................................. 6
    tree... 5
    layout.. 17
    viewable and unviewable 7

window manager
    decorations..491
    icons...491
    Motif..14
WM_DELETE_WINDOW...................... 173, 488
WmShell widget class 172
work procedures 275–277

X

XA_PRIMARY 468
XAllocColor() 297
XAllocColorCells() 299
XAllocNamedColor() 302
XAnyEvent.. 250
XAPPLRESDIR.. 59
XChangeGC()... 322
XChangeProperty() 457
XCharStruct........................... 364, 365
XCirculateEvent 259
XCirculateSubwindows() 259
XCirculateSubwindowsUp() 259
XCirculateSubwindowsDown() 259
XClearArea() 339
XClientMessageEvent.......................... 462
XClipBox() 331
XConfigureEvent 259
XConvertSelection()........................... 464
XCopyArea() 335
    and graphics expose..............258, 329
XCopyPlane() 336
    and graphics expose.......................329
XCreateBitmapFromData() 334
XCreateColormap() 294
XCreateFontCursor()........................... 408
XCreateGC() 319
XCreateImage() 343
XCreatePixmap() 333
XCreateRegion() 329
XCrossingEvent() 254, 255
XDeleteProperty() 458
XDestroyImage() 344
XDestroyRegion() 330
XDrawArc() 410
XDrawArcs() 411
XDrawImageString() 367

XDrawLine() 404
XDrawLines() 405
XDrawPoint() 383
XDrawPoints() 383
XDrawRectangle() 410
XDrawRectangles() 410
XDrawSegments() 404
XDrawString() 366
XEmptyRegion() 330
XENVIRONMENT.......................................60
XEqualRegion() 330
XEvent 250
XExposeEvent 258
XFetchName() 459
XFILESEARCHPATH..................................59
XFillArc() 412
XFillPolygon() 412
XFillRectangle() 411
XFillRectangles() 412
XFontStruct 364
XFreeColormap()................................... 294
XFreePixmap() 334
XGCValues...................................320, 321
XGetAtomName() 456
XGetGeometry() 376
XGetImage() 343
XGetPixel() 344
XGetSelectionOwner()......................... 463
XGetStandardColormap() 296
XGetWindowProperty()......................... 458
XGrabButton() 407
XGraphicsExposeEvent......................... 258
XIconifyWindow() 490
XImage 342
XInternAtom() 456
XIntersectRegion() 330
XKeyEvent......................................252, 253
Xlib 1–10
    and widgets 39
    graphics functions 39, 382–454
XLoadFont() 364
XLoadQueryFont() 364
XLookupColor() 301
XLookupString()................................... 253
XLowerWindow() 259
XmAddWMProtocolCallback()................ 489
XmAnyCallbackStruct.............................93

XmAPPLICATION_DEFINED scrolling policy ... 155
XMapWindow() 490
XmArrowButton widget class 95
XmArrowButtonGadget 123
XmAS_NEEDED scrollbar display policy 155
XMatchVisualInfo() 295
XmAUTOMATIC scrolling policy 155
XmBROWSE_SELECT 114
XmBulletinBoard widget class 46, 48, 129–130
    support for dialogs 231–232
    resources 129
XmC prefix 21
XmCascadeButton widget class 96
    used in menus 184
XmCascadeButtonGadget 123
XmChangeColor() 316
XmClipboardCancelCopy() 480
XmClipboardCopy() 480
XmClipboardCopyByName() 481
XmClipboardEndCopy() 480
XmClipboardRetrieve() 482
XmClipboardStartCopy() 479
XmCommand widget class 158
XmCOMMAND_ABOVE_WORKSPACE 158
XmCOMMAND_BELOW_WORKSPACE 158
XmCONSTANT visual policy 155
XmCR_DRAG_MOTION_MESSAGE 498
XmCR_DROP_MESSAGE 497
XmCR_DROP_SITE_ENTER_MESSAGE 498
XmCreateDragIcon() 513
XmCreateErrorDialog() 225
XmCreateFormDialog() 240
XmCreateMenuBar() 191
XmCreatePopupMenu() 184
XmCreatePulldownMenu() 184, 191
XmCreateQuestionDialog() 226
XmCreateScrolledList() 112
XmCreateTemplateDialog() 246
XmCvtCTToXmString() 381
XmCvtXmStringToCT() 381
XmDESTROY 173, 488
XmDIALOG_CANCEL_BUTTON 233, 241
XmDIALOG_FULL_APPLICATION_MODAL228,232
XmDIALOG_HELP_BUTTON 233, 241
XmDIALOG_MESSAGE_LABEL 241
XmDIALOG_MODELESS 228, 232
XmDIALOG_NONE 233

XmDIALOG_OK_BUTTON 233, 241
XmDIALOG_PRIMARY_APPLICATION_MODAL228,
    232
XmDIALOG_SEPARATOR 241
XmDIALOG_SYMBOL_LABEL 241
XmDIALOG_SYSTEM_MODAL 228, 232
XmDialogShell 173, 224
XmDO_NOTHING 173, 488
XmDragStart() 508
XmDrawingArea
    displaying a pixmap 336
XmDrawingArea widget class 383
XmDrawnButton widget class 96
_XmDrawShadows() 551
XmDROP 504
XmDROP_COPY 497
XmDROP_LINK 497
XmDROP_MOVE 497
XmDROP_NOOP 497
XmDROP_SITE_INVALID 497
XmDROP_SITE_VALID 497
XmDropProcCallbackStruct 497, 498
XmDropSiteRegister() 496
XmDropTransferEntryRec 504
XmDropTransferStart() 504
XmEXCLUSIVE_TAB_GROUP 177
XmEXPLICIT 173, 176
XmEXTENDED_SELECT 113
XmFileSelectionBoxCallbackStruct ... 237
XmFileSelectionDialog widget class 236–240
XmFONT_IS_FONT 368
XmFONT_IS_FONTLIST 368
XmFontList 368
XmFONTLIST_DEFAULT_TAG 24, 368
XmFontListAppendEntry() 368
XmFontListEntry 368
XmFontListEntryCreate() 368
XmFontListEntryLoad() 368
XmForm widget class 137–150
    resources 137–139
XmFrame widget class................................... 150
    resources 150–151
XmFRAME_TITLE_CHILD 151
XmFRAME_WORKAREA_CHILD 151
XmGetColorCalculation() 316
XmGetColors() 316
XmGetPixmap() 344

634

XmHORIZONTAL 131
XmInstallImage() 346
XmLabel
    displaying multiple lines 89
    displaying text and pixmap at once 375
XmLabel widget
    displaying a string 24
XmLabel widget class 86–90
    common resources 87
    used in menus 184
XmLabelGadget 123
XmList widget class 113–119
    callbacks 113
    common resources 112
    convenience functions 115–117
XmListAddItem() 115
XmListAddItems() 115
XmListCallbackStruct 114
XmListDeleteAllItems() 116
XmListDeleteItem() 115
XmListDeleteItems() 115
XmListDeletePos() 116
XmListDeselectItem() 116
XmListGetSelectedPos() 116
XmListItemExists() 116
XmListItemPos() 116
XmListReplaceItems() 116
XmListSelectItem() 116
XmMainWindow widget class 157-159
XmManager widget class 128, 560, 586
XmManagerClassPart 563
XmManagerClassRec 563
XmManagerPart 564
XmManagerRec 564
XmManagerWidgetClass 563
XmMenuPosition() 187
XmMessageBox widget class 233–236
XmMessageBoxGetChild() 240
_XmMoveObject() 574
XmMULTIPLE_SELECT 113
XmNarrowDirection 95
XmNactivateCallback 44, 91, 95
    XmText widget 102
XmNadjustLast 131
XmNadjustMargin 131
XmNalignment resource 87, 89
XmNallowOverlap 129

XmNallowResize 167
XmNallowShellResize 172
XmNancestorSensitive 85
XmNanimationMask 496
XmNanimationPixmap 496
XmNanimationPixmapDepth 496
XmNanimationStyle 496
XmNarmCallback 44, 91, 95, 98
XmNarmColor 90
XmNarmPixmap 91
XmNautoUnmanage 232
    and XmFileSelectionDialog 239
XmNbackground 85
XmNbackgroundPixmap 85
XmNbaseHeight 172
XmNbaseWidth 172
XmNblendModel 508
XmNblinkRate 102
XmNborderColor 85
XmNborderPixmap 85
XmNborderWidth 84
XmNbottomAttachment 138
XmNbottomOffset 139
XmNbottomPosition 138
XmNbottomShadowColor 86, 128
XmNbottomWidget 138
XmNbrowseSelectionCallback 114
XmNbuttonFontList 130
XmNcancelButton 232
XmNcancelCallback 234
XmNcancelLabelString 233
XmNchildHorizontalAlignment 151
XmNchildHorizontalSpacing 151
XmNchildren 127
XmNchildType 151
XmNchildVerticalAlignment 151
XmNclipWindow 155
XmNcolormap 85
XmNcolumns 102
XmNcommandWindow 158
XmNcommandWindowLocation 158
_XmConfigureObject() 574
XmNcursorBackground 509
XmNcursorForeground 509
XmNcursorPosition 102
XmNcursorPositionVisible 102
XmNdestroyCallback 44

XmNdecimalPoints............................. 161
XmNdecrementCallback 122
XmNdefaultButton.............................. 232
XmNdefaultButtonType 233
XmNdefaultPosition............................ 232
XmNdeleteResponse 173, 488
XmNdestroyCallback.............................. 84, 86
XmNdialogStyle............................... 232
XmNdialogTitle.............................. 232
XmNdialogType.................................. 233
XmNdirectory 237
XmNdirSpec 237
XmNdisarmCallback 44, 91, 98
XmNdragCallback
    and XmScrollBar 121, 122
    example................................164
    XmScale widget class 162
XmNdragInitiatorProtocolStyle.......... 495
XmNdragOperations 509
XmNdragProc 496
XmNdragRecieverProtocolStyle........... 495
XmNdropProc 496, 497
XmNdropRectangles 496
XmNdropSiteOperations........................... 497
XmNdropTransfers....................................504
XmNeditable 102
XmNentryAlignment 131
XmNentryBorder.............................. 131
XmNentryClass 131
XmNentryVerticalAlignment 132
XmNexportTargets...................................509
XmNexposeCallback 96
XmNextendedSelectionCallback............ 113
XmNfillOnArm 91
XmNfillOnSelect 98
XmNfocusCallback............................... 102, 129
XmNfontList..................................... 87, 102, 113
XmNforeground.............................. 85, 128
XmNfractionBase 138
XmNgeometry................................. 172
XmNheight................................ 84
XmNheightInc 172
XmNhelpCallback 86, 128, 217, 234
XmNhelpLabelString.............................. 233
XmNhighlightColor 86, 177, 179
XmNhighlightOnEnter............................. 85, 86
XmNhighlightThickness........ 86, 177, 179, 181

XmNhorizontalScrollBar.......................... 154
XmNiconic.................................... 174, 490
XmNiconName.................................. 174
XmNiconPixmap................................ 173
XmNimportTargets................................. 497
XmNincrement................................. 121
XmNincrementCallback................................ 122
XmNindicatorOn.................................. 97
XmNindicatorSize 97
XmNindicatorType 97
XmNinitialFocus................................... 177
XmNinitialState............................ 172, 174
XmNinsensitivePixmap............................87, 88
XmNinvalidCursorForeground 509
XmNisAligned................................... 131
XmNisHomogeneous 131
XmNitemCount............................. 113, 115
XmNitems 113, 115
XmNkeyBoardFocusPolicy.................. 173, 181
XmNkeyboardFocusPolicy......................... 176
XmNlabelFontList............................... 130
XmNlabelPixmap............................87, 89
XmNlabelString................................. 87
XmNlabelType.................................. 87
XmNleftAttachment.............................. 137, 138
XmNleftOffset 139
XmNleftPosition............................ 138
XmNleftWidget 138
XmNlistMarginHeight............................112
XmNlistMarginWidth 112
XmNlistSpacing.............................. 112
XmNlosingFocusCallback.......................... 102
XmNmapCallback.............................232
XmNmappedWhenManaged.......................... 85
XmNmarginBottom.............................. 87
XmNmarginHeight.............................87, 101
XmNmarginLeft 87
XmNmarginRight.............................. 87
XmNmarginTop.............................. 87
XmNmarginWidth............................87, 101
XmNmaxHeight............................... 173
XmNmaximum.............................. 121, 161
XmNmaxLength.............................. 102
XmNmaxWidth 173
XmNmenuBar............................. 158, 159
XmNmessageAlignment.................................. 233
XmNmessageString..................226, 233, 246

XmNmessageWindow 159
XmNminHeight 173
XmNminimum 121, 161
XmNminWidth 173
XmNmodifyVerifyCallback 103
XmNmotionVerifyCallback 102
XmNmultipleSelectionCallback 113
XmNmwmDecorations 173, 491
XmNmwmFunctions 173
XmNmwmMenu 173
XmNnavigationType 177
XmNnoneCursorForeground 509
XmNnoResize 232
XmNnumChildren 127
XmNnumColumns 131
XmNnumDropTransfers 504
XmNnumExportTargets 509
XmNnumImportTargets 497
XmNnumRectangles 496
XmNokCallback 234
XmNokLabelString 233
XmNoperationCursorIcon 509
XmNorientation 121, 130
    of XmScale 161
XmNpacking 130, 131
XmNpageDecrementCallback 122
XmNpageIncrement 121
XmNpageIncrementCallback 122
XmNpaneMaximum 167
XmNpaneMinimum 167
XmNpattern 237
XmNpopdownCallback 172
XmNpopupCallback 172
XmNprocessingDirection 121, 161
XmNpushButtonEnabled 96
XmNradioAlwaysOne 132
XmNradioBehavior 131, 132, 135
XmNrecomputeSize 88
XmNrefigureMode 167
XmNresizable 138
XmNresizeCallback 96
XmNresizeHeight 131
XmNresizePolicy 129
XmNresizeWidth 131
XmNrightAttachment 138
XmNrightOffset 139
XmNrightPosition 138

XmNrightWidget 138
XmNrubberPositioning 137
XmNsashHeight 167
XmNsashIndent 167
XmNsashShadowThickness 167
XmNsashWidth 167
XmNscaleHeight 161
XmNscaleWidth 161
XmNscrollBarDisplayPolicy 155
XmNscrollBarPlacement 155
XmNscrolledWindowMarginHeight 155
XmNscrolledWindowMarginWidth 155
XmNscrollingPolicy 155
XmNselectColor 98
XmNselectedItemCount 113
XmNselectedItems 113
XmNselectionPolicy 113
XmNselectPixmap 97
XmNsensitive 84
XmNseparatorOn 167
XmNset 97
XmNshadowThickness 128, 129, 151
XmNshadowType 96, 129, 151
XmNshowArrows 121
XmNshowSeparator 159
XmNshowValue 161
XmNsingleSelectionCallback 113
XmNsliderSize 121
XmNsourceCursorIcon 509
XmNsourcePixmapIcon 509
XmNspacing 97
    XmScrolledWindow 155
XmNstateCursorIcon 509
XmNsymbolPixmap 233, 246
XmNtearOffModel 197
XmNtextTranslations 130
XmNtitle 173
XmNtitleString 161
XmNtoBottomCallback 122
XmNtopAttachment 138
XmNtopItemPosition 113
XmNtopOffset 139
XmNtopPosition 138
XmNtopShadowColor 86, 128
XmNtopWidget 138
XmNtoTopCallback 122
XmNtransferProc 504

XmNtraversalOn.................................. 176, 181
XmNtroughColor................................... 121
XmNunmapCallback........................... 232
XmNuserData.............................. 86, 128
XmNvalidCursorForeground.................... 509
XmNvalue.......................... 101, 121, 161
XmNvalueChanged
    and XmScrollBar...............................121
XmNvalueChangedCallback................ 98, 102
    and XmScrollBar...............................122
    XmScale widget class.........................162
XmNverifyBell................................. 102
XmNverticalScrollBar........................ 154
XmNvisibleItemCount.......................... 113
XmNvisibleWhenOff............................. 97
XmNvisualPolicy 155
XmNwidth 84
XmNwidthInc 172
XmNworkWindow........................... 155, 159
XmNx 84
XmNy 84
XMotionEvent 254
XmPACK_COLUMN 130, 131
XmPACK_NONE 131
XmPACK_TIGHT 130, 131
XmPanedWindow widget class 166–168
XmPIXMAP 87
XmPOINTER.............................. 173, 176
XmPrimitive widget class 85–86, 530
XmPrimitiveClassPart 531
XmPrimitiveRec................................ 532
XmProcessTraversal() 180
XmPushButton widget class........................ 90–95
    callbacks 91
    common resources 90
    used in menus 184
XmPushButtonGadget 123
_XmRedisplayGadgets() 575
XmR prefix 21
XmRepTypeRegister()........................ 80
XmRepTypeValidValue........................ 80
XmRESIZE_ANY 130
XmRESIZE_GROW 130
XmRESIZE_NONE 129
_XmResizeObject() 574
XmRowColumn widget class 130–137
    alignment of children........................132

resources 130–132
    used in menus 184
XmScale widget class...........................160–166
    callbacks 162
    picture 161
    resources 161
XmScaleCallbackStruct.........................162
XmScrollBar widget class.......................120–122
    callbacks 121
    common resources 120
XmScrollBarCallbackStruct 121
XmScrolledWindow widget class 153–157
XmSeparator widget class 119–120
    used in menus 184
XmSeparatorGadget 123
XmSHADOW_ETCHED_IN...........................129
XmSHADOW_ETCHED_OUT 129, 151
XmSHADOW_IN..................................129, 151
XmSHADOW_OUT 129, 151
XmSINGLE_SELECT 113
XmSTATIC scrollbar display policy 155
XmSTICKY_TAB_GROUP...........................177
XmSTRING.....................................87
XmStringByteCompare()........................369
XmStringCompare() 370
XmStringConcat().............................370
XmStringCreate().............................369
XmStringCreateLocalized()...................369
XmStringCreateLtoR() 25, 369
XmStringDraw()...............................372
XmStringDrawImage() 373
XmStringEmpty()..............................370
XmStringExtent().............................370
XmStringFree() 26, 369
XmStringGetLtoR() 373
XmStringGetNextSegment() 374
XmStringInitContext()........................374
XmTAB_GROUP.................................177
XmTEAR_OFF_DISABLED 197
XmTEAR_OFF_ENABLED..........................197
XmText widget class...........................101–112
    callbacks 102
    common resources 101
    convenience functions 105–108
    using XmNmodifyVerifyCallback........108
XmTextBlock...................................103
XmTextBlockRec 103

XmTextClearSelection() 107
XmTextCut() 107
XmTextField widget class 101–112
XmTextGetInsertionPosition() 106
XmTextGetLastPosition() 106
XmTextGetSelection() 106
XmTextGetString() 106
XmTextInsert() 106
XmTextPaste() 107
XmTextRemove() 107
XmTextReplace() 106
XmTextSetInsertionPosition() 106
XmTextSetSelection() 107
XmTextSetString() 106
XmTextShowPosition() 107
XmTextVerifyCallbackStruct 103
    doit member 103
XmToggleButton widget class 96–100
    callbacks 98
    common resources 97
    convenience functions 98
    displaying pixmaps 100
    used in menus 184
XmToggleButtonCallbackStruct 98
XmToggleButtonGadget 123
XmToggleButtonGetState() 98
XmToggleButtonSetState() 98
XmTOP_LEFT scrollbar placement 155
XmTOP_RIGHT scrollbar placement 155
XmTrackingEvent() 217
XmTRAVERSE_NEXT_TAB_GROUP 180
XmUNMAP 173, 488
XmUpdateDisplay() 271
XmVARIABLE visual policy............................. 155
XmVERTICAL 131
xnlLanguage resource 58, 59
XNoExposeEvent 258
Xpm 353–362, 376
    format..354
    symbolic colors 360
    xlogo image 355
XpmAttributes 356
XpmColorSymbol.. 359
XpmCreatePixmapFromData() 355
XpmReadFileToPixmap() 362
XpmWriteFileFromPixmap() 362
XPointInRegion() 331

XPolygonRegion() 329
XPutImage() 344
XPutPixel() 344
XQueryColor() 299
XQueryColors() 299
XQueryFont() 364
XRaiseWindow() 259
xrdb 60
XRectInRegion() 331
XRestackWindow() 259
XRestackWindows() 259
XrmGetResource() 56
XrmOptionDescList...................................... 72
XSelectionClearEvent............................ 465
XSelectionRequestEvent........................ 464
XSendEvent()................................... 461, 464
XSetBackground() 324
XSetClipMask() 328
XSetClipOrigon() 328
XSetClipRectangles() 328
XSetFillRule() 327
XSetFillStyle() 326
XSetFont() 328
XSetForeground() 324
XSetFunction() 323
XSetGraphicsExposures() 329
XSetLineAttributes()........................... 326
XSetPlaneMask() 324
XSetRegion() 331
XSetSelectionOwner()........................... 463
XSetStandardColormap()........................ 296
XSetStipple() 327
XSetTile() 327
XSetWindowColormap()........................... 295
XSetWMColormapWindows() 296
XStoreColor() 300
XStoreName() 458
XSubImage() 343
Xt Intrinsics................................... 10–14
    basic functions 23–50
    programming model.............................. 28
XtActionsRec... 41
XtAddCallback()................................. 44, 47
XtAddEventHandler()............................ 261
    non-maskable events 462
XtAddExposureToRegion() 331
XtAllocateGC() 322

XtAppAddActions() 41, 43
XtAppAddInput() 278
XtAppAddTimeOut() 272
XtAppAddWorkProc() 275
XtAppContext() 25
XtAppCreateShell() 29
XtAppInitialize() 29–30
    arguments to 25
XtAppMainLoop() 26, 40
XtAppNextEvent() 39, 250
XtAppPeekEvent() 270
XtAppPending() 270
XtAppSetFallbackResources() 59
XtArgVal 32, 36
XtAugmentTranslations() 44
XtConvertArgList 76
XtCreateApplicationContext() 29
XtCreateManagedWidget() 37
XtCreatePopupShell() 174
XtCreateWidget() 31
    use with gadgets....................................123
XtDestroyWidget() 38
XtDisownSelection() 468
XtDispatchEvent() 39
XtDisplay() 39
    use with gadgets....................................123
XtDisplayOfObject() 123
XtDisplayStringConversionWarning() 78
XtExposeCompressMaximal 521
XtExposeCompressMultiple..................... 520
XtExposeCompressSeries 520
XtExposeNoCompress 520
XTextExtents() 365
XTextWidth() 364
XtGeometryAlmost 555
XtGeometryMask 555
XtGeometryNo 555
XtGeometryResult 578
XtGeometryYes 555
XtGetApplicationResources() 69
XtGetGC() 321
XtGetSelectionValue() 467
XtGetSubresources() 219
XtGetValues() 36
XtGrabExclusive 175
XtGrabNone 175
XtGrabNonexclusive 175

XtInputExceptMask.................................278
XtInputId 278
XtInputNoneMask....................................278
XtInputReadMask....................................278
XtInputWriteMask..................................278
XtIsRealized() 38
    check before drawing into widget window 382
XtMakeGeometryRequest() 578
XtMakeResizeRequest() 578
XtManageChild()......................................37
XtManageChildren() 38
XtMoveWidget() 574
XtName() 187
XtNumber() 33
XtOffset() 68
XtOpenDisplay().......................................29
XtOverrideTranslations() 44
XtOwnSelection() 466
XtPopdown() 172, 175, 224
XtPopup() 172, 174, 224, 231
XtQueryGeometry()..........................554, 576
XtRealizeWidget() 38
XtRemoveTimeOut() 272
XtRemoveWorkProc() 275
XtResizeWidget() 574
XtResource.......................................68, 69
XtScreen() 39
XtSetArg() 33
XtSetValues() 34
XtToolkitInitialize() 29
XtTranslations.......................................41
XtVaCreateManagedWidget().......................37
XtVaCreateWidget() 32, 34
XtVaGetValues()................................37, 47
XtVaSetValues()......................................35
XtVaTypedArg..34
XtWidgetToApplicationContext()..........39
XtWidgetGeometry 555, 578
XtWindow() 39
XtWorkProcId..275
XUSERFILESEARCHPATH................................59
XVisual 294
XYBitmap 343
XYPixmap 343

To Order Example Source from P T R Prentice Hall:

Please make a copy of the form below and fill in the necessary information to receive a copy of the software containing the example source for a nominal fee. See pp. 621-22 in the text for more information and directions on unpacking these files.

Mail form to:

P T R Prentice Hall / NEODATA
Order Processing Center
P.O. Box 11071
Des Moines, IA 50336
Tel. (515) 284-6751
Fax (515) 284-2607

Please send the item checked below. The publisher will pay all shipping and handling charges.

_____ Sample software to accompany *The X Window System™ Programming and Applications OSF Motif® Edition* (second ed.) (ISBN 0-13-148743-4)

_____ $12.95 Payment Enclosed

Name _____

Title _____

Name of Firm _____

Address _____

_____

_____

I prefer to charge to my _____ VISA _____ Mastercard

Card Number _____

Expiration date _____

Signature _____